VIOLENCE GOES TO COLLEGE

Second Edition

VIOLENCE GOES TO COLLEGE

The Authoritative Guide to Prevention and Intervention

By

JOHN NICOLETTI, PH.D.

Nicoletti-Flater Associates
Lakewood, Colorado

SALLY SPENCER-THOMAS, PSY.D., MNM

Executive Director
Carson J Spencer Foundation
Westminster, Colorado

CHRISTOPHER BOLLINGER, PH.D.

Assistant Professor, English & Communication
Texas Lutheran University
Seguin, Texas

CHARLES C THOMAS • PUBLISHER, LTD.
Springfield • Illinois • U.S.A.

Published and Distributed Throughout the World by

CHARLES C THOMAS • PUBLISHER, LTD.
2600 South First Street
Springfield, Illinois 62794-9265

© 2010 by CHARLES C THOMAS • PUBLISHER, LTD.

ISBN 978-0-398-07909-3 (hard)
ISBN 978-0-398-07910-9 (paper)

Library of Congress Catalog Card Number: 200030005

*With THOMAS BOOKS careful attention is given to all details of manufacturing
and design. It is the Publisher's desire to present books that are satisfactory as to their
physical qualities and artistic possibilities and appropriate for their particular use.
THOMAS BOOKS will be true to those laws of quality that assure a good name
and good will.*

Printed in the United States of America
UB-R-3

Library of Congress Cataloging-in-Publication Data

Nicoletti, John.
   Violence goes to college: the authoritative guide to prevention and in-
tervention/by John Nicoletti, Sally Spencer-Thomas, Christopher
Bollinger. – 2nd ed.
      p. cm.
   Includes bibliographical references and index.
   ISBN 978-0-398-07909-3 (hard) -- ISBN 978-0-398-07910-9 (pbk.)
   1. Campus violence–United States–Prevention–Handbooks, manuals,
manuals, etc. 2. Universities and colleges–United States–Safety
measures–Handbooks, manuals, etc. 3. Universities and colleges–
Security measures–United States–Handbooks, manuals, etc. 4.
Conflict management–United States–Handbooks, manuals, etc. I.
Spencer-Thomas, Sally. II. Bollinger, Christopher. III. Title

LB2345.N53 2010
303.6'9–dc22
                                                    2009030005

This book is dedicated to
Tanner Johnson Thomas
Nicholas Rex Thomas
Jackson Thomas
Theresa Tafoya
Richard Tafoya
Chen Tafoya
Isaac Tafoya
Christopher Wilson

May they someday have
violence-free college experiences.

CONTRIBUTORS

Darby Dickerson
Vice President and Dean
Stetson University College of Law
Gulfport, Florida

Rebecca Flintoft, M.A.
Director, Auxiliary Services and Housing
Colorado School of Mines
Golden, Colorado

Jina Jensen, Psy.D.
Assistant Director
Office of Counseling and Personal Development
Regis University
Denver, Colorado

Heather Morris, Psy.D.
Lakewood, Colorado

Hank Nuwer, M.A., DH.L
Franklin College
Franklin, Indiana

Rae Sandler Simon, Psy.D.
Denver, Colorado

Kyle Wych, M.A.
Director of Residence Life
Texas Lutheran University
Seguin, Texas

FOREWORD

Over the past 26 years I have dealt with inappropriate behavior, demonstrations, crime, and violence on three different university campuses in three different states. My perspective has changed over that time as my career progressed from the street to the chief's office. The wide range of behavior, problems, and challenges that confront today's leaders in higher education, in securing and policing these institutions, has never been more complicated. Unfortunately, today there are some who still hold the notion that universities and colleges are exempt from violence found elsewhere. Even following the tragedy at Virginia Tech, the largest mass casualty murders in the United States, some are slow in learning there is no campus exemption from violence.

Violence Goes to College is an invaluable resource for understanding, preventing, and interrupting violence on college campuses. This resource recognizes that all violence is not the same. The causes of one form of violence vary from the next. Therefore, the manner in which violence is prevented or dealt with must vary as well.

This book reviews many forms of violence on campus. The authors provide a background for understanding the causes of violence. The research further provides how alcohol, peer pressure, and the need to be accepted socially motivates young adults to occasionally act out in unacceptable ways. Certain forms of violence are the end result of a discernable process that when recognized can be interrupted, redirected, or decreased.

By de-bundling the different types of violence the book clarifies ways in which professionals can act to prevent or reduce problems, crime and violence in the first place. Examples are factually based and cover some of the most difficult complex incidents and circumstances higher education professionals may confront.

Violence Goes to College is a complete guide for the professional in looking for real solutions, both immediate and long term, to reducing violence and keeping students, staff, and faculty safe as they learn, teach, and work. From environmental factors, reporting mechanisms, threat assessment, policy documents, alternatives to violence, intervention strategies, consequence management, and handling the aftermath of actual incidents, this is a comprehensive guide that is a must read.

Using the information and strategies found in *Violence Goes to College*, the institution I work to safeguard is better prepared to confront and resolve many of the challenges we face. These strategies have helped to reduce our institution crime rate to a 35-year low. If you believe in prevention rather than reaction, community policing and problem-solving policing, this guide will help you achieve your goals of providing a safe learning and work environment for your institution.

Susan Riseling
Associate Vice Chancellor and Chief of Police
University of Wisconsin-Madison

Vice President At Large
The International Association of Chiefs of Police 2005-2009.

PREFACE

ALMOST A DECADE has passed since we wrote the first edition of *Violence Goes to College*, and with this time, major violence has redefined the landscape of our nation. Most notably, the experiences of 9/11 and the tragedy of Virginia Tech will go down in history as two of the worst days in the United States. The Elizabeth Shin case, University of Oklahoma suicide bombing, and the Northern Illinois University shooting further increased anxiety on campuses. On the positive side, however, great strides have been made in understanding violence and how to prevent, interrupt, and respond to both internal and external threats; we have reflected this growth in our revisions. Not only have increasing numbers of campus leaders awakened to the real potential of many forms of violence, but our legislators are also paying attention. Technological advancement has expanded and altered communication mediums, leading to potential for greater violence as well as greater prevention, both of which have been significantly nuanced. Another milestone that passed in the last decade was the Garrett Lee Smith Suicide Prevention Grant funded by the federal government's Substance Abuse and Mental Health Services Administration (SAMHSA).

The three original authors have grown as the field has grown and as their lives have changed. Dr. Nicoletti continued to provide numerous trainings on preventing, detecting, interrupting, responding to, and surviving campus violent incidents across the nation. He also has worked with various campuses on developing vortexes and policies in addition to conducting risk assessments. He participated in an International Association of Chiefs of Police commission to review the Virginia Tech shooting, served on the National Association of Attorneys General Campus Safety Task Force, following the Virginia Tech tragedy, and was on the front lines of developing recommendations for the final publication presented by the Department of Justice.

Dr. Spencer-Thomas lost her younger brother to suicide in 2004, and subsequently her family and a network of supporters started the Carson J Spencer Foundation (www.CarsonJSpencer.org), a nonprofit "sustaining a passion for life" through suicide prevention. In 2006, she applied for and received funding from the Garrett Lee Smith Suicide Prevention Grant, creating a partnership between her family's foundation, Regis University, and the BACCHUS Network to develop comprehensive suicide prevention strategies for campuses.

Dr. Chris Bollinger received his Ph.D. in Communication after completing a dissertation exploring the ways in which hate is conceptualized, formulated, practiced, and resisted within our educational systems. He is currently an Assistant Professor in the Department of English and Communication studies at Texas Lutheran University. He routinely facilitates workshops and programs on recognizing and working against hate and on occasion works as a consultant for student affairs programs.

Collectively, the three of us have also mentored a number of graduate students in the work of violence prevention and have made wonderful new connections with other experts in the field. We have brought these new voices to this revised edition as well. Rather than edit out the individual voices to one unifying voice, we have chosen to have their styles shine through. We welcome your comments and offer further collaboration as the field continues to grow and change.

Over the course of the last few decades, violence has infected new areas of society such as the workplace, schools, malls, and religious sanctuaries. As violence prevention experts, we and others have been observing and intervening as the violence spreads to these new locations; despite their peaceful facades, college campuses are not immune. In fact, the recent tragic campus shootings have fundamentally changed how campuses operate – security is not on the forefront of many minds.

Since our first edition of the book, progress has been made:

- Many national associations published reports, adopted position statements, developed collaborations, held forums, and promoted safety legislation:
  - National Mental Health Association and the Jed Foundation (2002). *Safeguarding Your Students against Suicide: Expanding the Safety Net.*
  - American College Health Association (February 2005). *Campus Violence White Paper.*
  - National Association of Attorneys General (September 2007). *Task Force of School and Campus Safety: Report and Recommendations.*
  - NASPA (n.d.) *In Search of Safer Communities: Emerging Practice for Student Affairs in Addressing Campus Violence.* NASPA also developed a collaborative campaign called "Enough is Enough" in 2008, designed to empower all campus stakeholders in the effort of violence prevention in our society.

- In 2005, the U.S. Senate recognized September as National Campus Safety Awareness Month.
- Bureau of Justice Statistics shows that violence against college students decreased 40 percent while violence against nonstudents of the same age fell 44 percent during 1995–2002.[1]

When violence occurs on a college or university campus, the entire community is impacted. The ripple effects of one rape, one hate crime, or one riot spread rapidly and significantly contaminate the learning environment. Concentration and creative thought are stifled when fear is overwhelming. In order to deal with violence, campuses must not only treat the symptoms of the virus, but they must also inoculate and prevent further infection.

When the first edition of *Violence Goes to College* was published in 2001, it became the first violence prevention and intervention guide for college communities designed to prepare concerned individuals with up-to-date information and strategies to address campus violence. This now revised publication continues to be a user-friendly resource providing busy college personnel, students, and parents with directed, well-researched strategies to prepare for the possibility of tragedy before it strikes. Collectively, we bring decades of experience in both higher education and violence prevention to the task of developing these effective tactics. In addition to authoring three books on violence prevention, our violence experience includes consulting with the FBI and serving on national prevention panels.

Many of you may have picked up this book because you are interested in the threat of the mass casualty shootings that have rocked institutions of higher education. While these tragedies have dominated headlines, they are exceedingly rare – actually considered by many to be anomalous forms of campus violence.[2] All things considered, college campuses continue to be one of the safest places for people to be – motor vehicles, off-campus violence, family violence, and self-harm are often far bigger dangers. In fact:

- The murder rate off campus is about 28 times higher than on campus.[3]
- According to the National Crime Victimization survey, 93 percent of the crimes that students experience happen off campus.[4]
- Other way to look at it: with about 4,200 colleges in the U.S. and an average of 16 murders per year on college campuses, the average college can expect a murder on campus about once every 265 years.[5]

Nevertheless, when we are faced with the continuous barrage of images of violence, we tend to forget these facts and resort to a reactive response, best articulated by risk management expert Brett Sokolow:

> If you believe the pundits and talking heads in the aftermath of the Virginia Tech tragedy, every college and university should rush to implement text-message-based early warning systems, should install loudspeakers throughout campus, should perform criminal background checks on all incoming students, should allow students to install their own locks on their residence hall room doors, and should exclude from admission or expel students with serious mental health conditions. We should profile loners, establish lockdown protocols and develop mass-shooting evacuation plans. We should even arm our students to the teeth.

In the immediate aftermath, security experts and college and university officials have been quoted in the newspapers and on TV with considering all of these remedies, and more, to be able to assure the public that WE ARE DOING SOMETHING.[6]

Sokolow goes on in his op-ed piece to emphasize as we have here that our best protection against violence is strategic and comprehensive prevention – much of it through mental health promotion and communication strategies.

The book is organized into three sections: The first addresses broad campus violence concerns and violence conceptualization. The second explores general prevention strategies. The third looks more in depth at particular forms of campus violence including sexual assault, rioting, hate crimes, hazing, homicide, nonsexual assault, arson, and bombing.

Violence Goes to College offers hope that somewhere between Pollyanna and paranoia, campuses can find a healthy balance between reasonable protection and personal freedom.

J.N.
S.S.T.
C.B.

ACKNOWLEDGMENTS

OUR THANKS TO Anna Reishus for her help in organizing the bibliography. Regis University's Dayton Memorial Library for their research assistance; Susan Richardson and Jerene Anderson for their mentoring and support; Diane Cooper for her helpful feedback and encouragement; Clark Newman, Alice Reich, Frank Lavrisha, Rebecca Flintoft, Allan Blattner, Steve Vrooman, the TLU works in progress group, Kevin Bollinger, and David McInally for their review of the manuscript; Heather Morris, Rae Sandler, and Jina Jensen for becoming violence/suicide prevention scholars; NASPA Task Force on Violence for their insights; the BACCHUS Network for shared aims; the Clery Family and Security on Campus, Inc. for their assistance in the research process, their relentless commitment to preventing campus violence, and their permission to share the story of their daughter Jeanne; Eileen Stevens and Hank Nuwer for their review of the manuscript and permission to share the story of Chuck; Darlene and Robert Krueger and their lawyer Brad Henry for their suggestions and permission to share the story of Scott; the Suicide Prevention Resource Center, SPAN, American Association of Suicidology, the American Foundation for Suicide Prevention, SAMHSA, and those who have supported the Garrett Lee Smith Memorial Act; all of our contributing authors; and Randy Thomas, Lottie Flater, and Denise Menchaca for their patience and love.

NOTE TO THE READER

ALL THE INFORMATION provided herein is general in nature and designed to serve as a guide to understanding. These materials are not to be construed as the rendering of legal, management, or counseling advice. If the reader has a specific need or problem, the services of a competent professional should be sought to address the particular situation.

For more information or consultation, contact Nicoletti-Flater Associates at:

Nicoletti-Flater Associates
3593 South Teller St.
Suite 310
Lakewood, CO 80235
303-989-1617 or (toll free) 1-877-989-1617
www.n-fa.com

CONTENTS

Part I

LEAVING "IT-WILL-NEVER-HAPPEN-HERE": HELPING COLLEGE COMMUNITIES ACKNOWLEDGE VIOLENCE POTENTIAL WITHOUT CREATING PANIC

Part II

DEVELOPING ANTIBODIES: GENERAL PREVENTION STRATEGIES FOR THE COLLEGE COMMUNTIY

Part III

STRAINS OF CAMPUS VIOLENCE

VIOLENCE GOES TO COLLEGE

Part I

LEAVING
"IT-WILL-NEVER-HAPPEN-HERE":
HELPING COLLEGE
COMMUNITIES ACKNOWLEDGE
VIOLENCE POTENTIAL
WITHOUT CREATING PANIC

Chapter 1

SEEING VIOLENCE AS A VIRUS

JOHN NICOLETTI & SALLY SPENCER-THOMAS

"I NEVER THOUGHT it would happen here." We hear this statement repeatedly in the aftermath of tragic incidents. Most people want to believe that they are immune from harm, and that their learning and working environments are safe havens. When violence occurs, they often feel blind-sided, but in retrospect, they can usually identify subtle and sometimes not-so-subtle warning signs.

In order to understand the current state of campus violence, one must look to two sources of information – the factual and the theoretical. We must start by taking a look at what we know. This can be accomplished both by looking at our history and by looking at what current research is telling us. When we examine the impact high-profile cases have had on the campus culture over the past several decades, we can learn a great deal. While these cases may have only directly impacted a small number of individuals, their legacy continues to influence how many colleges think about violence. So, the first step is to look at our history to understand where we are today. Then we can appraise what credible sources are telling us about the prevalence and trends of violence on our campuses.

The second step is to develop a conceptualization that is relevant and useful to college campuses. We have found that a particularly effective conceptualization is achieved by thinking about violence as a virus. By

using this analogy, we can examine the many different "strains" of violence hosted on college campuses.

WHAT CAN WE LEARN FROM CAMPUS VIOLENCE HISTORY?

The following list of high-profile cases of college violence is not intended to be an exhaustive account of all devastating tragedies college communities have faced. Rather, certain cases were selected to illustrate how various forms of violence can forever change campus culture.

High-Profile Cases: History and Impact

- **July 13–14, 1966: Chicago Massacre South Chicago Community Hospital – residences for student nurses in training Chicago, Illinois**

On this July night, Richard Speck brutally murdered – stabbed, strangled and sexually assaulted – eight nursing students in their Chicago townhouse.[7] The 24-year-old sailor broke into the townhouse through a mesh screen door armed with a pistol and a knife. Initially he stated that his motive was robbery, but after taking his victims' money, he proceeded to tie up the women. Over the next several hours, he murdered each victim, except one who hid terrified under a bed. She would later be a crucial witness, leading to his eventual capture and conviction. This "crime of the century" is not usually thought of as a campus crime per say, but it was. From this tragedy of mass murder involving college women sprang a new genre of horror – a story that would be repeated in multiple novels, films, and reality in the upcoming decades.

- **August 1, 1966: The Texas Sniper**
  University of Texas
  Austin, Texas

Charles Joseph Whitman, a former Eagle Scout and Marine Lance Corporal, was a student at the University of Texas.[8] In the early morning hours of August 1, 1966, Whitman stabbed his mother and wife to death in their homes. Later that same morning, he bought ammunition and a shotgun. When he arrived on campus, he had an arsenal of weapons and knives that he brought to the top of the Tower, a University landmark that overlooks most of the campus grounds. On his way up, he killed the receptionist and two other people who were touring the Tower. From an elevation of 231 feet, Whitman shot at people crossing the campus.

The siege lasted 92 minutes, an eternity for this type of crime.[9] Finally, Whitman was shot to death by two Austin police officers. In the end, 17 people were killed, including Whitman and an unborn child, and 31 were wounded. An autopsy of Whitman's body indicated that he had a brain tumor, but experts remain unclear as to the extent to which this tumor affected his behavior.

In September 1999, the University of Texas moved to reclaim this landmark by reopening the Tower.[10] All visitors to the observation deck must pass through a metal detector and are prohibited from bringing any packages with them. Thus, the legacy of this one terrible act of violence still haunts the University of Texas today. With two major massacres impacting college campuses during this violent one-month period in the summer of 1966, the image of college campuses as ivory tower sanctuaries sheltered from violence was shattered.

- **May 4, 1970: Kent State Riots**
  Kent State University
  Kent, Ohio

In late April 1970, the United States invaded Cambodia, escalating the Vietnam War. Shortly after, protests emerged on college campuses across the country.[11] At Kent State University, antiwar gatherings became increasingly intense. Students began by peacefully burying a copy of the Constitution, then built bonfires in the streets of Kent, and eventually clashed with police. Because of this escalation, the mayor declared a state of emergency and called in the Ohio National Guard. On May 2, the ROTC building was set ablaze in the presence of over 1,000 demonstrators. By Sunday, May 3, the campus looked like a war zone and most of the campus assumed that the university was in a state of martial law.

On the morning of Monday, May 4, 3,000 people began to gather in the Commons area for an antiwar rally scheduled for noon.[12] Initially the rally was peaceful, and the accounts of the following events are still subject to debate. Just before the rally was about to commence, officials made the decision to disperse the demonstrators. What ensued was an escalating confrontation between demonstrators and enforcement, and in the end, 28 guardsmen fired over 60 shots, wounding nine and killing four Kent State students. This event is critical to appreciating campus violence history for two reasons. First, the politically driven campus protests of that era can be compared and contrasted to rioting that many campuses are experiencing today. In understanding potential rioting triggers and diffusion tactics, we need to ask, "What are the similarities and differences in the campus culture now and then?" Second, the community response in the aftermath of the tragedy can serve as a model for other schools facing such violence. At Kent State, at that time and for years to come, students, faculty, and staff all participated in the recovery and the future direction of the campus.

- **January 14, 1978: The Chi Omega Murders
  Florida State University
  Tallahassee, Florida**

Ted Bundy is probably the most notorious serial killer in American history.[13] His modus operandi: preying on young women and luring them in with his charm and perception of vulnerability. On the night of the Chi Omega murders, Bundy apparently walked right in the front door of the sorority, leaving it wide open after he entered. He then attacked the sorority sisters in their rooms while they slept. He beat them, raped them, bit them, and strangled them. Two victims died and two survived. Like Richard Speck's attack on the nurses a decade earlier, this event magnified the vulnerability of women living on campus and perpetuated a perception of college women as accessible sexual prey.

- **February 24, 1978: Chuck Stenzel
  Alfred University
  Alfred, New York**

Hank Nuwer, hazing expert, describes the following tragedy in his books *Broken Pledges* and *Wrongs of Passage*. February 24, 1978 was Tapping Night at Alfred University's Klan Alpine fraternity.[14] Chuck Stenzel had recently re-enrolled at Alfred. His mother thought, in hindsight, that he probably chose to join the fraternity to increase his chances for making the lacrosse team (several brothers played the sport) or to get closer to his existing friends. The "Klan" had a reputation of being an "animal house," and ironically, the theme for this particular Tapping Night was, "Don't Stop til You Drop." Sometime after 7:00 P.M.,

a fraternity brother came to Chuck's room to congratulate him on his acceptance with a pint of Jack Daniel's whiskey. The brother then led Chuck to the car where he was to ride in the trunk. The temperature outside was below freezing. There were two other pledges in the trunk with Chuck who later testified that he chugged not only his pint, but also most of another pledge's pint of Scotch.

Chuck arrived at the fraternity house at some point before 9:30 P.M. at which point he drank more beer and wine in festive celebration and drinking games.[15] One of the goals of

Figure 1.1. Chuck Stenzel. February 28, 1978. Chuck Stenzel was a sophomore at Alfred University when his brothers at the Klan Alpine Fraternity locked him in the trunk of a car after giving him a pint of bourbon, a fifth of wine, and a six pack of beer, with orders to consume all before he would be released. He died of acute alcohol poisoning and exposure to the cold. Chuck's mother, Eileen Stevens formed C.H.U.C.K. (Committee to Halt Useless College Killings) in August of 1978 and has become a leading antihazing activist.

the night was to fill a trashcan up to a marked line with vomit. Chuck was given a shower at some point and when he began to pass out, he was placed on his side on an uncovered mattress. Chuck and another unconscious pledge were left in the room unattended until 11:30 P.M. when a fraternity brother came in to check on them and noted that Chuck's fingernails had turned blue. None of the three sober brothers on site knew CPR, and the rest of the brothers were too drunk to be of any assistance. By the time an emergency medical crew arrived, Chuck was dead. Chuck's blood alcohol content at the time of death was .46, a fourfold increase from the legal definition of intoxication. Two other pledges, one of whom the ambulance crew found in a locked closet, were close to death and were rushed to the hospital. They survived.

From that night on, Chuck's mother Eileen Stevens bravely chose to speak out against the dangers of hazing.[16] She founded C.H.U.C.K. (Committee to Halt Useless College Killings), a national anti-hazing organization. She speaks to groups on this issue sharing her personal experience as a mother of a hazing victim. Alfred University is now leading the cause to prevent hazing.[17] In 1999, Alfred helped orchestrate an NCAA study that exposed significant hazing activity in college athletics.

- **April 5, 1986: Jeanne Clery**
  Lehigh University
  Bethlehem, Pennsylvania

Just a few days after her parents dropped her off at Lehigh University following her spring break, Jeanne Clery was asleep in her unlocked room when she was brutally raped, beaten, and murdered by a fellow student.[18] Josoph Henry had easily gained entrance to the dormitory because the door had been propped open with empty pizza boxes. After the murder, he boasted about his attack to his friends. In 1987, he was sentenced to the electric chair.

Jeanne's parents thought they had been acting in her best interest when they encouraged her to attend Lehigh because it looked so safe.[19] What they did not know was that Lehigh had experienced 38 violent crimes within a three-year period. The Clerys filed a $25 million civil suit against Lehigh for negligence. The suit was settled out of court, and the Clerys used the settlement and their own money to begin one of the largest campaigns to stop campus violence to date. In 1988, they founded Security on Campus, Inc., and in

Figure 1.2. Jeanne Clery. April 5, 1986, Jeanne Clery was found dead in her residence hall room. She had been raped, sodomized, beaten, and strangled. Her attacker, Josoph Henry, bit her face and breasts, to make sure she was dead. The night of the murder, Josoph Henry walked through three security doors. In the months prior to the murder, students had lodged complaints about his behavior and threats to female students to administrators. Since this tragedy, the Clery family has developed a nonprofit organization called "Security On Campus" and is largely responsible for the passage of 27 campus safety laws.

1990 lobbied for the successful passing of the federal bill called the "Student Right-To-Know and Campus Safety Act" now known as the "Jeanne Clery Act." They continue to be very vocal and tireless in their pursuit to expose the truth about campus violence and to educate the public on how to prevent future tragedies.

- **August 1990: Gemini Killer University of Florida and Santa Fe Community College Gainesville, Florida**

The college town of Gainesville, Florida, experienced total devastation and panic when five bodies of brutally murdered college students were discovered within 48 hours. Three of the students were from the University of Florida and two were from Santa Fe Community College, both schools of Gainesville, Florida. On August 26, 1990, the day before classes were to start at the University of Florida, two freshmen women were found stabbed in their townhouse residence. The killer had raped and mutilated one of these victims; the other appeared to have been stabbed in her sleep. The next day, police found another female student naked and decapitated in her residence. On August 28, a maintenance man found two more victims, both college students. The 23-year-old female had been raped and stabbed in the back, and the 23-year-old male had been stabbed 31 times.

In the aftermath of these discoveries, the residents and students of Gainesville were terrified, and the town was in a state of siege. Many students purchased guns, creating a hazard to officers who were knocking on hundreds of doors to follow up on thousands of leads. It took investigators one year to track down and arrest serial killer Danny Rolling for the crimes. Rolling blamed the killings on his alter ego "Gemini," but profilers described him as a sexual predator who preyed upon women. He chose women who would most likely have no interest in him –

educated, beautiful, successful college women. In 1994, the jury gave him the death penalty. We believe that it is not a coincidence that four of America's most deadly and notorious serial and spree killers – Speck, Whitman, Bundy, and Rolling – chose college students as their victims.

- **June 3, 1991: *Time* Magazine Headline "Date Rape" College of William and Mary Colonial Williamsburg, Virginia**

In 1991, *Time* magazine put a face to date rape.[20] In that issue, they covered the story of Katie Koestner, a woman who dared to speak out against a silent epidemic. A graduate of the College of William and Mary in Williamsburg, Virginia, Katie testifies to her experience of being sexually assaulted by a fellow student, someone she met during her first week of school. Since then, she has become an activist for the issue, speaking to millions through college keynotes, inspiring an HBO documentary titled, "No Visible Bruises," and making television appearances ranging from "Oprah" to "Larry King Live" to "The NBC Nightly News." According to her audience, her powerful story humanizes a crime that few speak about and empowers both women and men to try to stop it.

- **September 29, 1997: Scott Krueger MIT Boston, Massachusetts**

Five weeks after the promising freshman Scott Krueger arrived on the prestigious campus of MIT, he died from an alcohol overdose.[21] Scott was a pledge at the Phi Gamma Delta house, better known as FIJI. Scott was not a big drinker, but on "Animal House Night" he and the other pledges were expected to drink two cases of beer, Jack Daniels whiskey, and Bacardi rum within a short period of time. He passed out, was carried to a basement room, and left alone after which he inhaled his own vomit into his

Figure 1.3. Scott Krueger, an 18-year-old MIT freshman died after lapsing into an alcohol induced coma as a result of a hazing experience at Phi Gamma Delta fraternity

lungs. According to his doctors, the critical point of the night was when his "big brothers" chose to leave him by himself so that they could go back upstairs for another drink. Scott's blood alcohol content was .41.

FIJI had very serious and well-known alcohol problems in the years before Scott's death.[22] Police and emergency medical personnel had been summoned to the FIJI house at least 15 times in the few years before Scott's death to deal with outrageously large parties, drunken fights, underage drinking, and to assist severely intoxicated students. MIT clearly knew of these problems and more.

Rather than indict the university for manslaughter and hazing, the district attorney indicted the MIT fraternity.[23] A sealed indictment was handed up from the DA's office on September 14, 1998, but was not made public to anyone until September 18, 1998.

Interestingly, MIT and FIJI National agreed to disband the local chapter between September 14 and the 18, and no individual showed up at FIJI's arraignment two weeks later. The indictment remains open and if the chapter ever reopens at MIT, it could be prosecuted. Despite the lack of closure on this case, the steps taken were groundbreaking in that the threat of a criminal indictment for a university or Greek association in the aftermath of a hazing death becomes viable.

The Krueger family prepared to file suit against MIT for the university's responsibility in the death of their son. In September 2000, MIT agreed to pay the Kruegers $4.75 million as compensation and $1.25 million for a scholarship established in the memory of Scott. In addition, the MIT president publicly apologized and accepted blame for MIT's role in Scott's death.[24]

Two weeks after the announcement of the MIT settlement, the Krueger family filed suit against the MIT fraternity.[25] The Kruegers' attorney, Brad Henry, was quoted in the *Boston Globe* (9/27/00) as saying, "They [FIJI] simply can't disband themselves out of accountability." Because of the intense media coverage in the aftermath of this tragedy, the deadly consequences of college hazing practices as well as binge drinking reached public consciousness.

• October 6, 1998: Matthew Shepard University of Wyoming Laramie, Wyoming

During October 1998, Matthew Shepard, an openly gay student at the University of Wyoming, met Aaron McKinney and Russell Henderson, two local roofers at the Fireside Lounge.[26] McKinney and Henderson lured Shepard into their truck by posing as two gay men. The two roofers robbed Shepard, pistol-whipped him repeatedly, and left him tied to a fence. He remained bound and unconscious for 18 hours in subfreezing temperatures. Shepard died five days later from the injuries. The brutal crime and dramatic trials brought significant media attention, and Shepard became a national symbol for gay rights and the effects of hate crimes. The University of Wyoming and the community of Laramie banded together in mourning by wearing or displaying yellow ribbons in his memory.

Along with a deluge of concern and activism came a backlash of hatred. Shepard's funeral and the ensuing trials brought antigay protests. McKinney's "gay panic" defense, claiming he snapped during a methamphetamine-induced fury instigated by memories of a childhood homosexual assault, brought additional media attention.[27]

In addition to learning about effective community response and the impact of campus hate crimes, the Matthew Shepard tragedy taught campuses another lesson: how to handle a media circus. During the ordeal, demonstrators representing all sides of the issues implanted themselves on campus in a national spotlight. Campus officials quickly learned that media parameters were necessary to protect the students and to control the dispersion of legitimate information.

- **March 27–28, 1999: Michigan State University Riots**
  Michigan State University
  East Lansing, Michigan

In stark contrast to the politically motivated riots of earlier days, the riots of the late 1990s have been dubbed "The Right to Party" movement. As colleges began to crack down on underage drinking and public drunkenness, students revolted in violent ways. The most notorious of these riots were a series of riots at Michigan State University in East Lansing. After school administrators put a ban on alcohol at a popular tailgate site, an estimated 10,000 students and townspeople torched cars, hurled bottles at police, set more than 60 fires, and caused up to $1 million in damage. While this particular riot at

MSU created a great deal of media interest, it was not the first riot MSU faced.

Since September 1997, there have been four alcohol-related riots at MSU. These incidents have negatively impacted the tenuous community relationship where the 43,000 MSU students significantly outnumber the 25,000 year-round residents of East Lansing. The university has spent a great deal of time trying to determine the underlying cause of the riots, to no avail. It seems to some that rioting has become trendy and fun; as one student commented, "It was a blast in all senses of the word. We came together as a school, burned some things, showed some skin and that's fine. It was Spartan pride." Interestingly, police are dismantling the anonymity that rioting brings by posting pictures of the rioters on the Internet.

- **October 2, 1999: University of Vermont Hockey Team Hazing**
  University of Vermont
  Montpelier, Vermont

On October 2, the University of Vermont (UVM) hockey team held its initiation party.[28] A freshman goalie, Corey LaTulippe, had warned university officials in September about the hazing party before it happened. Despite warnings from the Athletic Department, the party took place. Shortly after the initiation party, LaTulippe was cut from the team and subsequently filed a lawsuit against the university alleging assault and battery, invasion of privacy, and violation of his civil rights. Rookie players were ordered to arrive at the party with their pubic hair shaved, wearing thong underwear. Then they were forced to perform push-ups while dipping their genitals in cups of beer. Depending on the number they were able to perform, each athlete then had to drink his own glass or that of another rookie. During the evening, they were also instructed to walk around holding each other's genitals. During a deposition, the issue of Corey's consent was broached. Corey stated, "I didn't feel I had a choice (to decline the invitation to the initiation party)...this is what you had to do."

An initial UVM investigation concluded in disciplinary action against several players for their roles; however, LaTulippe's lawsuit renewed investigation by the university and the Attorney General. The Attorney General's conclusion was that the allegations were essentially true, and the entire team had lied to UVM investigators.[29] In January 2000, the UVM president made a bold move by canceling the remaining games of the team's Division I hockey season.[30]

The University of Vermont ended up settling the lawsuit for a payment of $80,000. One of the team's captains pleaded no contest to a charge of providing beer to a minor. He agreed to pay fines and court costs and was ordered to perform 50 hours of community service. He was also given a suspended 30-day jail sentence.

This case demonstrated what recent research has been telling us: hazing happens to athletes. The stance the UVM president took was unprecedented. Whether or not it will serve as a standard for future hazing violations remains to be seen.

- **April 10, 2000: Elizabeth Shin**
  MIT
  Boston, Massachusetts

A student heard a smoke alarm and cries coming from with a residence hall room. When police broke down the door, they found Elizabeth Shin engulfed in flames; she died several days later. Shin's family filed a wrongful death suit, claiming that despite numerous warning signs and notification of mental health problems and suicidal behavior, the University did not give her proper medical attention. Some of the evidence the Shins brought into court included[31]:

- A February 1999 overdose of Tylenol with Codeine resulting in a week-long

hospitalization and referral to campus Mental Health Services.
- October 1999, Elizabeth met with professionals from campus Mental Health Services stating she felt she was going crazy and was overwhelmed with negative thoughts.
- November 1999, Elizabeth meets with an Associate Dean to report she had become upset, smashed a glass vase, and cut herself. This prompted a referral to Mental Health Services, which she canceled.
- December 1999, Elizabeth emails a faculty member expressing a suicidal plan. This email is then forwarded to several MIT employees, including the Associate Dean. No action was taken in response to the email.
- March 18, 2000, students in her residence hall alert authorities that Elizabeth was cutting herself. Elizabeth is subsequently transported to Mental Health Services and is observed overnight in the infirmary.
- March 23, 2000, Elizabeth attends treatment at Mental Health Services and is given antidepressant medication. Elizabeth reports not eating or sleeping and having morbid thoughts about seeing herself bleed to death.
- Late March and Early April, Elizabeth continues to be seen on a walk-in basis and on April 5, 2000, she cuts her wrists and arms again. April 6, 2000, authorities discuss the option of hospitalization with Elizabeth. April 8, 2000, Elizabeth tells another student she wanted to kill herself by sticking a knife into her chest. A staff doctor determines she is safe to return to her room.
- On the morning of April 10, 2000, Elizabeth told other students she was going to kill herself and to erase her computer files. The students reported this and the news went all the way up to the dean. At 9:00pm that night, Elizabeth was found

burning in her room, and on April 14th she died.

The lawsuit continued for four years as campuses awaited the verdict of this landmark case. On April 3, 2006, almost six years after her death, the family of Elizabeth Shin settled for an undisclosed amount and the Shins released a statement saying, "We appreciate MIT's willingness to spare our family the ordeal of a trial and have come to understand that our daughter's death was likely a tragic accident. This agreement will allow us to move forward in the healing process."

- **October 1, 2005: Suicide Bomber University of Oklahoma Norman, Oklahoma**

At approximately 7:30 P.M., Joel "Joe" Henry Hinrichs III detonated himself with a homemade bomb just 200 yards from the Oklahoma Memorial Stadium, where 84,501 spectators were attending a football game. Many speculated about terrorism behavior as the crime mimicked both the July 2005 London bombings as well as the infamous shoe bomber; however, the FBI and local authorities concluded that Hinrichs worked alone. His father reported that Hinrichs did not have the ability to bond with other people. This case sparked tremendous interest in domestic terrorism and how campuses are vulnerable targets.

- **April 16, 2007: Virginia Tech Massacre Virginia Polytechnic Institute Blacksburg, Virginia**

In the early morning hours of April 16th, Seung-Hui Cho shot and killed two students in a residence hall. He then mailed writings and video recordings to NBC News and proceeded to Norris Hall where he killed another 30 people before taking his own life. An additional 23 people were injured. This massacre, currently the deadliest shooting rampage in U.S. history, received tremendous international coverage and sparked intense debate about

campus safety and gun policy. Details of this landmark case are elaborated in other chapters.

- **February 14, 2008: Northern Illinois University Shooting Northern Illinois University DeKalb, Illinois**

At about 3:05 P.M., a heavily armed Steven Kazmierczak entered a large lecture hall and fired into a crowd of about 200 students killing six people, including himself, and injuring 18. The former NIU graduate was attending graduate school in social work at the University of Illinois at Urbana-Champaign at the time of the shooting, and had allegedly became erratic after he stopped taking his medication. This second campus mass casualty considerably increased fears that Virginia Tech was not going to be just an isolated incident.

Fads and Trends of Violence

College campuses are generally viewed as safe places for individuals to go to develop critical thinking skills, learn about the world, develop social skills, and have fun. Recently, violence on campus has generated significant attention in the media. High-profile rioting and rape incidents have made national news and have caused increasing concern around the country.

Many wonder if these events are isolated situations hyped by the media or if they truly represent a trend in our society. Fads in American culture are very commonplace. They gain much attention in a short period and fade out just as quickly. Violence fads are often created by urban myths. For example, during the mid-nineties, many people thought they would be shot if they flashed their car's headlights at a car that was driving at them with no headlights in the dark. People feared that it was part of some rite of passage for gang members. For a few weeks, this myth circulated the Internet and grapevines. When this pattern of violence did not materialize, the fad dissolved.

In contrast to fads, trends are patterns of violence that alter the norms of our society. Fads can turn into trends because of what has been termed "copycat" behavior. Humans tend to learn from watching other people. When certain individuals see someone achieve a desired goal through violence without consequences, they begin to believe that the ends justify the means.

When threats and acts of violence are consistent over time, individuals adapt their way of living to minimize the impact. Soon, the adjustment becomes second nature and people consider the changes in the behavior to be normal. Current airport security is a consequence of a violence trend. Prior to the 1970s, safety checks were minimal. However, as terrorism, hijackings, and bomb threats increased in frequency throughout the early seventies, the airline industry took major counteractive measures. The current security strategies in airports can be quite intrusive and intense. Before this trend in violence, travelers would have thought a security guard rummaging through their bags was a major violation of privacy. Today, airline passengers have adapted to this practice and may even welcome it. If airports discontinued the security measures tomorrow, many people would likely be too afraid to fly.

Another example of a trend in violence involves product tampering. Not too long ago, stores sold over-the-counter medication and food products in relatively easy-to-open packaging. At most, childproofing caps existed. After the Tylenol® tampering incidents and the multiple copycat crimes that followed, products were protected with seals and plastic wrapping. This trend has resulted in an inconvenience and increased product costs, but the public does not seem to mind. In fact, most of us would not buy a bottle of cough syrup if there were not a protective seal wrapped around it. We have adapted to these security measures barely realizing a violent trend has changed the norm of our culture.

Violent mass killings in schools and workplaces are another trend in our society. At first, the instances were rare and isolated. Now it is clear that the trend is increasing in frequency and intensity. The killings are happening more often and there are more casualties. Furthermore, this form of violence is changing workplace and school culture. Schools and businesses are implementing metal detectors, increasing security, and improving identification procedures. Many are developing emergency plans to deal with a siege situation.

When trends are established, profilers can begin to develop psychological and behavioral indicators of common elements found in perpetrators. In essence, a profiler attempts to understand the "why" of the crime to get to the "who." By understanding the motives of the criminal, profilers can attempt to predict future directions of a crime trend.

A significant problem in identifying fads versus trends on college campuses is that our current knowledge base is inadequate. On one hand, there are many secrets hidden in campus life such as a preponderance of unreported acquaintance rape, and on the other hand, we are sometimes bombarded with information about overblown single cases of violence hyped by our sensation-driven media.

CONCEPTUALIZING VIOLENCE AS A VIRUS

Violence is like a virus with many different strains. Motives, perpetrator profiles, victims, and outcomes are diverse, and like a virus, these features of violence mutate when exposed to different hosting sites. Understanding violence in terms of its similarities to a virus can help prevention and intervention efforts. Violence is not static, and each time the virus mutates, those who seek to prevent it lag behind.

Too often, different strains of violence are lumped together when people attempt to develop prevention strategies. People assume that violence does not mutate. For instance, in the aftermath of the Columbine High School massacre, dozens of national "Violence Summits" emerged to find solutions to school violence. At these meetings hundreds of experts and concerned protectors gathered to discuss a multitude of violence issues including gang violence, bullying, hate crimes, sexual abuse, and more. Frequently, attendees left with increased confusion rather than clarity. Many sought the magical elixir; the one antibody to cure all, and found it did not exist.

One prevention strategy may be effective with a particular type of violence in a particular setting, but that tactic may lose its potency when the strain of violence moves to a different hosting site or to a different population. For example, domestic violence in the home presents a different set of challenges than when domestic violence spills over into the workplace or onto a college campus. For one, there are many more potential victims in a workplace setting or on a college campus. Furthermore, victims are affected differently; varying environmental factors impact how violence develops, and each situation demands tailored interventions.

The Host Site: Violence Impact on a Campus Community

Violence is threaded through many aspects of American life, but it is perhaps most out of place in an institution devoted to education and development.
                                                      – Mary Roark[32]

Unfortunately, in our society, we have grown accustomed to seeing violence in our inner cities and poorest neighborhoods. Media attention has made violence in our high schools and workplaces seem increasingly common. However, violence on college campuses is a concept that many people have difficulty reconciling with images of ivy-covered brick and sun-drenched, grassy quadrangles. College campuses are places for intellectual growth and developing civility, not rape, murder, and assault. Much of college violence happens behind closed doors, during the darkest hours of the night, or under sworn secrecy, and thus, many of us can continue to pretend that it is not happening. Or maybe we believe that it is happening on someone else's campus, but not ours. The truth is that all campuses are vulnerable to many forms of violence, an issue explored in greater depth in Chapters 3 and 4. We must be willing to acknowledge that it is happening before we can correct it.

Beyond Treating the Symptoms

While it is beyond the scope of this book to explore all the roots of violence in our society, it is safe to conclude that violence exists because of problems on many levels: personal, familial, social, and cultural. This is not just an issue for police or security to tackle. A reactive stance would tire the most competent enforcement department.

Proactive prevention is critical. All segments of the campus and surrounding communities have a role to play in preventing violence. Admissions, faculty, residence life, athletics, students, parents, alumni, counseling, public relations, student life, community leaders, neighbors, Greek life, human resources, and more need to play an active role. This guide is designed to provide relevant information to all those people committed to preventing violence on college campuses. Specific ways individuals can become involved are explored in Chapter 6.

CLASSIFICATIONS OF CAMPUS VIOLENCE

Violence Typologies

When we begin to think of violence not as a unitary concept, but in the form of multiple typologies, we discover many variations emerge:

Relationship-based	Street/Predatory
Bullying	Terrorist
Assassin	Suicide by Cop
(Suicidal) Avenger	Group-induced
Entrepreneurial	Road Rage

Some of these violence typologies are rarely seen on college campuses. Terrorist attacks, assassinations, and suicide-by-cop (provoking a law enforcement officer to use deadly force) seldom occur at institutions of higher education. Entrepreneurial (committing violence to gain a profit, e.g., robbery), road rage (e.g., aggression from parking shortage frustration), and bullying are common, but outside the scope of this book. Four of these general categories of violence seem to play out in various combinations on college campuses: predatory, avenger, relationship-based, and group-induced.

Predatory

For many violent offenders, the violent act is a means to an end. Violence is used to get something they want. A mugger attacks to get money. A terrorist holds others hostage to achieve a desired outcome. For the predator, the violence is the desired outcome. The thrill is in the kill or assault – the planning, execution, and aftermath. This is the primary goal predators are trying to obtain.

Several subtypes of predators exist classified by their methods of searching for prey and in their attack strategies. In searching methods, predators can be hunters, poachers, trollers, or opportunists. The hunter stays within a familiar area or neighborhood to locate prey. The poacher will survey an area away from the home territory. A troller will wander around to areas of vulnerability searching for viable prey. For instance, a troller might make the rounds at several bars looking for intoxicated potential victims. The opportunist builds a sense of trust with potential victims because

of a role he or she has managed to obtain. For example, a child molester who works at a day care center is an opportunist.

Predators also vary in their method of attack. The raptor uses the "swoop and scoop" tactic striking potential victims without warning. The stalker will track victims and get to know their habits from afar before attacking. The ambusher will take the Bundy approach of feigning vulnerability and weakness or manipulating victims with charm and seduction in order to lure them into a trap.

Avenger

For the avenger, violence becomes the only possible recourse for perceived grievances. Many of the workplace violence and school violence perpetrators personify this classification of violence. When we examine the pathways to violence in these cases, we find similar sequences. First, there is a string of perceived injustices ending with some form of rejection or discipline. A girlfriend ended a relationship, an authority figure doled out discipline, or peers taunted the perpetrator. Second, the perpetrator initiates a resolution. They may initially attempt to resolve the matter through appropriate channels, but they do not get the results they desire. Rather than drop the issue, the perpetrator becomes obsessed with the issue and moves into the third phase. During the third phase, problem solving narrows and the perpetrator begins to create a violent fantasy of retaliation. This fantasy becomes very satisfying to avengers as they can rework and replay the scene to play out as they wish. The details of these images interest the perpetrator – who is there, how are they responding, where do they go?

When the satisfaction from the fantasies begins to wane, avengers will start to act on their ideas. They may begin with threats or milder forms of violence such as graffiti. Without confrontation, avengers will escalate behavior to more dangerous levels. Avengers usually have particular targets in mind, although they may take down many others in their violent rampage. This often is because they see themselves on a suicide mission and do not think they have anything to lose.

Relationship-Based

This form of violence is unfortunately the most common and frequently the most devastating. Relationship-based violence involves a one-on-one attachment that is exploited. Relationships that have both power differential and privacy are most vulnerable – parent-child, husband-wife, pledge master-pledge. In relationship-based violence, the dominant partner has an "ownership" mentality over the submissive partner. Because the submissive partner is perceived as property rather than a person of equal standing, the dominant partner employs certain strategies to ensure that "the property" is maintained under current control. Often these strategies employ violent tactics.

Group-Induced

Group-induced violence occurs when a group of individuals are swept into a mob mentality. Because the violent act is not the work of one individual, they feel that they are not as accountable. The phenomenon is known as *diffusion of responsibility*. The larger the group, the more anonymous they feel. Group-induced violence can be contagious, in that the excitement of the moment may overpower the better judgment of the onlookers who chose to participate when they would have normally not behaved in such a fashion. Bystanders play a critical role in group-induced violence. Many spectators will watch in fascination as a group begins to engage in violence. By not acting in a way to diffuse the situation, bystanders perpetuate the problem. Others perceive the inaction of bystanders as passive approval of the violent behavior. With more people now involved in perpetuating the violence, the chance for anonymity increases,

and more people join in. Group-induced violence is often trigger-driven, that is, ignited by an external event or stimulus.

Malevolent Insider and Malevolent Outsider

Avenger perpetrators on campuses can be broken down in to two major categories. We have labeled them **Malevolent Insider** and **Malevolent Outsider**. Malevolent insiders are those individuals college campuses have on their radar, meaning one or more individuals in the college community has observed an individual engaging in concerning behaviors. These behaviors could be witnessed by professors, campus police, mental health providers, students, or any people involved with the campus. A malevolent outsider is somebody who is not known to the campus. Which means the campus does not have any behavior knowledge of this individual. The signs are still there with the malevolent outsider; however the signs are not seen by any individuals within the campus community.

Case Examples: In addition to the Virginia Tech case, which will be examined in depth later on in this book, there are several other case examples of malevolent insiders and outsiders impacting our educational institutions.

COLUMBINE HIGH SCHOOL. On April 20, 1999 in Littleton, Colorado, Eric Harris and Dylan Klebold shot and killed 13 and wounded 24 others at their high school. It is one of the most notorious avenger cases and it is well documented that a large majority of avengers idealized Harris and Klebold before committing their own acts of terror.

The observable avenger behaviors and avenger developmental characteristics of Harris and Klebold were evident several years prior to the massacre. They developed a website in 1996 that included several postings throughout the next few years about their growing anger towards society in addition to threats to kill students and teachers at Columbine. The website further included updates as to their progress in obtaining weapons and making bombs as well as a growing "hit list." A student told his parents about the website and authorities were notified.

A warrant was drafted to search their houses but for reasons unknown, it never got filed. If a search would have taken place, numerous weapons and journals detailing their plan would have been found in their bedrooms and the horrifying events of April 20, 1999 could have been prevented. Harris and Klebold also made a movie about killing students for a school project.

Harris and Klebold are both considered malevolent insiders as a result of the numerous observable behavioral data that was evident before the shooting took place. This case exemplifies the unfortunate reality that numerous people, including teachers, students, parents of students, and law enforcement knew about Harris and Klebold's concerning behaviors; however, at that time, their was little if anything known about this type of violence happening in schools and as a result, Columbine and local law enforcement had no idea of nor the ability to contemplate the seriousness of their behaviors. Additionally, there was not much known about how to handle such situations.

This case did prompt a ramped desire in schools, law enforcement, mental health professionals, and communities to learn more about this type of violence and more importantly how to prevent it. It is regrettable that so many lives had to be lost and many more lives negatively affected by this tragedy to learn about this type of violence; however, the lessons learned from Columbine have been utilized to prevent similar act of violence, thus many lives have been saved.

PACIFIC LUTHERAN UNIVERSITY. On May 18, 2001, Donald Cowan walked onto the Pacific Lutheran campus heavily armed, killing two before shooting himself in the head. Documented evidence indicates that he did have a vengeance against a university employee; however, he had no connection to the university. Unless the employee reported his concerns about Cowan to university officials, assuming he was aware that Cowan had a grudge against him, this incident is an example of a malevolent outsider because the university had no behavioral data on Cowan.

APPALACHIAN SCHOOL OF LAW. On January 16, 2002 in Grundy, Virginia, 43-year-old, former student Peter Odighizuwa shot and killed two faculty members and one student while wounding three others before several other students restrained him. There were numerous reports of Odighizuwa's poor academic performance and he had previously left the program voluntarily. There is evidence that he had made threats during his attendance. The day the shooting occurred, he had discussed his academic problems with a professor and during the conversation, Odighizuwa made what could have been consider a veiled threat. He returned later that same day with a semiautomatic handgun and began his shooting spree. Odighizuwa is considered a malevolent insider because professors and students had been aware that he had made threats in the past.

DAWSON COLLEGE. On September 13, 2006, 25-year-old Kimveer Gill shot and killed two and injured 19 before dying by suicide as officers showed up on scene at the Dawson campus located in Montreal, Quebec. He would be considered a malevolent outsider because he was not affiliated with the college and there is no documented evidence to suggest that the college had any behavioral data on Gill. However, there was documented evidence of his avenger progression. He was an author of an online diary that over 600,000 people had visited prior to the massacre. He further referred to himself as the "Angel of Death" and in numerous postings, he expressed his admiration of the Columbine shooters and was known by others as being a big fan of the horrific video game "Super

Columbine Massacre RPG." Furthermore, one of Gill's screen names on the website was "fatality666." In his web postings, which several thousands read, there was obvious evidence of suicidal and homicidal ideation.

PLATTE CANYON HIGH SCHOOL. On September 27, 2006, in Bailey, Colorado, 53-year-old Duane Roger Morrison entered Platte Canyon High School claiming to have a bomb and took six female students hostage, sexually assaulting them before killing one. As the Jefferson County SWAT advanced, he was shot several times before he took his own life. Morrison had no connection to the school and consequently, the school had no data on him; therefore Morrison is labeled a malevolent outsider. Jefferson County SWAT's tactical response probably saved the lives of the other hostages.

NICKEL MINES. In October of 2006, in Bart Township, Pennsylvania, 32-year-old milk truck driver Charles Carl Roberts walked into an Amish schoolhouse and took several students hostage before shooting 10, killing five students before committing suicide. Along with his gun, he also had tools to tie down his victims as well as other items to be used during the planned sexual assault; however, there is no evidence that any of the victims were sexually assaulted. Documented evidence confirmed that Roberts has been planning the attacks for days and had left several suicide notes. Since the school had no knowledge of Rogers, he is another example of a malevolent outsider.

YOUTH WITH A MISSION AND NEW LIFE CHURCH. On December 9, 2007, Matthew Murray opened fire and killed two staff members and injured two others on the YWAM campus in Arvada, Colorado before escaping. The following day, after several postings on religious websites detailing his intentions of more killings, he opened fire at a the New Life Church in Colorado Springs, killing two more and wounding several others before being shot by Jeanne Assam, a church security

guard. While on the ground wounded, Murray took his own life. This Avenger case is unique from others in that Murray is considered a malevolent insider for the first incident and malevolent outsider for the second. Murray had been expelled a few years before for "strange behavior" and performing violent rock music at an YWAM function. Murray began sending "hate mail" in the weeks prior to the shooting, which is the foundation for labeling him a malevolent insider. However, there is no evidence that the New Life Church had any data on Murray. The FBI was notified of the violent postings hours before the second shooting spree and notified the Arvada Police Department; however, as Arvada agents were investigating the threatening messages, the second shooting spree began. Though two lives were taken during the shooting spree, Murray would have had the opportunity to kill many more if it were not for the quick actions taken by the security guard. This is an example of the unfortunate but realistic fact that malevolent outsiders typically will have already begun their brutal attacks before an interruption takes place. However, with malevolent outsiders a quick strategic response can minimize the body count and save many lives.

Strains of Campus Violence

Combinations of the previously-mentioned typologies make up the specific strains of violence in our society. College campuses seem to be particularly susceptible to the strains of violence introduced below. The subsequent chapters will explore these areas in more depth and suggest strategies for prevention and intervention.

Sexual Assault

While stranger rape usually falls under the typology of predatory violence, acquaintance rape is usually a combination of predatory and relationship-based violence. The Higher Education Center reports that between 15 percent and 30 percent of college women have experienced acquaintance rape at some point in their lives. Gang rape is a combination of predatory, relationship, and group-induced violence. Stranger rape and gang rape are rarer, but also occur on college campuses.

Hate Crimes

First Amendment rights are often exercised liberally on college campuses. Sometimes they are abused, as in the case of many hate crimes. Perpetrators of hate crimes intentionally seek victims based on perceived differences in race, ethnicity, gender, sexual orientation, or physical/mental ability. The Anti-Defamation League (ADL) suggests college campuses are fertile grounds for spreading hate. According to *Link, The College Magazine*, there has been a significant increase in hate crimes against Asian-Pacific Americans and the gay and lesbian communities on college campuses in the last couple of years. Another trend fueling the fire of hate is the use of the Internet. Currently, the ADL monitors hundreds of hate-filled websites. Hate crime can be considered its own violence typology, but it shares characteristics with group-induced violence and avenger characteristics. Many hate crimes are committed in groups and perpetrators often believe they are "evening the score" for an injustice done to them.

Rioting

In the 1960s, campus riots erupted over civil rights issues and war protests. On today's campuses, riots are erupting over football victories and alcohol restrictions. The damage costs schools and communities hundreds of thousands of dollars. Many times the drunken rioters proudly pose before cameras only to have that evidence used against them in court. While riots often appear spontaneous, sometimes students plan for them by stockpiling bonfire kindling and by freezing beer cans to throw at windows. In the East Lansing riot of March 1999, T-shirts were even printed days before the riot took place. Antiriot community coalitions are surfacing in the neighborhoods of schools where riots have happened. Riots are generally group-induced violence with the exception of the group leaders. For them, avenger and predator characteristics also exist.

Hazing

While hazing is usually associated with college students who join a fraternity or sorority, it also occurs in military schools and with athletes. In the past, colleges have often turned a blind eye toward hazing incidents by excusing them as "traditions" and "rites of passage." In the wake of lawsuits and new legislation, schools are taking hazing more seriously. One concern is that most states have recently passed antihazing laws. A large-scale NCAA-supported study in 1999 found that hazing of athletes is more common and more severe than many had previously acknowledged.[33] Seventy-nine percent of the over 2,000 survey responders indicated that they were subjected to team initiation behavior that was humiliating, alcohol-related, dangerous, or criminal. Hazing perpetration combines elements of relationship-based violence and group-induced violence.

Suicide

Suicide is the second leading cause of death for college students, and with the support from the Garrett Lee Smith Memorial Act funding the Federal Campus Suicide Prevention Grant Program, campuses are now developing comprehensive and strategic approaches to this public health problem.

Despite the advances of treatment – both talk therapy and medication – campuses continue to report increased concerns about deliberate self-harm and significant mental illness on campus. Campuses find themselves having to navigate a delicate balancing act between student privacy and disability rights and minimizing disruption to a community that is often not suited to be a mental health treatment facility.

Mental health advocates become increasingly concerned about witch hunts on campus in the aftermath of the shooting rampages, which all point to mental illness as a root cause of the problem. Responding to this issue, the Director of public policy from the National Coalition of Mental Health Consumer/Survivor Organizations stated, "Reacting with judgment and labeling, fueled by the media, perpetuates misinformation and is a disservice to us all."[34] A recently published study from the *American Journal of Public Health* stated that when violent crimes committed by people with mental illnesses capture media headlines, stereotypes are reinforced, when by contrast, research supports the fact the people with psychiatric disorders are much more likely to be victims of violent crime than the perpetrators of violence.[35]

As campuses react to perceived increased threat of violence when presented with a suicidal individual, some rush to disciplinary action rather than treatment, and this has proved problematic. The most widely known example involved Jason Nott and the George Washington University. Nott checked himself into a hospital after experiencing depression and suicidal thoughts, and within hours, the university informed him in a letter that his "endangering behavior" was a violation of the code of conduct. The case was settled out of court but lead to intense debate about what were "foreseeable dangers" and what is "reasonable care to protect."

Darby Dickerson, Vice President and Dean of the Stetson University College of Law lists six steps to take to help find the balance between student privacy and campus safety:[36]

1. Ensure that campus policies and standard operating procedures are aligned with state and federal laws.
2. Apprise faculty and other key stakeholders of the truth about privacy laws and policies that protect student information.
3. Provide training on the limits of confidentiality so that all understand that serious health and safety concerns take priority over other privacy policies.
4. Inform students about the conditions under which private information may be released.
5. Appreciate the fact that some campus employees, especially in the mental health field, answer to more stringent levels of confidentiality under law and professional ethical codes.
6. Examine the restraints of HIPAA and develop compliant protocols.

Finally, the wise words of Gary Pavela, honors faculty at the University of Maryland at College Park and author of *Questions and Answers on College Student Suicide: A Law and Policy Perspective* (College Administration Publications, 2006):

"...colleges should not dismiss troubled students first and ask questions later. There are better ways to prevent campus violence than trying to predict students' future behavior, including mental-health support and thoughtful, responsible risk assessment. While no panacea exists, there are helpful, proven strategies: (1) Focus on actual conduct, not stereotypes, fears, or predictions; (2) Recognize that suicide prevention is violence prevention; (3) Create a cross-functional threat-assessment team; and (4) Encourage student involvement."[37]

Nonsexual Assault, Homicide, and Other Forms of Campus Violence

Campus interpersonal violence includes murder, beating, kicking, punching, slapping, and other violent behaviors combining any number of violence typologies. The most common offenders of simple assault are male athletes and fraternity members, and most of these crimes are closely linked to alcohol abuse. Relationship or dating violence also falls into this category of nonsexual assault; however, the distinctions between this form of violence and sexual assault are often blurry. Avenger violence resulting in homicide also has been experienced on college campuses in the aftermath of perceived academic and social grievances. Other forms of campus violence include bombing and bomb threats, arson, and property damage.

HIDDEN EPIDEMIC OR OVERBLOWN CASE? PROBLEMS WITH CAMPUS STATISTICS

What is the true extent of campus violence? We are just beginning to understand. There are several reasons for our ignorance, some understandable, some inexcusable. The controversy surrounding the issues underlying this uncovering process is heated. On one hand, there are violence prevention advocates who declare that the public has a "right to know" what goes on at college and that campus officials are trying to hide the truth. On the other hand, there are college administrators who are tirelessly attempting to ensure statistics are accurately reported while being bombarded with a host of complicating factors.

To some extent the reason that campuses underreport violence is because victims of campus violence frequently do not report their crimes. For some, they fear that they are partly to blame for the violence. As in the case of acquaintance rape and hazing, alcohol is usually involved, as is some degree of consent to events leading up to the violence. For instance, rape victims are clearly not responsible for being raped, but many victims are filled with self-blame for putting themselves in risky situations. Others question why they consented to being kissed or fondled before being raped. Victims of hate crimes may experience their own internalized self-hatred and may see themselves as deserving of violence on some level. These issues muddy the waters for the victims deciding whether to act against violence or not.

A second reason victims of campus violence do not step forward is because of fear of retaliation. For many, the perpetrators of violence hold positions of power or are associated with powerful groups – popular students, athletic departments, and Greek leaders. The less powerful victims fear that their accusations may be at best dismissed and at worst punished. They may be cut from an athletic team, blackballed from a fraternity, marginalized, trivialized, or ostracized.

A third reason why victims do not report campus crimes is that they do not believe anything productive will come from stepping forward. They may have heard stories on their campus or on other campuses where violence was either swept under the carpet or dealt with by a mere slapping of wrists. All too often, victims of campus crime will transfer or drop out of school because of the undue pressure of the violence aftermath. This outcome does not seem to justify the months of investigation and public display of their lives that often accompanies our campus and criminal judicial proceedings.

The problems with underreported campus violence statistics, however, do not all rest on the shoulders of the victims. Violence prevention advocates claim that many campuses have fallen into a pattern of "don't ask, don't tell." In 1990, President Bush passed a law to try to change that pattern. The Campus Security Act, now known as the Jeanne Clery Act, requires all colleges and universities to release annual crime statistics to the public. The Clery family, survivors of campus violence victim Jeanne Clery, who pushed for this legislation, claim some schools still blatantly cover up reported crimes as a means of protecting public relations. Some schools withhold relevant crime information in the report at the request of families seeking privacy. Other schools do not list all campus crimes because they were not reported to campus security, but rather to offices of residence life or rape crisis centers. The Clerys found that some schools even renamed crime categories to avert reporting. For example, one school renamed "rape" as "advances without sanction." According to the Clerys, another tactic schools have employed is to call land surrounding the campus as "off-campus," thereby legally omitting crimes committed there.

When violence has occurred on a college campus, public statements by university officials are sometimes misleading or overly vague. The public record might state that an athlete "violated the student-athlete code of conduct" rather than calling the behavior "hazing" or "sexual assault." When the behavior is not directly labeled, the perpetrator is not truly held accountable and the public gets a distorted view of what is going on.

In 1997, the Clerys found 63 schools who were not in compliance with the reporting law. There were no consequences for these schools. In 1998, Congress passed an amendment to the law tightening up reporting obligations and increasing penalties for noncompliance. These changes went into effect during the summer of 2000, and schools are now receiving fines for noncompliance.

On the other side of the debate, many campus administrators state they are doing their best to comply with the laws and deeply resent the accusations that they are being intentionally misleading. Reporting officials on campuses adamantly state the laws are confusing, constantly under revision, and so detail-oriented that they become meaningless. Some claim that so much data is being generated, the purpose of the laws has been lost.

The lack of standardization with other law enforcement reports increases the complications. There are different definitions for crimes like sexual assault and different time frames to calculate the data (e.g., academic year or calendar year). This leads to multiple reports and confused interpreters.

Many campus administrators are highly frustrated with the idea that people who are on Capitol Hill can make sweeping decisions about how campuses will function without understanding how life works from the inside. Much controversy exists on who should report, what information gets reported, and how to maintain privacy of the victims.

Most campus officials agree that having an accurate picture of campus violence is in everyone's best interest. Because there is so much at stake when dealing with such highly charged issues, campuses have learned to partner together to look for solutions. These coalitions will hopefully bring increased consistency and a higher standard for violence prevention.

One controversial solution to the problem of gathering campus violence statistics is to have an objective party look at the data. Campuses are in a bind when they police themselves. On one hand, they have a duty to the institution they are protecting, and on the other, they have an obligation to uphold federal expectations. Sometimes these demands conflict and objectivity is compromised. Recently, an agency outside of higher education, APB news, began the task of predicting campus neighborhood crime risk. The system does not track actual crime, but estimates the risk of crime from a high-tech computer model that takes into account past crimes and socioeconomic data. The intent of the crime risk report was to give prospective students and their families comparative information about the rates of violence at various campus communities so that they can make informed decisions about the safety of those campuses. Their first published report in the fall of 1999 caused a great deal of controversy as schools that were poorly rated found APB's statistic gathering faulty and the report misleading.

Schools highly ranked for violence potential claimed that the risk of violence in the surrounding neighborhoods did not always reflect the level of violence within the campus. Nevertheless, it was a first attempt at someone outside the system of higher education attempting to report violence patterns in an unbiased fashion.

Because of these problems with our current statistics and reporting, we know we have just begun to scratch the surface of the truth about campus violence. As we begin to gain a clearer picture of what is going on, we will be better able to adapt our prevention and intervention efforts. For the most part, it is in everyone's best interest – institutes of higher education, students, families, and communities – to have a truthful picture of the nature of campus crime. The challenge that remains, however, is finding the best way to gather the pieces of the puzzle.

INSTITUTIONAL RESPONSES TO VIOLENCE STAGES OF IMPACT

A great deal of research has been conducted on individuals who undergo difficult changes in their lives. Quitting smoking, changing diet, and altering other lifestyle behaviors usually take a great deal of effort and failed attempts are as common as successful outcomes. James Prochaska and Carlo DiClemente have developed a trans-theoretical model for understanding individual change that we believe has relevance for institutions as well.[38] They call their model Stages of Change and describe the sequence of spiraling events that occur as an individual moves along a spiraling pathway from precontemplation (no change) to contemplation (thinking about change) to preparation to action to maintenance. The pathway spirals because often people need to repeat previous stages a few times in the process of moving forward.

When we look at stages of change or impact at an institutional level, the model still applies but becomes somewhat more complicated. Because the university or college is not a unified entity, different parts of the institution will move through these stages at different rates. Also, each strain of violence may be a different point along the pathway. For example, a college may have a very well developed strategy for dealing with sexual assault, but nothing in place to address hazing. A final drawback of "stage" models is that they assume everyone must pass through all of the stages. Thankfully, this is not the case. By sharing information and promising prevention strategies, campuses are able to help each other advance by jumping over earlier stages.

Denial or Precontemplation

At this stage, the institution of higher education is truly unaware of the problems of violence occurring. Perhaps, people have not reported the violence or potential reports have been discouraged. No one is assessing or addressing the problem, because it is thought not to exist.

Anger-Defensiveness

When people begin to come forward with information about violence, the initial reaction is often to find fault with the reporter or to otherwise discredit the information. Alleged rape victims are just trying to get back at perpetrators because they have morning-after regrets. Alleged hazing victims have sour grapes because they were not accepted into the group. Alleged hate crime victims are trying to get attention, more privileges, and so on.

Limbo

Limbo is the stage when, due to outside pressure, institutions can no longer deny or excuse away violence, but they do not know how to proceed. When increasing numbers of victims come forward, the mental gymnastics required to maintain denial become increasingly strenuous. For instance, when information was emerging about hazing, the initial response from some athletic departments was "That's a Greek thing, not an athletic thing." Then, "Well maybe it happens at other schools, but it doesn't happen here." Then, "Well I guess it happens on other teams, but not my players." Soon the evidence becomes overwhelming, and some level of problem contemplation emerges. The problem with the limbo stage is that resistance to acknowledging the violence still remains, so any attempt to address the problem is usually half-hearted. Quick-fix "Band-Aids" are applied in haste, usually more to show the public that "something is being done" rather than effective, comprehensive prevention. Very often, these attempts are phased out as soon as the public eye blinks.

Catalyst for Change

The catalyst for change is often an event, person, or group of people that show the true colors of the violence in a way that it cannot be ignored. The high-profile cases mentioned earlier provide many examples of catalyst events that forever changed the paths of their institutions of higher education. Fortunately, not every college has to experience a Matthew Shepard or a Corey LaTulippe to fully face issues of hate crimes or hazing. Strong grassroots groups can have similar effects to committed top-down leadership. The factor tipping the balance from inaction or ineffective action to appropriate action is commitment.

Action

When many sectors of a campus community become determined to change, action results. The predatory form of sexual assault is one area that many campuses have committed to addressing. Most people within the campus community accept the fact that sexual assault happens at college. Thus, educational prevention and self-defense programs now abound. Policy and enforcement have improved significantly. Environmental safety strategies are considerable. Action dealing with acquaintance and gang rape is also getting attention, but lags somewhat behind "stranger" rape interventions. Nevertheless, in many ways this form of violence leads the way in the development of a comprehensive prevention plan.

Maintenance

Change can be difficult to maintain, and maintenance is not static. In order for change to continue to be effective, ongoing assessment of the situation must be undertaken and fed back into the system. Modifications in the strategies must be made accordingly. Again, this usually involves widespread effort and commitment. Sometimes a relapse into old patterns is inevitable, and the pattern of change recycles.

Chapter 2

VIOLENCE 101:
UNDERSTANDING THE BASICS

JOHN NICOLETTI & SALLY SPENCER-THOMAS

THE PURPOSE OF THIS CHAPTER is to give you a basic understanding of the elements of violence. In the latter chapters, we go into detail about how the various types of campus violence differ from each other. Here we draw on the similarities. We begin with some basic definitions of violence and then describe who are the participants in acts of violence. From there we outline a general formula for violence – what are the critical elements necessary for combustion – and we conclude with some ideas to keep in mind when responding to violence.

DEFINING VIOLENCE

Campus violence expert Dr. Mary Roark, former chair of the American College Personnel Association Commission I Task Force on Campus Violence, is an advocate for clear definitions. In the book *Campus Violence: Kinds, Causes, and Cures* (1993), she states, "once we name something, we can move beyond vagueness to clarity that favors efforts at prevention and control. Words are powerful, and naming gives us an ability to describe, to discuss, to understand, and to eventually make changes."[39] Dr. Roark goes on to make the case that before the terms "acquaintance rape," "sexual harassment," and "dating violence"

became recognized terms, people had a difficult time discussing and advocating for the prevention of these problems.

Some violence experts cited in Dr. Roark's writing define violence broadly and include not only physical acts but also verbal, psychological, symbolic, and spiritual attacks.[40] Clearly, violence exists on a continuum and all of these realms are affected; however, clarity is lost with definitions so broad. Other dimensions of violence to consider are (1) is the act of violence one of commission or omission? (2) is the act of violence offensive or defensive? and (3) is the act of violence covert or overt? We have chosen to endorse Dr. Roark's definition of violence for its simplicity and comprehensiveness: Violence is behavior that by intent, action, and/or outcome harms another person.

While violence can be both physical and verbal, we have chosen to focus mostly on the physical aspects of violence in this book. Thus, topics such as sexual harassment and intellectual violence will not be covered here. Violence against property such as vandalism also falls outside the scope of our definition, but may be an important warning sign for impending violence. In addition, many have considered suicide as a form of violence. While suicide is definitely a violent act, harm-to-self falls outside our definition of violence and thus, will also not be discussed here. Threats are another aspect of violence discussed in Chapter 5.

Even though there are many different forms of violence, common dynamics exist among them. By definition, violence has a perpetrator and victim or victims, and most premeditated violence follows predictable steps.

CAST OF CHARACTERS

The "cast of characters" are the people or groups of people usually involved in the act of violence or the response to it. This section is adapted from our previous works *Violence Goes to Work* (1997) and *Violence Goes to School* (2002).[41]

Targets

Targets of violence are the victims. In violence that impacts property, targets can also be buildings or cars. Targets can be intended or by chance; primary, secondary, or tertiary.

Victims of Choice

Victims of choice are chosen by the perpetrator for a reason. The reason may be revenge, easy access, or the victim's likeness to a violent fantasy. Ted Bundy chose women for his victims fitting a particular physical appearance. Avenger perpetrators will often choose the object of their revenge as their targets – professors, supervisors, or judicial officers. Rapists might look for the most impaired woman at the party. All these perpetrators systematically seek a particular victim or victim qualities to carry out their violent behavior.

Victims of Opportunity

Victims of opportunity are often in the wrong place at the wrong time. Rioting usually involves victims of opportunity. The rioters do not have any ill will toward the neighbors and businesses in their path, but the local people often suffer the most damages. Suicidal perpetrators sometimes take out victims of opportunity in their final act of violence believing they have nothing to lose. Sometimes well-meaning individuals who place themselves in the path of the perpetrator in hopes of deterring his or her progress end up being victims of opportunity.

Primary Victims

Primary victims are those individuals who have experienced the violence directly.

Secondary Victims

Secondary victims are the roommates, friends, witnesses, parents, rescue personnel, and others involved but not directly impacted by the violence. These secondary victims are often overlooked in trauma recovery efforts, but many of them may experience a posttraumatic response that is very upsetting.

Tertiary Victims

Tertiary victims are the helpers who also become affected by the violent event. In the aftermath of a violent incident, counselors may be flooded with individuals in crisis, needs for debriefing sessions, and requests for consultation. At the same time, these professionals may be dealing with their own reactions to the trauma. They also may be vicariously affected by listening to story after story from the survivors. In some cases, counselors may internalize another's pain and become overwhelmed. As a result, they may experience similar nightmares and distressing thoughts as their clients.

Perpetrators

Perpetrators are those who commit the act of violence. Contrary to popular belief, most violence on campus is not perpetrated by outside strangers descending on an otherwise safe environment. In fact, most campus violence experts agree that the overwhelming majority of violent incidents are perpetrated by students.

In the early 1990s, researchers at Pennsylvania State University asked residence hall staff what type of perpetrators committed the most serious offense in their careers.[42] The RAs responded: 80 percent residents; 6 percent guests; 8 percent unidentified; and 6 percent unknown visitors.

As you will see from ample case examples in this book, the overwhelming number of perpetrators of campus violence are students. But there are definitely cases involving strangers, faculty and staff, and students' loved ones.

Protectors

Protectors are those on campus who do what is in their power to prevent violent incidents from occurring or intervene when violent events are unfolding. All campuses have a security force or a sworn police department providing professional protection. But protectors also include residence life staff, often the first-line responders to campus violence. Coaches, faculty, and others frequently find themselves in situations where they are called upon to intercept violent threats or console victims in the aftermath of violence.

Bystanders

Historically, bystanders have not received a great deal of attention for their role in perpetrating and preventing violence. Regardless of their true feelings about the violent behavior, the silent presence of bystanders has a strong influence in continuing a violent incident. When bystanders do not stand up and confront perpetrators, their silence is interpreted as tacit approval of the actions taking place. The more people the perpetrator thinks support him or her, the more likely the violent act will continue. Most bystanders are fearful of stepping forward and getting involved because they fear they will become the next target of the perpetrator or peers will perceive them as a tattletale.

Bystanders play a critical role in campus rioting. Usually only a handful of instigators are needed to start a riot, but the hordes of curious on-lookers keep it going. The more bystanders present in a riot, the more intense the riot becomes and the more difficult it becomes for law enforcement to intervene. The sheer mass of bystanders becomes a roadblock insulating the violence.

Even though they usually are not physically present during violent acts of sexual assault, bystanders have a role in this crime as well. Bystanders can support attitudes that lead to sexual assault by linking sexual behavior to conquests and talking about potential partners as objects. Violence prevention experts from the Mentors in Violence Prevention (MVP) Program focus on these bystanders in their intervention efforts. They hold all-male workshops, usually through athletic teams, and talk to the men about what they will do if, for example, they hear or see a teammate sexually harass a woman.

FORMULA FOR VIOLENCE

In order for violence to occur, several factors must be present. The perpetrator or perpetrators must believe that access to the target is feasible. The assailant must have either an external catalyst or an internal emotional reaction that triggers the decision to act. Perpetrators must have the physical and mental ability to carry out the act, as well as ample time to complete the violent act. The formula used to assess the possibility of violence is identified by the acronym TOADS. This acronym stands for:

- Time
- Opportunity
- Ability
- Desire
- Stimulus

(Adapted from *Violence Goes to Work* and *Violence Goes to School*[43])

Each of these factors can be assessed and impacted by frontline responders (e.g., other students, professors, or security personnel), administration, or the outside professionals who assess the dangerousness of the situation. The components of this acronym are explained as follows:

Time

This refers to the time necessary for perpetrators to complete an act of violence. Violent individuals must have ample time to formulate and design a plan, overcome any inhibitions to engage in violence, gain access to the intended victim or victims, and execute the act. Protectors can remove the time factor from the equation by responding quickly to threats and other lower-level inappropriate behaviors.

Opportunity

Opportunity provides the chance or opening allowing the perpetrator access to the target. Often individuals can disable opportunities through swift intervention. Sometimes they are not even aware that they are doing so. In those instances where an individual can identify a potential perpetrator, security should attempt to control access to the campus. Campus safety officials accomplish this by posting a photograph of the suspect at entryways and, in cases of severe threat, calling for additional outside security.

Ability

The level of threat increases in direct proportion to the perpetrator's ability to commit a violent act. This involves both the requisite physical expertise and mental capability to formulate and execute a plan of action. When assessing a potential perpetrator's ability, one must take into account intelligence, creativity, experience with and access to weaponry, organizational skills, desensitization to violence, and hand-eye coordination.

Desire

The willingness to inflict injury or death on a person, or damage to property, must be present at a serious level in order for violence to occur. The desire usually builds within many violent individuals to the point that they perceive it as overwhelming, and they feel a sense of urgency to act out violently. The time frame during which this desire builds may be a matter of minutes or years depending on the situation.

For premeditated violence, revenge is a common theme. Like the avenger profile mentioned in Chapter 1, perpetrators who feel powerless often concoct elaborate fantasies of revenge. In these fantasies, they develop the details of the victims, witnesses, times, places, and the actual dynamics of the violent act. This fantasy becomes for them a primary coping mechanism and their ability to problem solve is increasingly narrowed. The satisfaction they receive from these thoughts only goes so far. Many perpetrators eventually act on their revenge fantasies. Threats, vandalism, and cruelty to animals are common before they attack their intended targets. In the end, the desire to act upon their fantasy becomes a mission.

Stimulus

The stimulus is the event, or series of events, which acts as internal or external triggers for the violence. The stimulus precipitates the violence, and can sometimes be anticipated, allowing protectors time to implement a prevention plan.

RESPONDING TO VIOLENCE

Pollyanna Versus Paranoia

The thought of violence occurring on a college campus is so distressing that many people respond in one of two extreme ways: Pollyanna or paranoia. Pollyanna responders see the world through rose-colored glasses. They believe in the inherent goodness of people and want to instill values of open-mindedness and acceptance. These responders are likely to believe, perhaps subconsciously, that if they do not talk about violence, it will not exist. This approach creates a situation where people naively enter dangerous situations without the awareness or skills to keep themselves safe. By contrast, paranoid responders are overly sensitive to the dangers of the world, and would prefer to keep schools in lockdown. Individuals under the guidance of these paranoid types are apt to rebel against the precautions, or become immobilized with fear.

People should be able to talk about violence in a realistic and balanced way. Given today's trend toward increased violence, protectors must consider violence preparation as important as fire prevention or other disaster preparedness. Most people do not think that disaster preparedness is over reactive or destructive. Each campus community will need to decide for themselves where they fall on the continuum from Pollyanna to paranoia and respond with interventions that best fit their culture.

One-Way Ticket

Responding to violence is a one-way ticket. Once you have implemented an intervention, you cannot go backwards. As mentioned earlier, there are defining events that change the fabric of our culture – airline terrorists, razor blades in apples, product tampering. These events cause "fence posts" or protective action to occur. Once the fence posts go up, they

cannot come down. Imagine how people would respond if tomorrow the Federal Aviation Administration declared that security measures were excessive and resources were better spent in other areas. Most people would be extremely concerned about airline safety.

Over time, security measures become safety signals. People see an armed guard at a bank and feel confident that robbers will choose to go elsewhere. Most people feel insecure when driving a car without a seat-belt fastened, even if it is just across a parking lot. Effective security measures provide a barrier between a potential victim and perpetrator, but none guarantees safety. Nevertheless, once a fence post goes up, it stays up.

Overreacting and Not Reacting Strongly Enough

Sometimes people worry that they are overreacting to a situation. Academically minded individuals tend to value trust and personal freedom. They become concerned about the ramifications of false positives. What if someone was identified as a potential perpetrator and he or she never meant to harm anyone? Would reputations be harmed? Would the wrongly accused sue? What if schools delegate resources to preventing violence, and the efforts are not warranted?

The truth is, protectors will never know if they have overreacted; they will only know if they haven't reacted strongly enough. In other words, if protectors take precautions and violence never occurs, they will never know – was prevention effective or was violence never going to occur in the first place? Effective protectors need to take those calculated risks when warning signs are present. They need to feel comfortable with the possibility of false positives.

The only workplace that consistently exercises a zero tolerance for threats of violence is the airline industry. Anyone who is even hinting at possible violence is taken seriously.

Thousands of false positives occur everyday. For some it is an inconvenience or a small embarrassment. Most find it reassuring that the airline takes these matters so seriously.

Giving Permission

An important part of responding to violence is to give the campus community permission to do what they need to do to keep safe without inflicting further harm. This may seem self-evident, but when violence plays out, breaking through these psychological barriers proves to be difficult for many. For instance, when training school children in how to respond during a school shooting, students became concerned that leaving the school building would get them in trouble because they had always been taught that as the rule. Generally speaking, we are rule-bound creatures. We may think twice in our evacuation efforts before going through an emergency-only door. We may hesitate before breaking a window while trying to escape. Students and campus employees must believe that if they act in good faith while trying to keep themselves or others safe, they will not be held accountable for breaking campus rules.

Planting Trees

Another metaphor useful in understanding violence prevention and intervention is to think of the violent individual as a skier. As perpetrators start down the "hill" of becoming violent, most tend to start slowly and build up speed. Sometimes they start with low-level threats or vandalism to test out how the system will respond. They continue to escalate until they hit a "tree" or barrier in their path.

Trees come in all shapes and sizes. Trees can be questioning. Sometimes the investigation process is enough deterrence. Confronting trees ups the ante. A warning is a confrontation tree. A security system is a confrontation tree. A police barricade is a confrontation tree. The next level of trees consists of implementing consequences. A range of consequences exists from probation to community service to suspension or expulsion/termination. Legal consequences are also an option.

Some trees perpetrators can see for quite a distance away and are easily averted. Some trees are easily identified as mirages, nothing real but just a symbol for others to see. Perpetrators sail right through these trees. Other trees are so large that perpetrators know they will not get around them, so perpetrators stop on their own. For those perpetrators determined to get down the hill, protectors must plant many trees to slow down the perpetrator. Most of the chapters of this book give readers ample suggestions on how they can plant effective trees.

Chapter 3

VULNERABLE TO INFECTION: RISKS TO COLLEGE COMMUNITIES

SALLY SPENCER-THOMAS & JOHN NICOLETTI

[Students] come to college in part for freedom and a sense of belonging, and a locked-down campus runs counter to that lifestyle.

– Report from D. Marcus, *U.S.
News & World Report*, 2/20/2000.

The dilemma faced by [college campuses] is similar to that faced by inner-city churches. Efforts to insulate the campus from intrusive crime and violence defeat its purpose as an interactive, societal resource.

– John Schuh,
Violence on Campus, p. 19.[44]

CAMPUSES STRIVE TO PROJECT an impression to the community and prospective applicants. Among other things, campuses want to appear friendly, accessible, and community-oriented. Most campuses operate as both a workplace and a home to thousands of people. Sometimes these dual roles can come into conflict when issues of safety are of concern. Because of these and other unique features of the campus environment, values, people, and traditions, many colleges are vulnerable to violence. Campus violence experts such as John Schuh of Iowa State University and Mary Roark of State University of New York College at Plattsburgh have written about such vulnerabilities, and we draw from their observations and add our own. We call these factors the setting, the psyche, the society, the substances, and the sacred cows.

THE SETTING

Campuses are often caught in the crossroads between making their campuses welcoming and making their campuses safe. In their effort to make their environments welcoming, certain safety hazards are inevitable.

Access

Most campuses want their facilities and grounds to appear pleasant and friendly to their employees, students, and visitors. Guidebooks frequently feature color photos of people walking in and out of pleasant looking buildings and strolling through open walkways. While access to buildings and campus grounds might not actually be that easy, the pictures are generally accurate.

Who is to say who belongs on campus and who does not? When we consider the number of people who can walk onto the campus grounds with a legitimate reason for being there, the numbers can be staggering. Current students and current staff clearly come and go at will. Prospective students can also drop in at any time. Consider too the number of former students and former staff, friends and family members of all of the above, and the list goes on exponentially. Any number of these individuals can descend upon a campus without any prior warning, at any time. Colleges usually make some facilities like libraries and fitness centers open to the public as a way to build ties with the local community. Thus, the campus doors are more or less open to all who want to enter. These features are fairly unique to the college setting. The permeable boundaries of the campus make predator infiltration all too easy.

Despite residence hall and security attempts to restrict access to buildings, it is an impossible task to monitor the constant ebb and flow of people. Students often rebel against security locks and codes on their residence halls and will frequently prop the doors open with whatever they can find. Propped doors make student life convenient, but they pose challenges for safety.

Permanence of Location

One unique feature of the campus setting is that most campuses cannot relocate. Given the expensive and specialized infrastructure, few would want to purchase campus property for other types of businesses. Furthermore, many campuses build their identity in part from their surroundings. Relocating the campus would most definitely change the climate of the school. The downside of the permanence of campus location is that if the criminal activity in the neighborhoods surrounding the campus increases, the campus is stuck.

At Regis University in Denver, Colorado, houses in adjacent neighborhoods began showing signs of gang activity. Graffiti tags were seen spray painted on walls. Concerned about the safety of the school, campus officials decided to erect a black iron fence around the perimeter of the campus. As an obstacle, the fence did possibly deter graffiti from migrating onto campus buildings. As a symbol to the community, it set up barriers between the campus and the neighborhood, an indication that the surrounding families were not welcome on the other side of the fence.

Hours of Operation

Colleges operate 24 hours a day, 365 days a year. The day is not over when classes are finished. Sports events, concerts, evening programs, all-night study sessions, and parties keep much of the college community out and about on the campus grounds long after most workplaces are locked down for the night. Even faculty and staff are known to work long hours, often isolated in their offices. Much of the student-related violence occurs during these evening and weekend hours when professional staff such as counselors and administrators may be less accessible.

Predictability

Another environmental vulnerability is that colleges operate on a predictable schedule. Anyone trying to target an individual or group of people would have an easy time anticipating the location. In the Columbine massacre, this predictability factor was a crucial element in the perpetrator's planning. They timed their siege on the high school to correspond to the time when the greatest number of people would be congregating in the cafeteria and library. The movement of college students and staff can be similarly foreseen.

Throughout the year, the activity on college campuses also ebbs and flows in predictable ways. Holidays, summer vacation, and spring breaks usually bring a lull of activity on campuses. Because there is not as much commotion to attend to, people are more likely to let their guard down.

Perhaps the greatest predictable phase of vulnerability for college campuses is the first few weeks of school. During that time, a large group of new faces, mostly young and inexperienced in the world, descend upon unfamiliar territory. A great number of these students are living away from home for the first time; many have not yet learned the social cues for danger; they have not had experiences to figure out how to handle an emergency; and they do not know how to set limits on alcohol consumption. Many parents and school staff hold their breath during this time, in the hopes that the students will successfully negotiate these weeks without incident.

Crowding

Crowded residences make adjustment to college life very difficult for many students. Most are not used to sharing bathrooms with dozens of people and become annoyed over the lack of privacy residence halls offer. Even within the rooms, personal space is limited and irritates those who are used to having their own rooms.

With crowding comes noise. Even with designated "quiet hours," noise is a continuous problem in most campus residences. Students who like their music loud at 2:00 A.M. neglect to consider their neighbors who are studying for their organic chemistry test the next day. Disruption to sleep due to fire alarms in the middle of the night angers this group who tend to be sleep deprived most of the time anyway.

Parking on most campuses can be another trigger for rage. Students tend to outnumber parking spaces and the race to find the space before the 9:00 A.M. exam begins makes blood boil. Mini campus road rage clashes erupt as they cut each other off. When drivers get creative by parking in nondesignated areas, the tickets they receive do not do much to quell the anger.

THE PSYCHE

Certain values of an academic institution may place individuals at a greater risk for danger. Colleges tend to foster trust, respect, independence, freedom of expression, and debate. Under certain circumstances these attributes become catalysts for violence. To be clear, these values are assets to campuses, and to discourage their existence would alter campus life for the worse. They do, however, open opportunities for violence that do not exist in institutions where these beliefs are not as widely held.

Unlike other institutions, trust is cultivated on college campuses. Trust is essential when people who have never met each other are forced to share a living space. There is also a general feeling on most campuses of being a community where everyone is expected to treat their neighbors as they would want to be treated. When new faces appear on campus, most witnesses do not think much about it and trust that these people have a legitimate reason for being there.

If someone is questioned about the whereabouts of another person, they are usually not suspicious of the motive and will give the needed location without thought. When partying together, students trust that fellow students will not hurt them because they are all just out to have a good time. Trust is an asset in most instances on college campuses. Living in such confined quarters would be difficult without it. But when a person decides to become violent, the trust factor works in the perpetrator's favor.

Most schools have a code of conduct for both students and staff that stresses personal integrity and accountability. Campus community members are expected to uphold a standard of behavior that is representative of the mission of the school. They expect to be treated with honor and respect, and when these codes are broken it often comes as a shock to the recipient.

In classrooms and many staff meetings on college campuses differing points of view are encouraged and valued. Diverse perspectives make discussions lively and creative ideas are brought to fruition. Debate and controversy are not suppressed. The First Amendment rights are expressed freely in most cases. Sometimes, however, the topics become too hot and peaceful protests turn angry and violent. Sometimes, First Amendment rights are abused and hate crimes result.

Independence and personal freedom are strongly held values on college campuses. Students experiment widely with personal choices involving appearance, sexual behavior, alcohol, and drugs. And when these choices are not harming other people, many faculty and staff are reluctant to step in the way. Even when personal choices run the risk of self-harm, the value of personal freedom is so strong that people who are in a position to make a difference often look the other way. Faculty members are sometimes the greatest upholders of personal freedom. They will see students drag themselves to their 8:00 A.M. class hungover day after day, but they will not confront them because they believe it is not their place to confront this choice of self-abuse.

While security is important, it is not the main mission of most campuses. Therefore, it is understandable why some security measures take a backseat to the above-mentioned values. Nevertheless, the campus community should be aware of the many ways traditional campus values place them at risk for opportunities for violence.

THE SOCIETY

The campus society is comprised of a diverse group of individuals with varying backgrounds and goals. Students, faculty and staff, and community members all contribute to the tapestry of campus life. And each group potentially brings a threat to campus safety.

Students

By far, those most at risk for becoming victims and perpetrators of violence are the traditional age students. According to the Higher Education Center for Alcohol and Drug Prevention, students perpetrate 70 percent of violent incidents on campuses. These individuals face significant developmental challenges during a time when things are changing all around them. For many, they either learn to develop effective coping strategies, or they begin to develop dysfunctional patterns that will impact their future.

Some violence experts have suggested the increase in high school violence, specifically high-profile school shootings, is an additional risk factor to consider on college campuses. In *Schools, Violence and Society*, A. M. Hoffman calls this trend a "rising tide of violence" in America's elementary and secondary schools, and suggests this rising tide may be spilling over onto college campuses.[45] Others argue that there are enough filtering processes in place that weed out these types of violent offenders from ever reaching campus grounds. In any event, the wave of violent shootings in schools across America has emotionally impacted incoming freshmen in a different way than previous classes have had to deal with, and these students are possibly more aware of potential violence than their predecessors.

Developmental Issues

Adolescents often behave as though they are invulnerable. As children, we often take at face value what authorities have told us is dangerous. As adults, we have often experienced enough negative consequences to know how to make better decisions for ourselves. As adolescents, there is a drive for many to test out what we have been told is true and to believe that we will live forever.

Even when tragedy strikes, such as a drunk-driving fatality, many students still believe that it will never happen to them. Too often in the aftermath of an unexpected, violent campus tragedy, a brief period of shock is followed by a gradual slide back into denial. In one case we experienced firsthand, a popular, well-liked student had died as a result of alcohol-induced recklessness on a spring break trip. The campus experienced significant grieving. However, the way some students chose to grieve seemed incongruous to the tragedy. A small group of his friends chose to celebrate his life by getting drunk at the local bars.

Freed from the constant supervision of parents, many college students spend a great deal of time exploring areas that were previously forbidden. Alcohol and sex usually top this list. As students attempt to figure out what role they want alcohol and sex to have in their lives, many struggle with setting limits. The combination of these exploratory pursuits can sometimes have unwanted outcomes resulting in many forms of sexual assault and alcohol-related violence.

College is a stressful time. Much of the stress is because students have large amounts of unstructured time and multiple long-term demands, and they have not learned appropriate time management skills. In addition to time management, many are dealing with financial strains and must juggle one or more jobs on top of their demanding academic schedule. A recent report of the American Freshmen Survey, a collaborative project between the American Council on Education and UCLA's Higher Education Research Institute, found that 30 percent of freshmen are

feeling "frequently overwhelmed" at college. These stress levels have almost doubled since the researchers first conducted this survey in 1985. Grades constantly remind students of their status in their goal to obtain their degree. Each unsatisfactory evaluation given reminds them that their dreams may go unfulfilled. The process of chasing this dream can often seem ethereal.

Many students are poor regulators of stress. They switch into "all-or-nothing mode." Rather than find a way to balance their lives, letting their engine idle at a steady pace, students often slam on the accelerator then the brake then the accelerator then the brake. They avoid studying all semester and then stay up for four consecutive nights. They do not drink all week, and then feel they "deserve" to get outrageously intoxicated on the weekend.

Being "on-schedule" versus "off-schedule" can add to feelings of stress and self-doubt. When students progress in college as anticipated, finishing a four-year program in four years, they are considered "on-schedule." This progress is no longer the norm. Students switch majors, take time off to work or travel and experience medical and emotional setbacks that often delay graduation anywhere from one semester to several years. This sense of being "off-schedule" is difficult for many. They become out of sync with their friends, school debts accumulate, and the destination of reaching a degree and prosperous career feels out of reach.

Transitory Population

For the most part, college students are a transitory population during their time at school. Most will not stay in one residence for more than one year, and sometimes students relocate several times in one year. Because of their short-term relationship with these residences and to a lesser extent, the college, students provide less consideration for the long-term effects of their behavior on the campus environment.

Rioting and vandalism are prime examples of this lack of consideration. Many get caught up in the excitement and do not think about the effect the destruction will have on those who have longer-term commitments to the institution and surrounding community. East Lansing residents for example spent many years in conflict with Michigan State University students who rioted in the community. Many townspeople criticized the students for their lack of respect for the people who lived there.

Dealing with Diversity

One of the biggest transitions for new students is dealing with diversity. Campuses tend to be diverse places, and differences often bring conflict. Students often come from homogeneous communities with cultures they knew and understood. When they arrive on campus, they are thrown together with students from around the country and the world, who look and act in very different ways. Intolerance for certain groups may have been supported in their home cultures, but is not supported on college campuses. Coming to terms with these differences can be challenging for some students. Some may choose to subvert to hate crimes as their way of dealing with the uncomfortable feelings this process brings them.

Different cultures also have varying norms for acceptable behavior. This includes violent behavior. What may be an innocuous gesture in one culture may offend another. What may seem like strong discipline in one culture is considered violence in another. Raised voices and heated arguments may be common in one culture and a signal for danger in another. These differences make developing a common language about violence difficult.

Many campuses offer special housing options for students. From Greek residences, to substance-free housing, to international students, to families, these residences are designed for the purpose of bringing like-minded individuals together to share common experiences. Sometimes, however, this plan backfires when "in-group, out-group" polarization evolves. This divergence leads to increased misunderstanding and segregation of the groups.

A Word about "Nontraditional" Students

While an explosion of "nontraditional" students has erupted in the last decade, this population still represents a minority of students. According to the book *Violence on Campus*, the "typical" nontraditional student is a woman, over age 30, who is a part-time student and a commuter.[46] Nontraditional students are less likely to get involved in social activities that revolve around alcohol. In fact, nontraditional students actually spend little time on campus outside of classes due to the many other obligations they juggle. These students tend to be very concerned about family finances and their children.

For these and other reasons, nontraditional students are less likely to be either perpetrators or victims of campus violence. Nevertheless, nontraditional students, like faculty and staff, may experience violence at home that will clearly affect their campus life and academics. In some cases, violent partners may follow students to school and stalk or attack them there. In addition to being affected by violence in the home and in the general community, nontraditional students are also affected by the violence perpetrated and inflicted upon their traditional-aged peers.

One other issue to consider is the fact that some students have had violent histories, including arrests and jail time, before enrolling in college. In Chapter 7, we discuss legal issues and policy implications in more depth. There we explore the difficult decisions schools have had to face denying or accepting the enrollment of known felons, even murderers. To complicate matters further, individuals who committed violent crimes in their youth often have their records sealed and admissions may not gain access to these important potential violence indicators. Nevertheless, colleges that cater to nontraditional students are finding themselves facing these issues as those who have served jail time attempt to start a new life. Comprehensive databases do not exist giving schools pre-enrollment violence statistics for nontraditional students, so the true extent of the problem remains speculative.

One hot topic that has emerged since our last edition is the establishment of the 2000 Campus Sex Crimes Prevention Act that provided for the tracking of convicted, registered sex offenders enrolled as students at institutions of higher education or working or volunteering on campus. Those who were opposed to the registry laws are concerned about the violation of due process and possible double jeopardy for a punishment already served. However, because sex offenders are more likely to reoffend than other violent crimes, lawmakers often feel this treatment is justified.

Brett Sokolow,[47] a leader in campus violence and the president of the National Center for Higher Education Risk Management, states that campuses view the registered sex offender as a fox in a henhouse and recommends that those who have been convicted of violent sex offenses use the option of online distance education to remove the temptation of a residential population.

Faculty and Staff

Colleges and universities are workplaces, and like other workplaces they are not immune to workplace violence issues such as the disgruntled employee and the vengeful student. In Chapter 14 on homicide and physical assault, two high-profile cases of workplace violence are described – one involving a professor who murdered his colleagues, and the other a graduate student who murdered his professors. Both perpetrators were "avenger" types; harbored injustices turned to blind rage.

University faculty and staff are not immune from the issues of domestic violence. Employers of many types of workplaces have come to the realization that violence that starts at home can often follow employees to work. In rare, but terrifying cases, male perpetrators stalk and sometimes even kill their girlfriends or wives in the workplace. According to the Family Violence Prevention Fund, approximately 13,000 acts of domestic violence against women occur in the workplace each year. When women attempt to protect themselves by moving to a shelter or changing their phone number, their partners still know where to find them eight hours a day.

Universities may have difficulty preventing this type of violence because victims of domestic violence usually do not come forward voluntarily with their concerns. Instead, supervisors can sometimes pick up on cues that domestic violence is occurring from increased absenteeism, clothing worn to conceal bruises, or incessant harassing phone calls from the partner.

Faculty members are especially vulnerable targets on college campuses. They are usually very accessible and predictable, having open office hours and regular class schedules. Faculty members often work in isolated areas and sometimes work late into the night. In contrast to senior leaders of major corporations, faculty are on-site and do not have frontline buffers of administrative staff to work as gatekeepers for their visitors. Faculty members are also common targets of anger as they control major decisions in students' lives. Therefore, grading and exam time can be vulnerable times for faculty safety if there is a particular student who has given them trouble during the year.

Surrounding Community

As mentioned earlier, the campus community involves the larger society in which it resides. Athletic events, concerts, museum exhibits, special lectures, theater performances all bring community members on campus in large groups and as individuals. Outside guests are often invited to campus too as speakers, conference attendees, or for other programs hosted on campus grounds. For the most part, colleges and the towns they live in enjoy a symbiotic relationship – each benefits greatly from the other. But sometimes the outside community can perpetrate extensive violence on campuses and vice versa.

Rioting on campuses is an example of this problem. A large number of individuals engaged in the campus rioting were either from visiting schools or the community. Some of these individuals might even have had feelings of revenge motivating their attacks on campus property. Students from a visiting campus who are present to watch a sporting event might perpetrate violence in the case of an upset or even a victory.

"Pre-frosh" or students who visit during their senior year of high school to become acquainted with the campus are sometimes very vulnerable to violence. In an effort to show them a good time, many college hosts offer these often-inexperienced drinkers large amounts of alcohol. In their naivete, some of the female high school students can find themselves in dangerous acquaintance rape situations while they are totally unfamiliar with the campus and security resources.

THE SUBSTANCES

Because the next chapter is dedicated to the relationship of alcohol abuse and campus violence, we will just underscore the issue briefly here. Alcohol is a prime catalyst to most forms of campus violence. Clearly, there is not a cause-and-effect relationship. Many people get drunk and do not inflict violence, and many people who are not drunk do cause harm to others. Nevertheless, alcohol has biological and social effects on people that increase the probability that violence will occur to individuals under its influence.

Besides alcohol, other drugs can also contribute to campus violence. Much of the relevant literature from the past three decades has been comprehensively reviewed by Robert Parker and Kathleen Auerhahn in their 1998 publication *Alcohol, Drugs, and Violence* and has served as the basis for much of this section.[48] Adapting from one resource cited in this work, there are three ways in which drug use may be causally related to violence:

- "DRUG" or Psychopharmacological Violence is related to the actual chemically induced properties of the drug itself. Drugs can cause agitation and paranoia in a perpetrator, and can also cause sedation and memory loss in victims.
- "SET" or User-Based Violence encompasses internal expectations or needs of the user. One example of this form of violence is economically motivated crimes. Illicit drugs often are expensive, and because of this, users may often engage in other illegal behaviors to obtain the drugs. Others may use drugs to drum up a false sense of courage before committing a violent act.
- "SETTING" or Culturally Influenced Violence is violence shaped by expectations or traditions of the social group using the drug separate from the actual effect of the drug. Of these three factors, the setting is often the most powerful predictor of violence. Parker and Auerhahn conclude, "Our review of the literature finds a great deal of evidence that the social environment is a much more

powerful contributor to the outcome of violent behavior than are pharmacological factors associated with any of the substances reviewed here."[49]

Illicit drugs affect judgment and emotions in different ways. When individuals are under the influence of mind-altering substances, their ability to find alternative ways of coping in social situations can become limited. Some users of drugs rationalize under-the-influence behavior as being acceptable since they were not in their right minds. These cognitive acrobatics reduce personal responsibility and give users a socially acceptable excuse to engage in otherwise prohibited behavior.

The other issue with illicit drugs is that they involve dealing the substances illegally. Students often end up in places that they would not otherwise be to get drugs, and they become easily identified as targets for street violence. Additionally, when students deal drugs out of their on-campus residences, they run the risk of spreading a new virus of violence originating from a different hosting site. In other words, street violence – robbery, gang activity, and other forms of violence usually perpetrated off-campus – can infiltrate the campus boundaries when drug activity is at hand.

The presence of illicit drugs can also influence the climate of the social environment. Social rules of behavior are often discarded when certain drugs are present as the atmosphere becomes increasingly permissive. Because drugs are used in private or semiprivate environments, the chances of outside enforcement or social control is slim, and an "anything goes" sentiment can prevail.

According to "Monitoring the Future Study," published by the University of Michigan's Institute for Social Research, the annual prevalence rates for youth drug use for most illicit substances appears to be gradually declining since the mid-1990s.[50] Most notably,

inhalant use and crack cocaine use dropped significantly during this time. Ecstasy use seemed to be increasing toward the end of the decade. This research focused on eighth, tenth, and twelfth graders, not college students. Nevertheless, the data can be used to predict incoming trends to college campuses.

Not all illicit drugs that make their way to campus are created equal. Some drugs with a sedating effect minimally impact violence, while others increase violence potential under certain circumstances. Contrary to popular opinion, however, most recent research concludes that it is not the drugs themselves that cause physiological changes leading to violence, but it is the context that drugs are used in that leads to violence. The 1992 Bureau of Justice Statistics indicated that only 5.6 percent of violent perpetrators had positive urinalysis findings of illicit drug use at the time of the offense. Study after study supports the fact that alcohol is overwhelmingly the substance most frequently implicated in most forms of violence.

According to the Higher Education Center, marijuana is the most frequently used illicit drug in the United States and on college campuses.[51] Data collected by the Core Institute indicates that the annual usage of marijuana has steadily increased since 1990. The specific effects of marijuana depend on the strain of marijuana used, the method of ingestion, the environment in which it is taken, the expectations of the user, and whether or not other drugs are used at the same time. It is generally accepted, however, that the use of marijuana actually suppresses hostility while the user is high.

Heroin is a drug rarely used on college campuses, but one that has recently been making a comeback in the 1990s. A significantly sedating drug, heroin is not usually associated with violence, with one exception. There is some evidence that heroin is associated with economically motivated property crimes. Another comeback drug, LSD, seems to have found its place with some college students. LSD is relatively inexpensive, and does not produce compulsive drug-seeking behavior as more addicting drugs such as nicotine and cocaine. The strength of LSD has declined in the last 30 years, and there is no substantial evidence linking LSD to violence.

"Rave" or "club drugs" have been increasing popular in recent years. Ecstasy and GHB (Gamma hydroxy butyric acid) are two of the most common. Ecstasy acts like a stimulant and a mild hallucinogen, and has been shown to turn off brain cells responsible for memory and sleep. Rave participants usually take the drug to induce a warm sense of well-being accompanied by heightened senses. The drug helps keep them awake during these all-night dance parties. While ecstasy is related to dehydration and may cause long-term brain damage, it is not associated with violence. In fact, one of the stated ideologies behind the raves is called PLUR – peace, love, unity, and respect.

GHB is another story. We explore the effects of GHB and another party drug with potential violent consequences, Rohypnol, in the Sexual Assault chapter of this book (Chapter 10). GHB has been historically used by bodybuilders for its ability to stimulate growth hormone release. Over the Internet, individuals can receive kits giving instructions on how to make it in their homes. The actual extent to which GHB and Rohypnol are used in cases of rape is unknown because the necessary urinalysis testing in the immediate aftermath of rape is rare. GHB overdose is another concern when unconsciousness, coma, or even death results as was the case for actor River Phoenix. This consequence usually occurs when individuals take GHB with large amounts of alcohol. Proponents of GHB state that the drug is a less violent alternative to alcohol and may even serve as a helpful sleep aid and nutrient.

There may be a pharmacological link between amphetamines and violence. When use is sustained over long periods of time or when acute doses of speed are extremely heavy, users can experience a "toxic psychosis" that is essentially indistinguishable from schizophrenia. A complicating factor of this research is that users who have shown violent behavior before using amphetamines are more likely to engage in violence after ingestion of amphetamines. Similarly, cocaine use is linked to violent behavior. Because cocaine use can lead to paranoid feelings, some users act out violently to irrational fears while under the influence of this drug.

Methamphetamine is another stimulant popular with the club crowd. It is very inexpensive to make using over-the-counter materials. Abusers usually show signs of agitation and increased physical activity levels. The direct association with meth and violence is unknown and an area for future study. A recent review by the National Institute of Justice revealed the surprising finding that methamphetamine users were less likely to be charged with a violent offense than other drug arrestees.[52] Nicotine and caffeine, while stimulants, are not associated with aggression, and may in fact reduce aggressive tendencies by giving agitated people a "time out."

PCP or phencyclidine is often associated with violence, but this assertion is usually based only on single cases. While PCP has not had great popularity on college campuses, its close cousin ketamine has recently been perceived as a recreational drug of choice for some students. "Special K" and PCP are both considered "dissociative anaesthetics" because they diminish the sensation of pain while distorting reality. Despite the reputation these drugs have for causing violence, at least one researcher cited in Parker and Auerhahn's review believed that emotionally stable people under the influence of these drugs would not tend to act differently than their normal behavior.[53]

Anabolic steroids also have raised concern in relation to violence. Anabolic steroids are

related to male sex hormones and promote
skeletal muscle development. They are
legally available in the United States by prescription. Case studies have called the impact
"'roid rage," and have suggested that increased levels of male hormones can lead to
homicidal impulses and other forms of violent crime. Others suggest that those who
engage in violence while under the influence
of steroids are fulfilling an expectation perpetuated by extensive media attention to the
issue. Anabolic steroid use by student athletes is currently at its lowest levels since
1985.[54]

Polysubstance abuse (using several different drugs at the same time) adds increased
risk for violence and other negative outcomes for several reasons. First, drugs can
have a number of interacting effects with
each other when consumed simultaneously.
One of these interaction effects is called synergy whereby one drug accentuates the effects of another. This problem can be seen
with the combination of alcohol and some of
the so-called "date rape drugs." The date
rape drugs amplify the effect of the alcohol
making the victim feel much more intoxicated than they usually would with the same
dose of alcohol alone. Second, with increased drug activity and impaired mental
state, individuals begin to lose their ability to
cope with life stressors effectively. They may
begin to resort to antisocial behavior as a
means of solving problems and obtaining
more drugs.

In summary, alcohol is the only drug
whose consumption has been shown to commonly increase aggression. This issue will be
comprehensively explored in the next chapter. The data on the other drugs remain in-
conclusive. Large doses of some drugs
including amphetamines, cocaine, and PCP
may lead to violent episodes in individuals
who are predisposed to psychosis. Illegal
drugs are more likely linked to violence
through drug marketing and distribution.

THE SACRED COWS

Sacred cows are those groups or individuals that are treated by a different standard
than the rest of the campus community. The
violent behavior of these people may be excused from consequences due to their perceived importance or influence of powerful
stakeholders. Sacred cows can be athletes, or
even whole athletic teams, sons or daughters
of influential alumni or board of trustees, student body presidents or other campus leaders.

Traditions are also sacred cows. Initiation
into college life is an important transition,
and initiation practices create bonding and a
sense of belonging. Some traditions have existed on campuses for generations and give
campus life a sense of history. Lately the
values of some of the more dangerous rituals
have been thrown into question. Most notably, the recent tragic situation of the col-
lapsed Texas A&M bonfire that killed 12
students challenged the existence of a 90-
year-old ritual. Some claim that the accident
was inevitable as each year's students tried to
outdo the previous year by building even
bigger structures. Campus officials, critics
say, turned a blind eye toward the inherent
dangers just because the event was a piece of
campus history. Supporters claim the tradition was an organized event, scientifically en-
gineered by students and supported by
university administration. Even some of
those students who lost friends in the tragedy
support the continuance of the ritual.

Another tradition at Princeton University
was put to an end in recent years. "Nude
Olympics" began decades ago with a small
group of men doing naked jumping jacks in
public areas in the middle of winter. This
event evolved to 400 naked students and organized events such as wheelbarrow races.
The university became concerned about the
negative image these events were having on
the institution as many intoxicated students
engaged in these events, some even urinating

and having sex in public. In February 2000, in subzero temperatures, Princeton University Nude Olympians were greatly outnumbered by administrators, campus security, emergency medical personnel, and the media. The event was a total flop.

Yet another tradition was changed after the Virginia Tech tragedy. At Bowling Green State University, one of the highlights of Zombie Week was a game where students carried Nerf guns for a week shooting the zombies before the creature could tag them. Most of the participants were considered "harmless nerdy kids" who like role-playing, but the game no longer was funny when the guns triggered fears among students and parents. Administrators suggested the students substitute the guns with marshmallows, but it didn't go over well with the participants who circulated a petition to reinstate the tradition.[55]

Recently the media has targeted athletes and fraternity members as the sacred cows in college violence. Some view this scrutiny as unfair stating that athletes and fraternity members are only marked because of their high visibility. Others say the investigation into this issue is long overdue. According to the Higher Education Center, 92 percent of documented gang rapes were committed by members of fraternities or intercollegiate athletic teams. The Higher Education Center also reported that male athletes and fraternity members are also overrepresented in nonsexual assault violence such as fist-fights.

Jeff Benedict, former director of research at the Center for Study of Sport in Society at Northeastern University, suggests that people tend to minimize the seriousness of violence committed by student athletes. According to Benedict's research, athletes comprised only 3.3 percent of the student body but were responsible for 19 percent of the reported sexual assaults. In 1995, he found that no fewer than 220 college athletes were subject to criminal proceedings; more than half of those crimes were sexual assault or incidents of domestic violence.

The NCAA (National Collegiate Athletic Association) states that scholarships can be revoked if athletes are found to have engaged in serious behavior warranting disciplinary action. Often determining the correct course of action is complicated in these circumstances. Benedict notes that during investigation, a process that can take months to complete, athletes are often allowed to continue playing their sport. He suggests that institutions should immediately remove from play any athlete arrested or otherwise formally charged with a felony or a misdemeanor involving an aggressive act against another student. Furthermore, Benedict recommends that coaches should be careful in choosing who they give scholarships to and avoid rewarding athletes with violent histories.

At the University of Minnesota, independent investigators reviewed 40 cases where athletes have been accused of sexual and domestic assaults in order to determine what if any systematic interference occurred to impede a fair judicial process. They determined that only in one instance did an athletic official interfere with the criminal investigation. Nevertheless, investigators did conclude that there was a "pattern of favoritism" among athletic officials toward the accused student athletes, and that many of the alleged victims were treated insensitively.

Others outside of the athletic department have pressured colleges to show leniency to accused student athletes. At Florida State University, President Talbot D'Alemberte suggested that a star football player serve a jail sentence for a $600 shoplifting crime before returning to play. One alumnus wrote, "How dare you treat Athletic Director Hart and Coach Bowden as mere subordinates. I will never give another penny to the university as long as you are president of the institution." In the end, this student worked out a deal to do community service instead of jail time, and he was allowed to return to the football team. The team later went on to win the Sugar Bowl, largely due to this player's performance.

Student athletes are not the only sacred cows of the athletic department. Bob Knight, the fired Indiana University basketball coach made headlines with his history of abusive behavior. He was even caught choking a player. But he was not immediately dismissed from the university. First, he was fined $30,000 and suspended for three games. The university president, Myles Brand, indicated that the university played a role in allowing this behavior to continue by either ignoring inappropriate behavior or by letting Mr. Knight off with light sanctions. When a local paper polled Indianapolis residents about their views on the matter, 55 percent stated they supported the decision to keep Mr. Knight as coach while 39 percent disagreed. One faculty member stated, "[The decision] sends the message that athletics are more important than academics, that marketing and revenue streams mean more than scholarships."[56]

Greek life has long been treated as a sacred cow on many campuses. Recently increasing numbers of students have exposed dehumanizing and sometimes life-risking practices they were pressured to endure. Consequently, the Greek system is currently under close scrutiny. Many campuses are asking themselves, "Are the benefits of fraternities and sororities outweighing the consequences?" On a parallel course, many athletic departments are also being closely examined and regulated in attempts to deter hazing rituals.

In conclusion, some areas of campus vulnerability we cannot do much about. Nor do we want to. Most campuses cannot change their location, and will not change the policies and practices that make campus life an open community. However, becoming aware of potential areas of weakness in campus safety can give campuses an awareness that will hopefully lead to early detection of developing violence.[57]

Chapter 4

ALCOHOL: A VIOLENCE CATALYST

SALLY SPENCER-THOMAS

Any concerted effort to reduce campus interpersonal violence or crimes against property must address the use and abuse of psychoactive substances.

– T. Rivinus and M. Larimer[58]

A UNIVERSITY OF CALIFORNIA, Davis, senior celebrated his twenty-first birthday by slamming shot after shot for 90 minutes. He mixed tequila with bourbon and whiskey on this rite of passage frequently referred to as "21-for-21." For this tradition, individuals drink one shot for every year of their life. It often amounts to suicide. This student passed out soon after his twenty-first drink. By the time his friends got him to the hospital, his lips were blue. His blood alcohol content was .50, but his official cause of death was choking on his own vomit. Drinking traditions common on college campuses can leave a trail of death and violence in their path.

Georgetown University experienced back-to-back, alcohol-related violence and death during the winter of 1999–2000. In December, a Georgetown student vandalized a Jewish menorah while drunk and in February, David Shick, a 20-year-old junior, died four days after receiving a severe head injury during an alcohol-fueled fist-fight. The death was ruled as a homicide by the medical examiner's office. Physical assault is probably the most frequent alcohol-related form of violence; however, the effects of alcohol play a critical role in many sexual assaults, hate crimes, riots, and hazing.

A tradition at the University of Virginia is called "fourth-year fifth" – in which seniors attempt to consume a fifth of alcohol during the last home football game. When asked about this tradition, one student commented, "Come on, all of college is about binge drinking."

Scott Krueger is the person most associated with alcohol-related death on a college campus. As part of an initiation rite into his pledged fraternity, Phi Gamma Delta (FIJI), Scott died after consuming a significant amount of alcohol during a short period of time (see Chapter 1 for his story). The case brought national attention because it occurred at a place where alcohol and hazing are not even supposed to be issues.[59] According to MIT, the Institute's high-risk drinking rate is half the national average – 23 percent compared to the 44 percent national rate. Yet, Scott's death showed the nation that if a promising student like he could die from alcohol-related hazing, then it could happen anywhere.

In the aftermath of his death, Krueger's family expressed criticism with the policies and practices of MIT. Among other things, the family felt that the Institute's housing policies played a significant role in Scott's death. To avoid overcrowding its dormitories, MIT required about 60 percent of all freshman males to choose fraternity housing. This factor undoubtedly contributed to Scott's decision to pledge a fraternity, thus placing an unnecessary risk of his subjection to hazing practices. The family was also troubled by the fact that a formal acknowledgment from MIT, and an apology for their role in Scott's death, was slow to come, and that no one has yet been held accountable for Scott's death.

To MIT's credit, the school responded to the tragedy in many ways.[60] Enforcement and disciplinary proceedings stepped up, housing provisions improved, and prevention and education increased. ABC's "20/20," A&E's "Investigative Reports," CBS's "48 Hours," and Court TV have all featured special programs on the tragic death of Scott to increase awareness of the dangers of hazing and high-risk drinking. Scott's death and the ensuing media coverage put a human face to the national issue of college alcohol abuse and hazing practices.

The media attention surrounding Scott's death was soon amplified by additional headlines during the spring of 1998. During this time, the Harvard School of Public Health released a second wave of publications on "binge drinking." This intense media focus on alcohol abuse created an uproar of concern with college administrators and a backlash among many students. Protests and riots after colleges crack down on drinking behavior make some campuses leery of enforcing strict alcohol abuse prevention policies. "Chicken and egg" questions arise: is alcohol leading to violence or are the alcohol abuse prevention measures leading to rioting?

Many college drinking hangouts are losing their fear of student retaliation. On South Padre Island, the violence and social problems associated with alcohol abuse have become so disturbing that local residents are trying to lose the 300,000 college tourists they attract each year. Most spring break vacation spots have found that the costs of hosting thousands of drunken college students outweigh the meager dollars they spend while in town. During one spring break season, the South Padre Police Department arrested 530 people, a multifold increase from the normal 15 to 20 monthly arrest rate. Fort Lauderdale, Florida, learned this lesson long ago and changed its marketing strategy from targeting rowdy college students to attracting families, resulting in a huge increase in revenue and decrease in headaches for the area.

HIGH-RISK DRINKING ON COLLEGE CAMPUSES

Alcohol is clearly the drug of choice for most college students. Drinking games have a long history on college campuses. Quarters, chugging races, beer bongs, and many other contests often lead to large quantities of alcohol consumed in a short period of time. With these types of games, drinkers easily lose track of how much alcohol they are consuming, becoming increasingly vulnerable to alcohol poisoning.

What We Know

In the last decade, some researchers investigated the campus phenomenon they labeled binge drinking. This catchphrase, used to describe high-risk drinking, is defined by researchers as five drinks or more in a row for men and four or more for women. As Dr. William DeJong, Director for the Higher Education Center for Alcohol and Other Drug Prevention, notes, the problem with this term is that four or five drinks over a several-hour period does not relate to the commonly held image of a drinking binge, especially for college students.[61] Thus, for this book we choose to use the terms "high-risk drinking" or "heavy episodic use" to describe a large amount (e.g., 5+ drinks) of alcohol consumed in a short period of time (e.g., 0–2 hours) or otherwise drinking that exceeds the "injury dose" for a person. Injury dose means the amount of alcohol that typically results in negative consequences for the consumer (e.g., vomiting, severe hangover, fights, falls, blackouts, etc.).

Dr. DeJong also notes that responsible drinking is a confusing term as well. Most people, despite where they fall on the drinking continuum, consider their drinking responsible. From our focus groups on campus, we discovered many students believed that responsible drinking meant getting a sober driver to take you home. Dr. DeJong supports this notion and cites research that indicates that even heavy drinkers view their own level of drinking as "responsible." Because of this confusion, we choose to use the term low-risk drinking to describe standard guidelines for decreasing consequences related to alcohol use. The 0-1-3 guidelines suggest for some situations no alcohol is appropriate. Zero alcohol consumption is important for those dependent on alcohol, pregnant women, and most high-risk tasks such as driving. Otherwise, for most people, one drink per hour with meals, and no more than three in any sitting will usually minimize consequences.

According to research conducted by the Harvard School of Public Health sponsored by the Robert Wood Johnson Foundation, high-risk drinkers on college campuses tend to be white, live in a fraternity, and have a history of heavy episodic drinking in high school.[62] From this research, it appears that frequent heavy episodic drinking is on the increase. In 1993, the rate was 19.8 percent and in 1999, the rate moved up to 22.7 percent. High-risk drinkers such as this group have increased rates of missing class, getting into trouble, and getting hurt.

Recent studies conducted by the Core Institute indicate that Greek leaders actually consume more alcohol than lower-level members.[63] Furthermore, as groups, athletes and Greeks drink more than the rest of the college population. According to the National Interfraternity Conference (NIC), alcohol is the number one risk-management concern.[64] Alcohol was involved in 95 percent of falls, 94 percent of fights, 93 percent of sexual assaults, and 87 percent of automobile accidents. The NIC also reports that in almost nine out of ten fraternity deaths, alcohol played a role.

Hank Nuwer, the national hazing expert, calls one frightening pattern of fraternity response to alcohol poisoning, "Greek-think." In the moment of crisis when an individual has become hurt or is critically impaired by alcohol, there is a devastating pause. At the time when first responders should be racing to get appropriate medical attention, these individuals who are often fairly impaired themselves think, "oh shit." They pause because they are concerned about getting in trouble, about covering up evidence, and about taking care of the problem themselves. This pause often leads to lifesaving minutes lost.

A secondary analysis of the Harvard study presented for the American Public Health Association looked at multidrug users. The subjects of this study were students who drank heavily and consumed two or more illicit drugs. Researchers found that multidrug users were at an even greater risk for alcohol-related accidents, for engaging in unprotected sex, and for getting in trouble with the law than either the binge drinkers (who did not use drugs) or the exclusive substance users (e.g., people who only used marijuana). Another trend these researchers discovered was that close to 60 percent of the multidrug users were regular heavy drinkers in high school, about a twofold increase than among any other drug use subgroups.

Unfortunately, despite the level of consequences and duration of these problematic behaviors, very few high-risk drinkers consider their behavior an issue. Even when they do consider their behavior a problem, very few consider getting help. Evidence from the Harvard Study indicated that only one in five students who recognized they had a drug or drinking problem had ever sought counseling for it.

On the opposite end of the continuum, the Harvard Study reports another trend: the percentage of nondrinkers is also on the rise. In 1993, this rate was 15.4 percent and in 1999, the rate rose to 19.2 percent. Low-risk drinkers tended to be black or Asian, over 24 years old, and married. This trend actually reflects a larger trend in America towards decreased consumption of alcohol and an increased number of abstainers. In a later chapter we will discuss the rise of rioting on college campuses as a result of this "Right to Party" agenda. In essence, students are expressing outrage of tighter policies and tougher consequences for underage drinking and drunkenness by wreaking havoc on their campuses. The thought is that if enough damage is done, campus officials will regret their enforcement decisions and become more liberal with their policies. According to Nuwer's interviewees, the students report feeling empowered by gathering together and demonstrating.[65] They state that their efforts show that campus administrators are very "out of touch" with the student body. If anything, the way this "Right to Party" protest is currently going, the opposite effect is taking place. Many colleges do not want to be bullied by violence and are holding to or increasing the strictness of their policies.

Many agree that the issues of freedoms and responsibility underlying this outrage are valid, but believe the methods of protest are counterproductive. In many countries, drinking alcohol is a symbolic claim to independence and rebellion against authority. These cultural beliefs can be powerful motivators to challenge established rules. A former sorority national president, paraphrased in Nuwer's book, *The Wrongs of Passage*, states, "...in a democracy, students who felt strongly that the state drinking laws were passed in error could take their case to legislators and to the press for an amendment. Those committed to protecting the rights of students must give a little too and consider the rights of their fellow citizens..." (p. 78).

Institutional Denial

In *Wrongs of Passage*, Nuwer indicates that many colleges are in a state of denial when it comes to admitting their institutional drinking problem, very much like an alcoholic. He calls these colleges "addictive organizations" and lists many "enabling" behaviors colleges engage in to allow the students' out-of-control drinking to continue without consequences. Enabling, an addictions term, occurs when one person or group of people minimizes the short-term consequences for an addicted person without addressing the long-term problems. For example, between individuals enabling occurs when a friend or spouse calls into work for someone who is incapacitated by a hangover.

Nuwer suggests that on an institutional level enabling is happening when colleges require their Greek houses to hold "dry rushes." Nationals and school administrators will require the undergraduate officers to sign off on contracts stating they will not serve alcohol to minors, but no one ensures these contracts are enforced, and they are often perceived as a joke. When campus authorities conduct house inspections with Greeks, they often announce their visits well enough in advance for members to hide any incriminating evidence. When investigations are conducted, they usually meet the legal requirements, but are not comprehensive enough to uncover what is really going on. Similar practices occur on athletic teams for initiation and recruit hosting practices.

For the general population of college students, there sometimes exists a mentality of "boys will be boys" that can lead to relaxed standards of accountability. According to many alcohol experts cited in *Campus Violence*, this process of thinking often relocates the origin of the problem not with the intoxicated individual, but the substance itself: "The beer made me do it." Those who buy into this line of thinking often excuse otherwise inexcusable behavior with the "drunkenness defense," and thereby promote the continuance of violence.

> The mere belief that drunkenness can be used to excuse violent behavior is perhaps the most straight forward sociocultural risk factor affecting intoxicated violence....
> – Kai Pernanen[66]

College alcohol use expert Henry Wechsler and others wrote an article for *The Chronicle of Higher Education* on this topic as well.[67] They discuss the tendency of parents and school officials sometimes have of turning the other cheek because they too engaged in alcohol abuse during their college years. The difference is that today lethal sexually transmitted diseases, easy availability of guns, and overcrowded highways make the consequences of alcohol abuse more deadly. The authors sum up this issue with this quote:

> Those in denial act as if they believe that this deep-seated American problem can be changed by someone, able and dedicated, working part time in a basement office at the student-health service.[68]

Too many colleges are still in denial about alcohol abuse (*The Chronicle of Higher Education*, Opinion & Arts Section).[69]

Alcohol and Advertising: A Blessed Curse for College Communities

More universities are giving up big-time revenue from alcohol advertising and sales in an effort to separate themselves from the public relations problems high-risk drinking is causing. Athletic events can bring in significant revenue from the alcohol industry – scholarships, apparel, radio programs, scoreboard ads, as well as consumption of their product. As alcohol-induced unruly student behavior becomes increasingly frowned upon in the public eye, many schools are faced with a dilemma. What, if any, relationship with the alcohol industry is appropriate for a college campus?

Jean Kilbourne, social commentator on advertising practices in the United States, makes convincing arguments in her video "Calling the Shots" on how the advertising industry targets young adults in the college-age range, and promotes heavy consumption of their product.[70] In particular, she describes several media campaigns linking alcohol with sexual behavior and the objectification of women. She considers these practices highly irresponsible given the significant co-occurrence of sexual assault and alcohol impairment.

In his book *Beer Blast* (1998), alcohol-advertising insider Philip Van Munching, former advertising director for Heineken, gives several examples of beer advertising imagery designed to appeal to young drinkers. The most infamous example, of course, is Spuds MacKenzie, the "Party Animal" and Bud Light spokesdog. During his reign, Spuds was frequently shown skateboarding and dancing and helped increase Bud Light sales 21 percent. The fact that Spuds was also very attractive for children caused an uproar among parents across the nation.

On the other side of the argument, many believe that it is in the alcohol industry's best interest to lower the risk to their consumers for improved public relations and longevity of their market (you cannot buy their product if you die from an alcohol overdose). As Trish Bonnell, an educational director for Anheuser-Busch commented, "The problem isn't alcohol, but rather alcohol abuse." Anheuser-Busch funded a $2.7 million grant for alcohol abuse prevention programs on college campuses. Anheuser-Busch sponsors "T.I.P.S." training for servers of alcohol to reduce underage and problematic drinking and an educational program for high schools featuring a "Flight-for-Life" nurse who talks about the grizzly details of drunk-driving accidents.

Likewise, other beer companies have made efforts to enforce underage drinking laws and to increase education about responsible serving of alcohol. For example, Coors launched a campaign designed to encourage underage individuals to wait until they were of legal age before drinking. Many companies now add tag lines to their advertising spots encouraging "responsible drinking" and discouraging impaired driving. Again, the term responsible drinking remains problematic, but the message is a step in the right direction. The Century Council, a national prevention task force funded by America's leading distillers, created "Alcohol 101," an interactive CD-Rom educational tool designed to teach college students about the consequences of high-risk drinking.[71]

Nevertheless, with so many colleges working hard to discourage alcohol abuse, many feel the alcohol advertising on their campuses sends a mixed message to students. Many have banned alcohol advertising or sales from athletic events, school newspapers, and campus celebrations. Other campuses take advantage of the beer industry's educational and prevention opportunities but control the dissemination of the sponsorship. For example, the National Collegiate Alcohol Awareness Week Awards are offered every year to colleges demonstrating outstanding substance abuse prevention strategies. Award applications are under the direction of Fort Hays University, but a little known fact is that the thousands of dollars in prize money are actually funded by Coors. Clearly, the issue of alcohol advertising and sponsorship on college campuses remains controversial

and unresolved for many campuses at this time.

HOW ALCOHOL LINKS TO VIOLENCE

There are clear links between alcohol and violence. Consider the statistics:

- Criminal violence and homicide are associated with intoxication by the aggressor and victim in 60–70 percent of documented cases.[72]
- The Core Institute reports that almost half of all college students experience violence on campus and alcohol is almost always involved.
- Gun possession at college is significantly more likely among students who drink five or more drinks in one sitting.[73]
- Studies of sexual violence on college campuses estimate that 75 percent of victims and perpetrators had been using alcohol at the time of the crime.[74]
- A 1998 study published in the American Journal of Health Studies found that alcohol was involved in almost 60 percent of nonsexual assaults perpetrated on college students.[75]
- One study indicated that 27 percent of women had experienced rape or attempted rape after being given alcohol or other drugs by the perpetrator.[76]

Dr. Timothy Rivinus, a Harvard researcher, summarizes some of what we currently know about the relationship between alcohol and violence in the edited book entitled *Campus Violence* (1993).[77] We know that alcohol decreases pain sensitivity, anxiety about future consequences, and frustration tolerance. Flexible problem-solving ability decreases with intoxication. We also know that witnessing or engaging in prior alcohol-related violence plays a major role in the connection between alcohol and violence. Finally, alcohol abuse has a built-in denial mechanism: blacking out. Two studies have shown that alcohol abusers who committed violent acts have little or no memory of their behavior.

We also know that alcohol directly affects the brain. All parts of the brain are eventually impacted with excessive consumption of alcohol, but it is the frontal lobe that plays a critical role in judgment and behavior inhibition. The frontal lobe is one of the first areas of the brain to be affected by alcohol, and thus, appears to lead to increased impulsivity and "acting out" behavior. The frontal lobe is also responsible for long-range planning, and when it becomes impaired, short-term objectives become more pronounced. Thus, in the case of sexual violence, the immediate gratification of forced sex may supercede any fear of long-term legal, emotional, or health consequences.

With violence, not all alcohol is created equal. Research conducted by the Alcohol Related Injuries and Violence (ARIV) project, funded by the Robert Wood Johnson Foundation (cited in Join Together Online, 2000), has shown that beer is overwhelmingly associated with violence.[78] According to these findings, 80 percent of beer is consumed in a hazardous way as compared to 16 percent of liquor and 4 percent of wine. This may be due to the fact that beer is relatively cheaper and is perceived as less harmful than other types of alcohol beverages.

Anger expert Dr. Jerry Deffenbacher suggests that alcohol and anger have a synergistic effect in that anger and alcohol each individually lead to negative consequences, but together in high doses, the problems are exponential. In his research, Deffenbacher differentiated low and high trait anger individuals by Speilberger's Trait Anger Scale and then analyzed any differences in their experienced consequences. As reported in Table 4.1, angry individuals were much more likely to experience negative consequences from alcohol than were their nonangry peers.

When thinking about the relationship of alcohol and violence, some wonder again about chicken and eggs. Which comes first? Some argue that decreased inhibitions of the drinker can lead normally nonviolent individuals to act on aggressive impulses. Clearly, alcohol affects judgment. People are much more likely to say and do things when intoxicated that they normally would not say or do when sober. Intoxicated people also distort what they hear other people saying. Thus, alcohol impairment can lead to social misunderstandings or an overreaction to a perceived threat, and can evolve into anger.

Table 4.1
PERCENT OF COLLEGE STUDENTS DRUNK IN THE LAST MONTH
AND SUFFERING ALCOHOL CONSEQUENCES
IN THE LAST THREE MONTHS

	Males		*Females*	
	Low Anger	*High Anger*	*Low Anger*	*High Anger*
Broke something	3%	30%	4%	17%
Felt like hurting others	16%	57%	2%	16%
Felt like hurting self	7%	9%	2%	13%
Vomited	22%	50%	18%	37%

Source: Adapted from an unpublished manuscript (2000). Used with the permission of J. Deffenbacher.

On the other side of the argument, some state that alcohol increases risk-taking in those already prone to anger, and becomes their excuse to act violently. We know that alcohol consumption tends to promote aggression because people expect it to. A person who intends to engage in a premeditated violent act may get intoxicated to create the "liquid courage" to act out.

RECOMMENDATIONS

Despite heightened awareness of the dangers of alcohol abuse, some college administrators are still somewhat hesitant to create and enforce effective policies that restrict alcohol access and discourage overindulgence. Some hesitate because they fear student backlash against their decisions. After passing an alcohol ban on their Greek organizations, Michigan State University (MSU) and Southern Illinois State University at Carbondale (SIUC) both succumbed to student pressure to reverse the decision. The students argued that morale and recruitment at the Greek houses had dropped significantly since the ban and that some organizations were consequently suffering financial problems. Campus officials conceded to reverse the original decision when the Greek organizations promised to uphold strict alcohol policies stating that they had learned from their mistakes and could prove

to be responsible. Time will tell how the decisions to reallow alcohol in the fraternities will play out. We are not particularly optimistic, knowing that Greek members tend to be the heaviest drinkers of all. According to Dr. Henry Wechsler, 81.1 percent of those living in fraternity or sorority houses binge drink as compared to the national 44 percent rate.

It is true that there is a subpopulation of college drinkers that are very committed to defending their "right to party," but as Dr. Henry Wechsler of Harvard points out, it really depends on who is asked. More than four out of five nondrinkers support the prohibition of kegs on campus, the strict enforcement of the rules, and the crackdown on underage drinkers and abusive Greek drinkers. The majority of low-risk drinkers and many occasional high-risk drinkers also agree to these measures, as well as the idea of holding party hosts responsible for their guests.

Gather Accurate Information

In order to be able to address the problems of alcohol abuse, each campus must assess where the problems are. This can be accomplished by several needs assessment strategies. Student focus groups give small groups a chance to answer structured questions about the who, when, and where of alcohol misuse. Focus groups give rich qualitative data, especially groups that represent diverse

Table 4.2
STUDENT SUPPORT FOR TOUGHER POLICIES[79]

Policy	Nondrinkers	Drinkers/ Nonbingers	Occasional Bingers	Frequent Bingers
Prohibit kegs on campus	86.4%	67.7%	48.6%	34.6%
Enforce rules strictly	93.2%	75.0%	54.2%	35.2%
Crackdown on Greeks	90.1%	69.5%	47.1%	28.2%
Hold hosts responsible	81.1%	59.9%	45.3%	33.3%
Crack down on underage drinkers	93.5%	76.9%	56.6%	37.1%

aspects of campus, but responses can be biased because of a lack of anonymity. Surveys can free students to state the truth without fear that their answers will be traced back to them, but sometimes the statistics generated from surveys raise more questions than they answer. Colleges seeking to understand the prevalence of these behaviors often use standardized questionnaires such as the Core Instrument, but surveys such as these do not address the issues of change and motivation. Clearly, a combination of strategies will give colleges the most accurate picture.

When alcohol-related violence occurs, some experts suggest taking Blood Alcohol Content (BAC) levels from both victims and perpetrators. This information can help determine issues of consent in cases of sexual assault. When a sexual assault victim appears impaired, but the BAC is low, medical providers can be alerted to screen for date rape drugs such as Rohypnol. When we have better evidence linking alcohol to campus violence, we have better leverage to impose appropriate restrictions on the access to alcohol and have better information from which to offer relevant prevention tactics.

Community-based Approach

Because a problem such as substance abuse is so entrenched in the campus community, a comprehensive strategy for change is appropriate. Such a strategy must involve a committed cross-section of campus representatives who are up to the task of challenging these behavioral and attitudinal norms. Many campuses have created a task force representative of the following groups of individuals for the purposes of generating effective change strategies.

Presidents

Top-down support is critical to the success of a prevention program requiring a community-wide embrace. The Director of the Higher Education Center for Alcohol and Other Drug Prevention, Dr. William DeJong, states, "...college and university presidents must address problems related to student drinking....Many of the things college presidents worry about – student death and injury, weak academic performance, property damage and vandalism, strained town-gown relations, negative publicity – are linked to student alcohol use."[80]

In 1999, The Presidents Leadership Group, sponsored by the Robert Wood Johnson Foundation, urged college presidents to "Be Vocal, Be Visible, Be Visionary" in their response to alcohol and other drug problems on campus. The report suggests that colleges do not need to return to prohibition, but do need to determine the appropriate role of alcohol in a learning community.

One direct way college presidents can demonstrate their commitment to alcohol abuse prevention is to allocate a budget and staff reflective of such a communitywide problem.

Faculty

Because of their highly respected status and contact with students, faculty members have substantial potential for impacting student attitudes and behavior toward alcohol and its relationship to violence.

Faculty can play many roles in dealing with this issue. They often witness the effects of post-partying consequences as students come to class hungover with a laundry list of excuses why their work is not done on time. They are in an excellent position to confront and refer students who are in trouble. Classrooms provide captive audiences for discussion and lecture on this topic that so many fear to face head-on.

In the mid-1990s, curriculum infusion became a big prevention buzzword. The movement made attempts to get alcohol issues and other drug topics integrated into almost every syllabus. Several schools found that curriculum infusion had a ripple effect in alcohol abuse prevention. From the process, faculty became more invested and informed about what students were doing. Students seemed more open to the topic when it was presented as an "academic topic" rather than through the assumption that they were all problem drinkers. Issues gained importance to the community at large when funneled through the minds of the most elite thinkers around.

Student Life Staff

Personal counseling services, health services, residence life offices, student activities, security officers, judicial officers, and other administrators all have vital roles in alcohol abuse prevention and intervention. Many of their roles are discussed in other sections of this chapter and throughout this book. Another excellent sourcebook, *Promising Practices*, compiled by David Anderson and Gail Milgram, provides additional information for professional student life staff.[81]

Parents

A sensitive discussion of drugs and alcohol use can be even more difficult when discussed in the context of sexual behavior and violence. But, consider what you have to lose if you do not have this conversation. You could lose your son or daughter.
   – From the Syracuse University Substance Abuse Prevention & Health Enhancement Office

Of all the prevention influences, appropriate parental communication and role modeling is probably one of the most powerful. Parental influence can even overcome the power of television. A recent study at Washington State University demonstrated that the potential risk of frequent exposure to persuasive alcohol messages on television was significantly moderated by parental counter-reinforcement messages.

"Parental notification" has been a controversial movement in an attempt to determine who is responsible for student welfare. Some say that the students themselves are responsible for what happens to them and, as adults, have a right to privacy. Others say that since many parents are footing the bill for college, parents have a right to know if their son or daughter is in trouble. Under a federal law passed in 1999, campus administrators may disclose a student's disciplinary record without the student's consent. Supporters of this law favor the opportunity for early intervention with potentially high-risk behavior. An additional step that might improve the impact of this intervention would be to send parents information about helpful ways to talk to their son or daughter about alcohol.

Several experts have suggested open communication between parents and college students before the students even set foot on campus as a critical step in preventing alcohol abuse. The first six weeks of college often involve high consumption of alcohol as students are adjusting to having new freedoms while trying desperately to fit in. Kaiser Permanente advises parents to discuss issues of legality, high-risk behaviors such as impaired driving and sex under the influence, alcohol poisoning, and other consequences of alcohol misuse. Chris Wimmer, a substance abuse counselor at Kaiser stated, "Many parents treat this the same as they do discussions about sex – you have the talk with them, once, to explain the 'birds and the bees,' and that's it. Kids need an ongoing dialogue, especially once they are old enough to experiment on their own."[82]

The Century Council, a national, not-for-profit organization dedicated to reducing drunk driving and underage drinking problems (www.centurycouncil.org), recommends that parents share their own drinking experiences, both positive and negative, without glorifying alcohol abuse.[83] The first step in this

The Higher Education Center recommends eight points for parents speaking with students about alcohol:

1. Establish clear and reasonable expectations for academic performance. Research indicates that alcohol abuse is largely responsible for academic decline, and if students realize that parents expect their best, they may be more likely to devote more time to studying.
2. Stress that alcohol consumed in high quantities can be fatal. Discourage high-risk drinking activities such as drinking games and chugging practices. Encourage students to intervene if they see others putting their lives at risk with these risky behaviors.
3. Tell students what to do if they see someone who is in trouble with alcohol. Share with them the warning signs of alcohol poisoning and to whom they can turn for help in this crisis.
4. Encourage students to stand up for their right to a safe, sanitary, and sane living and studying environment.
5. Know the alcohol culture of the campus and confront students' misperceptions. Students tend to grossly overestimate the percentage of students who get drunk on a regular basis. Let them know that many students are making good choices for themselves, but it is the most out-of-control students who usually are visible.
6. Avoid telling tales about "the good old days" when your drinking was out of control. This clearly sends a confusing message.
7. Encourage your son or daughter to get involved in service work in the community. Being a productive volunteer helps structure the student's free time, gives students a broader perspective, and creates natural connections with others.
8. Emphasize the point that underage alcohol consumption and impaired driving are against the law.

process is becoming clear about one's own attitudes, values, and beliefs about alcohol and drinking. Parents should examine their own rituals and patterns around alcohol in order to recognize the influence their actions have on their children. Parents can talk about their own decision making related to how alcohol does or does not fit into their lives. Most importantly, parents must role model appropriate consumption of alcohol and live by example. If the student is involved in an alcohol violation, parents should avoid the tendency to react, and rather respond to the opportunity for dialogue on the issue.

Coaches

Like parents, coaches play an unbelievably powerful role in shaping student behavior. At Regis University, coaches are notified when students receive their second minor alcohol infraction or any major substance abuse infraction. The intent of the notification is not to increase opportunities for punishment, but for communication. Coaches requested this notification because sometimes they were the last ones to know when one of their starter players was being asked to leave school for disciplinary problems. Coaches felt that they were in a good position to influence their players to make better choices for themselves off the field.

Students

Students are on the front line of this issue and see firsthand the patterns and areas of risk developing on campus. In order for prevention and intervention efforts to be effective, the students' voices – on all points along the drinking continuum – must be heard. Student focus groups are especially useful in assessing the campus alcohol culture.

Peer education, now a regular prevention strategy on most campuses, has proven to help the peer educators themselves in addition to the larger campus community. A 1998 BACCHUS & GAMMA Peer Education Network survey found that peer educators tend to make healthier choices about substances use. Seventy-eight percent believed they had positively influenced their peers, and most indicated that being a peer educator had positively impacted their relationships with others.

Community

It has been called "town and gown" collaboration. Leaders from city government, neighborhood associations, community resource officers, owners of drinking establishments, and others combine efforts with the campus task force to devise a comprehensive strategy of prevention.

A critical segment of this joint effort is getting the support of local bars and clubs. Campus and local law enforcement can encourage community drinking establishments to uphold drinking laws by not serving underage patrons or overserving those of age. In addition, campus prevention groups can ask the local bars to become more responsible in their drink promotions and advertising. The Center for Science in the Public Interest offers a free community action guide to help colleges stop irresponsible alcohol promotion targeting college students (download a free copy of Last Call for High-Risk Bar Promotions That Target College Students by logging on to www.health.org/ pubs/lastcall/ index.htm).

Offer Attractive Social Alternatives

"We drink because there is nothing else to do." For many college students, alcohol is the cheapest thrill in town. For the price of a movie ticket or a night of bowling, students can get very intoxicated. Substance abuse prevention personnel must figure out what students are getting out of their high-risk drinking episodes and find other ways to accomplish the same goals. When asked, many students say they like to go drinking at parties or bars because it gives them opportunities to meet new people, especially those with dating potential. Student activities departments can host other types of social events on Fridays and Saturdays where meeting new people is also possible. Some students like the excitement of high-risk behavior; they get a rush out of living on the edge. For these students, other forms of risk-taking such as skiing, rafting, and rock climbing may be attractive. If drinking is part of the social activity offered, it should not be the sole focus. Students should be involved in other activities as well such as a casino night or bowling.

Stop Enabling

Campus alcohol abuse prevention groups should encourage faculty to hold Friday morning classes. Tests, too. Hangovers are natural consequences for overindulgence and performing poorly in a class might get students to reevaluate their priorities. Frontline individuals such as security officers and residence life staff are often critical decision makers when it comes to getting problematic drinkers appropriate help and deserved consequences. These staff members should receive training on why enabling perpetuates the problem and how to effectively confront the problematic drinker. Finally, those in positions of imposing sanctions must be prepared to act consistently, regardless of the size of the sacred cow. The son of a board trustee, the star basketball player, or the president of the student body all should be held to the same standards of behavior as the rest of the college community.

Restrict Access

Restricting access to alcohol has been shown to lower the prevalence of violence crimes and physical injuries linked to alcohol, according to a recent issue of Contemporary Drug Problems. Reduced availability of alcohol can take many forms – higher price, regulated serving, prohibited areas, and so on. The problem with restricted access of alcohol is that if the measures are unpopular with a large segment of the population, an illegal market will develop. This underground market adapts to the restrictions so that the type of alcohol favored will have a lower likelihood of being detected. Favored alcohol beverages will be higher in alcohol content so that they are easier to conceal and transport than large volumes of less potent alcohol. This means that students will be downing shot after shot of tequila rather than swigging from a keg. Students tend to have a more difficult time monitoring their intake of hard alcohol than they do beer. They are more likely to succumb to alcohol poisoning when ingesting numerous shots in a short period of time than bottles of beer over the course of an evening. Thus, when restricting access, campuses must take into consideration this tendency for the underground market to develop, and take additional precautions.

The National Bureau of Economic Research came up with a novel way to raise money for the states and prevent alcohol abuse at the same time: increase beer tax. According to these economists, there is a clear cause-and-effect between the price of beer and student trouble. In their analysis, they determined that for every 10 percent increase in the price of beer, the percentage of students who engage in problematic behavior such as fighting, sexual misconduct, and property damage decreases by 4 percent overall. In actuality, beer prices have fallen about 10 percent in the last ten years, and this trend may be contributing to college overindulgence.

Campus authorities have the power to regulate where, when, and how much alcohol is served. Banning alcohol from campus sporting events appears to be a current development on many campuses. According to the North American Interfraternity Conference, about 20 percent of fraternity chapters are going dry, and the number continues to increase. Sorority houses have always been dry and a new national rule will prohibit sorority members from attending fraternity functions where alcohol is served. Many residence halls are alcohol-free regardless of age of residents. Campus pub serving sizes and type of alcohol can also have an impact on how intoxicated students get.

Restriction policies must be well thought out in order for them to be effective. The University of Massachusetts, Amherst learned the hard way that sometimes the definition of a reasonable limit is complicated. Originally, the school had imposed a 24-beer limit for any of-age student to keep in his or her room. Then they increased this limit to 30 at the request of student government which noted that liquor stores were selling 30-beer cases. Upon reflection and substantial backlash from the alcohol abuse prevention community, the chancellor reversed his decision, which in turn caused student uproar.

Policies and Enforcement

Dr. Henry Wechsler of Harvard and the Department of Education suggests a "Zero Tolerance Policy" for alcohol-related violence including rape, assault, and impaired driving. Some schools go a step further and enforce a "Zero Tolerance Policy" for any underage drinking. Wellesley College has such a policy, and any underage student caught drinking by campus police is ordered to appear in court or is arrested.

Whatever policies campuses decide, the messages must be clear and consistent. Separate policies for of-age students and staff or alumni can send conflicting messages of "do as I say and not as I do." A "dry" campus drenched in lucrative alcohol advertising or event sponsorship is equally confusing for the community.

The law enforcement departments patrolling the area's neighboring campuses have begun various crackdown efforts to curtail harmful drinking habits. San Diego State University students now know what it means to be "CAPPed." This term emerged after the local police department developed the "College Area Party Plan" and started issuing written notices to students hosting loud, unruly parties. If the CAPP is violated, the residents face possible arrests, property seizures, and fines.

Many schools also enforce "minor in possession" (MIP) violations. Any underage possession and public consumption violating community standards leads to mandatory sanctions. Examples of first-offense sanctions include a monetary fine, mandated counseling, a semester's disciplinary probation, community services, and an alcohol educational workshop.

In Colorado, several schools have jumped on the Department of Transportation's prevention bandwagon with the "College Crackdown" movement. In 1996, the Colorado Department of Transportation started "The Heat is On!" DUI enforcement campaign involving multiple enforcement agencies and high-profile media tactics. In the past year, Regis University, the University of Colorado (Boulder), and the University of Northern Colorado have adopted similar strategies. During the week before traditionally heavy-drinking weekends, public announcements broadcasting the upcoming presence of DUI enforcement circulate the campus. With the heightened awareness of enforcement presence, many impaired individuals chose not to get behind the wheel. Throughout Colorado, DUI arrests have increased 29 percent and alcohol-related fatalities have decreased 23 percent since the program's inception.

Positive Social Tactics

In contrast to the usual "health terrorism" approaches many campuses have used in the past, many schools are finding positive results by focusing on what students are doing right. Scare tactics in the past played upon people's fears – fears of death, fears of rejection, fears of embarrassment, fears of incarceration. For many college students, fear is a short-lived emotion, especially when the risks for such outcomes are relatively low in their perception. Besides, most of them have been hearing about the dangers of alcohol abuse since elementary school days and tune out to such messages by their college years. The shift in today's alcohol abuse prevention is toward supporting non- and low-risk drinkers, challenging misperceptions students have about high-risk drinking, and highlighting protective behaviors.

According to Dr. Wechsler, seven out of eight low-risk drinkers have been negatively affected by another's drinking, but a very small minority ever formally complain. Students at Cornell University, the University of North Carolina at Chapel Hill, and the University of Arkansas at Little Rock recently combined efforts with the Center for Science in the Public Interest to develop a media advocacy website called "HadEnough." The site (www.cspinet.org/booze/hadenough) supports student involvement in reducing high-risk drinking on college campuses.

Another student-based group called the "CIRCLe Network" (College Initiatives to Reinvent Campus Life) states that its mission is "to promote the development of healthy, responsible, socially-conscious individual... (by) advocat(ing) social programming and social structures that foster true community and de-emphasize the role of alcohol on college campuses." The group started at Duke University and sought to provide students with social options that did not focus around alcohol. The CIRCLe founders were not satisfied with impacting just one campus, and began reaching out to other schools to challenge widely held perceptions of what college life is supposed to be like. Again, through the means of the Internet, this group hopes to disseminate information of "best practices" and ongoing consultation.

"Social Norms Marketing" is another idea related to positive social pressure that seems to be catching on. The idea behind this approach is based in the theory developed originally through the work of Wes Perkins and Alan Berkowitz. Stated simply, students typically overestimate alcohol and other drug use on campus. As a result this illusion creates a partially self-fulfilling prophecy. Social norms marketing is used to correct these misperceptions and decrease high-risk drinking.

Underlying these social norms is a theory called "pluralistic ignorance" or the belief that one's private attitudes and judgments are different from others. In terms of substance abuse issues, this notion translates to this: individuals who choose not to engage in high-risk drinking, assume that everyone around them is. These low-risk or nondrinkers then adopt a "bystander" position and "stay in the closet" about how they really feel about others' high-risk drinking and their own choice not to do so. This behavior perpetuates the misperception that everybody is being irresponsible because these bystanders become, in a sense, invisible.

Another group that adds to the problem consists of "carriers of misinformation." These people are students, faculty, staff, and even parents who, regardless of their own personal use or attitudes about alcohol and other drugs, pass on the misperceptions through conversation and comments. Through these carriers, the illusion gets reinforced.

When substance abuse educators continually focus on the problems of the minority of frequent high-risk drinkers, the misperception that all college students are problem drinkers gets perpetuated. Berkowitz and Perkins suggest

that strategies for changing these misperceptions are threefold: (1) misperceptions must be corrected through repetitive and visible messages reflecting the truth about campus drinking patterns, (2) bystanders need to come "out of the closet" and be public in their responsible behavior, and (3) educators and leaders should balance their emphasis on the problems of high-risk drinking with the acknowledgment and reinforcement of those who do not drink.

"Social Norms Marketing" approach uses traditional marketing techniques to promote healthy messages about student behavior to challenge the misperceptions. Mass market media approaches often are used including posters, campus newspaper advertisements, bus banners, and so on. Messages are carefully developed to be positive, inclusive, and empowering. Before mass circulation, they are pretested in student focus groups. Evaluation of impact is a continuous factor.

This "social norms" model of substance abuse prevention has resulted in consistent and impressive patterns of results at Northern Illinois University, Hobart and William Smith Colleges, the University of Arizona, and Western Washington University. After years of substance abuse prevention efforts that resulted in no change in student behavior, the social norming approach impacted misperceptions of student drinking and a 10 to 25 percent drop in high-risk drinking followed.

Intervention with High-Risk Drinkers

The idea behind this last step is to identify those on campus who are most at risk for experiencing consequences related to their alcohol misuse and give them brief, focused interventions that will hopefully redirect their thinking. Like the earlier mentioned concept of placing trees in the way of those practicing violence, this method attempts to place trees in the way of those practicing high-risk drinking.

Research by one of the leading experts in the field of substance abuse, Alan Marlatt, has found impressive results with these brief high-risk interventions. Dr. Marlatt heads the Addiction Behaviors Research Center at the University of Washington in Seattle and has demonstrated that his approach of "harm reduction" can reduce drinking-related problems five years postintervention. At-risk students identified as those with a family history of alcohol problems and those interested in joining a fraternity or sorority underwent 45-minute individualized motivational sessions in their freshman year. Students who went through this process were less likely to engage in high-risk drinking than students in the control group were. Marlatt claims that his program significantly accelerates "maturing out" of drinking behavior.

According to Marlatt and colleagues, harm reduction is referred to as indicated prevention (or in more formal circumstances secondary prevention) because it focuses on students who are somehow identified as high-risk and are already showing evidence of a problem. The primary goal of harm reduction is to have the student reduce risky behaviors and harmful effects from drinking rather than focusing on abstinence. The objectives of this brief intervention are designed to be student-chosen, realistic, and achievable. This approach realizes that allrisks will not be eliminated with this one intervention, but that lifestyle changes usually happen slowly over time through successive approximations.

Marlatt and colleagues designed the intervention model labeled BASICS (Brief Alcohol Screening and Intervention for College Students). This skills-based curriculum uses specific cognitive-behavioral strategies to guide students toward lower-risk drinking. The courses are nonconfrontational, nonjudgmental, and nonlabeling. For more information about this approach, read *Brief Alcohol Screening and Intervention for College Students: A Harm Reduction Approach*.[84]

Other campuses use the concept of "teachable moments" to intervene with high-risk drinkers. Students who are identified through the campus disciplinary system for alcohol abuse are sometimes mandated to the counseling center for a brief educational intervention. Effective intervention requires a combination of warmth, influence, resolution, and appropriate sanctions. Punishing, humiliating, or permissive interventions are not helpful and may make the situation worse. Those directing such interventions must carefully balance consistency with individualized approaches.

Brown University conducted a study of the effectiveness of this "teachable moments" approach conducted in emergency rooms. Again, medical providers conducted a 45-minute harm reduction session with teens being treated for extreme intoxication or injuries from an alcohol-related accident and compared the results to another group that received the standard ER intervention of assessment and referral. At a six-month follow-up, the group that received the "harm reduction" session had 32 percent fewer drinking and driving incidents, 50 percent fewer alcohol-related injuries, and far fewer alcohol-related consequences overall.

Other high-risk groups to consider are first-semester freshmen, especially those pledging fraternities or trying out for athletics, and high school students on recruitment visits. At Stanford University, campus administrators have experimented with another controversial approach. Prospective freshmen must sign a pledge that they will abstain from alcohol and drugs during their visit to the campus. Opponents of this strategy claim that it sends a very hostile welcome to potential new members of the community. The contract developers state that this is the most effective way to get the message across that the expectation is that all members of the community will be responsible, even if they are only visiting for a couple of days.

Many athletic departments are beginning to consider the value of "student host contracts" when bringing in high school athlete recruits. These contracts clearly outline expectations for student conduct in regards to alcohol and other drug use. Both the recruit and the student host sign the contracts.

In summary, the issues of alcohol and the college campus are too complex and broad to cover in one chapter. Rather, we have highlighted the emerging trends, the relationships between alcohol and violence, and the most promising intervention strategies currently known. For more information consult these resources:

The Higher Education Center
Education Development Center, Inc.
55 Chapel Street
Newton, MA 02158-1060
www.edc.org/hec

Dr. Henry Wechsler
Harvard School of Public Health
677 Huntington Avenue
Boston, MA 02115-6096
(617) 432-1137
www.hsph.harvard.edu/cas

Brief Alcohol Screening and Intervention for College Students (BASICS): A Harm Reduction Approach by Linda Dimeff, John Baer, Daniel Kivlahan, & G. Alan Marlatt (1999). Guilford Press.

The Century Council
www.centurycouncil.org

A Social Norms Approach to Preventing Binge Drinking at Colleges and Universities by Michael P. Haines (1996). A publication of The Higher Education Center for Alcohol and Other Drug Prevention.[85]

Part II

DEVELOPING ANTIBODIES:
GENERAL PREVENTION STRATEGIES
FOR THE COLLEGE COMMUNITY

Chapter 5

HEEDING THE SIGNS AND SYMPTOMS: WHAT ARE THE RED FLAGS FOR IMPENDING VIOLENCE?

JOHN NICOLETTI & SALLY SPENCER-THOMAS

IS VIOLENCE PREDICTABLE?

WHEN VIOLENCE OCCURS on a college campus, many respond by saying something to the effect of, "He (they) seemed so nice (quiet, normal, etc.). Who could have predicted this tragedy?" To be clear, violence is not predictable in the sense of being absolutely certain whether or not an individual will commit violence. There are too many intervening factors in our day-to-day lives that continuously influence decisions for behavioral science to ever be that accurate. But we can estimate violence potential based on a number of factors outlined in this chapter and throughout the book. Knowing these telltale signs can lead to effective prevention of violence; however, first we must overcome a basic myth many people hold about violent offenders.

MYTH: Violent perpetrators just snap.

FACT: Almost all violent perpetrators will give indications of violent intentions long before they act on them.

"He Just Snapped": Case Example at the University of Northern Colorado

On Tuesday, September 24, 1996, Joe Gallegos drove from Bayfield, Colorado to the University of Northern Colorado (UNC) in Greeley. Once there he held his ex-girlfriend and three other female students hostage for hours. He shot his girlfriend in the foot because he believed she had called the police. When negotiations with law enforcement began to deteriorate, Joe closed his eyes and stuck his head out the residence hall window. A SWAT marksman shot him. For 28 minutes Joe remained alive and fired back at police. He was taken to the local emergency room and was pronounced dead.

His girlfriend was interviewed by the *Rocky Mountain News* the following day and next to a large color photograph of her on crutches the paper quoted her as saying, "Joe was a nice person. He just snapped. He was kind and caring and considerate." The statement fed into the widespread myth that violent individuals experience a sudden unexpected change of character before acting out. It was also far from the truth.

Joe Gallegos began compiling a criminal record at the age of 13. His offenses included shoplifting, trespassing, criminal mischief, car theft, and assault. He was expelled from his high school because he participated in a food fight and set another student's pants on fire. Joe also had a problem with anger and alcohol. On one occasion, Joe and another youth visited the home of an acquaintance late at night. After breaking into the home through a glass window, Joe forced the victim to the floor and slashed him with a broken beer bottle. In 1995, he beat another man with a beer bottle. The assault resulted in a sentence of almost a year at a detention center, program for young offenders, halfway house, and supervised foster care.

Thirteen days before the UNC hostage situation in Greeley, Joe was paroled and claimed that he had found God. Joe went to visit his girlfriend on the day he was paroled, and she broke off the relationship. He told her, "I can't live without you. I love you too much."

Over the next few days, Joe began to show his true colors. He became violently jealous at a party and grabbed his ex-girlfriend, dragging her down some stairs. After returning to his home in southern Colorado, Joe obtained a 9mm semiautomatic gun previously stolen from the Cortez hardware store. On Monday, September 23, Joe called his girlfriend to attempt reconciliation, but she refused and he hung up on her. He then proceeded to dismantle and hide the kitchen phone of the home he shared with three young Christian men who took him in under the belief that Joe was turning his life around.

What happened over the next several hours is a matter of speculation and evidence interpretation as all of the witnesses are dead. Police officials surmise that Joe did not want any interference in his plan to kill his girlfriend. Furthermore, he needed a car. So he killed his three roommates, execution style, and took the truck belonging to one of them. He drove straight to Greeley, consuming more than 40 times the normal dose of ephedrine, a nasal congestion medicine with side effects of anxiety and impaired judgment. This pattern of behaviors was not indicative of a person who "just snapped," but rather one of an antisocial personality whose actions were premeditated and deadly.

ANALYZING THREATS

Threats, past interests and conduct, and current verbal and physical behavior can all serve as indications for violence potential. For many different strains of campus violence, perpetrators will make multiple threats before acting out. Therefore, it is imperative that protectors have some basic knowledge of analyzing threats. Understanding key aspects of three different types of threats – direct, conditional, and veiled – is a critical part of threat investigation.

When we look at certain forms of violence such as avenger and domestic violence, we find most perpetrators will make verbal or written threats before acting. For workplace violence and school avenger shootings, essentially all perpetrators made some sort of threat, before they committed violence.

When analyzing threats, verbatim reporting is critical. The exact wording of the threat will give you a clearer picture of the perpetrator's motive. Both written and verbal threats should be preserved exactly as they are made. Background noises, accents, tone of voice, and rate of speech also contain important information about who the perpetrator is and should be documented. Any envelopes or packaging of written threats should be kept for fingerprint or DNA analysis if needed.

Protectors must take all threats seriously, even if they sound ridiculous or are presented in the form of a "joke." Why should we take threats so seriously? Because generally speaking, people tend to reward those who threaten. Receivers of threats tend to either back down or retaliate. That is, they give in to the threat demand or they fight back in anger. Giving in to the threat is clearly a reward for the perpetrator. However, even if the receivers of the threat retaliate with lots of public negative action, the perpetrator is still reinforced with attention. Threats that are ignored give the perpetrator the message that he or she is not being taken seriously. All of these approaches lead to the likelihood that perpetrators will continue to use threats to get what they want.

Most threats are harmless, just individuals blowing off steam and not thinking before they speak. However, what has one learned about a person who makes a threat on a campus where no threats are allowed? They may have impulse control problems. They may be trying to manipulate or intimidate others. They may be defiant of rules, or the threat may be a cry for help or attention. In any event, all of these motives are potential indicators of future violence. If the individual continues to make threats after being warned to stop, one has learned much more. Investigators have a stronger case for an individual who is intent on committing violence unless sufficient impediments are put in place.

Threats should always be analyzed for credibility, seriousness, and lethality. Threats can be nonverbal, verbal, or written, and fall into three categories: direct, conditional, and veiled. The following descriptions of threats and cues are adapted from *Violence Goes to Work*[86] and *Violence Goes to School*.[87]

Direct Threats

A direct threat is a statement of clear intent to harm someone. There is no ambiguity or doubt in the statement. Examples are, "I'm going to kill you," or "I'm going to blow them away." A direct threat is punishable by law and the authorities should be contacted in this incidence. Individuals who make detailed threats regarding specific targets are more likely to become violent than those who make vague threats. Generally, the more specific the threat, the more concerned protectors should be. If the individual identifies types of weapons, names of targets, or an exact time or location of the violent act, immediate action should be taken. When individuals are that specific, we know that they

have thought about their violent fantasy for a long time and have worked out all the details to their satisfaction. The potential for threat to become reality at this point is very real.

Conditional Threats

A conditional threat is made contingent on a certain set of circumstances. These threats contain the word "if," or the word "or." These types of threats are designed to manipulate or intimidate the target into compliance. Examples of these types of threats include, "You better do this *or* you're dead," and, "If you don't give me what I want, you will pay." If these threats are not met with resistance and clear signs of intolerance, they are likely to increase as they are often powerfully reinforced.

Veiled Threats

Veiled threats are the hardest type to address because they are often vague and subject to interpretation. These types of threats are very real for the recipients, but feel like they lose some of their impact when repeated to others. The perpetrator easily minimizes this type of threat, by refuting the receiver's interpretation. For example, the perpetrator may say the recipient just blew the situation out of proportion, or that they only intended the threat as a joke. An example of a veiled threat is the student who says, "I can see how something like the Texas sniper can happen. I'm surprised more people don't go off the edge."

Veiled threats are often used as a form of harassment in stalking situations. These threats were a consistent theme in Richard Farely's letters to Laura Black before he hunted her down and killed four people at his workplace. He wrote, "You cost me a job, 40,000 dollars in equity taxes I can't pay, and a foreclosure. Yet, I still like you. Why do you want to find out how far I'll go? ... I absolutely will not be pushed around, and I'm beginning to get tired of being nice." Veiled threats are the most difficult to detect due to their vagueness and multiple interpretations. Again, the overall context and multiple signs are important when deciphering the significance.

In the aftermath of avenger-type violence, witnesses are often asked if they ever heard the perpetrator make any threats before the killings. These witnesses often say they "didn't know that they knew." In hindsight, these witnesses were able to say that the perpetrators often made comments or acted in ways that made them uncomfortable about possible violence, but they did not know they were dealing with veiled threats. Therefore, training for students and campus employees is critical to help them learn how to identify threats and how to report them.

A Note on Student Writing

When the dark and strangely violent writing of the Virginia Tech perpetrator emerged, increasing numbers of faculty became concerned about how to discriminate legitimate artistic exploration of a violent subject from a sign that the author might be expressing a veiled threat. One article in the *Wall Street Journal* stated, "... schools are trying to distinguish the dark musings of college fiction from deadly manifestos that foretell campus violence."[88]

One creative writing professor from Virginia Tech and his colleagues developed some probing questions to help faculty decide what to do with a violent essay (summarized here)[89]:

- Is the creative work excessively violent? Does the violence seem more expressive of range and anger than it does any literary aesthetic purpose?
- Do the characters question their violent actions or does the writing suggest unmediated venting of rage and anger?

- Is this the student's first piece of violent writing? Is violence the main theme of everything the student has written, "or does other writing suggest that violence is something the student is experimenting with for literary effect?"
- Are the violent actions and outcomes so disturbing or extreme they seem beyond the purpose of the larger narrative?
- Is the violence of the writing targeted at any one specific group that might pose a threat to other students?

However, even the author of these questions acknowledged they could be misused or could hamper creative freedom. Mostly the mantra for faculty has been "when in doubt, check it out." There are ways to protect student confidentiality and present the Behavioral Intervention Team with the data to determine whether or not a more invasive intervention is warranted.

NOTE: There is not a single variable capable of predicting violence. In the absence of disconfirming evidence, one can tentatively assume that the profile characteristics are additive. That is, the more traits or behaviors people have, the greater the probability that they may act violently.

DISTAL CUES: GENERAL INDICATORS OF VIOLENCE POTENTIAL

The following list of warning signs associated with violence is neither comprehensive nor exhaustive. Rather, the list intends to offer general guidelines to determine whether a situation warrants the evaluation of a violence prevention specialist.

History of Violence

Past behavior is the best predictor of future behavior. This maxim applies to violent behavior as well. The probability of future violence increases with each prior violent act. Seriously violent individuals often have histories that include mutilation, torture, and killing of animals. Violent campus offenders might not have such a disturbing violence history, but they may have a series of disciplinary offenses or run-ins with the campus police. When a student transfers to a new campus, violent offenses and disciplinary records usually do not follow. Military disciplinary action, prior arrests or convictions, and prior violent disciplinary action at a previous college are all areas for concern.

Poor Impulse Control

Many violent actions are precipitated by a deterioration of impulse control. From a developmental standpoint, by the time students are of college age, they should have a reasonable ability to inhibit unacceptable social behaviors. By nature, younger children have less capacity for impulse control since their mental capacity is not yet well developed. Older adolescents and adults should have a better sense to think before they react. In daily conversation, most people are able to screen out inappropriate things to say and do, even when the thought crosses their mind. Violent individuals seem to have a poorer ability to do this. Perhaps this is partly because so many of the campus violence perpetrators are under the influence of alcohol and other drugs at the time of the crime. Some indications of poor impulse control include a high number of moving traffic violations, destruction of property, or making terminal statements such as "I'm quitting" without much forethought.

Unsuccessful Personal History

Individuals who have repeated failures throughout their life may be at risk for developing low self-esteem. A person continuously confronted with unattained goals, rejections, and unfulfilled dreams may choose antisocial avenues to reconcile the imbalance they feel in their life. Clearly, this factor is not the case for all perpetrators of violence when one considers the number of high-profile athletes and popular fraternity members who are accused of sexual crimes, brutal hazing, and other forms of campus violence. This is just one variable of many to consider when assessing an individual's potential for violence.

Perceived Injustice History

A perceived injustice history is frequently evident in workplace violence situations. Often the perpetrator has filed a series of grievances before killing. On campuses, perceived injustice may take the form of an irate student denied a passing grade or a group of students denied their "right" to drink on campus. These self-righteous individuals feel justified in their anger and blame others for their violent actions. They find validation in their role as a victim in an unfair world. Usually, these individuals will start by filing grievances, making protesting phone calls, or writing angry letters filled with statements of blame such as, "Look what you have made me do!"

Obsession

Obsessions are persistent thoughts, impulses, or images that preoccupy the mind. Many types of campus violence perpetrators can have obsessions of one form of another. Avengers and predators can have obsessive thoughts as they became fixated on another person or activity. Stalking and persistent harassment are also forms of obsession.

Substance Abuse

As reviewed in Chapters 3 and 4, alcohol or drugs can interfere dramatically with reasoning ability, inhibition, anticipation of consequences, and the judgment to distinguish right from wrong. Alcohol has repeatedly been shown to have a strong link to violence on college campuses. Thus, someone with an alcohol or multidrug abuse history may be at higher risk for committing violence.

Fascination and Proficiency with Weapons

Extreme fascination with weapons, extensive gun collections, and shooting skills are indicators to consider when assessing the potential for violence. The individual who continually discusses or carries weapons, names their weapons, or evidences an unusual enthusiasm for semiautomatic or automatic guns presents a greater risk. This type of obsession may also apply to other forms of destruction, such as explosives and bombs.

A clear red flag for violence potential is the proficiency with explosives. While generally speaking our culture is not concerned with ownership of guns for hunting and target practice, there are no pro-social uses for bombs. In civilian society, there would be no reason for someone to have knowledge about how to build and detonate bombs other than for destruction.

Personality Disorders

Personality disorders develop as maladaptive patterns of behavior become deeply entrenched over a long time. With violent individuals, many precipitant and early warning signs of personality and emotional difficulties can be identified in childhood. Some of the early indications of antisocial tendencies include excessive lying, fire setting, bedwetting, and cruelty to animals. Narcissistic features also appear prevalent with this population, and their self-perception may vacillate between feelings of worthlessness and superiority. Personality problems can be identified

by explosive tempers, irrational thought patterns, manipulative conduct, and rapid mood swings.

Some Elements of Major Mental Illness

Major mental disorders include a loss of contact with reality, and can be manifested in paranoia and severe depression. Behavioral indicators are delusions, hallucinations, bizarre thoughts, or talking to oneself about irrational subjects. Extreme paranoia can sometimes lead to violence when an individual believes that others are unnecessarily spying on him or her.

Preoccupation with Violence

Individuals who evidence a preoccupation with violence will constantly talk about the subject, and find ways to expose themselves to further violence. Examples of this could include violent musical lyrics, movies, the Internet, and other media. Their ability to generate alternative solutions to their problems is diminished as they increasingly focus on details of violence and fantasies of violent rampages. Recently increasing numbers of violent and hate-filled websites are surfacing on the Internet. These websites fuel those who are obsessed with violence by giving them anonymity and a connection with other deviant individuals.

Other Situational Variables

An individual's overall "life context" is important in assessing his or her potential for violence. The individual who experiences multiple stressors appears to be at heightened risk to engage in violence. Specific factors to look for include:

- recent life and family stressors
- an inadequate or deviant social network

- medical or neurological disorders
- current psychological disorders
- a history of recent help-seeking behavior
- limited future opportunities

PROXIMAL CUES: VERBAL AND BEHAVIORAL INDICATORS

As humans, we are strongly verbal-oriented and tend to pay attention to what people say. Too often, however, we ignore the discrepancy between what is said and how it is said, and go only with the literal spoken word. When someone's verbal and nonverbal signals are incongruent, the nonverbal communication is almost always more reflective of the true emotional state. A person who says, "I'm not angry," but is red in the face and has clenched fists is showing nonverbal signs of anger. As people grow older, they find ways to control verbal behavior, but most are unable to control the physiological changes that accompany anger. Many times, people who are confronted about their anger are unaware of the messages their bodies are sending.

In addition to the discrepancy between the verbal and nonverbal, the *absence* of expected physical reactions to emotional situations can be an indication that the individual has serious emotional problems and may have little or no access to his or her feelings. We see these people in courtrooms yawning as they are given the death sentence. Or in the footage of the Columbine massacre when Eric Harris and Dylan Klebold seem to express intermittent icy and giddy demeanors as they perpetrate one of the most horrific crimes of our country. Individuals like this can commit heinous crimes because they lack empathy for others. In other words, they have no conscience. This type of discrepancy during violence is one of the most disturbing for most witnesses and others affected because it is so inconsistent with normal human responding.

Verbal Abuse Continuum

Language often reflects the emotional or mental state of an individual, and can warn of future behavior. Verbal statements can be placed on a continuum from compliant to assaulting. The following list explains the five categories on the verbal abuse continuum (see graphic below):

- *Compliant:* The least threatening verbal declarations indicate cooperation and compliance. The individual is not communicating any threat or resistance. This level reflects normal verbal interactions.
- *Negative:* This level of verbal communication is basically pessimistic. The individual frequently complains about a variety of things and responds negatively to helpful advice. This level of negativity is not necessarily dangerous, and some might argue it characterizes much of adolescence.
- *Abusive:* As the individual becomes more upset and distraught, the verbal

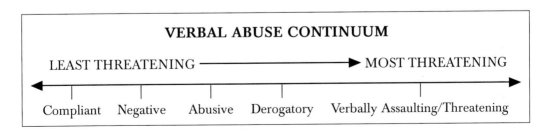

VERBAL ABUSE CONTINUUM

LEAST THREATENING ⟶ MOST THREATENING

Compliant   Negative   Abusive   Derogatory   Verbally Assaulting/Threatening

expressions escalate to abusiveness. This stage involves general nastiness and name calling. The individual appears intense, blames others excessively, and frequently uses the word "you" in an accusatory tone. For example, "You never understand," or "You don't know."

- *Derogatory:* The more the language deteriorates and becomes offensive, the greater the risk factor. At this level, the individual's conversation centers on making derogatory remarks, put downs, and harsh criticism of others' ideas. Language is marked by vulgar, racist, sexist, and slanderous words. For example, "You bitch," or "That dirty…" The purpose of this language is to dehumanize the target. By turning the person into an object, killers feel less connected to the consequences of their actions. This is a common defense mechanism during war when soldiers turn the individuals of the enemy forces into something subhuman, usually in the form of racial slurs.
- *Verbally Assaulting/Threatening:* This is the most serious verbal communication level. The individual is clearly threatening or attempting to intimidate others with language. Verbally assaulting behavior may include threats of physical assault and death. The more bizarre, destructive, and sadistic the language, the greater the risk of violence.

The lower levels of verbal abuse are designed to manipulate, intimidate, and otherwise control the behavior of others. These statements suggest the individual has minimal coping and/or interpersonal skills. While the lower levels of verbal abuse are not particularly dangerous, they do require attention and monitoring. The individual who makes verbally abusive, derogatory, or assaulting statements is a serious threat to the campus. This individual is likely experiencing an intense level of rage which could result in impulsive or destructive actions if timely intervention does not occur.

Physical Abuse Continuum

Physical behaviors are also rated on a continuum from least to most threatening. Physically destructive or abusive conduct could reflect a deteriorated internal state or poor impulse control. Either of these is a potential warning sign of violence (see graphic below).

- *Compliant:* A person who is fully cooperative demonstrates the least threatening form of physical behavior. This level reflects normal behavior.
- *Passive Resistant:* This type of behavior is also known as "passive aggressive" and is characterized by subtle defiance. Children and adolescents are masters at this type of behavior. They engage in resistive behaviors that are just under the threshold of noncompliance. They may follow directives but be extremely slow, putting forth only minimally acceptable effort. In a physical manner, they may use their body mass to impede another's effort by blocking a doorway for example. On college campuses, this form of resistance may manifest as "sit ins" or student strikes.

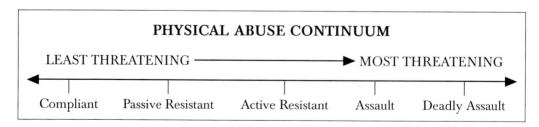

PHYSICAL ABUSE CONTINUUM

LEAST THREATENING ⟶ MOST THREATENING

Compliant   Passive Resistant   Active Resistant   Assault   Deadly Assault

- *Active Resistant:* This level of physical behavior involves a combination of actively resistant and passive-aggressive behavior. The individual actively resists any form of problem resolution or arbitration, and may engage in subtle or overt defiance or alternate between these styles. There is a noticeable shift in the scope and degree of resistance. The actively resistant individual is demonstrating signs of decreasing impulse control, and may show physical defiance toward authority figures. Examples of active resistance include slamming doors, turning over desks, or throwing objects. There is no actual bodily harm, but the threat of escalating violence exists.
- *Assault:* The physical threat at this level is high. The individual displays both verbally and physically aggressive behaviors, and is likely experiencing eroding impulse control resulting in a state of dangerousness. The individual's intention is to harm or destroy either property or people. Attempts to gain compliance at this point are met with hostile resistance or attack. For example, the individual may engage in an increased number of physical fights or attempt to hurt others with objects or vehicles.
- *Deadly Assault:* The final category is the most extreme of physical behaviors and represents the greatest level of danger to others. At this stage, the individual focuses on killing a specific target, harming a group of individuals, or committing suicide. The potential for critical harm or death to others is high

and immediate remedial intervention is necessary in order to thwart violence. NOTE: The above listed levels of verbal and physical compliance are provided for educational purposes only. A team of trained professionals should analyze the risk factors present in the individual's behavior.

PRACTICING

When violence is premeditated, the perpetrator will often engage in lower-level forms of violence to "test out the system" and his or her own courage. These practicing efforts can happen either mentally through violent fantasies or physically against "lower-level" targets. Without intervention, practicing efforts can escalate from fantasy to violence against property to harassment to deadly force. When practicing behaviors are noticed, protectors must work to create barriers to further escalation. As we discussed in Chapter 1, perpetrators often follow the analogy of skiing. At the top of the violence slope, the perpetrator begins slowly, but soon picks up speed. Increasing the intensity and frequency of violence, the perpetrator shoots down the mountain until he or she reaches a tree. When a tree is in the path, the perpetrator must make a decision. Do I slow down? Do I try a different trail? Do I turn a different way? The more trees or barriers in the perpetrator's path, the more difficult it is to continue on the violence mission. The rest of the chapters in this section are about "planting trees," or building barriers.

Chapter 6

BUILDING BARRIERS TO VIOLENCE
PART I: AMASSING THE ARMY

SALLY SPENCER-THOMAS & JOHN NICOLETTI

VIOLENCE IS AN ISSUE that almost everyone on campus is invested in preventing. Other hot topics on campus can come and go, or only light the passions of a few dedicated individuals, but violence touches the lives of many. There are many ways to channel this concern into effective action. A team approach is often the most effective tactic a campus can employ to prevent violence. Campus community members, whether they be students, faculty, or staff, are likely to be more committed to prevention and intervention policies if they help design them and put them into practice. A team approach also helps in the planning by allowing for an overall view of problem areas and potential obstacles. The following chapter lists many ways for campuses to assemble their most valuable asset: the campus community.

CAMPUS-COMMUNITY COALITIONS

In order to support a public health approach to violence prevention, we must go "beyond brochures," and start to cultivate teams broad and deep that can accomplish a wide range of goals far beyond the capacity of a single person or department.[90] Coalitions developed between the campus and community are likely to develop a "reciprocal influence" on each other while pooling resources and unifying messages to all those affected by violence.[91] Because they represent a wide range of interests from diverse stakeholders, the impact of a well-run coalition has the potential to be broad and self-sustaining. Campus-community coalitions consist of broad cross-sections of the university and surrounding neighborhoods. Campuses exist within larger communities, and as such, the larger community must be part of the solution when dealing with violence on college campuses. With campus-community coalitions, key stakeholders from the campus and community meet together to begin a discussion surrounding campus violence. This diverse group works toward the common mission of a safe campus and community.

The benefits of such a group are numerous. Members can get a very comprehensive picture of what is happening when so many interests are represented. Resources are shared and communication is enhanced to maximize the effectiveness of prevention efforts. Furthermore, cooperation is fostered when such diverse groups meet face-to-face. Credibility is enhanced when a wide range of individuals deems it an important issue.

Building and maintaining a coalition can be challenging. The reality of scheduling so many different individuals is daunting, and sustaining member motivation can be exhausting. Sometimes in such a large group, diffusion of responsibility settles in and getting things accomplished is difficult. Nevertheless, because of the benefits outlined above, a coalition is critical to the success of any prevention effort.

Effective coalitions share common characteristics, according to the Community Anti-Drug Coalitions of America.[92] This group studied the processes of eight successful coalitions and found them to be both highly flexible and structured. They concluded that the most successful coalitions operated with the following elements:

- a documented mission statement
- visionary and committed leadership
- willingness to share the spotlight
- a strategic plan
- a well-defined organizational structure
- an understanding of the local community leadership and volunteer networks
- representative membership and staff
- diverse partners
- recognizing accomplishments of member organizations
- clear expectations
- strong communication skills
- professional development opportunities
- diversified and relevant funding (often comes later in the process)
- up-to-date technology
- continuous evaluation

Potential coalition members may include:

- residence life
- health services
- personal counseling
- legal advisors
- upper-level administration
- campus security or police
- student leaders and other students
- athletics department
- faculty

- Greek life
- admissions
- public affairs
- alumni
- neighborhood and business associations
- local police
- alcohol retailers and bar owners
- city council
- feeder high school administrators

Presidential support for the work of this coalition can give it the momentum needed to generate successful outcomes. William DeJong urges senior leadership to, "Be vocal, be visible, be visionary"[93] when it comes to prevention issues. His article was focused primarily on the issues of alcohol and other drug prevention, but the message remains the same for violence prevention: "There is no shame in stepping forward, but there is great risk in holding back and just hoping for the best: higher insurance premiums, property damage, greater security costs, poor student retention, potential civil liability, and more seriously, an elevated risk of student injury or death."[94]

BEHAVIORAL INTERVENTION TEAM

Another step in addressing violence prevention is the development of a behavioral intervention team. This team is smaller and more focused than the campus coalition. The team usually consists of those individuals dedicated to taking action roles rather than just providing input. This team should consist of individuals trained in the evaluation of and intervention with threat assessment and potentially violent situations. Other specialties that would benefit the team are policy development, media and public relations, and human relations. While building this subcoalition, campuses should be selective in choosing the representatives. Solution seekers should be favored over status seekers. According to damage control expert Eric Denzenhall (2008, *Damage Control*), this lean and mean team ultimately should be "Benevolent dictatorships not democracies. A crisis team with too many people is not a crisis team, it is a committee. Committees do not solve crises."[95]

The Behavioral Intervention Team's objective is violence prevention and response.[96] Members are responsible for addressing threats and confronting violent behavior, and may assist in assessing potential for violence. They will serve as the primary decision makers in violent crises, and will be communication liaisons between internal and external responders. The team is responsible for making critical decisions quickly. They will develop the protocol in case of a threat or violent incident and establish a plan for the protection of students, staff, and other potential targets.

Of note, a college or university should carefully consider what to call this team. In earlier writings, campuses were encouraged to call these teams "Threat Assessment Teams," but have started to move away from this label because it automatically sets up a dynamic of opposition. Students and staff usually have a way of finding out these sorts of things and when they do, they are usually more than a little put off to know that they were the subject of such a committee. Instead, the term Behavioral Intervention Team does not carry such connotations and may imply that the committee is working toward the best interest of the community *and* the person of concern.

In the aftermath of violence, Behavioral Intervention Team members help coordinate affected parties such as victims, families, employees, media, government, or law enforcement. For this reason, they must have up-to-date knowledge about victim assistance and community service programs. They will

---

Maximizing the Effectiveness of the Behavioral Intervention Team

Due to the nature of the response duties of the Behavioral Intervention Team, the group must be more efficient and purposeful than the broader campus coalition. For this reason, the members must have a well-understood command structure and protocol. When campuses are developing this team, the groups should answer the following questions to clarify issues of command and response.

- Who assumes control when a dangerous situation develops? The Behavioral Intervention Team must establish an on-call leader who will activate the team when needed.
- At what point does the team begin activating the response plan? What happens to the chain of command at different points of responding to violence?
- How will information be communicated within and outside the organization?
- Who has final authority in decisions about the outcome for a violent or potentially violent student?
- Can the team negotiate with others?
- How will the team act as a liaison with all others involved?
- Who is responsible for the continuation of day-to-day business operations?
- Who will have the necessary information about students and staff (e.g., emergency contacts, phone numbers, addresses)?
- What alternative facilities are available if needed?

Adapted from *Violence Goes to Work*.[97]

be a primary referral source assisting victims with placement in immediate and ongoing counseling and support services.

The team must work in conjunction with local law enforcement to prevent guesswork in time of crisis. Authority and autonomy issues must be determined in advance. Specifically, when a campus is in a critical situation, law enforcement officials should be the incident commanders and assume authority. The scope of the other responsibilities of the group and particular individuals' tasks should be assigned. The Behavioral Intervention Team (see box) may also serve as the Crisis Response Team as described in Chapter 10.

SPECIAL FORCES

Special forces are campus groups who have additional impact on preventing and responding to campus violence, and consist of groups already in existence. These groups usually have multiple objectives, of which violence prevention is one. Nevertheless, they can have critical influence by connecting with high-risk individuals or situations not accessible by the Behavioral Intervention Team.

Upper Administration

Presidents and chancellors must be clear about their vision for their institution as a nonviolent entity. Ultimately, many difficult decisions are placed in the hands of these leaders. Many decisions lead to no-win situations. Expelling a violent student could lead to campus and alumni uproar in the short run and retaining that student could lead to future episodes of violence in time. Stricter policies regarding alcohol may provoke riots while lax policies may invite opportunities for many forms of campus violence.

In addition to being clear and consistent in their messages about violence prevention, campus leaders must be visible as well. Top-down support for violence prevention efforts can often trickle into a downpour of support from other campus departments. At some of the most active campuses, presidents have been involved in a number of ways. They have written letters to parents and alumni on these issues. They have also addressed the current campus community through compassionate yet hard-line speeches.

Faculty and Staff

Faculty members are natural participants in violence prevention efforts. Often they are the most highly respected individuals on campus. They also have daily access to students and can be a fundamental means to address violence prevention issues. As such faculty may be first-line responders to violence. In their classrooms, they may notice questionable student injuries or absenteeism. In writing assignments, professors may read about self-disclosed victims of rape or other assault. In these cases, faculty must be knowledgeable and comfortable in handling these difficult situations and summoning the help of others if necessary.

Curriculum infusion has been a buzzword of the last decade. It refers to the process of bringing current social issues affecting students into the classroom. Originally, curriculum infusion efforts focused primarily on drugs and alcohol. Faculty members were encouraged to integrate these topics with the course material at hand. Chemistry professors focused on the chemical structures of substances, history professors discussed changes in attitudes and policies dealing with substances over time, psychology professors talked about the impact of alcohol and drugs on relationships and emotions, and so on. Other professors developed entire courses to address the issues of alcohol and drugs.

Similarly, curriculum infusion has been used to increase awareness about violence and violence prevention. Emory University offers an interdisciplinary minor in violence studies.[98] This undergraduate course looks at the issues of violence from several different disciplines including history, sociology, biology, and literature. Beyond the classroom, students are required to complete an internship to gain hands-on experience with violence issues.

Many faculty members are also highly visible on campuses. They are well known by students and other staff, and their opinions are valued. When faculty share their own experiences with violence, the impact is powerful. At Regis University, faculty members joined students and other staff at an annual "Speak Out" on the library steps. During this forum, individuals voluntarily step up to a microphone and describe how alcohol and campus violence has affected their lives. Stories from faculty who talked about how they had been affected by these issues made a lasting impression on all those who witnessed the event.

Throughout this book, we speak to the numerous ways other campus staff can take a part in preventing violence. Most notably, counseling services, residence life, student activities, health services, athletics, campus ministry, and Greek life all play multiple roles in dealing with these issues.

Greek Life and Athletics

Greek life students and athletes are some of the most powerful students on campus. Many of them hold leadership positions and are respected role models. Others have charismatic personalities and are often in the spotlight. These groups also tend to have tremendous alumni support. For these and many other reasons, Greek life students and athletes can play a crucial role in violence prevention.

Because Greek life students, athletes, and respective advisors often feel scapegoated for all the problems of campus violence, they are often motivated to become part of a solution for change. Many Greek systems may be on the verge of being phased out, and thus, students who believe in the benefits of Greek life are actively trying to change the perception that all fraternity and sorority members are troublemakers. For example, some Greeks have formed chapters of GAMMA – a nationally organized peer-based health promotion organization designed to promote positive lifestyles.

Programs such as Mentors in Violence Prevention[99] (MVP) target student-athletes to empower them to become active bystanders to gender violence. The presenters also meet with the entire coaching staff and athletic director to make sure these leaders are also supporting violence prevention attitudes through their comments and behavior. Throughout the program, the facilitators focus on the social status of male student-athletes and the ways their leadership can create change in reducing all male violence against women.

Peer Educators

Peer education is an effective tool for creating awareness and supporting healthy lifestyle.[100] The BACCHUS Network has supported peer education efforts nationwide for decades and has demonstrated that peer education makes a difference. Campuses use peer educators to coordinate awareness weeks such as "Sexual Responsibility Week," "Alcohol Awareness Week," and "Safe Spring Break Week." Media campaigns, peer theater, interactive educational workshops, and informational displays organized by these students can have a positive effect on campus awareness and advocacy. Peer educators also work with students one-on-one by being active listeners and effective referral agents.

When asked how they made a difference[101]:

- 82 percent said they taught new information.
- 64 percent said they changed an attitude.
- 60 percent said they caused a positive behavior change.
- 55 percent said they confronted a risky behavior.
- 25 percent said they caused a change in behavior that resulted in saving a life.

Peer educators not only have an impact on their campuses they are also positively affected by their experience. Many peer educators claim that being in the public light supporting healthy choices holds one accountable for making good decisions. Across the board, peer educators make healthier decisions regarding substance use than do their peers.

Parents

As a result of the 1998 Higher Education Amendment Act, colleges can notify parents about disciplinary actions involving alcohol and drug violations of students under the age of 21. Many view this amendment as an opportunity to promote student health and individual responsibility by giving parents a chance to talk with their sons and daughters about the decisions they are making.

Parents can become active participants in preventing college violence. They are usually the most influential people in students' lives. Parents should ask for crime statistics of a campus before sending students. By law, colleges and universities must release the information. With this information, parents can warn their sons and daughters about potential dangers on college campuses by being well versed about the risks students face. Parents can also talk about the fact that according to national surveys, most students are not drinking to excess all the time and are not having multiple sex partners. Finally, parents can encourage effective coping and communication

skills, and support their daughters and sons through this transition.

A resource for parents of college students is College Parents of America, a national organization providing a voice for parents of college students. This organization can be contacted by calling toll free 1-888-256-4627 or by visiting their website at www.college parents.org.

Campus Law Enforcement

Campus law enforcement has taken great strides in the recent past to become a more effective presence on college campuses. According to research cited in *Violence on Campus*,[102] three out of four campuses have enforcement personnel with arrest powers. Campus law enforcement personnel frequently come into contact with many different segments of the campus population in their work as protectors and emergency responders. They are often responsible for public safety programs, violence containment, investigations, escort services, and other protective measures.

When it comes to addressing campus violence problems, the breadth of responsibility for campus law enforcement personnel remains under debate. Should officers have a community resource mentality and lots of direct community-building contact with the campus members on a daily basis? Or should the officers take more of a militaristic stance, wearing more formal enforcement attire and carrying weapons? Many departments struggle with the boundaries between their roles and the roles of local law enforcement. When is it all right to keep security concerns and investigations within house and when should outside enforcers be called in?

In any event, campus security and police play a vital role in preventing campus violence on many levels. They are often first-line responders to campus violence incidents and have eyewitness accounts of the situation.

Officers are often able to build rapport with students in a different way than faculty and other staff because security officers are present with students every day, all day long. Unlike most local law enforcement agencies, campus enforcers are frequently called upon to sit on committees and task forces where they have direct input to policy decisions and prevention initiatives. Additionally, security offices can serve as databases for campus crime information. Roles and responses of campus law enforcement are further discussed in Chapter 8.

TRAINING

A crucial component in violence prevention is the adequate training of students, faculty, and other employees concerning the dynamics of campus violence and effective preventive measures. Shared responsibility should be the emphasized message throughout the campus community. Three potential training seminars can help give the campus community an overview of the issues and potential solutions.

- **Campus Violence: What Is the Reality?** (2 hours)

Designed mainly for students, this workshop should help participants get a better understanding of the myths and realities of campus violence. Several different types of campus violence should be briefly discussed and broad potential solutions suggested.

- **Campus Violence: Become Part of the Solution** (4–6 hours)

This workshop should be designed for faculty, staff, student leaders, parents, and other concerned "protectors" who want to become more involved in preventing violence. Policies and prevention strategies should be covered in more depth and participants should leave with an understanding of what they can do to take the next step. This level of training is most appropriate for the campus-community coalition.

- **Campus Violence: Behavioral Intervention Team In-Service** (1–2 day seminar)

The program should be designed to train the small group of individuals who will be responsible for making the critical decisions before, during, and after a violence incident. In addition to the previous topics, the training should go into great detail about threat analysis, risk assessment, emergency preparedness, and crisis response. A critical part of training for this core team are "tabletop exercises" – exercises and drills that show officials any weak spots in protocols and should be conducted annually as new forms of violence and advancement in technology emerge.

Chapter 7

BUILDING BARRIERS TO VIOLENCE PART II: DEVELOPING POLICY AND PROCEDURES FOR THREATS AND VIOLENCE

JOHN NICOLETTI & SALLY SPENCER-THOMAS

To PREVENT VIOLENCE effectively, colleges need to develop specific and well-known violence prevention procedures. There is no cookie-cutter approach to violence prevention. Each campus must adapt the following recommendations to their unique situations and concerns. In addition, interventions for different types of campus violence (e.g., sexual assault, hate crimes, hazing, and so on) are more specific than strategies suggested here, and are dealt with in the chapters in the last section of this book. Campuses that have used the following general prevention and intervention strategies have been consistently more effective in dealing with campus violence than those that do not.

CONCEPTUALIZING PREVENTION AND INTERVENTION

Prevention and intervention occur at three levels:

1. *Detection and Awareness.* Protectors must have systematic ways of becoming aware of the signs and signals of potential violence. Anonymous tip lines and other streamlined reporting procedures can facilitate data gathering. Employee hiring practices, and to some extent admissions policies, must consider background patterns of violence when assessing the risk of bringing an individual to campus. Front-line responders must be aware of practice phenomena. They must be able to detect escalating threats and violent behavior to implement swift intervention before something more serious occurs.

2. *Delay and Insulation.* At this stage, "trees" and technology come into play. Protectors must be prepared with a range of trees or barriers as described in Chapter 2. Again, trees can question, confront, or implement consequences. The idea is to put a roadblock in the path of the violent individual. Technological approaches are designed to slow down the perpetrator and insulate potential victims. These include anything from ID cards to locked buildings to tear gas.

3. *Strategic Response.* Strategic responses must occur both on an individual level and on a campus-community level. Individuals must not only have the skills to escape or avoid violence, they also must be able to give themselves permission to act appropriately when the situation demands. On a community level, campuses must have well-coordinated response strategies both internally and with outside agencies.

GENERAL PREVENTION STRATEGIES

Multitiered Approach

All effective violence prevention strategies are comprehensive and broad-based. They go far beyond a single office or individual, and involve efforts on every level of the institution and many aspects of the community. Effective strategies target groups and individuals, employ large-scale and small-scale programming, and enact a host of different methods to create change. Each effort reinforces the next.

Clear Communication

Communication regarding violence, both written and verbal, must be clear and consistent. Messages must coincide with the mission of the institution and the image of the school. Catalogue descriptions, pre-enrollment experiences, and orientation events set first impressions of the university. All of these must give new students the incoming impression: We do not tolerate violence here.

Eric Hoover wrote April 10, 2008 in the *Chronicle of Higher Education*, "After the fatal shootings at Virginia Tech last April, colleges went shopping for hardware. They bought sirens, mass-messaging systems, surveillance cameras, and door locks. Some college armed their police departments for the first time. Others added assault rifles to their arsenals. "Active shooter" drills happened everywhere. As administrators responded to a new threat, however, they could not overlook one fact: Gadgets and guns might help colleges react to violence, but preventing it would require something else. Ultimately, prevention is all about communication."[103]

Evaluation

Both qualitative and quantitative evaluations are critical to the success of any violence prevention effort. Initially, a thorough needs assessment will give the prevention team a better picture of where the problems are and why. Focus groups and interviews with key stakeholders can flush out these descriptions and give important guidance on what might initiate change. Standardized questionnaires and university-developed supplemental surveys can be used to test pre- and post-changes in attitudes and self-reported behavior. Other indicators of campus violence such as disciplinary cases, personal counseling referrals, and campus security reports can be tracked to indicate trends in violence.

Not only are accurate campus incident records necessary to tally changes over time, this data can also relate important indicators of future violence or delayed violence impact. Violence does not happen in a vacuum. Ripple effects from one act of violence may lead to another related incident. Clustering of violent events during one period of time or around one general area may signify that new prevention techniques are needed.

Most importantly, in the evaluation process, the university must take a candid look at how certain systems or individuals may be contributing to problems of violence. This tactic is not done to lay blame, but rather as a place to start to take corrective action. If one area of the institution is working hard to make positive changes, it may be totally undermined if a more powerful segment of the university is sending a competing message.

Awareness and Skill-Building Efforts

Throughout this book, awareness raising and skill-building programs are suggested. The professional staff members in the counseling center are natural resources for these purposes. Most counselors are experts in conflict resolution, understanding the impact of violence on victims, and a host of other relevant topics. They can work with victims and perpetrators, individuals, and groups.

No violence prevention strategy will be effective without addressing the problems of alcohol abuse. Dealing with these issues must happen at many levels-individuals, high-risk groups, low-risk groups, and so on. A more comprehensive discussion of these issues is covered in Chapter 4.

As the Director of Prevention Institute in Berkeley, California, Larry Cohen advocates awareness programs because they effect the community on many levels, "Effective community education not only alerts individuals to new information, but it also builds a critical mass of support for healthier behavior, norms and policy change."[104]

Effective Response Mechanisms

Response mechanisms for violence or potential violence can run the gamut from mediation, to campus judicial codes, to civil and criminal action, to counseling and victim services. Mediation lets conflicting individuals or groups negotiate a resolution rather than resort to violence. This influential process allows participants to regain a sense of control in the situation.

Behavioral standards related to violence must be set and enforced. Once these codes are broken, the Behavioral Intervention Team may be called in to assess the situation and plan for further appropriate action. Emergency procedures must be spelled out and widely known. The first hour after a violent incident is most crucial for containing the situation, gathering information, and aiding the victim or victims. See Appendix for flow charts.

STANDARD OPERATING GUIDELINES

When it comes to rules and regulations, campuses seem to be coming full circle. The *New York Times* noted that before the 1970s, many campuses had housemothers, curfews, and even dress codes. In the post-Vietnam era, many campus rules were discarded and the notion of campuses *in loco parentis* (or campuses as substitute parents) died out.[105]

Today, the *zeitgeist* is shifting again. Possibly because of "boomer generation guilt," perhaps because of increased litigiousness, or maybe because of increased fears about dangers to students, policies and procedures are regaining popularity. Rules and regulations regarding many specific factors leading to campus violence are suggested throughout this book. Alcohol policies, hate crime policies, hazing policies, and so on are listed in their respective chapters. The following sections describe the necessary policies and procedures designed to monitor and detect potentially violent individuals. The prevention and intervention strategies listed below can assist colleges in developing a standard operating guide to avoid and respond to violence. Many campuses have implemented these and other techniques and have witnessed a positive response; however, there are no foolproof formulas for preventing violence. When people are 100 percent determined to carry out an act of violence, they will find a way. Fortunately, most violent individuals, like most suicidal individuals, experience some ambivalence. The more effective prevention and intervention techniques there are in place, the greater the likelihood that violence will be deterred because that ambivalence will be met with consequences and obstacles.

Much of the policy and investigation sections of this chapter were adapted from our book *Violence Goes to Work*,[106] while the emergency management section draws from our book *Violence Goes to School*.[107]

Bottom Line: Zero Tolerance

Campuses must be prepared to develop and enforce a zero tolerance stance against all threats and violence. What does zero tolerance mean? Does it mean that anyone who makes a joke about violence is automatically fired or expelled? No. What it means is that every questionable statement or gesture goes under the microscope. Every threat gets addressed, even if that only means investigation and documentation.

The airlines industry is currently the only trade that truly has zero tolerance for threats and violence. All threats or suspect behaviors are confronted. Even jokes. In the aftermath of the postal worker shootings of the early 1990s, many other workplaces have adopted zero tolerance programs involving tip lines and conflict resolution classes. The result? Homicides in the workplace have dropped significantly since 1993.

A zero tolerance message is clear and empowering. Creating the policy may seem relatively easy, but enforcing it becomes more complex. Campuses must think through what zero tolerance means for them. What is fair? What is legal? What fits with the mission of the campus as a learning environment? Does it mean, "One strike and you are out?" Many companies have learned the hard way that if you start shifting the line defining unacceptable behavior, the zero tolerance policy becomes worthless. When you enter situations where it's one person's word against another, zero tolerance can become confusing. Effective zero tolerance policies take these issues into consideration, create effective means of enforcement, and train those affected by the policy to enhance civility.

Legal Considerations

According to the Higher Education Center, before 1980, colleges were generally not held liable for crimes occurring on their campuses.[108] Today campuses are being held responsible for a number of violence incidents:

- The Nebraska Supreme Court ruled that the University of Nebraska had a duty to protect a fraternity pledge injured while trying to escape a hazing ritual. The court determined that the university had been aware of previous hazing incidents involving this fraternity and was therefore obligated to take reasonable steps to protect against future acts of hazing.[109]
- The mother of an Iona College freshman who died from alcohol poisoning sued the college and the owners of two bars. The suit stated that Iona administrators were negligent in their failure to control underage drinking and hazing activity.
- The Florida Supreme Court ruled that a university may be held liable for a student's injuries at an off-campus internship if the school knew in advance that the site was dangerous.
- The parents of John LaDuca have filed a wrongful-death suit against the fraternity and its alumni board. John hanged himself the day after the fraternity's initiation ended. Throughout the week leading up to initiation, John was subjected to multiple dangerous and humiliating hazing practices.
- Each of these cases calls into question a number of issues regarding campus liability. While this is not a legal manual per se, the following summary gives a brief overview of the concerns.

Definition of Campus

When people think about a college campus, they often think about the physical grounds of the school. But the boundaries of a campus are diffuse and permeable. Campus violence can involve visitors on campus grounds, students at an off-campus party or bar, individuals passing through campus property, Greek housing, interns at off-campus sites, and even study-abroad students. For example, in the aftermath of the campus riots, many schools found that their codes of conduct did not cover students' behavior in the local community. Many sought to rectify this problem by expanding the code to include behavior that was a reasonable distance from the institution. Then the question became what is a reasonable distance? Institutional responsibilities seem to be getting broader and broader.

What about student behavior that is so discrepant from the established code of conduct, but occurs during spring break or summer vacation? According to the *Chronicle of Higher Education*, a 1997 survey of 520 members of the Association for Student Judicial Affairs determined that more than three out of four institutions have expanded codes of conduct to include off-campus behavior.[110] What happens if a student or employee of the university is charged with a serious crime, but is awaiting trial? Should the school temporarily suspend the student or wait until the courts decide guilt or innocence? These are all difficult questions with which campuses have to struggle.

Negligent Hiring and Negligent Retention

Negligent hiring and negligent retention are legal terms that have received increasing attention in the wake of workplace violence incidents. The terms are usually used under certain circumstances when employees commit a violent act and employers are held liable. These situations occur when an employer has prior knowledge that people are at risk for committing violence but hires or retains them anyway. Thorough screening and background investigation, while not foolproof, can significantly reduce hiring risks. Swift and appropriate responses to threats and concerning behavior can minimize the potential of an escalating workplace violence problem. For more information regarding these issues, please consult *Violence Goes to Work: An Employer's Guide.*[111]

Violence Prior to Enrollment

At the time of this publication, no major case had demonstrated that a student's violent behavior prior to enrollment was cause for campus liability in a later act of violence while the student was at school. However, plenty of schools are concerned about such exposure. The best known case concerns a woman named Gina Grant who was offered an early admission to Harvard University in 1995. Later the school discovered that in 1990, Gina had testified to the court that she had bludgeoned her mother to death with a candlestick and stabbed her mother in the neck with a kitchen knife. Gina was charged with voluntary manslaughter and served six months in juvenile detention before moving in with an aunt and uncle. This information was omitted from her application to Harvard. When Harvard discovered her history, they rescinded their offer of admission.

Arizona State University chose to admit a convicted murderer. James Hamm shot and killed a Tucson man in 1974. He also scored in the 96th percentile on his law school admissions test, and he is married to a former justice of the peace. Understandably, his enrollment sparked a heated controversy. Some see him as a criminal justice success story, others as an institutional liability and an unfair decision to the thousands of applicants who were rejected.

Failure to Protect/Failure to Warn

According to *Violence on Campus*, when a university tries to control or prohibit dangerous behavior such as hazing or underage drinking, a court may find that the institution has a duty to protect those students.[112] Several suits against colleges have resulted in monetary awards for damages such as failure to provide adequate security or prevent foreseeable harm.

Policy Development

Policies reduce the chance factors in campus operations by establishing a common body of knowledge. Colleges that develop a Standard Operating Guide before it is needed are more likely to avoid panic and disruption when an event arises.

As with most important human relation issues, an antiviolence policy requires careful analysis and review before implementation. Policy developers should include only criteria that can be administered consistently. Commitment from the upper-level administrators to develop and enforce the policy is essential. Policies cannot promise to protect students or employees from physical harm since this is not absolutely possible.

The choice of words in policy development is important. Many legal advisors suggest that it is preferable to use words such as "strive" rather than a promise to promote and maintain a school environment free from intimidation and threats of violence. Similarly, policy developers should consider using the term "may" over the term "will" in the text of the policy. The use of the word "will" can be a promise to act. If a complaint is received and not investigated, the campus could face a negligence claim.

Who Develops Policies?

A violence prevention policy is most effective when it is created, implemented, managed, and evaluated by those who are directly involved with such assessments on a regular basis. A cross-section of the community should be involved to get varying viewpoints on the policy strategies. As always, legal council should be sought before any policies are put into practice.

What Policies Are Necessary?

Threat Policy. Campuses should create a written zero-tolerance policy that explains the position of the campus on intimidating, threatening, or violent behaviors. This policy should clearly define what constitutes threats (see Chapter 5 for a detailed description of

---

Sample Threats and Violence Policy[113]

Our policy is to strive to maintain a campus environment free from intimidation, threats, or violent acts. This includes, but is not limited to: intimidating, threatening or hostile behaviors, physical abuse, vandalism, hazing, sexual assault, hate crimes, arson, sabotage, carrying or use of weapons, or any other act, which, in the administration's opinion, is inappropriate to the campus environment. In addition, bizarre or offensive comments regarding violent events or aggressive behaviors will not be tolerated.

Campus employees or students who feel subjected to any of the behaviors listed above should immediately report the incident to _____ [name of designated campus representative(s)]. All complaints will receive prompt attention and the situation will be investigated. Based on the results of the inquiry, disciplinary action which administration feels appropriate will be taken.

Campus employees or students who observe or have knowledge of violation of this policy should immediately report it to _____ [the appointed campus representative(s)]. All reported events will be taken seriously. If an investigation is warranted, we will request the cooperation of all incident-related individuals. An employee or student who believes there is a serious threat to the safety and health of others should report this concern directly to law enforcement authorities.

various forms of threats), and establish appropriate procedures for investigating potential problems and determining appropriate consequences. One crucial component in the threat policy is the reporting procedure. Campuses must give students and staff clear instructions about what to do if they perceive a threat. An avenue for anonymous reporting should be implemented. Some prevention experts argue that language that guarantees strict confidentiality for reporting should be avoided for purposes of investigation.

Along these lines, campuses may consider developing the following additional policies:

- Search Policy
- Violence Communication Policy
- Hate Crime
- Hazing
- Sexual Harassment
- Sexual Assault
- Nonsexual Assault
- Rioting

The "Vortex": Communication Policies

A vortex or communication center should be established to provide a knowledge base for all investigations. A standard reporting form and procedure will help ensure that reporting is complete and contains consistent information. This system organizes all incidents of violence by keeping record of the details of the incident, interventions, and outcomes. Any consultations, referrals, or other outside intervention should also be noted in these files. This documentation will help investigators determine patterns in perpetrators, targets, means, or other factors in their assessment of dangerousness.

In addition to documenting critical or threatening incidents, the communication center also can be a resource center for those concerned with violence prevention. The communication can serve as a clearinghouse to distribute current literature and data on campus safety issues. The center also can house a list of local and national experts or others known to assist in solutions to campus violence problems.

INVESTIGATION

A formalized plan for investigation of threats or violence complaints is necessary to prevent campus personnel from being caught off-guard and unprepared when a prompt response is most critical. A carefully thought-out investigation procedure helps ensure that facts about the incident are collected and examined in an expedient and thorough manner. Effective investigation can often defuse further violence potential.

Who Conducts the Investigation?

Those in charge of the investigation must have training in violence assessment and intervention. They must keep a neutral and objective attitude toward all parties, and have the ability to manage the investigation in a professional manner. At various points, the administration may wish to use outside experts who have knowledge and experience in evidence collection, and in conducting investigations, interviews, and interrogations. An alternative is to designate appropriately trained members of the Behavioral Intervention Team to conduct the investigation.

A series of steps that involve planning, conducting, documenting, and evaluating the investigation are necessary for an effective, thorough analysis of the evidence.

Planning the Investigation

Campuses should draft investigation procedures prior to conducting any actual investigation. Consistent and comprehensive inquiries result when a detailed methodology is followed in each case. Multiple sources of data are essential in determining risk. Thus, investigation of collateral witnesses (e.g., parents, roommates, friends, and so on), academic and disciplinary records, legal history, and armament inventories all add critical information to complete the picture. The following step-by-step guide can assist investigators in their efforts to piece together the situation.

Step 1: Develop a preliminary list of witnesses or individuals involved in, or affected by, the incident.

Step 2: Specify the sequence of interviews and appoint interviewers.

Step 3: Determine what evidence the investigator can obtain for the investigation.

Step 4: Decide what, if any, action is necessary before beginning the investigation. For example, consider implementation of security measures to protect targets and property, or the temporary suspension of an accused student or employee until the investigation is completed.

Investigators must take necessary steps to ensure privacy of each interviewee to the best of their ability. This is critical to ensure that students and employees feel free to discuss the problem.

NOTE: The investigator(s) should be careful not to guarantee absolute confidentiality about the information gathered. Witnesses must understand that if the allegations are serious, their statements could be reported to others. Assure them that the statements are treated as discreetly as is practical.

When planning the interviews, investigators should determine the type of information needed from each person. Possible reactions or responses from the alleged perpetrator or witnesses need to be anticipated as best as possible. Investigators should develop a list of questions in advance to ask each party, keeping in mind the objective of the interview. In particular, pertinent questions concern who, what, where, when, and how.

When beginning the investigation, it is important to establish rapport by remembering to be empathetic and calm. Victims and witnesses may be in shock, and may need ample time to answer questions. Investigator patience is paramount. Questions should be contained to the matters related to the complaint or event, unless past patterns of this conduct have occurred in which case this history is open to questioning.

Investigators must be prepared to document what each party involved did, said, or knew. Follow appropriate questioning techniques such as:

- Ask open-ended questions, encouraging the individual to share more information.
- Listen to the response without interrupting the flow of details.
- Wait until the person has completed the narrative to ask for clarification.
- Keep each question brief and confined to one point or topic.
- Avoid leading questions that suggest or guide the answer.
- Keep questions simple, using words that are clear to the person being interviewed.
- Watch for nonverbal messages, and follow up with applicable questions to confirm or revise the received impression.

Conducting and Documenting the Interview

Begin the investigation with the individual who reported the occurrence. Ask for details regarding:

- What happened? What action did each party take? What did each person say? Where did it happen? Describe where the action took place.
- When did it happen? Get both the date and time of the incident.
- Who was present? List the names of any potential witnesses.
- What evidence exists to corroborate the story?

• Ask for a written statement summarizing the incident at the conclusion of the interview.

After this initial interview is completed, ask the same questions to the alleged perpetrator or perpetrators and any witnesses in an order appropriate to the situation. With witnesses or other involved parties, it is important to ask general questions first such as, "Are you aware of any problems that exist between students on our campus?" Investigators should then prepare a confidential report of the findings in case of a filed charge or lawsuit. The investigative notes and statements of witnesses may be used as an official record. Therefore, investigators must ensure there are no extraneous comments, opinions, or statements cited as fact. The report should stick to the objective, verifiable data of the event and not be embellished.

To compile the documentation, investigators should include all actual findings and their sources. Reports must be kept as confidential as practical. Only those with a legitimate need to know should have access to the report. No unnecessary copies should be made.

All those involved in the investigation must avoid defamation claims. Defamation is the unprivileged communication to a third person of a false statement intending to harm the reputation of another. To protect against the possibility of defamation, investigators should make the findings of an investigation and other pertinent documents available only to persons having a legitimate connection or interest in them. Precautions against needless publication of potentially defamatory statements minimize the exposure of the campus to liability.

Evaluating the Evidence and Taking Appropriate Action

The investigating team has an obligation to analyze the data collected and formulate a course of action. This is especially difficult when one person's word against another's is the only information available. Consultation with an outside violence assessment professional is often needed in evaluating the evidence.

To consider the credibility of the allegations, ask:

• When was the complaint made? If it was not immediately reported, find out why.
• Is the complaint specific and detailed? Are there any contradictions in the information collected?
• Are there things missing in the evidence that should be there? Is there any logical explanation for the missing data?

To consider the credibility of the accused, and any denials, ask:

• Has the student or employee accused simply made a blanket denial?
• Has the accused provided evidence that either supports or contradicts the allegations?
• Have other allegations been made about this person?

The type of corrective action needed depends on the nature of the incident and past practice. The more serious the allegation, the greater the need for law enforcement intervention. Failure to act can increase the liability of the campus. Overly severe discipline could lead to a legal suit from the accused or his or her family. When a campus needs to take immediate action to deal with a problem, suspending the student or employee provides time to investigate. As the team determines consequences, they should ask themselves, "Do the consequences fit the infraction?" Some examples of interventions include:

• Suspend student or employee pending investigation
• Individual is allowed on campus under close supervision

- Expulsion/Firing
- Probation
- Community service
- Psychological evaluation and/or mandated counseling
- Legal action

NOTE: If the campus plans to suspend or expel a potentially violent student or employee, escort the individual from the premises, deny the individual access to the campus, and take extra security precautions to impede attempted reentry. During this critical time, there should be a concerted effort to develop plans to keep the individual off grounds.

EMERGENCY MANAGEMENT

In addition to policy and procedures developed to prevent violence, emergency plans need to be designed as well. Each campus should develop systematic procedures for dealing with different types of crises. The purpose of these plans is to instruct key people on how to handle an actual crisis situation in an effective and efficient manner. In developing plans, take the following factors into consideration:

GENERAL CONSIDERATIONS

Emergency preparedness plans need to have both clarity and flexibility. Frequently, in the midst of a crisis, unforeseen obstacles will hinder the best thought-out plans. As much as possible, policy developers must attempt to identify any conditions or situations that can influence the emergency response and plan how these would be managed. These obstacles might include isolation or geographical location, critical functions the campus performs, or legal responsibilities.

We also have learned that the most effective plans are utterly useless unless people know them cold. The last thing campuses want at a time of crisis is key decision makers searching through file cabinets trying to find and then decipher the emergency manual. Campuses must evaluate the efficacy of the plan through regular "violence drills." While this concept may sound odd, it is no more outrageous than planned fire drills. As with most planning processes, what looks good on paper may be lacking in a real situation.

In addition to the identified Behavioral Intervention Team and campus and local safety and rescue personnel, campuses should consider whether or not they may need these additional resources on-hand depending on the nature of the crisis:

- Building maintenance personnel
- Additional cellular phones and two-way radios
- Professional negotiators
- Locksmiths
- Specialized victim assistance professionals to counsel people in sexual assault situations and secondary victims of the violence.

Tools for Emergency Response

Emergency Management Kit for Responders

One of the important lessons learned from the Columbine High School tragedy was that emergency personnel responding to the scene were slowed due to a lack of information. They could not get a sense of the school's layout because blueprints were not readily available. Precious time was lost because of this confusion. Because of this lesson learned, we recommend that campuses compile blueprints of campus buildings and give them to proper law enforcement. These blueprints of campus buildings should have exit routes clearly marked as well as any potential concealment locations. While reviewing these blueprints, be sure to examine exit strategies. Most exits have been designed for fire escape and not violence escape. In addition to these blueprints, the emergency management kit should also contain important phone numbers, for example members of the Behavioral Intervention Team, and if practical, a current list of campus residents. Having several kits stored in more than one place will increase accessibility in the time of crisis.

Emergency Response Procedures

Other aspects of the emergency management plan to consider are procedures for intruders, hostage situations, and catastrophic occurrences. Planners should identify off-campus locations where students and employees might be moved and triaged and investigate crisis transportation issues – early closings, traffic flow, parking, emergency vehicle access. The Behavioral Intervention Team must identify a responsible party for each portion of the emergency plan.

Emergency Communication Plan

When developing a communication plan, clear command responsibilities including alternates are essential. An effective communication plan must be able to inform students, staff, and the community of the campus' plans in case of catastrophe.

The criteria that determines whether a situation poses a significant and imminent threat is something the crisis teams needs to determine far in advance of a critical situation.[114] Communication strategies chosen to disseminate warnings must be multimodal (from old-fashioned phone trees and word-of-mouth to email, websites, fax transmissions, radio and television, sirens and horns, public address systems, and reverse 911 systems). Each communication strategy has a benefit and limitation and this multimodal strategy helps assure built-in redundancy. The goal is

to reach a "tipping point" of students, faculty, and staff in a very short period of time. Because of the chaos often experienced during crises, communication must be clear, concise, and action-oriented.

Timely Response

Because there was a two hour lag time between the first set of shootings and the second set at Virginia Tech, a large debate ensued regarding what is considered a "timely response" during a crisis. On one hand, in the immediate moments of a crisis, misinformation is often rampant – do campuses risk a warning that might be misinformed in the hopes of alerting students to be on guard knowing that in most active shooter situations the damage is often done in a matter of minutes. On the other hand, too many of these misinformed alerts might render the communication strategy a wolf's cry leading the community to question its reliability.

In February 2008, a provision in the Higher Education Act proposed that institutions notify people on their campuses within 30 minutes of a "significant emergency or dangerous situation."[115] Many are concerned that legislating the definition of "timely" could put campuses in a no-win bind.

Command Center

A command center serves as a communication vortex for an emergency. An easily accessible location and alternate must be determined in advance. One of the functions of the command center is to let people know who is where; thus, it is important to establish a procedure for creating a list of injured students and employees that includes their names and conditions. Procedures for alerting and providing supportive and counseling resources are also necessary. The command center also can serve as a location for reuniting students and employees with loved ones.

Telephone Use During a Crisis

- Consider installing additional lines or temporary 1-800 numbers to handle incoming calls demanding information.
- Consider opening one line just for media contact.
- Staff "information hotlines" with informed professional staff with scripted informational releases.
- If professionals cannot staff phones, consider recording information and updating as needed.
- Give people who are answering phones frequent breaks as they may need relief from handling ongoing emotional intensity and the inability to sometimes give answers that satisfy the callers.

The media liaison can gather and relay information obtained from the command center.

Particular importance must be given to communication between those within the campus and those outside the campus. Very often during a campus crisis, the telephone lines become jammed with incoming and outgoing calls of people trying to receive and relay information. For this reason, we have listed additional suggestions for telephone communication.

Disseminating the Emergency Plan

Again, all policies are in vain if no one knows them. Thus, it is essential that the plans be disseminated effectively. Informational brochures, special briefings, training videos, organizational newsletters, and staff meetings are some of the means of getting the plans out to the people who will be responding to the crises. But campuses should not rely on a one-shot approach to getting this information across. Regular reviews of the plan as conditions and staff change are necessary.

While these emergency preparedness plans are being disseminated, campuses must be sure to cultivate a supportive climate and not a panic climate. Violence prevention campaigns and recognition awards can help create a positive climate towards preventing violence on campus. Logos, slogans, and promotional items can help spread the message even further.[116]

Chapter 8

BUILDING BARRIERS TO VIOLENCE PART III: ENVIRONMENTAL PROTECTION AND SAFETY STRATEGIES

JOHN NICOLETTI & CHRISTOPHER BOLLINGER

As WE LEARNED in Chapter 3, most institutions of higher learning in good faith inadvertently lull their community members into a false sense of security. We open ourselves to the greater community by having our libraries, athletic facilities, and other facilities open for public use. Campus events are open to the public. Students are encouraged to be open to diversity. These are all very positive actions that should continue. However, we sometimes fail to recognize that there are some legitimate dangers in our community. By doing so, we fail to teach our community members how to identify dangers and take appropriate steps to keep themselves safe.

While colleges and universities are making efforts with physical improvements and developing safety programs, they are also fighting a battle to correct bad safety advice that has run rampant. The following are examples of such bad advice:

When being stalked, show the perpetrator that you are not afraid by remaining calm and collected.

Correction: You do not want to look like a target to a predator. Once the predator has identified you as a victim and is stalking you, you want to get away as fast as you can.

If you are cornered in an elevator, hit the Emergency Stop button.

Correction: This button will stop the elevator and entrap you with the perpetrator for the attack. Instead, you want to hit the buttons for every floor and get out of the elevator as soon as possible.

When you are being attacked, poke the attacker in the eye.

Correction: In a state of panic your fine motor skills become more difficult to use. Unless you are able to remain very calm in an attack, you need to depend on gross motor techniques. Another factor to consider is your psychological readiness to poke someone in the eye. The thought upsets most people, and yet in order to accomplish this effectively, there can be no hesitation.

If you are wearing high heels, jam the heel into the foot of the attacker.

Correction: A great deal of pressure is required to jam a heel into someone's foot. If you are actually able to do this, you have succeeded in connecting yourself to the attacker.

In the event that you are being chased, keep your keys in your hand so you can get into your car quickly and use the keys as weapons.

Correction: Again, when panicking, people often have difficulty with fine motor skills and sometimes experience blurred vision. When people attempt to put their keys in the keyhole, they find that the keyhole appears to shrink and move around. Unless you have a keyless entry system, these factors will make it difficult to get into the car. The better option is to run. Using a key as a weapon is also not a great idea, because in order to use the weapon you must get in close proximity to the attacker.

If attacked, talk to the perpetrator and help them understand what they are doing is wrong.

Correction: During an attack, perpetrators are past the point of being talked out their behavior. Again, the best option is to get away and get to help.

In addition to overcoming bad advice, colleges and universities often do not consider whom they are trying to protect and what violent behavior they are trying to prevent. For example, installing a blue light telephone for the purpose of helping someone who is being chased may not be effective. A blue light telephone is effective in those circumstances where people who are not in imminent danger can call in concerns. However, when people are being chased, they will not take the time to stop, figure out who to call, dial, and wait for an answer. They need to keep running. If the same blue light telephone were equipped with a single button that could be activated by a gross motor hit as the person ran by, that might make the telephone more effective. The phone would then provide a safety responder with the location of the person being chased.

In this chapter, we will examine guiding principles behind violent behavior and victim responses, how these principles influence prevention in environmental protection, safety services provided, and survival strategies.

GUIDING PRINCIPLES BEHIND VIOLENT BEHAVIOR AND VICTIM RESPONSES

Violence Is a Learned Behavior

As we mentioned in Chapter 5, people say things like, "He just snapped!" in the aftermath of violence. The reality is most violence perpetrators have a violence history and have worked up to the incident. Violence is a learned behavior. Perpetrators usually practice by engaging in behaviors that become increasingly violent. Practicing helps them feel more comfortable with the violent action. Most perpetrators provide veiled or direct threats before an incident occurs.

Responding Is Preferable to Reacting

Violent perpetrators have the upper hand because action is faster than reaction. Violent perpetrators are always one step ahead of potential victims because the victims cannot predict exactly what the perpetrator will do next. That leaves the potential victim in a position of guessing or waiting for the action. When people decide to become violent, they have crossed the line of social acceptability and the "rules" of human behavior are usually discarded. Because pro-social norms no longer apply, predicting the perpetrator's actions is challenging.

While violent individuals have an advantage, potential victims are not helpless. When potential victims are equipped with survival strategies, they become contenders. Responding is much more effective than reacting. When people react in a knee-jerk fashion when faced with violence, chances are they will make a decision that places them in greater danger. When people respond to a violent situation, they are able to pull from a repertoire of appropriate skills and options. These survival skills are well understood and practiced beforehand. While reacting can bring on escalating panic, responding helps the victim remain focused and flexible in problem solving.

Performance Under Stress Is Compromised

As we noted in our previous books, *Survival-Oriented Kids*[117] and *Violence Goes to School*,[118] under extreme stress, the human body prepares itself for fight or flight. Blood rushes from the extremities to the heart and large muscle groups. Senses become very sharp, sometimes to the point of distortion. Because of these changes, human beings often experience a set of difficulties that make responding to the stress challenging.

Fine Motor Skills Are Impaired

Under extreme stress, the blood is drawn to large muscle mass, and fingers fumble. For this reason, tasks such as unlocking car doors, punching in phone numbers, and poking people in the eye become difficult. Typing in codes for alarm systems is also unpractical at this time. Even dialing 911 can be a challenge. When building a response plan for violence, it is important to rely on gross motor movements like the arms and legs rather than the fine motor movement of the fingers.

Perceptions Are Distorted

When individuals are under extreme stress, the brain switches to a different mode of information processing called *cerebral acceleration*. The brain begins to sort through tremendous amounts of information quickly so that the best decisions can be made. The senses become very acute and amplified. The experience of this phenomenon is that it feels as if the world has turned into a very surreal, slow-motion movie. It appears as if the brain is on hyperdrive, but what is actually happening is that when a person is scared, the brain area responsible for making memories becomes more active so that the memories that are created are richer and denser.[119]

In this process, reality is altered. The brain attempts to make sense out of extreme circumstances. As a result, objects in the environment seem to appear and disappear. Gunfire sounds like firecrackers. What looks like a soda can is actually a gun. Victims sometimes recall that during an attack they thought the perpetrator was coming to shake their hand. In reality, the perpetrator was coming at them with an outstretched hand holding a gun.

Tunnel Thinking Limits Adaptive Problem Solving

When people are in traumatic situations, their thinking often gets locked into one mode. For example, in a violent situation on campus, people will try to call for help by dialing 911. On most campus phone systems, a 9 must be dialed first to obtain an outside line. They instinctively dial 911 as opposed to 9-911. This error may be repeated several times in frustration before the individual either gives up or figures it out.

Survival Instincts

People cannot rely solely on instincts to survive a dangerous situation. As people become more civilized and technically advanced, they rely less on instinctual survival skills. We have become more dependent on external alarm systems and less sure of internal alarm systems.

Some human instinctive reactions are inappropriate. For example, notice how crowds tend to behave when there is a fire in a movie theater. Typically, a mass of people will run hysterically toward the nearest exit, causing a big jam. Another example of poor survival instincts in people is indicated by how they run. When a predator is chasing prey in the wild, the prey will attempt to escape by running in a serpentine pattern. That is, running in zigzags or erratic movements. However, when people are pursued, they tend to run in a straight line. This pattern of attempted escape gives the pursuer the advantage because predicting direction of travel is easy. In order to survive a violent incident, people need to learn how to overcome such inappropriate instincts.

"The Bump"

The bump is a term that describes when a perpetrator engages a person to assess whether or not the potential victim will be a good target. Perpetrators may ask for the time when they are wearing a watch. By enacting this form of contact, perpetrators are assessing how friendly or passive the potential victim is. In another example, perpetrators feign weaknesses to lure in victims. Ted Bundy wore a fake cast and found young women to help him to his car.

When we are in these situations we instinctively know something is not quite right. Most of us, especially women, have been socialized to be friendly and helpful. Given the choice of listening to our internal fear alarm and potentially offending someone, many choose to override the fear and be nice. Perpetrators know this. We must retrain ourselves to listen to our instincts.

PERPETRATOR CHARACTERISTICS AND RESPONSE STRATEGIES

Predatory

Most campus security measures are designed with the predator in mind. Predators are motivated by the hunt and attack and do not want to bring attention to themselves. Like wild animals, predators target what they perceive as easy prey. They will seek out the most vulnerable, the most impaired, and the least assertive.

Prevention strategies should create barriers to the hunt and train potential victims to present themselves confidently. Locked doors, card key locks, adequately lighted campus areas, and frequent rounds of safety personnel all make the hunt more difficult. Individuals who appear strong and sure encourage the predator to seek other prey. Once a predator has honed in on a target, that target must then focus on escape. Knowing that the predator does not want to be noticed, any escape strategy should involve creating as much of a disturbance as possible to elicit help.

Avenger

Avengers are motivated by righting what they perceive to have been a grave injustice. Avengers will often threaten prior to their action. They will often plan for and fantasize about their attack in detail before acting it out. Unlike predators, avengers usually want to be noticed. Also, unlike predators, avengers may have greater access to and knowledge about the campus facilities because avengers have often been part of the system. Thus, barriers designed for predators often will backfire with the avenger.

Prevention strategies for the avenger are therefore somewhat different than for the predator. When an avenger type has been identified as a risk to the campus, his or her identity must be made known to those who will be in a place to intervene. If possible, the perceived injustice must continue to be addressed and resolution attempted. As long as avengers are engaged in a process of mediation, they are less likely to plot their revenge.

If the injustice is not able to be resolved to satisfaction, and the avenger continues to make threats, then the perpetrator must be removed from the community and blocked from return. This step is critical to preventing violence from an avenger. In many cases of workplace violence, disgruntled employees were allowed back on the work premises after termination or disciplinary hearings, and the results were deadly. Under these circumstances, campus-community members need to be made aware that the threatening individual is not permitted to return and that they should notify safety personnel if return is attempted. Any access codes or keys held by the potential avenger should be changed.

The escape strategies in an avenger situation are also different than the perpetrator. When an avenger attacks, victims should be advised to draw minimal attention to themselves. If they cannot escape, they should attempt to conceal themselves from the avenger.

Relationship-Based

Perpetrators of relationship-based violence are motivated by the needs to control and dominate. In extreme cases, they become totally myopic. They believe no one can understand their need for the relationship. Their world revolves around this other person, and they do not care about anything else. This ability to block out other priorities and a rational world makes them unpredictable and dangerous. For this reason, police officers often consider domestic violence their most dangerous type of call.

Only one approach effectively deals with relationship-based violence that has reached these extremes. One must break off the relationship completely. Any contact with the perpetrator serves to reinforce an ownership mentality. The immediate aftermath of this break in the relationship is the most dangerous time for victims. The temptation will be great to reestablish contact directly or through other people. See Chapter 14 for more information on intervening in relationship violence.

Group-Induced

Group-induced violence is based on diffusion of responsibility, herd mentality, and a need for belonging. Preventing group-induced violence can occur both from inside and outside of the group. For those in the group, members must feel comfortable setting boundaries. If the group pressures them to act beyond these boundaries, they must be willing either to confront the group or leave.

From outside of the group the following prevention strategies are recommended: (1)

Decrease anonymity. When individuals in a group realize they will be held personally responsible for the actions of the group, they are less likely to behave out of character. (2) Identify the leaders of the group and negotiate alternatives to violence. (3) Attempt to find different means of reaching goals group members perceive they are gaining through violent means.

ENVIRONMENTAL PROTECTION TACTICS: PROS AND CONS

As discussed in Chapter 2, perpetrators need time to plan and the opportunity to gain access and carry out violence. Physical and human barriers between the perpetrator and the potential victim serve to slow down the perpetrator and reduce opportunity. The following environmental barriers are effective in slowing or stopping some but not all types of campus violence perpetrators.

Campus Lighting

Adequate lighting helps prevent predator attacks and should be properly maintained. Good lighting means fewer places to hide and to stalk prey. Bright, well-lit areas can also draw more attention to potential attacks. Proper maintenance requires nighttime assessments and timely repairs. Community members should be made aware of the areas that are and are not illuminated. Some campuses publish night maps that provide directions through well-lit areas.

There are some lighting systems that are motion sensitive. These systems save money in electric costs. However, if the system breaks down or is undependable, the prevention tactic has failed. Because these lights are not on all the time, individuals will be delayed in reporting the malfunction to appropriate authorities. There are definite pros and cons to this new format.

Emergency Communication Systems

Call boxes are good because they provide a convenient place to contact security services; however, as mentioned earlier, they are not necessarily productive for someone who is being chased. Call boxes should transmit a location to safety responders. Call boxes should be able to be activated by running by and slapping a button. Personnel should be able to get to the location quickly. However, even with these provisions the chances are good that someone on the run will be long gone by the time help arrives.

Posting emergency information can improve speedy access to support and warn students of potential dangers. Numbers for primary support services should be posted in every building and near courtesy phones. Community alerts regarding potential dangers and reporting procedures should be disseminated when appropriate. This practice allows community members the opportunity to know when there is increased danger in their environment. This practice is extremely important in the case of a potential avenger who has been removed from the community. Finally, publicized information regarding what constitutes crime (such as hazing violations) can help community members by allowing them to make more informed decisions about when to intervene.

Routine Inspections

By conducting regular inspections of the grounds and buildings, potential danger points can be identified and resolved. Grounds inspections should be done in the evening as well as during the day. This enables staff to more accurately assess potential danger areas in the limited lighting. Rounds in residence halls should be done so that any lighting issues and locking difficulties can be identified and reported. Swift follow up on needed repairs is imperative. Sometimes the repairs may not

be obvious because they are not reported. Inspecting staff should make it a point to periodically ask students and staff if all grounds and building maintenance is up to par.

Peepholes

Peepholes in residential hall rooms are helpful because they give the potential victim added time to decide how to respond. A door can be an effective barrier between a perpetrator and victim. Witnesses are more likely to be concerned when they see someone hanging out in a hallway. Witnesses are left to guess what is going on behind closed doors. Inside the room, the victim is barricaded and may have access to protectors via the phone. Peepholes are not particularly helpful if people neglect to use them or do not lock their doors.

Security Cameras

If surveillance cameras are continuously monitored, they can be effective in preventing violence. Monitored cameras can help locate propped doors. They can also speed up response time when a known perpetrator has entered a building. However, if they are not monitored, they are more effective in catching people stealing or other criminal activity but not very effective at preventing violence. Predators often carefully hide their faces when they know a security camera is watching them. The avenger, relationship-based, and group-induced violence perpetrators usually will not care that their picture is being taken. Indeed, their presence on the monitoring screen may not be cause for alarm if the monitor is not aware of any potential danger. Cameras may be helpful in identifying perpetrators after the fact.

Building Lock-down

Card lock systems can be extremely helpful if the system is maintained properly. When cards malfunction, the locks slow down the potential victim in the same way they slow down the perpetrator. Desk systems with personnel in entryways can be helpful in this regard. However, propped doors continue to be a problem at many institutions.

Many campuses are moving to having their residence halls locked all the time. This practice does limit the ease at which guests can move through the building; however, it also limits the ability of a stranger to move through the building. Here again, this policy only helps if people do not prop open doors.

Appropriate key management is essential in promoting a safe environment. Key numbering systems should not be easily determined. As such, the numbers should not all fall sequentially and should not reflect room numbers. Lost keys should result in a lock change, not simply a key replacement. Master keys should be limited in number and issued only to essential personnel. Accountability for these keys should be strictly maintained.

SAFETY SERVICES AND PUBLIC SAFETY PROGRAMS

Campus Security and Law Enforcement

Different colleges and universities have used different security systems. Some have their own police departments, while others have security departments. Many security departments have sworn law officers who have arrest powers. Some schools have chosen to arm their officers while others have not. Depending on the size and culture of the campus, each school develops a system that meets its needs; however, one element to success is an effective officer recruitment and training program. Most successful programs run thorough background checks on their candidates. Routine professional development keeps officers' skills sharp. Specific training to rape sensitivity is essential.

Safety Education Programs

Safety education is paramount in creating safer environments. Orientation programs for new students regarding safety should be implemented. When students first arrive on campus they are very vulnerable to violence. They are unaware of their surroundings, unfamiliar with their neighbors, and often overwhelmed and distracted by social and academic demands. Concise and memorable safety awareness briefings can alert students to appropriate reporting mechanisms and safety services.

Orientation programs for new and current staff members are equally important. These programs not only notify people of their resources and their options, they also slightly change people's operational mindset in a positive way. Programs should be offered to the community throughout the year, including self-defense programs. Given the challenges people face attempting to respond in situations of extreme stress, programs that offer opportunity to practice new skills are the most effective. These programs allow people to feel more confident and become less of a victim.

Environmental Safety Conduct Codes

There are a few policies that are critical in order to promote a safe environment. For example, door propping allows perpetrators time and opportunity to commit violence. There have been multiple cases of violent crime happening after someone went through a propped door, the rape and murder of Jeanne Clery being a well-known example. A clear policy prohibiting door propping and consequences for violating this policy should be spelled out and enforced.

Another policy issue concerns guests. Campus guests are often the causes or the recipients of violence. Requiring guests to register increases their accountability and their host's accountability. A guest policy requiring registration and host responsibility for the actions of the guest should be created and enforced.

Everyone knows that a policy without enforcement is pointless, so adequate enforcement efforts are important. Many schools use central entrances with a staffed desk. Residence hall staffs make rounds checking for policy violations, propped doors, and other security breaches. Most hall staff members have radio access to security support services. Many campuses have security on foot or bike patrols. Thus, there are multiple options to provide adequate supervision and enforcement of policies.

Escort Services

Many campuses offer escort services; however, we caution people about providing this option. This service is very good in preventing a predator. However, in extreme relationship-based violence situations, the perpetrator only cares about regaining the "property" and will eliminate any obstacles to the control of the target. Nationwide, there have been several tragic cases of good Samaritans attempting to intervene in a domestic violence situation, only to be killed. Nevertheless, this service can be effective if personnel are trained to ask why the escort is desired. The officers must carefully assess the situation to determine the safest course of action. If the escort is armed with a firearm and capable of providing the necessary force to overpower the perpetrator, he should be prepared to do so.

Other Services

In addition to programming and enforcement, many security and law enforcement offices provide other services. By publishing the crime statistics required by the Jeanne Clery Act, they bring awareness of violence trends to the community. Officers also advise individuals of the legal options in a case. As referral agents, officers help victims get to needed counseling and other services. Most security officers provide response to emergency situations.

GUNS ON CAMPUS

According to a recent Harvard study, 3.5 percent or about 490,000 of the nation's college students own guns.[120] Put into perspective, this number is quite low considering approximately 25 percent of American households contain handguns. Nevertheless, most colleges and universities ban gun possession on their campuses. The fact that almost 90 percent of the schools involved in the Harvard study had at least one student who reported owning a gun on campus upsets many.

Harvard researchers estimated that two-thirds of student gun owners live off-campus.[121] By law, students age 21 and older have the right to keep concealed guns in vehicles in campus parking lots and garages. Research cited in the Harvard study indicated that 6 to 7 percent of students admit to carrying some form of weapon while on campus. Guns accounted for 14 percent of the weapons carried.

In the aftermath of the Virginia Tech and Northern Illinois University shootings, the gun bans have been seriously challenged, especially in states with strong gun rights attitudes. The supporters of the proposed legislation to allow guns on campus argue that in these states guns are allowed in most places, but not on campuses – an apparent violation of their second amendment rights. Opponents of the legislation, however, seem to have the upper hand for now and argue that liberalizing campus gun policies would make campuses much more dangerous.

Students who own guns are more likely to be male and white.[122] They are more likely to live in southern and western regions of the United States. They tend to attend public institutions in rural areas. Slightly more fraternity and sorority members owned guns than non-Greeks.

More disturbing findings from the Harvard study also emerged. Students were more likely to own a gun if they had damaged property as a result of alcohol consumption, been arrested for DUI, or driving after drinking five or more drinks.[123] Of the small number of students who said they needed an alcoholic drink first thing in the morning, 12 percent owned guns, a statistically significant finding. The Harvard study did not indicate that students were getting drunk and then firing their weapons. Nor is there any implication of a cause-and-effect relationship between alcohol and guns, but perhaps a third factor of sensation seeking or risk taking can account for the shared characteristics in this subgroup of gun owners.

While most guns are owned for hunting purposes or self-defense, some have resulted in campus homicide. Fatal campus shootings have been drug-related, while others were apparent revenge. Victims have been primarily students, but have also included professors, counselors, and other campus staff. Several of these cases are cited throughout the book.

Less known are the near misses involving guns on campus. For instance, in 1998, a student who said he needed an "A" in the class confronted a math professor at the University of Maryland at College Park. The student proceeded to lift his jacket, revealing a handgun in a shoulder holster. The student threatened that if the professor did not cooperate, the student would make him "disappear, leaving no evidence." The faculty member reported the incident to campus authorities who obtained search warrants and discovered the student possessed a loaded 9-millimeter semiautomatic handgun and three loaded ammunition clips on the seat of his car. Most college officials stand firm in their prohibition of guns in residence halls and other campus property. Bender and McGlaughlin provide recommendations for confronting people carrying weapons in their article.[124]

SURVIVAL STRATEGIES

The first survival strategy is preventing violence before it occurs. The following is a list of tips, many of which have been adapted from the Security on Campus website (http://securityoncampus.org/)[125]:

- Project confidence and power in the way you hold yourself and the way you talk.
- Beware of and report "bumps" or inappropriate interactions with strangers.
- Decline freshman photos. Freshman photo collections can unfortunately become a catalogue for sexual perpetrators.
- Study the campus and the local area (day and night). Know how to access the protectors on campus.
- Share your class schedule and activities with family and close friends.
- Set up buddy system. During parties, buddies can commit to making sure the other does not become isolated or find themselves in situations they do not want to be in.
- Travel in groups or shuttles during evening hours. Avoid shortcuts that lead you through poorly lit areas.
- Use alcohol moderately or not at all. Approximately 90 percent of campus crime involves alcohol and/or drug abuse.
- Do not leave valuables in open view.
- Know emergency telephone numbers and speed dial.
- Lock your doors while driving.
- Trust your feelings of fear and your instincts that things are not right.
- Avoid walking near bushes, trees, vines, shrubs, parked cars, or areas not visible.
- Be aware of your environment when you go to an ATM machine.
- Keep your keys with you; lock your door.
- Know your neighbors and report illegal activities or loitering.
- Let security know when you are in a location after hours.

- Attend safety programs and practice skills taught.
- Do not prop doors. Rather, remove props and report to the appropriate staff.
- Never admit strangers into a residence hall.

Unfortunately, prevention is not foolproof and learning escape methods is important. We learned earlier that under extreme stress, people encounter a number of difficulties. We also know that people cannot rely solely on their instincts to survive a dangerous situation. People need to learn to overcome inappropriate instincts, impaired senses and motor skills, and tunnel vision. People can learn a great deal about survival tactics from animals. Running, scanning, camouflaging, and distracting are all skills that animals use to escape their predators. Those specific tactics are included in four main strategies (also listed in *Violence Goes to School*: Get out, barricade, hide, play dead, and fight.[126]

Get Out

If there is enough distance between the potential victim and the perpetrator, this is the safest course of action.[127] While attempting to escape a violent environment seems like common sense, many potential victims are not effective in their efforts. In one case cited in research by Kelly Asmussen and John Creswell, a heavily armed gunman entered a classroom at a large public university. He pointed his rifle at the students, swept the barrel across the room and pulled the trigger. The gun jammed. The gunman attempted to dislodge the gun, but was unsuccessful. After about 20 seconds, a student was able to push a desk into the gunman and students ran out of the classroom. The gunman followed the students out of the building to a nearby car he had left running. Police eventually caught the gunman. In the weeks after the incident, investigators and researchers interviewed the witnesses

and discovered themes in their responses.[128] One of the main themes was denial. Students who were in the building and heard a gunman was present either ignored the warning or denied that the student could be a threat to them. For those students who exited the building, most just huddled together close to the exit doors rather than search for a safe place of protection. Curious on-lookers gathered too to see how the situation would play out.

Some of the following tactics are suggested to help potential victims overcome these unsafe tendencies.[129]

Scanning

When most people scan, they check quickly from left to right.[130] This method leaves many unchecked areas open for danger. All senses are important when trying to locate a threat, but humans primarily use vision. When scanning the environment, it is important to look for possible areas of concealment, shadows, or movement. Scanning a 360-degree circle is another valuable technique. By dividing the space into "pie slices," an individual can methodically check the entire space from floor to ceiling, one slice at a time. Sounds can also indicate areas of danger. Thus, potential victims can avert harm by cueing into any movement or breathing.

Distraction

The squid is known for its ability to distract its pursuer with an inky black substance.[131] Distraction is a very effective tool because it creates an opportunity to escape. Doing something unpredictable throws the perpetrator off guard. Perpetrators must first process the distraction before they can continue being aggressive. The pause may give the individual the opportunity to escape. In the above-mentioned case, one student was able to push a desk at the perpetrator to distract him. Visual distractions are especially effective because people are largely visually oriented. Eyes tend to follow the fastest moving object. Therefore, if a perpetrator is pursuing a potential victim and the victim throws something to the side, the aggressor's eyes will instinctively follow the object. Even if this is only for a second, the opportunity to escape may be provided.

Running

As mentioned earlier, many animals use running as a means of escaping their predators.[132] Darting back and forth makes it very difficult for pursuers to anticipate the next move, and thus slows the perpetrators down. Unfortunately, the natural tendency for people when they are fleeing is to glance over their shoulder. This can throw off the center of gravity and increase risk of falling or slowing speed.

Persist in the Pursuit of Protection

Once individuals are outside the immediate area of danger, they should continue running until they are in a protected area.[133] Sometimes, people get curious and want to stay in the periphery of the violent environment to see what will happen next. This choice could prove deadly. In the case mentioned earlier, the students who hung around the exit doors were lucky that the gunman did not return with another loaded gun.

Barricading

If it is impossible to get out of the environment, the next best thing is to barricade.[134] Barricading means putting as many obstacles as possible between the perpetrator and the potential victims. Perpetrators who are on a killing spree will not stop their momentum to tear down a barricade. Therefore, potential victims must close and lock doors and close blinds. When perpetrators are aimed at taking out victims of opportunity rather than victims of choice, "out of sight, out of mind" can help protect potential victims in the perpetrator's path.

Hide

The chameleon is known as the master of camouflage in the wild.[135] This animal blends in very well with the environment so that the predator will overlook it and not attack. The human predator is not an effective scanner and will most likely miss the person who is hiding above or below a straight line of sight. Within reasonable safety parameters, people should try to find hiding places that are not in direct view of the perpetrator. When hiding, it is important to remain still and silent. Individuals should check to make sure nothing is sticking out where it could be seen. Clothing, hair, limbs, shoelaces, strange lumps, or shadows may call attention to their presence.

Play Dead

If there is no other way to escape, playing dead is an option.[136] The individual must remain totally motionless. Controlled slow breathing and minimal startle response are difficult to achieve under extreme stress.

Fight

If getting out, barricading, and hiding are not options and playing dead is not feasible, the final alternative is to fight.[137] When fighting, an individual should fight to create an opportunity to escape. The end goal is not to beat up the perpetrator. If an option to escape becomes available, it should be taken. Given the difficulty with fine motor skills, gross motor skill movements should be used, such as kicking. Most important to fighting, people must give themselves permission to do what they need to do to escape.

PERSONAL SECURITY OPTIONS

Some individuals choose to protect themselves with nonlethal weapons of self-defense. People have purchased stun guns, pepper spray, body alarms, and other similar devices. But are these tools effective? Without proper training and practice, these devices can sometimes be more detrimental than helpful. Caution should be heeded using some of these devices. For example, perpetrators can take pepper spray from victims and use it against them. Furthermore, individuals who own these devices must be ready to use them at the appropriate time. Digging into a purse or backpack at the time of a crisis will only serve to slow down and fluster the victim. Pepper spray canisters clog and dry up without regular use, and so users must monitor these devices on a regular basis to maintain effectiveness.

Body alarms sound good in theory, but may not help the victim at all. We are so accustomed to hearing car alarms on a regular basis, most of us tune out such sounds and are not likely to respond.

SELF-PROTECTION FOR INDIVIDUALS WITH DISABILITIES

Individuals with disabilities are often even more vulnerable to campus violence than others. The term disabilities encompasses a multitude of impairments: physical disability resulting from injury, chronic disease or congenital conditions; sensory impairments (e.g., hearing or visual); cognitive impairments (e.g., mental retardation or brain injury); or mental illness. Individuals with disabilities may be targets of hate crimes, or they may experience miscommunication that escalates into conflict.

Only a few North American studies have investigated this issue, mostly in regards to violence against women with disabilities. In many ways the results are reflective of violence against women without disabilities. Most notably, perpetrators of violence against women with disabilities are largely spouses or other partners. There are significant differences, however, that are important to consider. Many women with disabilities reported being abused by service providers, and many did not report violent episodes because of fear and dependency. Treatment services for these women were often inadequate. Programs were architecturally inaccessible, interpreter services were lacking, and so on.

Often campus violence prevention strategies are devised with the able-bodied individual in mind. Consideration and accommodation must be made for those campus-community individuals who have disabilities as well. Escape routes must be planned to be accessible to wheelchairs. Panic buttons must be available and comprehensible to those with motor and sight impairments. Campus call boxes must be equipped to handle calls from the hearing impaired.

Students with disabilities can be coached in adapting behavioral and sensory safety strategies to work from their functioning abilities. For example, when scanning a room the blind can scan with their ears rather than their eyes. Those in wheelchairs can learn to equip their chairs with safety devices such as pepper spray (as long as they follow the suggestions listed earlier).

Many of the general prevention strategies can easily be adapted to working with individuals with disabilities. Nevertheless, violence prevention with individuals with disabilities remains an underresearched area. Increasing numbers of students with disabilities will continue to enroll and colleges and universities must be prepared to ensure that their safety is met.[138]

Chapter 9

LAW AND CAMPUS VIOLENCE

DARBY DICKERSON[139]

ALTHOUGH THE LAW can rarely be used to cure violence, it can be an important and effective part of the treatment regime. But to be used effectively, universities and their officials must learn to view the law as a tool that empowers them to use their professional judgment and discretion, and not a force to be feared and avoided. By understanding the law and messages that courts are sending to the higher education community, we can use the law as a positive force in our request to control violence on our campuses.

NEGLIGENCE ACTIONS

Violence enters our campuses in myriad ways, but this chapter will address student-on-student violence, because students tend to be both the primary victims and perpetrators of on-campus crime. As noted in earlier chapters, students may pose a danger to others in different ways: some threaten to injure others, some intentionally injure others without warning, and others bully or stalk. When a student is injured or killed as the result of another student's conduct, suits filed against the university most frequently found in negligence: negligent supervision, negligent failure to provide security, and negligent failure to warn, to name just a few.

In a negligence action, the plaintiff – often the injured student or the deceased student's parents or estate – bears the burden of proving that the university or its officials owed the plaintiff a duty, that they breached that duty, that plaintiff's injury was caused by an act or omission of the university or its employees, and that the plaintiff suffered damages as a result of that act or omission.

"Duty" is an obligation, recognized by law, that requires a person to conform to a certain standard of care to protect others against unreasonable risks. In most instances, the standard of care requires that a person act like a reasonably prudent person would act under the same or similar circumstances. The second part of this standard – under the same or similar circumstances – is critical, because it means that actions taken under emergency circumstances will be viewed from that perspective. It is important not to conflate "duty" with "liability." Duty is just one of five essential elements in the negligence equation.[140] Without the other four, liability will not attach.

"Breach" means that the defendant – the person sued – failed to conform to the standard of care. Thus, "breach" is the alleged misconduct.[141] As noted above, under the breach element, the analysis focuses on whether the defendant acted reasonably under the circumstances. Accordingly, universities and their employees are not insurers

105

of students' safety. Instead, they must provide a reasonably safe environment for students and employees, and must act reasonably under the circumstances presented.

"Cause" refers to two distinct elements of a negligence claim. First, "actual cause" or "but-for cause" refers a factual link exists between the plaintiff's acts or omissions and the defendant's injuries. The separate concept of "proximate cause" involves a policy analysis about whether the defendant should be held liable or whether its actions were too remote to impose liability. That analysis includes asking whether the defendant's conduct is "too attenuated."[142] As one law professor has explained: "So, if the plaintiff is injured in a fall from slipping on the vomit of a friend who was nauseated by a smelly plate of shrimp, the injurious consequences may simply seem too far outside the foreseeable risks of serving foul food to hold the restaurateur responsible for plaintiff's harm."[143]

In addition, the unforeseeable acts of third persons, like criminals, may in some instances insulate the defendant from liability.[144] So, too, may legislative actions. For example, in many states, social hosts are not liable for injuries caused by their intoxicated adult guests because state legislatures have concluded that "legal responsibility, as a matter of policy, should be borne alone by the intoxicated guest."[145]

"Damage" means the actual injury suffered by the plaintiff.

Two other concepts that are critical in any negligence action are reasonableness and forseeability: in most contexts, courts hold that the university and its officials must use reasonable care to protect students from foreseeable danger. What constitutes reasonable care and foreseeable danger are fact-intensive questions; thus, the outcomes in cases differ, with some resulting in liability and others resulting in no liability.

If a plaintiff is able to establish all four essential elements, liability will attach unless the defendant can prove a valid affirmative defense. Although a variety of defenses to negligence exist, one of the most common is that the plaintiff was contributorily negligent: that is, the plaintiff's actions contributed to his or her injury or loss. Because tort law is typically controlled by state law, the consequences of this defense may differ from state to state. However, many now hold that if a jury determines that the plaintiff is as or more culpable than the defendant, the plaintiff may not cover, or may recover only for the percentage of negligence assigned to the defendant.

LEGAL EVOLUTION

The law of negligence as it relates to campus violence has evolved over time. For decades, universities were immune from most negligence actions. Public universities were protected by the doctrine of sovereign, or governmental, immunity, and private universities were protected by charitable immunity. While remnants of immunity protection remain, the application has become extremely narrow.

Another concept that precluded negligence liability was causation. Traditional tort doctrine held that there could be only one legal cause of a tort, and that cause was the most culpable individual or organization. For instance, when a person was injured by an intoxicated individual, it was that individual – and not the person who supplied or served the alcohol – who was culpable. Modern tort law, however, recognizes multiple causes of injuries, which means that universities and campus officials are more frequently named in lawsuits.

Following the decline of these protective concepts, we can view the evolution of negligence law regarding universities in three phases. The first phase focused on facilities – keeping buildings and parking lots "safe." During this phase, courts often concentrated on issues such as whether universities had appropriate campus safety departments and safety devices such as lights, fences, and locks. Later, the focus shifted to the university's knowledge regarding potentially dangerous persons on campus and its role in protecting one student from the aggression of other students. The current phase also involves student-on-student crime, but focuses heavily on issues such as violence associated with alcohol and other drug use, mental health, or hate crimes.

A landmark case from the first phase is *Mullins v. Pine Manor College*.[146] In *Mullins*, a female student was raped in her dorm room by an unidentified assailant. In a shift from prior law, the Massachusetts Supreme Judicial Court held that the college had a duty to exercise reasonable care to protect students from the criminal acts of third parties.[147] The Court based this conclusion on a variety of grounds, including determinations that criminal behavior on campus was foreseeable and that the college controlled key aspects of campus safety, such as installing a security system, hiring security guards, setting a patrol policy, installing locks, etc.[148]

In *Nero v. Kansas State University*[149] – a case from the second period – the rule in Mullins was extended to require a university to reasonably protect students against the dangerous acts of other students. In *Nero*, a male student was accused of raping a female student in an on-campus, co-ed residence hall in which they both lived.[150] Following the rape accusation and pending resolution of the criminal case, the University reassigned the male student to live in an all-male dorm on the other side of campus; the University also directed the student not to enter any co-ed or all-female dormitory.[151] The student registered for spring intersession, and the University assigned him to a co-ed residence hall, which was the only dormitory open.[152] A few weeks later, he sexually assaulted Shana Nero, a female dorm resident. Nero sued the university in negligence for failing to protect her from the sexual

assault or warning her about the male student and his past conduct.[153]

The *Nero* court emphasized that a university can never insure students' safety, but also concluded that a university "has a duty [to use] reasonable care to protect its students against certain dangers, including criminal actions against a student by another student or a third party if the criminal act is reasonably foreseeable and within the university's control."[154] Because the university was aware of the prior rape charge, moved the perpetrator to an all-male dorm, and prohibited him from entering co-ed and all-female dorms, the court determined that the attack on Nero could have been foreseeable, and that the issue of foreseeability in this context was a jury question.[155]

Although a university may have a duty to use reasonable care to protect a student from foreseeable harm, the student must also take reasonable steps to protect himself. In *Lloyd v. Alpha Phi Alpha Fraternity*,[156] a student's negligence action against Cornell University for injuries suffered during fraternity hazing was dismissed, in part because the student failed to alert the university about the alleged abuse and actually concealed the activity by lying to campus officials about the true source of his injuries. The court stated that if the university was unable to learn about the hazing through the individual student or others, "then it is contrary to common sense to think a duty could be imposed upon the University to protect persons against these unknown activities."[157]

In the 2007 case of *Love v. Morehouse College, Inc.*,[158] one student was severely beaten by another in the dormitory shower. The perpetrator initiated the attack because he believed the victim was homosexual and looked at him inappropriately. The injured student sued the College for negligence, alleging the College failed to use reasonable care to keep him safe because the attack was foreseeable and the College did not act. In addressing whether the College should have known about a hostile atmosphere against homosexuals, the court found that Morehouse had failed to address the harassment of students believed to be homosexual; had fostered an atmosphere of hatred and violence toward such students; had "approved and ratified the disparate treatment" of those students; and had failed to take disciplinary action as to the students who perpetrated such behavior.[159]

REASONABLE CARE

These and other cases instruct universities that they have a legal duty to exercise reasonable care to protect students and others on campus from foreseeable danger. "Reasonable care" is a flexible concept that requires a fact-finder, such as a jury, to balance the probability and potential seriousness of an injury against the burden of avoiding the harm, under the same or similar circumstances. So, while the legal responsibility to provide a safe and secure environment is settled, what actions are reasonable under the circumstances will vary. For this reason, some try to anticipate the bare minimum that will be required. But instead of guessing about minimum legal requirements, institutions of higher education would be better served by allowing their officials to follow their professional judgment and discretion, in addition to the law, and focus on what is best for our campus communities.

JUDICIAL TRENDS

Judicial trends reinforce the notion that courts prefer for universities to act in ways that reflect their care for students' well-being rather than in ways designed to circumvent legal liability. For example, in *Mahoney v. Allegheny College*,[160] the parents of a deceased student sued the College and several administrators for negligence following their son's suicide. In refusing to impose liability, the court emphasized the importance of a "humanistic" approach: "We believe the 'University' has a responsibility to adopt prevention, programs and protocols regarding students['] self-inflicted injury and suicide that address risk management *from a humanistic and therapeutic as compared to just a liability or risk avoiding perspective.*"[161]

Another judicial trend, as identified by Professor Peter F. Lake of Stetson University College of Law is the concept of "riskscapes." Today, courts are less concerned with issues of geography – where the campus borders begin and end – and more concerned about foreseeable pockets of risk, whether on or off campus. Courts recognize that danger can flow on and off campus. Cases have described situations where a fraternity prank started on campus, then shifted off campus.[162] Similarly, the media have reported situations when off-campus drinking resulted in on-campus sexual assaults. Moreover, the reality that today's students live much of their lives in a virtual world with its own set of dangers – including cyber-bullying and cyber-stalking – means that universities can no longer focus safety and risk-management efforts just on the physical campus borders.

In addition, especially with regard to issues related to alcohol and other drug use, courts are beginning to insist that universities use techniques that are "evidence based" and supported by science. This trend highlights the importance of hiring individuals who have been trained in the area in which they are assigned to work, supporting regular training and professional development, and empowering them to use their professional judgment and discretion when handling issues regarding campus safety and security.

POST-VIRGINIA TECH CONSIDERATIONS

The shootings at Virginia Tech, Northern Illinois, and other campuses are likely to impact negligence law in the area of campus safety. More specifically, these tragedies – and the many task force reports that followed – are likely to impact what "foreseeable" and "reasonable" might mean.

For example, given the increase in campus shootings, coupled with the calls to abolish "information silos," courts and juries in the future may find it unreasonable if a university has not developed a way to share, collate, and act upon information regarding disturbing student conduct. Post-Virginia Tech, higher education has seen a surge in universities creating at-risk student concern teams to facilitate communication and action. Similarly, a campus that has not developed appropriate levels of cooperation with local law enforcement and the local mental-health system might be found not to have acted reasonably under the circumstances if a student with a documented, serious mental health condition slips through the administrative cracks and later injures another person.

Also, it will be difficult to claim that a university acted reasonably if it failed to share information about a potentially dangerous student internally or with appropriate law enforcement due to FERPA or similar privacy laws. When campus safety is at issue, it will trump privacy concerns. Stated differently, it's always better to be defending a suit for violation of privacy than for wrongful death.

SUGGESTIONS

To use the law in a way to help fight the virus of campus violence, a university should focus on the risks most likely to occur on its campus. Every campus is different, and – given most institutions' limited resources – each must focus on the most likely risks that can result in the most serious injuries. For most schools, this means focusing significant resources on high-risk alcohol use and providing a variety of mental-health services.

Universities should also strive to create a culture in which everyone on campus understands that he or she has a role in health and safety. In this regard, universities should provide regular training and empower individuals to report concerns. Without continual encouragement, many will be reluctant to raise difficult issues and questions.

Next, universities should not fear FERPA. When the choice is between campus safety and privacy, campus safety should prevail. In addition, if the 2008 proposed amendments to FERPA are enacted, the statute will no longer be strictly construed, and the Department of Education will not initiate an investigation if the school identifies an "articulable and significant threat" to the health and safety of a student or other individuals.[163]

Similarly, universities should not confuse privacy under FERPA with the confidentiality rules by which mental-health and medical professionals are bound. Educators can and should share information that relates to campus safety. And while the medical and mental-health professionals may not be able to provide specific information, universities should still include them in meetings and conversations. They can listen and potentially use what they hear, and they can share general observations, such as whether more students need help for depression, or whether the school might consider increasing patrols in an area of campus.

Finally, universities should encourage faculty and staff – educators – to act based on their professional judgment, training, and discretion, instead of acting solely to avoid legal liability. If universities and their staff focus on the institution's mission and core values, they will tend to make the right decisions and create a culture and environment that is reasonably safe for students to live and study.

Chapter 10

PREPARING FOR THE VIOLENCE AFTERMATH: A COMMUNITY AFFECTED

CHRISTOPHER BOLLINGER & SALLY SPENCER-THOMAS

THE ROLE OF THE UNIVERSITY community after a violent incident is just as critical as in early interventions. Initially, most of the attention in the immediate aftermath is focused on the victims and perpetrators. Secondary and tertiary victims are often overlooked. Beyond these groupings, most campus community members are affected by known campus violence, and they need support systems in place. Grieving and healing as a community can have a synergistic effect, pulling the community together and reminding them of some of their better qualities.

When violence impacts our campuses, it disrupts the community like an earthquake. The immediate victims fall in the epicenter receiving most of the original impact. From there, the impact radiates outward affecting people based on their physical or emotional proximity to the event. Many are affected, even people who did not know the victims. In some cases, memories of their own traumatic experiences were triggered. Emergency responders may be affected because of the youthfulness of the victims or the atrocity of the violence. Depending on the media coverage of the event, the impact could be nationwide or even international. The depiction of the ripple effect is illustrated

in Figure 10.1 inherent in a violent event. This diagram shows the overwhelming number of people that can be affected by just one incident.

This chapter will explore four areas which need to be considered in the aftermath of a crisis. When the violent event occurs, the first area of concern is **Communal Management**. Communal management focuses on providing the immediate responses to victims and perpetrators and coordinating efforts to help the community deal with the incident in the best way possible. After responding to immediate processing needs, **Counseling Support** needs to be considered. Counseling support addresses both the short- and long-term needs of those suffering trauma resulting from the violent incident or that is triggered by the violent incident. Campuses frequently find themselves surprised by the long-term support needed for survivors of violent incidents, which is surprising as we can almost always anticipate some level of need in this area. As we have relearned with every violent event, **Media Management** remains a constantly evolving yet crucially important area which requires our attention. Finally, after a violent event slowly comes to an end, **Evaluation** and **Future Planning** should be considered.

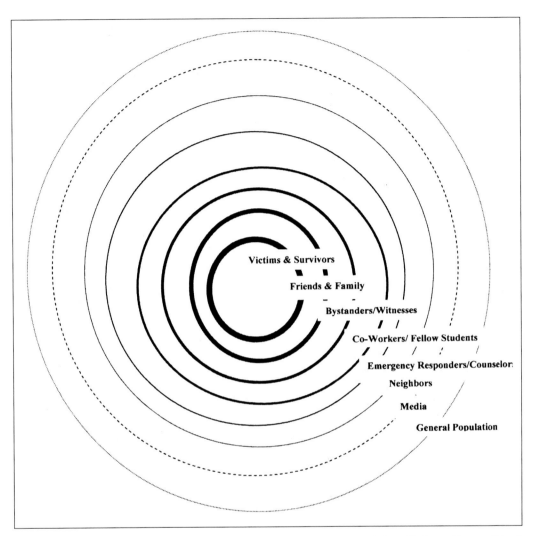

Figure 10.1. Violence Impact. This model is adapted from a model in *Violence Goes to School*. Nicoletti, J., Zinna, K., and Spencer-Thomas, S. (1999). *Violence Goes to School: Lessons Learned from Columbine*. Denver, Colorado: Nicoletti-Flater Associates.

COMMUNAL MANAGEMENT

After experiencing a violent incident or trauma, many people are immobilized by the shock and uncertain what to do next. The following guidelines are to help survivors know what to expect and what to do to effectively manage community needs in the days and weeks following. A critical incident analysis of colleges and universities that have successfully dealt with violence revealed the following factors and themes in their approaches.

Presence of Leadership

Presidents, faculty, key administrative personnel, and student leaders should be highly visible and demonstrate intense personal

involvement. In the aftermath of highly publicized violence, people not directly involved
begin to make assumptions about the community in which the perpetrator resided. For
example, the murder of Matthew Shepard at
the University of Wyoming led to misperceptions about the entire Laramie, Wyoming
community and rampant homophobia. While
Laramie certainly dealt with homophobia in
their community, it was not so different than
most communities in the United States.
Much of the Laramie community was not as
homophobic as it was often perceived to be.
Perceptions such as these are sometimes unfounded and become detrimental to the survivors. A truthful message from the leaders of
the community must override such misperceptions. Leaders must repeat with clarity
and conviction what the campus stands for
and what it will not tolerate.

On November 1, 1991, two professors and
one graduate student were shot and killed at
the University of Iowa. In a summary of the
crisis, Gerald Stone, the Director of the University Counseling Service, described the importance of campus leadership uniting the
community.[164] The President and the Vice
President for Academic Affairs defined the
tragedy as a community experience. The
campus leadership spoke of healing as a community and set the tone for the teamwork that
would be required to deal with the tragedy.

Leaders also need to provide opportunities within the community for members to
offer support for targeted groups. Often in a
violent event, targeted groups are made to
feel afraid of their own community. In a
workshop on coping with hate conducted in
2006, participants expressed concerns over
their campus leadership's response to an anti-
Semitic incident on campus. Staff and students had received letters notifying them that
the incident had occurred, that their leadership did not condone such actions, and that
the incident was being investigated. They appreciated that their leaders were concerned

but felt as though they were left out in the
dark alone and unsupported by their broader
community. It is important for leaders to set
the tone, but it is also important for that leadership to encourage broader community support in standing against those perpetrating
the violence and for those being targeted by
the violence.

Crisis Response Team

In the aftermath of a tragedy, a predetermined team can be instrumental in addressing the needs of affected individuals and the
community. The Crisis Response Team usually consists of a cross-section of university
representatives who are highly invested and
trained in handling critical incidents. This
team may have significant overlap or may
even be identical to the Behavioral Intervention Team (BIT) described in Chapter 6.

A common experience after a violent
tragedy is a search for direction. In Stone's
description of the tragedy at the University of
Iowa, he remembered hearing "Who is in
charge?" "What can I do?" and "Where is the
plan?"[165] Responses like these are common.
The Crisis Response Team can serve as a locus
of control for communicating with departments, community members, survivors and
the media as well as for planning and organizing the many post-incident events. The team
should be representative of the community
affected including faculty, staff, administration, students, and local community members when appropriate. The team should be
flexible in membership to meet the needs of
the violent crisis.

In his About Campus article on the
Matthew Shepard tragedy, Dr. Jim Hurst,
Vice President for Student Affairs at the
University of Wyoming, cited this kind of
flexibility as being a critical contribution to
the healing of the community. For instance,
professional staff members gave up offices
and resources to student groups who were

facilitating memorial planning for Matthew. The Crisis Response Team may be responsible for organizing the debriefing and victim's assistance needs described below.

Debriefings and Victim's Assistance

The purpose of debriefings is to bring people together so they may discover what has actually happened and/or is still happening, understand what that means for them and others, and learn about what resources might be helpful and/or are available to them. Debriefings are provided as a form of crisis intervention with the goal of minimizing the psychological disturbance resulting from the traumatic event. When a violent event happens, people's understanding is often fragmented and illusive. In a debriefing, participants come together to discuss their roles, experiences, thoughts, reactions, and symptoms.

So how does a debriefing work? A facilitator, usually a professional mental health care staff member, will lead the group in a discussion of what happened. Frequently, voicing the perceptions of the events, in a chronological order, helps participants piece together a coherent account. The facilitator will work with the group on recognizing normal stress reactions, symptom management, and when to seek additional help. The facilitator will also help the group focus on survivor strengths, coping skills, and social support. The facilitator should also provide community referrals and readings for further assistance and information. Debriefings should be timely and repeated as necessary. When scheduling debriefings, we need to consider other related events, such as memorial services for the victims of the crime. On-campus experts may be more likely than outside experts to understand the social circumstances and organizational factors particular to the participants.

Debriefings are often easier to facilitate face to face. Given the technological proficiency and preference of many of our contemporary students, campuses should consider also offering on-line debriefings. Before engaging in such practices, we should be attentive to a few issues. First, we need to know if our infrastructure can support the practices. Losing a connection during a debriefing could prove to be tragic. Second, our professional staff needs to possess the necessary technical, facilitation, and health care proficiencies to appropriately facilitate the debriefing. If a community member begins to have a breakdown on-line, intervening becomes more challenging. Our health care professionals and our student affairs professionals should be trained and well practiced in dealing with the nuances of this medium of communication. Third, we need to be attentive to our interaction with the larger community in these mediums. While press releases should be distributed over the internet, debriefings should be conducted within intranet spaces with greater security safeguards. Many schools have gone to creating Facebook like spaces for their first-year students that are in a more secure environment. Extending this model for the larger body might be wise for responding to crises.

Managing Experts and Helpers

A trend in postviolence situations is the flocking of "helpers" to the scene of the incident. Some are well meaning; others are sensation seeking. Few are invited. In the Iowa tragedy, Dr. Stone shared that the number of phone calls he received from experts offering support was overwhelming.[166] He went on to share that some of the agendas of the experts were questionable. This is not uncommon. Following the crash of TWA Flight 800, back in July 1996, the American Red Cross announced they had gathered almost 500 volunteers, mostly mental health counselors to help families. At the same time, another welfare agency was sending their grief counselors to the airport. Counselors ended up outnumbering victims at the scene.

Crisis tends to attract people who are excited by the event and not always motivated by genuine concern to help others. Many inexperienced counselors will abandon the situation when the novelty wears off or when they realize that they are in over their heads. Survivor needs in the immediate aftermath are more mundane such as transportation, medical assistance, or financial resources. Rushing past appropriate first response needs (practical assistance, debriefing, referrals) in the hope of fixing the problem does not necessarily help and sometimes hinders the grieving and healing process.[167] Much of the needed professional counseling will follow in days, weeks, months, and in many cases years to come. In the cases that do require extra psychological assistance, having identified qualified professionals (and ideally having worked with them) prior to the crisis can save a great deal of time and energy screening out the not so helpful experts from the needed qualified and committed supporters.[168] Community members are likely to have a variety of support and style needs. The Emergency Support Network recommends providing a "menu" of services from which victims and their families can choose. Such services can include a 24-hour crisis hotline/information line, psychological debriefings, educational seminars on "how to help someone who has been through a trauma," posttrauma counseling, follow-up debriefings or telephone contact, and trauma-anniversary assistance.

Working with Victims' Families

Both in the immediate aftermath and over the long term, families play an important role. Families can be an integral part of the campus healing and campus life can help families heal as well. The first question to answer is what if any connection between the campus and family is appropriate given such tragic circumstances.[169]

To determine this, family members must be found and contacted. In some cases, such as in extended blended families, this is not an easy task and everyone might not be agreeable to the involvement.

One or two campus contacts should provide a link between the family and the campus to facilitate communication and help coordinate memorial services if needed.[170] These contacts should stress that their role is one of a caregiver and not a legal advisor. Depending on the circumstance, families may want to have varying degrees of connection with the campus after the tragedy. They may wish to have their own written statements distributed via letter or newspaper editorial. They may be interested in speaking at rallies or services held on campus. They may desire to set up scholarships in the name of their son or daughter. Families may also need help from the campus contacts. They may want to get information from sources on campus such as faculty members, roommates, and student life officials. They may require help gathering their child's personal belongings from his/her living space. In essence, these contacts are there to ask the family members the question, "How can I help you right now."

Re-establishing a Sense of Security: The Role of Law Enforcement

Increasing security efforts in the weeks and months post-incident will help reassure the community that serious efforts are being implemented to prevent tragedy from reoccurring. To deter copycat violence of high profile cases such as the Florida A&M University bombing or the avenger massacre at Concordia University, security and law enforcement officers should be highly visible and readily available to provide positive information quickly. They should be prepared to quickly examine any rumors regarding potential acts of further violence. Law enforcement officials should interact with the campus community informally on a regular basis in order to build trust. While community outreach of this kind routinely happens on many campuses, it needs to be magnified even further in the aftermath of a crisis.

In order to work effectively with law enforcement agencies outside of campus, campus officials must establish and nurture an on-going contact with their local department prior to the emergence of and during a crisis. Usually, a community resource officer can be a good liaison between the two institutions. This contact person must be familiar with the procedures and key personnel at the university and be able to communicate effectively the needs of each agency.

When a violent crisis occurs on campus, it is important to note that law enforcement officials may have different objectives than other campus administrators. Usually, law enforcement is focused on tracking down and stopping the perpetrators while other groups on campus are focused on responding to the needs of the victim. Sometimes these roles collide. For example, in the instance of sexual assault, campus security officers work to build a case against the perpetrator while residence life and counseling staff members strive to empower the victim and ensure privacy. Law enforcement professionals are trained to take control in crises. Victims may not be willing to surrender that control, and in some cases such as sexual assault, they probably should not be expected to do so. As long as the different agencies responding to the crisis are aware of the potential conflict of roles and are willing to work through them, the interference to an appropriate outcome should be minimal.

Constructive Outlets

Often, people can find a sense of purpose and meaning in terrible events if they can channel their sorrow or anger into action. Additionally, tangible symbols of the tragedy can provide a sense of solidarity for the community. In the weeks after the Matthew Shepard tragedy, students distributed yellow ribbons to symbolize the community's loss.[171] These yellow ribbons were still noticeable months later on students' backpacks. Community retail stores became involved by donating ribbon materials to the students. The yellow ribbons became work that helped with the grieving and healing process for the community.

In the aftermath of the Florida A&M University bombings, students organized a march demonstrating their fears and concern over the safety of their campus. Similarly, in the aftermath of assaults at the University of Massachusetts, students gathered to protest what they perceived as an underresponse by the university.[172] These gatherings empowered students and gave them a tangible way to become part of the solution so quickly after the event.

Limiting Destructive Outlets

Following a major incident, many people will experience a rush of emotions. People enhanced by zealous and competing media outlets very quickly move to assigning blame. There is a time and place for appropriately levying responsibility. This should be a thoughtful and well reasoned process and not a reaction in the heat of the moment. The media can be and often is a catalyst for pursuing appropriate accountability. However, given the speed and force of our media competing for our attention, blame is frequently assigned very quickly and without a great deal of consideration. We need to be aware of this process and how it might affect our students.

Blaming can deteriorate into socially constructing monsters for other monsters to compete with. Following 9/11, hate crimes against Middle Eastern appearing Americans vastly increased. Following the Virginia Tech shootings, the press quickly put out stories blaming the shooter's English teacher for not recognizing danger signs in a creative writing class as well as administrators and campus police for not responding to the first death (which at the time did not appear to be the beginning of a murder spree) quickly enough. These speedy assignments of blame can make it difficult for our campus community to stay focused on moving through the crisis. The blame did not stop there though. Stories printed in papers specifically marked his Asian status and one alluded to the spree emerging from frustrations in his secret gay life. Anger, misinformation, and a desire for swift retribution can lead to more violence. Premature blaming and the creation of enemies is unfortunately a very routine process and will likely need to be dealt with in the event of a campus crisis.

Follow-Up Services

For the most part, society responds well immediately after a crisis, but once the fanfare dies down, the victims are left wondering, "Where did everybody go?" Periodic check-in points for students, faculty, and staff will let survivors know they are supported in their continued struggle and healing. Be prepared for significant dates for the survivors: graduation, birthdays, special events, the beginning of the school year, and especially the anniversaries of the trauma (e.g., one week, one month, six months, annually, and so on).

COUNSELING SUPPORT

Not every person who is victimized by a life-threatening situation is necessarily traumatized. Responses to emotionally intense experiences are strongly influenced by past history and personality makeup. As such, it is not reasonable to expect everyone who endures the same traumatic experience will exhibit symptoms and posttrauma reactions. In

fact, suggesting there is something wrong with people who are not grossly affected may prove detrimental. People should be encouraged to "feel what they are feeling." The truth is, there is no standard way to respond to extraordinary events, and each person will have an individual reaction. The following sections of this chapter are based on our own experiences and observations and a combination of sources: *Trauma Recovery Handbook* (Slover and Tasci), *Violence Goes to School*, the American Psychiatric Association's *Diagnostic and Statistical Manual of Mental Disorders*, and *Trauma and Recovery* (Herman).

Trauma Symptoms

A violent incident is certainly a traumatic event and can cause strong physical and emotional reactions in those involved. These aftereffects are considered, *normal responses to very abnormal events.* During this time, the mind and body are trying to adapt and cope with a life-threatening situation. People can remain in survival mode for a prolonged period of time. The defensive guard remains up and ready for action at all times. Irrational fears, discomfort with previously enjoyed activities, worries about family members and loved ones, are examples of the unwillingness of the body and psyche to be victimized again.

In addition to this activation of survival instinct, there is the impact of shattered assumptions. All people hold assumptions about the world and themselves. These fundamental beliefs are often not conscious, and they are quite resistant to challenge and change. According to trauma specialist Dr. Janoff-Bulman, these assumptions usually fall within three themes: "The world is benevolent," "The world is meaningful," and "I am a good and worthy person."[173] Most people believe the world is a safe and fair place, and people are moral. From these core beliefs, people derive the adaptable sense of trust, security, and invulnerability. These traits enable us to go through the day and interact with others without distress.

When a person experiences a traumatic event, these assumptions are dramatically challenged and often shattered. This is especially true when traumatic events are perpetrated by another human being. Research has consistently shown that trauma inflicted by another person, as opposed to those resulting from natural disasters such as hurricanes, tornadoes, and floods, is more damaging and tends to complicate and prolong recovery. The disillusionment and "depressive realism" that can stem from such events can be paralyzing. In other words, the individual's sense of trust, security, and invulnerability is gone. The survivor becomes aware of the reality of surrounding danger and loss potential. The implications can be overwhelming.

In the process of trauma recovery, survivors learn to rebuild their assumptions by integrating the new traumatic experience. Talking with others, or writing about the event, is a very effective way to impose order on a chaotic event. By nature, humans are very verbal creatures, and need to put words to experiences. This is even truer for emotionally loaded incidents.

Another phenomenon associated with trauma is "survivor guilt." When survivors blame themselves for what happened, it is often in an attempt to find some degree of control over an out-of-control situation. "If only I had done this…" or, "If only I had not done that…" or "Why did I survive when others didn't?" are statements often heard repeated by the victims of a traumatic incident. This attempt to regain control and predictability over one's life reestablishes a sense of fortitude and the belief that a people can control their own destiny.

Finding some benefit or purpose in the experience can also assist with the "meaning-making" process for survivors. It is important to know that the event had a purpose. The benefits found in the aftermath of a crisis often involve a rediscovered appreciation for life, one's family and loved ones, and oneself. This drive for resolution can be aided by the community activities previously discussed.

According to the American Psychiatric Association's Diagnostic and Statistical Manual (DSM-IV), *Post-Traumatic Stress Disorder* (PTSD) is a psychological syndrome that affects individuals who have experienced a critical incident. The cluster of symptoms including nightmares, flashbacks, hyperarousal, dissociation, depression, and avoidance, was first noticed in WWI veterans returning from combat. It was initially labeled "shell shock," and then later "battle fatigue." Over the last several decades, research in the area of psychological trauma has discovered that other life-and-death situations, earthquakes, rape, domestic violence, airplane crashes, car accidents, and violent crime can produce similar effects.

For many individuals, the symptoms gradually disappear with time, but for others, the symptoms can persist with varying intensity for decades. Many people experience a traumatic reaction that spans from two days to four. This is known as an *Acute Stress Disorder*. People experiencing Acute Stress Disorder report "feeling in a daze" and the symptoms they experience cause significant impairment in their functioning. Usually, these symptoms resolve after one month.

In order to be diagnosed with PTSD post-trauma symptoms must have persisted for at least four weeks. The symptoms of PTSD fall into three categories:

(1) *Intrusive symptoms:* These symptoms occur when the images, sounds, smells, tactile or taste sensations related to the traumatic event unexpectedly "intrude" into the person's consciousness. These vivid memories may be manifested during sleep in the form of nightmares. Others are "triggered" by internal or external cues that resemble

some part of the trauma. When this happens, the trauma is repeatedly reexperienced. These experiences can be quite distressful to the individual. In fact, many survivors report that these "flashbacks" make them feel like they are going crazy. The intrusive memories are part of the normal healing process. The brain is desperately trying to make sense out of an unfathomable situation by searching memory banks for any related information. This is an unconscious process that often shocks and deeply upsets victims.

(2) *Avoidance Symptoms:* Reexperiencing the traumatic event is usually painful. So many individuals develop avoidance patterns to dampen the intensity of the uncomfortable feelings. For example, an individual with PTSD may avoid situations that are reminiscent of the traumatic event. Others may become numb to emotions altogether. Depression and a loss of pleasure in life are common results of the withdrawal and "emotional shutting down" that occur.

(3) *Hyperarousal Symptoms:* Individuals with PTSD often demonstrate "hypervigilence," as they feel constant pressure to be on guard for danger. Hypervigilance is the constant scanning of the environment for danger cues. Victims who have hyperarousal symptoms also experience exaggerated startle responses, irrational and new fears, increased irritability, and sometimes explosive anger. They may have difficulty concentrating or remembering new information. Sleep disorders and disrupted appetites are common. It is commonly believed that the survivor of a trauma remains in hyper-alter mode to prevent future danger. All systems are revved at full throttle in case the individual should need to react again to a life-challenging event. After a while state of hyperarousal begins to wear and tear on the individual's body and mental capacity.

There are several associated symptoms that may be present when one develops PTSD. These include:

- Alcohol or drug abuse (the individual's attempt to "self-medicate" painful feelings)
- Anxiety and panic attacks
- Suicidal thoughts, gestures, or attempts
- Extreme guilt
- Feelings of alienation or intense loneliness

If these or other symptoms persist for longer than one month, and interfere with the individual's life, professional counseling services with a therapist who is well versed in trauma should be sought.

Trauma Recovery Phases

Individuals who are traumatized proceed through different phases during the recovery process. While each person may vary widely in their clinical presentation and array of symptoms, the general process among individuals is similar. Sometimes traumatized individuals will recycle through earlier stages when their traumatic experience is triggered. Others will proceed through the stages sequentially. There is not necessarily a right or wrong way to go through this process, and all time parameters mentioned here are general guidelines. Some people may move quickly through the phases while others may take years to come to resolution.

1. *Shock:* The first phase begins at the onset of the traumatic event and can continue for up to a week. The perceived threat of death or injury is very real. Sensory information floods the brain. Sights, smells, sounds, and feelings overwhelm the individual's entire being. The brain is unable to process it all, and emotional numbness sets in. At the time of the traumatic event, there are often distortions in time and space, as well as auditory and visual misperceptions. The experience of events is in "slow motion," there is an unreal or dream-like quality to them. Sounds may be intensified, muted, or absent. Things may look different and unfamiliar, and there may be an intense focus on

only one part of the visual field. There may be a strange sense of calm due to a survival mechanism of extreme denial in the presence of overwhelming danger. There may be some physical symptoms, including agitation, hyper-alertness, overactivity, or biological disruption (e.g., sleeping and eating patterns).

2. *Impact:* This phase often begins when an individual leaves the location of the critical incident and can persist from a few days to several weeks. This phase frequently triggers confusion and a sense of being overwhelmed as full realization of the extent of the danger, damage, death, or injury is made conscious. The individual may become highly emotional when leaving the scene of a disaster. They will likely feel a strong need to isolate, but should be with others for support and to ensure a reconnection with people.

3. *Recoil:* This phase begins with return to a near-normal routine pattern, accompanied by stable days. There will be a decrease in the symptoms of the impact phase, and attention, concentration, reasoning ability, recall, and emotional expression gradually return. This phase often resembles an emotional roller coaster with good days and bad days interspersed. At this stage, individuals often feel as though they will never regain a "normal" life. Each time they begin to get on their feet, another wave of memories sets in.

4. *Posttrauma Resolution:* This phase occurs after returning to one's routine pattern. Here the trauma's impact will show longer-term changes in behavior, thought patterns, beliefs, emotions, and perception. These changes may be irreversible. There are two possible outcomes of this phase: positive resolution or negative reaction with no resolution. The positive course will lead to acceptance of the event and the individual's actions, along with a positive reevaluation of goals and values. Keep in mind, this may be a lengthy process and the continuum of resolution is broad. Without any trauma resolution, there is a strong likelihood of a chronic struggle throughout life with distress, family problems, job difficulties, chemical dependency, and potential suicide.

Counseling Approaches with Survivors

At the first stages of shock and impact, when the victims are feeling a lack of control in the situation, the most effective counseling approach is crisis management. At this time, the goals of crisis management are to restore some sense of order to the person's life and to initiate referrals for help. This process might involve finding a safe place to stay, addressing physical and health issues, or initiating any investigation procedures. During this time, the victim may need support and someone with whom to discuss important decisions. The victims may remain highly symptomatic throughout these stages.

The second level of counseling occurs during the impact and recoil stages. The goal is to move the individual from victim to survivor. Here counseling addresses the unwanted symptoms and underlying causes. This may be achieved in a number of ways. Social support networks are often the most powerful healing mechanisms. Social support can be obtained through family and friends or through support groups. These caring helpers may have good intentions, but they also must have sensitivity and awareness about what victims are experiencing and how best to support them. Thus, counselors can have family sessions or consult with other significant others in the victim's life. Counseling can also help survivors unlearn maladaptive thinking processes and behaviors and work through upsetting emotions.

Trauma recovery work, while very rewarding, can be very complicated and draining for the counselor. Counselors with specialized trauma intervention training are best qualified to work with more difficult cases. As mentioned earlier in Chapter 2, counselors can sometimes become vicariously affected by the trauma themselves. It is essential that these therapists receive on-going support and supervision for this demanding work.

The final level of counseling survivors is maintenance. Inevitably, new situations may trigger past traumatic memories, and survivors may need to check in with counselors periodically for booster sessions. The purpose of these sessions is to help remind the survivor of the strengths they have built from the experience and that set backs do not mean they have to relive the whole process again.

Some Basic Coping Strategies

Recovering from a traumatic event can be a difficult process. Some survivors find they are able to use the following coping strategies to get through the tough times. Others find that professional counseling is most beneficial. Each survivor must determine the most helpful course of action. The following strategies are also recommended for the victim's significant others.

- *Education.* There are many excellent self-help books on the market today which describe the course and treatment of Post-traumatic Stress Disorder (see Notes section for resources).
- *Understand that healing occurs in stages over time.* After a traumatic event, life may not return to the way it was due to permanent losses and changes in views of the world and the self. Many assumptions about life have been destroyed, and developing a new set of beliefs will take time. Don't expect the traumatized individual to just "snap out of it."
- *Get support.* Victims, their families, and others affected by the violent event should talk about their experiences and feelings with others who are supportive. An organized psychological debriefing or support group could be arranged to

help with this process. If there were others involved in the traumatic experience, it may help to establish regular contact when dealing with life after the event. Professional counseling should be considered if symptoms persist.
- *Empowerment.* After the turmoil and intense emotional processing has passed, many people find they can derive strength from the knowledge gained from the trauma. Some people volunteer to help other trauma survivors. Others write about and publish their experience. Some pursue legal avenues for compensation as an avenue for their empowerment.

MEDIA MANAGEMENT

Media has grown far beyond newspapers, radio, and television. We now live in a world of laptops; instant messaging; cell phones that allow you to text, film, record, and send e-mail as well as old fashion talking; not to mention Facebook, MySpace, and the ever popular YouTube. Media can have positive and/or negative influences on the community in the aftermath of a violent tragedy and require management. On a positive note, media can provide a quick and efficient way to inform the surrounding community and concerned others far away about what is happening. Parents who cannot reach their children have means by which they can find out information during the intense stages of a crisis. Likewise, the media can help inform the community on ways to keep safe during a time of crisis and alert them to resources for help. On the flip side, media can also take an already tragic event and make it far worse.

The News Media

Without doubt, many violent incidents on campuses attract the full force of the press. In the case of rioting, campuses' reputations have been damaged by the highly publicized footage of a few out-of-control individuals. Alcohol-poisoning deaths and hazing cases have also received close scrutiny by the media. Therefore, it is important to have a preplanned strategy to handle this phenomenon, and to know the rights campus community members have with the media.

Much of the information included in this section is adapted from the National Association of Student Personnel Administrators (NASPA) Task Force on Violence and the book *Campuses Respond to Violent Tragedy* (Siegel, 1994). General guidelines for media management include the following goals:

1. Vigorously communicate that which you know to be accurate.
2. Keep errors to a minimum and correct each of them immediately.
3. Prevent media from becoming part of the crisis.

As we have mentioned earlier in Chapter 7, a "Communication Vortex" is a critical factor in controlling communication that goes out to the community as well as assessing and organizing information coming into the campus. This vortex, or communication center, should be known by the media as the keeper and sharer of information. Highly visible representatives should be located in the main traffic pattern on campus so that media personnel can find them easily. These appointed communication representatives must diligently verify all incoming and outgoing information for accuracy. If the information cannot be verified, it should not be released. Speculation of any kind is discouraged.

Once accurate information is established, it should be vigorously promoted both within and outside campus. Campus officials should not wait until inaccurate information has surfaced. Periodic information sheets, letters from the president, or mass email can help keep the campus up to date on developments. Key individuals who will be most likely sought

after for quotes and perspectives on the situation should be coached and given written scripts to be communicated to ensure that a consistent message is being sent from university officials. To avoid a "No comment" response to a question that cannot be answered, provide the reason that answer cannot be given at this time. Appropriate campus officials should always return media calls, even when the tone may be hostile.

Well-trained spokespeople can be a tremendous asset to the campus in these circumstances. Each campus should identify one spokesperson and an alternate to handle the press in the aftermath of a crisis. All inquiries should be directed to this spokesperson to minimize confusion and contradictory statements. The Crisis Response Team should establish guidelines for sharing appropriate information prior to releasing it. The spokesperson should be well practiced, having engaged in role plays of possible crises prior to a violent event. We live in diverse communities. The spokesperson should be prepared to respond to questions presented in the languages appropriate to our regions or have a qualified translator working with them. For example, in the southwestern United States, a spokesperson or translator should be fluent in Spanish.

This appointed spokesperson must be prepared to clarify questions before speaking into the microphone. To avoid potential distractions, the spokesperson should select a time and location based on comfort level, not the convenience of the reporter. Cold call interviews in the home or during the normal business day are unacceptable. In order to prepare for the interview, the interviewee should ask beforehand what questions will be asked and what direction the interviewer is planning to take.

Most reporters and other media personnel appreciate courtesy and professionalism and will often reciprocate this treatment. That being said, it is appropriate to put parameters on what is allowable for media coverage. For privacy reasons, campus administrators should prohibit the media from access to residence halls and classrooms. Campus community members can be advised as to limits they can impose on the media. For example, campus officials can give community members permission to tell the media, "I don't want to talk to you." See Figure 10.2 for more suggestions.

Message Outlets

Following the Virginia Tech tragedy, in which a young man gunned down several students, there was a series of security experts calling into question how we get messages out to students. One popular media suggestion has been the text-message warning systems. Campuses would pay an outsourced company for the privilege of sending a message to every student with a cell phone with information about the crisis and directions regarding what they should do. Brent Sokolow, President of the National Center for Higher Education Risk Management, has cautioned rushing into contracts for these services.[174] He raised concerns about the likely return of student apathy with respect for voluntarily turning over their cell phones to college administration. Such an implementation will also create a cost for the bureaucracy we would need collecting and inputting the data. Would our investment be better served in getting loudspeakers like those which were effectively used at Virginia Tech? Furthermore, he cautioned the types of directions that would be sent out as the perpetrator would also likely have a cell phone. Text messages would serve well for weather emergencies, but violent incidents work differently than weather threats, although they should not be taken lightly either. Following a crisis, campuses are under great pressure to do something to show they are on top of the problem. Choices regarding where our monetary resources are invested and what will best serve the campus community should be carefully scrutinized. While text-based message systems suggest that we are safer to the general public, they have yet to be shown to be a prudent use of resources that might be placed somewhere else with greater benefit. Posting vetted information and pod casts on the main website have proven effective for campuses but requires the

---

The campus community has the following rights with the media. While they may not all be granted, they should be requested to protect the campus and victims.

- The right to grieve and recover in private.
- The right to say "no" to an interview.
- The right to request a specific reporter.
- The right to refuse an interview with a specific reporter even if the interviewee has granted interviews to other reporters.
- The right to avoid a press conference atmosphere and speak to only one reporter at a time.
- The right to refrain from answering any questions with which the interviewee is uncomfortable or feels are inappropriate.
- The right to ask to review quotations in a story prior to publication
- The right to demand a retraction when inaccurate information is reported.
- The right to ask that offensive photographs or visuals be omitted from airing or publication.

Figure 10.2. Rights with the Media. Adapted from Slover, C., and Tasci, D. (1999). *Trauma Recovery Handbook*, published by Nicoletti-Flatter Associates.

same media management vigilance as dealing with the news media.

Video Cameras

Compact digital video cameras, cell-phone video cameras, convenient editing software, and YouTube, have put the prospect of making famous movies directly in the hands of most students today. On the one hand, when the public has the opportunity to bring hidden abuses to the larger public perception, justice can be better served. On the other hand, students and staff can put themselves and others in greater danger while attempting to record something interesting for the sake of spectacle. Last year, we were hosting a high school scholars' camp. We were at a community event when a police chase broke out on foot. I was working with my college student staff to help evacuate the high school students away from the area. Meanwhile one of my student staff began videotaping the chase with his phone. Of course, this meant he was not helping to evacuate the high school students from the area. At another school a few years prior, one of the residence halls caught fire. The students were immediately evacuated to the student center. A student from another building got his video camera, went to the student center, and started interviewing them on how they felt about losing all of their possessions as their building burnt to the ground. This was not helpful as the campus staff was attempting to attend to the victims of the crisis. Our most responsible community members can get caught up in the moment. In these moments, they need to be managed just like the news media. Schools should consider adapting policies to deal with these kinds of practices.

EVALUATION AND FUTURE PLANNING

After the intensity of the crisis has passed, all parties involved in violence prevention, intervention, and response should conduct a tactical debriefing as a group. This is an opportunity to evaluate what worked well and to plan for the future. Consider the following questions for the debriefing. What happened? How did our prevention, intervention, and response strategies work? Consider application of the strategy as well as the strategies themselves. What were the challenges presented to these strategies? Consider the following "Safety Net" tool for both evaluation and future planning.

Consider the impact model we presented in the beginning of the chapter. Begin listing the parties involved in violence prevention, intervention, and aftermath at your institution along the outside of the ripples as seen in image "10.3." If we extend a line from the center of the inner most ripple to the outer most ripple, the intersections provide us with an idea of potential areas of interaction during the crisis. For example, if we follow the line from the Crisis Response Team, there are eight intersections, indicating eight potential areas of interaction. If we examine the location marked with a star in Figure 10.3, we would consider the ways the Crisis Response Team may need to interact with institutional neighbors or the media. While it may not be appropriate for every responding group to interact with each of the affected groups, this *Safety Net*[175] model provides an efficient way to identify points of interaction for evaluation and future planning. The model is also quickly and easily tailored for individual campus structures and unique crises.

CONCLUSION

When violent events occur, our community struggles with shock, grief, fatigue, and uncertainty amidst a whole host of other emotional and physical needs. While responding to such events is daunting, developing effective strategies for communal management,

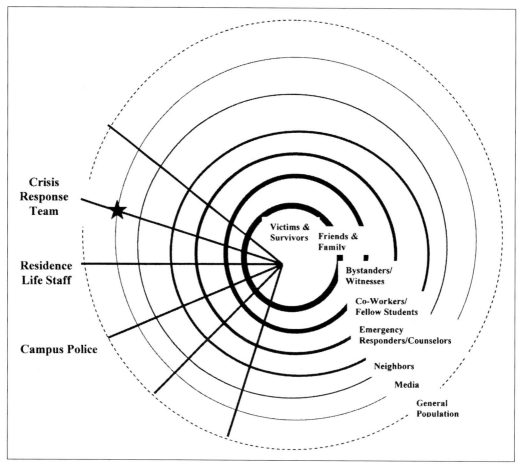

Figure 10.3. Safety Net Model. This model is adapted from a model in *Violence Goes to School* with the consultation of Rebecca Flintoft, Director of Residence Life at the Colorado School of Mines. Nicoletti, J., Zinna, K., and Spencer-Thomas, S. (1999). *Violence Goes to School: Lessons Learned from Columbine.* Denver, Colorado: Nicoletti-Flater Associates. See the appendix for a flow chart of violence aftermath responses.

counseling support, media management, and evaluation and future planning enhance our ability do so. Planning, practicing or simulating, and building necessary partnerships in each of these areas prior to a violent event is helpful. While simulations are never the same as real incidents, the relational bonds formed and the discoveries of potential improvement areas are well worth the effort. Every violent event is different and there is no magic formula. If there were one though, it would probably include knowledge of good practices, preparation, practice, relational support, and the will to experience, grieve, and heal from the tragedy together as a community.

Part III

STRAINS OF CAMPUS VIOLENCE

Chapter 11

SEXUAL ASSAULT

REBECCA FLINTOFT

Courtney, a new professional working as a residence hall director at a large public univer-sity, was attending an evening program in the building, when a resident, Melissa, ap-proached her and asked if they could speak privately. Melissa followed Courtney to her apartment, with her roommate Felicia in tow. It was early November, and Melissa and Fe-licia were first-year students who lived on the third floor. What they told Courtney, although terrible, was not a shock. She had learned in staff training sessions that sexual assault was common among college women, especially during the first semester of their college career. Melissa said, "Go on, Felicia. Tell her what happened to you. She can help, okay?" Felicia, with tears in her eyes, spoke in a quiet voice and said, "Something happened to me . . . on Halloween . . . at a party. It was off-campus . . . I'm so embarrassed, and it's probably my fault anyway . . . I had been drinking, and I know I'll probably get in trouble because I'm under 21, so I wasn't going to say anything at all . . . but something happened, and I don't know what to do." Melissa jumped in, "I told her it was important to come forward and get help, and that she could do something to make sure it wouldn't happen to someone else." Fe-licia continued, "I met this guy who is a friend of a friend. We hooked up once before, but it wasn't anything serious. This time was different. He was there at the party, and we were drinking, and one thing led to another . . . I didn't want to have sex with him. I told him I wasn't ready, that I didn't know him well enough yet. But he wanted to, and I was too drunk to stop him. I was crying, but I guess he didn't notice or didn't care. . . . Anyways, I didn't know what to do. But I don't want to talk to the police. And if my parents found out, they'd disown me. They think this kind of thing doesn't happen to good Latina girls . . . You know, Melissa said it was rape, but I'm not sure I'd call it that . . . Do you think I was raped?"

RAPE AS A SOCIAL EPIDEMIC

Sexual assault has been called a "silent epidemic" because of its high rate of preva-lence but low rate of reporting to authori-ties.[176] A recent national study indicated that there has been no significant decrease in the prevalence of rape in the last 15 years, despite efforts to reduce it. Further-more, the same report suggests that only 16 percent of all rapes in the U.S. were re-ported to law enforcement, and even fewer college rapes (12 percent) were reported to law enforcement.[177] The report indicates that 18 to 25 percent of women in the United States will be raped in their lifetimes. These staggering numbers support the notion that rape and sexual assault are ex-tremely common in our society, and also suggest an inherent conflict with reporting such violence to authorities. This discrepancy between prevalence and reporting will be addressed later in the chapter. Minimally, however, these numbers demonstrate the "epidemic" nature of sexual assault against women. Another aspect of sexual assault that has been less researched, less documented, and therefore less talked about in the general population, is the sexual assault of men. Lifetime rates of rape for men range from 3 to 16 percent.[178]

As with many other types of violent crimes, alcohol and other drug use is closely tied to most sexual assaults. Approximately one-half of all sexual assaults have been shown to involve alcohol use by the perpetrator and/or victim.[179] In order to understand sexual assault from a broad perspective, and especially as it impacts college students, it is crucial to explore this alcohol-related aspect of sexual assault. Likewise, in order to gain a full picture of the problem of sexual assault in society at large, as well as on college campuses, one must explore the connection of sexual assault to underlying social forces, such as sexism, heterosexism, and homophobia. Just as racism directly contributes to violence against people of color and homophobia to violence against gay and lesbian people, the sexism in society directly contributes to the prevalence of violence against women.

Lastly, in order to recognize sexual assault as an "epidemic," there must be evidence that sexual assault is, indeed, harmful to victims and to society. Unfortunately, some societal attitudes support the notion that sexual assault is a minor problem, or even suggests that victims of sexual assault deserved or were responsible for their own assaults. Such minimization of the impact of sexual assault, as well as victim-blaming attitudes, contribute to the social stigma of sexual assault, which in turn reduces the reporting of sexual assault, and thereby creates the perception that sexual assault is a minor societal problem.

This is the self-perpetuating cycle of the "silent epidemic" of sexual assault.

CHAPTER OVERVIEW

What would you do if you were Courtney, the residence hall director in the previous scenario? Would you be prepared to respond? Would you have the background to know that Felicia's incident is, unfortunately, common? Would your campus have the appropriate policies and procedures in place? Would a student like Felicia, or her roommate Melissa, have been educated on sexual assault enough even to know they could seek help on campus? Although the scenario is fictional, it is not unlike many college sexual assaults. The purpose of this chapter is to prepare you to answer these very questions.

We will, first, gain an overview of the broad topic of sexual assault by exploring current data on the prevalence of sexual assault, especially on college campuses. Second, we will examine the social complexities of sexual assault, including recognition of the sociocultural context of sexual assault, understanding of the problems and complexity for sexual assault reporting and disclosure, and recognition of the differential impacts of sexual assault on various social identity groups. Third, federal legislation and campus policies on sexual assault will be addressed. Fourth, this chapter will address the experience of victims of sexual assault, in the many commonalities they share, as well as the differences among individual experiences. Finally, since the purpose of this book is to examine violence on college campuses and prepare campus practitioners to both prevent and respond to violence, the chapter will give an overview of campus prevention efforts and will specifically address the role of campus practitioners and policymakers in preventing and responding to sexual assault on their campuses.

TALKING ABOUT RAPE AND SEXUAL ASSAULT

"Melissa said it was rape, but I'm not sure I'd call it that…"

The discussion of sexual assault is complicated by a variety of words used to describe these acts of violence and the people directly impacted by them. Words such as "rape," "sexual assault," "sexual violence," and "sexual abuse" are often misunderstood, confused, used incorrectly, or perhaps not used at all because of their insufficiency in describing particular acts of violence. Likewise, the words "victim" and "survivor" are often used interchangeably, and yet have dramatically different connotations to different people. Indeed, all of these words are emotionally charged and may be value-laden, depending on to whom you are talking. Certainly, words are powerful symbols in the important and sensitive discussion about sexual assault, and the way in which words are used is a valid and important concern. But how can we use language to broaden the discussion and increase understanding of sexual assault-related issues if we become inhibited in our willingness to have an honest conversation, concerned instead about the risk of offending, misunderstanding, or miscommunicating with others? We will explore the issue of definitions and language, and then attempt to move beyond word choice and, instead, use language to address the substance of the discussion on sexual assault for college and university practitioners.

A 2007 study titled *Drug-facilitated, Incapacitated, and Forcible Rape: A National Study* sampled 5000 women in the United States, ages 18 to 36, including 2000 college women, in order to assess the prevalence and consequences of rape in the United States. For the purpose of the study, the researchers defined three types of rape, for their research, as follows:

- "Drug and alcohol facilitated rape," defined as when "the perpetrator deliberately gives the victim drugs without her permission or tries to get her drunk, and then commits an unwanted sexual act against her involving oral, anal, or vaginal penetration. The victim is passed out or awake but too drunk or high to know what she is doing or to control her behavior,"
- "Incapacitated rape," defined as "unwanted sexual act involving oral, anal, or vaginal penetration that occurs after the victim voluntarily uses drugs or alcohol. The victim is passed out or awake but too drunk or high to know what she is doing or to control her behavior," and
- "Forcible rape," defined as "unwanted sexual act involving oral, anal, or vaginal penetration. The victim also experiences force, threat of force, or sustains an injury during the assault."

Obviously, these researchers chose to define these violent acts very specifically for the purpose of their study.

Such specific definitions of rape, as in this study, are useful for research purposes intended to quantify the prevalence of specific types of rape. However, most people who have either been the victim of a sexual assault or rape, and those who work frequently with victims, may find such definitions inadequate, limiting, counterproductive, or counterintuitive to their personal experiences or professional goals. We will explore some specific examples of different uses of language and definitions.

"Sexual Assault" vs. "Rape"

The term "rape" is a legal term, also commonly used by the general population, to describe a specific crime, defined differently by different states or agencies. In some cases, the term "first-degree sexual assault" may be considered synonymous with "rape." As noted in the previous definitions, "rape" usually refers to a specific act or acts. Various types of rape are commonly identified, including those mentioned earlier, as well as other subcategories, including stranger rape, acquaintance rape, date rape, familial rape, marital rape, and gang rape. The Rape Abuse & Incest National Network (RAINN) defines rape as "forced sexual intercourse, including vaginal, anal or oral penetration. Penetration may be by a body part or an object."[180]

Alternatively, the term "sexual assault" is commonly used among college and university practitioners, as well as in the fields of education, counseling, and victim advocacy and also in law enforcement, depending on different agencies' legal terms and definitions. Typically "sexual assault" is used as a more general, inclusive term to describe any unwanted sexual contact. Like "rape," however, it is also differently defined and used by various organizations or individuals. For example, RAINN defines sexual assault as "unwanted sexual contact that stops short of rape or attempted rape. This includes sexual touching and fondling." Many definitions of sexual assault are more general, such as the definition used by Waldorf College in Iowa, which defines it as follows: "Sexual assault involves any act of forced, coerced, or nonconsensual sexual intercourse or sexual contact. An individual is unable to give informed consent if they are asleep, intoxicated, unconscious, or in some other way physically or emotionally unable. Sexual assault is also the term used to define any unwanted touching of an intimate part of another person."[181] In general, most definitions of sexual assault are broader and usually encompass, but are not limited to, acts that meet the definition of rape.

Such a definition has its pros and cons. The term "sexual assault" was created during the feminist movement in order to draw attention

to the agency of the perpetrator and to extend the meanings of more specific terms relating to sexual violence by establishing a collective noun.[182] Indeed, the term sexual assault is preferable to many people for these reasons. The use of "sexual assault" to encompass more generally a variety of types of sexual violence may make it easier for some people to talk about the problem. On the other hand, it may minimize the severity of the encounter.[183]

"Victim" vs. "Survivor"

Two words that are often used interchangeably, but also have specific distinctions and are preferred by different people, are the words "victim" and "survivor," both of which are used to name the person who is the subject of sexual assault. The term victim "captures the sense of injury and injustice" felt by the subjects of sexual violence, whereas the term survivor is associated more with strength, recovery, and overcoming the trauma of rape, and emphasizes what happened after the incident not the incident itself.[184]

All of these terms can have a place in the discussion of this deeply complex issue, but it is also important to understand that for some victims, there are no specific words that adequately describe their experiences or how they define themselves. In research about how women who had experienced sexual violence labeled themselves and their experiences, most participants avoided static labels completely.[185]

Another important consideration is that victims of sexual assault may not describe their experiences as being a crime because they may not understand the legal definitions of rape or sexual assault, or because they do not feel their experiences otherwise deserve to be called sexual assault or rape. In a national study of college and general population U.S. women, 50 percent of the general population sample who had an experience which met the legal definition of drug- or alcohol-facilitated rape (DAFR) or incapacitated rape (IR) considered their experience to be "an unpleasant incident but not a crime" or "a crime but not rape."[186] Of the general population sample that had experienced forcible rape (FR), 25 percent defined the incident as "unpleasant but not a crime" or "a crime but not rape." College student rape victims were even less likely to describe their experiences as rape as compared to general population victims. Of those college women whose experiences met the legal definition of DAFR or IR, an overwhelming 71 percent of them described the experience as an "unpleasant incident but not a crime" or "a crime but not rape." For college students who were the victims of forcible rape, 47 percent defined it as "an unpleasant incident but not a crime" or "a crime but not rape." This data provides one rationale for why sexual assault is underreported – partly because victims may not identify their experiences as sexual assault – and it also provides impetus to raise awareness in the population in general, and especially on college campuses, of what constitutes sexual assault and rape so that victims may understand that they have legal recourse to report their experiences as crimes. This data also supports the previous assertion that static labels are insufficient to describe the experiences of sexual assault victims.

The language of sexual assault is understandably complex and important. Language is certainly powerful. For the purpose of the rest of this chapter, we will use the word "sexual assault" as an inclusive term to describe all unwanted sexual contact, including rape. Additionally, both "victim" and "survivor" will be used to describe the people who are subjected to sexual assault. Regardless of the word choice, it is most important to open the discussion and work to prevent and respond to sexual assault and other types of violence on college campuses.

PREVALENCE OF SEXUAL ASSAULT IN THE U. S.

The prevalence of sexual assault in the United States is high. Such data can be found through a variety of sources, including police reports, national random samples of crime victims, interviews with incarcerated rapists, interviews with victims who seek hospital treatment, general population surveys, and surveys of male and female college students. All of these are useful data sources, but none is completely comprehensive, and all are limited due to the significant underreporting of sexual assault. A 2007 national study surveyed 5000 U.S. women ages 18–36, including 2000 who were college students. The result of the study indicated that 18 percent of U.S. women will be raped in their lifetime. Furthermore, 11.5 percent of women currently attending U.S. colleges and universities have been raped in their lifetime, and more than 5 percent of college women were raped in the previous year. Another key finding of the study is the conclusion that, contrary to previous findings from other sources, there has been no significant decrease in the prevalence of forcible rape over the last 15 years.[187]

Another recent study of college sexual assault showed that 19 percent of undergraduate women had been the victim of at least one attempted or completed sexual assault since entering college.[188] More than half of rape victims experienced their first attempted or completed assault before the age of eighteen.[189] These findings support not only the emphasis on sexual assault prevention, but also necessitate the availability of skilled sexual assault counselors and therapists and other support programs for sexual assault survivors on college campuses. Campus practitioners need to be able not only to respond to and prevent sexual assault on current students, but they also need to be prepared to support those students who enter college already having been the victim of sexual assault.

The same study examined the prevalence of forcible rape, as well as that of drug/alcohol-facilitated rape and drug/alcohol-incapacitated rape. Among college women rape victims, the incidence of drug/alcohol-facilitated rape was 18 percent, and that of incapacitated rape for college women was 28 percent. That is, in nearly one-half of all rapes of college women, drug or alcohol incapacitation or facilitation was present, a finding that is consistent with previous studies of college sexual assault. In drug/alcohol-incapacitated and facilitated rapes, alcohol is by far the most frequently used substance. College women are at a greater risk of drug/alcohol-incapacitated sexual assault during college than before college (11 percent vs. 5 percent), a finding that indicates that the college environment creates additional kinds of sexual assault risk due to the common use of alcohol and other drugs.[190] Only one in five incapacitated sexual assaults against college women was the result of the victim being involuntarily drugged or given alcohol. Instead, the greater risk was the victim voluntarily using drugs or alcohol, and alcohol was by far more common than other drugs.[191]

A significant limitation of the research on the prevalence of sexual assault is the lack of data available on the prevalence of sexual assault on male victims, as well as on underrepresented women and men, including racial minorities, GLBT people, and people with disabilities. It has been estimated that 3 to 16 percent of men will become the victim of sexual assault in their lifetime, but also that only one in ten male rapes is likely to be reported to police.[192] Some racial groups have been shown to be at higher risk of sexual assault throughout their lifetime, including Native Americans, blacks, and whites, but contradictory studies have challenged these findings, and the overall scarcity of research on minority rape victims has left a significant gap in knowledge about how victims' race and ethnicity affect the risk of sexual assault.

WHO RAPES AND WHO IS RAPED?

"I met this guy who is a friend of a friend. We hooked up once before, but it wasn't anything serious. This time was different."

A common misconception about rape is that most rapes are perpetrated by someone who is a stranger to the victim. In fact, at least 80 percent of sexual assaults occur among people who know each other.[193] Different types of perpetrators have been shown to be more likely to commit forcible rape versus drug/alcohol-facilitated or incapacitated rape.[194] In a sample of general population U.S. women, 11 percent of forcible rapes and 19 percent of drug/alcohol-facilitated or incapacitated rapes were committed by strangers. In a sample of U.S college women, even fewer rapes were committed by strangers – just 6 percent of forcible rapes and 17 percent of drug/alcohol-facilitated or incapacitated rapes. Another study of college women showed conflicting results, in which college women reported that 23 percent of incapacitated sexual assaults and 12 percent of physically forced sexual assaults were perpetrated by someone they had never seen or talked to.[195] In either case, the standard of approximately 80 percent of sexual assaults occurring among people who know each other holds true. Among college women, over 50 percent of forcible rapes and about 70 percent of drug/alcohol-facilitated or incapacitated rapes were committed by classmates, friends, or boyfriends of the victims. Approximately 20 percent of college women who had been forcibly raped were victimized by a relative.[196]

There has been a fair amount of research on the prevalence of sexual assault perpetration among male college students. One study found that one in 12 college men had committed acts that met the legal definition of rape, but of those, 84 percent did not consider their actions illegal.[197] Risk factors for male sexual aggression on college campuses include negative gender-based attitudes, heavy alcohol use, pornography consumption, approval and use of sexually coercive behaviors, and peer pressure to have sex.[198] The sexual coercion employed is mostly verbal in nature, consisting of threatening, lying, and pressuring. Both physical force and verbal threats have been frequently reported by college women rape victims.[199]

IS THERE A TYPICAL SEXUAL ASSAULT?

We have started to answer the questions: Who is a typical rape/sexual assault victim? And who is a typical perpetrator? But another question persists: What is a typical sexual assault, in particular on college campuses? Like the previous two questions, it is difficult to answer because it requires balancing broad generalizations with individual experiences that may differ greatly. Current research suggests that most sexual assaults on college students occur off campus.[200] Previous research indicated that a typical college sexual assault occurs on a date, at either the man's or woman's home, and is preceded by consensual kissing.[201] We have already observed that alcohol is used in approximately 50 percent of campus sexual assaults. Perpetrators used a weapon in only 2 percent of sexual victimizations, data which corrects the common myth that most rapes are committed by a perpetrator who uses a weapon.[202] Another common misconception is that victims of rape or sexual assault are physically beaten or otherwise injured during their assaults. This is true for a minority of victims.

College campuses are dynamic cultures, and like American culture at large, they change with the times. Some relatively new characteristics of college campuses that may impact sexual assault in the college environment are the ubiquity of cell phones, camera phones, and text messaging; the popularity of online social networking websites such as Myspace and Facebook; and the increasingly common social practice among college students of "hooking up." Hooking up is commonly understood to be engaging in casual intimate acts that might include everything from kissing to a variety of sex acts, usually without a commitment to any relationship, and may be a one-time incident or a longer-term arrangement. In her book *Unhooked*, author Laura Stepp Sessions further explains, "Partners may know each other well, only slightly or not at all, even after they have hooked up regularly. A hookup often happens in a bedroom, although other places will do: dance floors, bars, bathrooms, auditoriums or any deserted room on campus." This is to say that a date may no longer be likely to be the typical venue for a college sexual assault. Recent research showed that college sexual assaults frequently occurred at parties – 58 percent of incapacitated sexual assaults and 28 percent of forcible sexual assaults.[203] Even among acquaintances – the primary relationship between college sexual assault victims and perpetrators – a traditional date is probably less likely to be the setting of a sexual assault. The term "date rape" may relate less to traditional age college students than it does to older individuals for whom dating was a common part of their adolescent and young adult experience, and perhaps the use of different language, such as "acquaintance rape" or another alternative, may be more helpful.

More research on the impact of these culturally significant changes is needed in order to understand their impact on sexual assault. Later in this chapter, the topic of sexual assault victims' experiences will be explored, and through that discussion it will be apparent that, although there are common characteristics of victims' experiences, there is no "typical" victim experience. Similarly, although there are common characteristics of sexual assaults, there is no "typical" sexual assault, although it is also an area which can continue to be researched.

UNDERSTANDING RAPE CULTURE

"It's probably my fault anyway."

Feminists and other sexual assault activists have given rise to the term "rape culture," and a discussion of the term and its meaning is necessary to understand fully sexual assault in the general population, as well as among college students. Rape culture describes a culture in which rape and other sexual violence is common, and the prevalent attitudes, norms, and practices of culture normalize, condone, excuse, encourage, or ignore rape and other forms of sexual violence. Rape culture can be conceptualized as an outgrowth of sexism, as well as homophobia and heterosexism, because it is perpetuated by sexist, homophobic, and heterosexist attitudes and practices. Some typical characteristics of rape culture are victim blaming, prevalence of rape myths, and the sexual objectification of women. Although there are some who criticize the concept of rape culture, and even challenge its existence, there are others who consider it critical to understanding sexual assault from a broad, societal perspective, in order to challenge and reduce sexual violence from all angles.

Another related way to conceptualize rape and sexual assault is as a subcategory of gender-based violence. This is directly related to the concept of rape culture, because both are based in the understanding of violence as a social phenomenon, not just an individual problem. According to Iris Marion Jones, "Many groups suffer the oppression of systematic violence. Members of some groups live with the knowledge that they must fear random, unprovoked attacks on their persons or property, which have no motive but to damage, humiliate, or destroy the person."[204] One definition of gender-based violence is "any attack directed against a (usually female) person due, at least in part, to a disadvantaged position within male-dominated social

systems."[205] From this perspective, a critical contributing factor to the prevalence of sexual assault is the widespread social support for violence against women, or against other people who do not meet typical norms of masculine identity, such as gay or bisexual men, transgender people, or heterosexual men who do not meet social standards of masculinity for one reason or another. Such support for violence against women and other underrepresented people is manifested in overt and covert ways. For example, an overt social manifestation of the support of sexual violence against women is violent pornography that depicts the sexual abuse of women. An example of a covert social manifestation of the support of sexual assault might be an unspoken belief that women are the sexual property of men.

Rape myths are beliefs that exist in society which typically support rape culture. They are commonly believed by a variety of people, across gender, race, sexual orientation, and class lines. The following are some common rape myths, most of which refer to the dominant paradigm of rape victims being female and perpetrators male:[206]

1. Rape is just rough sex.
2. Women "cry" rape to gain revenge.
3. Rape is motivated by lust.
4. Rapists are weird, psychotic loners.
5. Rape victims asked for it, so no harm was done.
6. Only bad women are raped.
7. Rapes are committed by strangers, who usually use a weapon and/or beat their victims.
8. If the woman doesn't resist, she must have wanted it.

These rape myths are associated with sociocultural messages regarding the strict assignment of gender roles to men and women. For example, a female gender role expectation of a "good" woman is not to wear provocative clothing. A male gender role expectation for a "normal" man is to have an uncontrollable desire for sex. These two ideals work in concert to create the rape myths that only "bad" women are raped, that rape victims deserved or asked to be raped, and that the rape was motivated by uncontrollable desire for sex. Society's adherence to such myths both punishes the victim and rewards the perpetrator, thereby further encouraging perpetrators to rape while discouraging victims from reporting their rape. There are also rape myths that pertain specifically to the rape of male victims, which we will explore later in the chapter.

In order to deconstruct rape culture and debunk rape myths for good, there must be a broader societal understanding of the dynamics of gender and sexism, as well as sexual orientation and heterosexism. Certainly, such a goal may seem lofty or even impossible, but just as attitudes are learned, they can also be unlearned. And what better setting is there for learning (or unlearning) than college campuses? We will explore educational efforts to promote awareness and prevention of sexual assault in a later part of this chapter.

FEDERAL LAW ON SEXUAL ASSAULT

A brief overview of federal laws related to sexual assault, in particular on college campuses, is in order. As discussed previously, state laws vary in how they define and respond to rape and sexual assault. Federal laws more often define requirements of law enforcement agencies, courts, and other institutions such as college and universities, and provide funding for particular efforts.

1972 Title IX of the Education Amendments of 1972

Despite more than 35 years that have elapsed since the passage of Title IX by Congress in 1972, the law has important applica-

tions regarding sexual assault and gender equality on college campuses today. Title IX is a comprehensive federal law that prohibits discrimination on the basis of sex in any federally funded education program or activity, and provides individual citizens protection against such practices as employment discrimination and sexual harassment. The law has been interpreted by some to include sexual assault as an extreme form of sexual harassment.[207]

In a 2007 court case settlement, the University of Colorado at Boulder settled out of court with former student Lisa Simpson for $2.5 million, the result of a lawsuit against the university that was filed in 2002 after she claimed she was gang raped at a 2001 party attended by football players and recruits.[208] The rationale for the university's responsibility in this case was that there had been ongoing reports of sexual harassment, abuse, and rape of women by football team players and recruits and that the university had been negligent in responding to such allegations, thereby creating a hostile environment for women, which ultimately resulted in Simpson's rape. Because the case was settled out of court, there was no final court ruling, but the settlement will likely be an important precedent for future interpretations of Title IX.

1990 Student Right-to-Know and Campus Security Act (CSA)

Known both as "CSA" and as the "Clery Act," this law was renamed in 1998 as the "Jeanne Clery Disclosure of Campus Security Policy and Campus Crime Statistics Act," in honor of a student who was sexually assaulted and murdered on her campus in 1986. The law mandates disclosure of campus crimes. It requires that colleges and universities track and annually disclose information about crime, including specific sexual crime categories, in and around campus.

1991 Campus Sexual Assault Victims' Bill of Rights

This amendment to the 1990 act requires the development of prevention policies and assurances of certain rights to victims by colleges and universities. The law was amended again in 1998 to expand reporting requirements. Specific provisions of these laws that most directly affect sexual assault prevention and response include the following:[209]

- A requirement that colleges collect, publish, and distribute in an annual campus security report (ASR) to students and anyone else who is interested a comprehensive set of campus crime statistics for the previous three years, including reported forcible and nonforcible sex offenses
- A requirement that every college must state in its ASR its policy on sexual assault and its disciplinary hearing procedures for sex offenses
- A requirement that colleges must include in the ASR a description of educational programs provided by the college to promote awareness of rape and other sex offenses
- An affirmative statement of student rights, including the following:
  - The right of both the complainant and the accused in a campus sexual assault hearing to have the same opportunity to have others present in support or advisory capacities
  - The right of the complainant to know the outcome of a campus hearing in which sexual assault is alleged (an amendment to the *Family Education Rights and Privacy Act* [FERPA] of 1974)
  - The right of students to be informed of their options to notify proper law enforcement authorities, including on-campus and local police, and the option to be assisted by campus authorities in notifying such law enforcement authorities, if the victim so chooses
  - The right of students to be notified of available counseling, mental health, or student services for victims of sexual assault, both on campus and in the community
  - The right to notification of and options for, and available assistance in, changing academic and living situations after an alleged assault incident, if so requested by the victim and if such changes are reasonably available
- A requirement that colleges make timely notification to the campus community of situations that pose a potential threat to student safety, when reports of such events or situations are received by any campus security authority
- A requirement that the ASR contain procedures that students should follow if a sex offense occurs, including whom should be contacted, the importance of preserving physical evidence as may be necessary to prove criminal sexual assault, and to whom the alleged offense should be reported.

In 1999, Congress asked the National Institute of Justice to study campuses' compliance with federal laws. In 2002, the results were published. The researchers found that institutions were complying with federal law unevenly. Overall, four-year and historically black institutions were in better compliance than other institutions. The report also found that only 37 percent of institutions fully comply with the Clery Act, indicating a great deal of confusion on college campuses and the need for better guidance in complying with the law. The study also discovered several campuses with best practices in the area of sexual assault response and prevention, which will be explored later in this chapter.

1994 Violence Against Women Act (VAWA)

In 1994, Congress enacted the Violence Against Women Act (VAWA), and a federal Violence Against Women Office was established. The act addressed violence against women on many different levels, including the following which are most relevant to college sexual assault work:[210]

- Education and training on sexual assault, domestic violence, and stalking for court personnel and judges
- Creation of a national research agenda on violence against women
- Appropriation of funds for and requiring the completion of a national baseline study on campus sexual assault

2000 Violence Against Women Act Reauthorization (VAWA 2000)

In 2000, Congress reauthorized the Violence Against Women Act, as part of the Victims of Trafficking and Violence Prevention Act of 2000. Some highlights of VAWA 2000:

- Inclusion of dating violence in several VAWA grant programs
- Increase of support for sexual violence programs and coalitions
- Provision of civil legal assistance grant money to sexual assault victims
- Reauthorization of grants for education and training for state and federal court judges and personnel on domestic violence, sexual assault, and stalking
- Extension of the federal stalking statute to include stalking via the Internet

2005 Violence Against Women Act Reauthorization (VAWA 2005)

In 2005, Congress enacted the Violence Against Women and Department of Justice Reauthorization Act of 2005, which funded and reauthorized the act from 2006 until 2010. Some highlights of VAWA 2005:

- Reauthorization of prosecutor and police training, to focus on collaboration with victim service providers, and to increase appropriate services for racial and ethnic minorities and ensure victim confidentiality
- Creation of a new program to educate court personnel in the areas of domestic violence, dating violence, sexual abuse, and stalking
- Protection of victim information collected by federal agencies
- Funding for U.S. Attorney offices to hire counselors to assist victims and witnesses in prosecution of domestic violence and sexual assault cases
- Creation of a separate, direct funding stream dedicated to sexual assault services
- Reauthorization and expansion of education, training, and services grant programs that address violence against women with disabilities
- Reauthorization of Grants to Reduce Violence Against Women on Campus, amending the existing campus program to a three-year grant cycle, providing more money and setting parameters for training of campus law enforcement and campus judicial boards
- Funding to train health care providers on recognizing and appropriately responding to domestic and sexual violence
- Provision to conduct a national baseline study on violence against American Indian women and the effectiveness of federal, state, local, and tribal responses.

SOCIAL IDENTITIES OF VICTIMS

"They think this kind of thing doesn't happen to good Latina girls."

Because sexual assault is so underreported, it is difficult to gain a completely accurate picture of its extent, its victims, and its perpetrators. The majority of the victims of sexual assault are women, but men are also victimized by sexual assault. Likewise, the vast majority of perpetrators are men, but women may also be perpetrators. Lastly, men and women from all races, sexual orientations, socioeconomic classes, and other social groups are potential victims of sexual assault, but each of these factors may have a differential impact on sexual assault prevalence. The purpose of this section is to explore the limited research on how certain underrepresented groups are impacted by sexual assault, both as victims and as perpetrators.

College women have been the frequent subjects of research studies on sexual assault, both because of interest in understanding the elevated risk of sexual assault among college students, and because of relatively easy access to college students for research studies. The predominant research available regarding sexual assault among college students is on women as victims. Several risk factors are predictive of sexual assault victimization among college women. They include prior sexual victimization, alcohol use, age, and year of study (women under 21 and first-year and sophomore women are at higher risk), on-campus residence in residence halls or sorority houses, sorority membership, dating violence history, and consensual sexual experience. Frequency of alcohol and marijuana use since entering college is a predictor of incapacitated sexual assault in college, although the voluntary use of other illicit drugs is not. Frequency of attendance at fraternity parties has been positively associated with higher risk of incapacitated sexual assault. The prevalence of sexual assault in the previous 12 months was highest among sophomores, indicating that the highest risk time for college women is early in their college career.[211]

Because people of color are often underrepresented on college campuses, there is limited research on the differential impact by race of sexual assault on college campuses. In one study of college women, black women reported the highest incidence of forced intercourse through verbal threats or pressure, and Asian women reported the lowest. Hispanic women reported the highest incidence of attempted rape, and black women reported the lowest. Black and white women were almost three times as likely as Hispanic women to have experienced incidents which met the legal definition of rape, although as is common with most rape victims, they did not describe their experience as rape.[212] Yet other studies have shown that the prevalence of rape in college is basically the same for women across racial groups. A recent study of more than 5000 college women showed no racial or ethnic differences in the prevalence of forcible sexual assault since entering college.[213] That same study did show, however, that nonwhite women had a higher likelihood of reporting both forcible *and* incapacitated sexual assaults since starting college, but there was no racial difference in prevalence when only one type or the other was reported. Several studies have shown a disproportionately high rate of sexual assault against Native American women.[214]

The predominant research on sexual assault victims has been on women, as they are most often the victims of sexual assault. In fact, research on male rape and sexual assault did not appear in the literature until less than 30 years ago, and then typically focused on children and not adult men.[215] Male sexual assault is believed to be extremely underreported, even more so than female sexual assault. In a 2007 survey, approximately 6 percent of college men surveyed reported experiencing an attempted or completed sexual assault, of which about half (3.7 percent of the total sample) had experienced a completed sexual assault since entering college.[216] Earlier research suggested that 16 percent of male undergraduates had been pressured or forced to have sex during their lifetime.[217] Another study indicated that 22 percent of male undergraduates were the victim of some sort of sexual assault, including 8 percent who were the victim of a "serious sexual assault." Obviously, the research on this topic is not consistent, with male sexual assault prevalence rates ranging from approximately one in five to one in 20. Because only one in ten male sexual assaults is reported to police, it is nearly impossible to know the real rate of male sexual assault. Reactions to male sexual assault victims by their community and by service providers are often dependent on the victim's sexual orientation and the gender of the perpetrator.[218] Negative reactions further stigmatize male victims and suppress reporting.

Like rape myths in general, male rape myths, which apply specifically to assaults in which men are the victims, contribute significantly to social stigma around sexual assault of men, and thereby contribute to a lack of reporting of sexual assault by male victims. Some male rape myths follow:[219]

- Men are too big or strong to be overpowered and forced into sex.
- Men initiate and control sexual activity and are not targets of sexual assault.
- Men who are raped lose their manhood or are gay.
- Male sexual assault is rare.
- Male victims should be able to tough it out and cope.
- Male rape cannot happen outside prison.
- Women do not rape.

Although men of all sexual orientations may be potential sexual assault victims, the rate of sexual victimization of gay or bisexual men dating or in a relationship with other men has been estimated at 12 to 28 percent.[220] Victim-blaming attitudes toward male rape victims have been shown to be more prevalent when the victim is gay rather than heterosexual. Adherence to male rape myths, such as those outlined previously, correlate to traditional male gender roles, including

negative attitudes towards gay men.[221] This connection among the belief in male rape myths, adherence to gender roles, and homophobic attitudes demonstrates the relatedness of sexism, heterosexism, and homophobia. Deconstructing these forms of social prejudice and oppression is one prevention technique that will be explored.

REPORTING SEXUAL ASSAULT

"I told her it was important to come forward and get help, and that she could do something to make sure it wouldn't happen to someone else."

The reporting or disclosure of sexual assault by victims is crucial to understanding the prevalence of sexual assault and is a key factor in efforts to enforce the law, hold perpetrators accountable, and support victims who often require significant treatment and support in their recovery from the trauma of sexual assault. For the purpose of this chapter, the word *reporting* refers specifically to informing police of a sexual assault or rape; the word *disclosing* will refer to informing anyone other than police, including friends, family, rape crisis counselors, medical professionals, or college staff members, of a sexual assault or rape.

Less than 5 percent of completed and/or attempted rapes were reported to law enforcement officials in a national study of college women.[222] In another study, 12 percent of college women rape victims reported their assaults to law enforcement, including 7 percent of drug/alcohol-facilitated or incapacitated rapes and 16 percent of forcible rapes. Overall, college student rape victims are less likely than their general population counterparts to report their assaults to police. Although disclosing an assault to a mental health professional is more likely than reporting to police, the rate of disclosure to mental health professionals is still relatively low at 16 percent. Over time, two-thirds of sexual assault victims eventually disclose their assaults,

most of the time (60 percent) to informal support sources like friends, family, or romantic
partners, instead of formal sources, such as
police, mental health professionals, medical
professionals, clergy, or rape crisis counselors.[223] Among college women, 70 percent
of forcible sexual assault victims and 64 percent of incapacitated sexual assault victims
disclosed their assault to a family member,
friend, roommate, or intimate partner.[224] This
data supports the need to train more potential responders beyond the typical formal resources for disclosing sexual assault.

Barriers to victims reporting to police include: (1) not having proof that the incident
occurred, (2) fear of retaliation by the perpetrator, (3) fear of hostile treatment by the authorities, (4) uncertainty that the authorities
would consider the incident serious enough,
(5) not knowing how to report the incident,
and (6) desire to prevent family and others
from learning about it.[225] Two common reasons that rapes and sexual assaults are not reported to police are that the victim was either
unsure if a crime was committed, or did not
think that the incident was serious enough.
This is consistent with the finding that most
women who experienced an incident that
met the legal definition of rape did not define
their own experience as rape.[226] At least one-
third of victims did not report their assaults
to police because they did not know how to
report or because they feared they would be
treated badly by police, lawyers, or other
parts of the criminal justice system. Other
reasons for not reporting to the police by college women included not wanting others to
know about the incident, lack of proof, and
fear of reprisal from the perpetrator. Some
negative predictors of reporting to police include alcohol use as part of the assault,
degree of intoxication, and lack of memory
of the incident.

The main reason for rape victims who did
report their assault to police was to prevent
crimes against others.[227] Positive predictors of
reporting to police among college women include use of physical force, verbal threat,
injury, perceived fear of death or injury
during the assault, and concern about their
family knowing about the assault.

There are some differences in reporting
and disclosure behavior of victims, based on
gender, age, sexual orientation, and race.
One study showed that nonwhite women
who had been sexually victimized were more
likely than white women to say they did not
report the incident to police because they
thought it would be viewed as their fault and
because they did not want the police involved, which suggests either real or perceived racial discrimination as a limiting
factor in reporting sexual assault by women
of color.[228] Likewise, white women have
been shown to be more likely to disclose a
sexual assault to mental health professionals
than nonwhite women.[229] In the same study,
older women were also shown to be more
likely to disclose a sexual assault to mental
health professionals than younger women,
and nonheterosexual women were more
likely to disclose to mental health professionals than heterosexual women. For male victims of sexual assault, there are a variety of
factors that contribute to the underreporting
of male sexual assault. Male rape myths, like
all rape myths, contribute to underreporting,
but due to the additional pressures of male
gender role expectations, there may be even
more perceived or real risk for male victims
to report.

Certain factors are believed to discourage
or encourage sexual assault victims on college
campus to report their assaults to authorities,
including police or campus administration.
First, the following policies and practices
may *reduce or discourage reporting:*[230]

- Campus policies on drugs and alcohol,
  which may inhibit reporting if the victim
  fears being charged with using drugs or
  alcohol

- Requiring victims to participate in adjudication of sexual misconduct/assault charges against another student
- Unintentional victim-blaming by institution's overemphasis of victim's responsibility to avoid sexual assault without balanced emphasis on the perpetrator's responsibility
- Trauma response, which may include psychological distress, shame, and self-blame
- Victim's avoidance of real or perceived stigma of victimization

Because of the multiple factors which discourage reporting of sexual assault by college students and sexual assault victims in society at large, campuses must implement a combination of positive approaches that *encourage reporting*, including the following practices and policies:[231]

- Support services for sexual assault victims
- Written law enforcement response protocols on sexual assault
- Coordination between campus and community resources regarding sexual assault response and prevention
- New student orientation sessions on sexual assault
- Campus-wide publicity about past campus crimes
- Prevention programs targeting high-risk groups (Greek students, athletes) to both prevent and encourage reporting of sexual assaults
- Both confidential and anonymous reporting processes for sexual assault and other crimes
- Sexual assault peer education programs

VICTIMS' EXPERIENCE OF SEXUAL ASSAULT AND ITS CONSEQUENCES

In addition to understanding factors that discourage and encourage reporting and disclosure of sexual assault, campus practitioners should also understand the common and very real traumatic outcomes for many sexual assault victims. Practitioners must understand these outcomes in order to formulate the best response protocols and procedures. Although there is a set of attributes that commonly affect sexual assault victims, there is no "typical" victim experience. Each individual experiences an assault and its consequences in his or her own personal way.

Of rape victims, 25 percent to 45 percent suffer from nongenital trauma; 19 percent to 22 percent suffer from genital trauma; up to 40 percent get sexually transmitted diseases (STDs); and 1 percent to 5 percent become pregnant, resulting in an estimated 32,000 rape-related pregnancies in the United States annually.[232] A national study on college sexual assault reported that college women victims experienced a physical injury in about 20 percent of the completed and/or attempted rape incidents, with the most common injury reported being "bruises, black-eye, cuts, scratches, swelling, or chipped teeth."[233] Another study of college women sexual assault victims reported that sustaining an injury was more common in forcible sexual assaults, in which 18 percent of victims sustained an injury, as opposed to incapacitated sexual assault, in which only 3 percent of victims reported sustaining an injury.[234]

The experience of sexual assault for most victims is not only a physical violation of one's body, but also a violation of a psychological nature, causing fear, distress, self-blame, loss of trust, and loss of self-esteem. Sexual assault significantly increases the risk of serious mental health problems. Rape victims are 13 times more likely to attempt suicide than noncrime victims and six times more likely than victims of other crimes.[235] College rape victims appear to be at a higher risk of mental health consequences than general population victims. The past-year prevalence of posttraumatic stress disorder (PTSD) among college rape victims was 34 percent, as compared to 9 percent of nonvictim college women and 23 percent of noncollege population rape victims. Past-year prevalence of depression among college rape victims was 33 percent, as compared to 11 percent of nonvictim college women and 23 percent of noncollege rape victims.[236] The higher risk of PTSD and depression for college sexual assault victims than for their noncollege rape victim counterparts demands significant mental health support availability for college student rape victims. Another common experience for victims is alcohol and drug abuse following their assault. Forty percent of college rape victims reported drug or alcohol abuse in the past year, as compared with 17 percent of nonvictim college women and 10 percent of noncollege victims. Furthermore, victims of alcohol/drug-facilitated or incapacitated rape were more than twice as likely to have abused drugs or alcohol in the past year as compared to victims of forcible rape.[237] Clearly, campus practitioners must be prepared to respond to the mental health needs of sexual assault victims, in particular with regard to substance abuse, PTSD, and depression.

Male victims of sexual assault experience many of the same consequences as female victims, but male victims have been found to be at even higher risk for some serious mental health consequences. Some research has also shown that male rape victims are more likely to endure physical injuries as a result of the assault, but this data may be skewed due to the severe underreporting of male sexual assault unless it is accompanied by serious physical injuries which would require medical treatment. Genital, rectal, and nongenital injuries are common among male sexual assault victims.[238] Other physical consequences for male rape victims, excluding injuries sustained during the assault include tension, headaches, nausea, ulcers, weight loss, and abdominal pain. None of these

symptoms are unique to men, and no particular combination of symptoms is indicative of sexual victimization. Other long-term consequences may include sleep difficulties, depression, substance abuse, suicide attempts, and violence. Again, because so few male victims of sexual assault seek medical services or report their assaults to police, the data available is limited and should not be generalized.

Regarding mental health consequences for male victims of sexual assault, there is no "typical" emotional or psychological response. There are studies that show male victims have higher rates of trauma, distress, and alcohol abuse than their female counterparts.[239,240] Other psychological consequences include shame, embarrassment, anxiety, depression, decreased self-esteem, self-harm, and rape-trauma syndrome, not unlike female victims. Male victims may also have higher levels than female victims of anger and hostility, as well as long-term sexual identity crises, sexual dysfunction, and problems with their sense of masculinity.[241] These consequences are likely related to societal gender role expectations of men, which also contribute to male rape myths and underreporting of male sexual assault.

CAMPUS POLICIES AND PROTOCOLS

American college and universities, often more proactive and progressive than local, state, and federal agencies, have led the way for effectively defining sexual assault and sexual misconduct.[242] Most college conduct codes use a consent-based definition of sexual assault or sexual misconduct. Using language of intoxication or impairment-based standards, not only physical incapacitation, is more inclusive of potential sexual assaults. Sexual assault may be achieved not only through force or physical incapacitation, but also through impairment which prevents a potential victim from giving informed consent. Additionally, some campuses have provisions for issuing campus-based restraining orders against students to prevent harassment or stalking, which may encourage reporting of sexual assault and provide better protection of victims and witnesses.

Not all colleges and universities, however, have the necessary policies in place to provide an effective response to sexual assaults. Some institutions may favor informal mediation that results in a slap on the wrist of perpetrators over a more formalized adjudication system. Indeed, some institutions refuse to adjudicate sexual misconduct on campus entirely, leaving a victim the only option of pursuing criminal charges, which may not best serve the victim or the campus community.

The National Institute of Justice compiled and published a list of best practices and recommendations for campus sexual misconduct policies and procedures based on eight institutions that it identified as having outstanding sexual assault policy and response practices. The following recommendations on reporting, victim support, investigation, and adjudication are borrowed directly from that publication.[243]

Sexual Assault Policy

The official sexual assault policy should be a reader-friendly, easily accessible, and widely distributed written statement of the school's definition of and expectations regarding sexual misconduct. This statement should include the following:

- Clear operational and behavioral definitions of what acts constitute sexual assault and consent
- Discussion of the prevalence of acquaintance sexual assault
- Description of circumstances in which sexual assault most commonly occurs

- Advice for what to do if a student or someone he/she knows is sexually assaulted
- A list of resources on campus and in the local community
- The name(s) of a specific person or office to contact when an assault occurs (preferably available 24/7) and when and where to file a complaint
- A statement strongly encouraging victims to report the crime to campus authorities and to the local criminal justice system
- A listing of reporting options, preferably including an anonymous report option
- An official statement prohibiting retaliation against individuals who bring forth reports of rape or sexual assault and the school's disciplinary actions for retaliation attempts
- A statement exploring that reporting, investigating the report, informal administrative actions (e.g., issuing a no-contact or no-trespass order), formal adjudication on campus and criminal justice prosecution are all separate actions
- A statement of the sanctions for violating the sexual misconduct policy

Definitions of Sexual Misconduct

Definitions of the various forms of sexual misconduct, including forms of sexual violence, should be provided to the student in the student code of conduct and/or the student handbook. It is critical for schools to define and illustrate actions that constitute gaining consent for mutually agreed upon sexual activity as well as sexual misconduct.

Victim-Centered Approach

Reporting and response policies that make a priority of the victim's need to control the pace of the process and be in charge of making decisions as she or he moves through the campus and/or community law enforcement system were found to be a promising practice.

Reporting Options

Students should have multiple options to file a report, including anonymous, confidential, and third-party reporting. The use of an anonymous reporting option is widely credited by administrators for increasing the reports of assault that are included in the school's annual security report statistics. The use of an anonymous option provides victims with the opportunity to seek out professional services while ensuring them that their confidentiality will be protected. This enables care providers and others to link the victim with counseling services, which are crucial to long-term recovery, and to give the victim information about the process of formally reporting and following through with an investigation. Even more crucially, it may enable the victim to come forward to get a sexual assault examination for time-sensitive evidence collection before she or he makes the decision to move further along in the reporting and adjudication process, which are confidential but not anonymous.

Response Protocols

Written protocols ensure a coordinated, consistent, victim-sensitive response to reports of sexual assault on campus. Written protocols are necessary to explicate (1) who will be notified after a formal report is filed, (2) what procedures will be implemented, (3) how confidentiality will be ensured, and (4) what the rights of the victim and the accused are and how they will be protected once a report of a rape or a sexual assault of a student on campus is made. As protocols are developed in collaboration with multiple offices on campus (e.g., law enforcement, dean of students, judicial services, counseling centers, women's center, residential life, etc.), all relevant staff should be trained in their responsibilities for carrying them out.

Investigation

Protocols to ensure confidentiality for the victim and the accused during the investigation are essential. Agreements between agencies should explicitly define their responsibilities and jurisdictions so investigations can be conducted promptly and may eliminate the need for the victim to repeat her or his experience multiple times to multiple individuals.

One of the most important promising practices is providing access to the services of a trained, certified Sexual Assault Nurse Examiner (SANE). SANE practitioners provide compassionate, state-of-the-art rape trauma treatment and forensic evidence collection, generally from a hospital or comprehensive hospital-based rape treatment center.[244] Particularly in nonstranger sexual assault cases, their documentation can corroborate a victim's account of the crime.

Adjudication

Colleges and universities provide victims with an alternative to the criminal justice system. Firmly established, documented, and consistent proceedings that balance the rights of the complainant and the accused are a key element of this basic practice. Complainants and accused students involved with these proceedings should be made aware of what to expect and how to ensure that their rights are protected. Schools should provide mandatory education and training to adjudication board members regarding the special circumstances of rape, the myths surrounding rape, particularly acquaintance rape, and other dynamics of sexual assault such as rape trauma syndrome and rape-related, posttraumatic stress syndrome.

Victim Support Services

The most promising practice in this area is the formation of partnerships between the school and community to provide student victims a comprehensive, coordinated network of service providers – medical, psychological, advocacy, safety, and legal – to meet a range of necessary services to meet her or his many needs for healing and justice after surviving the trauma of sexual assault.

THE ROLE OF PRACTITIONERS

Although many campuses have specific offices dedicated to serving the campus community broadly regarding sexual assault (e.g., taking sexual assault reports, coordinating campus education and prevention efforts, and providing direct support to sexual assault survivors), a truly transformative effort to respond to and reduce sexual assault requires a collaborative effort across campus and community constituents. Some colleges have no designated office to serve this purpose. Even for those who do have resources such as a victim services office, the responsibility of sexual assault education and prevention is a community responsibility, not that of an individual staff or faculty member, student organization, or campus office. Campuses with promising practices repeatedly emphasized the importance of collaboration among campus constituents and local resources.[245] Over and over, they emphasized the "comprehensive, collaborative effort," "team approach," and "community collaboration" of their institution's program. Sexual assault is a societal concern, not just the problem of individuals who are directly impacted. Campuses have a community responsibility to address sexual assault, and the most effective way to do so is through the joint efforts of a variety of individuals, organizations, departments, and offices.

Campus community members should be prepared to respond to victims of sexual assault. First, campuses should identify who is trained to respond to reports and disclosures of sexual assault. Second, campuses should assess whether those most likely to receive reports and disclosures have received adequate training. Few sexual assaults are reported to police or other official reporting agencies, and more often are disclosed to friends, family, and romantic partners. Students who are sexually assaulted are most likely to tell their friends first, and research shows that the response of those individuals to whom a victim discloses his or her experience can help a victim seek out necessary support and potentially report the assault.[246] In one study of college women, 21 percent of women reported that a friend had disclosed to them a drug/alcohol-facilitated or incapacitated rape, and 35 percent reported a friend had disclosed a forcible rape.[247] Students, faculty, and staff should be trained on what to do if someone discloses a sexual assault. In particular, staff and students in high-risk groups (i.e., sorority women and residence hall students) should receive focused training on how to respond to sexual assault disclosures. Such training is common for Resident Assistants on many but not all campuses, and similar training could be provided to other student leaders, such as sorority advisors and executive officers. In offices that have official reporting responsibilities, all staff members should understand the policy and protocol, have training on their specific responsibilities, and strictly adhere to the protocol.

Medical and nursing staff from campus and local health centers and hospitals, campus and local police, district attorneys, campus and community rape crisis centers, and court victim advocates should also be involved in the collaborative effort of sexual assault response. Due to the serious physical and mental health problems that are frequently consequences of sexual assault, campus and community physicians, nurse practitioners, and other medical providers should be trained on how to sensitively screen for past sexual assault in routine exams. They should then appropriately respond to and refer patients, in order to help them achieve optimum health outcomes.[248] Additionally, medical and nursing staff should be trained on the mental health consequences of sexual assault, including depression, posttraumatic stress disorder (PTSD), and substance abuse in order to help encourage referrals to sexual assault support networks. For recent sexual assault victims, access to a forensic sexual assault nurse examiner (SANE) is a best practice in providing adequate medical care for victims and crucial investigative data gathering for potential prosecution.[249] Campus and local police should offer this service to victims when they report sexual assaults to police, even if it means transporting the victim to a hospital that is perhaps not the nearest or most convenient.

College counselors and psychologists, as well as those in the community who serve college sexual assault victims, should be adequately educated in the most effective interventions to treat college sexual assault victims. Early intervention after an assault is important in preventing more severe reactions.[250] Some specific suggestions for college counselors include:[251]

- Establish formal policies regarding referrals to other support resources when a student presents immediately following an assault, particularly if the student may want to pursue legal action at a later date
- Coordinate services on behalf of the student within the college community (i.e. academic excuses from the Dean of Students for missed classes or assignments)

Although there is only limited theoretical basis and almost no empirical research specifically on the most effective interventions for college sexual assault survivors, some suggestions for interventions include:[252,253]

- Pyscho-education efforts, such as accurate information (i.e., bulletin boards, website, programs) to normalize the experiences of sexual assault victims and reduce the social stigma of sexual assault

- Cognitive behavioral therapy
- Cognitive restructuring
- Exposure therapy
- Prolonged exposure

In addition to training community members and campus practitioners to respond in person to sexual assault victims and work collaboratively with each other, institutions should be prepared to respond to victims through alternative technologies, including online and telephone resources. Telephone counseling and cybercounseling account for most crisis intervention work done in the world.[254] Online communication methods such as information websites, survivor chat rooms, personal blogs and web pages, and email or online counseling can facilitate healing and empowerment for survivors, as well as provide emergency support to individuals experiencing immediate crisis surrounding sexual violence. Additionally, such technological resources can serve traditionally underserved groups, such as people with disabilities and adolescents, by making important support services more accessible. There are some complications and concerns with providing online or telephone support to survivors. First and foremost, service providers must ensure the safety and confidentiality of their clients, and second, they should ensure they have the technological and human resource capacity to handle the potential client load.[255]

PREVENTION

Services to support sexual assault victims and efforts to increase reporting on college campuses are crucial in responding to sexual assault on campus, but a comprehensive program must include prevention as well. Prevention efforts can include efforts aimed at the entire student body or those targeted at specific groups, on- and off-campus efforts, awareness efforts and student activism, bystander training, and perpetrator reduction.

All of these efforts have some application and effectiveness. This section will explore prevention goals, types of prevention programs, specific interventions, and suggestions for developing a campus prevention program. The key to success is collaboration and comprehensiveness.

General Education

General campus education should focus on increasing awareness of sexual assault through providing accurate information on the prevalence of sexual assault, what constitutes sexual assault and consent, and the campus sexual assault policy. In particular, campus education efforts should focus on acquaintance rape and the role of alcohol in sexual assault, since both are highly relevant in the college setting. It is important to stress that even though many sexual assaults involve substance use by the victim, this fact should not be interpreted to blame victims for their sexual assault.[256] Since other students are the most likely people to whom sexual assault survivors will disclose their assault, it is important to raise general awareness levels regarding typical rape characteristics and victim responses, how to support sexual assault survivors, and campus and community support resources and reporting options. General education should also be used to combat and correct rape myths, so that students have correct information and will hopefully contribute to the reduction of the stigma of sexual assault. To reach the entire student body, educational messages should be disseminated in many forms, including posters, websites, orientation sessions, open training sessions, and campus events.

Environmental Approaches

An environmental approach to sexual assault prevention involves changing campus culture regarding attitudes and behaviors that support sexual assault. One aspect of an environmental approach is known as a "social norms" approach. Social norms are the perceived values, beliefs, and attitudes of a group that shape the behavior of individuals within a group, such that individual behavior matches what the individual perceives to be the normal beliefs and behaviors of others in the group. Social norms regarding sexual assault are skewed because most people, especially men, misjudge the attitudes and values of others in their peer group. For example, research on social norms suggests that most men are uncomfortable with behavior by other men that is sexist or degrading toward women, yet most men also underestimate other men's level of discomfort with the same behavior.[257] A social norms approach to sexual assault prevention involves correcting such misperceptions, thereby encouraging positive behavior that is in line with the true group values instead of the incorrect perceived values.

Another type of prevention effort that falls within the scope of environmental approaches is a "public health" approach. Public health approaches seek to change culturally-accepted behaviors that are unhealthy and have been used successfully to encourage seat belt use and reduce cigarette smoking in the general population. Similar to social norms approaches, the public health strategy focuses on changing widespread public attitudes and long-standing habits in favor of healthier behavior.

Social Justice Approaches

Social justice is the value that all people, regardless of their social identities such as race, class, gender, sexual orientation, and ability level, should have full and equal participation in society, an equitable distribution of resources, and physical and psychological safety and security.[258] Violence is in direct opposition to the goals of social justice. In particular, when one views sexual assault through the lens of gender and sexual orientation, in which "rape culture," sexism, homophobia, and heterosexism perpetuate sexual violence against all its victims, social justice education can become an important tool in a comprehensive sexual assault prevention program. One way in which a social justice approach can be used to prevent sexual assault is in programs with men and women to dismantle rape myths and gender roles that encourage and perpetuate sexual violence. The social justice approach not only involves groups that have been historically oppressed in bringing about change (i.e., nonwhites to fight racism, or women to fight sexism), but it also involves those who have privilege and power within the paradigm of oppression to join the fight against oppression by taking responsibility for their privilege. For example, men have gender-based privilege that gives them both the influence and the responsibility to help reduce gender-based violence, including sexual assault.

Role of Women

Women traditionally have spearheaded sexual assault response and prevention efforts on college campuses and in society at large. Indeed, sexual assault awareness and prevention originally grew out of grass-roots feminism. Women are the most frequent victims of sexual assault, and therefore have an enormous stake in reducing sexual assault. Women can raise awareness, create policy change, educate their peers, promote victim services, and learn to better protect themselves. Women's self-defense training emerged from the feminist activism of the 1970s, 80s, and 90s as a way for women to strengthen their capacity to defend themselves against assault. Tactics in self-defense programs should be practical, simple, and effective in common situations. Research has shown women's self-defense programs to have therapeutic benefits for sexual abuse

survivors, including reducing psychological distress, fear, vulnerability, anxiety, avoidance behaviors, and helplessness; it also increases self-efficacy, perceived control, self-esteem, and ability to set boundaries.[259] In this way, women's self-defense may serve as a both prevention and response effort. Another important factor to note is that ongoing, multiple-session interventions and educational opportunities have been shown to be more successful than single interventions, with both men and women.

Role of Men

The role of men in sexual assault prevention has grown largely out of the social justice movement. Through the lens of social justice, it is imperative for men to accept responsibility for their privilege in the area of gender, and therefore fight against the sexual victimization of women. Additionally, men have a significant amount of influence on one another. In particular, the desire of most men to meet the societal expectations of masculinity is largely judged by other men. The majority of men have historically been perceived as bystanders and even encouragers of sexual assault against women.[260] A social justice approach simultaneously demands that men take ownership and responsibility for their role in perpetuating sexual assault, and recognizes the potential of men to serve as allies with women in the fight against sexual assault. Additionally, both men and women should be made aware of the prevalence of sexual assault against male victims, both to prevent it and to respond to male victims more effectively.

All-male peer group interventions have been shown to be effective venues for educating men on sexual assault. Based on certain risk factors for increased likelihood to perpetrate sexual assault, targeted efforts have been tailored to meet the needs of fraternity members and male student athletes, two groups that have higher risk of sexual assault perpetration than average. In these all-male environments, participants can freely discuss topics including:[261]

- Men's responsibility for preventing sexual assault
- Sexual activity as a choice
- Relevant local laws and policies
- Role of alcohol and drugs in sexual encounters, in particular that an intoxicated person cannot legally give consent
- Sexually coercive behaviors that men are socialized to employ
- Male gender roles and their relatedness to rape myths
- Men's false fear of false accusation
- Bystander interventions among men
- Empathy for victims and understanding the impact of rape
- Male victims of sexual assault
- Understanding what constitutes consent for sexual activity, and educating that they are responsible for determining if their partner is (1) capable of consenting, and (2) has freely given consent.

Research on men-only sexual assault prevention programs has shown that participants gained a new awareness of gender, deeper understanding of homophobia and GLBT issues, increased empathy for women, awareness of sexism and rape-supportive culture, and learned bystander intervention strategies and skills.[262]

Effectiveness of Prevention

With a variety of prevention approaches available to campus practitioners and students but limited time and resources, choosing effective prevention approaches is critical. Measuring the actual prevalence of sexual assault victimization as an outcome of prevention programs has been rare. A 2007 study was the first to show that a prevention program actually reduced sexual assault among participants who had no prior history of sexual assault.[263] The program had no effect in reducing sexual assault rates among participants with a prior history of sexual victimization. The study suggested more intensive prevention programming specifically for sexual abuse and assault survivors due to their higher risk of sexual assault in college. One clear recommendation regarding prevention effectiveness is that one-time programs do not appear to have long-term effects on individual attitudes and behaviors or rape-supportive cultures.[264] Effective programs are ongoing, comprehensive, and multifaceted. Additionally, single-sex and peer-to-peer formats have been successful.

Developing a Prevention Program

The following four basic elements of sexual assault prevention program are adapted from *Men's Violence Against Women: Theory, Research, and Activism* by Christopher Kilmartin and Julie Allison, a recommended resource for any campus or organization developing a prevention program:

1. Programs should be *comprehensive* and create connections among relevant community, campus, state, and national entities.
2. Programs should be *intensive, interactive, and sustained over time.*
3. Programs should be *relevant to the audience*, and tailored to the specific demographics of the participants.
4. Programs should be *positive*, characterizing men as part of the solution.

Additionally, some suggestions for starting new programs include:

- Providing incentives for participation
- Seeking out leaders from across campus
- Seeking a diverse membership
- Creating gender-aware programming.

CONCLUDING THOUGHTS

Students like Felicia in the opening scenario of this chapter are common on our college campuses, but they rarely tell us their stories. The stigma and shame of sexual assault may prevent them from accessing real options for support, but we have the power to create change on campus and in society at large. Each person who speaks up against sexism, who confronts homophobia, who challenges the dominant culture that perpetuates sexual assault, or who supports a survivor has the power to make a difference. If we work together – men and women, students and administrators, campus and local resources – we can reduce sexual violence. But we must open our eyes to see the reality of sexual assault, raise our voices to make this epidemic silent no more, and create change to prevent the harm of sexual assault for all our students.

Chapter 12

SUICIDE

SALLY SPENCER-THOMAS, RAE SANDLER, & JINA JENSEN

ALBERT EINSTEIN FAILED his freshman liberal arts exam. What if he had died by suicide instead of going on to study physics? Marie Curie lost her mother at an early age. She was so devastated by this she lost her faith in God and was hospitalized for depression as an adult. What if she had taken her own life instead of going on to win two Nobel Prizes in science? Martin Luther King certainly lived in violent and oppressive times when many were hopeless. What if he had died by suicide instead of being a major catalyst to fuel the civil rights movement? Even William Shakespeare – "to be or not to be" – he got his unwed girlfriend pregnant at age 18. What if he had taken his own life instead of writing his masterpieces?[265]

The above mentioned statements are part of a social marketing campaign developed by the University of California, Irvine in partnership with A Better World Advertising. The goals of this campaign were to shift the culture around suicide from one of avoidance to one of assistance and to connect college student with resources to help. In 2007, this campaign won the Best Electronic Media Award from the American Public Health Association, and it has since been replicated on several other campuses. This campaign was one of many turning points around the issue of suicide prevention and campuses began to shift their thinking. Not only is suicide a mental health problem, but it is also a public health problem that requires a comprehensive strategy that goes beyond counseling, adding many other strategies and stakeholders to the efforts.

Suicide prevention efforts on campuses in the U.S. have been drastically altered in the last few years, largely by the work of one man and his determination to make this work a federal priority. On September 8, 2003, Garrett Lee Smith, son of Senator Gordon Smith and a 21-year-old college student majoring in culinary arts, took his life in an apartment in Utah where he was attending school. Gordon Smith subsequently wrote a book entitled *Remembering Garrett, One Family's Battle with a Child's Depression*, and developed legislation to fund campuses, states and tribal communities. In 2004, President George W. Bush signed the Garrett Lee Smith Memorial Act, authorizing $82 million for suicide-prevention and awareness programs at colleges. Because of this funding, hotlines, resources, research, and comprehensive programs have emerged in almost every state and we now know so much more about how to prevent suicides among our students. This chapter will start with a downward and inward look at suicide in our country and on our campuses. The second half of the chapter will offer a comprehensive blueprint for suicide prevention on campus.

OVERVIEW OF SUICIDOLOGY

Suicide in the United States: Facts at a Glance

- There are over 30,000 suicides in the United States each year: about one completed suicide each 16 minutes and one attempt every minute.[266]
- Internationally, about one million people die by suicide each year – more than war and homicide combined.[267]
- Two thirds of suicidal deaths occur on the first attempt.[268]
- While men complete suicide four times as often as women (17.7 per 100,000 for men versus 4.6 per 100,000 for women), women attempt suicide twice as often as men.[269]
- About 5 percent of people who engage in deliberate self harm (e.g., cutting) die by suicide within five to 10 years.[270]
- More than 90 percent of persons who complete suicide have a mental disorder at the time of death, most commonly depression, alcohol abuse, or both.[271]
- Almost 75 percent of suicides are completed by white males, who have a twofold higher risk for suicide than black males (19.1 per 100,000 versus 10.4 per 100,000).[272]
- The average medical cost per completed suicide: $3,875; The average work-loss cost per completed suicide: $1,178,684.[273]
- Native Americans also are at higher risk for suicide, but this rate varies greatly by tribe (12.9 per 100,000).[274]
- 972,264 years of potential life lost to suicide each year.[275]
- It is estimated that each suicide death intimately and profoundly affects at least six people.[276]
- During the previous 12 months, more than one-fourth of adults reported having symptoms that would qualify them for a diagnosis of a mental disorder; and most of those disorders can be classified as serious or moderate.[277]
- More Americans suffer from depression than coronary heart disease (7 million), cancer (6 million), and AIDS (200,000) combined.[278]

A Note about Language, Suicide, and Mental Health

Few would disagree that issues of mental health and suicide have been stigmatized over the course of history, and one of the ways we challenge stigma is by watching our use of language. Thus, throughout this chapter, we will use the phrases "die by suicide" or "took their lives" rather than "committed suicide," as the latter phrase emerged during a time when suicide was thought of as a crime or a mortal sin. Likewise, the terms "completed suicide" and "successful suicide" are often frowned upon because they give a positive status to a negative outcome.

In the field of suicide prevention, those who are impacted by a loved one's suicide are interchangeably described as "bereaved by suicide" or "suicide survivors." The latter term here is often confusing to the lay public whose first impression is that "suicide survivors" are those who have lived through a nonfatal suicidal behavior, thus to clarify, the latter group is often referred to as "suicide attempt survivors." Currently, there is much debate about the phrase "suicide attempt" because this too indicates that one "failed" in their intention to die; however, to date, the language to replace this phrase remains in flux. One of the more endorsed replacements is nonfatal deliberate self-harm, but that is quite a mouthful and does not make clear the intent to die that is not always the case with deliberate self-harm, but is the case in a suicide attempt. Thus, as the field of suicide prevention continues to grow, issues of language will continue to evolve.

In the field of mental health, there is also debate. When describing diagnostic categories of mental and emotional distress, some people prefer the term "mental illness" because it underscores the biological basis for the diagnoses and people can make the connection of having to manage a chronic disease just as they would diabetes or high cholesterol. Others find this term conjures up images of people in straight jackets and is usually associated with extreme forms of distress. Others find that the idea of a chronic mental illness is not comforting, but feels like a life sentence of despair, and thus, some of these people prefer the term "mental disorder" because it feels like a more temporary state. Dis-order — something that is out of order and can be put back into order but does not define one's whole life. To others, the term "mental disorder" also evokes negative feelings of being disturbed or deranged. Even the phrase "mental health issues," often used as the most inclusive of the three terms because everyone has mental health, is often seen with skepticism. Because of these issues in language, this chapter will interchange these three terms throughout.

SUICIDE AS A PUBLIC HEALTH PROBLEM

Each year, approximately 30,000 people die by suicide with 32,637 people dying by suicide in 2005, the most recent year for which data is available).[279]

A Model of Suicide Risk

Why Do People Attempt Suicide: Escaping the Flames

The main thing that most people who kill themselves have in common is a belief that suicide is the ONLY solution to their unbearable situation. Many of us have etched in our memories the images of people jumping out of the World Trade Center on 9/11. These

people did not want to die. They were leaping to get away from the flames at their back. In a similar manner, people who contemplate suicide are trying to escape some type of peril in their own lives. Many of us find it difficult to truly appreciate the flames that consume the minds of people who contemplate suicide.

Ed Shneidman, a founder of suicidology, coined the term "psychache" to describe the unbearable psychological pain suicidal people experiences that often blocks the ability to see other potential solutions to problems.[280] Despite the fact that pervasive sense of hopelessness stifles the ability for many to seek help, most people are very ambivalent about taking their lives – they don't want death, they just want the pain to stop.

In his book *Why People Die by Suicide*, Thomas Joiner[281] brings together several theories of suicide that have emerged over the past two centuries in developing his model of suicide risk. In his theory, Joiner says that those who kill themselves not only have a desire to die, they have also learned to overcome the instinct for self-preservation (see Figure 12.1).

That is, wanting death, according to Joiner, is composed of two psychological experiences. The first is a perception of being a burden to others (*perceived burdensomeness*). When people are in this state they feel that their death is worth more to the people who love them than their life is because they have let people down. The word *perceived* is emphasized because frequently these thoughts are significantly distorted by the impact of depression or other mental disorders. The second is a social disconnection to something larger than oneself (*thwarted belongingness*). People in this state feel that they have lost key relationships – partners, children, colleagues, and friends. In other words, they have become socially isolated and have lost their sense of purpose.

By themselves, however, neither of these states is enough to move a person to act on

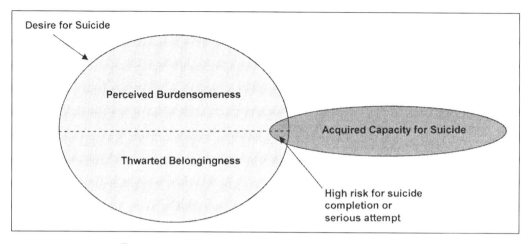

Figure 12.1. Thomas Joiner's Model of Suicide Risk.[282]

the desire for death, but together with the ability and fearlessness to inflict self-injury, they become high risk for suicide. Thus, repeated exposure to painful and provocative experiences, familiarity and access to lethal means, and a disposition to reckless behavior can increase the risk of suicide when combined with someone who is experiencing a strong desire to die.

What Are Risk and Protective Factors for Suicide?

According to the Suicide Prevention Resource Center, "Risk factors may be thought of as leading to or being associated with suicide; that is, people 'possessing' the risk factor are at greater potential for suicidal behavior. Protective factors, on the other hand, reduce the likelihood of suicide. They enhance resilience and may serve to counterbalance risk factors."[283]

RISK FACTORS[284]

Biopsychosocial Risk Factors

- Mental disorders, particularly mood disorders, schizophrenia, anxiety disorders, and certain personality disorders

- Alcohol and other substance use disorders
- Hopelessness
- Impulsive and/or aggressive tendencies
- History of trauma or abuse
- Some major physical illnesses
- Previous suicide attempt
- Family history of suicide

Environmental Risk Factors

- Job or financial loss
- Relational or social loss
- Easy access to lethal means
- Local clusters of suicide that have a contagious influence

Social-cultural Risk Factors

- Lack of social support and sense of isolation
- Stigma associated with help-seeking behavior
- Barriers to accessing health care, especially mental health and substance abuse treatment
- Certain cultural and religious beliefs (for instance, the belief that suicide is a noble resolution of a personal dilemma)
- Exposure to, including through the media, and influence of others who have died by suicide

PROTECTIVE FACTORS[285]

- Effective clinical care for mental, physical and substance use disorders
- Easy access to a variety of clinical interventions and support for help-seeking
- Restricted access to highly lethal means of suicide
- Strong connections to family and community support
- Support through ongoing medical and mental health care relationships
- Skills in problem solving, conflict resolution and nonviolent handling of disputes
- Cultural and religious beliefs that discourage suicide and support self preservation

Warning Signs

People who are in danger of taking their own lives may try to reach out to others — sometimes directly, sometimes indirectly. Rarely will at-risk individuals immediately volunteer the information that they are thinking of harming themselves. Instead they might exhibit some of the following warning signs:

- Talking or writing about suicide, death, or preoccupation with dying. Suicidal people might say:
  - "I wish I were dead"
  - "People would be better off if I am not around"
  - "Soon you won't have to worry about me"
  - "I just can't take it anymore. I am done."
  - "I wish I could go to sleep and never wake up."
- Developing a suicidal plan and the means to carry it through (note: many attempts, especially in youth are impulsive. Thus, absence of a plan is not evidence of absence of risk)
- Exhibiting trouble eating or sleeping (sleeping all the time, unable to sleep at all, not able to eat or overeating)
- Showing intense signs of distress and agitation accompanied by depression.

- Displaying significant changes in behavior and/or personality
- Withdrawing from family and friends
- Losing of interest in activities, work, school, hobbies, or social interactions
- Deteriorating physical appearance
- Giving away prized possessions and saying goodbye
- Previous suicide attempts
- Increasing drug and/or alcohol use
- Making statements about hopelessness, or worthlessness or feeling like a burden to others
- Taking unnecessary risks
- Displaying sudden happiness or calmness following a depressed mood (this may indicate that they have come to peace with their decision to end their lives)
- Exhibiting an obsession with suicidal means (guns, knives, hanging materials)
- Increasing problems in school or work performance
- Experiencing chronic pain or frequent complaints of physical symptoms
- An inability to concentrate, trouble remembering things
- Stockpiling medications
- Buying a gun
- Taking a sudden interest or losing interest in religion
- Getting one's affairs in order – paying off debt, getting a will, getting life insurance
- Scheduling medical appointments for vague symptoms

The American Association of Suicidology developed a mnemonic to remember these warning signs:[286]

IS PATH WARM?

I	Ideation		
S	Substance Abuse	W	Withdrawal
P	Purposelessness	A	Anger
A	Anxiety	R	Recklessness
T	Trapped	W	Withdrawal
H	Hopelessness		

SUICIDE ON CAMPUS

Among the 15 million university students in the United States, approximately 24,000 suicide attempts and 1,100 deaths by suicide occur every year, or an average of three per day.[287] In addition, one in ten college students report seriously considering suicide.[288]

According to Centers for Disease Control and Prevention (CDC), suicide emerges as a significant problem during the high school years, increases among young adults 20–24 years of age, and continues to increase marginally over the next two decades of life.[289] The CDC states that the rate of completed suicide has quadrupled for males ages 15 to 24 and doubled for females of the same age over the past 60 years.[290] In 2003, suicide was the third leading cause of death among young people ages 15 to 24, surpassed only by unintentional injury and homicide.[291] "Whereas suicides account for 1.3 percent of all deaths in the U.S. annually, they comprise 12.3 percent of all deaths among 15–24 year olds."[292] When we focus just on young adults on campus, we find that suicide is the second leading cause of death for college students.[293]

These numbers do not account for deaths attributed to accidental injury that may, in fact, have been suicides. Experts estimate a "considerable proportion" of suicides among youth are ascribed to accidental injury, the leading cause of death among young people.[294] Making a determination between suicide and accidental injury can be extremely difficult as the difference frequently comes down to the intent of the individual's actions, which is often difficult to determine post-mortem.

In spite of these statistics, there is some indication that being at college is protective against suicide for some. The suicide rate for young adults attending college is roughly half (7.5 per 100,000) of the national suicide rate of young adults not in college (about 15 per 100,000).[295] Rates for subgroups of college students fluctuate from 30 percent of the national rates for 17–19-year-old male and female students to 169 percent of the national rate for women ages 25–29."[296] Making estimates even more difficult is the time-limited nature of being in college, with individuals able to discontinue their studies at any time. Given the nature of mental illness and suicide and the negative impact these struggles may have on academic performance, it is important to consider whether students are more likely to drop out of college when experiencing suicidal ideation, which could have an impact on the actual rates of suicide within this population. Of additional consideration is when to classify someone as a "student." For example, is an individual classified as a student while on winter and summer break? Because of these complications of this population, researchers struggle with such questions as:

- If a student takes his or her life over spring break does this count as a campus-related suicide?
- What if the student fails out and then dies by suicide a week or two later?
- If the student goes home for Thanksgiving and dies by suicide at home, does this count as a campus-related suicide?, and so on...

Regardless of the methodological struggles that make comparing college students and the general U.S. population difficult, suicide is an issue on college campuses. In the U.S., approximately one in ten college students have seriously considered suicide in the past 12 months.[297] Additionally, the Division of Adolescent and School Health estimate that one in 14 U.S. college students have made a specific plan and 1.5 in 100 U.S. college students have attempted suicide in the past 12 months.[298]

College students who admit to suicidal ideation represent a high-risk group of individuals who report other risky behaviors at increased rates. Students reporting suicidal ideation are more likely to report the use of alcohol, and illegal drugs,[299] which can result in suicidal ideation becoming suicidal intent. Students who reported suicidal ideation were significantly more likely than other students to engage in high-risk behavior:

- carry a weapon
- engage in a physical fight
- boat or swim after drinking alcohol
- ride with a driver who had been drinking alcohol
- drive after drinking alcohol
- rarely or never use seatbelts[300]

Student mental health and suicide impact all levels of a campus: administration, community, student services, and student development. For example, "confidentiality issues, including those stemming from the Family Educational Rights and Privacy Act (FERPA) and the Health Insurance Portability and Accountability Act (HIPAA) regulations, also have implications for the management of mental crises."[301] These regulations influence what information about a student is considered confidential and thus may not be shared with parents. Many high-profile institutions, including Brown, Harvard, and MIT, have been the target of lawsuits alleging inadequate or negligent treatment of mental health problems, some of which have involved the perceived failure of these institutions to inform parents of situations involving the mental health of their student.[302]

Obviously, being suicidal also has a negative impact on academic performance, retention, and graduation rates of college students. National Survey of Counseling Center Directors, in which 274 institutions participated, indicates that "eighty-nine percent of centers had to hospitalize a student for psychological reasons and 10 percent reported a student suicide,"[303] showing that many institutes of higher education are dealing with the mental health crises of their students.

College Contributes to Both Risk and Protective Factors

As mentioned earlier, those who come to college have a lower suicide rate than those who do not attend college of the same age. Why then are college students getting so much attention in the world of suicide prevention? Often, it is because people have difficulty fathoming why a young, healthy adult at the precipice of so many opportunities and with access to so many resources would consider suicide.

The protective factors of college abound and provide an opportunity for prevention efforts unique to small communities like universities. The campus community (e.g., resident advisors, faculty, mental health service providers) are usually highly trained individuals, aware of risks and warning signs for emotional distress. Most campuses also have policies prohibiting firearms, the number one method of suicide in the U.S. Recent research at Harvard indicates that when lethal means are less accessible, suicide rates decline.[304] Additionally, campuses are very keen to the impact of alcohol abuse on self-destructive behavior and over the past 20 years have improved their ability to identify and intervene with students who may be prone to substance abuse. Nevertheless, the fact remains that suicide is the second leading cause of death for college students, and thus, additional exploration examines what else might be putting students at risk.

When examining how college life may actually contribute to students' stress disorders and suicidal behaviors, despite the presence of protective factors, several factors emerge. First, the onset of a first experience with mental illness and suicidal ideation often coincides with late adolescence, and this fact has often been attributed to the stress of transition during this time of life. The "diathesis-stress" model of mental illness explains that psychological disturbances are the interaction of a vulnerable hereditary presdisposition and stressful events in the environment.[305] When we consider the fact that stressors may be positive or negative, few would deny that the transition to college represents a large upheaval in daily routine and challenges to students' identities. This stress may increase as parents create pressure to succeed while economic commitments create pressure to do well in classes in a shorter period of time.

The first few weeks of college often bring these issues of stress to the forefront, and thus it is not surprising that at least one study found a spike in college suicides during the first six weeks of a new school semester.[306] Each new academic term thrusts students into a chaotic, pressure-filled, and sometimes unstructured social and academic life. Although students have a tendency to report increased levels of anxiety related to academic pressures, at least one study[307] finds that while students at one prestigious university frequently related their academic struggles to their mood, they were typically struggling in school as a result of being depressed rather than being depressed as a result of academic difficulties. Thus, although academic struggles are commonly associated with students who report depressed mood and suicidal ideation, the academic difficulties may be a symptom rather than a cause.

Some students have difficulty adjusting to this momentous change in lifestyle, become overwhelmed, and begin to feel isolated from family and friends from home. The uncertain social and academic college climate makes students with psychological illnesses even more vulnerable to mental health challenges and can be a catalyst for manic, depressive, or suicidal states. In addition to stress, sleep deprivation is considered "normal" to most college students, their professors, and their parents. Lack of sleep, however; may also trigger mania that increases the likelihood for depression, mixed states, and suicide.[308]

Many students are already coming to the university setting already diagnosed with pre-existing mental health conditions.[309] While feeling hopeless or depressed does not necessarily mean an individual is contemplating suicide, having thoughts of suicide frequently does involve these feelings. The American College Health Association[310] states that 33.4 percent of students who report feeling depressed had "seriously considered suicide."

The National Mental Health Association and The Jed Foundation's landmark "Expanding the Safety Net" report[311] identified several trends that enable students with previous mental health conditions to seek a college education whereas this may historically have been more difficult. These factors include more effective treatment of mental illness during high school, "decreased stigma associated with mental illness and help-seeking on college campuses" (p. 10), mental health resources becoming more available on college campuses, and better recognition of mental illness by university faculty and staff. Together all of these factors result in students receiving treatment and services that increase their retention in college despite a major mental health issue. Another factor may be that psychotropic medications are more easily accessible and have more manageable side effects than in the past. Thus, children who would have struggled significantly with social interactions and academics due to mental health issues may not have been able to attend college previously. Now, however, disability services, tutoring, medication, and support from their parents and teachers enable them to be accepted by and attend college.

Although many students with mental illnesses thrive, for others, the transition to college is stressful, and places risks on their ability to maintain their mental health. Some students who arrive at college may want to "start clean" and may intentionally stop taking medication. Others become less diligent about taking their medication or regularly seeing a mental health provider without their parents' physical presence or because the mental health systems are too complicated to navigate. Many students increase their consumption of drugs or alcohol upon arriving to college, especially during the first few weeks of school; this behavior can prove to be a dangerous combination with psychotropic medications. When students' mental illness are not managed well at school, they may become vulnerable to manic or depressive states, feel frustrated by their inability to perform as well academically as in high school, and may become extremely depressed and possibly suicidal.

In addition to having a difficult time adjusting to a college campus and managing previously or newly-diagnosed mental health illnesses, college and university students are faced with problematic binge drinking on campuses across the United States. The American Psychiatric Association's *Diagnostic and Statistical Manual of Mental Disorders*, 4th Edition (DSM-IV) defines "binge drinking" as "consuming five or more drinks on the same occasion on at least one day in the past 30 days." The Office of Applied Studies reports that more than one in ten young adults between 18 and 24 years old are heavy drinkers, and almost two in five are binge drinkers.[312] Drug and alcohol intoxication increases risk-taking and impulsive behavior, many times moving someone from depressive thoughts to suicidal ideation, attempt, or death.[313]

Gender and age also appear to be risk factors for suicide. Silverman, Meyer, Sloane, Raffel, and Pratt[314] report a higher rate of suicide among female graduate students as compared to female undergraduate students as well as the general college population. Silverman et al. also suggest that the highest rate of suicide among both male and female college students occurs in the age range of 20–29. This correlates to upper class undergraduate and graduate students, indicating that students further along in their education are likely at higher risk. Among increased stressors for all graduate students are increasing financial burdens, time spent away from a career and out of the workforce, and uncertainties about the future job market.[315] Graduate students who are female may be more likely to face additional pressures associated with having a family and motherhood.

The Suicide Prevention Resource Center[316] also suggests that gay, lesbian, bisexual, and transgender (GLBT) students are at increased risk for suicide. However, tracking rates of death by suicide among GLB individuals is extremely difficult as "sexual orientation is not a question on the death certificate, and to determine whether rates are higher for GLB persons, we would need to know the proportion of the U.S. population that considers themselves gay, lesbian, or bisexual, " states National Institute of Mental Health.[317] It is very difficult to estimate the prevalence of GLB individuals as any estimate relies on the self-report of individuals who may or may not feel safe reporting such information. Laumann, Gagnon, Michael, and Michaels[318] estimate that up to 5 percent of the adult male U.S. population identifies as gay. This percentage is lower than previously thought and, if accurate, would indicate that the rate of suicide among GLB people is even higher than previously believed as the number of completed suicides remains steady for a smaller number of individuals, resulting in a higher percentage of GLB individuals who have died by suicide. Because the rate of completed suicide is difficult to determine, suicidal ideation and suicide attempts, risk factors for completed suicide, are instead focused upon.

Another reason for the difficulty assessing the relationship between sexual orientation and suicide is that relatively little research has focused on this area, and the studies that have are not completely consistent.[319] One group of researchers[320] compared 16 different studies and concluded that rates of suicide attempts among GLB individuals range from 20 percent to 53 percent. Another group of researchers[321] explored the differences among twins in which one twin reports having had a same-sex sexual partner and the other does not. This group reported a higher rate of suicidal ideation and suicide attempts among the gay and lesbian twins (15%) as compared to the heterosexual twins (4%). Additionally, Bagley and Tremblay[322] indicate that gay and bisexual males are at 14 times greater risk for attempting suicide than heterosexual males.

Overall, although the data are not entirely consistent, they do suggest that GLB individuals have higher rates of suicide and suicidal ideation than heterosexual individuals.

SUICIDE PREVENTION AND INTERVENTION

Best Practice: U.S. Air Force Suicide Prevention Program

We have a responsibility to our active duty members and their families to provide a safety net of support services that ensures a healthy and fit force and assistance to those in need. This is the foundation underlying the Air Force Suicide Prevention Program. Now more than ever, we need to remind ourselves that our Air Force is only as strong as those who serve.

– General Jumper (http://afspp.afms.mil)

Many campuses are looking for best practices to help guide their strategies in developing a comprehensive suicide prevention program. The National Registry of Evidence-based Programs and Practices currently lists only two programs; one is for adolescents (Signs of Suicide or SOS program) and the U.S. Air Force Suicide Prevention Program. This National Registry uses a panel of experts to judge each program's quality of supporting research and readiness for dissemination.[323] Thus, the Air Forces' model is the leading model for the campuses today.

After a five-year period of rising suicide rates, the U.S. Air Force committed to implementing a comprehensive suicide prevention program, knowing that, as the above General

indicates, the Air Force had a shared responsibility to address this public health issue. This decision occurred even though the Air Force rates were comparatively lower than that of the U.S. population overall. Strong and visible support from the Air Force Chief of Staff provided the top down endorsement that encouraged other leaders to discuss the various aspects of suicide prevention and reminded leaders about their roles as suicide prevention gatekeepers. The intervention consisted of five components (http://afspp.afms.mil):

1. Changing social norms through marketing community awareness.
2. Educating community members through education, training, and preventive services.
3. Improving surveillance through the development of a well-integrated database and community action information board.
4. Critical incident stress management
5. Integrated delivery system for human services that coordinated efforts and training among Chapel program, mental health services, financial counselors, career counselors, health providers, and others.

When the Suicide Prevention Program started, suicide was the second leading cause of death for the 350,000 Air Force members (suicide rate of 15.8 per 100,000). Since the implementation of the program, the suicide rate fell to 3.5 per 100,000, the lowest rate on record. Interestingly, the rates of violent crime, family violence and deaths due to unintentional injures have also shown statistically significant declines at the same time as the interventions.[324]

Leadership: Involving Senior Administrators

In the aftermath of the Virginia Tech Tragedy, campus administrators are even more worried

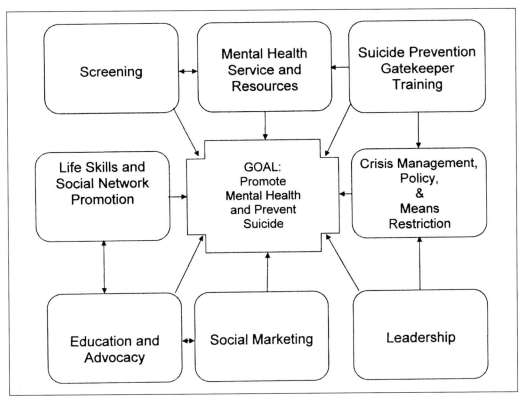

Figure 12.2. Comprehensive Suicide Prevention Program. This model is adapted from the Best Practice Air Force Model and the Jed Foundation.

about making the right decisions when it comes to mental health and their students. Some are fearful of liability, wondering where the balance is between discipline, confidentiality, and support. Senior administrators are in critical positions to make informed decisions that influence the culture of campus life and can be a major catalyst around the major public health issues of mental health and suicide prevention. Finding a nondiscriminatory and nonpunitive approach to students in mental health crisis is the goal.

Having a mentally healthy campus not only affects the students' lives, but the faculty and staff as well. Knowing that mental disorders are one of the leading causes of attrition today, senior administrators can help retain highly productive and engaged students by

supporting the vision for a comprehensive mental health campaign.

Adapting from the best practice of the U.S. Air Force, the standard is clear: in order to develop a comprehensive suicide awareness and prevention program, a strong message needs to be sent from those in top positions: "suicide prevention is a priority." Leaders on campus have the power to set the tone, establish policy, and involve a wide variety of individuals and departments in the efforts.

Setting the Tone

Senior administrators can use their visibility and influence to set the tone for suicide prevention. Preferably, this leadership happens *before* a suicide crisis has occurred. In order for senior administrators to become involved, they must know what is going on and where the opportunities are for leadership. Some suggestions for senior administration involvement are:

- Invite senior administrators to make welcoming remarks at campus programs on mental health promotion and suicide prevention.
- Keep senior administrators up-to-date with brief (one page) and factual, outcome-oriented memos sent about once a semester.
- Send senior administrators notices of accomplishments (e.g., media publications, awards, notices of accolades).
- Ask senior administrators to write letters of support to other campus stakeholder (e.g., faculty) to encourage participation.
- Interview senior administrators for campus media.
- Nominate senior administrators who are doing exceptional work in the area of mental health promotion for awards related to the cause.
- Connect senior administrators from like-minded institutions to share best practices on policy and crisis management.
- Thank senior administrators for any support given to the cause.

Establishing Policy

By developing protocols in a methodical manner prior to crisis situations, you minimize the need for *ad hoc* decision-making during a crisis. Ideally, your college's protocols should be broad enough to cover many potential situations while allowing for case-by-case flexibility; they should also be sufficiently well-defined to remain meaningful and emphasize how decisions are made and by whom.

– The Jed Foundation, *Framework*, p. 9

After conducting a roundtable discussion of policy issues, The Jed Foundation published

a document known as "The Framework" to assist senior administrators in crafting the following policies most effectively:

1. Developing a Safety Protocol
   a. Responding to the acutely distressed or suicidal student
   b. Addressing issues around voluntary or involuntary psychiatric hospitalization
   c. Developing a post-crisis follow-up plan
   d. Documenting encounters with the acutely distressed or suicidal student
2. Developing an Emergency Contact Notification Protocol
3. Developing a Leave of Absence and Re-entry Protocol

Establishing a Suicide Prevention Coalition

One way to help ensure success of a comprehensive suicide prevention campaign is by involving campus stakeholders and creating partnerships. The basics of building a coalition are covered elsewhere in this book; however, specific issues apply to a coalition that oversees suicide prevention. By bringing together a variety of individuals with unique perspectives, stakeholders can explore:

- What mental health services are currently available on campus?
- Which departments provide each available service? Are these departments coordinated in any way?
- How are students made aware of these available services?
- Does current marketing of available services reach the college student population?
- What services/programs would help to increase mental health awareness and support?
- How can partnerships be developed to help support and improve services?

- What policies and procedures exist to guide our decision-making?
- Who may come in contact with suicidal students or who might pick up on behavior changes related to suicidality? Are these individuals trained on identifying risk and making appropriate referrals?

One way to promote mental health awareness on campus is by appropriately educating key players. This means that members of the coalition and campus community should be provided an overview of current campus standards and procedures, recognizing when a student needs help, and knowing how to make a referral.

Education and Advocacy

Raising awareness and promoting mental health advocacy are important and challenging tasks; however, many approaches that mean well might actually be doing more harm than good. Campuses that have been indoctrinated into the "social norms" approach for substance abuse prevention have realized that when you only talk about the problem, you actually reinforce its existence. For instance, many campus programs address the stigma of mental disorders – this approach may actually inflate the idea that mental disorders are shameful. Thus, mental health education and advocacy must be done with care – to open dialogue, engage appropriate involvement, entice critical thinking, and encourage help-seeking – all without reinforcing stereotypes.

Some schools have had success getting students involved in suicide prevention by framing it as a social justice issue. Students critically examine the issues around injustice related to funding for mental health and disparities in access to services. Sometimes they participate in or volunteer at community walks for suicide awareness. Others have worked on promoting state and federal legislation related to suicide prevention. Still others work with campus, local and national media to help educate the public about facts related to suicide and resources that are available to help.

Peer Education: Developing a Student-Run Grassroots Mental Health Advocacy Group

Increasing numbers of campuses are creating grassroots advocacy groups to promote mental health and prevent suicide. One organization fueling this movement is called Active Minds on Campus (www.ActiveMinds

---

Suicide Prevention Education and Advocacy Activities

- Faculty panel exploring a number of perspectives (e.g., psychology, sociology, neuroscience, philosophy, epidemiology) on mental health and suicide
- Articles and editorials in the student newspaper
- Public Service Announcements "There is hope, there is help."
- Awareness tables or mental health fairs – Suicide Awareness and Prevention Week is the second week in September
- Poster campaigns that encourage friends to support each other and promote positive methods for dealing with emotional distress. Messages that promote positive norms around help-seeking
- Mental health speakers – especially those with a hopeful story to share that models recovery
- Bulletin boards or bathroom stall newsletters
- Art shows that depict recovery from emotional pain

onCampus.org), and it develops and supports student-run mental health awareness, education, and advocacy chapters on college campuses across the country. Each student group's mission is to engage the young adult voice in promoting mental health among peers and to help put a face to "mental illness" by normalizing mental health disorders.

Another helpful resource for student groups and their advisors is the BACCHUS Network (www.bacchusnetwork.org). In 2008, BACCHUS launched its *Building Bridges* campaign designed to let students know "what a difference a friend makes." This mental health campaign distributed nationwide includes a program manual and a number of awareness tools to encourage students to help each other through emotional difficulties.

Educational Programs and Suicide Prevention

Mental Health Awareness and Suicide Prevention programs should occur all year long and be integrated into the overall suicide prevention strategy. Making programs timely is helpful in garnering interest. Use the following list of timely issues to jumpstart planning for programs on campus:

Fall

- First week of school – social anxiety
- Greek Life rush activities
- Awareness Events
  National Suicide Prevention Week
  National Mental Illness Awareness Week

National Collegiate Alcohol Awareness Week – alcohol and self-medication
World Mental Health Day
National Depression Screening Day
Great American Smokeout – relationship between smoking and suicide

Winter

- Programming focusing on holidays and dealing with grief and loss
- Stress reduction programs preceding midterms and finals
- Awareness Events
  Holiday Healing Candlelight Ceremony (for those bereaved by suicide)
  Sexual Responsibility Week – Post-traumatic Stress Disorder
  National Eating Disorders Awareness Week

Spring

- Stress reduction programming preceding finals and graduation
- Awareness Events
  Alcohol Awareness Month
  Counseling Awareness Month
  National Alcohol Screening Day
  National Mental Health Month
  Anxiety Disorders Screening Day

Summer

- New student orientation – homesickness, adjustment issues, importance of staying on medication and establishing support systems at school
- Residence Life staff training – suicide prevention gatekeeper training

---

Mental Health Movie Nights: Spark a Dialogue

Movie nights are an excellent way to help students deconstruct issues related to mental health and suicide. Some great films for discussion include:

The American Foundation of Suicide Prevention published an excellent resource for ready-made campus programming entitled *The Truth about Suicide: Real Stories of Depression in College*. The goal of this 27-minute film and its accompanying facilitator's guide is to present a recognizable picture of depression and other problems associated with suicide, as they are commonly experienced by college students and other young adults.

Social Marketing

Definition of Social Marketing: (noun) the application of marketing techniques that change behaviors with the ultimate goal of contributing to a social good.

Social marketing blends the social sciences with business marketing techniques. Social marketing strategies are essentially the same marketing principles that are used to sell products to consumers, but instead are used "sell" ideas, attitudes, and behaviors. Social marketing seeks to influence social behaviors that do not benefit the marketer, but rather benefit the target audience and the larger society. The "product" might be an idea ("It's okay to ask for help.") or a service (mental health screening). The "price" relates to what the participant must give up in order to get the product – time, effort, embarrassment, and or fear of rejection. When the costs outweigh the benefits, the experienced value of the offering is low, and most likely, the "product" will not be adopted. By contrast, when the benefits outweigh the costs, the likelihood of a trial adoption of the product increases.

> Education and awareness are necessary but not sufficient strategies for changing behavior. Social marketing uses psychological tools to increase motivation to change.

When using a social marketing strategy for suicide prevention, campuses must consider what idea, attitude, or behavior they trying to alter: one that normalizes mental disorders, one that encourages helping friends through tough times, one that promotes the suicide prevention lifeline, or one that refers students to the on-campus counseling center. Messages in a social marketing campaign need to be simple, repeated, and memorable. One of the most successful campaigns in this regard is the one mentioned at the opening of the chapter: "Don't Erase Your Future."

Life Skills and Social Network Promotion

Suicide prevention is about reducing risk factors: debilitating mental illness, isolation, access to lethal means, substance abuse, etc. But campuses cannot stop there. Suicide prevention is also about mental health promotion. Colleges and universities will function best when we have mentally resilient people. In other words, we need to find ways to boost psychological hardiness in a world that seems increasingly confusing and isolating.

> *Definition of resiliency:*
> re·sil·ien·cy (rI%-zI%l'y@n-se$): the ability to recover from (or to resist being affected by) some shock, insult, or disturbance or a self-righting tendency.

Resiliency is evident when there are: (1) positive performance regardless of high-risk status, (2) constant competence under stress, and (3) recovery from trauma.[325]

Student Life offices have often been forerunners in developing community and offering programs on personal development. By focusing two major strategies, campuses can optimize resiliency:

1. *Increase Positive Coping Strategies*
Our students are reporting increasing amounts of stress every year and need tools to handle time management, stress management and conflict.

2. *Increase Social Integration*

Social integration research tells us that Americans are losing confidants at an alarming rate. That is, on average people have fewer close relationships they can turn to when they have a problem. In the 1980s most people had at least three confidants; now the modal number is one.[326] Campuses looking to bolster resiliency might consider how to better foster a sense of belonging and reduce isolation, especially in the high tech age when the number of friends you have on facebook counts more than how close you are to each of them.

Suicide Prevention Gatekeeper Training

The Surgeon General's National Strategy for Suicide Prevention[327] defines a suicide prevention gatekeeper as anyone who is in a position to intercept information about another person's suicidal ideation or intent, identify these intentions, and refer someone to a mental health professional. For example, a Resident Advisor, college faculty member, or most likely a peer could be a potential gatekeeper for a suicidal college student. Studies have shown that 25 percent to 40 percent of male youths and 40 percent to 60 percent of female youths know someone who has attempted suicide; however, only approximately 25 percent of this age group actually tells an adult about their suicidal peer and hardly any have received any formal training in suicide prevention.[328]

Some mental health professionals may recoil at the idea of training lay people, especially youth, the basics of such a complicated clinical skill as suicide prevention, and they should be reassured that gatekeeper training only provides the essential skills to identify when a person may be at risk and know how to refer that person to a professional for appropriate care. In other words, suicide prevention gatekeeper training is like CPR for a mental health crisis: the training provides individuals with the skills to identify warning signs and to sustain the lives long enough to link people to the help they need.

There are many models for gatekeeper training. The Suicide Prevention Resource Center has created a matrix of the possibilities to help organizations choose which program best fits their needs.[329] One of the most common models for gatekeeper training on campus is the "QPR" – or Question, Persuade, Refer model. The QPR Institute offers programs to institutions who want to increase their care-giving efforts and reduce mortality by suicide in their organizations. The QPR Institute was established after Spokane Mental Health (in Spokane, Washington) and Paul Quinnett, Ph.D., QPR Institute Founder and CEO, launched a national suicide prevention training program in July of 1999. Training recipients learn three steps to help prevent a suicide. Similar to Cardiopulmonary Resuscitation (CPR), QPR is a three-step life-saving technique. It trains people to recognize the warning signs of a crisis and how to "question, persuade, and refer someone to help." People can become Certified QPR Gatekeeper Instructors through a self-study course; locate a Certified Instructor in their area to train themselves or groups of friends, families, coworkers, or community members; or learn QPR through the *QPR Online Gatekeeper Training*. Although QPR is not specifically geared towards the college students, it has a general usability for any population.

Other models of suicide prevention gatekeeper training are two programs provided by Living Works Education (ASIST and SafeTalk) and the Yellow Ribbon program.

Goals and Objectives of Suicide Prevention Gatekeeper Training:

1. Bolster knowledge surrounding suicide and mental health
2. Address obstacles (prejudice and discrimination) to help-seeking

3. Give practical skills for what to do when someone is suicidal (Question, Persuade, Refer)
4. Offer people a safe place to discuss mental health crisis and suicide

Target Audience:

Students, staff, and faculty

Program Format:

The trainings are a combination of lecture, video, discussion, and role play.

Training components include the following:

- Mental health and suicide stats related to the general public and campus-specific information
- Suicide facts
- How to ask "The Question" (what to say & not to say)
- How to persuade someone to stay alive and get help
- How to refer and who to refer to for help

Screening

Like most public health problems, the prognosis for mental disorders is best when they are detected early in their course of development and subsequently treated appropriately. Unfortunately, sometimes mental illness festers because people are too ashamed to admit they need help. During this time, the illness can become catastrophic, like a metastasized cancer. Treating a highly suicidal individual is much more invasive and complicated than treating someone early on in the development of the problem. Thus, just like breast and testicular cancer, frequent and regular screening can help catch problems early.

Campuses can develop their own online screening tool by partnering with Mental Health Screening: *http://www.mentalhealth-screening.org* or the Jed Foundation's ULifeline *http://www.ulifeline.org.*

Campuses can also increase awareness by participating in the national screening days:

National Depression Screening Day (October)
National Alcohol Screening Day (April)
National Anxiety Disorders Screening Day (May)

Mental Health Services and Resources

Mental Health Services for suicidal people often include some combination of medication and therapy aimed at changing the underlying causes of suicidal thinking. Experts estimate that 90 percent of people who die by suicide have some form of a diagnosable mental disorder. Mental disorders such as depression and substance abuse are highly treatable, and yet are often the most common forms of mental disorders found in suicidal people.

Suicide Risk Assessment

Only professional mental health service providers trained in the area of suicide prevention should attempt the process of assessing suicide risk. Because completed suicide has such a low base rate, it is not possible to predict suicide with any accuracy. The goal of a suicide assessment is not to predict suicide, but rather to place a person along a risk continuum and note changes as a person moves up or down that continuum to allow for a more informed intervention.

Figure 12.3 outlines the standards for assessment of suicide risk used by crisis call centers in the network of the National Suicide Prevention Lifeline. The four columns represent four areas of assessment: suicidal desire, capacity, intent and protective factors.

Suicidal Desire

- Suicidal ideation – killing self and/or others, fantasies, imaginal rehearsal, habituation

Suicidal Desire	Suicidal Capability	Suicidal Intent	Buffers & Connectedness
Suicidal Ideation	History of suicide attempts	Attempt in progress	Immediate supports
Psychological Pain	Exposure to someone else's death by suicide		Social supports
Hopelessness	History of/current violence to others	Plan to kill self/other	Planning for the future
Helplessness	Available means of killing self/other		Engagement with helper
Perceived burden on others	Currently intoxicated	Preparatory behaviors	Ambivalence for living/dying
	Substance abuse		Sense of purpose
Feeling trapped			
	Acute symptoms of mental illness	Expressed intent to die	Core values/beliefs
Feeling intolerably alone	Extreme agitation/rage		

Figure 12.3. Suicide Risk Assessment Standards.[330]

- Psychache/feeling trapped – extreme distress diminishes ability to problem solve
- Burdensomeness – "my death is worth more than my life"
- Feeling alone – thwarted belongingness
- Hopelessness

A prospective study of 1,958 outpatients found that hopelessness, as measured by the Beck Hopelessness Scale, was significantly related to eventual suicide. A scale cutoff score of nine or above correctly identified 94.2 percent of the people who eventually died by suicide, thus replicating a previous study with hospitalized patients. Researchers determined that the high-risk group identified by this cutoff score was 11 times more likely to die by suicide than those whose cutoff score was lower, and

thus, the Beck Hopelessness Scale appears to be a sensitive indicator of suicide potential.

> Desire for suicide alone is a necessary but not sufficient condition for suicide risk.

Suicidal Capability

- History of suicide attempt, particularly multiple suicide attempts, increases the risk for suicide significantly. These behaviors represent that the individual has a certain fearlessness when facing death and that self-harm is a primary way of coping.
- History of/current violence to others may indicate that he or she is capable of self-inflicted violence and comfortable with violence means.

- Exposure to/impacted by someone else's death by suicide. Grief and trauma caused by another's suicide might make a person more vulnerable. Sometimes when someone close dies by suicide, a person may consider suicide because of the contagion effect (copycat). Others will not have considered suicide before their loved one died and because of this experience, this option has entered their consciousness.
- Availability of and familiarity to lethal means.
- Current intoxication.
- Tendency toward frequent intoxication.
- Acute symptoms of mental illness – agitation, insomnia, recent dramatic mood change; command hallucinations (hearing a voice telling one to kill oneself); extreme rage.

Suicidal Intent

Aaron Beck investigated the validity and reliability of the Suicidal Intent Scale as a measure of the seriousness of a suicide attempt. All of the 194 people who had died by suicide had higher scores on the scale than the 231 people who had a suicide attempt. In addition, 19 people who attempted suicide and then reattempted suicide within one year of discharge had greater suicidal intent than attempters who did not.[331]

- Plan– to hurt self or others
- Expressed intent to die – ambivalence
- Some studies have documented a low association between intent and lethality of method

Buffers/Connectedness

- Perceived immediate supports (can the person list five people to call, who can help the person remove the lethal means? Who will take the person to the ER?)
- Planning for future – long-term and short-term

- Engagement with helper – openness and disclosure; clinicians sense of collaborative connection
- Ambivalence
- Religion/spirituality
- Children

Suicide Assessment Scales

"Suicide assessment scales may be used as aids to suicide assessment but should not be used as predictive instruments or as substitutes for a thorough clinical evaluation."[332] Several assessment tools have been developed to help clinicians assess suicidal risk with their clients. These tools should always be used in conjunction with a comprehensive clinical interview and collateral data. It is beyond the scope of this book to cover all of these issues; however, the assessment tools with the best predictive validity include:[333]

- Scale for Suicide Ideation (Beck)
- Suicide Intent Scale (Beck)
- Hamilton Rating Scale for Depression (Suicide Item)
- Beck Hopelessness Scale
- Beck Depression Inventory (Suicide Item)

Suicide Intervention

A number of therapeutic interventions for suicide have been supported in clinical research trials and are listed here as promising practices for suicide intervention.

Cognitive-Behavioral Therapy (CBT)

Cognitive-Behavioral Therapy is a structured, time limited, directive and change-oriented form of psychotherapy that emphasizes the important role of thoughts and assumptions in guiding how we feel and what we do. According to a 2005 randomized controlled trial by The University of Pennsylvania Center for the Treatment and Prevention of

Suicide (Gregory Brown, Aaron Beck, et al.), cognitive therapy can reduce repeat suicide attempts by 50 percent. This form of therapy focuses on cognitively mediated processes such as hopelessness and reducing impulsivity. In a study published in a 2005 issue of the *Journal of the American Medical Association*, these researchers reported that the CBT group had a significantly lower reattempt rate, diminished severity of self-reported depression on the Beck Depression Inventory II, and less self-reported hopelessness on the Beck Hopelessness.[334]

Dialectical Behavioral Therapy (DBT)

Dialectical behavioral therapy is a form of psychotherapy developed by Marsha Linehan to treat people with borderline personality disorder; however, it is used for people with other diagnoses as well. DBT attempts to balance change/problem solving with acceptance/validation and attempts to move those with suicidal ideation out of an either-or to a both-and framework. An NIMH funded study found that DBT reduced suicide attempts by half compared with other types of psychotherapy among people with borderline personality disorder.[335] Personality disorders are estimated to be present in more than 30 percent of individuals who die by suicide, and 60–70 percent of patients with borderline personality disorder make suicide attempts.

Lithium Treatment

A 2003 study published in the Journal of Clinical Psychiatry concluded that, "major reductions of suicidal risks (attempts > suicides) with lithium maintenance therapy in unipolar ≥ bipolar II ≥ bipolar I disorder, to overall levels close to general population rates."[336] In other words, lithium appears to have a specific antisuicide effect for people with mood disorders.

Clozapine Treatment

Approximately 50 percent of people with schizophrenia or schizoaffective disorder attempt suicide, and approximately 10 percent die of suicide.[337] A 2003 study results suggest that clozapine therapy significantly reduces suicidal behavior in these patients.

Crisis Management, Policy, and Means Restriction

In establishing a network of mental health awareness and support, campus professionals must first understand policies that influence these issues. The following are a list of questions that are important to review as a campus or coalition.

- Does the campus have a policy surrounding procedures for identifying students who may require mental health services?
- What are the responsibilities of campus personnel who may refer students for mental health services?
- What are the responsibilities of campus personnel surrounding follow-up with students who have been referred for mental health services?
- Does the campus currently have a policy in place to ensure the health and safety of an individual student as well as the overall health of the classroom? For example, what protocol is in place if a professor receives a student assignment that indicates a student is at risk for suicide or violence?
- What legal issues may influence the student and campus? For example, does the campus currently have a policy surrounding providing medical leave for students needing mental health treatment? Can the university require that a student receive treatment and what legal issues are present?

- How do current policies take into account the Americans with Disabilities Act?
- What is the campus policy on involving a student's family and how does this impact confidentiality?
- Is there a policy in place that addresses academic issues such as allowing for make-up exams for students experiencing a significant mental health crisis?
- Does the campus currently have an anti-discrimination policy detailed in the student Code of Conduct? What is this policy and how does it take into account the complexity of disciplinary issues?

For more information on legal and policy issues, please review the article "The Emerging Crisis of College Student Suicide: Law and Policy Responses to Serious Forms of Self-Inflicted Injury" by Peter Lake and Nancy Tribbensee (2002). A summary of this article is located in the Helpful Reports on Campus Mental Health section of this manual.

All policies should be reviewed by the University Legal Council prior to being implemented.

Emergency Response

In creating a campus environment of mental health awareness, it is necessary to review current emergency response procedures. As a coalition or campus community, these policies should be frequently revisited to ensure the health and safety of all students and campus personnel. In examining your campus emergency response procedures, be sure to address the following questions.

- What are the current policies in place for the identification and referral of students who are at risk for self-harm?
- What steps should be taken if a student attempts or completes suicide in a residence hall?
- What immediate support services are available for fellow residents and/or

students impacted by the suicide attempt or completion of a peer?
- What current policies are in place to address a threat or act of violence on campus? How will information be released, what is the chain of communication, and what areas of campus may be closed?
- If violence is threatened or takes place on campus, what support services will be made for students to help ensure their mental health?
- If an event of local, state, national, or global significance occurs and directly impacts the mental health of students, what services will be made available?

Means Restriction Matters

Limiting access to lethal means of self-harm can be an effective strategy for suicide prevention. Sometimes suicidal behaviors are impulsive and by making access to means more difficult, campuses can give people more time and space between a suicidal crisis and an irrevocable decision. One study asked people who survived nearly-lethal suicide attempts: "How much time passed between the time you decided to contemplate suicide and when you actually attempted suicide?" 24 percent said less than five minutes.[338] If campuses can get people through their suicidal crisis by preventing them access to lethal means, the chance of recover is great: 90 percent of survivors of near-lethal suicide attempts do not end up completing suicide.[339]

In the general population, firearms are the common method of suicide completions in the United States, followed by suffocation, poisoning, and falls. Several studies have indicated that having a firearm in the home significantly increases the risk of completed suicide, and stricter gun control laws have been followed by a decrease both in homicide and suicide.[340] The suicide rate may be lower for college students because campuses prohibit firearms.

SUICIDE POSTVENTION

Definition: Suicide Postvention

The American Association of Suicide Prevention defines suicide postvention as the "provision of crisis intervention, support and assistance for those affected by a completed suicide."

Traumatic Grief – The Initial Impact

There are many *symptoms of trauma* that suicide survivors often experience in the immediate aftermath of a loved one's suicide:

1. Shattered sense of order and trust
2. Increased feelings of vulnerability
3. Difficulty sleeping and eating
4. Disorientation – feeling like you are in a fog
5. Flashbacks or intrusive recollections of the trauma
6. Nightmares
7. Uncontrollable crying or intense anger
8. Feeling numb
9. Denial and disbelief

SUPPORT FOR SURVIVORS OF SUICIDE

Survivors of another's suicide often fall into one of three clusters:

1. *Quick Recovery*

Those who recover quickly without assistance and can return to functioning as before. Some of these people are not impacted because they had only superficial contact with the deceased, while others are often internalizing and suppressing pain, anger, or guilt. Oftentimes, in the latter case, maladaptive strategies of coping emerge such as substance abuse or work-a-holism.

2. *Modest Support Needed*

Most people who were functioning well before the suicide need only a modest level of support for a period of time that might span a month to a couple of years. This level of support might include outpatient therapy or support groups.

A Word on Language: Like most sensitive issues, language matters when discussing issues of suicide. The term "successful (or unsuccessful) suicide" is considered a poor choice because they connote something positive with a tragic outcome. Similarly, the phrase "committed suicide" is frowned upon because it referred back to an era when suicide was considered a sin or a crime. Lastly, the idea of choice or free will is often discouraged when talking about suicide because thinking is often very impaired that they would not be considered competent to make a rational choice. The following phases are recommended alternatives:

- Died by suicide
- Took his/her own life
- Completed suicide
- Died by his/her own hand
- Suicided (using suicide as a verb)

A person dying of suicide, dies as does the victim of physical illness or accident, against his or her will. People die from physical heart attacks, strokes, cancer, AIDS, and accidents. Death by suicide is the same, except that we are dealing with an emotional heart attack, an emotional stroke, emotional AIDS, emotional cancer and an emotional fatality.

– Rev. Ron Rolheiser (1998)

3. Psychiatric Disability

Some people may develop a mental disorder in reaction to the trauma and loss and may require extended or intensive treatment.

Support from other suicide survivors is one of the most powerful connections one can make in the aftermath of a suicide. Many people find great relief in being able to talk openly and honestly about the range of complicated experiences they are going through with people who really understand. Survivor support groups offer a safe haven to share and build new healing relationships. Some survivors go weekly; others go when they need it most – around birthdays, anniversaries, and other difficult times.

THE GOALS OF SUICIDE POSTVENTION

Why Should We Consider Postvention on Campus?

The true essence of leadership and the real character of a campus are often revealed when faced with adversity. When a campus's coping skills have been overwhelmed by a critical incident, such as a suicide, an effective well-organized response can restore a campus to a state of well-being and bolster a sense of trust that fosters resiliency against future dark times.

> "Faced with a crisis, the man of character falls back upon himself."
> – Charles De Gaulle

Goals

1. **To stabilize the campus community and help people at all levels of the organization (and related family/community) cope with the trauma and grief.**

The emotion pain and disruption of suicide is significant in any system. Suicide survivorship if not supported well, may lead to other psychological conditions such as depression, posttraumatic stress disorder, anxiety, and substance abuse. The initial hours and days following a suicide can make a big difference for survivors and their subsequent emotional healing; however, longer-term support may also be needed.

2. **To prevent further suicides.**

Suicide contagion, or the copycat effects of suicide, are often seen in younger high-risk adolescents, but can also happen among vulnerable adults. Postvention practices work toward minimizing the factors that might make copycat suicide more likely.

3. **To help the campus return to normalcy and the pursuit of its mission.**

Rumors, second guessing, and blame can create critical rifts in the campus family; thus, containment is needed to help reassure people and give them appropriate means to express their feelings. A balance is often needed between providing support for those who need it and letting people get back to their regular lives. For most, after an initial expression of grief, a campus may be able to return to a normal routine more quickly than for campuses that are denied an opportunity to express openly.

Special Issues

Contagion

The contagion effect (otherwise known as the copycat effect) of suicide is real. Several studies have documented cases of suicide clusters that have been partially explained by imitative behavior. Contagion is defined as suicidal behavior by additional people that is influenced by a previous attempt or completion. The contagion effect is more common in younger people who are more prone to impulsive behavior. Contagion behavior, while rare, is a central concern in suicide postvention work; many strategies are cognizant of trying to reduce identification with the victim and discourage modeling of suicide behavior. Practices that help prevent the contagion effect are:

- Providing appropriate and accurate information about suicide
- Avoiding glamorizing or romanticizing suicide
- Avoiding idealizing the person who died by suicide or by offering simple explanations for the death.

Cultural Issues

Because cultures vary in their beliefs about and levels of acceptance regarding suicide, those directing suicide postvention must possess a degree of cultural competence and sensitivity. Some cultures believe that suicide might be permissible under some circumstances (e.g., in instances when honor is at stake or at the end of life when the pain of living is intolerable). Other cultures may regard it as a sin or even as a crime. Some cultures may be very open in the grieving process, while others cultures might need more privacy. For cultures that have strict moral sanctions against suicide, bereaved families may feel isolated in their grieving process; however, with these strong values against suicide comes a diminished risk for the contagion effect. On the other hand, cultures that are less stigmatizing of suicide may provide more comfort for a bereaved family, but may also communicate permissiveness that increases the risk for the contagion effect. If in doubt about the best way to bridge cultural differences, consult with someone more familiar with the culture to help guide you through the most appropriate aftermath process.

Suicide on Campus

In the aftermath of a suicide on campus, special care must be taken to assess the impact on friends, witnesses, responders (especially public safety professionals internal to the organization who might know the deceased), and campus stakeholders (those who need to respond to the campus and community at large). As the organization becomes the first to know in a situation such as this, an appropriately appointed person should notify family members in a timely way. Clean up of the death scene should be handled by an external organization with extreme sensitivity to those who knew the deceased and without the expectation that it will appear as "nothing ever happened."

At the same time, memorializing the death site should be avoided. One campus decided that the room where a student hung himself was not suitable as a living space, so they turned it into a library. Several years later when the collective memory of the student body in new again, students wonder why there is a library in the residence halls and the story of the suicide resurfaces in an inappropriate way, when it could have subsided with the passage of time. Likewise, the planting of trees or any permanent markers of suicide may be misinterpreted as glorifying the act and thus could encourage a vulnerable student to make a similar decision to be thus remembered.

Homicide-Suicide

This type of campus tragedy is explored more fully in other sections of this book, nevertheless, people often forget that these horrific crimes were caused by a suicidal avenger who may not have taken others' lives if he did not feel he had anything to lose himself. Emotional distress under these circumstances is often contagious and self-amplifying. For these reasons, rapid and honest campus-wide communication is needed to discourage damaging rumors.

CONCLUSION

In summary, suicide is a public health issue that is impacting our campuses. Fortunately, there are evidence-based models of prevention, intervention, and post-vention for campuses to adapt. With the availability of the Garrett Lee Smith Suicide Prevention Grants offered by the Substance Abuse and Mental Health Services Administration of the federal government, we shall continue to see emerging best practices over the next decade. The important paradigm shift that has developed in the last few years is that campuses have come to realize that everyone can play a role in suicide prevention, and that together we can build a strong safety net to help those suffering through the long dark night of the soul see the light of a new day.

Chapter 13

HATE CRIMES AND LESSER FORMS OF HATEFUL VIOLENCE

CHRISTOPHER BOLLINGER & KYLE WYCH

SEPTEMBER MORNINGS in northwest Ohio were always a little brisk. She was walking to school the same way she did every other day. Today was not any other day though. September 11th was the anniversary of the attacks on the World Trade Center. Today would be a day of remembering and mourning. When the attacks had happened, she was devastated by the tragic loss of so many lives. So many people were drawn to each other on some deeper level that terrible day. She, too, reached out to the people around her but found their responses ambiguous, if not cold. She was raised in the United States all of her life, but she looked as though she could be from the Middle East. Each anniversary of the event met her with a similarly cool response from those around her. As she walked, a small group of white men came up on her. She feared for her life as they began circling her, shouting racial slurs and spitting on her. She didn't know any of her attackers, and there was nothing distinctive about them. She didn't know who she could trust. She may still not know (Report made to author).

It had been a long day, already, in the second week of school. He was having a difficult time fitting in with the other men on his floor. Although, he tried to get to know people, he was concerned they may not understand him. He had good reason to be concerned.

In high school, he knew a guy who was jumped and beaten for acting too feminine. He was on his way back to his room to drop off his books when saw it. Someone had written "Die Faggot Die!" on his door. How did they know? He had been so careful. He wasn't sure what to do or whom to trust. It could be any or all of the people whom he lived with. He would live the rest of his semester worried that someone was going to hurt him, a fear justified by frequent abuse enacted against people who are not heterosexual (Report made to author).

At Penn State, several black, Asian, and Latino students received an e-mail message directed at black students. The author described minorities as "savages." The message also stated, "Every time you scan your ID to the dorm, every time you eat on campus, and every time you log into your computer – we are watching." The message was signed, "Long Live Amerikka."[341]

He walked into work already frustrated by an earlier class discussion about racism. Growing up a black man in the United States, he had no question that racism existed. He began sharing his frustrations with one of his colleagues when another student worker, a young white man, interrupted the conversation, "I don't know what your complaining about; we paid for your boat ride over here."[342]

He grew up in Kenya and had been in the United States for only a few months. He was one of the top students in his major and was quickly accepted into the graduate program. When he first arrived, students told him not to be surprised if he was pulled over for "driving while black." He did not believe this really happened. He was driving home after an evening shift at work one night when it happened. The state trooper pulled him over, told him to exit the car, searched him, and then released him. The officer gave no reason for pulling him over. Later when recounting this story, he was visibly hurt as he stated, "I can't change the fact that I am black."[343]

He walked around the college fair excited and a little nervous. He was a young Hispanic male from an upper middle class background. As he approached the recruiter representing a school he liked, the recruiter greeted him by saying, "We have a GPA requirement here." Startled by the abrupt greeting he said, "I have a 3.7," and walked away feeling a little smaller (Report made to author).

These varied accounts of hateful violence affecting our college students were all true and unfortunately not so uncommon. While only some of them would be classified as hate crimes, all of them should be understood as violent and hateful. In this chapter, we will provide a model for understanding how hate is produced and practiced in our communities and how we can work toward better preventing, intervening, and responding to hateful violence.

CONCEPTUALIZING HATE

The FBI identifies hate crimes as crimes that were motivated in whole or in part by a "bias against a particular race, religion, sexual orientation, ethnicity/national origin, or physical or mental disability."[344] According to the 2006 Hate Crimes Statistics report, 7,722 incidents involving 9,080 hate crime

offenses were reported to the FBI. While this collection of data is extremely helpful in providing us with some sense of the magnitude and scope of criminal hate in our country, it provides us with a very limited picture of how hate is understood and practiced on our college campuses. Hate crimes, by definition, are criminal activities that are committed with bias against race, religion, sexual orientation, ethnicity, or disabilities. Not all hateful violence is legally deemed criminal.

Hate is often misunderstood as only a heightened emotional state in which one engages in an extreme act of violence. Understanding hate this way gives us a false sense of containment and allows us to think of it as unrelated to our daily practices. In these moments, we believe that hateful violence is a rare and uncommon action. While the most extreme violent actions, such as beating, torturing, and murdering people, are less common, the less physically violent actions, such as racist comments and homophobic jokes occur with far greater frequency. While people acting in the most violent ways are often in a more enraged state, in most cases they did not simply snap into that state. They progressed to that state through an ongoing practice of prejudicial learning.

To better grasp how to prevent and respond to hateful violence, we need to consider a more complex and nuanced understanding of how hate works. Hate might be understood as an embodied experience, fleeting or continuing, of varying emotional/physical magnitude, in which one person or group of people is/are discomforted or anxious about the existence or presence of another person or group who is/are culturally recognizable as different from them. This difference is usually understood in terms of race, socioeconomic class, gender, sexual orientation, religion, or (physical or mental) ability. We borrow the term "embodied" from feminist literature to recognize that cognition (thought), affect (emotion), and physical experience are inextricably tied together. As we work toward our better understanding, we will first consider what drives perpetrators within our sociocultural contexts.

Motivation

Multiple scholars have found that perpetrators often indicate they were acting in self-defense of some perceived threat. In her study, *Psychosocial Motivations of Hate Crime Perpetrators: Implications for Prevention and Policy*, social psychologist Karen Franklin found that participants acted because they perceived that a person of a different sexual orientation made a pass at them. Imagine a world in which a woman attacked every man she believed made a pass at her and made her uncomfortable. The participants have embraced the homophobic idea that a simple social interaction with a person of a different sexual orientation will harm them, or at least their reputation. This fear is rooted in the erroneous ideological belief that homosexuality not only is morally wrong, but also endangers the values and lives of heterosexual people. They see the interaction with a person of a sexual orientation different from their own as a threat to their way of being, to their ideology – a set of cultural values and understandings of how the world is and/or ought to be. Franklin also found that participants believed they had a moral obligation to dole out justice for their wrong behavior. In these cases, their ideology justified them to punish others who possessed an ideology different from their own. Ideologies are produced, practiced, and perpetuated within sociocultural fields. Later in this chapter, we will provide a deeper explanation of the ways in which ideologies are formed.

In their book *Hate Crimes Revisited: America's War on Those Who Are Different*, sociologists Jack Levin and Jack McDevitt also found that people were motivated by perceived threats. Whereas Franklin delved into perceived ideology threats,[345] Levin and McDevitt also discussed **perceived physical and socioeconomic threats**.[346,347] Perceived physical threats might include erroneous beliefs such as "Black men are violent criminals who will hurt me" or "Muslims are terrorists who want to kill me." Perceived socioeconomic threats might include erroneous beliefs that unqualified Mexicans are trying to take away white people's jobs. These fears, while invalid, are grounded in sociocultural ideology.

Another motivation commonly found is **thrill-seeking**. In Franklin's study, participants thought engaging in the act would provide some excitement. Interestingly, participants did not go and find a straight person to beat up for fun. They didn't go cliff diving. They chose to harm a person different from them. Where they channeled their need for excitement is also socioculturally entrenched. We need to consider why they chose to act on the need for a thrill in this way. While thrill-seeking has been an identified category within the research, we will focus our attention in this area on the ideologies that suggest these violent acts are accessible and/or acceptable forms of fun.

Both Franklin's and Levin and McDevitt's studies addressed **perceived needs for inclusion in and support from a valued group** as a motivation for hateful violence. In Franklin's study, participants indicated their desire to prove themselves to their peer group. Picking on someone your group sees as different to gain favor with your group is not a new or surprising phenomenon. Levin and McDevitt focused more on the influence of organized hate groups. Though different in magnitude and perhaps focus, the peer groups and organized groups identified in these studies provide a sense of belonging, safety, and fear of retribution if crossed. They also usually provide ongoing education that is prejudicial and unchecked.

To summarize our discussion so far, we have discussed the following types of situations that motivate people to be hateful: (1) Perceiving a person or a group as an **ideological threat** (e.g., Gay people are trying to turn straight people gay and ruin moral heterosexual families). (2) Perceiving a person or a group as a **physical threat** (e.g., Muslims are terrorists who will attack me, black men are criminals who want to hurt me). (3) Perceiving a person or a group as a **socioeconomic threat** (e.g., Mexicans and women are taking the jobs from more qualified white men; students of color are taking my scholarship money). (4) Perceiving a **need to marginalize a person or group different from you to gain acceptance and support from a valued group** (e.g., suggesting a woman got promoted by sleeping her way to the top to get a laugh from your male buddies).

Different prevention strategies might be employed to help neutralize different types of threats. For example, in cases where people perceive physical threats, learning that Muslims don't want to kill them may be enough to reduce the vulnerability. Similarly, in cases where people perceive socioeconomic threats, learning to question why women on average are paid less for similar work done by men or why people automatically assume that a minority who has been hired for a job was unqualified in relation to their white counterparts may be enough to reduce this vulnerability. In many cases though, multiple motivations are interacting, and one of those motivations is frequently perceived ideology threat. When dealing with people who are motivated by perceived ideology threat, traditional teaching methods of disseminating information fail because people perceive this as proof of the threat. For example, just telling people that racism exists is perceived as the Race agenda at work. Yet racism does exist, as do ethnocentrism, heterosexism, ableism, sexism, and classism, and people need to become aware of them in order to work against them.

So how do we deal with multiple motivations that usually include a perceived ideology

threat? This is complicated. Culture is understood as the framework that helps one know how they ought to be in a given community. Culture is closely linked with ideology, a set of ideas and values that helps you make sense of the world. For example, your ideology helps you understand what is right, wrong, nice, mean, or relatively unimportant. As a diverse culture, different groups work from different ideologies. Our family traditions on holidays are shaped by our ideologies – what we celebrate, how we celebrate it, what roles we play, what traditions we enact, what meaning they have for us, etc. Ideologies are not necessarily bad. In fact, we all have them, and our larger culture is full of competing ideologies. Typically, the ideology that holds strongest in our larger culture is often thought of as the dominant ideology. An ideology becomes dangerous when it is exclusive to other people's humanity. When an ideology marks the value of another person's existence as inferior or less human and justifies treating the other person as inferior or less human, then it becomes dangerous.

For reducing our vulnerability to multiple motivations, we recommend working toward shifting cultural values away from values that justify hateful violence toward a group of people for simply existing and engaging in their cultural beliefs and practices. Should we follow this recommendation, the fear some perpetrators possess of having their ideology altered is a justifiable fear. To be clear, our intention is not to convert everyone to our ideology, but rather to move them away from those that value a group of people as less than human and justify hateful violence against that particular group of people for existing as human beings.[348] Traditional educational methods of disseminating information (e.g. telling students they should change their values) will likely be perceived as proof of ideological threat and draw out greater resistance. Prevention will require conceiving our educational efforts differently. We suggest two tactics. First, proceed incrementally rather than through immersion. Second, address the issues by presenting critical questions to real life situations. In order to develop strategies that can accomplish these tasks, we need to understand the cultural conditions in place that lead to hateful ideologies.

CULTURE AND IDEOLOGY

So how does such an exclusive and violent ideology come into existence? As human beings, we categorize information and store it away for future use. Even though we are constantly engaging new and different situations, we make use of these categories a great deal. On the one hand, categorizing is very helpful. We wouldn't want to have to rediscover what a cup is and how to use it everyday. On the other hand, when we get away with using negative stereotypes to understand our world and the people around us, categorizing is deeply problematic. We formulate our understanding of what fits into which categories and the value of those categories through our communicative interaction. This interaction may be reading, intellectual discussion, sharing stories, playing games, surfing the net, wearing clothes, walking down the street, rolling your eyes, hitting a person – that is to say just about anything in which you make meaning.

We are constantly communicating meaning, and we are constantly negotiating who we are in relation to those around us. When this negotiation, in some way, takes the form of marking others within a particular group as having less human dignity and worth, then it is working toward an exclusive and violently imposed ideology. In our culture this is often achieved through the use of stereotypes. For example saying, "You throw like a girl," to a young boy who just threw the ball badly begins to form a harmful structure. First, the statement marks girl throwing as bad. Second, it situates the category of girl as

inferior to the category boy. In this way, the communicative interaction has just served to reinforce an ideology that privileges males over females. Of course, this comment being said once in all of history does not make an ideology. This comment, along with many other communicative interactions reinforcing the same hierarchy within a social group over a period of time, makes an ideology.

Let us dispense with a misperception before moving forward. There is a belief that all stereotypes began with at least one circumstance in which it was true. This belief is inaccurate. While some stereotypes began that way, many have been manufactured and publicized as having some truth. Every few years, some pseudo scholar puts out an unsubstantiated claim that white people have more natural intelligence than _____ (insert marginalized group here). When we track the scholars and follow the evidence, we find they are printed in some journal that is produced by a pro-white group and are supported by vague findings fraught with methodological and interpretive error. Let's consider the real way stereotypes and ideologies are formed.

Language

In his article *Political Discourse and Racism: Describing Others in Western Parliaments*, Van Dijk mapped out the ways in which "othering" occurs within political discourse. Othering is a term that comes out of research that focuses on how we come to know or understand ourselves in relation to an "other," someone outside of our self. The term has come to be used to describe when a member of one group communicates (verbally or nonverbally) in such a way as to position their group as superior to an "other" group.

According to Van Dijk,[349] **positive self-representation** occurs when one presents oneself positively in comparison to others. This would not be a problem if it were positively recognizing the contributions of many groups. However, this move positions the other by comparison as lacking the positive quality and permits the presenter to see his/her practices as beyond the challenges others may make. For example, "I deserve the job over her because I work really hard and have the qualifications." By comparison, the other is perceived as not working really hard or having the qualifications. **Negative other-presentation** occurs when one presents the other in a degrading or less favorable way directly. Frequently an anomalous occurrence is discussed as if it is the norm for all others who fit into the classification. As an RA of mine once said, "I wrote her up for being loud. Those people are just like that." All people in a group are now considered to be loud. More obvious examples would include things like, "She's a B___" or "Poor people are lazy." **Denial of racism** occurs when one denies their prejudices and then follows that denial with a prejudicial statement. The classic example is "I don't have anything against people of color, but..." Fill in the blank with a degrading stereotype. **Apparent sympathy** occurs when one supports a prejudicial practice by declaring they are doing it for the other's own good. Consider an admissions committee saying, "I want to help him out, but given where he is from, he is going to have too many barriers to overcome. Maybe he should go somewhere less demanding for a few years." **Top-down transfer** occurs when one blames their need to mistreat others on the constituents being served by them. For example, a school may blame their students or their donors for not being able to address issues of systemic oppression. **Justification: The force of facts** occurs when someone presents a litany of "good reasons," that may be questionable in the first place, as a series of facts requiring mistreatment of others. For example, "They are trouble. I lost my position on the team because of one of them. I didn't get a scholarship because of them. I didn't pass my algebra

test because they were loud in the hall the other night."

These strategies are deployed in such a way as to dehumanize the "other" and reinforce hate. Much like the ball throwing example provided earlier, these communication practices reinforce a hierarchical ideology by assigning positive values to the "self" and/or negative values to the "other." Now that we understand how some of these patterns work, we can work with our communities in recognizing, considering the effect of, and correcting these patterns in our communication.

Sharing Stories

Stories are another way in which hateful practices are reinforced and ideologies justifying violence are perpetuated. Levin and McDevitt[350] indicated that people who engage in hate often believe the target group has or will harm them physically, economically, morally, or otherwise. People are not born with fear targeted toward any particular group of people. We learn this fear. We sometimes learn through our own personal experiences of a situation. In the case of hate crimes against marginalized groups, we more frequently learn our fears through exposure to fictional stories told by members of our communities or by messages observed in our popular culture. False rumors spread within a community, intentionally or unintentionally, carry their own violence. As Levin and McDevitt have well demonstrated with account after account, when false rumors go undisputed they frequently increase and end in extreme violence enacted against the marginalized groups targeted in the rumors. In these cases, names not only do hurt you, but they also have a way of bringing out the sticks and stones that hurt you even worse.

Popular Culture

Popular culture has played an ominous role in creating resentment or fear. There are countless studies challenging portrayals which reinforce and justify racism, sexism, heterosexism, and classism. Television has helped to teach us everything from "no really means yes" and "women want a strong hand" to "be afraid of the big black man who the police are currently looking for in a neighborhood near you" and "Muslims are terrorists." In his book, *Culture of Fear*, sociologist Glassner demonstrates with statistical clarity that black men are shown to be perpetrators disproportionately higher and victims disproportionately lower in news media portrayals. In *Can't Buy My Love*, nationally recognized media analyst Kilbourne demonstrates in case after case how the $250 billion advertising industry sells a particular misogynistic and violent ideology of the relationship of men to women as it continues to sexualize women in subservient ways. One needs to look no further than the nearest beer commercial to find proof of her argument. In *White Lies: Race, Class, Gender and Sexuality in White Supremacist Discourse*, sociologist Daniels provides compelling evidence to the echoes of extremist rhetoric in the stereotypes perpetuated in mainstream communication. The media wasn't particularly helpful when it showed footage of Middle Eastern people in celebration following 9/11, which incidentally was footage taken prior to 9/11. America's youth thought all of the Middle East was jumping for joy at the tragedy. Unfortunately, given the way many of our students have been sheltered, popular culture may be the only experience they have had of people who appear to be different from them.

Academic Culture

As teachers and administrators, we sometimes fail to examine the messages we send in our courses or our programs. What authors are represented in our courses? Are they all white men? What kinds of examples do we use in our classroom conversations? Do we

sacrifice real dialogue about issues in favor of a quieter space? With what local groups do we establish connections? Are the programs we offer on our campus culturally diverse? What messages do we send in our residence hall programs? What messages are on the posters in our buildings? Whom do we hire as faculty, staff, or administrators? Where do we put our funding? As higher education professionals we are called to ask the question, "Just how diverse is our ivory tower?"

PREVENTING AND/OR WORKING AGAINST HATE

Through our communication, whether it is how we say something, the stereotypes we rely upon, the stories we share, the media and popular culture we consume, the academic culture we perpetuate, or the physical interactions we enact, we are constantly producing and practicing cultural ideologies. These ideologies guide how we understand ourselves, others, and the relationships among and between us. When these ideologies justify hateful violence against a group of people for simply existing as valued human beings, we are challenged to engage and alter our communication to formulate ideologies which do not.

As we mentioned earlier, reducing our vulnerabilities will require a multi-tiered effort. Formulating an understanding of what hate is and how it functions in all the facets of our institution is important. Such a formulation should take place through collaboration. We recommend creating a task force representative of multiple institutional and community constituencies, including a diverse selection of students, staff, faculty, and administration. The task force should develop a plan that addresses the following: Educating the community about what hate is and how it works; identifying the greatest vulnerabilities present in the community with respect to hate; developing appropriate policies in relation to recognizing and supporting diversity within the institution as well as policies in relation to identifying and responding to hate; creating short- and long-term prevention, intervention, and response strategies; and assessing the success of these strategies. Such a plan should consider the multiple arenas of interaction on campus: Residence halls, campus programs, academic courses, student groups, staff meetings, etc. We offer the following strategies as potential areas of consideration for the task force.

Becoming Critical Practitioners and Consumers of Communication

As hateful ideology is at the root of most motivations, we need to teach people how to be critical practitioners and consumers of our communication. When people engage in hate, they look for social support of their actions. By teaching people to become critical practitioners and consumers of our communication, they become equipped to recognize and choose which ideologies they wish to support and which they wish to work against. They can choose to socially stand against the hate and stand instead with those being marginalized. By standing with the targets of hate, people will develop more empathy. Equipping people to intervene in the more routine violence can help to deter the occurrence of more extreme violence. As more of society resists hateful violence and supports the humanity of the targets of that violence, there will be fewer opportunities for hate to thrive.

We need to teach people to ask questions about the messages they send through their communication choices. Do these messages represent some groups as less human than others? Do these messages create a hierarchy in which a group of people are considered subservient to another group? Do these messages unfairly privilege me over another group? These are difficult questions to ask

and even more difficult to answer. Creating a critical consciousness that is aware of the plight of others is necessary if we want to eliminate hate.

Group Engagements

In his book *The Nature of Prejudice*, Allport asserted that intergroup contact, in which *all four*[351] of the following conditions were met (1) both groups are given equal status, (2) the groups must have a common goal, (3) there must not be any competition between the groups, and (4) the interaction between the groups needs to be sanctioned by an authority, then prejudice between the two groups would decrease. This theory, more commonly known as the Contact Hypothesis, was published in 1954. While some concern has been raised that the model fails if the two groups behave in ways which reinforce the other groups' prejudices about them, Allport's theory, for the most part, has been shown to be successful in many studies since its origin.

In his books *The Jigsaw Classroom* and *Nobody Left to Hate*, noted psychologist Aronson builds on Allport's[352] understanding as he offers Jig Sawing as a method of education to reduce prejudice. In this method, students are put into groups with other students who are different from them. They are given a common objective to complete. Each group member is given information to which the other group members do not have access but will need to complete their objective. Giving each group member something the other members need gives help to promote a more equal status for the project. They have to rely on each other and work together to achieve the objective. If they want to do well, they need to learn how to communicate effectively with each other. To accomplish this, they begin to learn about each other's needs and to some degree how to accommodate those needs. The activity must be sanctioned by a recognized authority or they may choose to leave the situation when they become a little frustrated. This model has had success with reducing prejudice, developing empathy, and teaching collaboration.

Chosen Communal Grouping

Most schools have some form of communal grouping opportunities for their students where people can live or enjoy space with a particular group to which they belong, such as Black Student Union, GLBT house, Woman's Center, etc. Some authors have described this as voluntary separatism. While the groups are separate, many minority students join these groups so they can be understood on their own cultural terms instead of another group's. They choose the community for support and not necessarily to be separate. The effect of such choices, however, is still separate from the community mainstream and has been related to increased tension and hate on many campuses. Many of our campuses are predominately white in population as well as in curriculum. For minorities, this often serves as a constant barrage of assimilation. The ability to go some place where you and your culture are recognized as the norm can be very empowering. In the opinions of these authors, until we can grow the diversity on our campuses so we truly do have integration, the support benefits of these programs outweigh the potential tension increases. Integration needs to be a supported choice if we desire it to not become assimilation. This recommendation does not negate the need for better integration.

Creating Dialogue in Classroom Communities

In her book *Teaching to Transgress*, Hooks reinforces Freire's work in *Pedagogy of the Oppressed* as she maps out how dialogue and praxis are imperative for meaningful learning.

Praxis is a term used to describe practices in which one is simultaneously engaging in critical reflection about one's choices and practices in relation to the larger world community. Dialogue is to be distinguished from competing monologues in that people actually listen to, playback, and consider multiple points of view. For Freire and Hooks, praxis and dialogue are necessary for a deeper learning of the material that also recognizes and honors the inherent human dignity of the class participants. Similar to Allport's[353] efforts, praxis and dialogue require empathy and critical engagement of the self.

To work toward praxis and dialogue, Hooks encourages us to have students critically examine their real life everyday personal experiences in relation to the course material, to each other, and to the larger social world.[354] A first step toward this endeavor is building a classroom community. Students are more likely to honestly engage if they recognize the classroom community as a trusted space of learning which includes both support and challenge. We have had good results by creating class agreements, what many people call class covenants. In these agreements, the instructor works with the class to negotiate some ground rules for sharing. For example, you might discuss what the common purpose of classroom engagement should be, what respectful sharing looks and sounds like, how people want to be challenged by each other, or how the group will check each other when someone violates the ground rules. Some teachers have recommended distinguishing "responding" as more favorable than "reacting" and sharing informed experiences or arguments as more favorable to uninformed or unsubstantiated opinion.

From the assignments we give to the social issues we explore to the authors we choose, we make choices about the diversity of knowledge and experiences we use in our classrooms. Assignments can be structured that encourage students to identify personal experiences and put those experiences in conversation with the theoretical course material and/or in conversation with other students' papers. This approach is more effective when the class is held responsible for understanding each others' positions (e.g., tests, response papers, group papers, etc.). As we have already discussed in the section addressing Allport's Contact Hypothesis, carefully constructed group projects can help work toward this goal as well. Choosing diverse social issues to explore can be a way to bring in multiple voices as well. Service learning can be a key ingredient in helping students to recognize and critically examine their social position in relation to their larger community. Finally, there has been much criticism of courses over recognizing white contributors of knowledge at the expense of other diverse yet credible authors. This critique has been well supported in research. We can better diversify our course topics, the texts we choose to engage, and the representation of teachers in our classrooms. These changes too bring in a broader range of voices.

Structural Programs

While diversity has multiple meanings for multiple people, it continues to be one of the most discussed and debated issues in campus programming. Some universities have committed extensive departments focused on dealing with diversity issues and implementing programming on their campus. One such example is the Center for the Prevention of Hate Violence at the University of Central Maine. Their mission is too train and educate schools, businesses and other organizations to prevent bias, harassment and violence (http://www.preventinghate.org/).

Some schools have chosen to focus their efforts into a few large scale initiatives. One popular choice has been implementing ally programs or Safe Zones for LGBT students. Not only does this program work with the

LGBT populations on campus, but it also focuses on the students, staff, and faculty who want to be allies. According to the Consortium of Higher Education[355] (http://www.lgbtcampus.org/index.html), more than 200 colleges and universities across the United States have Save Zone/Allies Programs for students. Often people desire to become an ally because they want to be supportive, but they may still not recognize what being an ally might mean. Employing some level of screening for allies is extremely important. LGBT people have a great deal of community issues with which they must struggle. If an ally is unprepared or unwilling to support them through those struggles, he/she can cause a great deal of harm, even if unintentionally.

Many of these programs have training seminars that help those that what to be Allies understand the role they will actually play. Not everyone who puts in an application becomes an ally. The University of Florida for example has several different nights of training that a person can attend and go through a curriculum style class to be better educated on services to the LGBT population on their campus. U of F also requires the person to fill out a questionnaire that encourages people to consider why they want to be a friend or ally of LGBT students.

Educational Activities

There are hundreds of activities available to people wanting to help their departments, students, or staff understand diversity. When exploring activities, consider your goals and how the activities may or may not work toward those goals. The facilitation and processing of these activities is crucial. Consider one popular activity, "Walk Apart...Walk Together." This activity is intended to show how hard it is for people to look beyond the obvious visible differences between them. Two volunteers stand back to back. Members of the audience then name things different about the two volunteers. For each difference the volunteers take one step away from each other. Once they are on opposite ends of the room, the volunteers turn around and face each other. Now the audience has to name things that are common between the two people. The activity demonstrates the way differences are often observed visually, maybe one has glasses, different color hair, etc. By contrast, the similarities might not been as easily seen. The students may come from the same state, share class together, or even have similar viewpoints. This exercise points out the ways in which we note and value difference or similarity.

While this exercise encourages dialogue about low key issues of difference, there are some inherent challenges in using this exercise. First, if not facilitated well, the exercise can lead us to the conclusion that difference, visible or otherwise, is bad and similarity is good. We need to be cautious about encouraging a same/difference dichotomy. In many ways, we are similar as human beings, but the ways we are different generally should be recognized and celebrated for what we all bring to the table. Assuming everyone is the same is tantamount to assuming everyone, including all minority group members, should express themselves in the same way as the dominant cultural group, which is assumed to all express themselves in the same way. We are both similar and different, neither of which is inherently right or wrong and neither of which should exclude the other. This exercise can be very effective in beginning dialogue but should be carefully facilitated.

Another popular activity is the "Scavenger Hunt." With this activity, it is up to the organizer to come up with questions for the participants to either seek out others in the room. This can pose problems for those people who are not really talkative or shy, but it encourages them to learn about people whom they do not already know. For example, a question may direct them to find someone in the room who is very excited about their academic major. By having a question that requires participants to go beyond scanning the room to locate an answer, it forces them to interact and learn something about someone else that is not driven by visual recognition of difference or similarity.

Living Learning Communities

Academic courses are a great place to talk about diversity, but what about outside the classroom? A great opportunity for conversation might be in the residence halls. Many colleges have turned to living learning communities that help bridge the academic and social worlds of a college campus. One of the key developments "over the past two decades has been to take the 'learning community' with a new sort of inquisitive seriousness by asking how *do* students learn best".[356]

It is these living learning communities (LLC) that can help promote our understanding of diversity from student to student, student to staff, and student to faculty. The University of Denver defines their LLC as "...a unique environment in which a select group of students share common residential and academic experiences."[357] There students can choose from a variety of LLC options including one which is a social justice community. Throughout the course, students engage in conversation, attend seminars and retreats, and write for a newspaper on campus. The students get to engage with people sharing the same interest, creating an atmosphere that Shapiro and Levine say is student learning by doing.[358]

LLCs can be understood as "any form of curricular design that links together existing courses to enable subgroups of students and their teachers to achieve a deeper understanding and integration of the course material."[359] Similar to our previous discussions

on creating reflexive dialogue in the classroom and creating group interactions that
reduce prejudice, we need to be strategic
and intentional about the kind of curricular
and cocurricular interactions we design for
our LLCs.

WHAT HAPPENS WHEN WE COMMUNICATE HATE

Every communicative interaction we have,
regardless of the medium, has a way of calling forth and simultaneously reconstructing
our communal relations, those of the past,
the present, and the potential future. Judith
Butler, well known philosophy and gender
scholar, eloquently captures this phenomenon in her book *Excitable Speech: A Politics of
the Performative* which explores the politics
and practices of hate speech.

> The racial slur is always cited from else-
> where, and in the speaking of it, one
> chimes in with a chorus of racists, produc-
> ing at that moment the linguistic occasion
> for an imagined relation to an historically
> transmitted community of racists. In this
> sense, racist speech does not originate with
> the subject, even if it requires the subject
> for its efficacy, as it surely does. Indeed,
> racist speech could not act as racist speech
> if it were not a citation of itself, only be-
> cause we already know its force from its
> prior instances do we know it to be so of-
> fensive now, and we brace ourselves
> against its future invocations. The iter-
> ability of hate speech is effectively dissim-
> ulated by the 'subject' who speaks the
> speech of hate.[360]

History matters. We experience life through
our bodies. All of our cognitions and affects
are intertwined within our physical experiences. Our experience of history is also
embodied. Our embodied experiences of
ourselves being mistreated are not the same
as our embodied experiences of others being

mistreated; however, they may reinforce
similar messages. So when a person is
marked as an "outcast," to borrow the termi-
nology from a student once interviewed,
their embodied experience is not only con-
stituted by that marking, but also by that
marking in the context of history as well as
the possible future. They may remember all
of the times they were personally hurt in this
way in the past, and in some cases may
relive that pain. They may remember how
they felt when others like them were
harmed. They may also fear what might
happen to them in the future and probably
constrain their future choices. Could they be
resented, taunted, beaten, tortured, or killed
as others like them have in the past and unfortunately still are in the present? All this
may be considered in conjunction with the
pain of the actual moment.

The fears people will likely perceive are
not irrational like those often perpetuated by
popular culture (e.g., the erroneous belief that
black men are gangsters and will steal from
you). The fact that marginalized populations
are frequently targeted for hateful violence is
not simply a historical fact but also a contemporary one. People targeted by hate wrestle
with these embodied experiences all the
while knowing they are being targeted not
for something they have done but rather for
their existence, because it happens to be dis-
comforting to someone with a different ideology about who should be counted as human
beings. They can attempt to hide who they
are and often do, but they cannot change
who they are. In the words of another interviewed student, "I can't change the fact that I
am black."

Given what we have learned about perpetrator motivations, the formation of hateful
ideologies, and the experience of the target
groups, we can see that the past, present, and
possible future all influence how hate is experienced. As hate is about the classification of
groups of people into superior or subordinate

communities, hate is always experienced on not just an individual but also a communal level. In our discussion on motivations for hate, we noted that perpetrators seek to honor their ideology as superior and to establish their position in a community they value. These motivations highlight the communal aspect of hate. Their cultural ideologies, which in this case are exclusive to the existence of "others," are formed and reinforced through their valued community. In our discussion about what happens when we communicate hate, we noted the ways in which a person can feel targeted by the awareness of others like them being harmed. Hate is experienced differently by every individual, but it is always experienced by the entire community of members aware of the occurrence. Understanding the communal nature of hateful violence and how that violence is situated in and influenced by history, we should not be surprised to learn that researchers have suggested in their respective studies that the duration of stress, anger, and fear produced by hate is longer than the duration of stress, anger, and fear produced by a nonbias motivated violence.[361]

INTERVENTION AND RESPONSE

Reporting

Perpetrators look for a reaction from the community after they have committed hateful violence. If the hate is ignored, they will interpret the inaction as implicit support for their beliefs. Thus, a swift acknowledgment and response by campus officials is crucial. A first step in this process is to have an effective reporting procedure. Most hate activity goes unreported. This is in part due to the fact that most victims are not aware of or do not have access to proper resources that can offer assistance.

Anonymous reporting is helpful in many cases, and some universities offer e-mail reporting. Furthermore, reporting does not necessarily have to go directly to campus security. Sometimes students have built relationships with other departments on campus such as the Dean of Students or an advisor and may feel more comfortable reporting the incident there first. These staff members can support the victim and direct them to the appropriate resources.

How Should We Respond

So, how should we respond once hate is recognized and/or reported? As we work with our communities to prevent and respond to hate, there are three guiding principles that will be helpful. The first, **Recognizing Affect**, reminds us to remember that the affect hate produces is done so in the context of cultural history and perceived possible futures. Similar to responding to sexual assault, responders need to be well trained in how hate functions, in particular the influences situational and historical contexts may have on both the immediate target and the broader target groups. As was noted earlier, hate affects communities in complex ways that differ from similar nonbias motivated violence. The second, **Restoring Agency**, reminds us that targets have had their sense of control and security in their environment ripped away from them. Responders need to work to help both the immediate target and the larger target group regain their control by making choices on how to move forward. In more traumatic cases where victims have lost most of their capacity to make choices, providing them with the opportunity to make simple decisions, such as whether they would like to sit or stand, and moving to more complex decisions can be helpful. The final principle, **Rebuilding Communities**, is often overlooked but incredibly important. Because of the nature of hate crimes, victims often fear even the immediate community which surrounds them, effectively cutting them off from support. The hateful violence continues to cause damage as long as these communities remain divided. A first step in rebuilding communities is for the recognized leadership in the community to make a public declaration which comes out against the hateful violence and in support of those who have been targeted. Perpetrators feel a sense of group justification in their actions and perceive silence to be supportive.

For example, in a workshop on hate, participants shared frustrations with their administration's response to an anti-Semitic event that happened on their campus. Someone mailed out anonymous hate mail to some Jewish members of the community. It did not take long for news of the hate mail to circulate throughout the community. The workshop participants, of whom some were Jews, felt a great deal of anxiety and fear even though they did not personally receive the hate mail. Following the incident, their campus leadership sent out a letter to the community indicating they were investigating the incident and did not condone the sentiments expressed in the hateful message. While the workshop participants said they appreciated the letter, they felt distant from the authors and alone in their communities. As the hate mail was anonymous, almost everyone became potential threats to the target group.

Clearly in this situation, the group affected was much larger than the few letters sent out. While the administration's response denouncing the letter was helpful, the workshop participants felt they needed more. Their community had been restructured to be an unsafe community, not knowing who was targeting them. The reality of cases like these is that we may never be able to identify the anonymous perpetrator. However, more can be done with the community. Localized conversations with the communities about

the hate mail may have prompted others in their communities to respond against the letter and come out in support of the marginalized group. Such conversations are delicate but can and have on many campuses proven to be very supportive.

We recommend the following approach to these discussions.[362] (1) Ask the victims if they are willing to have the meeting. (2) Share what has happened and how it has affected their fellow community members. If the victims feel capable and willing, they should be the ones sharing the information. However, if they do not feel up to sharing themselves but are agreeable to the facilitator sharing, this works as well. (3) The leader or facilitator should share how they feel about their community members having been harmed. (4) The facilitator should ask if other members of the community also had concerns about the event. Usually, people are willing to respond supportively between the second and third step. In situations where people are unlikely to come out in support of the targeted group, identify smaller groups that will be supportive and then work your way outward into the larger community. Engaging in these conversations begins to rebuild communal relations. While we cannot take away what happened, we can reunite divided communities in working against the hateful action, an action that will remain at work until it is addressed as a community.

For a comprehensive response to violence, please refer to Chapter 10. For responding to hate specifically, we offer a review of the University of Wyoming's response to the tragic murder of Matthew Shepard. This case brought national attention to hate issues and serves as an exceptional model for responding to a tragedy of this magnitude.

Case Review

Matthew Shepard was a gay man attending the University of Wyoming.[363] He was brutally murdered by two men who were made uncomfortable by his existence. Matthew was tied to a fence post, brutally beaten and pistol whipped, and left to die in a remote area on October 6, 1998 in Laramie. This extreme act of hate threw the small community into upheaval. The massive media presence that followed for months made the grieving even more difficult. Dr. James Hurst, Vice President for Student Affairs at the University of Wyoming, wrote a deeply personal article in the July–August edition of *About Campus* that discussed how the University of Wyoming and the Laramie community moved through this tragedy. This article demonstrates how the way we respond to an incident can provide tremendous help to the healing process a community must move through after such a horrific event. What follows is a summary of the areas highlighted in Hurst's article that were crucial to the healing process.

Campus Leadership

The campus leadership was visible and involved with the work of the crisis response team and other key planning groups (e.g. memorial services, vigils).[364] Throughout the tragedy, their public support demonstrated to the campus that valuing difference in their community was important. The leadership also made themselves visible and available to the media, standing by their message that their university and community were about compassion not hate.

Crisis Response Team

Their crisis response team served as the focal point coordinating various efforts to meet the multiple needs of the community.[365] These needs included coordinating media management, internal and external communication, memorial and vigil services, roles of varying community members, and the interactions with the Shepard family. When the

tragedy occurred, the existing team was expanded to include a mix of students, staff, faculty, and Laramie community members. The flexibility for this expansion was important for responding to a crisis with such a wide impact.

Flexibility of Staff

Hurst credited the flexibility of the staff as being crucial to effective management of the crisis.[366] For example, staff members in the student union turned over their offices and resources to the LGBTA (Lesbian, Gay, Bisexual, Transgender Alliance) membership. As the media converged on those offices the ten days following the attack on Matthew, staff and students commonly worked 18-hour days to help with the crisis. The students felt empowered and validated by this recognition, and they demonstrated above and beyond to turn the tide on a tragic situation.

Involvement of Student Organizations

Not long after the stories began, the media had portrayed the University of Wyoming and the Laramie community members as comprised mostly of people who hate gay people. The LGBTA played a significant role swaying that misperception.[367] Their leadership provided accurate information to their community and the larger public. The group also played a key role in getting people to talk about the difficult issues this tragedy provoked. While the community was often surrounded by loud and hateful protesters throughout the ordeal, the LGBTA provided a quiet and calming presence during the trial, funeral, and memorial service. Multiple other student organizations from across the campus also provided leadership to the community. One example of this leadership was the creation of the yellow armbands.

Symbols

The yellow armbands served as a powerful symbol of remembrance which unified the community.[368] The Matthew Shepard armbands were decorated with green circles reflecting the international symbol for peace. Student groups worked tirelessly creating and distributing the armbands. Upon learning what the materials were for, local storeowners refused payment for them and even helped make them.

Management of the Media Presence

Most reporters were professionals and acted in good taste.[369] Some of them, though, sought out sensational statements and constructed stories around them. This experience makes it clear that centralized communication across campus with the media is imperative if an accurate picture is to be portrayed.

Discussion Forums

Half the student body had at least one day of their classes set aside by faculty to talk about the tragedy.[370] There were also a series of university-wide faculty teach-ins addressing the tragedy from scholarly perspectives. The teach-ins were provided over the noon hour during the weeks after the incident.

Counseling Center

Although the counseling center was prepared and services were made available, fewer students than anticipated requested help regarding the tragedy.[371]

Planning the Memorial Service

On October 19th, the University held the memorial service for Matthew Shepard.[372] The planning for this highly emotional event was conducted by a committee selected to ensure appropriate representation of the constituencies interested in helping with the memorial service. The speakers included the president of the university, a friend of Matthew's from LGBTA, and a local poet. By the time this event was held, the intense critical media pressure seemed to have passed.

Involvement of the Spiritual Organizations

Several campus based religious and spiritual organizations were helpful throughout the process.[373] The Canterbury House coordinated the communication between the university and the Shepard family. Great care was taken to ensure that university activities and plans were consistent with the desires of the Shepard family.

Police Department

The UWPD was instrumental in dealing with threats from organizations and people from all over the country.[374] One antigay group made threats of attending the campus memorial service with signs degrading Matthew and suggesting he is in hell and hated by God. Although the group did not attend the memorial service, the UWPD was thoroughly prepared. Finally, they were attentive to meeting the safety needs of LGBTA members and others during Gay Awareness Week.

A Commitment to Continue Life without Forgetting

The tragedy occurred days before homecoming.[375] Campus officials decided not to cancel homecoming, but rather to note the tragedy and its impact on the campus. Throughout the week, participants at the events paused for a moment of silence reflecting upon the tragedy. Additional floats were added to the parade as tributes to Matthew. Members of the University and Laramie community gathered at the end of the parade behind a yellow banner with green circles. Participants and spectators wept openly as the parade progressed.

CONCLUDING THOUGHTS

While a tragic event that has occurred can never be undone, The University of Wyoming demonstrated that a collaborative communal response to hate can not only help to prevent further escalations of violence but also serve to reunite and heal affected communities under extreme pressures. This chapter has been devoted to unpacking the complexity of how hate is produced and practiced, what motivations trigger hateful actions, how hate affects individuals and communities, and how we might work toward better prevention and response. Learning about the prevalence and complexity of hate can feel overwhelming. We now know, though, we can make a positive difference. Working collaboratively, we can employ some of the strategies outlined in this chapter to reduce our vulnerability to different motivations for hate, recognize and work against the negative stereotypes formed through communication practices, alter ideologies that justify hate, and rebuild communities that recognize and appreciate diversity. Together, we do have power to work against the production and practices of hate.

Chapter 14

HAZING

HANK NUWER & CHRISTOPHER BOLLINGER

THE STATE OF HAZING TODAY

WHEN RIDER UNIVERSITY STUDENT and Phi Kappa Tau pledge Gary DeVercelly died of alcohol poisoning following a so-called chapter party in 2007, the news was sickening, disheartening, and damaging to a Greek system largely dedicated at the executive level to hazing reform, but hardly unexpected. After all, as the Hazing Deaths and Information web site <hanknuwer.com> grimly observes, a hazing death had occurred on some college campus (and often more than one annual death on college campuses) each year from 1970 to 2007. For more than a decade, an attorney named Douglas Fierberg who had conducted numerous successful civil cases against hazing participants on behalf of the families of hazing victims, had argued that fraternities and universities were doing far too little to counter a widespread collegiate hazing culture. Eileen Stevens, a hazing activist whose son had died at Alfred University in a hazing incident, argued in 2008 in favor of passage of a toughened New York law which would increase penalties for criminal hazing in that state to a felony. "As Security on Campus has shown, too many institutions and organizations avoid bad publicity at any cost...and do not sufficiently educate or punish when hazing occurs," stressed Mrs. Stevens. "My prayer is that New York finally puts a law into place that is a stiff law, that will stop hazers in their tracks...or have them imprisoned to carry a permanent record as felons."

What was newsworthy was that a prosecuting attorney agreed that colleges were doing too little too late to stop hazing and charged two Rider University administrators with aggravated hazing – along with three fraternity members – for the DeVercelly death. The charges against two of their own sent shudders through college administrators and staff members, particularly those charged with overseeing fraternities, athletic clubs and teams, and miscellaneous student organizations.

Although the prosecutor dropped the charges, and the case became tangled in civil litigation, he nonetheless sent a message to higher education. That message was that it may not be enough for colleges to publish a hazing policy or to kick out hazing groups caught redhanded while abusing their newcomers. The message was that universities had to take a proactive stance to address and to eliminate hazing conditions on campus, particularly those involving alcohol (since like DeVercelly's demise, nearly nine of every ten hazing-attributed deaths since 1970 have alcohol directly or indirectly listed as a cause of death).[376]

Significantly, in a handful of club and intercollegiate athletic incidents, college coaches either were present at a hazing, participated in a hazing, or did far too little to discourage such annual wrongs of passage, causing speculation among observers of the hazing culture that eventually it might be a coach who would face charges similar to those levied briefly against the Rider administrators.

Had the trial for the two administrators gone ahead, there is no question that attorneys for the prosecution and defense would have done what lawyers always do in hazing criminal cases. Namely, they would have argued and argued about the legal definition of hazing, as well as what constitutes proof that a dangerous hazing condition preexists on a campus prior to a death.

The 44 state laws on the books in the United States differ slightly in wording, but, in some cases, significantly from one another in terms of punishment options. While aggravated hazing trials in California and Florida have resulted in felony convictions for a fraternity death and a fraternity beating respectively, other trials in other states allow only a misdemeanor conviction or merely the opportunity to pursue civil litigation in a noncriminal court. Six sparsely populated states (Alaska, Hawaii, Montana, New Mexico, South Dakota, Wyoming) do not have a hazing law. Wyoming's state Senate in 2007 rejected a bill that would have made hazing a crime.

On the other hand, Stevens had seen immense positive changes in hazing awareness at the college level over the three decades since her son perished in 1978 during a series of mandated drinking events required of initiates by Klan Alpine fraternity in what she calls "the misguided name of tradition." Many Greek national and international organizations used the Internet as a base to disseminate information and to promote awareness activities. Nationally, activist Tracy Maxwell spearheaded the formation of the Hazingprevention.org website and organization to promote the group's well-received and well-attended annual National Hazing Prevention Week and National Hazing Symposium. The Higher Education Center with Associate Director Linda Langford, identified hazing as a violence and school safety issue, using social norms training and bystander awareness as two weapons to educate collegians on the risks associated with hazing. In Indianapolis, the National Collegiate Athletic Association put hazing education, health, and safety on the table as one of its major policy concerns in 2008 and sponsored a Hazing Summit in January 2008 packed with college presidents and athletic directors under the direction of NCAA Assistant Director of Education Outreach Mary Wilfert. And Security on Campus, the national campus crime watchdog, expanded its focus on criminal hazing targeting campuses it regarded as failing in a duty to protect students from harm and violence.

A Common Definition of Hazing

Even with a standard definition of hazing, what a university or international fraternity regards as a clear-cut hazing violation, an undergraduate or alumnus may and frequently does term a hazing-free "tradition." Two of the few indisputable facts about hazing are that such initiations carried to extremes can result in deaths, and that both women and men can and do haze, although the number of hazing deaths of women over time is significantly less than the number of male deaths by hazing. Moreover, as many experts argue, while hazing deaths may grab headlines, it is actually the unethical, demeaning daily occurrences of hazing that cause dishonor to higher education, even if these do not result in an actual death.

Until the Rider case made headlines it was common for some coaches or bandleaders or fraternity alumni to turn their heads to reports of "initiation" rituals that almost certainly would have gotten a fraternity or sorority

chapter in hot water. The list of rationaliza-
tions was long but generally followed a similar self-serving pattern. Such hazing ought to
be tolerated, it was argued, because it contributed to school spirit, or was harmless fun
that let undergraduates blow off a little steam,
or made the group and its members a little
better and tougher. Often, with the definition
of hazing either unclear or disputed, acts of
initiation were labeled with euphemisms such
as horseplay, pranks, stunts, and traditions.

Consequently, when hazing researchers
from Alfred University, the University of
Maine and elsewhere have asked students in
formal surveys if they had been hazed, the
number of positive responses usually has
been relatively low. However, when athletes
or group members are asked whether or not
they have experienced specific hazing behaviors, the overall number is quite high. In a
1999 study of athletes, for example, researcher Norm Pollard found that 80 percent
of all NCAA male and female athletes had
endured at least one type of hazing ritual or
occurrence.[377] Of that number, about one in
five had participated in something dangerous
or potentially dangerous or illegal.

In 2008, University of Maine researchers
Elizabeth Allan and Mary Madden conducted a survey entitled "Hazing in View:
College Students at Risk" that concluded not
only had more than half of all college students been hazed but that 47 percent of all
high school students coming to college already had experienced hazing.[378] That being
said, for comparison sake here is one commonly cited definition of hazing. From the
January 2008 National Collegiate Association
definition of hazing distributed at its national
convention in Nashville, Tennessee: "[Hazing
is] any act committed against someone joining
or becoming a member or maintaining membership in any organization that is humiliating, intimidating or demeaning, or endangers
the health and safety of the person. Hazing
includes active or passive participation in

such acts and occurs regardless of the willingness to participate in the activities. Hazing
creates an environment/climate in which dignity and respect are absent."

Even so, debates over acceptable parameters exist among even the best known hazing
researchers and authors. Dr. Norm Pollard,
coconductor with Nadine Pollard of the 1999
Alfred University study, stopped short of referring to the common practice of having
"rookie" athletes carry balls as a hazing occurrence, although he personally recommends more sophisticated teambuilding
exercises in place of such traditions.[379] However, Dr. Susan Lipkins, author of a book on
hazing, opines that the practice does single
out players for unusual treatment.[380] The
Chico State women's soccer program coach
agreed and banished the tradition of freshmen carrying balls in 2005. Pollard and
others recommend that schools institute positive teambuilding activities in place of cancelled traditions such as carrying balls lest
students themselves invent a hazing activity
to take place of the banned event.

Thereby lies the problem for educators
trying to convey the definition of hazing. The
term "hazing" now applies to all incidents as
the same term whether a group makes a newcomer or rookie chug a fifth of alcohol or
endure a brutal paddling (clearly dangerous,
even criminal in most states) – as opposed to
carrying balls to and from a practice field or
wearing a pledge pin (neither dangerous nor
illegal). Far more frightening, many groups
(fraternity and athletic team members especially) downplay even the most dangerous
hazing practice – "encouraging" members to
drink copious amounts of liquor – on the argument that the decision to drink is a personal choice on the part of a newcomer. Yet,
slightly over half of all state hazing laws and
nearly 100 percent of all school hazing policies recognize that peer pressure and other
pressures upon a newcomer trying to join a
group make it irrelevant whether or not a

pledge, rookie athlete, or other neophyte "agrees" to undergo silly, demeaning, or dangerous activities in order to gain acceptance. Notably, many who haze are notoriously more creative in devising new rituals than they are in attempting to devise safe and acceptable alternative ways to welcome newcomers to a group that involve no hazing. An activity may be demeaning and dangerous, but the following examples may prove instructive.

Examples of Hazing

Silly

- Requiring pledges to wear silly clothing, diapers, or foolish costumes as many college and professional sports teams do. Such customs often are followed by requests that rookies purchase a team meal in which veterans order anything and everything on the menu to run up a bill that costs thousands of dollars.
- Blindfolding pledges and telling them that they will be required to show their loyalty by enduring a dangerous or unpleasant task such as removing an object from a toilet with their hands or teeth. The pledge is made sport of when the object turns out to be a banana, although educators also point out the hygiene dangers in such stunts.
- Ordering pledges to carry large painted rocks, stuffed animals, and other objects on campus and even to class.
- Locking pledges in a room and requiring them to smoke cigars.

Demeaning

- Asking sorority women to streak on campus and, in an inebriated state, and to knock on a fraternity house door, as occurred at DePauw University in Indiana. This particular incident escalated to

a dangerous activity when a member asked two pledges to accept a cigarette burn on their inner thighs.

- Asking pledges or new athletes to disrobe, to watch or to be touched by a stripper or to submit to the writing of crude vulgarisms on their bodies or clothing – often with alcohol present to reduce their inhibitions.
- Tying up a pledge or athlete.
- Ordering acts of servitude such as mindless errands.
- Forcing pledges into lineups where they are asked to touch genitalia of another pledge or athlete inappropriately as occurred during a University of Vermont hockey hazing – a well-publicized incident that led to the cancellation of one season of play.
- Forcing rookies to run with cookies in their buttock cheeks. Asking pledges to sit on blocks of ice, an event that could get out of hand and lead to hyperthermia.
- Asking newcomers to wear costumes that insult racial minorities or women, or which include the writing of slurs on the bodies or clothing of such persons.

Dangerous

- Locking initiates in a room and ordering them not to come out until the supply of alcohol has been consumed such as occurred in the death of a University of Maryland pledge.
- Ordering first-year students in a group to drink enormous amounts of alcohol along with a small serving of food. Such an initiation killed a pledge for a now banned athletic fraternity at American International College in Massachusetts.
- Ordering pledges to drink enormous quantities of water, thereby interfering with the normal chemistry of their bodies. Such a ritual led to the deaths of Matt Carrington, a Chico State fraternity

pledge, and Walter Dean Jennings, a pledge from Plattsburg State in New York.

- Ordering pledges to fill a trash can with vomit, as was the case with an alcohol overdose at a State University of New York school in the north-central part of the state.
- Ordering pledges to walk single file on a darkened or dark and remote highway, a practice that killed four members at a western Pennsylvania school and another pledge in Louisiana.
- Asking athletes to consume tremendous amounts of beer and liquor from a pretzel barrel and caused the nearly fatal overdose of a University of North Carolina soccer player. Such requests are especially dangerous since hazers and the hazed alike lose track of precisely how much alcohol has been ingested. Consequently, blood alcohol levels in hazing deaths run the gamut from lower .30 levels on up to .5 and above.
- Requiring pledges or athletes to accept blows, punches, or hits with paddles, canes or fists, as led to the deaths of young men at Morehouse College, Tennessee State, and Southeast Missouri State University. A number of high school athletes have been injured when punched in the groin.
- Requiring or strongly suggesting to pledges that they should swim or enter a body of water. Drowning victims during a hazing or alleged hazing include two California sorority pledges, a University of Miami pledge, and a University of Nevada pledge.
- Requiring pledges, rookies, or new members or to wear little or no clothing and to endure freezing temperatures outside or in a car trunk, as once threatened the life of a University of Michigan hockey player.

These are only a few examples of silly, demeaning, or dangerous practices.

Two other forms of hazing frequently encountered by Greek advisors, coaches, and administrators are mental and sexual hazing incidents. *Mental* hazing is usually silly or mindless but can also be hazardous since not all pledges react in the same way to such activities and others bring life experiences that may cause them to react in unexpected negative ways. One nationally known speaker, Travis Apgar of Cornell University, silences audiences of Greeks and athletes when he tells them how he reacted in an extreme fashion after fraternity males expected him to handle a pistol during a mental hazing exercise. Unbeknownst to the hazers, Apgar's father had committed suicide with a firearm, traumatizing him prior to the hazing he was asked to endure.

Sexual hazing was rarely reported before an Arizona high school baseball team made headlines in 1983. The number of incidents slowly increased in the late 1980s and early 1990s. After 1995, such incidents became fairly common among high school athletes and to a lesser extent among college athletes. Like hazing laws themselves, such incidents can be interpreted in widely varying ways by local prosecutors. While some prosecutors charge athletes who place their genitals or bare buttocks on another's face or person as sexual offenses, other prosecutors have argued that these cannot be sexual offenses since they were intended to be gross events, not events designed to give the alleged hazers sexual pleasure. Families of several high school victims in Missouri were protesting such a call for reduced charges asked for by a prosecutor in a 2007 hazing incident that took place just over the state line in Arkansas at a sports camp. The survey by the aforementioned Maine researchers Allan and Madden uncovered large numbers of students saying they had to perform or simulate sex acts with the same gender. Methodist College in North Carolina, McGill University in Canada, and the University of Vermont are three schools that have had to investigate charges or allegations of sexual hazing amongst undergraduate groups such as athletes.

As numerous writers and reporters have observed, hazing has grown increasingly more brutal and violent in terms of high school, athletic, and fraternity incidents reported on sites as http://hanknuwer.com and http://insidehazing.com and http://stophazing.org.

The issue also has drawn headlines as more and more hazing on the job gets reported in the press. These go beyond school into the workforce. For example, a hazing death of a laborer in Texas was treated as a homicide, resulting in 18- and five-year sentences for two men convicted in the case. A settlement was reached in a racially tinged hazing of a firefighter in Los Angeles who was made to eat dogwood, resulting in more than a million-dollar settlement payoff, one of two such large payments made by taxpayers locally in Los Angeles firefighter hazing cases. Other brutal occupational cases in recent years have seen involvement by police, restaurant chefs and employees, oil rig workers, and even ambulance team members (an 18-year-old young female died after being pressured into drinking a bottle of alcohol in the back of an ambulance). In 2008, three University of Medicine and Dentistry of New Jersey paramedics were accused of coercing interns into wearing simulated Ku Klux Klan sheets.

COUNTERING A TOXIC CULTURE

As bleak as the hazing picture is in terms of the large numbers of perpetrators seemingly eager and willing to flout criminal laws and organizational rules, anti-hazing activist and past Executive Director of the National Pan-Hellenic Council Michael W. Gordon likes to say that he takes comfort from the equally determined army of fellow activists, journalists, researchers, and educators lining up against the practice in ever-increasing numbers. Through the mid-1990s, the one determined group against hazing with any kind of solidarity at all were the parents – mainly the mothers – of young men who had died from fraternal or athletic rites gone wrong. Chief among these was the aforementioned Eileen Stevens who in 1978 founded a fledgling group called CHUCK – the Committee to Halt Useless College Killings – which made her a force for national fraternities at first to fear, and then over time, to ally themselves with as the reasonableness of her arguments against hazing (and the continuing string of Greek deaths) won her many converts in the fraternity and sorority movement. By 1990, her story had been told in the book *Broken Pledges: The Deadly Rite of Hazing*[381] and, slightly fictionalized, in a 1994 television movie starring Linda Gray as Stevens. Also by 1994, Stevens was joined in the fight she had taken to the media by articulate and outraged mothers Alice Haben, Edith Davis, Rita Saucier, Ruth Harten, and Adrienne Harris, whose sons had died in hazings respectively at Western Illinois University, Southeastern Missouri State, Auburn University, the University of Texas, and Morehouse College. When these activists retired, the parents of more recent hazing victims made their presence known nationally. William Meredith (father of a fraternity hazing death victim at the University of Miami) and his attorney David Bianchi worked with Florida legislators to gain passage of a felony hazing statute known as Chad's Law. In California, Debbie Smith and Edie Heideman (mothers of Chico State victims) raised their voices in support of Matt's Law, named for Smith's son Matt Carrington. In Colorado, Leslie Lanahan (mother of University of Colorado deceased pledge Gordie Bailey) gained national attention when a powerful documentary about her son's death was released as a DVD in 2008 (Hazethemovie.com).

Also in the field of higher education, there were other well-organized individuals and organizations that often used one another's resources and members to promote hazing education. Elizabeth Allan, a University of Maine associate professor and cofounder of Stophazing.org, teamed with colleague Mary Madden and an advisory team to undertake a groundbreaking study of hazing with results published in 2008 at http://hazingstudy.org. In New York, Buffalo State College in 2007 announced the formation of "The Hazing Collection" in its library's special collections – the first institution to serve as a clearinghouse for all dissertations, theses, books, video documentaries, and journal articles dedicated to the study of hazing behaviors. In Greek affairs, the Association of Fraternity Advisors, under then-president Dan Bureau, launched an ambitious taskforce targeting hazing in fraternities and sororities that continues today at this writing under the auspices of hazingprevention.org. Finally, in 2008, a company called The Human Equation hired Nuwer and Jeff Meltzer to develop an online education course to train students, administrators, and coaches to reduce risks associated with hazing (for more information see http://www.profraternity.org/the-human-equation.htm).

Additional serious books, studies, and articles addressing hazing were turned out by Pan-African Studies chair Ricky L. Jones at the University of Louisville; journalism professor Hank Nuwer at Franklin College; sociologist Stephen Sweet at Ithaca College; psychologist Susan Lipkins; Human Kinetics professor Marjorie Holman; University of Toronto graduate student Jay Johnson; and the editors of this volume, John Nicoletti, Sally Spencer-Thomas, and Christopher Bollinger. Additional important studies, book chapters, or monographs were published by researcher Shelly Campo, now at Iowa; Indiana University Education professor George Kuh and graduate student James A. Arnold,

and State University of New York sociologist and men and masculinities professor Michael S. Kimmel.[382]

PUTTING INITIATION PRACTICES IN PERSPECTIVE

To conceptualize hazing, think of it as a phenomenon that resides somewhere in the cross-section of three dimensions or continuums. The first continuum, Rites of Passage, deals with self-growth. Where one end of the continuum might be characterized by coming to know yourself and overcoming new obstacles, the other end might be characterized by inflicting pointless harm of some kind on yourself or another. The second continuum, group development, deals with group team building. While one end of this continuum might include group team building in which all group members overcome shared challenges as equal team members, the other end might include social deprivation exercises working toward brainwashing and wiping out individual identity and accountability. The third continuum of power or influence deals with degrees of empowerment or disempowerment. Where one end of this continuum focuses on enabling people to feel confident and supported in who they are and the choices they make, the other focuses on controlling the group member's choices. Together, the cross-section of these continuums could represent initiation rites as a whole. Hazing is a subsection of this whole picture of initiation practices, one subsection that can cause harm to individuals and destroy the unity and reputation of an organization.

Rites of passage take on many forms in cultures, religions, communities, and organizations marking a significant transition in an individual's life. These rites are often characterized by a period of challenge followed by a period of celebration. Most religions have some form of ceremony and celebration as young people take on their adult faith, and it is not surprising that research from Pollard and others points to church groups as a harbinger of hazing practices. Members of the military endure and complete boot camp, which can include hazing practices, such as the banned but continued practices such as "blood-pinning" (insertion of awards directly into the chests of airmen) or "Crossing the Equator" kangaroo courts. Greek organizations have pledging processes and induction ceremonies. High school, college, and professional athletes frequently hold annual initiation events to induct new team members.

One of the arguments for hazing is that it fosters group development and loyalty, a lofty sounding argument ignoring the evidence that newcomers are asked to sacrifice their personal identity, dignity, and will in the pursuit of group homogeneity. Some of the commonly cited techniques within this dimension are sleep deprivation, abusive treatment, and forced dependency. Sleep deprivation limits individuals' ability to concentrate and make decisions. Once their inhibitions are reduced, they need to depend on senior group members to provide them with direction and upon one another to make it through the hazing activities and abuse imposed upon the newcomers. A consequence of this technique is that it limits people's ability to make sound and independent decisions as well as their ability to accept the consequences of their decisions. The intent behind abusive treatment is to create a negative experience that a group has to live through together, thereby creating a tighter and stronger group of initiates. Some unspoken consequences of abusive treatment are the division created between the abusers and the abused and the reduced self-esteem of the abused. Inevitably cliques get formed and resentments build that never actually go away even after the newcomers become senior members themselves.

Forced dependency is a technique where members are taken away or prohibited from associating with people outside the group. They may sleep in a confined space such as a bathroom or wear unclean or conspicuous costumes that keeps perceived outsiders at bay. They may be forced to parade across campus in a so-called "line" or be called down to a basement to be berated or physically manhandled behind closed doors in a so-called "lineup." These techniques get excused and explained away by group leaders because enforced isolation allows members to commit to learning about each other and their purpose. All the while new members also learn to flout institutional regulations and state laws, begin to lose their ability to function productively outside of the group, and often watch their grades plummet as their time to focus on their academics and their access to professors and other students is severely limited. Published research by Nuwer and James C. Arnold refers to the work of psychologist Margaret Thaler Singer concerning cults when it points out banned but all too-common practices among collegiate fraternities that use cultlike "systematic" manipulation and coercion to effect "psychological and social influence."[383]

Power and influence may be exercised in many forms of which empowerment and control are on opposite ends of the spectrum. In the process of empowering, an individual's choices or options are expanded and discussions are held to assist the individual in decision-making. The motivation in empowerment is principle oriented, choosing to act a certain way, because it appears to be the most "right" choice. In the process of control, an individual's choices are limited, so the decision is no longer entirely one's own. When there is only one way to achieve a desired goal, an individual must choose to follow the direction of another if she or he wants to achieve the goal. The motivation in control is consequence oriented. Newcomers must give up choice and act a certain way to achieve a specific outcome or to avoid punishment, humiliation, or shunning that might lead to expulsion or so-called "blackballing" votes by the senior membership.

In our review of the issues concerning initiation, we have noted two common factors in hazing activities: (1) While forms of hazing can and do differ from one another in duration, severity, and construct, they all rally around the argument, often rationalized, that a group's status quo will be threatened by the admission of perceived "weaker" members unless hazing practices weed out weaker members and continue to enforce solidarity. (2) The perception of what constitutes hazing held by group members, those inside the culture, varies considerably with perceptions of those outside of the group. This lines up with separate surveys of college students conducted by Pollard and Allan in which a very large number of surveyed students acknowledge that they have endured specific hazing activities, but nonetheless insist in follow-up questioning that they have not been hazed. Author Stephen Sweet uses symbolic interactionism theory to conclude that group members legitimize subcultural definitions of their experience that essentially rationalize away hazing events because newcomers and members alike accept these as ordinary and necessary rites that have been accepted by prior members and must be experienced by all future members.

Many groups still see hazing as an integral part of creating group trust and loyalty, and proponents of bystander and social norms theory such as Alan Berkowitz try to change attitudes by getting members to see what is all-to-obvious to nonmembers – that hazing is humiliating, pointless, and risky. These varying perceptions challenge us with questions of needs and power: What is it about group bonding that groups are seeking to achieve with these practices? What is it about the actual practice of hazing that is unhealthy? How can educators persuade groups to abandon their belief that without hazing

their group solidarity may crumble as the doors to membership get thrown wide open? How can educators help groups to learn how to build orientation programs that develop group bonding in healthy and nonharmful ways?

In this chapter we focus on these questions with regard to hazing. First, we examine how hazing plays out in different contexts. Second, we examine the motivations behind hazing. Third, we explore how hazing relates to individuals and institutions. Finally, we offer recommendations on ways to address hazing.

HAZING IN DIFFERENT CONTEXTS

Greek Life

Although hazing practices happen in many different groups, fraternities and sororities have received the most public attention over the years, obscuring the more positive aspects of Greek life. While detractors dismiss fraternities and sororities by arguing that member selection is based too often on appearance instead of shared values, for many other people, these social networks provide a sense of history and connection going back to the start of fraternal collegiate groups in the eighteenth century. By providing a training ground for leadership and service, fraternities and sororities have sought to uphold worthy principles. They have served students by helping them find their places in society and to develop social skills and connections. National Greek organizations and their alumni continue this service by providing connections and role modeling in the postgraduate world.

Fraternity and sorority legacy also has a less positive aspect. To wit, years of tradition and principle have been accompanied by years of deceptive hazing that make a mockery out of the values formally acknowledged by respective Greek groups. According to Nuwer, fraternity fatal hazing incidents date back to 1873 when a brother of the Kappa Alpha Society fell to his death in a gorge after being required to find his way back home in the woods.[384] From this point onward, fraternity and sorority hazing has received increasing press coverage to the present day. The more drastic and lethal initiations in which initiates have fallen to their deaths from on high, drunk themselves to oblivion, been burned alive, drowned, or otherwise demeaned provide sensational newspaper reading that social norms advocates remind us constitute the exception, not the norms. Even if it were not true, as Nuwer reminds us, that hazing deaths have continued unabated each year for nearly four decades, hazing still should be abolished because it is an abhorrent practice that has no part in an educational system charged with civilizing and enlightening each and every student.

Some recent cases of Greek life hazing have captured media attention. All resulted in school and national group intervention and some have spurred legal action. The first cases involve female hazing. This is not to say that sororities do not haze, but Nuwer's collected list of hazing deaths demonstrate that males die in hazing events significantly more times than women do. In 2008, Missouri State University and Sigma Sigma Sigma stripped its MSU chapter of recognition after an investigation found evidence that some pledges had been allowed to illegally drink, be taken blindfolded into a cemetery, and asked to perform certain demeaning tasks. In 2007, three members of the historically black Zeta Phi Beta sorority found themselves in legal hot water facing third-degree assault and hazing after their national organization and Southeast Missouri State University claimed pledges were hit and made to eat disgusting foods. At Plymouth State University in New Hampshire, where the campus already was reeling from the death of a blindfolded sorority pledge in an SUV crash, five students from an unrecognized sorority in November 2006 were charged with miscellaneous offenses connected to an alleged hazing of new members.

Other recent cases making headlines of late involved fraternities. In 2008, the University of Texas Lambda Phi Epsilon chapter settled the alcohol-related hazing death of Phanta (Jack) Phoummarath for $4.2 million and paid for the filming of an antihazing video (www.inmemoryofjack.com). In 2008, Rider University found itself defending against a lawsuit brought by the parents of pledge Gary DeVercelly who died of acute alcohol intoxication following a fraternity party. In Boulder in 2008, individuals connected to the fraternity chapter at Colorado University where pledge Lynn Gordon "Gordie" Bailey died of alcohol poisoning found themselves in court facing a civil suit brought by the deceased pledge's parents. In Texas, law enforcement officials tapped the email of pledges to find that hazing was connected to the death of University of Texas fraternity pledge Tyler Cross, and at this writing, officials were looking into the possibility of criminal charges being placed. Because of the death of sleep-deprived Texas A & M pledge Clay Warren at Texas Tech, the state of Texas in 2008 passed House Bill 2639, mandating student activities' administrators on all campuses to attend an annual risk management course.

The irony of students willing to risk life, limb and reputation by engaging in hazing was not lost upon attorney Douglas Fierberg, involved in numerous suits against fraternities and members, representing the families of DeVercelly, Bailey, and fraternity pledge Daniel Reardon at the University of Maryland. In a letter to *USA Today*, Fierberg charged that the fraternity industry has known since at least the mid-1990s . . . that it plays a lead role in an unparalleled number of fatal incidents of binge drinking and hazing.

We established in the litigation involving Daniel Reardon's death that fraternities have a steadfast desire to keep alcohol available to members and guests, and they – unlike any responsible business in this country – rely on underage, untrained students (often intoxicated) to implement and manage alcohol policies that can mean the difference between life and death. We also established that the industry has long known that this method of managing alcohol is dangerous, and that it refuses to change because it fears losing membership and revenue."

On the other hand, Tracy Maxwell and Dan Bureau of Hazingprevention.org point out that while fraternities and sororities most often are the groups connected with a hazing culture by the general public, with the exception of a handful of activist mothers whose sons died in hazing, the best-known antihazing leaders all have Greek backgrounds as these two do. In an attempt to combat hazing behaviors, the North American Interfraternal Foundation and a host of national Greek groups have contributed heavily to the funding of research by Elizabeth Allan for her surveys connected with the "Examining and Transforming Campus Hazing Cultures" project. Ironically, the outspoken antihazing messages delivered by Charles Eberly of Sigma Phi Epsilon, David Westol of Theta Chi, and Marilyn Fordham of Delta Gamma underscore a calculated, prolonged attempt by a number of undergraduates in miscellaneous chapters everywhere to disobey and deceive their elders by not only hazing but also covering up their activities to avoid certain punishment mandated by antihazing regulations that virtually every Greek group now posts on official websites. Moreover, a hazing task force begun by Bureau, past president of the Association of Fraternity Advisers, has ensured that virtually every campus in the nation with an organized Greek system and formal adviser will run one or more antihazing educational events each year.

Athletics

While the Greek systems have been in the public eye for hazing, the 2008 Hazing Summit sponsored by the NCAA has demonstrated that organized college athletics clearly wants to combat dozens of alcohol-fueled hazing parties reported by national media. With the support of the NCAA, Elizabeth Allan at the University of Maine has included athletic teams and clubs in her survey of collegiate hazing practices. Her findings show a need for resolve by coaches and athletic directors who by and large have lagged behind Greek groups in terms of offering antihazing education or formulating policies with clearly designated punishments for teams and individual athletes who haze.

The list of schools and prominent teams ensnared in bad publicity over hazing continues to grow longer and more troubling each year. McGill University cancelled a football season following allegations of sexual abuse by a first-year player. Other schools that have followed suit include the University of Vermont (hockey), Kent State University (hockey), and Manhattan College (women's lacrosse). Other schools such as Alfred University (football) and Northwestern University (women's soccer) have suspended operations for a time in response to hazing allegations. And individual teams and members have been sanctioned at the University of Maine, University of Michigan, Harvard University, Miami of Ohio, Catholic University, and the University of Georgia – a small list of schools that is just the tip of the iceberg of those in the news.

The results of the 1999 Alfred study conducted on behalf of the NCAA were categorized as acceptable, questionable, alcohol-related, and unacceptable activities. Acceptable activities included activities that form team unity but do not degrade or humiliate new members such as preseason training, dressing nicely for team functions, completing a ropes course together, keeping a specific grade-point average, doing community service work as a team, and signing team standards agreements. Questionable activities included activities that were humiliating or degrading, but not potentially dangerous or illegal. These activities include yelling, swearing, wearing embarrassing clothing, tattooing, piercing, head shaving, branding, sleep deprivation, food deprivation, and not allowing association with people outside the group. Unacceptable activities included activities that had a high probability of danger or injury, or the potential to result in criminal charges. Such activities include making prank calls and harassing people, destroying or stealing property, being confined, beating, kidnapping or abandoning, and other illegal activity. Alcohol-related activities include drinking contests and alcohol consumption on recruitment visits.

Preliminary reports demonstrate that students generally have little idea of the definition of hazing and tend to brush off the danger of drinking games, in particular, as potentially violent in themselves or offering the possibility of harm post incident to participants. Allan's research at the University of Maine found that a disturbing fifth of all athletic hazing incidents to have been conducted with the knowledge of one or more coaches. While 81 percent of all athletes had gone through one or more hazing rituals, merely 7 percent defined themselves as having been hazed.[385]

The Alfred and Allan studies have generated a media-frenzy, not all supportive of the findings. Richard Hoffer wrote an article published in *Sports Illustrated* titled, "Praising Hazing." Hoffer highlights a difference between "good clean fun and felonious assault." He contends that the idea behind hazing is the destruction of status to foster teamwork. His downplaying of high school hazing practices which include touching buttocks or genitals to the faces of rookie players brought an onslaught of criticism right up to and including the NCAA Hazing Summit in 2008.

While hazing deaths in athletics are far less common than in Greek groups, they have occurred, causing heartbreak and dismay at these campuses. For example, football player John Davies died pledging an athletic club at the University of Nevada, Texas Cowboys athletic club pledge Gabriel Higgins drowned in an unsanctioned University of Texas athletic booster club initiation, and lacrosse club rookie Nicholas Haben died at Western Illinois University.

At the Hazing Summit, one consistent message sent over and over to the constituents was that high school hazing incidents involving assault and sexual abuse or even activities legally defined as rape were growing in number, quite probably increasing the likelihood that similar incidents would be carried to future colleges by victims and hazers alike. The only organized athletic association targeting the phenomenon of high school hazing has been the National Federation of State High School Associations, a rules and procedures governing body. Under director of Educational Services Elliot Hopkins, the NFHS addresses hazing with attending coaches and hundreds of high school delegates in at least one session every international convention drawing high school athletes from the United States, Canada, and countries as far away as Israel.[386]

Miscellaneous Campus Hazing

Incidents involving university bands have included allegations of harassment and vulgarity during initiations. Unlike fraternities and athletes, no organized attempt to combat band hazing has ever transpired nationally. Attempts to educate members occur on specific campuses only, and they often follow media-publicized incidents or threats of lawsuits.

In October of 2006, University of Wisconsin Chancellor John Wiley publicly chastised band director Michael Leckrone who has been in charge of the acclaimed band for four decades. An incident aboard a bus trip to the University of Michigan, which was revealed on ESPN and National Public Radio, involved head shaving and coerced disrobing of new band members forced the chancellor's hand. The band was placed on probation but allowed to continue playing while Leckrone addressed criticisms.

The more prestigious university bands have endured and paid off costly civil suits brought by members who have been hit, beaten, shaved, or accosted sexually by older members. The most publicized award was $1.8 million paid by five band members to Florida A & M band member Marcus Parker in November 2004. He was so badly paddled that one of his kidneys failed, according to court records. Another band member settled out of court. Nonetheless, in 2006, Florida A & M was again in the news when campus police asked the state of Florida to pursue formal hazing charges against four band members. The state declined, citing lack of evidence needed to produce a conviction.

Military Campuses

Although athletics has been the recent focus of the press, military campuses have had their own long-standing tradition of hazing. During the nineteenth and early twentieth centuries, reports of military hazing were a frequent source of media scandals. The purpose in military hazing is commonly accepted as an effort to break someone down, so as to build him or her back up stronger, more confident, and more committed to the unit. Preparing military personnel for combat readiness is the primary objective; therefore, the ability to follow orders blindly and immediately is required. The task of military authorities clearly is to establish a mindset that since hazing is outlawed, these are illegal orders that cadets are following. Hazing in military organizations internationally has been problematic. Deaths in Russia from hazing brutalities or related

suicides have been particularly high. In February of 2008, soldier Roman Rudakov died of a blood disease, but his nearly fatal beating 13 months earlier had embarrassed the military and led to an all-out attempt to stop the savagery and human rights abuses. In 2007, 15 suicides were related to hazing brutality, according to Russian military records.

The purpose of this book is to help the reader understand violence, how to prevent it, and how to respond to it; this contrasts with the purpose of the military. Becoming combat-ready requires soldiers to learn how to be violent. Our hope for educational institutions is that students are being taught how to prevent violence. The military teaches blind obedience, whereas, our hope is that institutions and students critically reflect upon what they are asking or being asked to do. These purposes are at odds.

The intent in this book is not to debate the need for and the purpose of the military. Nor is the intent to disregard the choices we are privileged to make because of the military's existence. That being said, military academies have hazed in ways that General Douglas MacArthur, himself, has found to be inappropriate and not in accordance with the purpose of the military.

In a previous edition of this book, hazing incidents at the various prestigious academies, the Citadel and Virginia Military Institute, were reported due to a high number of well-publicized incidents. In recent years, as a result of stepped-up awareness programs the number of hazing scandals has dwindled dramatically, particularly as all institutions have adjusted to the incorporation of female cadets into the various academies. In 2005, VMI's so-called rat line was embarrassed when a series of highly sexualized photographs depicting a bound cadet in a shower room were widely distributed over the Internet. The threat of pulling an upperclassman's rank for hazing has been particularly effective. Whether less direct and less physical hazing still continues behind closed institution doors is a matter of debate, but what is clear is that the number of media scandals involving the academies is clearly down by 2008.

HAZING AND THE INDIVIDUAL

The dynamics of hazing vary somewhat as it relates to individuals and institutions. As such, we will explore these dynamics in greater depth in the next two sections.

The Vulnerable New Member or Recruit

People who haze rarely consider the physical or psychological state of being of the people they are hazing. People who haze often assume all recruits are well-adjusted people, both physically and emotionally, capable of "being broken down to be built back up" as the saying goes. Reality suggests that recruits are drawn from a wider population yielding a group of people with all kinds of issues and vulnerabilities. Some recruits have medical conditions while others may be highly stressed and possibly suicidal. Hazing is not an activity that yields positive outcomes with these issues. Even the healthiest people can suffer the negative consequences of hazing, stresses hazing speaker Travis Apgar, who candidly shares with campus audiences his own breakdown following a hazing.

Physical and Emotional Consequences

Hazing can and has resulted in serious physical and emotional damage. Many pledges and recruits have been hospitalized following physical abuse such as paddling or beating, many with punctured eardrums, kidney failure, or flesh wounds to the buttocks area. Many have been hospitalized due to intoxication or other dangerous results of alcohol hazing

such as automobile accidents. Some victims of hazing such as Jessica Zimmerman, a Kappa Kappa Kappa pledge at DePauw, had a painful recovery from post-traumatic stress disorder (PTSD), a clinical mental disorder that is highly debilitating. Zimmerman suffered burns on her inner thigh from a cigarette and was encouraged to perform highly humiliating tasks under the influence of alcohol.[387]

Those like Zimmerman who choose to report hazing are subjected to negative attitudes and behavior from the peer group and are often ostracized and harassed both physically and emotionally, similar to the ordeal faced by a workplace whistleblower. For example, in the workplace, when a person reports illegal or unethical activity being conducted by the company, he or she is often fired and blackballed from any similar employment. In the college setting, the group member is usually expelled from the group and the word is put out that the individual lacks loyalty and should not be allowed in any similar social circles. A second pledge with Zimmerman who also was diagnosed with PTSD dropped out of school.

HAZING VIOLENCE TYPOLOGIES

Most hazing falls into one of two violence typologies: group-induced violence or relationship-based violence. In group-induced violence there is a diffusion of responsibility. People just follow the crowd. In relationship-based violence, an individual is seeking control over another person. Both of these types of violence have the potential to lead to great physical harm.

Examples of Group-Induced Hazing

In 2004, at Colorado University, Gordie Bailey was a Chi Psi fraternity initiate. He was asked to consume large amounts of alcohol. At the end, as he lay dying, fraternity brothers wrote epithets all over his body and attempted to scrub these clean after he was found dead. Hazing educational film information connected to this incident available at (http://hazethemovie.com/).

Two other notorious cases include the deaths of Walter Dean Jennings at Plattsburgh State University in New York and Matthew Carrington at Chico State University in California. Both were subjected to various tortures including the consumption of many gallons of water, throwing each's body chemistry out of whack. In addition, Carrington was abused in a cold, damp, and wet basement. In 2007, a judge awarded the family of Jennings a $1.5 million judgment for the pain and suffering their son endured, and in addition, some members served a small amount of jail time and were asked to participate in the Public Television documentary titled "Unless a Death Occurs" (film available at www.mountainlake.org). Fraternity members involved in the Carrington death also were sentenced to terms of up to one year in jail.

For Nuwer's research, he interviewed Yale Professor Irving L. Janis who applied his well-known "Groupthink" theory to hazers in fraternities. In the interest of group unity and harmony, members of hazing chapters will recklessly require pledges to perform stressful and even dangerous tasks in the misguided belief that the latter are invincible. When the risky behavior inevitably results in an injury, death, or public disclosure, the groupthink factor will lead to denials that any wrongdoing occurred and even outright lies and pressure upon fellow members and pledges to cover up the hazing. Janis's theory explains why pledges will allow themselves to endure the unendurable in harm's way for the sake of camaraderie. "All of us are very hungry for that sort of thing," Janis said to Nuwer about such group-induced dynamics. "None of us can get enough of it."[388]

In 2007, Chico State's Beta Theta Pi allegedly was involved in an incident according to a pledge complaint. Yet just a few months later in 2008, not one Beta Theta Pi pledge was willing to testify as the case moved through the California court system.

Example of Relationship-Based Violence

There are multiple examples of control via personal servitude and humiliation. This kind of abuse often leads to greater physical abuse. In his 2004 book *The Hazing Reader*, Nuwer published a revealing interview with a pledge who stressed the physical and mental brutality that was done to him by a pledge "education" officer and an alumnus with the apparent support of the greater membership at a small Pennsylvania liberal arts college. "The minute you walked into the house, and the minute your foot crossed that door, you were in a prison, you were theirs," he said, noting that he still suffers headaches from a blow to his head that floored him though he was a ranked heavyweight wrestler. "Your spirits get crushed, and you're always someone's – I don't have a real good [term] – someone's bitch. All the time, you got to do this and you got to do that. Then someone would come up and say, "The brotherhood – they never said 'they', just 'the brotherhood' – The brotherhood's really impressed that you're here all the time. It's been taken note of. I can't lie – it made me feel good. I felt I was a part of it."[389]

HAZING AND THE INSTITUTION

Duck and Cover

People create and operate institutions; thus, the instinct of self-protection is very strong. This instinct can lead to denial and avoidance, neither of which is necessarily intentional. Earlier, we noted Allan's survey of athletes who often reported that their coaches were aware hazing was occurring on their teams, although it is safe to say most coaches would argue that what was occurring failed to meet their personal definition of what was meant by hazing. In judicial and criminal case after case, testimony from victims of hazing demonstrate that some Greek and athletic leaders downplay or even lie about their lack of knowledge with regard to hazing. Institutions, as a whole, are no different, and several administrators have been accused in court of turning their heads to blatant hazing. Hazing researcher James C. Arnold, a Ph.D. graduate of Indiana under George D. Kuh, refers to schools and groups who haze while proclaiming themselves hazing free as "addictive organizations."[390]

Blaming an institution and proving culpability are two very different things, of course. In 2008 the eyes of the academic world focused on Rider University and a civil suit by the family of deceased Phi Kappa Tau pledge Gary DeVercelly whose blood-alcohol content was an astounding .426 at the time of death. The suit claims that the school failed to give the chapter the same level of oversight that it gave residence halls. Given the nature of such lawsuits, it could drag on for many years before a verdict is rendered or be settled without any revelation of details or admission of culpability by the institution. "Greek organizations present unique dangers, real dangers, to students on campus. And Rider specifically chose to manage them with less supervision and to give them control over their own activities despite the risk," Douglas Fierberg, attorney for the family, told a reporter. Rider officials in turn either issued denials or pointed to years of hazing education programs they claim were offered in good faith to Greeks.[391]

It is very rare for an institution to lose litigation brought by a victim who charges that an institution has done too little to protect students. One of the exceptions was the case of *Jeffrey J. Knoll v. Board of Regents of the University of Nebraska* in which the Nebraska Supreme Court ruled that liability does exist if the college fails in its duty to protect against an incident that in the court's judgment could or should have been detected. The court awarded a monetary payoff after finding that the Lincoln administration had prior knowledge of other hazing activity by its Phi Gamma Delta chapter. In court, Knoll testified that he had been asked to drink and was injured in a fall when he tried to get away from chapter members hazing him. Needless to say, this was regarded as a landmark decision by many observers of hazing litigation.

Sacred Cows and Sacred Herds

Every institution has a "sacred cow" to protect. At some institutions, the sacred cow is the star athlete who takes the team to a higher level filling the stands, making money for the institution, and providing a great deal of alumni support. The sacred cow is often protected and rewarded by the institution. Rewards come in the forms of camouflaged gifts and privileges from boosters even if such clearly are illicit under NCAA rules and regulations. Protection comes in the forms of institutional blind spots when these star students violate school policy or the law. Universities may conduct substandard investigations into the actions of these students and issue lesser consequences to these students.

In addition, institutions protect their "sacred herds." These may take the form of a sports team, a Greek organization, or another not as popular group that has the support of the board of trustees. Why would an institution protect individuals or entities like these? There are at least two reasons: money and politics. Sacred cows often bring in money or offer an alliance to an individual or organization that has considerable political strength.

These two reasons often accompany each other but not always. The money may take the form of revenue generated from games, alumni support, affluent potential donors, and potential lawsuits. Political strength has the potential to make the jobs of institution officials more difficult or easier. For these reasons, officials are often reluctant to harm the sacred cow.

Civil and criminal case decisions have many officials rethinking their philosophies on their sacred cows and sacred herds. College officials are no longer faced with the straightforward choice between acting, possibly leading to lawsuits and monetary loss, and not acting in hopes the problem goes away. Civil and criminal case decisions suggest that you may be sued for not acting appropriately with regard to an incident.

Following the death of Phi Delta Theta pledge Chad Saucier at Auburn University involving an exchange of bottles with his big brother at a traditional Dead-Day party, the school's handling of not just this incident but also other incidents was scrutinized when legal action was brought against the fraternity by the Saucier family. As it turned out, the school had warned or disciplined the fraternity over various complaints and infractions no less than 12 times in the years leading up to that fatal night.

Regulations and Laws

Hazing can result in both judicial and legal consequences. As noted, 44 states have adopted hazing laws and California and Florida have increased certain kinds of hazing to the level of a felony. Many laws undoubtedly will come under scrutiny, as has the New York State law at this writing. Media attention and broader legal influence has put colleges and universities under the looking glass by evaluating their policies and their judicial follow-through. Case law addressing an institution's responsibility for the prevention of dangerous hazing continues to be made, as is clear in the suit brought by the family of Gary DeVercelly against Rider University.

Increased attention to hazing has certainly elevated accountability; however, many maintain that simply adopting laws is not enough. The issues of enforcement, consistency and consent need to be addressed. In his time on the bench, Judge Mitch Crane has seen very little use of antihazing laws and believes there needs to be greater enforcement. "To further protect the university official, I suggest reporting the alleged activity to law enforcement officials and sending a report to a superior university official," he wrote in an opinion for the Association of Fraternity Advisors.

As Crane noted in the same opinion, there is considerable variance from state to state on what is criminal hazing and what is not, and attorney David Bianchi has said there is a need for greater consistency when legislators pen these hazing laws. Hazing activists such as Stevens or Debbie Smith fight for amendments to these state laws that acknowledge that hazing yields negative consequences with or without consent of the victim. At this time, only about half of all state laws contain such a provision, according to research published by hazing legal expert R. Brian Crow.[392]

The Issue of Consent

Hazing expert Fierberg argues persuasively that there is no way a victim truly gives informed consent when under pressure to perform for members of a group who have the power to include or exclude a prospective member. The debate of what constitutes consent and whether or not it mitigates hazing is a powerful one and is similar to the argument fought by prosecutors in sexual assault cases. Investigation often shows that the person hazing and the person being hazed share different viewpoints on whether or not consent was given. In many sexual assault cases, the person who exercised power over another viewed the consent or lack of consent differently than the person who did not have the power.

Consent has been an issue of confusion for sexual assault situations, and recently this issue has been clarified: the absence of refusal does not imply consent. The victim who is coerced into drinking may be too impaired to refuse, and this debilitated state must be taken into consideration when determining consent. Hazing laws still are clouded on this issue. About half of all state hazing laws inadequately reflect the notion that consent provided when the victim was sleep-deprived, intoxicated, or subjected to massive peer pressure is different from consent provided under normal circumstances. Activists in Florida and California successfully persuaded lawmakers to reform hazing laws in a way that protects potential victims from perpetrators who would take advantage of an altered mental state and the chaos that often marks a hazing incident.

To take the analogy one step further, we are faced with the issue of progressive consent. Some states consider individuals who consented to one part of hazing and not to another to be less victimized. The assumption is made that if the person was comfortable with one form of hazing, the person must have been comfortable with all forms of hazing. In sexual assault cases, assumptions are often made that women who consented to fondling also consented to intercourse.

In one oft-quoted ruling cited in *Broken Pledges: The Deadly Rite of Hazing*, a South Carolina court ruled against Sigma Nu in a civil suit brought by Ray and Maisie Ballou following the alcohol-related hazing death of their son L. Barry Ballou. Boiled down, the court ruled that Ballou did consent to some activities, but being of sound mind he would not have agreed to consume all that he did had he known fully beforehand that what he was consuming could and would prove lethal to him.

WHY DO PEOPLE HAZE?

Diffusion of Responsibility

The group dynamic involved in hazing interferes with members' ability to reason. Group members fail to recognize inappropriate activity for what it is when they see a whole group of people they trust acting in the same way. Group members also experience a diminished sense of responsibility for the consequences of their actions since multiple people were involved. There is a sense of anonymity in a group; members just follow along doing what everyone else is doing. Understanding such a mentality is critical to combating it, according to Berkowitz and other proponents of using a Bystander Model to awaken a conscience in lesser-involved members seeing a hazing incident. If bystanders can be awakened enough to protest or call hold enough, goes the theory, then others witnessing the event will also be conscience-stricken enough to realize the inappropriateness of an action and to call for an end to an activity.

Reciprocity

For all the loyalty development and personal growth rhetoric spouted by people who haze, some of the reason they haze is clearly, "This happened to me, now it's going to happen to you." While few group members enjoyed being hazed, most do not believe that the goals of hazing can be accomplished in a less abusive way or they lack the intellect to step back and see the abuse they endured for what it really was. Such an acknowledgement would require them to believe that what they experienced did not really need to happen. This pattern is seen in the cyclical patterns of abusive families. Abused children can grow up to be abusive parents unless they are able to come to an understanding that something was wrong with the way they were raised. The process of diverging from those you have loved and trusted can be very challenging.

In addition to bystander training, most hazing educational programs offer new and senior members training in creative confrontation. Nearly all Greek Life offices either offer such training or post the need to learn creative confrontation skills on their web pages. See, for example, the Texas A & M website at http://orgmanual.tamu.edu/Hazing.htm.

Badge of Loyalty

Another reason people haze is because they have convinced themselves that they are doing a service for the people they are hazing and for the group. The philosophy is, "I am willing to get my hands dirty to make the group stronger and more loyal." Other members of the group value this commitment to the group and revere the hazing leader as a sort of guardian of the group. In return, the group members themselves start to believe that hazing makes them stronger and more loyal. Their philosophy is "I must be committed and loyal if I am willing and strong enough to endure this from the group."

Even after he came close to death in a soccer initiation, player Gregory Belanger berated himself for his team being punished – or he did so until he quit the team and was able to gain a little perspective he wrote in an essay for *The Hazing Reader*.

> I was crying out for help, but it didn't seem to me like anyone at North Carolina cared. No one asked me how I was doing, not my coaches, not the players, not anyone at the University. Moreover, coaches and players continually blamed me for bringing disgrace upon the team. Upperclassmen would literally come up to my face and blame me for all the bad press. I was repeatedly ridiculed and given nicknames like "Detox" and "Pump." The initiation did bring everyone closer together, but they

were now close together – against me. I felt blacklisted and blackballed. It seemed I was the only one around with the plague, and everyone avoided me.

> Most coaches and players could not even look me in the eyes. Even many of my fellow freshmen distanced themselves from me.

> Yet, oddly perhaps, I didn't blame them. They wanted to play just as much as I did, and siding with me would have jeopardized their chances, so I couldn't blame them. So instead, I continued blaming myself.[393]

WHY DO PEOPLE ALLOW THEMSELVES TO BE HAZED?

One of the most basic needs of human beings is to belong to a community, to have yourself validated by other members within your community. When people enter new environments that sense of belonging is often lost. For new students in college, this need is particularly strong. They are frequently faced with living with new people they do not know, learning where everything on campus is located, struggling with more difficult classes, and learning how to manage their time in a completely new way. For many, it is the first time they have been away from their family and friends. They find themselves in need of a new support system. Most students suffer from a sense of insecurity when they arrive on campus and organizations present a perceived immediate solution with a built-in social group. On some campuses, they are the primary social group. The need for acceptance, particularly for first year students, when so much of life is in flux, is enormous. In order to gain acceptance and social status, students are willing to endure a great deal more than they would under normal circumstances.

> Hazers are in effect extremists; they justify actions that are outside the range of normal human behavior. People join extremist groups because they crave relationships and

acceptance, not primarily because they respond to a group's particular ideology. People who are friendless, who move to a new locale, who lack focus, or who need a romantic attachment are vulnerable to the recruiting efforts of extremists. Fraternities and sororities 'rush' predominantly first-year male and female students who find themselves in unfamiliar settings, away from family and childhood friends, and who seek a feeling of belonging. Part of the exhilaration some students experience upon their arrival at College involves their ability to choose a Greek group that offers them friendship, some of which are likely to endure for life. To these young people, enduring hazing beats the pain of loneliness.[394]

RECOMMENDATIONS

We developed the following intervention model, drawing from what we know of group-induced violence and relationship-based violence and from recommendations from the Alfred University study, Hank Nuwer, Judge Mitch Crane, Eileen Stevens, multiple focus articles on hazing, interviews with Greek members and advisors, and interviews with administrators and coaches.

Work to Convince Legislators to Enact Enforceable and Consistent Hazing Laws

There are currently three major concerns with hazing laws. One, there is not a high degree of consistency in the laws from state to state; consequently, clear messages are more difficult to communicate. Two, the question as to whether consent mitigates hazing is still highly debated. Activists continue to fight for greater recognition of the roles that social pressure, sleep deprivation, and vast alcohol consumption play with consent to hazing. Three, there are limited consequences for hazing resulting in death or severe injury.

The reason 44 states now have hazing laws is because of continued efforts of activists, increased public attention, and more legal action. Continued efforts such as these will be important for the development of stronger laws.

On the other hand, one of the dangers of the passage of laws following a specific incident is that the wording of such legislation may be too narrowly focused on the past hazing death or incident. This has led subsequent hazing charges in states such as Florida, Illinois, and South Carolina to be contested heatedly by lawyers for the defense representing accused hazers.

Stop Sheltering

Despite the demise of the "in loco parentis" doctrine, institutions still retain some responsibility for protecting students from foreseeable harm. Police departments and local law enforcement are often willing to allow colleges and universities to deal with illegal behavior internally. This partnership can unintentionally permit the inappropriate sheltering of "sacred cows." In an effort to help our students grow in a more protected environment, sheltering can prevent our students from feeling the full weight of appropriate consequences, and as a result, inhibit their ability to learn. Judge Mitch Crane has suggested that in the future, hazing will be eliminated as serious offenders are jailed and offending organizations are closed. As long as offenders are sheltered, this level of accountability cannot be achieved.

In courts of law, those accused of hazing are often attractive, well-spoken individuals dressed for a performance by their attorneys. Again and again, courts are told the effect a conviction will have upon a fraternity member accused of hazing and reminded what a bright future this person could have. Ironically, charges Eileen Stevens and other activists, slick defense attorneys somehow manage to move the jury's sympathies from the victim or family of the deceased onto the group of individuals who would not be viewed as quite so attractive if they could be seen in the minutes and hours they were engaging in acts of criminal hazing.

Improve Communication

The first step in communicating a clear antihazing message is creating and communicating a hazing policy. The policy should include clear definitions, appropriate consequences, and a clear reporting policy. The policy should articulate the roles community members (staff, faculty, coaches, and students) should play in hazing prevention and reporting.

The second step in communicating a clear antihazing message is for such information to be made available to students and to quiz or check them in some way to be assured the materials have not only been signed but also read and understood. There is a need for Greek Life and Judicial Affairs to keep accurate records of hazing and to make the hazing records of groups available to potential recruits or their parents upon request. For example, if a chapter was disciplined or suspended two years ago for hazing, that fact should not be concealed from potential pledges during recruitment. There is a need to educate students about Bystander Interaction and group norms theory. Outside consultants such as Alan Berkowitz can be called in if necessary to train staff, Greeks, or athletes.

New students must be taught that they do not have to consent to being hazed. It must be made clear to all Greeks, athletes, band members, cadets, and others that actions will be taken against groups who expel, harass, or blackball students for refusing to being hazed.

The third step in communicating an antihazing message is establishing a clear method of reporting allegations. In addition to identifying the method of reporting in the hazing policy itself, students should know who has

been designated a hazing compliance officer. It is important to give the reporting and advising process a home. Many schools such as George Washington University offer students an 800 number that allows for anonymous reporting of hazing accusations, while taking caution that the rights of the accused be absolutely protected and not abused. In addition, the law firm of Manley Burke in Cincinnati, publisher of the Fraternal Law Newsletter, also operates a national hazing hotline (1-888-Not-Haze) and promises to refer allegations to the proper authorities. Other places to report include the Security on Campus organization and The Higher Education Center for Alcohol and Other Drug Prevention, which has explored social ecology models and partnered with alcohol use experts to change the hazing culture and find ways to encourage and to support bystander interventions.

The fourth step in communicating an antihazing message is establishing a record for strong action against hazing. Institutions need to establish a zero-tolerance policy that leads to a review of all suspected hazing actions followed by appropriate consequences if verified. It is important that consequences reflect the seriousness of the situation and that other factors such as a chapter's philanthropies not obscure the actual hazing that has occurred. Today, nonaction is as likely if not more likely to result in a damaging lawsuit since a school's turning a blind eye may violate a perceived duty to care; consequences can be even more severe in athletic hazing where a school actually recruited and invited an athlete to its doors.

Often administrators, coaches, and advisors do not know with certainty when hazing is going on until it is too late and someone is injured, and if they do know and do nothing, the institution then gets placed in a tenuous legal situation. Student leaders and team captains must be convinced to make and uphold these changes and to be responsible and inform an administrator or coach when a hazing incident comes to their attention.

Behavior accountability should be incorporated into advising and coaching. Students need to be convinced that accountability is a key to growth and that ethicality is not only desirable but also expected in a values-based educational environment. If inappropriate actions are not challenged, passive approval is assumed by hazing perpetrators. If the end goal is to develop and educate students, accountability for actions is paramount.

It is also recommended that a school set a philosophy and policy for recruitment visits, and that the school train its staff and hosts on this philosophy and policy. The Alfred University study clearly showed a problem with recruit visitations, and subsequent scandals at Colorado University show a pattern of veteran players and cheerleaders abdicating social host responsibilities by serving alcohol to recruits as a common occurrence. The study has recommended that clear guidelines be established, exercised, and enforced. The study also suggests that coaches screen potential recruits thoroughly for past behavioral concerns.

Education

The first step in educating the community is to provide training on hazing prevention. Experts recommend creating a structured format to discuss the hazing policy and the institution's philosophy on hazing with students, staff, faculty, and coaches to increase understanding of what hazing is and what can be done about it. The campus speakers network Campuspeak (303-745-5545) and Contemporary Issues Agency (800-843-2179) host several experts on the topic of hazing, including Judge Mitch Crane, Hank Nuwer, Rick Barnes, and Travis Apgar to help campus groups become more aware of the dangers and liabilities hazing presents. In addition, qualified NCAA sports programs are eligible for a $500 hazing speaker grant (Contact Mary Wilfert of the NCAA for a list of approved speakers at mwilfert@ncaa.org or 317/917-6313).

Alcohol education and support programs are important to educating the community. All the research indicates that alcohol is a significant factor in hazing and in hazing deaths. Focusing attention on the issue of alcohol education will also have a clear impact on reducing the worst dangers associated with hazing. At the same time, it is important that schools provide accurate information on the actual dangers of hazing and not exaggerate the number of deaths or incidents in a misguided attempt to raise awareness.

Enhanced community awareness also helps education. Major changes have occurred in hazing laws and institutional practices toward hazing in the past ten years. These changes are the result of increased awareness and attention. Greater numbers of civil cases are resulting in $1 million awards and more for hazing abuse to families such as those of Chad Saucier, Nicholas Haben, and Walter Dean Jennings. Criminal penalties also are escalating to recent sentences of one and two years for hazing, but have not yet reached the seriousness of hazing death sentences in the Philippines which have put fraternity members in jail for life. Activists against hazing continue to present and educate. Media attention keeps institutions on their toes regarding their practices. Critics suggest that greater law reform still needs to occur and many institutional practices still beg for reform. Awareness and attention of the issue remains important.

Encourage Alternative Initiation Rites and Focal Points

Providing alternative initiation rites that have no hazing will require education and effort. Educating faculty, staff, coaches, and students on the importance of initiation rites helps people recognize realistic needs of groups. Integrating initiation philosophy and goals into group or team goals empowers groups to be a part of the solution as opposed to part of the problem. Identifying positive initiation rites provides groups with examples they can emulate. Role modeling team building by creating and implementing positive initiation rites shows groups that you take the issue seriously and are willing to do the work necessary to help them meet their needs in positive ways.

For Greek life, a shift in focus to academics, leadership development, career connections, and service may draw individuals away from hazing traditions. The emphasis on such activities may through natural selection create an atmosphere where hazing is less prevalent.

Provide Appropriate Leadership

Leadership provides united support for addressing the issue of hazing and requires four components: Top-down support, role modeling, utilization of campus leadership, and a strong connection with students. Addressing issues of hazing without unified support from campus leadership is ineffective. In order to make real cultural change, campus leaders need to be active participants in discovering and providing new direction. Without support from higher-level administration, students will ignore the issue. Without student involvement, student acceptance and support will be very difficult to achieve. When deaths from first-year student hazing were the major concern of administrators in the 1920s, what turned the tide to end such hazing deaths (only one after 1929) was the collective voice of campus leaders such as Branch McCracken at Indiana University who called for an end to nonsensical, dangerous rites of passage.

As we discussed earlier in this chapter, we are faced with questions of needs and power. We have the responsibility to take the time to build teams in healthy ways. In a student culture, perception is often equal to reality. We need to take care that our actions are beyond reproach.

The involvement of campus student leaders is very important. There are many leaders on campus who can deliver a message, sometimes more potently, than a written policy. Once these people are on board, cultural change can come more quickly. Without the involvement of student leaders, the ordinary rank-and file of students will be more reluctant to follow.

Advisors and coaches must connect with students and gain their trust and respect and confidence in their leadership. Authority does not instantaneously equate to trust and respect in a relationship. Trust and respect are developed as people feel they are being heard, understood, cared about, and treated fairly. Support and accountability are two forms of interaction that occur with students that highly contribute to trust and respect. There is no substitute for spending time with people and listening to them. Accountability needs to be consistent, appropriate, and compassionate. Compassionate does not mean looking the other way or issuing a "slap on the wrist" for a serious behavior. Students have a strong sense of justice and expect that you show care for all the people involved when issuing just consequences. Compassionate sometimes means being willing to suspend a student or organization in a caring way.

In conclusion, we recognize that none of the perceived positive intentions behind hazing practices advocated by students can ever justify the death or injury suffered by even one student in a hazing. Group members and athletes need to be convinced, often and emphatically, that there are other, better ways of accomplishing the same bonding goals without the negative consequences. They need to hear the message that challenging experiences exist that do not include the abuse of new members. There is merit in having a group focus on its members for a period of time.

Chapter 15

AVENGER VIOLENCE ON COLLEGE CAMPUSES

JOHN NICOLETTI & HEATHER MORRIS

IN THE LAST DECADE, there have been several high profile incidents of violence in schools and on college campuses, with Columbine and Virginia Tech being the most notorious. These incidents and the mayhem they cause have given rise to much debate about whether or not violence could be predicted. The purpose of this chapter is to identify a type of violence that occurs in schools and on campuses, discuss risk assessment approaches that have been designed to predict and prevent this type of violence, and to utilize the Virginia Tech massacre as a case example to illustrate this information.

There are several types of violence with diverse motives, perpetrators, and victims including predatory, entrepreneurial, domestic, workplace/schoolplace, gang, stalking, terrorism, and alcohol/drug-related. As a result, one must first identify which type of violence is in question before devising prevention and prediction strategies because prevention and prediction methods for one type of violence may not work for another. For example, if someone was attempting to kidnap you, the best strategy would be to scream and call attention to yourself; if you did that during a workplace or school shooting, you are likely to become a victim. In addition, security cameras are likely to deter several types of violent perpetrators; however, if a perpetrator is out for revenge, the cameras are likely not going to prevent it because revenge perpetrators are not deterred by cameras. Moreover, a risk assessment approach designed to determine if someone is at a high risk to commit a sexual crime cannot determine if an individual is at risk to commit robbery. Therefore, it is necessary to determine what type of violence one would like to prevent before deciding what prevention and/or prediction strategies to utilize.

The violent incidents that occurred at Columbine and Virginia Tech can be categorized as avenger violence. Avenger violence is defined as a type of violence where the perpetrator perceives violence as the only possible recourse for a perceived injustice. In other words, the individual feels inadequate and insignificant, which incites a need to right the perceived wrongs against him through violence. An avenger mass murder is rare; however, the devastation it causes and the media attention that it gains have schools and campuses scrambling to find a way to predict and prevent this type of violence. As a result, several risk assessment approaches have been developed or generalized from other types of violence to meet this need, including profiling, guided professional judgments/structured clinical assessments, actuarial tools, automatic decision-making computer programs, and the threat assessment approach.

Regrettably, most of these approaches have significant limitations and will not be effective in predicting or preventing avenger violence. The threat assessment approach has been revered as the most promising method to prevent avenger violence, but it, too, has several weaknesses. For that reason, an approach that addresses these limitations, the Impact Behavior Assessment of Risk (IBAR©) will be presented and discussed. In addition, an in-depth analysis of Seung Hui Cho and Virginia Tech will be presented followed by a practical system risk management approach that schools and campuses can utilize.

AVENGER VIOLENCE

In cases where students and/or faculty have been killed on a college campus, at least 70 percent of those cases were planned and can be described as *avenger violence*. Another term widely used in the literature to describe this type of violence is targeted school violence, which is defined as "violent incidents where both the perpetrator and target(s) are identified or identifiable prior to the incident."[395,396] For the purpose of this chapter, *avenger violence* is used because it better describes the nature of the perpetrator and further implicates a specific type of violence. Many types of violent individuals can choose a target for a number of reasons, but in avenger violence situations, the reason is specific: *to avenge a perceived injustice.*

One difference between avenger violence and other types of violence can also be comprehended by understanding how paranoia plays in the mind of some violent perpetrators. In general, most people can understand why some people commit violent acts if the cause is just. For example, violence is sometimes honored: the soldier, the shopkeeper who fought back, the little boy who slugs the bully, the father who reacts against the man

who molested his daughter, etc. However, what is just for one person may not be considered just to another. Of concern are situations where someone, usually a man, interprets his situation as just when most of society would not and, as a result, he feels victimized. The hallmark of paranoia is the sense that feelings of insignificance are caused by malevolent forces and a sense of importance can be resorted by righting the wrongs that the individual perceives as being done to him. In other words, the individual feels wronged, and the only way he perceives that he can save face is through violence.

Feelings of perceived injustices come from paranoia which stems from sex-role inadequacy. In other words, men are made to feel unmanly, women made to feel unwomanly, which helps explain why men get paranoid and violent about losing their jobs and women in our culture get paranoid and violent about losing their kids, and both get paranoid and violent about losing their mates (Wolowitz 1971; Karson, 2001).[397] In addition, paranoia can cause great feelings of inadequacy and induce a feeling of being victimized, which can lead to an individual feeling that to restore his sense of self, he must avenge the injustices against him. Regrettably, the method he chooses can sometimes be violent.

In recent years, avenger violence has gained much media attention with Virginia Tech being the most recently publicized case. Avenger violence can be one of the more destructive types of violence. The target is usually a workplace, school, or college campus, where innocent people die and the aftermath results in not only the family and friends of the victims feeling devastated, but it also causes the community to be in a paralyzing state of shock and confusion. Even those who survive such a horrifying experience will struggle with the overwhelming effects of trauma. Therefore, an in-depth discussion of avenger violence is provided so that schools and colleges can learn how to detect and interrupt an avenger situation.

Types of Avengers

Avenger perpetrators can be broken down into two major categories: Malevolent Insider and Malevolent Outsider. Malevolent Insiders are those individuals on the system's radar, meaning that one or more individuals in the school or campus community have observed an individual engaging in troubling behaviors. These behaviors could be witnessed by teachers/professors, campus police/school resource officers, mental health providers, students, parents, or anybody involved with the campus. A Malevolent Outsider is somebody who is not known to the system, which means the school/campus does not have any suspicions about this individual. The behavioral signs are still there with the Malevolent Outsider; however, the signs are not seen by any individuals within the campus community.

Malevolent Insider and Outsider Cases

An annotated list of cases from 1936 through 2007 that we perceive as Avenger Violence can be found in Appendix A. The following section, however, provides a more detailed analysis of recent key Avenger incidents that have occurred on campuses or in primary schools.

Columbine High School

On April 20, 1999 in Littleton, Colorado, Eric Harris and Dylan Klebold shot and killed 13 and wounded 24 others at their high school. It is one of the most notorious Avenger cases and it is well documented that a large majority of Avengers idealized Harris and Klebold before committing their own acts of terror. The observable Avenger behaviors and Avenger developmental characteristics of Harris and Klebold were evident several years prior to the massacre. They developed a website in 1996 which included several postings throughout the next few years about their growing anger towards society in addition to threats to kill students and teachers at Columbine. The website further included updates as to their progress in obtaining weapons and making bombs as well as a growing "hit list." A student told his parents about the website and authorities were notified. A warrant was drafted to search their houses but for reasons unknown, it never got filed. If a search would have taken place, numerous weapons and journals detailing their plan would have been found in their bedrooms and the horrifying events of April 20, 1999 could have been prevented. Harris and Klebold also made a movie about killing students for a school project. Harris and Klebold are both considered Malevolent Insiders as a result of the numerous observable behavioral data that was evident before the shooting took place. This case exemplifies the unfortunate reality that numerous people, including teachers, students, parents of students, and law enforcement knew about Harris and Klebold's concerning behaviors; however, at that time, there was little if anything known about this type of violence happening in schools and as a result, Columbine and local law enforcement had no idea of nor the ability to contemplate the seriousness of their behaviors. Additionally, there was not much known about how to handle such situations. This case did prompt a ramped desire in schools, law enforcement, mental health professionals, and communities to learn more about this type of violence and more importantly how to prevent it. It is regrettable that so many lives had to be lost and many more lives negatively affected by this tragedy to learn about this type of violence; however, the lessons learn from Columbine have been utilized to prevent similar act of violence, thus many lives have been saved.

Pacific Lutheran University

On May 18, 2001, Donald Cowan walked onto the Pacific Lutheran campus heavily armed and killing two before shooting himself in the head. Documented evidence indicates that he did have a vengeance against a university employee; however, he had no connection to the university. Unless the employee reported his concerns about Cowan to university officials, assuming he was aware that Cowan had a grudge against him, this incident is an example of a Malevolent Outsider because the university had no behavioral data on Cowan.

Appalachian School of Law

On January 16, 2002 in Grundy, Virginia, 43-year-old, former student Peter Odighizuwa shot and killed two faculty members and one student while wounding three others before several other students restrained him. There were numerous reports of Odighizuwa's poor academic performance and he had previously left the program voluntarily. There is evidence that he had made threats during his attendance. The day the shooting occurred, he had discussed his academic problems with a professor and during the conversation Odighizuwa made what could have been considered a veiled threat. He returned later that same day with a semiautomatic handgun and began his shooting spree. Odighizuwa is considered a Malevolent Insider because professors and students had been aware that he had made threats in the past.

Dawson College

On September 13, 2006, 25-year-old Kimveer Gill shot and killed two and injured 19 before committing suicide as officers showed up on scene at the Dawson campus located in Montreal, Quebec. He would be considered a Malevolent Outsider because he was not affiliated with the college and there is no documented evidence to suggest that the college had any behavioral data on Gill. However, there was documented evidence of his Avenger progression. He was an author of an online diary that over 600,000 people had visited prior to the massacre. He further referred to himself as the "Angel of Death" and in numerous posting he expressed his admiration of the Columbine shooters and was known by others as being a big fan of the horrific video game "Super Columbine Massacre RPG." Furthermore, one of Gill's screen names on the website was "fatality666." In his web postings, which several thousands read, there was obvious evidence of suicidal and homicidal ideation.

Platte Canyon High School

On September 27, 2006 in Bailey, Colorado, 53-year-old Duane Roger Morrison entered Platte Canyon High School claiming to have a bomb and took six female students hostage, sexually assaulting them before killing one. As the Jefferson County SWAT advanced, he was shot several times before he took his own life. Morrison had no connection to the school; consequently, the school had no data on him; therefore Morrison is labeled a Malevolent Outsider. Jefferson County SWAT's tactical response probably saved the lives of the other hostages.

Nickel Mines

In October of 2006 in Bart Township, Pennsylvania, 32-year-old milk truck driver Charles Carl Roberts walked in to an Amish schoolhouse and took several students hostage before shooting 10 and killing five students before committing suicide. Along with his gun he also had tools to tie down his victims as well as other items to be used during the planed sexual assault; however, there is no evidence that any of the victims were sexually assaulted. Documented evidence confirmed that Roberts has been planning the attacks for days and had left several suicide notes. Since the school had no knowledge of Rogers, he is another example of a Malevolent Outsider.

Virginia Tech

On April 16, 2007, 23-year-old Virginia Tech Student Seung-Hui Cho killed 32 students and faculty and wounded 25 more before committing suicide, in what is the worst mass murder in United States History. Cho's Avenger development was evident as early as middle school when he wrote a paper following the 1999 Columbine shooting and the teacher referred him for psychological help due to the suicidal and homicidal ideations present in that paper. As a result, Cho was closely monitored throughout his high school years by school officials, his family, and a psychiatrist. This early intervention and continued monitoring most likely interrupted Cho's Avenger development and probably prevented an Avenger situation at his high school. However, Virginia Tech was unaware of this history; therefore he was not closely monitored while in college. Throughout his two years at Virginia Tech, Cho was well known to teachers and students for hostile and violent writings as well as threatening behaviors. For that reason, we consider Cho a Malevolent Insider. Later in the chapter, an in-depth analysis of the lessons learned from this horrific tragedy will be discussed.

Youth With a Mission and New Life Church

On December 9, 2007, Matthew Murray opened fire, killing two staff members and injuring two others on the YWAM campus in Arvada, Colorado before escaping. The following day, after several postings on religious websites detailing his intentions of more killings, he open fired at the New Life Church in Colorado Springs, killing two more and wounding several others before being shot by Jeanne Assam, a church security guard. While on the ground wounded, Murray took his own life. This Avenger case is unique from others in that Murray is considered a Malevolent Insider for the first incident and Malevolent Outsider for the second. Murray had been expelled a few years ago for "strange behavior" and performing violent rock music at an YWAM function. Murray began sending "hate mail" in the weeks prior to the shooting, which is the foundation for labeling him a Malevolent Insider. However, there is no evidence that the New Life Church had any data on Murray. The FBI was notified of the violent postings hours before the second shooting spree and notified the Arvada Police Department; however, as Arvada agents were investigating the threatening messages, the second shooting spree began. Though two lives were taken during the shooting spree, Murray would have had the opportunity to kill many more if it were not for the quick actions taken by the security guard. This is an example of the unfortunate but realistic fact that Malevolent Outsiders typically will have already begun their brutal attacks before an interruption takes place. However, with Malevolent Outsiders, a quick strategic response can minimize the body count and save many lives.

Psychological Development of the Avenger

Using paranoia as a model, the first psychological development stage of an avenger is disappointment or frustration that then develops in to a *perceived injustice.*[398] The word perceived is extremely important in this developmental stage because the injustice may not be a reality or it may be a minor injustice to those individuals observing the avenger.

However, to the avenger, the injustice is real. As this perceived injustice stays in the mind of the avenger, it grows like a cancer. The avenger obsesses over the perceived injustice to the point where he feels greatly victimized.

The perceived injustice and a sense of victimization continue to fester and then develop into a grudge against those whom the avenger feels are victimizing him.[399] During this stage, the avenger externalizes responsibility and feels that his behaviors are justified because they are not his fault. At this point, the avenger begins obsessing with the idea of retaliation and revenge.[400] During this phase, the avenger also begins to idealize past avengers who have committed mass murder. As a result, an avenger begins to feel a kinship with those who have felt similar to him and have acted on their grudges; they are heroes in the mind of this beginning avenger.

Once the avenger has begun to harbor this grudge against those whom he believes are victimizing him, he then begins thinking about how to avenge these perceived wrongs against him. At this point, the obsession to avenge leads to two choices. The first is a good pathway, usually through the legal system, such as lawsuits or other forms of grievances.[401] This choice is actually a rational choice, because from what has been indicated in past cases, is that as long as he is suing you, he won't be shooting you. The other choice is for the avenger to right the wrong himself. Sometimes an avenger begins by using the legal system or the media, but if he does not get his desired outcome, he can move to his other option: violence.

Behaviors of an Avenger

An important observation about an avenger is that he will broadcast his intentions. Broadcasting is any behavior, verbal or written, that causes concern that the individual is thinking about avenging. Part of the avenging process is to broadcast his intent

because he is avenging a grudge and he wants people to know about it. An avenger is also obsessed with getting even and when persons are typically obsessed, they will talk and write about whatever they are obsessed about. In addition, broadcasting is a milder form of the behavior of doing it and a stronger form of behavior than simply imagining it. Moreover, broadcasting is concerning, as it indicates that the avenger is desensitizing. Furthermore, broadcasting places a bind on the avenger because once a threat has been made public and the main issue becomes about saving face and not just about getting revenge. Additionally, the more one talks or writes about something, the more it becomes easier to do, plus the current level of expression loses its appeal. In most avenger cases, there was a written and/or oral threat; however, it is important to note that the threat is not always given to the target.[402] However, in many cases, the written and oral threats are witnessed by a third party.[403]

An avenger typically broadcasts his intentions in a number of ways. He will usually use direct threats, conditional threats, or veiled threats. A direct threat is not ambiguous, it is a clear statement to harm someone.[404] A conditional threat is a statement made that is contingent on a certain set of circumstances and is designed to manipulate or intimidate the target. Veiled threats are often vague and subject to interpretation, but can be very serious. Furthermore, the avenger will write about his desires to avenge in a journal, for a class assignment, on the Internet, or a combination of all of these. In some cases, broadcasts have been written on walls or even stalls in the bathroom.

A number of people may witness an avenger's broadcast.[405] It could be fellow students, roommates, friends, professors/teachers, counselors, parents, law enforcement, acquaintances, someone just surfing the Internet, and so on. Regrettably, when people do hear or see something concerning, they typically do a unilateral threat assessment, i.e., they decide on their own that the broadcast is not a real threat. In addition, they take the information and usually minimize it to the point where they do not think it is something that needs to be reported. One reason for this is that usually the person making the threat has a nonviolent history with the individual who witnesses the threat. Another reason is the person witnessing the threat usually does a *who* and not a *what*.[406] This means that the person who is privileged to the information will minimize the behavior by justifying it as being the result of a characteristic of the person. Some typical *who* characteristics are mental disorders, ethnicity, race, sex, being introverted, etc. Some examples of someone focusing on a *who* would be, "He wrote that because he's just depressed and he's just looking for attention" or "He's just acting that way because he has ADHD," or "He's saying that because he's just venting his anger." Focusing on the *what* means to only look at the behavior of the person. If someone is engaging in violent verbalizations, writings, or behaviors, it does not matter if the person is depressed, a loner, or has ADHD – the behaviors are still of a serious nature.

The other disheartening occurrence that happens when people hear or see an avenger broadcast is that they do not know to whom they should report it. Or they assume it is an isolated event and is not worth causing a stir over. This was evident in many avenger cases, with Columbine and Virginia Tech being the most notorious examples. The point is that in most avenger situations, the avenger does broadcast and people are aware of it.

Another important behavior that is observable in avengers is suicidal and homicidal ideations.[407] This can be observed in their writings as well as in statements they make to others. In most cases, if not all, the avenger is using homicide to avenge his perceived injustice and as a catalyst for suicide. In many of the cases researched, the avenger had been

in counseling or had a mental health professional conduct a suicide assessment on him. Therefore, it is important for mental health professionals doing a suicide assessment to also take into account the individual's homicidal ideations through *collateral data.* Typically, only self-report is used and it is rare that an individual will admit to wanting to kill others. It is also helpful for clinicians to fully understand the extent to which suicide is a form of murder in which the perpetrator and victim happen to live in the same skin. Furthermore, many acts of suicides are revenge for failure.

Other important behaviors an avenger engages in are practice sessions.[408] A practice session is when the avenger progresses from an obsession to an action. Practice sessions can be observed through a number of behaviors including: behaviors that are beyond the realm of normal, boundary probing behaviors, attack-related behaviors, and attack behaviors. Normal behaviors are the expected behaviors for a particular environment. Furthermore, it is important to note that some behaviors are normal in some contexts but are not considered normal in another. A typical example that colleges and schools deal with would be defining normal behaviors in a creative writing class. The concern schools and colleges have is how do they know whether or not an individual is a budding Steven King or if the individual is using the class as a stage for his/her avenger manifesto? If the writing causes other students or the professor/teacher to feel intimidation or fear, chances are the writing is beyond the normal expectation of the class, unless the student has been primed for expressing fear and intimidation by the teacher/professor. With any writing that is of concern, the best practice approach is to have it reviewed by a risk assessment professional.

One aspect of practice sessions is boundary probing behaviors. Boundary probing is pushing the limits to see what one can get away with and also to see what the consequence will be for his/her actions.[409] Boundary probing is acceptable in many situations. For example, young children will boundary probe against their parents throughout their development. If the boundary probe is for acceptable or independent behaviors, parents typically reinforce the behavior. If the boundary probe is negative behavior, parents will typically push back or deter the behavior. Boundary probes, whether with children, students, employees, or customers need to be addressed, whether positively or negatively, as soon as they are recognized. In many avenger cases, the individual tested the limits and received no push back from the professor/teachers or other school/campus officials. If nothing is done, the lack of action allows the avenger to gain confidence and he will continue to escalate to more serious behaviors. Furthermore, lack of action sends a subtle signal that the boundary violation is acceptable, and even sends a subtle signal that the perceived injustice is real. Additionally, the avenger may interpret the acceptance of the boundary violation as confirmation that the system deserves the retaliation.

Another element of practice sessions are attack-related behaviors. These are defined as behaviors that precede an attack. Attack-related behaviors specifically include dehumanization and desensitization. Dehumanization is the mental process of turning a person into an object so that the attacker feels less connected to the consequences of his/her actions.[410] Dehumanization has been used throughout history; specifically, it is taught to soldiers in times of war. Name-calling or referring to someone or a group of people to something other than human is the typical way to dehumanize. Desensitization can happen mentally or physically. Talking about violence, writing about it, watching it over and over on TV, or playing violent video games are just a few ways one can become desensitized.[411] Regrettably, an avenger will take it one step further and begin to fantasize

about the horrific violence he wishes to commit.[412] In addition, an avenger will not only write and talk about these violent ideations, but he will also begin to obtain his weapons of choice and start to practice and enhance his skill-set for using these weapons.

Attack behaviors are the most serious form of practice sessions, and are defined as any physically destructive behavior to people or property. Physical violence against people needs no explanation regarding the seriousness of the behavior. However, a discussion on destruction of property is warranted because colleges/schools typically minimize property destruction, which can be an important sign that an individual is on a progression to becoming an avenger. Property destruction is a type of desensitization and should be treated seriously. For instance, there was a recent case in Colorado, where a student set off a homemade bomb in the cafeteria. No one was hurt or injured, therefore the discipline of the student was much lighter than it should have been. Regrettably, there are many examples of cases where a student punches a wall or vandalizes the building and it is not treated seriously because no one was injured. It is important to realize that property destruction itself may be less damaging than hurting someone; however, if someone is capable of property destruction, next on the continuum of violence is hurting people.

Not every student who turns in a paper that includes violence or every student who vandalizes property is on a pathway to becoming an avenger. Therefore, the big picture must be analyzed as a whole before that determination can be made. In addition, it is important to investigate all areas the college/school has access to so that ample data can be used to put together the big picture. However, it is even more important to not assume that one paper or one incident of dormitory graffiti is an isolated incident. Moreover, writing a violent story is protected in our legal system, but once a threat is made or vandalism incurs, there is no civil right.

One important factor to consider with avenger behaviors is that they cause significant social and psychological disruption. Social disruption is defined by disruptive behavior that impacts the day-to-day activities of the school/campus. Psychological disruption is defined as any behavior that creates reasonable fear, intimidation, or exorbitant psychological distress in others. An easy way for schools and campuses to separate avenger behavior from normal goof-off behavior is to look at the impact of that behavior. More importantly, when the individual's behavior causes significant social and psychological disruption, and when the behavior is not protected by civil rights laws, and when the behavior lacks prosocial elements, then the behaviors should be investigated. If there is evidence that the behaviors are on the avenger continuum, than a risk assessment should also be conducted.

Successful Interruptions

In order to understand the development of an Avenger, it is important to analyze documented cases of Avenger Violence. It is equally important to look at near misses or what we term **Successful Interruptions**. Some success cases rarely get any publicity because campuses sometimes believe that they maybe overreacted and nothing was ever going to occur. Reality is that you never know if you've interrupted a violent act or not, and campuses obviously can't conduct research studies with control groups of potential Avengers and wait and see who actually commits a violent act and who doesn't. Therefore, it is important to focus on the fact that a concerning behavior occurred, the campus took action, and the situation deescalated. There could have been a situation on your campus and you never knew about it because Avenger Behaviors were interrupted.

This is a tough stance to take because when a campus takes an Avenger situation seriously, they get push back from the individual, parents, or the legal community. The push back usually comes along the line of "I didn't intend on following through with the threat" or "you're overreacting" or "you're profiling this individual because he is a loner and depressed." However, if the campus focuses on documented observable behaviors, then they have every right to protect themselves.

Table 15.1 summarizes several Successful Interruptions that did occur, but by all means, it is not an inclusive list. These cases are examples of Avengers who were all extremely progressive in terms of the psychological development of an Avenger as well as advanced in their Avenger Behaviors. In all of these cases, someone reported their concerns and the police took appropriate action. These cases also raise little if any questions about whether or not an intervention should have taken place. It should be noted that when Avengers are so advanced, the report should go directly to law enforcement for immediate intervention and interruption. Furthermore, these cases are proof that people do not just snap or that Avengers chose random targets. Their targets are very methodically chosen, and the individuals who would have been present would have been victims of opportunity, not random victims.

An important point about the following cases of near misses is that they are all examples of Successful Interruptions at the high-school level. One hypothesis for the lack of college exposed Avenger plots is that colleges typically try to keep such situations from the public for many reasons. The main reason is that when parents and teens look at possible choices of colleges to attend, one area they typically inquire about is safety. If a college advertises that they interrupted an Avenger situation, parents and teens tend to believe, "Oh, they must have an issue with violence on their campus." Along the same line, if colleges let it

Table 15.1
SUMMARY OF SUCCESSFUL INTERRUPTIONS

Date	Location	Description
January 30, 2001	Cupertino, California, United States	De Anza College student Al DeGuzman planned a Columbine-style school shooting at the school. An employee at a Longs Drug store developed pictures of DeGuzman posing with his guns and homemade bombs. She and a coworker called police. DeGuzman was arrested when he returned for his photos. A search of Deguzman's bedroom found numerous sophisticated handmade bombs and a map of De Anza College, marked with locations where bombs would be placed.
September, 2004	Clinton Township, Michigan, United States	In an Internet chat with a friend Chippewa Valley High School student Andrew Osantowski revealed his plans for a Columbine-style massacre at the school. The friend alerted police, who found a number of stolen weapons, including an AK-47.
March 2, 2006	Muscatine, Iowa United States	On March 1, 2006, Muscatine High School student, Joseph Titus, was arrested at his parents' home after he sent a message to a friend on the internet that said he planned to bring a bomb to school. Law-enforcement officials found materials that could be used to make a bomb in the young man's home.
April 20, 2006	Riverton, Kansas United States	Five students were arrested for suspicion of committing a school shooting. Documented evidence indicates that they had a well-developed plan and were only stopped as a result of one of the boys discussing their intentions on a website. They were arrested just hours before their planned shooting spree.
September, 2006	Green Bay, Wisconsin United States	Two teenage boys amassed a cache of guns, ammo, bombs, and other weapons at their homes and had planned to attack their high school. A school resource officer became concerned about their behavior and initiated an investigation, which lead to a search of the boys' homes where the weapons were found. Consequently, the boys were arrested.
March, 2007	Sydney, NSW, Australia	Three 15-year-old boys were arrested at Ambarvale High School after one of the boys had told the school counselor that he and two other students were going to commit a Columbine-style massacre. An investigation found that the three boys had been planning the attacks and had made maps of the school.
April 10, 2007	Westminster, Colorado United States	Adams County Sheriff's deputies arrested two students from Ranum High School after they had made threats to "shoot up the place." Subsequent, evidence verified that the threats appeared to be plausible.
October, 2007	Norristown, Pennsylvania United States	Dillon Cossey was arrested when he tried to recruit another boy to help him stage a Columbine-style attack. The friend told his parents who notified police. When the police came to the Cossey home, he admitted to planning the attack. Several guns and explosive devices where found in his home.

be known that they have a BIT, the same thought crosses the minds of potential students and their families. It is a tough line to walk for colleges. However, would you rather attend or have your child attend a college that is prepared or one that would rather roll the dice and have the attitude of "it won't happen here."

In our experience, we have dealt with several Avenger situations that have occurred on college campuses. There are numerous campuses that have already received or plan to receive training on developing a BIT, developing a Vortex, and how to respond to individuals who may be on the pathway to Avenger Violence. Virginia Tech opened the public's eye to an unfortunate but realistic possibility, and colleges need to respond with an attitude of "we are as prepared as we can be, for the safety of our students and our staff." With the right polices, procedures, and trainings, colleges can feel confident that they are prepared to handle and interrupt an Avenger situation.

System Time Considerations

There are two key time considerations that schools and campuses should consider when dealing with an avenger: the event threshold and the event horizon.[413] The event threshold is the moment in time when the individual enters the awareness of the school or campus as a concern. The event horizon is when the avenger engages in an act of violence. In addition, with a malevolent insider, there will be plenty of time to interrupt violent behavior between the event threshold and the event horizon. In both the Columbine and Virginia Tech tragedies, there were at least two years between the event threshold and the event horizon. However, with a malevolent outsider the time between the event threshold and the event horizon is very minimal or they can occur at the same time, which means the goal becomes fast tactical

response to decrease the amount of destruction engaged in by the avenger. More importantly, the key ingredient to reducing the severity of an avenger is training and preparation focused on recognizing avenger behavior and how to interrupt the individual.

Risk Assessments in Schools

Events like the shooting at Columbine and Virginia Tech are rare; however, when they do occur, the lives lost combined with the psychological impact on the community is devastating. In addition, between 1991 and 2003, the number of students who do not attend school because they felt too unsafe to attend significantly increased.[414] Moreover, almost a decade later, people in Littleton, Colorado and the surrounding areas are still dealing with the aftermath of the Harris and Klebold mass murder. Regrettably, in an attempt to avoid similar situations, school and college campuses rush to implement strategies that often times result in ineffective measures. For example, after Virginia Tech, many schools and campuses focused on a number of preventive measures such as increasing security, installing cameras and developing tactical plans for active shooter situations; however, these responses alone are not effective in preventing avenger violence.[415] Other interventions that many schools and colleges rushed to implement after the latest headline of avenger violence included the following: implement a text-message warning system, perform criminal background checks on all incoming students, allow students to install their own locks in their dorm rooms, allow students to carry weapons, exclude from admission or expel students with mental health conditions, and profile depressed loners.[416] Again, these interventions are also not going to effectively prevent an avenger situation from occurring.[417]

What can schools and campuses do to prevent themselves from being the next headline?

A good risk management plan that is informed by an effective risk assessment is the most useful intervention method.[418] However, there are different types of threat and risk assessments methods, some having major flaws that make them inappropriate for avenger violence situations. This section will review and discuss several types of risk assessments that schools and campuses have ineffectively utilized for avenger situations. In addition, a risk assessment approach that is much more effective and can be easily adapted by many schools and campuses will be proposed.

There are four main approaches to risk assessments in schools and on campuses: profiling, guided professional judgments/structured clinical assessments, automated decision making (actuarial tools and computer programs), and the threat assessment approach.[419] All four have the best intentions in mind, to prevent avenger violence from occurring; however, all have limitations which impede them from reaching their goals of effectively preventing avenger violence.

Profiling is the use of demographic or behavioral characteristics shared by previous school shooters to identify students who are likely to become the next school shooter without any behavioral evidence that raises concern.[420] The original use of profiling was developed by the Behavioral Science Unit of the Federal Bureau of Investigation (FBI) to come up with a set of hypotheses of certain characteristics of the person who committed a crime to narrow down the list of suspects.[421] This type of technique has been used successfully when used from a behavior, such as a murder, to identify characteristics of the perpetrator; however, when used prospectively (from a person to predict a behavior), the technique has numerous problems.[422] One problem is the high rate of false positives, meaning the overwhelming majority of students who fit the profile will not engage in violence.[423] In addition, profiling students based on characteristics not only excludes students who pose a significant risk but do not share the demographics of previous school shooters, it also marginalizes students and produces bias against students who seem different from normal students.[424] Also, stigmatizing students and unfairly labeling students as dangerous can impair their civil liberties.[425] Furthermore, this approach does not produce risk management recommendations. It simply focuses on the characteristics that past school shooters have shared, and share with millions of teens, and unfairly labels them as being at risk to kill without any behavioral evidence.

Another approach that is utilized in schools is guided professional judgment, also referred to as structured clinical assessment.[426] Guided professional judgment tools are instruments or checklists that help the evaluator structure the interview and evaluation of the person of interest and helps organize the collection of relevant information.[427] This type of approach typically uses a checklist or a list of warning signs that was developed for a particular type of violence among individuals with similar characteristics.[428] One main limitation of this approach is that the prevalence of avenger violence is so low that even if a student exhibited a number of the warning signs, the chance of the student becoming violent would be low due to the low probability baseline of actual occurrences.[429] Furthermore, there is simply not enough empirical research on avenger violence to have a sufficient knowledge base from which to draw statistically significant characteristics to formulate a guided professional judgment or structured clinical assessment tool that would be statistically successful.[430] Another weakness with this approach is that typically it requires an interview, evaluation, and extensive review of all school and mental health records. The time it would take to carry out this approach is not only financially costly, but also when the concern is that a particular student poses a risk to become violent, a speedy risk assessment is imperative so that the appropriate risk management recommendations can be activated.

The next approach to be discussed is what Reddy et al. termed automated decision making.[431] This type of approach includes actuarial tools and computer programs that produce a decision concerning the violent potential of the individual in question without any discretion of the evaluator. Actuarial methods are "based on supposedly validated relationships between measurable predictor and outcome variables and ultimately determined by fixed, mechanical, and explicit rules."[432] Automated decision-making approaches are derived from empirical research on a certain type of violent behavior and are usually standardized for a certain population. This approach requires a "sufficient knowledge base of known variables that contribute to the outcome" along with a "sufficient frequency of occurrence of the event/outcome to permit statistically derived prediction."[433] Here, as with guided professional judgment, the limitation is that avenger violence is rare; therefore, the sufficient knowledge base of risk factors that is needed to derive a meaningful statistical equation has not yet been created, resulting in the inability to create reasonable accuracy in the prediction of avenger violence.[434] Even if a knowledge base of risk factors did exist for avenger violence, the low base rate of occurrence still would limit the usefulness of an actuarial tool in this area. Furthermore, any equation derived from such a low base rate could never sufficiently minimize the number of false positives or false negatives.[435] Another weakness with this approach is that the main goal is prediction not risk management. For many types of violence, such as sexual crimes, predicting the likelihood of recidivism is very useful in terms of determining the level of supervision; however, with avenger violence, a risk assessment approach is more effective if risk management is the goal – this point is elaborated below. Furthermore, with automated decision-making approaches, the evaluator has no discretion in terms of the final risk prediction, which is problematic when relevant behavior data is known to the evaluator but is excluded from the actuarial tool or computer program. For instance, an individual may score low on the actuarial tool due to lack of risk factors, but the evaluator is aware that the individual has vowed to commit a violent act if a certain event takes place. Moreover, if an individual has scored high due to exhibiting many risk factors but the evaluator has become aware of a situation that would make the possibility of the individual committing violence lower, such as the individual being incarcerated or the trigger events that escalated the individual having dissipated.

The most promising risk assessment approach for avenger violence as of yet, according to the literature, is the threat assessment approach.[436] The threat assessment approach is based on empirical research on assassinations and attacks on public figures, and incorporates three elements: identification of persons who pose a risk, assessment of them, and risk management strategies.[437] A positive aspect of this approach is that it does not focus on characteristics that are shared among similar perpetrators but on the facts of the particular case in question.[438] Furthermore, this approach integrates collateral data from several sources in conjunction with an analysis of the progression of ideas and behaviors over time to evaluate the risk with the goal of managing the posed risk.[439] In addition, an underlying assumption with this approach is that individuals who commit avenger violence do not just snap, but engage in an observable pattern of thinking and behaving that escalates to committing a violent act.[440]

In the response to the escalation of avenger violence in school in the 1990s, the Secret Service's National Threat Assessment Center, the Department of Education and Drug-Free Schools Program, the Department of Education and several leading experts combined their resources in the *Safe School Initiative (SSI)*, a collaborative project that included in-depth research on avenger violence in schools and focused on the potential for adapting the threat assessment approach to school violence.[441] The SSI provided much-needed empirical research on avenger violence and implies that the threat assessment approach is the most effective with avenger violence in schools. However, this risk assessment approach has its limitations. One is that only proponents of the threat assessment approach – Reddy, Fein, Vossekuil, and Borum, just to name a few – were the leading experts collaborating in the SSI. Even though the threat assessment approach is very promising and the aforementioned experts are extremely knowledgeable on the issue, the lack of additional experts on other risk assessment approaches limited the possibility to produce an even more effective risk assessment approach. Furthermore, the threat assessment approach is generalized from a different type of violence, namely assassinations and attacks on public figures, which though similar to avenger violence is still a different type of violence. In addition, the two major weaknesses of the threat assessment model are the amount of time needed to gather the information to address all of the factors included in the threat assessment approach and the need to interview the individual in question along with various other individuals (see Fein et al., 2002 for an in-depth description of all the factors included in the threat assessment approach). If time permits, and the individual is compliant, this approach very well could be the best possible risk assessment approach. However, in many situations, time is of the essence, especially if there is behavioral evidence to suggest that the individual has engaged in serious behaviors that indicate the individual is well progressed in the continuum of avenger thoughts and behaviors, and immediate intervention is needed. Furthermore, individuals who are the subject

of the investigation along with their guardians are likely to not cooperate or be defensive.

In light of the limitations of these risk assessment approaches, a risk approach that incorporates the positive aspects and addresses these limitations is greatly needed for addressing avenger violence. Avenger violence is different from the types of violence that the aforementioned approaches were originally developed to address. Moreover, the seriousness of this type of violence calls for an effective and timely response that incorporates a risk assessment that gives a practical assessment of risk in a reasonable time frame, which in some situations can be almost immediate, combined with risk management techniques that are individualized to the case in question. Therefore, a risk assessment that can be done with collateral data that is available, without the need to interview or evaluate the individual in question or without the need to do extensive information gathering would be the most useful in avenger situations. Below is a summary of a risk assessment approach that meets these requirements and has been utilized successfully in avenger situations.

Impact Behavioral Assessment of Risk (IBAR)©

John Nicoletti, a police psychologist who specializes in avenger violence, has developed a risk assessment model that utilizes an IBAR) approach. IBAR stands for Impact Behavioral Assessment of Risk. If the initial evidence implies that an individual is exhibiting a behavioral spectrum that indicates violence or disruption, then the data is organized into observable behaviors with an emphasis on the impact of the behavior. Furthermore, the IBAR can be done without interviewing the individual in question because the analysis is done on the documented behavioral data that initially elicited the concern; therefore, no consent from the individual in question is needed. Moreover, this protects the mental health professional from resorting to "reading tea leaves" to predict future violence. In addition, the IBAR is not intended as a medical or psychiatric evaluation and as a result, no mental diagnosis is provided.

Conducting a risk assessment on a potential avenger should not be limited to evaluating risk but must also include system risk management simultaneously. The IBAR is a consistent way to evaluate the behavior in context and the impact of the behavior, on a case-by-case basis; therefore, the risk management strategies will be catered to that particular case and the seriousness of the situation. The IBAR was developed by researching numerous avenger cases where violence did occur and categorizing the behaviors those individuals engaged in, as well as the impact of those behaviors, before their final act of violence. In addition, the IBAR has been utilized on several avenger cases with great success. A success in an avenger situation is when there is documented evidence that an individual has progressed through the avenger psychological developmental stages, engaged in avenger behaviors, and a risk assessment was performed, which included a risk management plan that was followed, and the situation deescalated.

An effective and timely risk assessment is only one step in addressing avenger violence. The other major step is the system response to individuals who pose a risk. Later in this chapter, a practical system response that schools and campuses can incorporate into their daily operations will be discussed.

VIRGINIA TECH: A CASE STUDY

On April 16, 2007, Seung Hui Cho shot and killed 32 students and faculty at Virginia Tech, and wounded 17 more, before killing himself. In the days following the tragedy, Tim Kaine, Governor of the Commonwealth of Virginia, appointed a panel to review and investigate the events leading up to the tragic deaths of 32 innocent students and faculty. The panel reviewed thousands of pages of documents, and conducted over 200 interviews. The in-depth report yields important findings that help put together the pieces of the big picture that led to the events of that day.

The information unveiled in the report clearly depicts several concerning incidents that, with appropriate intervention and continued monitoring, could have prevented the violence. It is unfortunate, to say the least, that 32 people lost their lives; however, using the Virginia Tech tragedy as a case study can help other universities and colleges prevent a similar tragedy. This is not an attempt to blame Virginia Tech in any way. Furthermore, knowledge of avenger violence and how to prevent it is simply something that many colleges and schools lack. Therefore, an analysis of Cho's behaviors and Virginia Tech's response is useful to illustrate the two main angles of avenger violence: the individual perspective regarding the perpetrator's psychological development and behaviors, and the systems perspective regarding how Virginia Tech responded to Cho's behaviors.

Cho's Avenger Development and Behaviors

Cho's avenger development and behaviors existed before he attended Virginia Tech. In 1999, following the Columbine avenger murders, Cho wrote "a disturbing paper"[442] that expressed suicidal and homicidal ideations. In that paper he indicated that he wanted to repeat Columbine. In response, Cho's school took immediate action and contacted his parents and arranged for a psychiatric evaluation. In addition, Cho and his family began and continued therapy throughout his high school years with coordination between the therapist, psychiatrist, and the school. This multifaceted approach seemed to mitigate any risk of Cho becoming violent. Unfortunately, Virginia Tech was unaware of his violent writings or the amount of monitoring he received while in high school.

In his freshman year at Virginia Tech, Cho took introductory classes and ended the year with a 3.0 GPA. There is no documented evidence that he engaged in any avenger behavior in his first year. In his sophomore year, he began taking English and Literature courses, as he became more interested in writing. He did not do well in these classes, but it was not until the beginning of his junior year that his demeanor changed and he began engaging in avenger behaviors. Table 15.2 lists a summary of Cho's behaviors, beginning in the fall of 2005, and the avenger behavioral label that these behaviors fall under.

Discussion

Cho clearly had a grudge against people he perceived as being wealthy. In his manifesto video that he sent to NBC he stated:

> You had everything you wanted. Your Mercedes wasn't enough, you brats. Your golden necklaces weren't enough, you snobs. Your trust fund wasn't enough... You had a hundred billion chances to have avoided today... but you decided to spill my Blood... You forced me into a corner and gave me only one option... Now you have blood on your hands that will never wash off.[443]

These quotes also depict his feelings of victimization and the thought that violence is his only way to avenge these perceived wrongs against him. In addition, Cho's perceived injustice and anger towards others was also evident in some of his writings; however, it is unclear if he specifically spelled out a particular person or group in his writings. Cho's family recalled that after his freshman year, he became excited about writing and stated that he wanted to become a writer. He received a rejection letter from a New York publishing house (he had submitted a topic and outline for a book) late in his sophomore year. This rejection could have been a triggering event that enhanced his perception of injustice.

In Cho's case, the event threshold began in the fall of 2005 when he stabbed the carpet with a knife in front of several students in a dorm room. This behavior is considered an attack behavior because it was reactive violence against property. In addition, this behavior also caused psychological disruption, which was evident in the reaction the witnesses experienced. Throughout 2005 all the way to April 16, 2007, Cho engaged in many avenger behaviors including boundary probing, attack-related behaviors, attack behaviors, behaviors that cause social and psychological disruption and suicidal and homicidal ideations. Moreover, all of these behaviors were observed by someone, either by students, RAs, professors, or others. Even the campus police were aware of several incidents regarding Cho's behaviors. However, there is no evidence to support that someone was aware of all his behaviors, resulting in each behavior appearing to be an isolated incident.

Virginia Tech's Response

Several individuals in different departments including academic, administration, mental health, public safety, and student affairs were concerned about Cho and were aware of his concerning behaviors and writings. In this section, a more in-depth discussion of how these departments and individuals responded to Cho is specified. A number of factors impeded the Virginia Tech campus community in detecting Cho as an avenger and interrupting his behaviors. These factors include lack of understanding of avenger behavior, lack of communication, lack of understanding of privacy laws, and failed attempts to intervene.

In the fall of 2005, the English Department did make several attempts to address Cho's

Table 15.2
SUMMARY OF CHO'S BEHAVIORS

Fall/Winter 2005 *Summary of Incidents*	*Avenger Behavior Label*
Cho's suitemates took him to a party during which they all went back to a female student's room. Cho took out a knife and started stabbing the carpet.	Attack behavior (violence against property) Social and psychological disruption
Cho's roommate said that Cho would watch movies and play video games that seemed dark.	Attack-related behavior (desensitization)
Cho is assumed to have written dark lyrics on the wall of his suite and later in the halls of the dorm.	Social and psychological disruption Attack behavior (property damage)
There are several incidents in which Cho's suitemates smelled something burning. One time they discovered burnt pages under a sofa cushion.	Attack behavior (property damage)
In a poetry class taught by Nikki Giovanni, Cho showed a lack of cooperation and disruptive behavior.	Social and psychological disruption
Dr. Giovanni reported that she would have to take time away from teaching at the beginning of *each* class to have him remove his reflector glasses and hat. She would stand by her desk and not start until he complied.	Social and psychological disruption
Then Cho began wearing a scarf around his head and Dr. Giovanni felt bullied by him.	Psychological disruption Dehumanization
Cho was uncooperative in class by reading his writings in class in a voice that couldn't be heard and when asked to make changes, he would present the same thing the following week.	Social and psychological disruption
One of the papers Cho read aloud was titled, "So-called Advanced Writing-Poetry." Students remember it as very dark, with violent emotions. Cho wrote about his anger with the class for discussing eating animals instead of poetry one day. He wrote, "you low-life barbarians make me sick to the stomach that I want to barf over my new shoes…I hope ya'll burn in hell for mass murdering and eating all those little animals." [Note – Cho denied being a vegetarian when asked later by Dr. Giovanni about his anger towards the class.] Students began to not to attend class due to being afraid of Cho.	Attack-related behavior (desensitization, dehumanization) Social and psychological disruption
Dr. Giovanni contacted the head of the English department and warned that if Cho was not removed from her class she would resign.	Social and psychological disruption
There are reports from female students complaining of Cho's "odd behavior" and "stalking." Cho was caught taking pictures with his cell phone of female students in class.	Social and psychological disruption Attack-related behavior (dehumanization)

(Cont'd.)

Table 15.2
SUMMARY OF CHO'S BEHAVIORS *(Continued)*

Fall/Winter 2005 *Summary of Incidents*	*Avenger Behavior Label*
Cho began to work independently with Dr. Roy due to his disruption in class. One of Dr. Roy's updates stated that things were going "reasonably well, though all of his submissions so far have been about shooting or harming people because he's angered by their authority or by their behavior."	Social and psychological disruption Attack-related behavior (desensitization, dehumanization)
VTPD followed up on an incident report made after a female student complained about Cho. He had been text messaging a female student identifying himself as "question mark." Cho had shown up in the female's room wearing dark glasses and a hat pulled down, covering most of his face. The student "freaked out" and called the police. The officer warned Cho not to bother female students.	Social and psychological disruption Attack-related behavior (desensitization, dehumanization)
Cho's resident advisor said that Cho "was strange and got stranger." She further stated that his suitemates told her that they had found a very large knife in Cho's desk and discarded it.	Social and psychological disruption
December 12 VTPD received a complaint from a female student regarding Cho (this is the same woman whose carpet Cho stabbed with a knife repeatedly at a party). She had received instant messages and postings to her Facebook page throughout the semester from Cho. She stated that the messages were self-deprecating. She also believes Cho left a disturbing quote on her white erase board outside her dorm room.	Social and psychological disruption
Following a police contact regarding his contact with a female student, Cho sent an instant message to one of his suitemates stating, "I might as well kill myself." The suitemates contacted VTPD and Cho was placed on a 72-hour hold.	Suicidal ideations
Spring 2006 *Summary of Incidents*	*Development and Behavior Label*
Cho continued to not participate in classes and turn in violent writings. Robert Hicok, one of Cho's professors, consulted with Dr. Roy regarding his concerns but decided to keep Cho in the class.	Social and psychological disruption
In one of the writings Dr. Hicok was concerned about, Cho wrote, "I hate this! I hate all these frauds! I hate my life . . . This is it . . . This is when you damn people die with me." He further wrote about entering the empty halls "and goes to	Social and psychological disruption Suicidal and homicidal ideations Attack-related behavior (desensitization, dehumanization)

(Cont'd.)

Table 15.2
SUMMARY OF CHO'S BEHAVIORS *(Continued)*

Spring 2006 *Summary of Incidents*	*Development and Behavior Label*
an arbitrary classroom" where "everyone is smiling and laughing." Cho wrote about meeting a "gothic girl" and telling her "I'm nothing. I'm a loser... I was going to kill every god damn person in this damn school..." Cho wrote that he and the girl obtain two handguns, a sawed off shotgun and an automatic rifle. The story concluded with, "You and me. We can fight to claim our deserving throne."	
Cho encountered problems in another class. In a Technical Writing class, Cho's behaviors of wearing sunglasses and a hat pulled down and not participating are again problematic. Professor Carl Bean confronted Cho on these behaviors. Professor Bean also made some suggestions regarding an upcoming assignment. He had asked Cho to write about George Washington and the American Revolution. Cho turned in a paper discussing *Macbeth* and correlated it to serial killings.	Social and psychological disruption
Professor Bean confronted Cho again after class telling him the work was not satisfactory and the topic of his last paper was not acceptable. Professor Bean recommended to Cho that he drop the class. Without invitation, Cho followed Professor Bean into his office. Cho proceeded to argue loudly with him. Cho was asked to leave the office and return when he regained control. Cho never returned and eventually dropped the class.	Social and psychological disruption
Fall Winter 2006 *Summary of Incidents*	*Development and Behavior Label*
In a playwriting workshop taught by Professor Ed Falco, Cho's behaviors continued. He did not participate and wrote pieces that were angry. A student in that class had reported to a follow student that Cho "was the kind of guy who might go on a rampage killing."	Social and psychological disruption
Cho's resident advisor had been warned by the previous RA about his unwanted advance toward female students and that he had been suspected of writing violent song lyrics on the dorm walls and those same lyrics were posted in his website.	Social and psychological disruption
In an Advance Fiction Workshop, Professor Norris was concerned about Cho's behaviors and lack of participation. She checked with the dean's office to see if it was "safe" to have Cho in class and asked to have someone intervene on his behalf.	Social and psychological disruption

(Cont'd.)

Table 15.2
SUMMARY OF CHO'S BEHAVIORS *(Continued)*

Spring 2007 *Summary of Incidents*	*Development and Behavior Label*
Cho began to buy guns and ammunition. He began going to a nearby shooting range to practice. His class attendance began to fall.	Attack related behavior
April 16, Cho committed the nation's most notorious avenger mass murders. At 7:15 am, Cho shoots two victims at West Ambler Johnston. At 9:40 am, Cho begins shooting victims in Norris Hall.	Attack behavior

disruptive behavior in class and his violent writings. After several attempts to address concerns directly with Cho to no avail, Dr. Nikki Giovanni contacted the head of the English Department, Dr. Roy, due to a number of students refusing to attend class because "everyone's afraid of him,"[444] as well as her own fear. She further told Dr. Roy that she would resign if Cho was not removed from her class. Dr. Roy contacted the Dean of Student Affairs, Tom Brown, the Cook Counseling Center, and the College of Liberal Arts in regard to some of Cho's writings. The psychologist at the counseling center determined that there was no "specific threat" in the writings and Judicial Affairs stated that his disruption does fall under behaviors that meet the threshold for adjudication. Dr. Roy was advised to refer Cho to the counseling center in her upcoming meeting with him and to advise him that any further disruptive behavior would be referred to Judicial Affairs.

The matter was further brought to the attention of the Care Team, which is comprised of individuals from Student Affairs, Student Health, Resident Life, Judicial Affairs, with other individuals from other agencies and departments attending meetings occasionally. However, at this point in time his behaviors in his English classes were the only behaviors discussed. As a result, the English Department decided to handle the matter; therefore,

the Care Team assumed the situation was taken care of resulting in no other referrals, interventions, or any further discussion of Cho in the future. Judicial Affairs further stated in interviews following the tragedy that they received no communication from the female students or the Virginia Tech Police Department (VTPD) regarding his harassment and stalking, and if they had been aware of these behaviors, Cho would have been discussed with the Care Team again.

To address the situation with Cho, Dr. Roy contacted him via email to schedule a meeting. Cho replied with an "angry two page letter"[445] but agreed to meet. Dr. Roy and another colleague met with Cho and in the meeting transcription he was described as being very depressed and troubled. The intent of the meeting was to discuss his writings and his disruptive behavior in class. In regard to his writings, Cho stated that he was "just joking."[446] In the meeting, Dr. Roy proposed an alternative, which was for Cho to work independently with her and another professor, and he accepted. Twice during the meeting Dr. Roy recommended that he talk to a counselor at the student mental health center, but Cho never committed to going. Dr. Roy told the Review Panel during the interviews that she was obligated to offer Cho an academic alternative that was equal to what he would receive in class. For the rest of the fall semester, Dr. Roy met with Cho and occasionally wrote updates regarding his progress to colleagues. In one update, she wrote that the meetings with Cho were going "reasonably well, though all of his submissions so far have been about shooting or harming people... I have to admit that I am still very worried about this student."[447] Throughout the remainder of the meetings, Dr. Roy continued to offer to take him to counseling, but again he would not go and she eventually gave him an "A" for a grade.

In late November of 2005, VTPD followed up on a complaint from a female student who lived on the fourth floor in the West Ambler Johnston dormitory regarding some of Cho's unwanted communication with her. He had been text messaging her and eventually had gone to her dorm room wearing a hat pulled down low and reflector sunglasses and stated, "I'm question mark."[448] The police officer confronted Cho and told him not to bother her anymore and that the case was going to be referred to Judicial Affairs.

Three days after the police contact, Cho called the Cook Counseling Center and spoke with a licensed professional counselor. The counselor stated in the interview with the Review Panel that she collected the necessary information needed to decide the level of intervention; however, her notes from the phone triage are missing from Cho's file. There was a note in the file that stated Cho had specifically asked to schedule an appointment with Dr. Betzel, the psychologist that Dr. Roy had previously had a conversation with regarding Cho's writings. Cho failed to show up for the appointment and Dr. Betzel conducted a brief phone interview with him; however, the notes from this phone call are also missing from Cho's file. There is evidence to support that Dr. Betzel was unaware that Cho was the individual that she and Dr. Roy discussed earlier. Regrettably, no referral or future appointment was made.

In December 2005, VTPD was again contacted by another female student regarding receiving text messages and Facebook postings from Cho that she described as "self-deprecating."[449] The police again instructed Cho to have no further contact with her. Following the police contact, Cho sent a text message to a suitemate stating, "I might as well kill myself."[450] The suitemate contacted VTPD and they returned. Cho was considered an imminent danger and involuntarily hospitalized. During his hospitalization, he did admit to having access to a firearm but denied any prior violent history. The psychiatrist who conducted his evaluation stated that Cho denied having any previous mental health treatment or problems. The psychiatrist further stated that he did not gather collateral data due to privacy laws that impede in the information gathering. The special justice overseeing the court hearing regarding Cho's involuntary hospitalization ruled that Cho "presents an imminent danger to himself" and ordered him to outpatient treatment. An appointment was made at Cook Counseling Center. Cho was discharged shortly thereafter from the state hospital. No one knows how Cho got back to campus; however, he did make it to the scheduled appointment at the counseling center. The notes from that appointment are also missing from Cho's file. No follow-up appointment was scheduled. The Report of the Review Panel stated that Cook Counseling Center's policy is to allow patients to decide whether or not to schedule follow-up appointments.

In the spring of 2006, Cho's problems in class continued. His writings were violent and another professor expressed his concern. Dr. Hicok consulted with Dr. Roy about Cho but decided to keep Cho in his class. It was in his class that Cho turned in writings that had suicidal and homicidal ideations, including shooting students in a classroom, but it is unclear if Dr. Hicok shared the specific details of these writings with Dr. Roy. Another professor stated in the report that he was concerned with Cho's demeanor and writings. This was also the professor that when he confronted Cho about his writings and classroom behavior Cho followed him into his office and raised his voice at the professor. The professor asked Cho to leave and return when he had gained control of himself. Cho never returned and eventually dropped the course. Professor Bean did not discuss any of these incidents with Dr. Roy and was also unaware of the problems other professors were experiencing.

At the start of his senior year, fall of 2006, Cho continued to turn in writings that were angry in nature, and one student in the class had told a friend that Cho was the type of person "who might go on a rampage killing."[451] Cho was also suspected of writing violent song lyrics on the walls in his dormitory, but no one confronted him. In another class, Cho's professor had checked with the dean's office to see if it was safe to have him in class and asked to have someone intervene on his behalf. It is unclear how this request was handled, if it was handled at all. The only statement regarding his academics in the spring semester was that his attendance began to fall.

On February 2, 2007, Cho ordered his first handgun online. On March 12, 2007, Cho bought another gun from a gun store near the university. The gun store did the required background check but found no record of any mental health issues. The next few weeks, Cho purchased additional ammunition and practiced at a local shooting range. On April 14, 2007, Cho was seen by a faculty member wearing a hooded sweatshirt in Norris Hall. This faculty member also stated that a student had informed her that doors had been chained impeding entry and exit from Norris Hall. On April 16, 2007, the doors were also chained. It is unclear if they were still chained from two days earlier or if Cho had rechained them before he began his shooting spree.

On April 16, 2007, at approximately 7:00 am, Cho entered West Ambler Johnston dormitory, went to the fourth floor, and killed his first victim. There is no evidence that Cho had any relation with or knew the victim. After hearing a disturbance, the resident advisor went to investigate and became Cho's second victim. When the police arrived, they gained information that led them to believe the first victim's boyfriend was a "person of interest" and it was assumed he had left the campus. The report stated if VTPD suspected the murderer was on campus, precautions would have been ordered and the campus closed; however, due to the assumption that the murder was a result of a domestic disturbance and the belief that the suspect was no longer on campus, the university did not shut down. However, local emergency response teams were immediately placed on alert. The university Policy Group was also contacted. The Policy Group met around 8:30 am to discuss how to notify students of the homicides. Local public schools initiated a lockdown after hearing of the homicides at the Virginia Tech campus via police radio. At approximately 9:30 am, the Policy Group and VT administration decided to email students, staff, and faculty about the homicides at West Ambler Johnston. At 9:40 am, Cho began his shooting spree at Norris Hall. Within minutes, a 911 call reached VTPD and they responded, arriving at Norris Hall at 9:45 am but could not get in due to chained doors. It took several minutes for VTPD officers to shoot open the chained doors and gain entry. Just as police reached Cho, he shot himself in the head. In just over 11 minutes, Cho killed 30 people plus himself and wounded 17 more.

Summary and Discussion

There were several incidents that occurred that were clear warning signs that Cho was on the pathway to avenger violence; however, these incidents were perceived as isolated incidents because there was no open communication between all relevant departments, and no one person was aware of all of Cho's concerning behaviors. Moreover, Cho was labeled as a depressed loner and not correctly identified as a young man engaging in avenger behaviors. There were several attempts made by the English Department to intervene; however, Cho's behaviors and violent writings continued. Several professors stated that they were unaware of Cho's problems in his other classes. In addition, there was a lack of appropriate mental health assessment and treatment as a result of insufficient resources. Cho had several phone conversations with the campus counseling center on several occasions; however, the mental health staff only utilized self-report and no collateral data was gathered. Additionally, he never received individual therapy. The mental health staff available to Virginia Tech students were not trained on how to deal with students exhibiting the concerning behaviors Cho engaged in; therefore, the necessary precautions and monitoring of Cho was not initiated. As a result, he was simply dealt with as a depressed loner with possible suicidal ideations. Open communication between faculty, the counseling center, the campus police, resident advisors, the hospital where Cho was committed, and other key individuals did not occur. Moreover, Cho purchased guns even though a federal law prohibited anyone who had been judged a danger to self and others from buying a gun. The VTPD assumed that the first murders at West Ambler Johnston residence hall were an isolated incident; therefore, no campus-wide notification was initiated until two hours had passed. The campus-wide notification system that was finally initiated failed at reaching all students and staff because it relied on email as the sole communication. In addition, there were no locks on the classroom doors to delay Cho's entry, and no way to communicate to

the rest of the building what was happening. As a result, as Cho was shooting in one classroom, other students and staff in other classrooms were not aware and no attempt to escape was made. Fast thinking by several students and faculty in barricading the doors did save lives. However, other students were simply in shock and did not know what to do. There had been no previous training or discussion on what to do during an active shooting situation.

Given the above key findings, several important lessons were learned. Developing a Behavioral Intervention Team (BIT) that acts as a vortex is crucial for colleges so that all concerning behaviors can be reported to one entity and the big picture can be analyzed. Furthermore, the main goal of the vortex is to organize all reports of concerning behavior to ensure that records of the incident, interventions, and outcomes are documented. Another important responsibility of the BIT and vortex is deciding appropriate interventions and monitoring of how that individual is responding to those interventions. Open communication between all key players on campus (professors, resident advisors, campus police, etc.) is crucial. In addition, the BIT should initiate and continue this communication.

Relying on a campus counseling center is not a remedy in situations where the individual has engaged in avenger behaviors nor should counseling be the only intervention. Getting the individual psychological help is necessary; however, the mental health professional should be aware of all the concerning behaviors, have knowledge on how to handle avenger situations, and be willing to report on the progress or lack of progress made in treatment to the BIT.

With avenger situations, lack of communication between the different entities involved is a major problem. One reason is each individual or department assumes that the problems are isolated to their specific situation. Another problem is the custom of not disclosing information to others due to privacy laws. There are two main privacy laws hindering the sharing of vital information: privacy laws guarding mental health records Health Insurance Portability and Accountability Act (HIPAA) and educational records, the Family Educational Rights and Privacy Act (FERPA). In Cho's case, there was widespread lack of understanding of privacy laws which impeded open communication between the necessary individuals and departments. Privacy laws are intended to be a balance between protecting an individual's privacy and sharing important information when necessary. These laws do permit disclosure of information in certain situations, especially when needed to protect the health and safety of students.[452] Although FERPA is widely misunderstood, it does grant college and university discretion. For instance, FERPA allows colleges to contact students' parents if there is concern regarding their well-being or public welfare. FERPA even permits but does not require colleges and universities to notify parents of certain drug and alcohol violations.[453] Decisions to not disclose minor offenses is a policy choice not a legal one. Furthermore, FERPA only limits the disclosure of records about the student and does not limit disclosure or discussion of personal observations. In addition, FERPA permits appropriate communication under circumstances in which the student may be at risk of harm, including self harm and/or harm to others. This is a fairly low threshold of good faith for determining when disclosures are needed. There is a great need for legislation at the state and federal level, as well as policies at the collegiate level to address this issue and clarify what situations permit disclosure so that there is no confusion regarding open communication when there is sufficient documented evidence that an individual poses a danger to self and/or others or evidence of the lower threshold to support that the safety of students may be at

risk. It is a fine line, in terms of balancing privacy rights; however, as a college or university administrator would you rather deal with a privacy lawsuit or a wrongful death lawsuit?

Cho's behaviors clearly met the threshold under FERPA for notifying his parents. Furthermore, the report stated that if Cho's parents were contacted at any time regarding any of his behaviors, especially his involuntary hospitalization, they stated that they would have pulled him immediately from VT and initiated treatment with the therapist and psychiatrist that he had seen throughout his high school years. Throughout the investigation, Cho's family stated that they would have fully participated with any investigation and expressed tremendous regret.

The fact that Cho was able to purchase a gun even after a judge found him to be a danger to self and others is frustrating. The reason Cho was not in the national background database was due to the fact that the judge presiding over Cho's involuntary hearing referred him to outpatient treatment with the counseling center on Virginia Tech's campus rather then committing him to an institution. The law in Virginia did not clearly require persons recommended to outpatient services to be reported, so no report was made. This is an issue that must be dealt with at the state and federal level; however, campuses can utilize a "Zero Tolerance" rule with guns on campus. This would mean that any evidence that a student has a gun or has recently purchased a gun and is keeping it in his dorm room, is sufficient for the BIT to initiate an investigation to see if the individual has engaged in any other serious behaviors.

In regard to the VTPD believing that the first murders were an isolated incident, any violence of that nature on campus should warrant a campus-wide alert, especially if the police believe the suspect is still on the loose. Murders rarely occur on campus, so any justification about not initiating an alert so the day-to-day activities of the campus are not disrupted is simply not a good choice. It has been common practice for law enforcement to lock down schools when a violent situation occurred nearby and a suspect is on the loose. Colleges should be no exception, particularly if the violence occurred on campus.

Campus-wide alert systems should not rely on email or text messaging alone. There are many reasons for this, the main one being that it will not alert students who are walking to class or already in class, who are typically the ones in the most danger. Campuses should utilize both high-touch and high-tech warning systems. An example of high-touch would be placing either officers or trained faculty, armed with radios for fast updates, throughout campus informing students on what's going on and what to do. High-tech examples of warning systems include text messaging, a loudspeaker, and digital information boards, which should be placed in high traffic areas. Additionally, students and faculty need to be educated on what to do when such alerts are initiated so that panic does not ensue.

If classes are already in session and an active shooter incident occurs, having classroom doors that lock is one of the most effect methods of delaying entry into the classroom. An intercom system to alert other classrooms in the building should be in every classroom. These intercom alerts can also be wired to go directly to campus security so that they can know exactly what's going on and respond immediately as well as initiate a campus-wide alert.

A SYSTEM RISK MANAGEMENT APPROACH

The system response to an avenger situation is different from how schools and colleges would handle other types of violence because the type of prevention and intervention strategies used to prevent other types of violence in schools and on college campuses will be ineffective with avenger violence. In light of the Virginia Tech tragedy, a new approach to dealing with avenger violence situations at schools and college campuses is presented: a system risk management approach. Typically, risk management has been used to manage the individual. For example, if a student is engaging in concerning behaviors, a risk assessment is done and risk management strategies are used that typically focus on the individual and what interventions that individual needs. System risk management involves strategies for the school/campus to implement and do not focus solely on the individual in question.

An imperative first step to a system risk management approach is to be proactive instead of reactive, meaning that several prevention methods need to be developed and integrated into the school's daily activities. Policies and procedures that pertain specifically to how to handle an individual who has engaged in avenger threshold behaviors are an important first step in a system risk management approach. All students and parents of students should be aware of these polices and procedures. Good polices and procedures should specifically spell out what behavior is not accepted and what will happen if such behaviors are exhibited. For example, if a student engages in behaviors that cause significant social and psychological disruption, the BIT and parents will be notified. However, the BIT should balance civil rights and the safety of students and only report to parents if there is significant evidence that indicates the student is engaging in unacceptable behaviors.

Organizing a BIT and training BIT members is easy to do and is the most important element to preventing avenger violence. The BIT should consist of individuals who are dedicated to being trained on the psychological development of an avenger and avenger behaviors. These individuals should be representatives from several different school/campus departments. The BIT's objective is avenger violence prevention and response. More importantly, the BIT acts as the vortex. The vortex is the person/persons whom all information regarding the individual engaging in avenger behaviors flows through so that the big picture is seen. For instance, if a professor/teacher is concerned after a student turns in a violent essay, the BIT would be notified. Another example would be, if a resident advisor becomes aware of a student who may be suicidal or engaging in other concerning behaviors, the BIT should be notified. A practical and timely risk assessment, such as the IBAR should be utilized and the BIT should be trained in risk assessment and have access to an individual who specializes in risk assessment for consultation. Additionally, the risk assessment should include system risk management strategies in conjunction with individual risk management strategies.

Once the BIT has been notified and the initial risk assessment indicates a concern, intervention and interruption will be activated. Intervention and interruption can take place in a numbers of ways, and focus on the specific needs of the school and campus in terms of how to protect the system. System risk management includes disciplinary actions that the school/campus can utilize such as suspension pending a more in-depth investigation (when such a suspension does not abrogate the student's civil rights). In addition, other strategies such as notifying staff and faculty of the situation and a review of how to protect a class in an active shooter situation are also examples of system risk management. If the risk assessment does not indicate an immediate threat, other system risk management strategies can be utilized such as a "knock and talk," which is nothing more than approaching the student and discussing the seriousness of the action and notifying them that first, they are being monitored and second, what

will happen if the behavior continues (as long as the statement of what will happen does not abrogate the student's civil rights). Monitoring as well as specific interventions for the individual will be activated. For example, if a student is engaging in concerning behaviors but is also suspected of having mental health issues, referral to the mental health center or a mental health professional in the community is important; however, there needs to be clear understanding that the mental health provider must report back to the BIT regarding treatment status. The key to intervention is to continue to monitor the individual's progress or lack thereof. If the individual's behaviors continue despite intervention, other more serious steps need to be taken. These steps should be clearly spelled out in policies and procedures to ensure fair treatment of all individuals. It is also recommended that the BIT consult with the school's/campus' legal counsel to insure that student's first amendment rights are not being violated.

Another imperative preventative piece is to train all relevant individuals. Specifically, professors and staff need to be educated on avenger behaviors. Furthermore, the training should also include how to contact the BIT if they observe any concerning behaviors, written or verbal. In addition, the campus police or local police, the student mental health center, student life, academic and other departments should all be trained on what behaviors are worthy of reporting and how to report to the BIT. A discussion of privacy laws and what behaviors are considered reportable should also be a part of the training.

If an active shooter situation arises or the individual engages in violent behavior, system response and neutralization begins. The system response involves immediate notification of all individuals in the school or on campus as well as notification to relevant departments such as law enforcement and emergency response teams. Notification systems should have already been designed and tested. Schools/campuses should utilize a number of internal notification methods, including high-tech and high-touch. High-tech notification systems include intercoms, loud speaker systems, a specific alarm only used for active shooters (not just an all inclusive alarm), text messaging warnings, email warnings, phone warnings, and any other technology that can be used to notify all individuals in the school or on campus. Classrooms and offices should have a panic button to notify the designated external response departments such as law enforcement and it should be clearly known that any pranks will be harshly punished. In addition, training on what to do after these options have been utilized is imperative. High-touch notification would include having designated individuals to notify others located in the building or on campus. Moreover, setting up delay systems to delay entry of the avenger into classrooms and offices is important. The most proven delay system is to have doors that lock from the inside. In all avenger cases, not one has taken the time to shoot open a locked door.

Students and faculty should be given personal survival strategies on how to strategically respond to avenger situations. These include, depending on the location and type of violence occurring: getting out of the building, barricading, finding concealment, playing dead, and actively resisting. If a good notification system is in place and people are aware of the exact situation, getting out of the building is the best survival technique. In the avenger shooting at Northern Illinois, several students were able to escape when the shooter entered the auditorium, thus saving their lives. However, if there is no information of where the shooting is taking place or no easy exit is available, then barricading the door is the next best option. In the Virginia Tech incident, some students were able to barricade the door keeping Cho from entering, even though he tried several times to enter. If the door cannot be barricaded, if it opens to the

outside, for example, then hiding is the next option. If the shooter is in the room and shots have been fired, playing dead has been a proven survival technique in many incidents including Virginia Tech, Columbine, and several other cases. The last option if faced with an active shooter is to actively resist, which means to attack the perpetrator with whatever means are available. In the avenger incident that occurred in Springfield, Oregon in 1998, several students tackled the avenger, ending the shooting spree. In Grundy, Virginia, during the Appalachian School of Law avenger incident, students also subdued the avenger. Again, active resistance is a last resort and should only be utilized if there are no other options.

What a System Risk Management Approach Would Have Looked Like with Cho

If a system risk management approach was utilized with Cho, the events on April 16, 2007, could have been prevented. For instance, the BIT would have been notified by either the concerned students or the students would have notified their resident advisor who would have notified the BIT after the first few incidents where Cho stabbed the carpet with a knife, wrote dark lyrics on the dorm walls, and set things on fire in his dorm room. At this point, the BIT could have employed the "knock and talk" techniques as well as require that he begin therapy, with updates from the therapist to the BIT. If a system risk management approach was used, the professors in the English Department could have reported Cho's violent writings and his other concerning behavior in class to the BIT. The BIT, still aware of Cho's other behavior, would realize that they were dealing with more than a disturbed student and would have initiated more intervention; that would have probably included harsher disciplinary action, more monitoring, and contacting his parents. Once the VTPD contacted the BIT regarding Cho's stalking behavior and harassment even more intervention and interruption would have been initiated. For instance, a suspension until a specified risk assessment specialist considered Cho safe to return. When the BIT became aware of his involuntary hospitalization, much more could have been done, especially since the BIT would have been aware of many of his other concerning behaviors, and Cho would more than likely not have been able to return to campus until a specified risk assessment specialist considered Cho safe to return. If a system risk management approach had been utilized, specifically, if a BIT had been formed, appropriate policy and procedures had been developed, and all the relevant people been trained on what behaviors to report and who to report them to, interventions with Cho could have begun in the fall of 2005.

CONCLUSION

Avenger violence is a rare but serious type of violence. When it does occur it instigates shock in schools, campuses, and the surrounding communities. Experts have vigorously debated if violence can be predicted and prevented. There are several risk assessment tools and approaches that have been developed in an attempt to predict and/or prevent different types of violence, with varying success. However, when it comes to avenger violence the threat assessment approach has garnered the most attention. Though it is a very solid approach, the time

and effort into conducting a risk assessment using the threat assessment approach can be costly. The IBAR is a proven technique that addresses the limitations of the threat assessment approach. Together, the IBAR and a practical system risk management approach, can be a successful approach at preventing avenger violence.

As knowledge about avenger violence grows, so will the need to conduct more research on this type of violence so that prevention methods can continue to be developed. Specifically, research on why some individuals report serious or concerning behaviors and others do not. In addition, empirical studies on the success of risk assessments utilized in avenger violence situations would be a great addition to the growing literature on avenger violence. Furthermore, the more knowledge there is available about avenger violence and the techniques used to prevent it, the more likely this type of violence can be interrupted thus, preventing situations like Virginia Tech.

Using Virginia Tech as a case example, one can clearly see that avenger violence does not occur at random, but is a long behavior progression in which the individual begins with a perceived injustice and eventually escalates into more concerning behaviors. These behaviors are often witnessed by several people but are seen as isolated incidents if there is no communication system in place to monitor these individuals. More importantly, if schools and campuses are prepared to handle avenger situations and have a strategic risk management system in place, tragic events like the one at Virginia Tech can be avoided.

Chapter 16

RIOTING

SALLY SPENCER-THOMAS

PERSPECTIVES: HERE'S WHAT PEOPLE ARE SAYING ABOUT CAMPUS RIOTS

For all activists who seek drastic social change, the university is an obvious target and a potential instrument of the greatest value. It is filled with young people whose natural idealism is as yet untempered by the patience and tolerance of maturity. These students are at a time of life when a normal feeling of revulsion against all authority easily can be diverted into violent antagonism toward existing political and economic institutions and policies.... The noisy clamoring of a handful of students may capture the headlines, but the vast majority of their fellows is either indifferent or even hostile toward them....

> – Columbia University President Grayson Kirk, June 1, 1965

Tired of a few skittish cops turning a mildly out-of-control party into a life-threatening riot? Do your tear ducts still burn after last weekend's big soiree? Well, dammit the cops are going to bust up your party anyway so you might as well validate their aggression. Just follow the steps below to ensure a proper riot. By the time you're done the EPD won't be using tear gas, they'll resort to Napalm....

> – The Official Commentator Riot Guide, Featured in University of
> Oregon's *Oregon Commentator*, October 2, 1997

They treat us like animals, we'll act like animals.

> – Freshman at University of New Hampshire (UNH), May 8, 1998

If everyone is so puzzled as to why UNH students are rioting, I think the answer is pretty simple – they're fighting back.... We seem to have this understanding with the national press now: UNH = trouble....

> – Cathleen Genova, student at UNH, The New Hampshire Forum,
> October 7, 1997

Over the years, colleges tended to wink at the alcohol policies, and then they started enforcing and changing policies without involving students in the decisions. It was the ideal set of circumstances to bring about these riots.

> – Arthur Levine & Jeanette Cureton, authors of *When Hope and Fear
> Collide: A Portrait of Today's College Student*[454]

245

I think the police made an utter mockery of the state, as well as the nation. We disagree with what's happening here. We think the students of UNH should stand up for their rights.

– UNH Senior, September 1997

The thing that is stupid is they did it for no reason other than to go into the street and set trashcans on fire. It's like their parents never taught them anything better to do.

– Athens Police Chief about the Ohio University riots, April 2000

When you have 23 officers injured, some of them with broken bones, and you see the size of the objects being thrown ... We're not out there for fun and games.

– Pullman Police Chief Ted Weatherly, Commenting on
the Washington State University riot, May 4, 1998

It was a blast in all senses of the word. We came together as a school, burned some things, showed some skin and that's fine. It was Spartan pride.

– Michigan State University junior March 29, 1999

What I have to say to East Lansing is that the riot is a symbol of freedom and we deserve it.

– Michigan State University senior September 9, 1997

We're all moving out. I don't think you'll find any other permanent residents around here after this thing's over.

– Beth Van Liere, East Lansing resident and former Chairperson
of the Bailey Neighborhood Association about the MSU riots,
September 1, 1997

"Students Demonstrate for Their Right to Bear Beers"

– Times Union (Albany, New York) headline May 13, 1998

"College Protests are Sophomoric: All We Are Saying Is Give Beer a Chance"

– *Cincinnati Enquirer* headline May 13, 1998

CAMPUS RIOTS OF TODAY

The above perspectives on rioting demonstrate the wide range of conflicts campuses and communities are currently facing. Finger pointing abounds and emotions run high. The students blame administration, the police, and the media. Administration blames the students' upbringing and irresponsible attitudes. The media obtains dramatic photos and catchy headlines. The police find themselves in a no-win situation. The community residents and alumni of these schools are disgusted. What is going on here?

Many students involved in today's rioting liken the uproar of the 1990s to the campus unrest during the 1960s and 1970s. Some believe that their rights have been violated and they are protesting unfair university and law enforcement policies. One Michigan State University student wrote an editorial to *The State News* drawing similarities between the student rioting and the Boston Tea Party stating students may have a voice, but not a vote,

"Clearly, we the students of Michigan State are being taxed without representation. Sound familiar? The founders of this great country also threw a party, and it was even more costly than a few windshields and a street light...."

Table 16.1 offers some similarities and differences between the riots of the 1960s and 1990s:

Table 16.2 profiles some of the major riots affecting our campuses from 1996 to 2000. In this analysis we chose only the riots that either caused major damage or resulted in numerous arrests. Many other lower intensity incidents occurred on these and other campuses that still had a significant impact but were not included. Several campuses experienced "anniversary rioting" that occurred at lower intensity either before or after the more intense riot included in this chart. For instance, a couple of the campuses had annual riots around Halloween, some years worse than others. The riots analyzed here involved between 500 to 10,000 people and resulted in damage estimates ranging from $5,000 to $500,000.

Intriguing observations emerge from this chart. Geographically, the rioting campuses seem to be clustered together indicating that copycat behavior may be occurring. Two schools were in New Hampshire, two in Colorado, and three in Ohio. Interestingly, so far, no major riots have occurred in the South, a part of the country known for civil rights campus rioting in the 1960s and 1970s.

While it is difficult to pinpoint possible triggers for the riots, student interviews shed some light on the climate before behavior became out of control. "Alcohol restriction" rioting occurred after campus officials imposed a tighter reign on underage drinking, banned tailgating, or developed other drinking restrictions on the students. Police crackdowns on unruly parties also fell into this category. Limiting access to alcohol seems to be the biggest trigger for rioting at this time. There are many perspectives on this controversy, and we will address them later in this chapter.

Athletic victories or defeats also triggered rioting on several campuses. On large campuses where athletic teams are the source of school pride and identity, wins or losses of important games can result in an outpouring of out-of-control fans. Sometimes the athletic match does not even have to involve college

Table 16.1
RIOTS OF TWO GENERATIONS

1960s	*1990s*
Challenge values of authority	Challenge values of authority
Located on campus, heavy student involvement	Located on campus, heavy student involvement
Peaceful and violent demonstrations	Peaceful and violent demonstrations
Alcohol intoxication not a major contributing factor	Most participants drunk
Race and War central issues	"Right to Party" central issue
Targets of destruction – R.O.T.C. buildings, police	Targets of destruction – College towns, police
Media focal point – Four students killed at Kent	Media focal point – "Real TV" footage of MSU riot

Table 16.2
CHARACTERISTICS OF CAMPUS RIOTS 1996–2000[455]

Number of Campuses Analyzed = 11, Number of Riots Analyzed = 20				
Geographic Location	South		0	0%
	Northwest		2	18%
	Northeast		4	36%
	Midwest/West		5	45%
Possible Triggering Event	Alcohol Restriction		10	50%
	Athletic Victory/Loss		6	30%
	Tradition		4	20%
Time of Year	August–October		8	40%
	November–February		1	5%
	March–May		9	45%
	May–July		2	10%
Town-Gown Dynamics	Students Outnumber Permanent Residents		3	27%
	Students Roughly Equal to Permanent Residents		5	45%
	Permanent Residents Outnumber Students		3	27%
Characteristics		Unknown	# Yes	# No	%
Alcohol major contributing factor		0	20	0	100%
Campus enrollment 10,000+		0	10	1	91%
More than 15 people arrested		5	11	4	58%
Police injured/ Police cars		7	9	4	45%
More than one riot at the school		0	6	5	54%

sports. Many campuses in Colorado experienced student riots and disturbances after the Denver Broncos' Superbowl victories.

Sometimes the rioting becomes a tradition. Schools tend to have annual big party weekends, and rioting can evolve out of these celebrations. As mentioned earlier, Halloween rioting seems to be a particularly favored pastime at some schools. Costumed rioters are especially difficult for investigators to identify and prosecute. With traditional rioting, students anticipate that rioting will occur at these times, and they prepare ahead of time, stockpiling bonfire kindling and spreading rumors of the riot repeat. Out of curiosity, groups of students will turn up just to see what will happen. Once the crowd has gathered a few instigators act outrageously and the riot is on.

The time of year also seems to have an important influence on rioting. Springtime seems to be the most popular time for campus riots. Many occur around the last days of school or spring party weekends. The beginning of the school year ranked second with Halloween weekend coming in a close third.

The campus and community relations or "town-gown dynamics" may be a critical factor. In many of the most destructive riots to date, the student population outnumbered or closely matched the population of the permanent surrounding community. Michigan State University, Penn State University, University of Connecticut, Washington State University, and Ohio University are large schools in small towns or cities. In some ways, this setup may give students an inflated sense of "owning" the town and doing what they please. Often the students have an educational and economic advantage over many of the residents. Community members may be reluctant to confront students as the university may employ townsfolk, or local businesses may heavily depend on student patronization. Building resentment and tensions can easily escalate into fuel for the riots. One East Lansing resident commented on the MSU students' rioting by saying, "These kids do not seem to get the picture of what it means to be a resident in a community."

College students are not the only ones participating in these campus riots. High school students, alumni, and community residents have all been involved. In the aftermath of a big sporting event, rival college students are also present. Nevertheless, we look at arrest rates as an indication of who is causing the trouble; college students of the campus where the riot took place usually account for about 75 percent of the arrestees.

The subsequent chronology details some of the more devastating riots on campuses in the last few years.

University of Colorado (CU)
Boulder, Colorado
May 2-4, 1997

Just before midnight on Friday, May 2, police were called when two house parties at 14th Street and College Avenue overflowed into the street.[456] A crowd of 400 to 500 people gathered around a bonfire in the middle of the street. They greeted police by throwing bricks, rocks, and bottles. The mob moved into the commercial area of University Hill and began smashing store windows and vandalizing cars. By dawn the crowd had swelled to more than 2,000 people and 100 officers were called to the scene. Police wore riot gear and used tear gas and rubber bullets to disperse the crowd.

The rioting continued into early Sunday morning when University Hill bar patrons left their establishments after "last call" and entered the streets to find police officers positioned and ready.[457] Another clash ensued. Damage estimates from the two nights was $300,000. Twelve officers and many students were injured including some head injuries.

The history behind this incident involves a chain of events familiar to many campuses.[458] First, in 1994 the university experienced an alcohol-related tragedy. A sophomore woman was killed in a drunk-driving accident. This unfortunate event combined with numerous community complaints regarding unruly student parties led to a law enforcement crackdown on underage drinking. The police targeted big parties, usually those within the Greek system. Resentment and tension began to build. At the same time, the university beefed up its campaign to address alcohol problems on campus and increased educational and enforcement initiatives within the campus system.

In the fall of 1996, campus officials boldly decided to ban the sale of beer at football games and restrict alcohol use at tailgate parties.[459] At the same time, fraternities and sororities agreed to ban alcohol-related parties in their residences. Less than a year later they retracted that agreement, causing further conflict between students, the community, and the police.

In the aftermath of the riot, town meetings were held and four task forces were formed to address issues of police-student relations, community building, violence, and alcohol. Despite campus-wide involvement in dealing with this event, smaller riots have plagued the CU campus for the last few years.[460] Halloween disturbances have occurred annually for as long as people can remember. In 1999, CU experienced a post-Superbowl outbreak after the Broncos' victory, and in the fall, CU and Colorado State University students were involved in a major disruption at Mile High Stadium after the football upset. During August 2000, a riot involving up to 1,000 people erupted after a block party got out of control. A large bonfire threatened trees and one-hundred-year-old structures in the neighborhood. This latest riot led CU to form a "three strikes and you're out" alcohol discipline policy. Coincidentally, the same week of the riot, the *Princeton Review* revealed that CU ranked number 5 on their list of top party schools in the country.

Because all of this rioting has cost the school and city of Boulder hundreds of thousands of dollars, local leaders and campus administrators are floating around the idea of developing a "rioting fee" likened to the annual student fee to help pay for the damages.[461] The latest policy suggested by administrators has been called the "film and fine" policy. This tactic would involve hiring private contractors with video cameras and halogen lights to film student bystanders at riots. These bystanders would then be charged a stiff fine – up to $1,000 each in hopes spectators begin to view rioting more as a crime to stay away from rather than a sporting event to revel in.

Ohio University (OU)
Athens, Ohio
April 5, 1998

Ohio University has the dubious distinction of having the most bizarre rioting trigger of all – daylight savings time. When the clocks were set to "spring forward" on April 5, 1998, 2,000 OU students and others protested the fact that bars were forced to close an hour earlier.[462] The 1998 riot marked the one-year anniversary of a spontaneous protest against the early closings the previous April. After the 1997 incident, which involved about 1,000 people and was much less violent than the 1998 riot, police invested in costly riot gear because they felt the safety of the officers was in jeopardy.

In preparation for the 1998 riot, camera crews were set to capture the action as students chanted "CNN! CNN!"[463] Because of this, many blamed the media for creating a self-fulfilling prophecy. OU prides itself as an outstanding journalism school, and many have remarked how effectively OU students staged a sensationalized media event.

Police began by shooting foam bullets at the crowd, but the plan backfired as students goaded police to fire at them.[464] The police then moved to wooden bullets. The students fought back with bottles, asphalt, and bricks. One student commented, "It's a year after the big riot and people will probably celebrate this every year. We came down because we knew the cops would be here overreacting if something did happen. It's been great to watch."

University of Connecticut (UConn)
Storrs, Connecticut
April 25, 1998

During the annual "University Weekend," a crowd of 2,000 people taunted police and hurled bottles, cans, and rocks at them while 80 officers stood their ground on the perimeter of the dirt parking lot.[465] A couch was set on fire. A Honda Accord was overturned. Still the police were motionless. According to the university police chief, the police were told to take the approach of, "You can have a party, and you're clearly going to break the law – just don't break it on a massive scale." When the rioters attempted to put the couch on the Honda, police moved in with pepper spray to disperse the mob. By the end of the night, 27 police cars had been vandalized.

The traditional party weekend occurs during the last couple of weeks before finals each year and had a reputation for getting out of control.[466] Police were prepared to step in if they were needed, but their mere presence enflamed the situation for those who saw it as a violation of students' right to have a good time. The university tried to provide alternative entertainment for students, but their plan failed miserably. Only 100 students attended the university-sponsored party. Students claimed they were not interested because beer was not available to underage students.

By the end of the ordeal, UConn and state police arrested 101 individuals and the university disciplined 92 students.[467] Six people received criminal convictions resulting in jail sentences and probation, 13 people received criminal convictions that included suspended jail sentences and probation, 17 people were placed in programs for first-time offenders, and 44 people paid fines for noncriminal offenses. From the university disciplinary side of things, two students were expelled, six were suspended, 12 were removed from the residence halls, and scores of others received warnings and probation.

Washington State University (WSU) Pullman, Washington May 3, 1998

May 1–3, 1998 was the worst weekend for campus rioting for several decades. Plymouth State College in New Hampshire, University of Kansas (Lawrence), and Michigan State University in East Lansing all experienced fire-setting, rock-throwing, glass-smashing, police-clashing disturbances involving large crowds of students.[468] The weekend's most violent riot was at Washington State University.

The riot began with a party at the notorious "Golf Patrons Only" house, a rental residence on Greek Row nicknamed by a stolen sign.[469] Police were originally called to the party in response to an unfounded report of a drunk-driver-pedestrian accident at 12:30 am When the two officers arrived on scene, they were greeted by 200 rock-throwing partygoers. The officers quickly retreated while several bonfires were set in the street. The crowd grew as curious onlookers began to gather.

Other Pullman police were called in to close the three bars in the area.[470] Subsequently, several hundred more students joined in the gathering in the street. At 1:30 am, the Pullman police chief divided his 37 officers into two teams of 22 and 15 officers. The plan was to have the teams confront the crowd from opposite directions and meet in the intersection. The plan failed. Communications efforts were hampered because the two teams were using different radio frequencies. Aggressive, intoxicated students drastically outnumbered the officers. Hostile bottle-throwing individuals halted the larger team. Students surrounded the smaller team.

Police supervisors did not anticipate that students would charge the officers.[471] But they did. Carrying sections of chain-link fence as shields, kegs, bricks, frying pans, and even a manhole cover were projected at police. An officer was knocked nearly unconscious when a chunk of concrete struck his riot helmet. All 15 officers in the smaller team were injured, many of them seriously. A state of emergency was declared and the crowd ordered to disperse.

By 5:00 am, an additional 60 officers were dispatched to WSU.[472] Nine state patrol officers responded ill equipped for a riot because they did not possess riot shields. Eight of the nine were seriously injured by thrown objects. A small National Guard contingent was activated but not used. By 6:00 am, the riot was over and 23 officers were in the hospital. Five of the officers were awarded a Purple Heart distinction for their injuries.

Police confiscated cameras and videos of bystanders for their investigation over the next several days.[473] With this evidence, police declared to the student body, "We know who you are!" Students quickly proceeded to dye their hair and alter their looks in other ways to avoid arrest. Flyers circulated the campus making jokes about the incident such as, "Top Ten Reasons to Start a WSU Riot."

Two years later, WSU was still feeling the hangover of the riot. On March 3, 2000, several hundred students gathered outside the Golf Patrons Only house.[474] Six officers responded and some individuals began throwing bottles. The police acted swiftly by setting up a command center and calling for backup law enforcement agencies. Chanting emerged from the crowd and rumors flew – there's going to be a riot. Onlookers began to gather. Six individuals attempted to agitate the crowd. Approximately 150 officers in riot gear gathered behind the scenes. But it was probably student leadership that snuffed out the riot before it began. Greek leaders circulated the crowd telling people to go home. By 3:30 am, all was quiet again.

WSU suffered a major public relations problem in the wake of the riot.[475] Enrollment has dropped since 1998, and the footage of the riot continues to roll. WSU alumni Randy Stegmeier was quoted on spokane.net, "Once it's (the bad public image) spread across TV screens especially, that damage is done and it takes a lot to undo because anytime you have an incident that even slightly mirrors that, it's like peeling the scab off. There it is again."[476] Others speculate that WSU is under the microscope for being the center of attention in a small town.

Nevertheless, campus officials and Greek leaders have attempted to change the culture of WSU and prevent future riots from happening.[477] Task force members developed a 40-page plan to systematically deal with the problems. Examining alcohol policies, expanding education, restructuring Greek residence, and enhancing student leadership training are some of the strategies. Student affairs faculty members participate in a walking patrol of College Hill every weekend. Alternative activities are being developed to offset the large street party attraction.

Pennsylvania State University (Penn State)
State College, Pennsylvania
July 12, 1998

The Penn State riot is unusual because it occurred during the time of year most students were not in class. During a weekend in July, the State College community hosted the annual Central Pennsylvania Festival of the Arts, but a combination of too much alcohol and a crowd of 1,500 turned this event into a disaster.[478] By the time the riot was over, 16 police officers were injured, 20 people were arrested, and $150,000 worth of damage had taken place.

The riot took place in a section of town nicknamed "Beaver Canyon" because student high-rise apartment buildings line both sides of the street.[479] Police state that within ten minutes a Frisbee game involving 150 people swelled to a rowdy crowd of 1,500 after the bars closed at 1:30 am. Three storefronts were damaged, 33 streetlights were broken, and at least one student was burned when the crowd pushed him into the bonfire. By some reports, police stood back initially, hoping the mob would wear itself out. Instead, it just gained momentum. Rioters got right in the officers' faces, challenging them to take action. Some students stripped naked and threw their underwear in the fire. The balconies of the high-rises became a public safety hazard as people threw objects from their apartments and cheered on the rioters. Some balconies held up to 30 people. One high-rise spectator commented he was so grateful to have "front-row seats for a major sporting event."

Police had difficulty identifying the rioters.[480] Many of them left town after the event because school was not in session, and they were living elsewhere for the summer. Shortly after the riot, State College police began purchasing thousands of dollars worth of riot gear and received special training in crowd control. Penn State President Graham

Spanier received criticism for not expelling the 11 Penn State students who were arrested. He was quoted in the *Lancaster New Era* as saying, "To kick somebody out of college is a life-changing event." During the same event in 1999, students were planning on heading over to Beaver Avenue just to see what would take place, but this time, State College was ready for them and the weekend went smoothly.

The Festival of the Arts 2000 did not have such a good outcome.[481] Once again, police used pepper spray and other riot tactics to disperse a crowd of 2,500 who inundated Beaver Avenue. The high-rises again were cause for concern as beer bottles were thrown into the crowd from seven stories above. Police moved quickly and contained the riot within an hour. Because of this swift response, extensive property damages were avoided. After the riot, police requested video footage taken by witnesses, and many voluntarily turned in their videos. Campus leaders voiced their disappointment publicly given the effort and planning that had gone into both the Festival of the Arts and the riot prevention.

Michigan State University (MSU) East Lansing, Michigan March 27–28, 1999

The largest and most damaging campus riot to date occurred at MSU in March 1999.[482] This riot was MSU's fourth in two years, but rioting history at MSU dates back to the 1980s. On September 7, 1997, the "Gunson Riot" erupted after MSU beat Western Michigan University's football team on opening day. About 500 people participated and $5,000 worth of damage was inflicted. In late April 1998, email messages spread across campus urging people to gather at Munn Field to protest the recent school officials' decision to ban alcohol there during football season. On May 1, 1998, 3,000 people showed and the peaceful protest evolved into a riot (known as the Munn Riot). Shortly after

MSU was ranked in a national survey as one of the leading "party schools" in the country. On March 21, 1999, 1,000 people took to the streets after MSU defeated Kentucky to enter the Final Four competition (known as the Kentucky riot). After Duke beat MSU in the final four championship on March 27, 1999, 10,000 people swarmed the streets of East Lansing causing up to $1,000,000 in damage (known as the Duke riot).

The mayor of East Lansing said March 27 was the worst night of his life.[483] Everyone knew the probability for a riot that night was high. MSU basketball coach Tim Izzo taped a message to the students asking them to celebrate responsibly; however, when the segment was aired to the 3,000 students in Munn Arena the sound was not turned on. The university had arranged for a pep rally and fireworks display after the game, but too many students descended on the site. Chanting began and someone threw a police barricade in the fire. The riot was on. Seventy fires were lit across town, one three stories tall. A group of people stood on top of the local Taco Bell and tore the tiles off the roof.

MSU had perfected rioting by the time the Duke riot erupted.[484] In preparation for the event, students froze beer cans to throw through windows, stockpiled kindling, and even had T-shirts printed with the logo "Absolut Riot" (a spoof on the vodka's advertising). They also learned that anonymity is difficult to maintain in the age of videotaping and the Internet, so a few wore ski masks. Still a riot website containing more than 100 photographs led to the identification of 33 defendants before hackers entered the site to uncover informants' names. Through meticulous and undying determination, investigators arrested 132 individuals of which 113 were convicted of their crime. Seventy-one of those arrested were MSU students. Of those convicted, 94 went to jail and many were ordered to pay back the owners of property that was destroyed.

Not only had rioters and investigators perfected their skills by the Duke Riot, the campus community developed innovative approaches to prevention as well.[485] Community residents and students banded together to attempt to stop the rioting. A community group called the "Peace Team" consisted of a handful of brave East Lansing citizens wearing yellow jackets who roamed the streets during the riot and confronted rioters who were trying to flip cars and start riots. A small group of students who call themselves "SPARTY" (Students Pissed About Riots This Year) in recognition of the school mascot, attempted to sell T-shirts to raise money to help pay back East Lansing for riot damages. In the year 2000, MSU beat Iowa State in the NCAA Basketball Tournament, and the celebration was peaceful. The East Lansing mayor credits strong education and the multiple convictions of the previous year's riot as determining factors in deterring a riot. A new ordinance passed by the city council gave police authority to establish police lines and safety zones, which prevented people from entering a designated area. Another ordinance passed making standing within 300 feet of an illegal fire a disorderly conduct misdemeanor. Continued efforts are being made to mend the torn relations between East Lansing residents and MSU students. The local University Lutheran Church sponsored a community-wide conference called "No Future Without Forgiveness" to begin the reconciliation process.

WHAT IS A RIOT

Definitions and Dynamics

Throughout the history of America, rioting has been a catalyst for social change. The perspective of the individual largely determines what constitutes a riot. What may be a peaceful demonstration or, more relevant to today's riots, a wild party to one person may be seen as a riot to another. We choose to abide by the definition suggested by historical rioting expert Paul Gilje in his book *Rioting in America*, "a riot is any group of 12 or more people attempting to assert their will immediately through the use of force outside the normal bounds of law."[486] "Force" refers to both violence and the threat of violence and the determination of what constitutes "force" is often circumstantial. The concept of spontaneity is absent from the definition as many riots are premeditated by a small group of people.

Retired U.S. Lieutenant Colonel Rex Applegate adds to this definition in his landmark book *Kill or Get Killed: Riot Control Techniques, Manhandling, and Close Combat, for Police and the Military*.[487] He makes the distinction that a crowd is not a riot because members of a crowd think and act as individuals. When agitators manipulate a crowd, members begin to lose their identity and merge into a primitive cohesive group.

The larger the group the more the anonymity is protected and the more normal moral restraints break down. For instance, many women participating in the college riots of the 1990s flashed bare breasts or took off their shirts entirely. Simultaneously, members gain strength knowing that large numbers of people support their actions. When riot offenses begin to happen in rapid succession, the rioters can easily overwhelm police who are usually scrambling to react. As Northwestern University Professors David Haddock and Daniel Polsby comment in their article, "Understanding Riots," "There comes a point at which the police pass from inadequacy to impotence."[488] During some campus riots, police have had to retreat because they were so outnumbered. As noted in the Washington State University riot, police ended up being surrounded by rioters. At the Penn State riot, one man allegedly grabbed a police officer by the collar and shouted, "What are you going to do?!"

Rioters tend to act like a stampede. A triggering event sends a few noticeable leaders in a direction, and the rest of the group blindly follows. The triggering event can range from an athletic victory to bars closing one hour early for daylight savings time.

Once the starting signal is given – a rock through a car window or a couch in a bonfire – most of the crowd knows a riot is imminent. Haddock and Polsby emphasize that crowd psychology is crucial in the early stages of the riot because usually people who are looking to commit violent crimes do not want to be in the presence of hostile bystanders. Thus, a critical mass of the crowd must expect and desire the riot to begin.

According to Haddock and Polsby, the location of the riot is usually not determined by chance. Usually one or more logical focal points exist, and people instinctively know where to congregate. At CU Boulder, riots have started in front of the Golf Patrons Only house. At Penn State, they commenced at Beaver Canyon. Sometimes the location is symbolic of the cause for the riot itself. The Munn riot at MSU started there because of protests on alcohol restrictions during games at Munn Field.

First Amendment: Rights and Responsibilities

College protesters, like other American citizens have the rights of freedom of speech and assembly. College administrators and enforcers must take these rights seriously. Nevertheless, students and other protesters must be aware that they relinquish these rights when they break the law. According to Col. Rex Applegate, when the crowd begins to block entrances or exits, prevent free passage of individuals, use physical force on a person, throw matter, disturb the peace, use offensive instigating language, or commit any criminal act, the demonstration then becomes an "unlawful assembly." After announcing this state

of unlawful assembly to revelers and demanding individuals disperse, law enforcement officers are then empowered to use reasonable force to restore order.

PLAYING A PART: ROLES IN A RIOT

There are many different ways people contribute to the outcome of a riot. Some get it going. Others sustain it. Often a large group watches and a small group tries to extinguish it.

Agitators

When we look across different riots in our nation's history, the agitators of riots tend to be young adults (average age 20) with prior offenses and almost exclusively male. Agitators often plan for the riot and plant the seeds for the uprising long before the event takes place. They will spread rumors through email and by word of mouth to pique the interest of the masses. When the climate is right and the crowd has gathered, they will be the ones to take the risk of throwing the first bottle or flipping the first car in hopes that others will follow. During campus riots, the agitators are usually outrageously intoxicated.

Haddock and Polsby suggest that agitators are often motivated by their need to uphold their reputation. Some students pride themselves on having reputations for hard partying or acting crazy. Witnesses may be surprised by who eventually gets sucked into the riot as these often unlikely participants have acted out of character, but they usually are not surprised by the ringleaders. Some agitators are chronic troublemakers who are looking to jump on the bandwagon of creating mischief or cashing in on crime opportunities (e.g., looting). Many of these individuals are not even college students, but local residents who want to get into the action.

In the aftermath of the riot, agitators and their lawyers will use a host of excuses to blend in with the "innocent bystanders." As we will discuss in the solutions section of this chapter, campuses cannot be seduced by this rhetoric if they are going to be effective in stopping agitators. A felony committed under the influence of alcohol is still a felony. If it only takes five seconds to commit the felony, it is still a felony. If you apologize for the felony, it helps, but it is still a felony.

Bystanders

Bystanders play a critical role in keeping the riot going. Curious on-lookers usually outnumber the agitators exponentially. Sometimes they will cheer on the destruction and treat the riot like a sporting event. Many are there because they just want to see what will happen next. In effect, they serve as an audience for the agitators. As the crowd grows and their chances of getting

Table 16.3
AGITATOR EXCUSES

Common Excuse	Agitator Quote	*Additional Information*
Authorities have blown this way out of proportion.	"I am not a bad person. The costs of my five seconds of stupidity are far overboard."	MSU rioter ordered to pay $5,000 for standing atop an overturned car.
Do I look like a rioter?	"Can we really look at [student] and say he is what a burglar looks like or what a rioter looks like? And I'd have to say he's not."	Attorney for Penn State rioter who defended his client on the basis that his actions resulted from recklessness not harmful intentions.
Wrong Place, Wrong Time	"I feel badly for [client]. It was just an unfortunate set of circumstances."	Attorney for another Penn State rioter who pleaded no contest to a misdemeanor charge of resisting arrest.
I don't remember what happened. I was too drunk.	"I was very intoxicated, more than I've ever been before in my life. I don't remember where we went or what happened to me."	WSU rioter's testimony during his trial for assaulting an officer. While he did not remember being actively involved in the riot, he did recall getting pepper-sprayed by police. Video cameras caught him pushing a dumpster toward police. He was eventually acquitted of the assault charges.
He said he's sorry. What more do you want?	"He apologized to his parents, for the grief he's brought them and the embarrassment they feel and the stress. Then he said he was very regretful and remorseful for participating in the so-called riot.... He wasn't out there yelling and screaming and leading a group of people with flags of anarchy, saying smash the machine. He just happened to be standing on the edge of a crowd when someone said help us tip this police car over."	Attorney for MSU student who pleaded guilty to flipping a police car. The student came forward after police posted a photograph of him on their Website. The crime is considered a 10-year felony, of which this student served 47 days.

caught decreases, some will join in with the agitators.

Bystander apathy has long been an interest with social scientists, beginning with the Kitty Genovese case in 1964 when 38 witnesses saw her being raped and murdered during an attack that lasted more than half an hour, and no one intervened. Initial research indicated that bystander apathy was an effect of the number of people present when an event was occurring. That is, a person would be more likely to give help if he or she were the only bystander present, than when there was a group. The larger the group the less likely any one person was to assume personal responsibility. This effect was labeled "diffusion of responsibility."

Later research by psychologist Mark Levine at Exeter University indicated that social presumptions of bystanders also play a role in the lack of intervention. In other words, people viewing violence will internally make a judgment as to whether or not the violence is legitimate. In the Kitty Genovese case, many witnesses assumed that the man beating and raping her was her husband or boyfriend and it was not their place to step in. With campus rioting, we would argue, a similar social excuse crosses the minds of those who might otherwise step in. "Boys will be boys," or "college students are just having the time of their lives" are common comments that excuse normally inexcusable behavior.

In addition to cheering on agitators and failing to intervene, bystanders add to the riot by their sheer mass. Assistant City Attorney for East Lansing commented, "Once the fires started [during the riot] they became a point of congregation. The streets became so crowded and people became so unruly that the crowd impeded emergency vehicles. Not all the 10,000 people were acting unruly, but the problem is that there were 10,000 people."

For these reasons, we make the bold statement that there are no innocent bystanders during a riot. The few brave counterrioters are not bystanders because they are actively involved in the resolution. Like the old saying goes, "If you are not part of the solution, you are part of the problem." We also support the notion that bystanders should be held accountable in part for the riot and should receive consequences.

Thin Blue Line

Many campus security officers and law enforcement officers of small towns are not prepared to handle a riot. Eugene Methvin, author of *The Riot Makers: The Technology of Social Demolition*, states, "Inexperienced and undermanned for riots [paralyzed law enforcers] fuel the fires, first by bumbling or inaction and then by overreaction."[489]

Even if the departments are adequately prepared for a riot, they remain paralyzed because they know their every move will be documented on someone's video camera. Witnesses at the Ohio University riot filmed officers spraying a student in the face with mace six seconds after he apparently complied with the arrest. The footage was aired repeatedly on news broadcasts.

Attempting to contain a riot is extremely stressful work for officers. Monitoring students' parties is not nearly as gratifying as other lines of police work. Students and other participants harass police officers and often attempt to embarrass them in order to get the attention of the media or to bait them into aggressive action. Officers are always outnumbered, and the power of the faceless mob can be overwhelming. In more than one campus riot, officers suffered serious injuries and were hospitalized.

Increasing numbers of campus security and police officers are receiving training and equipment to improve their crowd control tactics. Many of these strategies are listed in the recommendations section of this chapter.

Media

One need only look at recent history and the tremendous social changes that have occurred during the past thirty-five years to see how and why demonstrations are increasing. Extensive television coverage came into being at the same time these changes were occurring and service to communicate the turmoil of the times to the country.
– Capt. Charles Beene, Ret. 1992 *Police Crowd Control,* p. 14

The role of the media in campus rioting has hit the spotlight as both instigating the problem and providing evidence for intervention. Some campus administrators blame the media for creating a self-fulfilling situation by making such a big deal out of the anniversaries of riots. When the cameras show up, the students do, too. In some ways, the media attention to campus rioting has helped make it a trendy thing to do.

Students compete for media attention by providing on-scene interviews and violent performances for the news crews. When the camera is on, the audience increases from a couple thousand to potentially millions. The power of this attention is too much to turn away. Often the footage of riot performances comes back to haunt the participants.

In East Lansing, the issue of using journalism footage as crime evidence caused a great controversy. A local newspaper objected to a judge's order requiring the paper to hand over 300 unpublished photographs of the March 1999 riot. The newspaper claimed that this form of evidence gathering interfered with journalistic integrity. Student journalists were the most vocal in their objection. They claimed they would be violating trust they had with students who let them record the riot from their apartment windows and gave them interviews because they knew the reporters as fellow students. Prosecutors stood their ground and claimed that journalists have a legal obligation to testify to the court what they witnessed. Just because these reporters are students, they are not excused. They are journalists who witnessed crimes taking place and should not take sides in the issue. Some student reporters and photographers felt so strongly about the issue, they agreed to spend time in jail, if necessary.

The East Lansing Police posted 50 photographs confiscated by a freelance photographer on a special task force website. They hoped to ask the public for help in identifying the people in the pictures. More than 60,000 people accessed the site over the course of a month, and police received over 500 tips. However, they closed down the site because hackers had found their way into a file that revealed confidential tip-offs from informants. The photographer, armed with three pro bono attorneys from Washington D.C., demanded the site cease existence due to copyright infringement. Despite the fact that the site helped lead to the successful convictions of dozens of riot participants, it was taken down.

There is another issue some people have with the media. Many see the coverage of the campus riots as a race issue. While the overwhelming majority of participants are white, no one has made note of this. Astute observers argue that if people of color were represented in larger numbers, the incidents would be called a "race riot." But because it is mostly young white men, the incidents are often described as "disturbances," "frat parties gone bad," and "youthful melees."

Counterrioters

Fraternity brothers stand guard over a neighborhood business to protect it from rioters. Student leaders urge spectators to go back to their homes. Community residents attempt to distract rioters by engaging them in everyday conversation during the riot. Many stories emerge of brave individuals who attempt to take the speed out of the raging stampede.

Eugene Methvin calls this group "the decent majority." He claims in many riots counterrioters outnumber rioters, but that police fail to back up the counterrioters in the early stages of the riots.

RIOT STAGES

While riots appear spontaneous and unpredictable, most tend to develop in apparent stages over time. Much of our understanding of riot stages comes from Eugene Methvin, author of *The Riot Makers: The Technology of Social Demolition*, and others who have analyzed decades of riots in our country.[490] While they have not typically included campus riots in their investigation, many similar patterns can be identified. In describing these stages we have likened the riot process to a wildfire, because the analogy is compelling.

Stage I: "Drying the Tinder" – Preconditioning

Let's Get Gassed!
Spectator chants at the Colorado State University versus University of Colorado football game riot
September 1999

CNN! CNN!
Rioter chants during the Ohio University riot
April 1998

In the weeks, days, and hours before a riot, events take place that set the stage for violence to occur. Rumors pique curiosity. Agitators gather potential missiles (e.g., frozen beer cans) and bonfire kindling (e.g., old couches). A sense of in-group and out-group is fostered by editorials in the campus paper and social discussion. "Look at all the (administration, police, etc.) are doing to interfere with our rights," is the general theme. Gossip about impending restrictions

and consequences can become highly exaggerated during this time.

Tension and excitement start to build as students anticipate what will happen next. Music and chanting can help fuel the emotion. During several of the campus riots, students blasted the Beastie Boys' lyrics "You've gotta fight for your right to party" out of apartment windows. Many participants baited law enforcement by shouting "F*** the police." One Penn State student called the catchy chants "infectious." When Penn State president Graham Spanier arrived on scene, the chants became "Graham, Graham." Chants filled with loaded language and repetition have been known to have a hypnotic effect on some rioters. The emotional intensity of the chanting moves people to get caught up in the moment. Some have likened riot chants to war cries.

Stage II: "Striking the Match" – Precipitating Event

The precipitating event is the signal to all that now would be the appropriate time to get things going. In several cases, the precipitating event has been a campus athletic event or an annual party. In one case, the riot was precipitated by a peaceful protest on alcohol restrictions. Students anticipate something big is going to happen with the buildup leading to this upcoming event. This anxious awaiting further sets the stage for the next phase of rioting.

Stage III: "Igniting the Fire" – Instigating the Riot

Someone has to make the first move. If the climate setting has been handled well by the instigators, it usually will not take much – an anonymous bottle thrown in the direction of the police officers, furniture dragged out of apartments onto bonfires, a rock thrown through a window. The behavior confirms what the spectators have been waiting for. The riot has begun.

The next few moments can be tenuous for the riot depending on how authorities handle the situation. If the police cannot or do not respond, the crowd reads anarchy and the situation becomes a "moral holiday." Most of the violence will take place within the first couple of hours of the riot.

Stage IV: "Feeding the Flames" – Magnet to Mayhem

At this point, the riot becomes a wildfire out of control. Law enforcement officers become quickly overwhelmed by the sheer mass and power of the mob, and usually must retreat or call for reinforcement. The riot takes on a life of its own as hoards of people are drawn into the chaos. As when handling a fire (real or symbolic), the enforcers can only hope for one of two things at this time – it rains (an outside force changes the momentum), or the fire loses its fuel (the students get too tired to participate anymore).

Stage V: "Wild Fire Containment" – Reestablishment of Order

At some point, the riot begins to lose its muscle and law enforcement moves into a better position to take over. When this shift of power occurs, rioters tend to jump ship quickly as the anonymity becomes diminished.

PREVENTION, INTERVENTION, AND POSTRIOT STRATEGIES

The following suggestions are a compilation from several sources including Captain Charles Beene,[491] Col. Rex Applegate,[492,493] David Haddock and Daniel Polsby,[494] and interviews describing "lessons learned" from campuses where riots have taken place.

Prevention

According to deterrence theory, there are two tactics that effectively discourage potential criminals. First, there must be an increased probability that the perpetrator will be caught and the means for doing so must be visible and widely known. Second, the consequences must be harsh enough to make the costs of committing the crime outweigh the benefits.

Effective Code of Conduct and Appropriate Consequences

The student handbook must explicitly detail the type of rioting behavior that students will be held accountable for within campus policies. Many campuses have found themselves in a difficult position in their attempts to discipline students who were riot participants because the code of conduct did not take into consideration off-campus behavior. These schools then found themselves in the position of having to reinstate suspended and expelled rioters because their code of conduct did not encompass off-campus rioting. One MSU student was caught on videotape at an epicenter of the 1999 riot, was arrested for unlawful assembly, and did admit that what he did was wrong. Nevertheless he disagreed with the university's decision to suspend him because he was not convicted in a court of law. He stated to the *State News*, "It was really against my constitutional rights. They basically kicked me out of school for nothing." MSU, like other schools, found rioters were indeed a "clear and present danger" to the campus and were able to hold them accountable to established conduct codes.

Students have admitted that being suspended or expelled from college is a far worse fate than any legal consequences they would most likely face. They know that when an individual is expelled from an institute of higher education, it becomes virtually impossible to get readmitted somewhere else.

Finally, campuses must determine their stance on bystanders. As we have indicated, there are no innocent bystanders at a riot. If you are not actively trying to counteract the problem, you are part of the problem. However, handling bystanders is even a more difficult issue than disciplining rioters. At the very minimum, campus policies should indicate that those witnessing or encouraging riot activity will be held accountable for contributing to the riotous climate. Bystanders should then receive consequences appropriate to their behavior, from letters of warning to probation or more. Bystanders who refuse to disperse should have more severe consequences.

Training Student Leaders

Many campuses have found that student leadership is a very effective method for taking the steam out of an escalating situation. People tend to follow directions of others with whom they are familiar and who symbolize the interests of their group. The WSU riot fizzle of 2000 supports this claim. Here Greek leaders effectively convinced their fellow students to go home without incident.

Building Bridges

Conversations around the conflicts at hand can help minimize misunderstandings between parties. Schools should attempt to find mutually agreeable arrangements between students and campus officials that are legal, moral, and effective. This last part must be stressed. "Agreeable arrangements" does not mean accommodation to student demands. Some schools retracted appropriate policies because of student pressure. Others altered enforceable policies so that they became loopholes. When negotiating with

disconcerted parties, campus officials must be able to stand by their bottom line.

One school had a particularly difficult time with the rowdy section of their athletic stadium. The fans perceived the college crackdown on their section as unfair and the enforcement measures fuelled their anger. This school chose to have a conversation with some of the student participants and found that the students just wanted to have a good time. The officials replied along the lines of "we will not get in the way of your having a good time as long as you don't involve alcohol or destruction of property." This interaction became a first step in building bridges between these two usually adversarial groups.

If students are not open to a discussion with campus officials about potential solutions and no tangible roadblocks are identified, the prognosis for a positive outcome is poor. These students should seriously consider why they will not cooperate with efforts to prevent further destruction and bloodshed on their campuses.

Professional Development and Equipment for Law Enforcement and Campus Security

Depending on the size of the campus and each campus's potential for rioting, enforcement officials may need minimal protection and training or may need full riot preparation. As first-line responders with the need to take action quickly and decisively, campus enforcers cannot always depend on local authorities' ability to mobilize forces as quickly as needed. At a minimum, most at-risk campus enforcers should receive basic training in crowd management and control.

From there, tactics for intervention become increasingly invasive, and campuses will have to weigh the pros and cons of having such equipment at their disposal. Nonlethal riot control methods offer several options for officers. Tear gas canisters can be an effective means of dispersing the crowd, but often these canisters are thrown back at the officers. Plastic or rubber pellets fired at the rioter's torso can bring offenders into pain compliance, but drunken individuals can sometimes be immune to pain, so this technique might also backfire. Other strategies are outlined in the intervention and aftermath sections.

Protective gear for officers is essential if they are going to be handling riot situations. Multiple unprotected officers were seriously injured during campus riots because they lacked basic riot protection gear. Shields have proven to be one of the most effective protection devices in campus riots due to the brutal nature of the projectiles launched by students. As mentioned in the case studies earlier, officers have been hit not only by bottles and rocks but by manhole covers and concrete bricks as well. Other protective gear include riot helmets with visors, fire resistant jumpsuits, and body armor to protect knees, groins, thighs, forearms, and shoulders.

Intervention

At some point, campus enforcers must make a decision to move from crowd management to crowd control when a riot situation is escalating. Two signals help officers make that decision. The first is the tone of the crowd. When celebratory exuberance turns into angry chanting, enforcers need to begin a different tactic. The second has been called the "upping the ante" phenomenon. This occurs when revelers begin to try to outdo each other through increasingly outrageous activity. When this behavior crosses the line of putting people in danger, especially the officers, crowd control is needed. Throwing of missiles is a good indicator that the crowd is getting unruly.

As mentioned earlier, as Americans, we have the right to demonstrate peacefully, but we lose that freedom when criminal activity takes place. At that time, enforcers must make it known that the gathering has become an "unlawful assembly" and that those who do not disperse immediately will face possible arrest. These announcements should be made slowly, deliberately, and repeatedly. The information should contain the reasons for the announcement and what students can expect if they do not disperse. Announcements should be repeated every three minutes and also be posted on highly visible banners. Photographs of the banners will serve as evidence that the police did declare the situation as a riot before acting.

The following list contains brief descriptions of interventions campus enforcers can use to bring an out-of-control crowd back into containment. For a more comprehensive review, the reader should consult Captain Charles Beene's *Police and Crowd Control: Risk-Reduction Strategies for Law Enforcement*.[495]

Show of Force

Once the riot has been declared, officers must be prepared to act swiftly. One of the first lines of offense is to present the crowd with an authoritative show of force. Large numbers of riot-prepared officers assembled in riot formation give many the intimidating presence needed to leave the area. Officers should remain as machine-like as possible, not showing any expression on their faces and definitely not retaliating with remarks or threats.

Divide and Conquer

As officers begin to take control of the crowd, they should move to divide the group into smaller and smaller subgroups. Through the use of roadblocks and barricades, officers can direct rioters in a direction that makes it more difficult for them to assemble as a large group. Officers should also limit access by outsiders to the riot area. These tactics are along the lines of herding sheep. At all times, officers must be aware of an escape route for both themselves and the group they are trying to direct. A mob that is cornered will come out fighting. Pullman officers who responded to the Washington State riot learned that large mobs can easily surround small groups of officers, making for tragic consequences.

Decreasing Anonymity

Anonymity is a factor that fuels an out-of-control mob. Rioters do not believe that they will be held accountable for their actions, and thus, they are free to act without a social conscious. When we are able to put a face and a name to the rioters, the game changes. Photographs and videotapes have become instrumental weapons in the efforts to combat rioting. Plainclothes officers can mingle with the crowd or be posted on rooftops to detect the instigators behind the scenes. Anyone in the role of recording the events of the riot must be prepared to become targets of violence themselves as rioters attempt to destroy the evidence.

Take Out the Leaders

Just a few agitators are responsible for creating the energy that eventually involves thousands of people in destruction. Most rioters are ambivalent about their participation, and would not engage without the urging of the instigators. When these leaders are no longer in a position of influence, the followers drop out. As Eugene Methvin stated, enforcers must act by, "pinching off the criminal spearheads with precise and overwhelming force."[496]

Effective Communication

During the escalation of a riot, clear lines of communication and command must be established. Most agencies will need to simplify their command structure to give appropriate individuals authority to make decisions quickly.

Riot Aftermath

During the riot aftermath several strategies can help expedite the investigation and assist in damage control.

Handling the Media

Campus authorities must be savvy in their reactions to the media. On one hand, several campus leaders have been criticized for their public minimization of the campus violence. Pictures of students flipping cars and hurling bottles does not fit in with the public's perception of a mild campus disturbance. On the other hand, visible outrage and mass condemnation of the student body will further alienate the fragile student-administration relationships. Negative buzzwords like "catastrophic" and "devastating" can create a very damaging image for the campus.

Campuses should appoint a well-trained spokesperson to get accurate facts about the riot to the media before others fill in the holes with misinformation. The spokesperson must refrain from saying "no comment," as this phrase has been associated with covering up a larger story. Bluffing and lying to the media never works as experienced journalists often can discover the truth very easily. Comments to the media should be contained to short sound bites of 20 to 30 seconds that fall into one of two categories. Either, "We are very concerned about what has happened, and we are doing the best that we can under the circumstances," or "We are trying to gain cooperation on this matter to get a better understanding of what has happened and what we can do to prevent it from happening again."

Investigation

In addition to the investigation tips suggested in Chapter 7, campus officials may consider additional tactics when facing rioting. Many campuses have had great success in identifying perpetrators by posting photographs on websites. Tipsters are even more forthcoming with information if reward money is tied to the eventual conviction of a rioter. However, anonymous means of reporting must be ensured so informants do not become targets of revenge. Conducting door-to-door interviews in the neighborhoods where the riots have taken place has also helped investigators. Very often these informants are motivated to seek justice on the individuals who destroyed their property and community.

Clean-Up

Some believe that immediate clean-up is necessary to remove the negative image of destruction from campus consciousness. Others suggest that those who have been identified as contributors to the riot work toward putting back together what they have torn apart. In any event, the clean-up process, while sad, can help bring communities back together by working hand in hand on a common goal.

Chapter 17

HOMICIDE AND NONSEXUAL ASSAULT

JOHN NICOLETTI & SALLY SPENCER-THOMAS

IN PREVIOUS CHAPTERS we have constructed patchwork themes in campus violence – sexual assault, hazing, hate crimes, and rioting. The last two chapters attempt to pull together the leftover pieces – physical assault, homicide, bombing, and arson.

Some of these violence types are common. Some are rare. In comparison to the previous topics, few experts have written on these issues. Our attempt is to begin to sketch a picture of what we know on these topics to help guide future prevention strategizing.

HOMICIDE

While the straightforward definition of homicide is relatively simple – the killing of one person by another – the permutations of campus homicide are multiple. Campuses have faced student-on-student, student-on-staff, staff-on-staff, stranger-on-student, student-on-stranger, and other combinations of homicide. The victims are more equally distributed than other forms of campus violence. In other words, students, staff, and strangers all have about an equal chance of being either perpetrators or victims of this form of violence. While men still outnumber women in being perpetrators, women perpetrators are represented in greater numbers here than in other forms of campus violence.

In fact, they are highly represented in one form of campus homicide: infanticide.

Strategies for dealing with one form of homicide do not necessarily protect against others. The following analysis of clustered case examples lists the possible typologies off-campus homicide and type-specific recommendations.

Predatory Homicide

Predatory homicide occurs when perpetrators stalk down victims with whom they do not have a prior relationship and murder the victims for no other motive than the satisfaction they get from the killing. The Florida cases described in Chapter 1, Ted Bundy and the Gemini Killer, are two of the most notorious mass murder perpetrators in our country's history, and both preyed on college students. The 1986 murder of Jeanne Clery, also described in Chapter 1, was also a predatory murder. Predatory murders are usually what people think of when they think of a campus homicide, scary drifters lurking in the bushes, commonly known as "stranger danger." These types of homicide do occur on college campuses, and they are rare. However, most security tactics are designed to deter the predator and not other types of perpetrators. Predatory homicides are not the only form of homicide campuses face –

avenger, relationship-based, and other forms are also possible.

Avenger Homicide

While avenger homicides are also rare on college campuses, they do occur. When they do occur, the sequence of events is virtually indistinguishable from other forms of workplace violence:

- An individual has experienced a series of perceived grievances.
- Previous attempts to resolve the problem through pro-social means are not adequate.
- The perpetrator begins to develop fantasies of violent revenge.
- Often perpetrators will make veiled or direct threats about the plan of violence.
- Finally, they execute their plan following a well-scripted plot and murder their intended victims without much concern for witnesses or their own outcome. Again, the permutations of who seeks revenge on who are multiple. Students have sought revenge on disciplinary officers and on faculty members. Faculty members have sought revenge on colleagues.

Two prominent cases of avenger homicide demonstrate this pattern of violence. Each case was a mass murder by a disgruntled individual whose premeditated actions targeted the source of his anger. Both perpetrators chose to execute their victims in a public area during a workday, without concern for observers. One perpetrator was suicidal, another hallmark of the avenger. In the aftermath, copycat behavior was apparent in one of the cases.

Concordia University

In August 1992, Dr. Valery Fabrikant, a Russian-born engineering researcher at Concordia, walked into the Henry F. Hall Building on campus, concealing a 7.65-mm Argentinean Bersa pistol, a snub-nosed Smith & Wesson revolver, and a 6.35-mm semiautomatic pistol.[497] He proceeded to fatally gun down four of his professor colleagues and injured a secretary before taking two people hostage. After an hour-long standoff with police, he was overpowered and arrested.

During his 13 years as a professor at this large Canadian university, Dr. Fabrikant had been involved in a series of disputes surrounding his contract and allegations he filed against his colleagues.[498] He claimed that the top echelon of faculty was engaged in significant academic and financial fraud. In the aftermath of the murders, his allegations were proven true, but before the murders, he was simply known as a troublemaker. A head administrator at Concordia commented in an interview with *Maclean* magazine, "He was always complaining about something."[499] The administrator also noted that Dr. Fabrikant had made a series of veiled threats such as, "Don't you want to search my bag to see if I have a gun in it? I might have a gun." Concordia officials claimed they warned police about these threats and Dr. Fabrikant's potential for violence. One repercussion of the murders was a redrafting of gun control laws in Ottawa.

San Diego State University

During the summer of 1996, master's candidate Frederick Davidson allegedly killed three professors at his second thesis defense.[500] Mr. Davidson failed the first defense several months earlier, and police speculate that he expected to fail this defense as well, a decision that would have led to a dismissal from the university. On the morning of the killing spree, Mr. Davidson planted his 9-mm handgun in a first-aid kit in a laboratory. When his thesis review committee was assembled, Mr. Davidson reached into the first-aid kit and began firing, killing all three professors. Three other students were in the room at the time, and they claimed that Mr. Davidson did not attempt to kill them. When police officers arrived on scene, Mr. Davidson begged them to kill him. They apprehended him and took him into custody.

Three months later, a copycat threat occurred.[501] An unnamed black faculty member at San Diego State University received a death threat. The anonymous flier allegedly stated that a bomb would be placed in the professor's car and included racial insults. The notice made veiled references to the earlier Davidson murders.

Recommendations

While comprehensive strategic suggestions are made throughout Part II of this book, the following list highlights particularly relevant issues for an avenger situation:

1. Zero Tolerance for Threats. Unlike other forms of violence, avengers usually make multiple veiled, conditional, and direct threats before carrying out their violence. All threats should be taken seriously, and at a minimum investigated and documented.
2. Track Injustice History. The perpetrator usually has a reputation as a complainer or troublemaker. He rarely takes responsibility for his own actions (the overwhelming majority of the perpetrators in these cases are male). They can often reach harassing levels of pursuing their complaints, such as constant letter writing and phone calls.
3. Notice Interest in Weapons. Avenger perpetrators often collect guns and exhibit intense interest in violence. By taking note of the potential perpetrator's discussion of his weapon collection, assessors can determine the lethality of the perpetrator's threats.
4. Fitness for Duty Evaluation. If enough evidence exists to warrant concern, universities should consider what has been labeled in workplace situations as a "Fitness for Duty Evaluation." For students it might be labeled "Fitness for Enrollment Evaluation." This evaluation, conducted by an outside, independent violence expert, takes into consideration all the factors for violence potential and makes recommendations for the campus to minimize risk.
5. Warn Potential Targets. When an avenger names a targeted individual, this potential victim should be notified immediately. In addition, law enforcement should be alerted and reasonable measures should be undertaken to protect the victim.

Relationship-Based Homicide

Relationship-based homicide occurs when a one-on-one relationship, such as romantic partnership or friendship, becomes obsessive.[502] When the submissive partner attempts to leave the relationship, the dominant partner begins to think: "If I can't have you, no one will." When the mindset of partner-as-property is so strong, the threat of relationship termination becomes unfathomable to the perpetrator. No one will get in his way when he attempts to repossess what is rightly his (again, the majority of perpetrators are male). For this reason, relationship-based homicide is one of the most dangerous, especially during the initial period of separation.

The acts of relationship-based homicide tend to be horrifying acts of rage.[503] A relationship-based homicide is more likely to be a stabbing or strangling, much more intimate forms of violence, than other forms of homicide. In addition, the perpetrator is much more likely to involve more force than necessary to kill someone. For instance, a relationship-based perpetrator might stab the victim dozens of times and beat the victim severely around the face.

Unlike the avenger, the relationship-based perpetrators will not take out many victims of opportunity. But like avengers, they are not usually deterred by barriers of any sort. Perpetrators often start their quest to regain the relationship through harassment and stalking, and later escalate their behavior to violence. Police presence, witnesses, and security devises are often ineffective in stopping a determined relationship-based perpetrator. In many cases, perpetrators feel that they have nothing to lose and are suicidal.

The next several cases presented represent both the wide variability and common themes in this type of violence. The first two cases are examples of intimate partner violence on college campuses. Both of them are male perpetrators murdering female partners, a pattern that matches national trends. "In the U.S., estimates from the Bureau of Justice Statistics (BJS) are that more than three women a day are killed by their intimate partners. Women are killed by intimate partners more often than by another acquaintance of stranger. Most of these murders involved were preceded by physical and psychological abuse."[504] Other experts consider this fact to be a gross underestimate and suggest that the true figure is closer to 50 or 70 percent. Both cases presented here also resulted in the perpetrator's death – one a clear suicide, the other an apparent suicide-by-cop.

The second set of cases illustrates apparently nonsexual relationship-based violence, those homicides committed by obsessive friends and roommates. These cases also follow patterns of relationship-based violence.

University of Michigan

On September 23, 1997, Kevin Nelson brutally stabbed his girlfriend Tamara Williams, a University of Michigan senior, multiple times with a kitchen knife while neighbors watched in horror.[505] Unlike the infamous Kitty Genovese case (see Chapter 2)

decades before, bystanders this time became actively involved. Many neighbors attempted to intervene and twenty-five 911 calls were made. One neighbor even threw a baseball bat at Kevin to get him to stop attacking Tamara. When an officer arrived on scene and ordered Kevin to back off, Kevin refused and the officer shot him twice. Both Kevin and Tamara died in surgery. The autopsy report indicated that Kevin had several horizontal "sharp cuts" on his inner wrists, suggesting that he might have been suicidal on the day of the murder.

The history of their relationship is also typical of relationship-based violence.[506] Tamara and Kevin had had an on-again, off-again relationship for a few years. In 1995, Kevin was convicted of a domestic assault on Tamara. In her letter to the court, Tamara stated, "...June 20, 1995 was not the first time that Kevin Nelson had been abusive to me. He has hit me many times before and once he even hit my infant daughter in his attempt to strike me. My main concern is that every time Kevin Nelson has been in trouble he has only received a tap on the wrist...." This time Kevin was sentenced to eighteen months probation. According to Tamara's friend, the two "got over their differences" and Kevin moved back in with Tamara. Witnesses, however, reported that during the attack, Kevin shouted, "She won't have me. And I love her."

Columbia University

On February 5, 2000, Timothy Nelford allegedly stabbed his girlfriend Kathleen Roskot in the neck.[507] Her body was found hours later when her lacrosse teammates became concerned at her absence from practice. Kathleen was a well-liked sophomore at Columbia. Timothy dropped out of Columbia in 1998 due to academic difficulties possibly stemming from drug abuse. According to friends, the two dated since the prior semester, although some thought they might have split up in recent months.

On the night of the murder, security cameras recorded Kathleen and Timothy entering the residence hall together.[508] Kathleen signed in her guest, and he left his photo ID, standard security procedures. An hour or so later, neighboring suites heard noise coming from Kathleen's room, but did not think anything of it, since loud parties were common. Kathleen was found naked on the floor of her bedroom. The apparent murder weapon, a kitchen knife, was found in the bathroom.

Shortly after Kathleen's body was found, Timothy threw himself in front of a subway train.[509] Police found Kathleen's wallet on his body. Acquaintances claimed they had no warning signs of violence potential in Timothy.

Harvard University

In 1995, during the final days of their junior year Sinedu Tadesse, a biology major from Ethiopia, fatally stabbed roommate Trang Ho 45 times. Sinedu then hung herself in the bathroom of their suite.[510] Five days before the killing, the *Harvard Crimson* received an anonymous envelope containing a photograph of Sinedu and a computer-printed note reading "Keep this picture. There will soon be a very juicy story involving the person in this picture."

Trang Ho was a premed student born in Vietnam who had been profiled in *Boston* magazine as one of "25 Who Can Save Boston." In the aftermath of the deaths, the press painted the picture of two quiet international students whose problems were "no different than thousands of disagreements that happen between roommates at every college."[511] Many asked, who could have predicted such a tragedy?

One reporter, a Harvard graduate who had actually met Sinedu years before, dug deeper. In her book *Halfway Heaven: Diary*

of a Harvard Murder, Melanie Thernstrom uncovered what actually took place during the months that led up to the murder-suicide, and all the telltale signs were there.[512] The summer after her freshman year, Sinedu wrote a long letter about herself and sent copies to strangers whose addresses she had found in the telephone directory. Here are some excerpts from that document:

> Well, why am I writing this letter? Because I am desperate.... My problem is that I am not bonding with people. I do not make friends even with my relatives.... I live in my own shell, afraid to reveal my personality and to express my opinions.... As far as I remember my life as been hellish.... Year after year, I became lonelier and lonelier. I see friends deserting me. They would take every chance to show me that they did not have any love or respect for me.... You are one of the very few people who see me struggle... All you have to do is give me a hand and put into words what you already know.... I am sure one of your concerns, if you have gotten this far in the letter is, what if I am one of those criminals lurking around. But believe me, right now I am not strong enough.... I anxiously wait to hear from you.[513]

One woman who received this letter knew an administrator at Harvard and passed it on.[514] The letter eventually reached the Freshman Dean's Office and was forwarded to the Dunster House, where Sinedu would be living in the fall. It was then placed in her file.

In her sophomore year, Sinedu moved in with Trang and became obsessed with her one-sided friendship. She referred to Trang as "a girl I would make the queen of my life." Trang was "spunky" and had lots of friends, and this angered Sinedu as she felt her bond with Trang slipping away. When Trang would invite friends over, Sinedu would sit in her room festering with jealousy. At the end of their sophomore year, Trang reluctantly agreed to live with Sinedu the following year and immediately regretted her decision.

Sinedu became increasingly disorderly and Trang began spending less and less time in the room. During the second semester, Trang decided she would move in with another woman for her senior year. At this point, Sinedu stopped speaking to Trang and became increasingly difficult. As indicated by her journals, Sinedu's violent fantasies began at this time: "The bad way out is suicide & the good way out killing, savoring their fear & then suicide."

Thernstrom concludes in her book, "Through her single act of violence, Sinedu's reality became the ultimate one, linking the two girls through death in a common fate, so that in memory they are bonded in a way in which Trang has no choice, and which in life never existed."[515] If I can't have you, no one will.

Johns Hopkins University

People Weekly called it a "fatal friendship."[516] During their time at Johns Hopkins University, students Bob Harwood and Rex Chao had an intense friendship and some wonder if it bordered on a sexual relationship. Rex, a nineteen-year-old sophomore, called Bob, a twenty-two-year-old senior, "the older brother I never had." But when Rex developed a relationship with a woman, Bob became increasingly obsessive, demanding to know where Rex was at all times. Rex became so distressed by the rambling emails and accusations made by Bob that he filed a grievance with the Dean of Students. Rex felt that he was being stalked and told the dean that Bob owned a gun.

Bob proceeded to pass out flyers defaming Rex when Rex ran for chairman of the College Republicans club.[517] On the night of April 10, 1996, Rex won the election. After the meeting, Bob followed Rex and his girlfriend outside and shot Rex in the head with a .357 Magnum. Bob then stepped over Rex and fired a second shot into Rex's chest.

Bob then ran for a security guard to call for an ambulance and immediately requested a lawyer.

Bob was sentenced to 35 years in prison.[518] Bob later sued the university for withholding his degree. The Maryland Court of Special Appeals supported the rejection of the lawsuit stating that Bob had violated the university's code of conduct, thereby breaking the contractual obligation to award a degree for completed academic requirements.

Understanding Relationship-Based Homicide as End-Stage Stalking

Stalking is legally defined as "willful, malicious and repeated following and harassment combined with the credible threat intended to make the victim fear death or serious injury." Experts estimate that one in 20 women will become stalking targets at some point in their lives. According to the National Victims Center, both men and women can be either perpetrators or victims of stalking, but the overwhelming majority of cases involve men stalking women (75–80 percent).[519]

Psychologists have identified two categories of stalking behavior: (1) "Love Obsession Stalkers" represent about 20 to 25 percent of all stalking cases.[520] These stalkers develop a love fixation on another person with whom they have never had any personal relationship. Some choose to stalk celebrities; others develop obsessions with regular, ordinary people. (2) "Simple Obsession Stalkers" represent about 70 to 80 percent of all stalking cases. These stalkers are differentiated from Love Obsession Stalkers in that they have had a personal or romantic relationship with their victims before the stalking behavior began. In most instances, the victim has become the stalker's sole source of self-esteem. When the victim tries to break off the relationship, the perpetrator's thinking evolves from "If I can just prove how much I love you" to "I can make you love me," to "If I can't have you, nobody else will." Stalking cases which developed from domestic violence patterns are the most common and potentially lethal.

Stalking usually progresses through predictable stages[521]:

Mental Obsession

At this level, the stalker is preoccupied with intrusive thoughts regarding the victim. The stalker is unable to stop thinking about him or her. This type of obsession often occurs at the beginning of a relationship during the infatuation stage, or at the end of a relationship when the stalker feels rejected.

Surveillance

At the next level, the stalker follows the victim to collect information. Surveillance allows the stalker to watch the victim in his or her natural habitat. Information about the victim is collected from various sources – observation, coworkers, friends, family, and unsuspecting others. Direct approaches range from reading the victim's mail to going through the victim's trash.

Harassment

During harassment, the stalker attempts to either seduce or intimidate the victim into compliance. The stalker crosses the line from observation of to interaction with the victim. In the beginning, the stalker may attempt to be attentive, charming, or even romantic. The stalker remains congenial as long as the victim responds favorably. However, if the victim rebuffs or ignores the stalker's attempts at courtship or control, a more negative campaign of harassment may result.

Extermination

This is a lethal phase of stalking because the perpetrator has now realized no possibility exists for any relationship with the victim. The stalker may not see any alternative but to kill the victim and frequently him or herself. While the progression of these levels is common, no stalking case is completely predictable.

It wasn't until 1990 that California became the first state to pass a law that made stalking a crime. This gave law enforcement officers legal leverage to intervene in stalking cases *before* offenders took action. Since that time, all 50 states have made stalking a crime.

When people file a complaint under the stalking statute, they must have sufficient evidence to establish "probable cause." In other words, the stalking victims are put in the position of having to prove their case to law enforcement before they are allowed to take their case to court. It is essential, therefore, to document every stalking incident very thoroughly. For example, victims should be advised to collect phone answering messages, letters, photos of the stalker, videotapes, audiotapes, photos of property damage, affidavits from witnesses, and any objects the stalker may have left.

Victims may seek to obtain a restraining order from the local court. These orders require the offender to stay away from the victim, and, if violated, the stalker may be punished by a fine or jail time. Nevertheless, restraining orders are not foolproof and may create a false sense of security.

Victims may also use the arm of the law when they have determined that the perpetrator has broken the law by entering the victim's residence without permission, by stealing property, by destroying property, or by physically assaulting the victim.

Recommendations

Homicide is the worst case scenario of obsessive relationships. Unfortunately, there is not much campus administrators can do to prevent it from happening. This is especially true if the perpetrator is a part of the campus community and continues to have a relationship with the victim. Victims, however, are in a position to prevent violence, although it is usually a complicated and difficult endeavor. The following recommendations for victims are adapted from the National Victims Center guidelines. They are presented in order of escalating danger from preventive measures to responding to imminent danger.[522]

1. Notify the stalker to stop. You or your attorney can send a registered letter to the stalker requesting that the behavior cease. Treat all threats as serious and notify law enforcement immediately.

2. Tell everyone you know what is going on. Give residence hall directors, campus security, friends, coworkers, relatives, and neighbors a description or picture of the stalker and vehicles, and have them document everything they see. Warn them not to give the stalker any information about you. Have coworkers or family members screen visitors and calls. Give your address and phone number to as few people as possible.

3. Document everything carefully. Take pictures of destroyed property, injuries inflicted on the victim, or other evidence. Save all letters or notes written by the stalker. Save answering machine messages. Log dates and times of all unwanted contact.

4. Secure the residence. Change locks and secure spare keys. Install solid doors with deadbolt locks. Post a "no trespassing" sign on the edge of your property. Improve lighting and visibility around your house. Change your phone number to unlisted. Obtain a post office box.

5. Vary your behavior. Don't follow the same routine every day. Change your driving routes and times when you usually do things. Limit or eliminate walking or jogging alone. Try to stay in public places.

6. If you move don't leave a "paper trail" by having mail forwarded to your new address. Take all records (medical, financial, school) with you.

7. Take care of yourself. Join a support group or consider therapy to help you deal with stress. Develop your support system.

8. Develop a safety plan.
   a. Memorize or have quick access to important phone numbers including:
      i. law enforcement
      ii. safe places (friends, shelters, etc.)
      iii. attorney
      iv. Trusted people to help you when safety is secured (childcare, pet care, etc.) Be ready for a quick departure:
         1. pack a small suitcase for yourself (and children)
         2. have reserve money stashed
         3. gather critical documents (birth certificates, prescriptions, social security information, passports, creditors' numbers)
   b. Alert critical people of your situation:
      i. family and friends
      ii. law enforcement/security
      iii. employers/coworkers

9. Victims in imminent danger:
   a. Attempt to locate a safe place:
      i. police stations
      ii. residences of family or friends
      iii. shelters or local churches
      iv. public areas (stalker may be less likely to create a public disturbance)
   b. Call 911 or other emergency number.

NOTE: The above information is not intended to be a strict set of guidelines, but rather to give victims options. Unfortunately, there is no guarantee that if you follow any or all of these suggestions that you will be safe.

Infanticide

Infanticide is a form of homicide that is often overlooked as a potential type of campus violence. There are numerous cases across the country where female students, sometimes with the assistance of their partners, kill their unwanted newborn babies. Amazingly, most of these women were able to hide their pregnancies from others, and thus, college officials are unable to reach out to these women to offer assistance. The women frequently claim that they are afraid to announce their pregnancy for fear that they will be asked to leave school. This fear seems to be pronounced at religious institutions.

These women often deliver their babies alone in their residence halls or nearby hotel rooms and can experience significant problems without medical assistance. According to an article in the *Chronicle for Higher Education*, a woman who was a junior at Claflin College delivered a baby in her residence hall room and was later found unconscious.[523] When doctors examined her and discovered she had just given birth, college administrators rushed back to her room to look for the baby. They found the baby dead in a gym bag under her bed. The housing policy at this particular school read, "Pregnant students...will be required to move out of the residence hall. The college is in no way responsible for any problem/complication that may arise out of this condition."

The highest profile case of college infanticide was "Baby Boy Grossberg." On November 12, 1996, Amy Grossberg, an 18-year-old freshman at the University of Delaware, gave birth in a motel with the assistance of her boyfriend Brian Peterson, Jr., a freshman at Gettysburg College. Autopsy findings revealed that the baby had been severely beaten before being wrapped in a garbage bag and thrown in the motel's dumpster. When Amy returned to school, she fainted and was taken to the hospital where they determined she had just given birth. Brian told campus officials where the baby was. While initially there was much talk about the death penalty for the two students, in July 1998 they were sentenced to brief prison terms (less than three years each).

Recommendations

Like many forms of violence prevention, colleges are again at the crossroads of protecting students' privacy and taking steps to intervene. Many schools see pregnancy as a moral issue as well as a medical issue, and these perspectives can complicate the picture further. Administrators are often at a loss as to how to intervene.

1. Colleges need to make sure that students know that medical treatment on campus is confidential.
2. Student conduct and residence policies should be reviewed to note any perceived punishments for pregnancy.
3. Campus communities must offer safe places where students feel that they can explore their medical options without consequences.
4. Residence hall staff must be trained on telltale signs of pregnancy and how to intervene effectively.

NONSEXUAL ASSAULT

Nonsexual assault is another heterogeneous category of campus violence. We have chosen to divide this section into two categories – physical assault between people not in an intimate relationship and dating violence.

Physical Assault

For the most part, physical assault that is not dating related usually occurs between male athletes or fraternity brothers who are under the influence of alcohol. In the *American Journal of Health Studies*, Nicholson et al. found 41 percent of college men surveyed reported nonsexual violent acts with those of the same sex.[524] Alcohol was involved in 60 percent of the incidents. Furthermore, over half of these men indicated that they were involved in more than one violent act, with alcohol present in almost 70 percent of these instances.

At the University of Rhode Island, football players smashed windows and doors at a fraternity house.[525] Campus administrators responded swiftly with significant consequences for the offenders. Ten days later 30 students, many of them football players, fought with fists and beer bottles. The university president punished the team by forfeiting the upcoming game against the University of Connecticut.

Virginia Wesleyan College suspended 23 male basketball players from participating in competition after a brawl that was allegedly ignited by a fight over a woman at an off-campus bar.[526] Shortly after, college officials reviewed the case and conceded to let some players seek reinstatement for some of the games for which they had been suspended. Instead, they were mandated to complete "meaningful community service." It was argued by proponents of this decision reversal that the suspensions could substantially hurt the basketball team's chances of a repeat NCAA Division III championship win.

Washington State University suspended two fraternities after a brawl involving golf clubs, flashlights, sticks, and other objects. The brawl apparently erupted after weeks of brewing conflict between the houses. Each house claimed that the other had damaged house property. During the fight, a half-dozen men from each house were injured and many required medical treatment.

In March 2000, the University of New Hampshire (UNH) experienced a bizarre case of drunken fighting.[527] Walter Wilson, a 21-year-old civil engineering senior got into a fight with another student. Hours later and intoxicated, Walter rounded up five fraternity brothers to seek revenge. Walter led his brothers to an apartment complex, barged through the door of Unit Cl, and attacked the man sleeping there. Soon they realized they had the wrong apartment and left. Then they went to the next door and broke in, attacking the two men sleeping there. One victim received a blow from a barstool. Again, they had the wrong apartment. It turns out the student Walter was looking for did not even live in that particular complex. The six men were arrested and faced disciplinary action by the school as well.

This UNH fraternity had quite a track record of violent offenses ranging from burglary to assault.[528] The university also has a history of trying to tame the fraternity system. In the 1990s, a campus administrator banned another fraternity for a number of violent allegations including hazing. Afterwards, this administrator received death threats, experienced car vandalism, and found drivers were attempting to run him off the road.

The most tragic case involved a man named David Shick from Georgetown University.[529] In a campus parking lot on February 18, 2000, David was involved in a drunken brawl involving five members of the school's soccer team. According to witness testimony, David was punched in the face and fell backward, hitting his head on the pavement. Georgetown's campus police sent the other students home without taking names or statements, and David went to the hospital. He died four days later. His death was ruled a homicide; however, no criminal charges were made.

In the aftermath of David's death, faculty urged the provost and other upper administrators to convene a panel of deans to examine the party culture at Georgetown.[530] Only half of the deans showed up for the first meeting; only one attended the second meeting.

While the majority of physical assault seems to come from athletes and fraternities, one unlikely group has also made the headlines: marching bands.[531] On September 19, 1998, two of the nation's most revered bands – Prairie View A&M and Southern University – battled it out, literally, during the halftime show. When Southern attempted to exit to the sideline the bands collided and 370 marchers got in a "full-on, 100-percent street brawl" for 20 minutes. Each band blamed the other, and three students were taken to the hospital. Both teams were suspended from the following two football games.

Given that nonsexual, male-on-male violence was such a common occurrence, one would expect to find a plethora of research and articles on the topic. There was scarcely any – another indication that our culture adheres to the "boys will be boys" mentality.

Recommendations

1. Swift and decisive action against all parties involved in physical assault. It seems that many colleges have a much lower expectation for acceptable behavior of their students on campus than we have for other individuals in other contexts. For instance, we would not excuse this behavior as "boys will be boys" if it happened in a church or a movie theater.
2. Address alcohol abuse (see Chapter 4).
3. Be prepared to slay the sacred cows and stand by a zero tolerance position on violence.

Dating Violence

Experts in women studies claim that the distinction between sexual violence and battering in relationships is rather artificial. They contend that relationship violence is often sexualized in nature because it usually takes place in the bedroom, is triggered by sexual issues, and is considered erotic subject matter to some. For this reason we conceptualize relationship violence and sexual violence as overlapping; however, we limit this section to nonsexual forms of violence.[532]

Dating violence can span a continuum from verbal abuse and threats to minimal injury contact to lethal force. Dating violence can take the form of physical abuse, emotional abuse, economic abuse, social isolation, and sexual abuse. As identified by domestic violence expert Lenore Walker, dating violence tends to pass through predictable distinct phases: tension building, explosion, and honeymoon.[533] These phases vary in time and intensity for each couple and between different couples. Tension building refers to the time when minor incidents occur, causing friction in the relationship. Explosion refers to the point where the tension building has reached uncontrollable levels, and the batterer explodes with an acute battering incident. The honeymoon stage, otherwise known as "hearts and flowers," is characterized by remorseful, loving, and contrite behavior by the batterer.

Verbal abuse is a category that often gets bypassed in discussions about dating violence.[534] Verbal abuse occurs when one uses words to attack or emotionally injure another person. Often disguised in the form of "harmless jokes," verbal abuse is often the first step in the progression of dating violence and can take many forms.

Heterosexual Couples

According to the National University Center for Law, Education and Public Policy, battering is the single greatest cause of injury to women in the United States. This cause of injury supercedes car accidents, muggings, and rapes combined. After reviewing several gender violence studies, Kay Hartwell Hunnicutt concluded that one-quarter to one-third of high school and college students have

Table 17.1
FORMS AND EXAMPLES OF VERBAL ABUSE[535]

Forms	*Examples*
Withholding Intimacy	"There is nothing to talk about."
Denying Victim's Reality	"No, that's not the way it is." (constantly saying the opposite)
Discounting Feelings	"You're too sensitive. You can't take a joke."
Shutting Down Conversation	"I don't see where this is going. Discussion over!"
Blaming	"I've had it with your complaining. You're just out to get me."
Judging	"Your problem is you never stop nagging."
Eroding Confidence	"You wouldn't understand. It's over your head."
Threatening	"Do what I want or I'm out of here."
Name Calling	Even "sweetheart" or "dear" when used with a sarcastic tone.
Convenient Forgetting	Promises, important occasions, agreements
Ordering	"Get over here and do this now." "You're not wearing that!"

been involved in relationship violence – as victims, perpetrators, or both.[536] Even more disturbing is the fact that approximately 70 percent of female college students found some form of dating violence acceptable. This probably helps to explain findings cited in Responding to Violence on Campus – 27 percent of college dating violence victims chose to continue the relationship with their abuser.

Like many forms of campus violence, the number of dating violence incidents reported to campus officials is significantly lower than the number reported by students. This pattern is largely due to either the reluctance of victims to come forward for fear of retaliation or the desire of the victim to continue the relationship.

According to a 1991 study published in the *Journal of Consulting and Clinical Psychology*, when we look at male violence against women, peer support of masculine hostility and abuse are stronger predictors of aggression than a remote history of a violent past. In addition, evidence exists to suggest other proximal influences like training in the military or violence on the streets "slip over" to affect personal lives.[537]

Most of this section focuses on male violence against women, but we acknowledge that women inflict violence against men. Research seems to indicate that this is an increasing trend. In 2000, a study published by Purdue University researchers found that females were significantly more likely to report using physical force than were male students.[538] "Physical aggressions" was defined as: throwing objects at partner; pushing, hitting, or grabbing partner; slapping partner; kicking, biting, or hitting partner with a fist; trying to hit partner with something other than a fist; beating up partner; choking partner; threatening partner with a knife or gun; or using a gun or knife on partner. Any endorsement of these items led to a categorization of "physically aggressive." It is not clear from this study what degree of violence was inflicted by the women.

It is generally understood by experts of gender violence that because of their greater height, weight, and muscular build, most males have a greater propensity to inflict harm on women than vise versa. Thus, most research to date has been focused on males perpetrating violence against women.

The media has placed a great deal of attention on male athlete violence against women. This trend has led to heated debates: Are athletes being unfairly scapegoated because they live in the spotlight or are athletes more prone to commit acts of violence against women because of strong aggression socialization and a hypermasculine culture? Recent evaluations by social scientists of athletic involvement and violence against women suggest that both sides of the debate have validity.

It is true that on occasion, the media has overly sensationalized the problem. Athletes are highly visible and their criminal activity makes for interesting news. That said, research indicates that male athlete involvement in violence against women is significant. Benedict and Crosset found that while male student-athletes made up 3.3 percent of the total male population at Division I institutions, they represented 35 percent of the perpetrators reported.[539] *Sports Illustrated* noted that in the aftermath of the Nicole Brown Simpson murder, college athlete domestic violence mushroomed. At the University of Florida alone, three football players were arrested for assaulting their wives or girlfriends, one of whom was pregnant. One of the players was expelled from school. For the other two, most charges were eventually dismissed and the Florida football program only suspended them for one game.

Researchers from Carleton University suggest the "DAD" model gives us insight as to why men perpetrate violence against their female partners.[540] DAD stands for dependency, availability, and deterrence. Dependency refers to the "addictive" quality of the relationship. Dependent partners will experience physical and emotional withdrawal pains when their significant other is absent. Likewise, many men who abuse their girlfriends or wives also abuse alcohol and drugs, and this substance abuse is often related to the trigger of the violent events.

Availability refers to the amount of access that a man has to his partner. Those men who live with their partners are more likely to be abusive than those who do not because there are more opportunities for abuse. Deterrence refers to how much the man conforms to social and legal conventions prohibiting violence. Social isolation plays into the level of deterrence – men who are isolated are less concerned with negative consequences of abusive behavior. Furthermore, the more violence a man has engaged in during the course of his life, the more his deterrence has worn down.

Recommendations

1. Develop disciplinary policies that specifically deal with the unique dynamics of partner violence to make sure cases are not dismissed as "lovers' quarrels." The consistent message must be repeated: violence is unacceptable and those who commit it will be punished. According to Rosemarie Bogal-Allbritten, Professor of Sociology, Murray State University, and William Allbritten, Director of Counseling and Testing Center, Murray State University, there exists a power differential in male-female violence, and thus, traditional disciplinary methods used in male versus male violence may not be appropriate in these cases.[541]
2. If danger is imminent make sure that the victim has an effective safety plan (see stalking section earlier in this chapter).
3. Depending on the circumstances, counseling and mediation between victim

and offender might prove beneficial in stopping the abuse. This would not be advisable in extreme obsessive relationships, but may be helpful in first-time low-level violence incidents to increase awareness before patterns develop.

4. Establish connections with services provided in the larger community, for example, support groups for victims or battering prevention groups for perpetrators. Assign someone on campus to serve as the liaison between the school and community agencies so that rapport is developed and referrals can be made more confidentially.

5. Provide educational programs for students on understanding patterns and consequences of dating violence. Include in these presentations a discussion on verbal abuse, a form of dating violence that often gets overlooked.

Gay and Lesbian Couples

According to *Violence in Gay and Lesbian Domestic Partnerships*, a book by Claire Renzetti and Charles Miley, domestic violence occurs at approximately the same rate in gay and lesbian relationships as it does in heterosexual relationships.[542] These findings clearly shatter many myths people have about same-sex partnerships. This research seems to indicate that partnership violence is less about gender and more about power and control. While very little is known about same-sex violence in the general population, even less is known about same-sex couples at our colleges and universities. Thus, the relationship between the findings reported and college life are speculative until future research is conducted.

Much of the dynamics of same-sex dating violence is similar to heterosexual violence.[543]

The types of abuse, the patterns, the consequences, and the reasons for staying in the relationship are all similar. Still, important differences exist. One form of psychological abuse for same-sex couples is the threat of "outing" the abused partner to family, employers, or others with "blackmail" potential. Another difference same-sex couples face is that the direction of violence can and often does go both ways between partners. Most state laws do not include language inclusive of gay and lesbian relationships, but rather use the terms "spouse" or "battered wife." Therefore, gay and lesbian victims do not have the same civil rights protection as heterosexual couples and their isolation from advocacy and other helpful resources is often magnified because of this.

Recommendations

The following recommendations are adapted from L. Kevin Hamberger's chapter in *Violence in Gay and Lesbian Domestic Partnerships*.[544]

1. Name the problem. Confront denial and challenge myths around same-sex dating violence. Community education regarding the incidence, prevalence, and dynamics of same-sex violence is essential.

2. Establish community networks. Task forces made up of local community and campus leaders, medical professionals, victim advocates, batterer therapists, law enforcement, and others can work together to advocate change, research the problems, and educate the community.

3. Safe-house resources must address the unique needs of same-sex couples.

4. Research campus same-sex dating violence.

Chapter 18

ARSON AND BOMBING

Sally Spencer-Thomas

WHILE THEY DO NOT ALWAYS make national headlines, arson and bombing happen on college campuses. Perpetrators who gravitate toward these crimes are becoming increasingly sophisticated in their ability to inflict tremendous damage without getting caught. Universities often have ample firepower materials available in science labs, and experimentation is the natural consequence of curious minds. Students of the computer era are very savvy in finding information about building bombs and setting fires with delay devices.

SIMILARITIES BETWEEN ARSONISTS AND BOMBERS

In their book *Bombers and Firesetters*, MacDonald, Shaughnessy, and Galvin noted some striking similarities between arsonists and bombers. The motives and agents of destruction are alike.[545] The destruction of evidence and cover-up of additional criminal activity causes similar frustration for investigators. Both compulsive bombers and compulsive firesetters can experience sexual excitement during their crimes, and many of these perpetrators return to the scene of their destruction. Few other crimes have the capacity to cause such widespread property damage and loss of life in one act. Like arsonists, bombers often seal their own fate. A large percentage of those who die from bombs are bombers themselves. In addition to intended victims and the perpetrators, arson and bombs often take the lives of innocent bystanders and rescue personnel.

ARSON

What We Know About Arson

- Each year, fire kills more Americans than all natural disasters combined.[546]
- Arson is the second leading cause of death by fire in the U.S. – surpassed only by smoking – and the leading cause of property damage due to fires.[547]
- Arsonists usually escape punishment. In 1997, only 19 percent of arson offenses led to arrest, and only 2 percent of those arrested were convicted.[548]
- Those 20 years of age and under account for about 50 percent of all arson fires in the United States.[549]
- The FBI Uniform Crime Reporting System definition of arson is, "Any willful or malicious burning or attempt to burn, with or without intent to defraud, a dwelling house, public building, motor vehicle or aircraft, personal property of another, etc." A recent campus crime

report published by the *Chronicle* indicates that arson happens more than most expect. In 1998, there were 539 cases of reported arson, a 16.9 percent increase over the previous year. This makes arson a more frequent crime than reported murders, manslaughter, nonforcible sex offenses, and hate crimes combined.[550]

- Arsonists are driven by a variety of motives. Curiosity, racial hatred, drunken vandalism, sexual excitement, copycat crimes, and revenge are some. The overwhelming majority of arsonists are male, and of the eight FBI Crime Index offenses listed in the Uniform Crime Report, arson has the highest percentage of adolescent involvement.

- As forensic expert John MacDonald notes, firesetting is a hazardous undertaking and can often take the life of the arsonist.[551] Arsonists often dump fire accelerant such as gasoline to help ignite their fire. Naive fire-setters do not realize that gasoline evaporates quickly and increases the risk for explosion. Young arsonists tend to light paper and trash as incendiary materials. Other flammable liquids used by arsonists include paint thinner, kerosene, turpentine, alcohol, and ether.

Effects of Alcohol

The crime of arson is often committed by persons under the influence of alcohol. As with other crimes, alcohol affects judgment and inhibition and increases the potential for violence. In a monograph published by the Institute of Psychiatry, forensic psychiatrist Ann Barker cited research stating 54 percent of solo arsonists and 40 percent of those with partners were intoxicated with drugs or alcohol at the time of the crime.[552]

Intoxication also significantly increases risks for victims of arson. Toxicological analysis of victims who have died in fires reveals that many of them had high blood alcohol levels, seriously affecting their ability to escape. Party pranks involving firecrackers and smoke bombs have sometimes turned deadly because of intoxicated victims. In 1996, at the University of Virginia in Charlottesville, fire officials speculate that senior Elizabeth McGowen died when a fire swept through her off-campus apartment because she was too impaired to respond.[553] The fire started when two of her friends threw smoke bombs into her apartment during a party. An autopsy indicated that Elizabeth's blood alcohol content was three times the legal limit for intoxication in Virginia.

Murray State and Other Campus Arson Cases

On September 18, 1998, Michael Minger, a sophomore music major at Murray State died in a residence hall fire that officials ruled as arson.[554] Fifteen other students were injured, including Michael Priddy who suffered major burns and brain injury from oxygen depletion. The fire was the second one set in Hester Hall that week; the former was quickly contained and caused only minor damage. Fire authorities surmise the fatal fire began from gasoline poured on a carpet in the hallway. Hester Hall did not have a sprinkler system despite repeated warnings from Deputy State Fire Marshals.

As the case has unfolded, it has taken many unexpected turns, complicating the investigation.[555] A couple of hours before the fire started, a group of rugby players and their friends decided to make prank calls to a freshman in Hester Hall. One of the calls recorded on an answering machine tape warned him that his door was on fire. A university police officer was summoned to talk to residents about the calls and reports of smoke. Sixty-eight minutes later, flames were visible and students began fleeing in their nightclothes. Some students were rescued from their windows, while others found themselves trapped in stairwells.

The university offered a $30,000 reward for information leading to a conviction of the firesetters.[556] In the weeks that followed, 100 students moved off campus. Toward the end of October, police indicted there were seven prank callers, five of whom were Murray State students. The charges ranged from capital murder and arson to complicity and conspiracy. All admitted to participating in the phone calls, but vehemently denied the firesetting charges. Predictably, these students were seen as guilty by many and ostracized from the campus community. When officials realized they did not have enough evidence to tie the students to the fire, they dropped the charges.

Nine months after the fire, another student was arrested.[557] Jerry Walker, a senior at the university and former member of a campus security unit, was charged with capital murder and first-degree arson. Ironically, Walker was one of the students injured and rescued in the fire. Police claim that after the fire, a letter written by someone stating to know the fire's source was found on the car windshield of Walker's girlfriend. Furthermore, a convenience store surveillance camera taped Walker buying a dollar's worth of gas on the night of the fire. Walker's trial was scheduled for October 2000.

Five of the seven previously accused students are filing suit alleging wrongful arrest on felony charges.[558] Four of the seven were nevertheless convicted of making prank phone calls, a misdemeanor. Murray State has since installed sprinkler heads in each room of Hester Hall along with a new evaluation system. In the aftermath of this tragedy, Michael Minger's mother, Gail Minger, championed legislation requiring public and private institutions of higher education in Kentucky to publicly disclose information about serious campus crimes and restates the fire marshal's jurisdiction over these campuses. In July 2000, the Michael Minger Act took effect.

Other lesser-known campus arson occurrences include the following cases:

- In 1995, three arson fires caused more than $1 million in damage to Clark Atlanta University buildings.[559] The fires were set over a five-day period during the university's spring break.
- In 1997, five fires ignited during one week at the University of Miami, Florida, one of them ruled as arson.[560] The arson fire was set before dawn in the offices used by the men's basketball coaches and caused more than $100,000 in damage.
- In 1998, seven minor fires were set at Benedict College, five of them occurring within a ten-hour span.[561] The arsonist lighted the fires in bathrooms and trash buckets.
- In 2000, a radical environmental group claimed responsibility for setting a fire that burned offices at Michigan State University.[562] The targeted offices were in charge of a controversial project bringing biotechnology research to agricultural scientists in Third World countries. The fire caused $500,000 in damage.

Arson Investigation

Arson is a difficult crime to solve because the crime itself erases most evidence. In fact, most campus arson cases remain unsolved due to this aspect of the crime. Thus, motives for campus arson are unclear. As Bernard Levin notes in his article "Psychological Characteristics of Firesetters," "Unfortunately, our knowledge about the psychopathology of firesetters is limited to those arsonists who are caught or give themselves up. In short, we know the most about the least successful arsonists."[563]

Generally speaking, arsonists light fires to create a financial gain, cover up a crime, inflict revenge, or bring themselves attention.[564]

However, according to a recent review of the psychiatric literature on arson, the largest category of motives is "pleasure or excitement, vandalism, boredom, or relief from tension." These latter experiences are common for college students.

During the investigation phase of arson, firefighters look for certain clues to help them determine the cause. John MacDonald, coauthor of *Bombers and Firesetters*, notes that fires that spread rapidly or irregularly are often suspicious.[565] The color of the smoke can indicate what set the fire. Distinctive odors of gasoline, diesel fuel, kerosene, or turpentine are other clues. Sabotaged fire safety equipment such as fire alarms and sprinkler systems and obstructed entrances are further evidence of arson. Many times the person who first reports seeing the fire is actually the firesetter.

Recommendations

The following recommendations were compiled from the www.fire-investigators .org[566] and www.fire.org.uk[567] and *Bombers and Firesetters*.[568] In general, arson prevention follows general burglar and fire prevention guidelines. One particular concern for college campuses dealing with arson is the high number of fire alarm pranks. The tremendous number of false alarms gives students, administrators, and even firefighters a sense of apathy. Some schools have a delay system when fire alarms are pulled to make sure the fires are real before fire crews are summoned. This delay can prove deadly. In the training video "How Fast It Burned," filmmakers demonstrate that fire from a lit candle can progress to engulf a residence hall room in three minutes.[569]

1. Illuminate campus property and exteriors. Arsonists, like burglars and predators, fear light and do not want to get caught.

2. Do not publicly announce when campus buildings will be vacant.
3. Most arsonists work at night, so surveillance cameras may be the best method of capturing evidence. Note that arsonists sometimes carry liquid accelerant, like gasoline, in an inconspicuous container. Acts of vandalism may precede arson.
4. Ensure that firefighting equipment is in good working order and is protected against sabotage.
5. University policies should require total evacuation of residence halls and notification of the fire department for every fire alarm.
6. Fire safety education provided by local fire officials can help students feel confident in using fire extinguishers and other fire safety techniques.
7. Take pictures of spectators who watch the fire burn. Arsonists often like to witness their act of destruction. If the fire takes place during normal sleeping hours, the arsonist may be the only spectator wearing normal street clothes instead of nightclothes.

BOMBS AND BOMB THREATS

Why should colleges be concerned about bombs and bomb threats?

- Because technology in the area of explosives has advanced tremendously and materials necessary to construct powerful devices are readily accessible via underground publications and the Internet.
- Bombing and bomb threats draw high media attention making these forms of violence susceptible to the "copycat" phenomenon.
- High school bombings such as at Columbine and bomb threats in high schools and workplaces are becoming

increasingly common and may spill over to the college setting.

- Today, bombers are very creative and bombs can be constructed to look like almost anything. Most bombs are homemade and are limited only by the imagination and resources of the bomber.

Bombs have appeal for sensation seekers. The power of the explosion, the magnitude of destruction and the deafening noise can be thoroughly exciting for some. Investigators can infer the motive of the bomber from the choice of target. A small toilet bowl explosion is probably a prank. A middle of the woods explosion is most likely out of curiosity. A targeted car or office would indicate revenge of some sort. In the few cases of college bombings that have been made public, the motives have ranged from revenge to curiosity to racial hatred to a burglary cover-up.

Campus Bombing

In 1996, a former student at the University of South Florida, Tampa, pleaded guilty to a bomb threat that essentially shut down the campus for three days.[570] The perpetrator mailed the threat to the student newspaper stating that he intended to bomb a building and kill a professor if the former professor Ramadan Abdullah Shallah did not receive an apology from campus officials. What specific type of apology was unclear to investigators.

In 1998, David Rose, a student at the California Institute of Technology, was killed when a homemade bomb he had built with friend Matthew Roesle, a sophomore at Rose-Hulman Institute of Technology, exploded. David was visiting Matthew and the bomb detonated in a wooded area on the campus of Rose-Hulman Institute. Police evacuated Matthew's residence hall to find a second explosive device in his room.

In April of 1999, campus police at Georgia Southern University arrested five students who allegedly attempted to set off a bomb to divert attention while they robbed a campus office.[571] The officers learned of the plan and defused the bomb minutes before it was going to explode. In the same month, three students at Brigham Young University were arrested for detonating a homemade pipe bomb outside their residence hall. The bomb's explosion shattered windows and injured the ear of a nearby student.

In a widely publicized case, Lawrence Lombardi, a 41-year-old white man, was convicted on six federal charges of setting off two bombs at the predominately black institution, Florida A&M University (FAMU).[572] Two small explosives detonated within a month during late summer of 1999. There were no injuries in either blast, but racist phone calls accompanied each and forecasted future attacks.

The evidence against Lombardi was staggering.[573] In the immediate aftermath of the bombings, Lawrence Lombardi called News Channel 27 and the Tallahassee Democrat to state that these bombs were "just the beginning." Later, government agents secretly taped him discussing his alibi with his wife on the phone. Lombardi was videotaped buying PVC pipe at a home improvement store. He later claimed this pipe was intended to build a lawn sprinkler, but the pipe was identical to fragments found at the crime scene. Lombardi had been a snack vendor and this position allowed him access to the campus and a FAMU photo identification card. When he stopped working for the food vendor, he did not turn in his photo ID. The men's bathrooms where the bombs exploded were 20 to 25 feet from the vending machines Lombardi serviced. Lombardi was known to make racial comments and visit racist websites. He also owned a manual on how to make bombs and had expressed interest in explosives to friends.

Understandably, the bombings set the FAMU campus in a panic.[574] After the first bombing, most students shrugged it off as a prank. But after the second bombing and subsequent racist phone calls, the campus community was terrified. In the days after the second bombing, students, faculty, and staff were required to wear campus identification around their necks to get access to the campus. The governor increased funding to take extra security measures on campus including increased law enforcement presence and security cameras. Campus officials immediately began detailing written evacuation plans to be distributed to classes. During the year of the investigation and trial, hundreds of students withdrew from FAMU out of fear.

Bomb Threats

Bomb threats, especially those in the immediate aftermath of a bomb incident, can cause intense fear and serious inconvenience for those who receive them and respond to them.[575] So many threats are made and never carried out that it becomes easy to dismiss them. Nevertheless, because of the significant damage bombs can inflict, all bomb threats must be taken seriously. Most threats are made via phone calls while a few are written or made in the presence of an intended victim. Schools are the number one target for bomb threats. Forensic expert John MacDonald estimates that two out of five callers of bomb threats give the time the bomb will explode. The time ranges from "right now" to a month away. Sometimes, the caller will give a location of the bomb or make taunting comments such as "Are you nervous?" MacDonald also notes that more than two-thirds of those who answered bomb threats were women.

The Bureau of Alcohol, Tobacco and Firearms suggests that there are only two logical explanations for a bomb threat. Either the caller has definite knowledge or the caller wants to create mayhem. If the caller has a strong suspicion that an explosive has been planted, he or she may want to minimize personal injury or property damage. In this case, the caller may be either the person who placed the bomb or someone who has become aware of the situation. An individual might become suspicious of a roommate's reading material or bomb-making equipment left in the room. In this "real" scenario (the threat of the bomb is real), the caller will present supporting information that can only indicate that the caller is legitimate. He or she may have detailed specifics about how the bomb was made or where the bomb was located. In the "fake" scenario, the person making the threat wants to create panic and disrupt normal activities. In this situation, the caller will not usually have verifiable information.

Recommendations

1. Do not touch suspected explosive devices under any circumstances. A burned fuse may be a trick designed to deceive the discoverer into believing the bomb was harmless.

2. According to the Bureau of Alcohol, Tobacco and Firearms (ATF), agencies benefit greatly from a bomb incident plan. Proper planning will instill confidence in those who must take charge of the situation and reduce the sense of panic. The bomb incident plan calls for a definite chain of command with provisions for alternates. Updated blueprints must be made immediately available to responding emergency personnel. Evacuation and communication procedures should be developed. Contact the police department or fire department for assistance in developing the specifics of the bomb incident plan.

3. Training is critical in helping those who answer phones deal with a bomb threat. It is desirable for more than one person to listen to a threatening call; thus, a covert signaling system can be

advantageous. Callers should be kept on the phone line as long as possible. Call recipients should have those making threats repeat their message several times. All words spoken by the perpetrator should be recorded verbatim. The following Bomb Threat Telephone Report Form was adapted from Stanford University.

4. With written threats, all materials including the envelope or container, should be saved for the investigation. Great care should be taken in handling the evidence so as not to hamper fingerprint analysis.

5. Residence halls and college administrators will have diverging views when it comes to the decision to evacuate a building after a bomb threat. The ATF states that agencies have three alternatives: ignore, evacuate immediately every time, or search and evacuate if warranted. Ignoring the threat is not prudent as a few threats do turn out to be real. Evacuating with every bomb threat can seriously disrupt the campus environment and certainly reinforces the person making the threat. Students can quickly learn a foolproof method for getting out of exams. The third approach, initiating a search after a threat is received and evacuating the premises after suspicious evidence is found is the most desirable approach according to the ATF.

6. Using area occupants to search their own areas is another recommendation by the ATF. Occupants' concern for their own safety motivates them to conduct a thorough search, and they are the most familiar with what belongs and what is out of place in their space.

Occupants should not move anything or attempt to investigate suspicious evidence; their only task is to search the area. If they have any doubt about this or are frightened, they should be instructed to leave the situation alone and let professionals handle it.

7. As suggested by the National Bomb Data Center and John MacDonald, investigation of witnesses of bomb explosions should include the following questions:

Questions to Ask a Bomb Witness

Before the blast:

- Where was the bomb?
- Were there any obstructions on the way to the bomb (stairs, doors, other hazards)?
- Are there alternative approaches to the bomb?
- What did the bomb look like? Smell like? Sound like?
- When was the bomb placed? Was there a telephone warning?
- Who might be the target?
- How long did it take the bomber to leave the bomb?

After the blast:

- How long were you in the area before the blast?
- Where were you when the explosion occurred?
- What did you see happening?
- What color was the flash and smoke?
- Was there more than one explosion?
- Did you notice any particular smell?
- What did the explosion sound like?
- Did you notice anything unusual in the area prior to the explosion?

EPILOGUE:
THE FUTURE OF CAMPUS VIOLENCE

JOHN NICOLETTI

O VERALL, OUR CAMPUSES are one of the safest places to be. Nevertheless, as violent crime continues to wreak havoc on our society, its effects will continue to wash up on the shores of our campuses. Many of these forms of violence are difficult to comprehend. They are even more difficult to control. Because the majority of campus violence cases occur among people who know each other and who are often under the influence of alcohol, there tend to be many mitigating circumstances that make reporting violence complex and adjudication complicated. From the aftermath of high-profile campus cases of the recent past and the new legislation dealing with campus violence, many colleges and universities have made violence prevention a priority. Campuses are more aware and prepared than ever before.

As campus officials begin to address the issues of violence, they are met with both support and backlash. Tighter controls and increased regulations are often met with resentment and, in some cases, outright rioting. Campuses should expect this and prepare for it. Rather than undoing effective long-term strategies in the face of immediate campus unrest, officials should seek to work collaboratively with all sectors of the campus community to find solutions that work for all. No violence prevention strategies will be successful without addressing the issues of alcohol abuse. This is an area that a small group of highly vocal students feels passionate about. They should be part of the solution-generating process.

The viruses of campus violence will continue to mutate. As campuses crack down on alcohol, students may move increasingly toward alternative drugs of choice – ones that are cheap, potent, and more easily concealed. We are already seeing the emergence of this trend through the growing attraction to the so-called club drugs. The proliferation of handguns in our society may work its way onto our campuses and into the hands of those seeking self-defense as well as perpetrators. As increasing numbers of students spend more time connecting with others via the Internet; we may see growing numbers of "cyberstalkers" affecting campus life. We bring up these possibilities, not to be doomsayers for campus violence, but to draw attention to the fact that violence changes. Campuses must be anticipating these changes so that they can stay one step ahead of the perpetrators. Or at least not be too far behind.

College and university campuses are inspirational places. They offer developmental experiences and challenges, community spirit and support, and under the right circumstances can offer a chemistry that can energize the nation toward better alternatives. A main motive in writing this book is our hope that they stay that way.

APPENDIX

VIOLENCE RESPONSE FLOW CHARTS

Plan A: Violence Potential Exists But No Immediate Danger

Plan B: Immediate Threat Exists

Plan C: Aftermath Situation

Plan D: Large Scale Violence Situation Adapted from *Violence Goes to School* (1999), Nicoletti, J. and Spencer-Thomas, S.

NOTORIOUS COLLEGE AND UNIVERSITY SCHOOL INCIDENTS

Plan A: Violence Potential Exists But No Immediate Danger

These situations develop when an individual uses abusive language and/or gestures and makes veiled or conditional threats without a death threat. In these instances, it is important to investigate, document, and confront the alleged perpetrator.

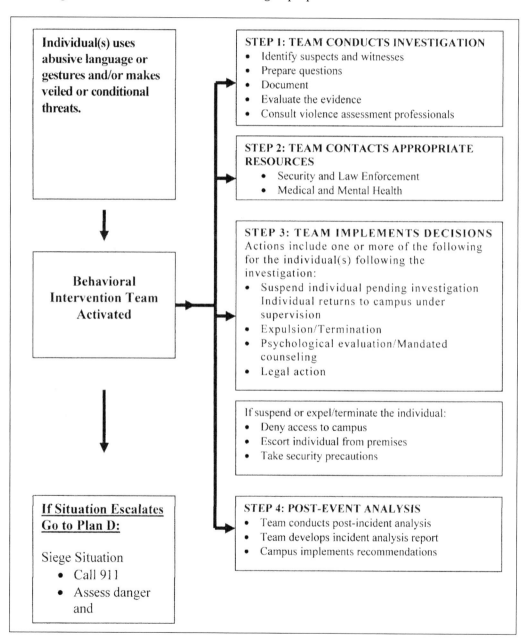

Individual(s) uses abusive language or gestures and/or makes veiled or conditional threats.

Behavioral Intervention Team Activated

If Situation Escalates Go to Plan D:

Siege Situation
- Call 911
- Assess danger and

STEP 1: TEAM CONDUCTS INVESTIGATION
- Identify suspects and witnesses
- Prepare questions
- Document
- Evaluate the evidence
- Consult violence assessment professionals

STEP 2: TEAM CONTACTS APPROPRIATE RESOURCES
- Security and Law Enforcement
- Medical and Mental Health

STEP 3: TEAM IMPLEMENTS DECISIONS
Actions include one or more of the following for the individual(s) following the investigation:
- Suspend individual pending investigation Individual returns to campus under supervision
- Expulsion/Termination
- Psychological evaluation/Mandated counseling
- Legal action

If suspend or expel/terminate the individual:
- Deny access to campus
- Escort individual from premises
- Take security precautions

STEP 4: POST-EVENT ANALYSIS
- Team conducts post-incident analysis
- Team develops incident analysis report
- Campus implements recommendations

Plan B: Immediate Threat Exists

Immediate threat exists when the situation involves direct or conditional threats ending with a death threat, evidence of aggressive behavior, including brandishing a weapon on campus. The goal at this time is to limit the access of the perpetrator to the campus. Notification to targets is crucial, as is a thorough assessment of the alleged perpetrator's dangerousness.

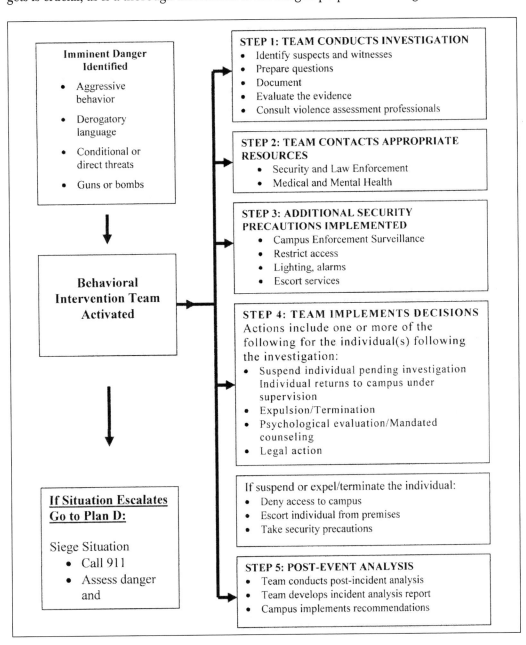

Imminent Danger Identified

- Aggressive behavior
- Derogatory language
- Conditional or direct threats
- Guns or bombs

Behavioral Intervention Team Activated

If Situation Escalates Go to Plan D:

Siege Situation
- Call 911
- Assess danger and

STEP 1: TEAM CONDUCTS INVESTIGATION
- Identify suspects and witnesses
- Prepare questions
- Document
- Evaluate the evidence
- Consult violence assessment professionals

STEP 2: TEAM CONTACTS APPROPRIATE RESOURCES
- Security and Law Enforcement
- Medical and Mental Health

STEP 3: ADDITIONAL SECURITY PRECAUTIONS IMPLEMENTED
- Campus Enforcement Surveillance
- Restrict access
- Lighting, alarms
- Escort services

STEP 4: TEAM IMPLEMENTS DECISIONS
Actions include one or more of the following for the individual(s) following the investigation:
- Suspend individual pending investigation Individual returns to campus under supervision
- Expulsion/Termination
- Psychological evaluation/Mandated counseling
- Legal action

If suspend or expel/terminate the individual:
- Deny access to campus
- Escort individual from premises
- Take security precautions

STEP 5: POST-EVENT ANALYSIS
- Team conducts post-incident analysis
- Team develops incident analysis report
- Campus implements recommendations

Plan C: Aftermath Situation

Violence has just occurred. The primary goal at this stage is to prevent further violence and get assistance to the victims.

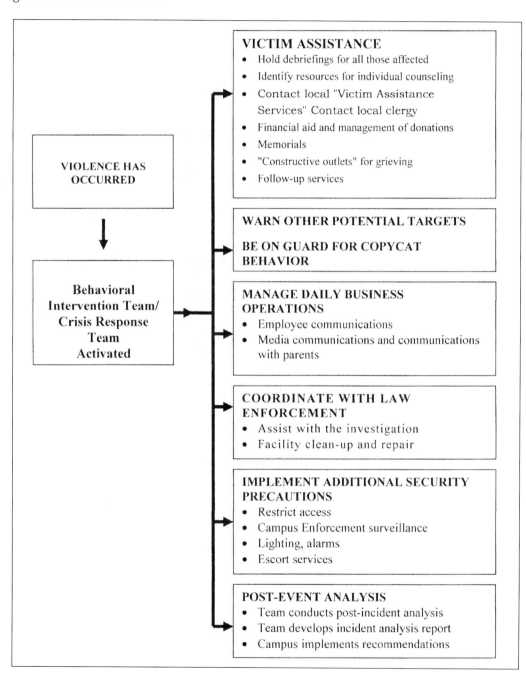

VICTIM ASSISTANCE
- Hold debriefings for all those affected
- Identify resources for individual counseling
- Contact local "Victim Assistance Services" Contact local clergy
- Financial aid and management of donations
- Memorials
- "Constructive outlets" for grieving
- Follow-up services

VIOLENCE HAS OCCURRED

Behavioral Intervention Team/ Crisis Response Team Activated

WARN OTHER POTENTIAL TARGETS

BE ON GUARD FOR COPYCAT BEHAVIOR

MANAGE DAILY BUSINESS OPERATIONS
- Employee communications
- Media communications and communications with parents

COORDINATE WITH LAW ENFORCEMENT
- Assist with the investigation
- Facility clean-up and repair

IMPLEMENT ADDITIONAL SECURITY PRECAUTIONS
- Restrict access
- Campus Enforcement surveillance
- Lighting, alarms
- Escort services

POST-EVENT ANALYSIS
- Team conducts post-incident analysis
- Team develops incident analysis report
- Campus implements recommendations

Plan D: Large Scale Violence Situation

Violence is occurring. The primary goal is to implement the previously developed safety and evacuation plans in order to contain the violence and reduce casualties. Law enforcement should be immediately notified and may direct many of these steps.

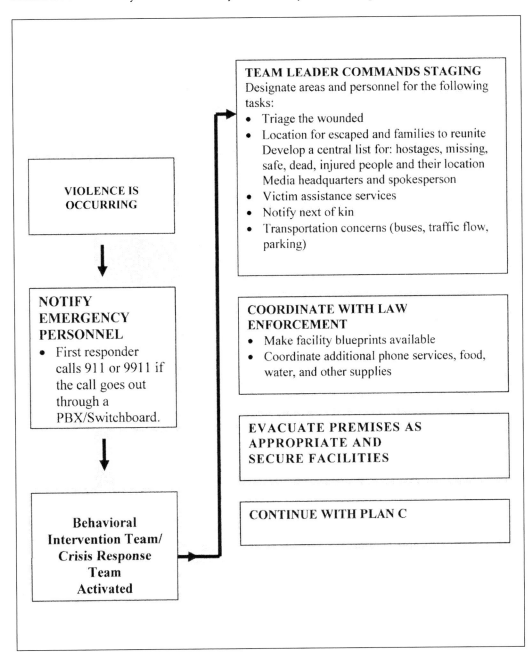

VIOLENCE IS OCCURRING

NOTIFY EMERGENCY PERSONNEL
- First responder calls 911 or 9911 if the call goes out through a PBX/Switchboard.

Behavioral Intervention Team/ Crisis Response Team Activated

TEAM LEADER COMMANDS STAGING
Designate areas and personnel for the following tasks:
- Triage the wounded
- Location for escaped and families to reunite
  Develop a central list for: hostages, missing, safe, dead, injured people and their location
  Media headquarters and spokesperson
- Victim assistance services
- Notify next of kin
- Transportation concerns (buses, traffic flow, parking)

COORDINATE WITH LAW ENFORCEMENT
- Make facility blueprints available
- Coordinate additional phone services, food, water, and other supplies

EVACUATE PREMISES AS APPROPRIATE AND SECURE FACILITIES

CONTINUE WITH PLAN C

NOTORIOUS COLLEGE AND UNIVERSITY SCHOOL INCIDENTS

From http://en.wikipedia.org

Date	Location	Attacker(s)	Number of Victims	Description
June 4, 1936	Bethlehem, Pennsylvania, United States	Wesley Crow	2 dead	Wesley Crow shot and killed his Lehigh University English instructor, C. Wesley Phy. Crow went to Phy's office and demanded that Mr. Phy change his grade to a passing mark. Crow committed suicide after shooting Phy.
August 1, 1966	Austin, Texas, United States	Charles Whitman	18 dead, 31 injured	University of Texas Clock Tower Shootings. After killing his wife and mother, Charles Whitman pointed a rifle from the observation deck of the University of Texas at Austin's Tower and began shooting in a homicidal rampage that went on for 96 minutes. He killed fifteen people and wounded 31 others before being shot dead by police. David Gunby was wounded in the shooting but died 35 years later after ceasing dialysis.
July 12, 1976	Fullerton, California, United States	Edward Charles Allaway	7 dead, 2 injured	California State University, Fullerton library massacre. A custodian opens fire on his fellow workers in the California State University, Fullerton library, killing seven and injuring two.
August 18, 1978	San Francisco, California, United States	Theodore Streleski	1 dead	Theodore Streleski murdered his mathematician professor, Karel deLeeuw at Stanford University by bludgeoning him with a ball-peen hammer. He was also found with a hit list containing deLeeuw's name.
April 5, 1982	Hot Springs, Arkansas, United States	Kelvin Love	2 dead	Kelvin Love, a student at Garland County Community College, killed an instructor and another student.

(Cont'd.)

NOTORIOUS COLLEGE AND UNIVERSITY SCHOOL INCIDENTS *(Continued)*

Date	Location	Attacker(s)	Number of Victims	Description
December 17, 1983	Ithaca, New York, United States	Su Yong Kim	2 dead	Non-student Su Yong Kim enters the Low Rise 7 dormitory and kills Cornell University freshmen Young Hee Suh and Erin Nieswand with a rifle.
December 6, 1989	Montreal, Quebec, Canada	Marc Lépine	15 dead, 14 injured	École Polytechnique massacre. Marc Lépine took a hunting rifle into École Polytechnique de Montréal, killed 14 women, wounded four men and ten women before committing suicide. It remains to this day the worst massacre in Canadian history. He believed that feminist were the reason his was not admitted.
November 1, 1991	Iowa City, Iowa, United States	Gang Lu	6 dead, 1 injured	After his dissertation did not win a certain academic award, Ph.D. physics student Gang Lu shot six people before committing suicide. Five were killed, including three professors. A student employee was paralyzed.
August 24, 1992	Montreal, Quebec, Canada	Valery Fabrikant	4 dead	Former professor Dr. Valery Fabrikant went on a shooting rampage at Montreal's Concordia University killing four. Was the second school shooting to happen in Montreal.
December 14, 1992	Great Barrington, Massachusetts, United States	Wayne Lo, 18	2 dead, "several" injured	Armed with a SKS carbine, 18-year-old Simon's Rock College of Bard student Wayne Lo killed a professor and a student and wounded several others. He was convicted of murder and sentenced to life imprisonment without parole.
April 4, 1994	Aarhus, Denmark	..., 35	3 dead, 2 injured	A 35-year-old student at Aarhus University entered the cafeteria of his University around 11 AM with a shotgun. He shot and killed two female students and wounded two others. Soon afterwards he went to the men's room where he committed suicide.

(Cont'd.)

NOTORIOUS COLLEGE AND UNIVERSITY SCHOOL INCIDENTS *(Continued)*

Date	Location	Attacker(s)	Number of Victims	Description
January 26, 1995	Chapel Hill, North Carolina, United States	Wendell Williamson	2 dead, 2 injured	Wendell Williamson, a law student and schizophrenic, opened fire on Franklin Street with an M-1 rifle, killing two and injuring two others, including a Chapel Hill police officer.
August 15, 1996	San Diego, California, United States	Frederick M. Davidson, 36	3 dead	Frederick M. Davidson, shot Dr. Chen Liang, Dr. Constantinos Lyrintzis, and Dr. D. Preston Lowrey during a meeting at which he was to defend his master's thesis. He pleaded guilty to three counts of murder and is serving a life term in state prison. [37]
September 17, 1996	University Park, Pennsylvania, United States	Jillian Robbins, 19	1 dead, 1 injured	Hetzel Union Building shooting. 19 year old Jillian Robbins opened fire on students walking to classes at The Pennsylvania State University, killing one student and wounding another.
October 16, 1996	West Lafayette, Indiana, United States	Jarrod Allen Eskew, 19	2 dead	On October 15, 1996 Jay Severson, 27 a Wiley Hall counselor at Purdue University caught Jarrod Allen Eskew, 19 of Crawfordsville, Indiana cutting cocaine in his dorm room. Severson called the Purdue Police Department but when they arrived Eskew had fled. Eskew returned the next day at 2:50 pm with a sawed off 12-gauge shotgun while under the influence of both marijuana and cocaine. Eskew went to Severson's Wiley Hall dorm room and fatally shot Severson in the head. He then barricaded himself in his third floor dorm room. A janitor found the body a short time later. SWAT and police took up positions around Wiley Hall. Police evacuated Wiley Hall, attempted to negotiate, fired tear gas, and stormed the room to find Eskew had taken his own life with the shotgun. [55][56]

(Cont'd.)

NOTORIOUS COLLEGE AND UNIVERSITY SCHOOL INCIDENTS *(Continued)*

Date	Location	Attacker(s)	Number of Victims	Description
June 28, 2000	Seattle, Washington, United States	Jian Chen, 42	2 dead	Jian Chen entered the University of Washington Medical Center around 3:45 PM and went to the office of his former supervisor, 57 year old Doctor Rodger Haggitt. Chen closed the door to Haggett's office and pulled out a gun and killed Haggett. Chen then turned the gun on himself and committed suicide.
May 18, 2001	Pierce County, Washington, United States	Donald D Cowan, 55	2 dead	Around 3 PM, Donald D Cowan walked onto the Pacific Lutheran University campus armed with a 9mm handgun and a .22 caliber handgun. Cowan saw music professor James D. Holloway standing outside a residence hall. Cowan fired four times, striking Holloway three times in the torso and once in the head. Cowan then walked over to his victim, dropped a 16 page suicide note, put the gun to his head and shot himself once. Cowan died later that day at Madigan Army Medical Center. Cowan was obsessed over a female faculty member at PLU and killed Holloway out of "personal animosity" towards the woman, who had tried for years to get Cowan to leave her alone. Cowan also had a criminal history in Hawaii for stalking, and was thought to be mentally ill.
January 16, 2002	Grundy, Virginia, United States	Peter Odighizuwa, 43	3 dead, 3 injured	Appalachian School of Law shooting. 43-year-old Appalachian School of Law student Peter Odighizuwa shot and killed the Law School Dean, Contracts Professor and another student; three others were wounded . The incident was ended when two students with personal firearms subdued the shooter. He was sentenced to multiple life terms in prison. Peter 'O' was a Nigerian student attending the school on a student visa. The school later settled

(Cont'd.)

NOTORIOUS COLLEGE AND UNIVERSITY SCHOOL INCIDENTS *(Continued)*

Date	Location	Attacker(s)	Number of Victims	Description
January 16, 2002 *(Cont'd.)*	Grundy, Virginia, United States *(Cont'd.)*	Peter Odighizuwa, 43 *(Cont'd.)*	3 dead, 3 injured *(Cont'd.)*	a lawsuit by some of the surviving victims and their families brought over the schools failure to take action when the student showed signs of psychosis and made threats.
October 21, 2002	Melbourne, Australia	Huan Xiang	2 dead, "others" wounded	Monash University shooting. Huan Xiang, a commerce student at the university, armed with five loaded handguns, opened fire in a tutorial room. Two students, William Wu and Steven Chan, were killed and others seriously wounded. Xiang was found not guilty of murder due to mental illness, and was ordered to be sent to a psychiatric hospital.
October 28, 2002	Tucson, Arizona, United States	Robert Flores, 41	4 dead	Three nursing professors were shot dead at the University of Arizona by a student failing the nursing program. Robert J. Flores, Jr., 41, shot and killed Robin Rogers, 50, Barbara Monroe, 45, and Cheryl McGaffic, 44 before turning the gun on himself. Two of the teachers were shot in a classroom and the gunman allowed the students to leave before killing himself.
May 9, 2003	Cleveland, Ohio, United States	Biswanath Halder, 62	1 dead, 2 injured	Biswanath Halder, a 62-year-old man, opened fire with an automatic weapon on his former school, Case Western Reserve University. He killed one student, seriously wounded two others, and kept over 90 people hiding for their lives for seven hours. After vigorous and bullet-ridden gun battles with school police and SWAT officers, Halder surrendered and was sentenced to life in prison.

(Cont'd.)

NOTORIOUS COLLEGE AND UNIVERSITY SCHOOL INCIDENTS *(Continued)*

Date	Location	Attacker(s)	Number of Victims	Description
September 13, 2006	Montreal, Quebec, Canada	Kimveer Gill	2 dead, 19 injured	Dawson College shooting. On September 13, 2006 at Dawson College, a CEGEP in Westmount near downtown Montreal. The perpetrator, Kimveer Gill, began shooting outside the de Maisonneuve Boulevard entrance to the school, and moved towards the atrium by the cafeteria on the main floor. One victim died later in the next day due to her serious injuries at the hospital, while another 19 were injured, eight of whom were listed in critical condition with six requiring surgery. The gunman later committed suicide by shooting himself in the head, after being shot in the arm by police. The Dawson incident was the third fatal school shooting in the city.
September 17, 2006	Pittsburgh, Pennsylvania, United States	. . .	5 injured	Shots are fired outside Duquesne University's Vickroy Hall after a dance party sponsored by the Black Student Union which several non-students were attending. Five members of the Duquesne Dukes basketball team were injured during the shooting including one who sustained critical injuries after an argument between 1 individual and 2 students.
April 2, 2007	Seattle, Washington, United States	Jonathan Rowan, 41	2 dead	Rowan entered Gould Hall on the University of Washington's Seattle Campus and headed to the fourth floor where he entered the office of his ex-girlfriend Rebecca Griego, 26, a program coordinator for the College of Architecture and Urban Planning. Rowan fired two shots, the first taking Griego's life and the second ending his own. Griego was aware that Rowan was tracking her

(Cont'd.)

NOTORIOUS COLLEGE AND UNIVERSITY SCHOOL INCIDENTS *(Continued)*

Date	Location	Attacker(s)	Number of Victims	Description
April 2, 2007 *(Cont'd.)*	Seattle, Washington, United States *(Cont'd.)*	Jonathan Rowan, 41 *(Cont'd.)*	2 dead *(Cont'd.)*	down and had alerted the authorities as well as co-workers to be on the lookout but nothing was done, raising questions about the UWPD and campus security.
April 16, 2007	Blacksburg, Virginia, United States	Seung-Hui Cho, 23	33 dead, 25 injured	The Virginia Tech massacre was the single most deadly civilian gunfire incident in American higher education history. It occurred at Virginia Polytechnic Institute and State University. Thirty-two people were killed by gunman Seung-Hui Cho in two separate locations, about two hours apart: West Ambler Johnston Hall, where two were shot dead, and Norris Hall, where the remaining 30 were shot in an attack lasting nine minutes. The gunman then took his own life. Police reported that 25 others were injured, some in the Norris Hall shooting, others when they jumped from second-story windows to escape.
September 21, 2007	Dover, Delaware, United States	Loyer D. Braden, 18	1 dead, 1 injured	Delaware State University shooting. An 18-year old student of Delaware State University opens fire of four to six rounds and wounds two 17-year old students, one injured seriously. 17-year old Shalita Middleton died from injuries sustained in the shootings 32 days later.

GLOSSARY

0-1-3 guidelines (Chapter 4) 0-1-3 guidelines are suggestions for low-risk drinking. These guidelines recommend that in some situations zero alcohol is appropriate. *Zero* alcohol consumption is important for those individuals dependent on alcohol, pregnant women, and most high-risk tasks such as driving. Otherwise, for most people *one* drink per hour with meals, and no more than *three* in any sitting will usually minimize consequences.

acquaintance rape (Chapter 11) A rape committed by someone the victim knows. The broad classification includes in its definition of rape forcing someone to have sexual intercourse with psychological pressure or threats of violence. This definition includes continual arguments or constant verbal harassment as part of psychological pressure. The stringent definition defines rape as forcing someone to have sexual intercourse using only threats of violence. This definition does not include those who use only psychological pressure.

active resistant (Chapter 5) A level of physical behavior that involves a combination of active and passive-aggressive behavior. Examples of active resistance include slamming doors, turning over desks, or throwing objects. There is no actual bodily harm, but the threat of escalating violence exists.

acute stress disorder (Chapter 10) A traumatic reaction classified as an anxiety disorder that spans from two to four days. Symptoms include "feeling in a daze," reexperiencing the trauma, avoidance of things that remind the individual of the trauma, and marked symptoms or increased anxiety. These symptoms cause significant impairment in day-to-day functioning.

agitators (Chapter 16) Agitators plan for and instigate riots. They are often motivated by their need to uphold their reputation. Some agitators are chronic troublemakers who are looking to jump on the bandwagon of creating mischief or cashing in on crime opportunities (e.g., looting).

ambusher (Chapter 1) A type of predator who takes the Bundy approach – feigning vulnerability and weakness or manipulating victims with charm and seduction in order to lure them into the trap.

anger-defensiveness (Chapter 1) A stage in an institution's readiness for change. It occurs when people begin to come forward with information about violence, and the initial reaction is often to find fault with the reporter or to otherwise discredit the information.

anniversary rioting (Chapter 16) Rioting that happens at predictable times each year. For example, Halloween rioting is a tradition on some campuses.

arson (Chapter 18) The FBI Uniform Crime Reporting System crime definition of arson is, "Any willful or malicious burning or attempt to burn, with or without intent to defraud, a dwelling house, public building, motor vehicle or aircraft, personal property of another, etc."

avenger (Chapters 1, 8, and 14) A type of violence perpetrator who perceives violence as the only possible recourse for perceived grievances. Avengers usually have particular targets in mind, although they may take down many others in their violent rampage.

avoidance symptoms (Chapter 10) A set of symptoms common in survivors of trauma that involve avoiding things that remind the victim of the trauma in order to dampen the intensity of the uncomfortable feelings. For example, an individual with PTSD may avoid situations that are reminiscent of the traumatic event. Others may become numb to emotions altogether.

barricading (Chapter 8) A survival strategy that involves putting as many obstacles as possible between the perpetrator and the potential victims.

binge drinking (Chapter 4) This catch-phrase, used to describe high-risk drinking, is defined by researchers as five drinks or more in a row for men and four or more for women.

bump (Chapter 8) A low-level behavior that perpetrators engage in to assess whether or not the potential victim will be a good target. By enacting this form of contact, perpetrators are assessing how friendly or passive the potential victim is.

bystanders (Chapters 2 and 11) People who observe violent or previolent behavior. Regardless of their true feelings about the violent behavior, the silent presence of bystanders has a strong influence in continuing a violent incident.

campus-community coalitions (Chapter 6) Campus-community coalitions consist of broad cross-sections of the university and surrounding neighborhoods. With campus-community coalitions, key stakeholders from the campus and community meet together to begin a discussion surrounding campus violence and to work toward the common mission of a safe campus and community.

carriers of misinformation (Chapter 4) Students, faculty, staff, and even parents who, regardless of their own personal use or attitudes about alcohol and other drugs, pass on misperceptions about campus substance abuse through conversation and comments.

catalyst for change (Chapter 1) Something that affects an institution's readiness for change. Often an event, person, or group of people that show the true colors of the violence in a way that it cannot be ignored.

cerebral acceleration (Chapter 8) A response experienced under extreme stress when the brain switches to a rapid mode of information processing. This occurs because the brain is attempting to sort through tremendous amounts of information quickly in order to make the best decision. Consequently, the senses become very acute and amplified. The experience of this phenomenon is that it feels as if the world has turned into a very surreal, slow-motion movie.

club drugs (Chapter 3) Drugs used recreationally at clubs or "raves" popular with teens and young adults. Ecstasy and GHB (gamma hydroxy butyric acid) are two of the most common. Rave participants usually take these drugs to induce a warm sense of well-being accompanied by heightened senses.

communication center (Chapter 7) Otherwise known as the communication "vortex," serves as a knowledge base for all investigations. This system organizes all incidents of violence by keeping record of the details of the incident, interventions, and outcomes. In addition to documentation of critical or threatening incidents, the communication center can also be a resource center for those concerned with violence prevention. The communication center can serve as a clearinghouse to distribute current literature and data on campus safety issues.

conditional threats (Chapter 5) A threat is made contingent on a certain set of circumstances. These threats contain the word "if," or the word "or." These types of threats are designed to manipulate or intimidate the target into compliance. Examples of these types of threats include, "You better do this or you're dead," and, "If you don't give me what I want, you will pay." If these threats are not met with resistance and clear signs of intolerance, they are likely to increase as they are often powerfully reinforced.

counterrioters (Chapter 16) The "decent majority" of a riot who is actively engaged in stopping or preventing further violence.

crisis response team (Chapter 6) In the aftermath of a tragedy, a predetermined team can be instrumental in addressing the needs of affected individuals and the community. The crisis response team usually consists of a cross-section of university representatives who are highly invested and trained in handling critical incidents. This team may have significant overlap or may even be identical to the Threat and Violence.

Behavioral Intervention Team (BIT) (Chapter 6) A team of campus professionals dedicated to taking action roles rather than just providing input. The BIT should consist of individuals trained in the evaluation of and intervention with potentially violent situations. The BIT's objective is violence prevention and response. BIT members are responsible for addressing threats and confronting violent behavior, and may assist in assessing potential for violence. They will serve as the primary decision makers in violent crises, and will be communication liaisons between internal and external responders. The BIT is responsible for making critical decisions quickly. They will develop the protocol in case of a threat or violent incident, and establish a plan for the protection of other students, staff, and other potential targets.

culturally influenced violence (Chapter 3) Otherwise known as the "setting" influence of drugs and violence. Violence shaped by expectations or traditions of the social group using the drug separate from the actual effect of the drug. Of the three factors, drug (biological effects of the drug), set (emotions or mental state of the user), and setting, the setting is often the most powerful predictor of violence.

curriculum infusion (Chapter 4) A substance abuse prevention practice attempting to get alcohol and other drug issues integrated into almost every syllabus. Faculty tie issues of substance abuse to their course topic. For example, "The Costs to Society" (Economics class) or "The History of Alcohol Advertising" (Mass Media class or History class).

cyberstalker (Chapter 10) A predator who finds and grooms prey via the Internet.

date rape drugs (Chapter 3) Drugs given to unknowing victims in order to induce a very impaired state. Rohypnol, GHB, and Ketamine are common examples. These drugs tend to cause profound "anterograde amnesia" or the inability to remember events that took place while under the effects of the drugs, making them very effective in preventing victims from coming forward after the fact. In 1996, Congress passed the Drug-Induced Rape Prevention and Punishment Act of 1996.

diffusion of responsibility (Chapters 1 and 14) The social psychology phenomenon of bystander apathy that occurs when a large number of people witness a distressing event. An individual would be more likely to give help if she or he is the only bystander present, than when there is a group. The larger the group the less likely any one person is to assume personal responsibility. Also contributing to this effect is whether the violent act is tacitly approved of by a majority of people. If there is some kind of consensus (usually unspoken and often misperceived) that a form of violence is legitimate, then few people in a group will step forward to stop it.

direct threats (Chapter 5) A statement of clear intent to harm someone. Examples are, "I'm going to kill you," or "I'm going to blow them away." Generally, the more specific the threat, the more concerned protectors should be.

dissociative anesthetics (Chapter 3) Drugs that diminish the sensation of pain while distorting reality. Ketamine and PCP are examples.

drunkenness defense (Chapter 4) A relaxed standard of accountability because "The beer made me do it." Those who buy into this line of thinking often excuse otherwise inexcusable behavior with the "drunkenness defense," and thereby promote the continuance of violence.

enabling (Chapter 4) An addictions term, referring to the situation when one person or group of people minimizes the short-term consequences for an addicted person without addressing the long-term problems. For example, between individuals, enabling occurs when a friend or spouse calls into work for someone who is incapacitated by a hangover.

entrepreneurial violence (Chapter 1) Committing violence to gain a profit (e.g., robbery).

fads (Chapter 1) Patterns or perceived patterns in violence that gain much attention in a short period and fade out just as quickly. They are often created by urban myths. For example, during the mid-nineties, many people thought they would be shot if they flashed their car's headlights at a car that was driving at them with no headlights in the dark.

forced dependency (Chapter 14) A technique often used in team building, brainwashing, or cults where members are taken away or prohibited from associating with people outside the group. The positive outcome of this technique is that it allows members to commit to learning about each other and their purpose. A possible consequence of this technique is that members' abilities to function productively outside of the group become more limited.

gang rape (Chapter 11) Sexual assault perpetrated by more than one person. Gang rape is a form of group-induced violence and has as its primary causes diffusion of responsibility, group modeling, and a need for belonging. Gang rapists are less concerned with the welfare of the victim or with the potential consequences of their actions because of the involvement of others.

GHB (Chapters 3 and 11) A popular "club drug," also considered a date rape drug, gamma hydroxy butyrate is a central nervous system depressant. When used in small amounts, the drug can produce the effects of being drunk. The drug is colorless, odorless, and salty. Other names for GHB include "GBH," "Grievous Bodily Harm," "Cherry Meth," "Liquid X," "Liquid Ecstasy," "Easy Lay," "G-Juice," and "Energy Drink."

Greekthink (Chapter 4) A term coined by Hank Nuwer who found the following behavior common among fraternities. During a crisis when an individual has become hurt or is critically impaired by alcohol, there is a devastating pause. At the time when first responders should be racing to get appropriate medical attention, these individuals, who are often fairly impaired themselves, think, "oh shit." They pause because they are concerned about getting in trouble, about covering up evidence, and about taking care of the problem themselves. This pause often leads to lifesaving minutes lost.

group-induced violence (Chapters 1, 8, and 14) Violence that occurs when a group of individuals are swept into a mob mentality. Group-induced violence creates the perception of decreased accountability through anonymity. Group violence can be contagious, in that the excitement of the moment may overpower the better judgment of the on-lookers that chose to participate when they would have normally not behaved in such a fashion. Bystanders play a critical role in group-induced violence. Group-induced violence is often trigger-driven, that is, ignited by an external event or stimulus.

harm reduction (Chapter 4) A treatment and prevention strategy developed by Dr. Alan Marlatt and colleagues designed to reduce dangerous drinking behavior through brief intervention.

hate crime (Chapter 13) Words or actions that are intended to harm or intimidate a person or group due to race, gender, sexual orientation, religion, or other group identification (according to *Violence on Campus*) (Hoffman, 1998).

hazing (Chapter 14) Any action related to an individual's admittance or membership in a group that produces mental or physical harm, embarrassment, harassment, or ridicule, regardless of the location of the activity or the individual's willingness to participate.

health terrorism (Chapter 4) Scare tactics that play upon fears of death, rejection, embarrassment, or incarceration. For many college students, fear is a short-lived emotion, especially when the risks for such tragic outcomes are relatively low in their perception.

high-risk drinking (Chapter 4) An alternative and preferred term to "binge drinking." High-risk drinking is a term that many people are still trying to operationalize. For some, it means a large amount (e.g., 5+ drinks) of alcohol consumed in a short period of time (e.g., 0 to 2 hours). For others, it is the quantity of alcohol required to get an individual legally impaired. Less specifically, drinking that exceeds the "injury dose" for a person. Injury dose means the amount of alcohol that

typically results in negative consequences for the consumer (e.g., vomiting, severe hangover, fights, falls, blackouts, etc.).

hunters (Chapter 1) A type of predator who stays within his or her own area or neighborhood to locate prey.

hyperarousal symptoms (Chapter 10) A collection of symptoms common in sufferers of PTSD (Posttraumatic stress disorder) including startle responses, irrational and new fears, increased irritability, explosive anger, problems concentrating or remembering new information, sleep disorders, and disrupted appetites.

hypervigilance (Chapter 10) Constant scanning of the environment for danger cues. Being constantly aware of potential danger.

impact (Chapter 10) A stage in posttrauma experiences when an individual leaves the location of the critical incident and feels confused and overwhelmed as full realization of the extent of the danger, damage, death, or injury is made conscious. This phase can last from days to weeks.

impulsive hate episodes (Chapter 13) A form of hate crimes defined by the search for excitement and spontaneity on the part of the perpetrators. The payoff for these types of hate crimes is mainly social. The perpetrator receives ample approval from like-minded peers who believe such action is fun.

injury dose (Chapter 4) The amount of alcohol that typically results in negative consequences for the consumer (e.g., vomiting, severe hangover, fights, falls, blackouts, etc.).

in loco parentis (Chapter 7) A notion of the 1960s that campuses were to act as substitute parents. A perspective that lost favor during the 1970s, 1980s, and early 1990s and is regaining support today.

intrusive symptoms (Chapter 10) A cluster of symptoms common in people who experience PTSD (Posttraumatic stress disorder). Intrusive symptoms occur when the images, sounds, smells, tactile or taste sensations related to the traumatic event unexpectedly violate the person's consciousness. These vivid memories may include nightmares, triggered memories, flashbacks, and obsessive thoughts.

Ketamine (Chapter 3) A "date rape drug" nicknamed "Special K." Veterinarians used this drug originally on farm animals. It usually comes in liquid form, but may also be found as a white powder or pill. According to National Institute on Drug Abuse (NIDA), Ketamine is a central nervous system depressant and a rapid-acting general anesthetic. Ketamine is usually snorted, but may be sprinkled on tobacco or marijuana and smoked. Some users describe intense hallucinations while using this drug. Other effects can include convulsions, potentially fatal respiratory problems, and delirium.

limbo (Chapter 1) A stage in institutional change when, due to outside pressure institutions can no longer deny or excuse away violence, but they do not know how to proceed. The problem with the "limbo" stage is that resistance to acknowledging the violence remains, so any attempt to address the problem is usually half-hearted. Quick-fix band-aids are applied in haste usually more to show the public that "something is being done" rather than effective, comprehensive prevention. Very often, these attempts are phased out as soon as the public eye blinks.

liquid courage (Chapter 4) A person who intends to engage in a premeditated violent act may get intoxicated to create the "liquid courage" to act out.

love obsession stalkers (Chapter 17) Represent about 20 to 25 percent of all stalking cases. These stalkers develop a love fixation on another person with whom they have never had any personal relationship. Some choose to stalk celebrities, others develop obsessions with regular, ordinary people.

low-risk drinking (Chapter 4) A preferable term to "responsible drinking," low-risk drinking describes standard guidelines for decreasing consequences related to alcohol use (e.g., 0-1-3 guidelines).

maturing out (Chapter 4) A substance abuse term referring to the developmental trend many individuals experience as they get older and do not find the need to get intoxicated as frequently or as intensely as they did when they were younger.

meaning-making (Chapter 10) A term coined by Sharon Parks (1991), in her book *The Critical Years*, identifying this critical developmental process college students experience when faith development is greatly impacted by creating order out of life occurrences, especially challenges to our core belief systems.

MIP (Chapter 4) Abbreviation for "minor in possession," a legal infraction for those under the legal drinking age who are consuming or possessing alcohol.

negligent hiring (Chapter 7) A legal term referring to the situation when employees commit a violent act and employers are held liable because they did not conduct an adequate background investigation to discover patterns of violent behavior in the individual's past.

negligent retention (Chapter 7) A legal term similar to negligent hiring where an employer retains a known violent or threatening employee despite ample evidence that the individual is a risk to the company.

off-schedule (Chapter 3) Students switch majors, take time off to work or travel, and experience medical and emotional setbacks that often delay graduation anywhere from one semester to several years. This sense of being "off-schedule" is difficult for many. They become out of sync with their friends, school debts accumulate, and the destination of reaching a degree and prosperous career feels out of reach.

opportunists (Chapter 1) A type of predator who lures in prey by placing himself or herself in positions of trust or authority.

parental notification (Chapter 4) A substance abuse prevention strategy gaining popularity among many schools (albeit controversial) to notify parents when their sons or daughters (under the age of 21) break alcohol policies on campus.

passive-resistant (Chapter 5) This type of behavior is also known as "passive aggressive" and is characterized by subtle defiance. These antagonistic behaviors are just under the threshold of noncompliance. Individuals using passive resistance may be extremely slow, putting forth only minimally acceptable effort. In a physical manner, they may use their body mass to impede another's effort by blocking a doorway for example.

pathways to violence (Chapter 1) Predictable patterns perpetrators engage in before becoming violent. Usually these patterns include testing limits and practicing out violence at lower intensity.

perpetrators (Chapter 2) Individuals who commit acts of violence.

pluralistic ignorance (Chapter 4) The belief that one's private attitudes and judgments are different from others. In terms of substance abuse issues, this notion translates to individuals who choose not to engage in high-risk drinking, assume that everyone around them is.

poachers (Chapter 1) A type of predator who surveys an area away from the home territory in order to find prey for violence.

posttrauma resolution (Chapter 10) A phase many people experience after a critical incident that is defined once victims return to routine patterns. Here the trauma's impact will show longer-term changes in behavior, thought patterns, beliefs, emotions, and perception. These changes may be irreversible. There are two possible outcomes of this phase: positive resolution, or negative reaction with no resolution. The positive course will lead to acceptance of the event and the individual's actions, along with a positive reevaluation of goals and values. Keep in mind, this may be a lengthy process and the continuum of resolution is broad. Without any trauma resolution, there is a strong likelihood of a chronic struggle throughout life with distress, family problems, job difficulties, chemical dependency, and potential suicide.

posttraumatic stress disorder (Chapter 10) A psychological syndrome that affects individuals who have experienced a critical incident such as combat, earthquakes, rape, domestic violence, airplane crashes, car accidents, and violent crime. The cluster of symptoms includes nightmares, flashbacks, hyperarousal, dissociation, depression, and avoidance.

practicing (Chapter 5) Behavioral and psychological precursors to violence imagined or acted out by perpetrators in an effort to prepare themselves for their violent act. These patterns may include elaborate fantasies, threats, vandalism, harassment, harm to animals, and so on.

precontemplation (Chapter 1) At this stage in readiness for change where an individual or institution is truly unaware of the problems. Some have called this stage "denial." When this concept is applied to campus violence, people in this stage do not believe violence is a concern because the violence is hidden or not believed. No one is assessing or addressing the problem, because it is thought not to exist.

predatory violence (Chapters 1, 8, and 14) A form of violence highly feared but relatively rare on college campuses in which a perpetrator commits an act of violence for the sole reason that it gives him or her a thrill. There is no other desired outcome than to experience the violence and another's suffering. Otherwise known as "stranger danger."

premeditated hate episodes (Chapter 13) In these cases, perpetrators actually declare "war" against another group of people. Usually, an organized group such as the KKK or the White Aryan Resistance supports these perpetrators.

primary victims (Chapter 2) Individuals who have experienced the violence directly.

protectors (Chapter 2) Individuals who do what is in their power to prevent violence incidents from occurring or intervene when violent events are unfolding. Protectors include security officers, law enforcement officers, residence life staff, coaches, faculty, and others.

psychopharmacological violence (Chapter 3) Drug-related violence caused by the actual chemically induced properties of the drug itself. For instance, drugs can cause agitation and paranoia in perpetrators, and can cause sedation and memory loss in victims.

PTSD (Chapters 9 and 13) – See Posttraumatic Stress Disorder.

rape (Chapter 11) Sexual violence defined by forced sexual intercourse using any of the following types of coercion: psychological pressure, physical force, or taking advantage of a person's inability to give consent due to intoxication, loss of consciousness, or mental impairment.

rape kit (Chapter 11) A medical exam given to victims after a sexual assault for the purpose of assessing needs for immediate medical attention (e.g., physical trauma, sexually transmitted diseases, pregnancy, or HIV) and for gathering medical evidence.

Rape Shield Law (Chapter 11) A law that precludes any testimony of the victim's sexual history that does not bear immediate relevance to the current sexual assault case. The law was implemented to keep the jury focused on the case at hand and not information that has no bearing on the rape being tried.

rape trauma syndrome (Chapter 11) A response some victims have to rape that occurs in three phases: acute, outward adjustment, and resolution stage. The acute phase often begins immediately after the rape and can persist from a few days to several weeks. Victims usually have difficulty concentrating, making decisions, or accomplishing everyday tasks. The outward adjustment phase begins with return to a near-normal routine pattern. Inwardly, there is still turmoil which can manifest itself in many ways: anxiety, sense of helplessness, fear, depression, vivid dreams, insomnia, recurring nightmares, physical ailments, variations in appetite, vomiting, nausea, preoccupation with safety, denial, hesitation to form new relationships, sexual problems, disruptions to everyday behavior. The resolution phase occurs when victims recognize that although they will never forget the rape or the pain and memories that go with it, it is a part of their life experience and they are choosing to move on.

raptor (Chapter 1) A form of predator who "swoops and scoops" victims without any warning or attempt to engage them socially.

recoil (Chapter 10) A phase many people experience in the aftermath of a critical incident that begins with return to a near-normal routine pattern, accompanied by stable days. During this time symptoms of the impact phase begin to decrease and attention, concentration, reasoning ability, recall, and emotional expression gradually return. However, this phase often resembles an emotional rollercoaster with good days and bad days interspersed. At this stage, individuals often feel as though they will never regain a "normal" life. Each time they begin to get on their feet, another wave of memories sets in.

relationship-based violence (Chapters 1, 8, and 14) A type of violence that involves an exploited one-on-one attachment. Relationships that have both power differential and privacy are most vulnerable – parent-child, husband-wife, pledgemaster-pledge. In relationship-based violence, the dominant partner has an "ownership" mentality over the submissive partner. Because the submissive partner is perceived as property rather than a person of equal standing, the dominant partner employs certain strategies to ensure that "the property" is maintained under current control.

responsible use (Chapter 4) A controversial term in alcohol abuse literature loosely defined as use that does not result in consequences to the user or others.

right to party (Chapters 4 and 16) A trend on many campuses based on the belief (held mainly by students) that college students have a right to drink alcohol when and where they choose. This perspective comes as a backlash against institutes of higher education that are attempting to crack down on underage drinkers and out-of-control drinkers. On some campuses, those who assert their right to party are sometimes the agitators of riots.

riot (Chapter 16) A large group of people attempting to assert their will with violence and the threat of violence outside the normal bounds of law. When agitators manipulate a crowd, members begin to lose their identity and merge into a primitive cohesive group. The larger the group the more the anonymity is protected and the more normal moral restraints break down.

Rohypnol (Chapters 3 and 11) Called a "date rape drug," Rohypnol is a benzodiazepine that produces a sedative effect, amnesia, muscle relaxation, and a slowing of psychomotor responses. Sedation occurs 20 to 30 minutes after ingestion and can last for hours. Other names used for Rohypnol include "the forget pill," "Mexican Valium," "R-2," "Rib," "Roaches," "Rope," "Roofenot," and "Roofers." Most often Rohypnol is found in tablet form stored in bubble packs. Sometimes the pills have been ground into powder and either taken recreationally to enhance an alcohol buzz or they are slipped in drinks of unknowing victims. Rohypnol is sold as a prescription drug in other countries and smuggled into the United States.

sacred cows (Chapters 4) Individuals who are treated by a different standard than the rest of the campus community. The violent behavior of these people may be excused from consequences due to their perceived importance or influence of powerful stakeholders.

secondary victims (Chapter 2) People involved but not directly impacted by the violence (e.g., roommate, friends, rescue workers, resident assistants, etc.). These secondary victims are often overlooked in trauma recovery efforts, but many of them may experience a posttraumatic response that is very upsetting.

shock (Chapter 10) The first phase many people experience in the aftermath of a critical incident. Shock usually begins at the onset of the traumatic event, and can continue for up to a week. During this time, sensory information floods the brain. The experience of events is in "slow motion," and there is an unreal or dream-like quality to them. There may be some physical symptoms, including agitation, hyperalertness, overactivity, or biological disruption (e.g., sleeping and eating patterns).

simple obsession stalkers (Chapter 17) A form of stalking that represents about 70 to 80 percent of all stalking cases. These stalkers have had a personal or romantic relationship with their victims before the stalking behavior began. In most instances, the victim has become the stalker's sole source of self-esteem.

When the victim tries to break off the relationship, the perpetrator's thinking evolves from "If I can just prove how much I love you" to "I can make you love me," to "If I can't have you, nobody else will." Stalking cases that develop from domestic violence patterns are the most common and potentially lethal.

social norms marketing (Chapter 4) A substance abuse prevention strategy (currently being adapted to address other campus issues) based on the idea that students typically overestimate alcohol and other drug use on campus. Consequently, this illusion creates a partially self-fulfilling prophecy. Social norms marketing is used to correct these misperceptions and decrease high-risk drinking. Social norms marketing approach uses traditional marketing techniques to promote healthy messages about student behavior to challenge the misperceptions.

stalking (Chapters 1 and 17) Willful, malicious, and repeated following and harassment combined with the credible threat intended to make the victim fear death or serious injury.

standard operating guide (Chapter 7) A set of procedures used in the prevention and intervention of violence on campuses.

stranger rape (Chapter 11) Sexual assault perpetrated by someone the victim does not know.

student host contracts (Chapter 4) Agreements between campus visitors and residents or campus hosts that, depending on the circumstances, all parties will either commit to a drug- and alcohol-free visit (as would be the case with high school recruitment visitors) or the hosts agree to take responsibility for the behavior of their visitors.

suicidal avenger (Chapter 1) A type of avenger (see above) who believes that he or she has nothing to lose and is willing to die during the violence rampage. Many of the school shooters and workplace violence perpetrators fall in this category.

suicide-by-cop (Chapter 1) A form of violence where individuals use law enforcement officers as weapons of suicide by provoking the officers to use deadly force against them. For example, a suicidal individual may threaten an officer with a plastic knife and the officer shoots the individual because the officer believes that he or she is in imminent danger.

survivor guilt (Chapter 10) In the aftermath of a violent tragedy, many people experience these feelings because they second-guess their actions or they wonder why they were not chosen as the victims.

synergy (Chapter 3) A term used in this book to describe drug interactions whereby two drugs that are used together have an additive effect and a more intense impact on the user than each drug's effect taken by itself.

targets (Chapter 2) The victims (or sometimes the property) harmed by the perpetrators.

tertiary victims (Chapter 2) Helpers who also become affected by the violent event. In the aftermath of a violent incident, student life staff may be flooded with individuals in crisis, needs for debriefing sessions, and requests for consultation. At the same time, these professionals may be dealing with their own reactions to the trauma. They may also be vicariously affected by listening to story after story from the survivors. In some cases these helpers may internalize others' pain and become overwhelmed. As a result, they may experience similar nightmares and distressing thoughts as the victims.

T.O.A.D.S. (Chapter 2) A "formula for violence" – Time, Opportunity, Ability, Desire, Stimulus.

trends (Chapter 1) Culture patterns that build slowly and forever change the fabric of a community, nation, or world.

trees (Chapter 2) A symbolic concept used to represent barriers placed in the way of practicing perpetrators to stop or slow them.

trollers (Chapter 1) A form of predators that wander around to areas of vulnerability searching for viable prey (e.g., campus bars).

user-based violence (Chapter 3) A drug-induced violence concept that encompasses internal expectations or needs or the user. One example of this form of violence is economically motivated crimes. Illicit drugs often are expensive, and because of this, users may often engage in other illegal behaviors to obtain the drugs. Others may use drugs to drum up a false sense of courage before committing a violent act.

veiled threats (Chapter 5) A type of threat that is hard to address because it is often vague and subject to interpretation. Veiled threats are statements made to communicate the desire or intent to commit violence, but when taken out of context are often minimized or misunderstood. For example, "I could see why someone would want to shoot a professor" is an example of a veiled threat.

victims of choice (Chapter 2) Victims who are chosen by the perpetrator for a reason.
The reason may be revenge, easy access, or the victim's likeness to a violent fantasy.

victims of opportunity (Chapter 2) Victims who are not intentionally targeted by perpetrators but are in the wrong place at the wrong time.

violence (Chapter 2) Behavior that by intent, action, and/or outcome harms another person.

Violence Against Women Act (VAWA) (Chapter 11) An act passed in 1994 that among other things allows rape victims to sue their attackers in federal court because, it is argued, rape impacts interstate commerce. There has been a great deal of debate about this act and its constitutionality.

vortex (Chapter 7) – See Communication Center.

zero tolerance (Chapters 4 and 7) An intervention stance used to address violent behaviors, meaning that every questionable statement or gesture goes under the microscope. Every threat or practice behavior is addressed, even if that only means investigation and documentation. Alcohol-induced violence is no exception.

ENDNOTES

1 Bureau of Justice Statistics (2003, December). Violent victimization of college students. Retrieved on July 20, 2008, from http://www.ojp.usdoj.gov/bjs/abstract/vvcs00.htm.

2 Greene, H., & Greene, M. (2008, April). What families think: Campus safety. *University Business.* Retrieved on August 17, 2008, from http://www.universitybusiness.com/viewarticle.aspx?articleid=1042.

3 Cornell, D. (2008). Threat assessment on the college campus. *Leadership Exchange,* 5(4), p. 10.

4 Ibid.

5 Ibid.

6 Sokolow, B. (n.d.) An op-ed on the media response to the Virginia Tech Tragedy. Retrieved on July 30, 2007, from http://www.ncherm.org/article-vtech.html.

7 Richard Speck: Born to raise hell. (n.d.) *Court TV Online.* Retrieved on March 14, 2000, from http://www.courttv.com/onair/shows/crimestories/q_z_.../richard_speck_born_to_raise_hell.htm.
Watkins, T. (n.d.) Terror in Chicago, 1996: Richard Speck's twisted world and the murder of 8 nurses. Retrieved on March 14, 2000, from http://home1.gte.net/deltakit/speck.htm.

8 Charles Joseph Whitman. (n.d.) *Find a grave.* Retrieved on February 27, 2000, from http://www.findagrave.com/pictures/5921.html.
Barr, A. (1999, February 15). *The handbook of Texas online: Charles Whitman.* Retrieved on February 27, 2000, from http://www.tsha.utexas.edu/handbook/online/articles/view/WW/fwh42.html.

9 Ibid.

10 U. of Texas tries to move beyond campus landmark's legacy of violence. (1999, September 15). *CNN.com.* Retrieved on 27 February 2000, from http://cgi.cnn.com/US/9909/15/texas.tower.ap/.

11 Mayday: Kent State. (n.d.) Retrieved on February 27, 2000, from http://www.emerson.edu/acadepts.cs.comm/chrono.html.
Lewis, J., & Hensley, T. (1998). The May 4 shootings at Kent State University: The Search for historical accuracy. *The Ohio Council for the Social Studies Review. 34(1):*9–21.

12 Ibid.

13 Ted Bundy: Murder on the run. (n.d.) *The crime library.* Retrieved on February 27, 2000, from http://www.crimelibrary.com/bundy/murder.htm.

14 Nuwer, H. (1990). *Broken pledges: The deadly rite of hazing.* Atlanta: Longstreet Press.
Nuwer, H. (1999). *Wrongs of passage: Fraternities, sororities, hazing, and binge drinking.* Bloomington: Indiana University Press.

15 Ibid.

16 Rogers, T., & Stevens, E. (1996, September 15). Anti-hazing activist. *New York Daily News.* Retreived on February 29, 2000, from http://www.alphaphi.org/Featured/Daily_News.html.
Stevens, E. (1996, September 15). Hazing – A Greek tragedy. *Alpha Phi: Eileen Stevens' message on hazing.* Retrieved on February 29, 2000, from http://www.alphaphi.org/Featured/tragedy.html.

17 Nuwer, H. (n.d.) Thank you survey! May I have another. And another? Retrieved on February 29, 2000, from http://stophazing.org/nuwer/sept99column.htm.

18 English, B. (1999, October 20). From a daughter's death, a life's work: After Jeanne Clery's murder at Lehigh University, her parents have worked to change laws and change minds about campus safety. *The Boston Globe.*

19 Ibid.

20 Katie Koestner. (n.d.) *Campus Speak.* Retrieved on February 28, 2000, from http://www.angelo.edu/~ucpc/kaite.htm.

21 Henry, B. (2000, September 28). "Revisions of the Manuscript." personal email.

Pratt, M. (2000, September 27). Mother of student who died drinking at MIT sues fraternity. *Boston Globe.*

[22] Ibid.

[23] Henry, B. (2000, September 28). "Revisions of the Manuscript." personal email.

Hussain, Z. (1998). Krueger's parents leave open option for civil suit against MIT, fraternity. *MIT News. 118(42):*1&27.

Pratt, M. (2000, September 27). Mother of student who died drinking at MIT sues fraternity. *Boston Globe.*

[24] MIT accepts responsibility in Scott Krueger's 1997 death. (n.d.) *Security on Campus Update #224.* Retrieved on September 13, 2000, from http://www.globe.com/news/daily/reporters/13/mit_settlement.htm.

MIT Statement on the ABC 20/20 program on Scott Krueger. (1999). *MIT News.* Retrieved on April 13, 1999, from http://web.mit.edu/newsoffice/nr/1999/alcohol2020.html.

[25] Henry, B. (2000, September 28). "Revisions of the Manuscript." personal email.

[26] Remembering Matthew Shepard. (n.d.) *MSNBC.com.* Retrieved on February 27, 2000, from http://www.msnbc.com/news/237387.asp.

Cullen, D. (n.d.) Killer: Shepard didn't make advances. *Salon.com.* Retrieved on February 27, 2000, from http://www.salon.com/news/feature/1999/11/06/witness/index.html.

[27] Dorin, R. (1998, October 11). Victim of anti-gay attack in Wyoming clings to life. *CNN.com.* Retrieved on February 27, 2000, from http://europe.cnn.com/US/9810/11/wyoming.attack/.

Hammer, J. (1999, November 8). The 'gay panic' defense. *Newsweek.com.* Retrieved on February 27, 2000, from http://www.newsweek.com/nw-srv/printed/us/na/a59700-1999oct31.htm.

Glover, P. (2000, February 27). Media circus back in Laramie. *Wyoming Tribune-Eagle.*

[28] Attorney general says Vermont failed in hazing investigation. (2000, February 3). Retrieved on February 27, 2000, from http://www.acmi.canoe.ca/HockeyNCAA/feb3_att.html.

UVM captain sentenced in hazing scandal. (2000, August 30). *USA Today.*

Denlinger, K. (2000, February 2). Vermont hockey team's hazing earns major penalty. *The Washington Post.* Retrieved on February 27, 2000, from http://www-wp9.washingtonpost.com/wp-srv/sports/daily/feb00/02/vermont2.htm.

Rosellini, L (n.d.) Unsporting athletics. *U.S. News Online.* Retrieved on September 3, 2000, from http://www.usnews.com/usnews/edu/college/articles/sthazing.htm.

Suggs, W. (2000, August 30). Hazed hockey player will receive $80,000 from the U. of Vermont. *Chronicle of Higher Education.* Retrieved on September 3, 2000, from http://chronicle.com/daily/2000/08/200083105n.htm.

[29] Attorney general says Vermont failed in hazing investigation. (2000, February 3). Retrieved on February 27, 2000, from http://www.acmi.canoe.ca/HockeyNCAA/feb3_att.html.

[30] Denlinger, K. (2000, February 2). Vermont hockey team's hazing earns major penalty. *The Washington Post.* Retrieved on February 27, 2000, from http://www-wp9.washingtonpost.com/wp-srv/sports/daily/feb00/02/vermont2.htm.

[31] (2002, January 30). Elizabeth Shin Chronology. *The Tech (Online Edition), 121*(70). Retrieved on August 17, 2008, from http://www-tech.mit.edu/V121/N70/70shin-timeline.70n.html.

[32] Roark, M. (1993). Conceptualizing Campus Violence: Definitions, Underlying Factors, and Effects. In L. Whitaker & J. Pollard (Eds.), *Campus violence: Kinds, causes, and cures.* New York: The Haworth Press, Inc., p. 4.

[33] Nuwer, H. (n.d.) Thank you survey! May I have another. And another? Retrieved on February 29, 2000, from http://stophazing.org/nuwer/sept99column.htm.

[34] National Coalition of Mental Health Consumer/Survivor Organizations (2007, April 21). National Coalition of People with Psychiatric Histories Responds to Virginia Tech Tragedy. Retrieved on April 25, 2007, from http://www.medicalnewstoday.com/articles/68481.php.

[35] National Coalition of Mental Health Consumer/Survivor Organizations (2007, April 21). National Coalition of People with Psychiatric Histories Responds to Virginia Tech Tragedy. Retrieved on April 25, 2007, from http://www.medicalnewstoday.com/articles/68481.php.

[36] Dickerson, D. (2006). Legal issues for campus administrators, faculty, and staff. In S. A. Benton & S. L. Benton (Eds.), *College Student*

Mental Health: Effective Services and Strategies Across Campus. NASPA.

37 Pavela, G. (2008). Fearing our students won't help them. *Chronicle of Higher Education, 54*(25). Retrieved on July 20, 2008, from EBSCOhost.

38 Porchaska, J. O., DiClemente, C. C., & Norcross, J. C. (1992). In search of how people change: Applications to addictive behaviors. *American Psychologist, 47*, 1102–1114.

39 Roark, M. (1993). Conceptualizing Campus Violence: Definitions, Underlying Factors and Effects. In L. Whitaker & J. Pollard (Eds.), *Campus violence: Kinds, causes, and cures.* New York: The Haworth Press, Inc., p. 6.

40 Ibid.

41 Mountain States Employers Council, Inc. & Nicoletti-Flater Associates (1996). *Violence goes to work: An employer's guide.* Denver, Colorado: Mountain States Employers Council, Inc. and Nicoletti-Flater Associates.
Nicoletti, J., Zinna, K., & Spencer-Thomas, S. (1999). *Violence goes to school: Lessons learned from Columbine.* Denver, Colorado: Nicoletti-Flater Associates.

42 Palmer, C. (1998). Violence at home on campus. In A. Hoffman, J. Schuh, & R. Fenske (Eds.), *Violence on campus: Defining the problems, strategies for action* (pp. 111–122). Gaithersburg, Maryland: An Aspen Publication.

43 Mountain States Employers Council, Inc. & Nicoletti-Flater Associates (1996). *Violence goes to work: An employer's guide.* Denver, Colorado: Mountain States Employers Council, Inc. and Nicoletti-Flater Associates.
Nicoletti, J., Zinna, K., & Spencer-Thomas, S. (1999). *Violence goes to school: Lessons learned from Columbine.* Denver, Colorado: Nicoletti-Flater Associates.

44 Schuh, J. 1998. Campus vulnerability. In *Violence on campus.* Gaithersburg, Maryland: Aspen.

45 Hoffman, A. M. (Ed.). 1996. *Schools, violence, and society.* New York: Praeger Publishers.

46 Palmer, C. (1998). Violence at home on campus. In A. Hoffman, J. Schuh, & R. Fenske (Eds.), *Violence on campus: Defining the problems, strategies for action* (pp. 111–122). Gaithersburg, Maryland: An Aspen Publication.

47 Lederman, D. (2006, January 19). A college's delicate 'balancing act.' Retrieved on May 2, 2007 from www.insidehighered.com.

48 Parker, R., & Auerhahn, K. (1998). Alcohol, drugs, and violence. *Annual Review of Sociology, 24*, 291–311.

49 Ibid.

50 Arbor, A. (1999, December 17). Drug trends in 1999 among American teens are mixed. Join Together Online. Retrieved on December 21, 1999 from http://www.jointogether.org/sa/de faultjtml?0=261301.

51 Marijuana use among students at institutions of higher education. (2000, July 11). *Higher Education Center.* Retrieved on August 10, 2000 from http://www.edc.org/hec/pubs/prev-updates/marijuana.txt.

52 NIJ Study questions link between methamphetamine use, violence. (1999, May 17). *Alcoholism & Drug Abuse Weekly, 11*(20), 7.

53 Parker, R., & Auerhahn, K. (1998). Alcohol, drugs, and violence. *Annual Review of Sociology, 24*, 291–311.

54 Survey shows steroid use on decline. (1997, September 15). *News and Features.* Retrieved on August 4, 2000 from http://www.ncaa.org/news/19970915/active/3432n01.html.

55 Young, J. (2008). Nerf guns strike a nerve on campus. *Chronicle of Higher Education, 54*(33), p. A1–A8.

56 McKinely, J. (2000, May 21). Decision on Knight shows the fine line that colleges walk. *New York Times.*

57 For further inquiry, the following are additional sources on college community risks:
Fenske, R., & Hood, S. (1998). Profile of students coming to campus. In A. Hoffman, J. Schuh, & R. Fenske (Eds.), *Violence on campus: Defining the problems, strategies for action.* Gaithersburg, Maryland: An Aspen Publication.
Hoffman, A. M. (Ed.). (1996). *Schools, violence, and society.* New York: Praeger Publishers.
Palmer, C. (1998). Violence at home on campus. In A. Hoffman, J. Schuh, & R. Fenske (Eds.), *Violence on campus: Defining the problems, strategies for action* (pp. 111–122). Gaithersburg, Maryland: An Aspen Publication.
Parker, R., & Auerhahn, K. (1998). Alcohol, drugs, and violence. *Annual Review of Sociology, 24*, 291–311.
Reynolds, L. (1997). Fighting domestic violence in the workplace. *HR Focus, 74*(11), 8.

Roark, M. 1993. Conceptualizing campus violence: Definitions, underlying factors, and effects. In L. Whitaker & J. Pollard (Eds.), *Campus violence: Kinds, causes, and cures.* New York: The Haworth Press, Inc.

Schuh, J. (1998). Campus vulnerability. In A. Hoffman, J. Schuh, & R. Fenske (Eds.), *Violence on campus: Defining the problems, strategies for action.* Gaithersburg, Maryland:Aspen.

58 Rivinus, T. & Larimer, M. (1993). Violence, alcohol, other drugs, and the college student (p. 106). In L.C. Whitaker & J. W. Pollard (Eds.), *Campus violence: Kinds, causes, and cures.* New York: Haworth Press.

59 Ritter, K. (1999, November 16). MIT frat disbanded for alcohol violation. *Boston Globe Online.* Retrieved on November 16, 1999 from http://www .globe.com/dailyglobe2/320/metro/MIT_frat_ disbanded_for_alcohol_violation+ .shtml.

60 What MIT has done to curb alcohol abuse. (1998). *MIT News.* Retrieved on April 13, 2000 from http://web.mit.edu/newsoffice/nr/1998/ factsalc2.html.

61 DeJong, W. (2000, January 28). Language matters. *Higher Education Center.* Retrieved on February 3, 2000 from http://www.edc.org/hec/ thisweek/

62 Wechsler, H. (1998, November 20). Getting serious about eradicating binge drinking. *The Chronicle of Higher Education Online.* Retrieved January 25, 2000, from http://www.hsph .harvard.edu/cas/test/articles/chronicle.shtml.

63 Nuwer, H. (1999). *Wrongs of passage: Fraternities, sororities, hazing, and binge drinking.* Bloomington: Indiana University Press.

64 Ibid.

65 Ibid.

66 Pernanen, K. (1998). Prevention of alcohol-related violence. *Contemporary Drug Problems, 25*(fall), 477–509.

67 Wechsler, H., Deutsch, C., & Dowdall, G. Too many colleges are still in denial about alcohol abuse. *The Chronicle of Higher Education.* 14 April 1995. Retrieved on January 25, 2000 from http://www.hsph.harvard.edu/cas/test/articles/ chronicle2.shtml

68 Ibid.

69 Alcohol-related death leads to debate over disclosure policy at Duke. (2000, March 3). *The Chronicle of Higher Education.*

70 Kilbourne, J. (1991). *Calling the Shots: Advertising and Alcohol* (2nd ed.). Produced by Cambridge Documentary Films. 28 minutes. Videocassette.

71 Anonymous. Parent's, you're not done yet. (n.d.) *The Century Council.* Retrieved on August 30, 1999 from http://www.centurycouncil.org/ parents/index.cfm.

72 Rivinus, T., & Larimer, M. (1993). Violence, alcohol, other drugs, and the college student. In L. Whitaker & J. Pollard (Eds.), *Campus violence: Kinds, causes, and cures.* New York: The Haworth Press, Inc.

73 Miller, M., Hemenway, D., & Wechsler, H. (1999). Guns at college. *The Journal of American College Health, 48*(1), 7–13.

74 Rivinus, T., & Larimer, M. (1993). Violence, alcohol, other drugs, and the college student. In L. Whitaker & J. Pollard (Eds.), *Campus violence: Kinds, causes, and cures.* New York: The Haworth Press, Inc.

75 Nicholson, M., Min Qi Wang, Maney, D., Yuan, J., Mahoney, B., & Adame, D. (1998). Alcohol related violence and unwanted sexual activity on campus. *American Journal of Health Studies, 14*(1), 1–10.

76 Rivinus, T., & Larimer, M. (1993). Violence, alcohol, other drugs, and the college student (p. 94). In L. Whitaker, & J. Pollard (Eds.), *Campus violence: Kinds, causes, and cures.* New York: The Haworth Press, Inc.

77 Ibid.

78 Addressing binge drinking in emergency rooms. (2000, April 18). *Join Together Online.* Retrieved on 19 April, 2000 from http://www .jointogether.org/sa/default.jtml?O=262751.

79 Wechsler, H., Nelson, T., & Weitzman, E. (2000, January/February). From knowledge to action: How Harvard's College Alcohol Study can help your campus design a campaign against student alcohol use. *Change: The Magazine of Higher Learning.*

80 DeJong, W. (2000, January 28). Language matters. *Higher Education Center.* Retrieved on February 3, 2000 from http://www.edc.org/hec/thisweek/.

81 Anderson, D., & Milgram, G. (1996). *Promising practices: Campus alcohol strategies sourcebook.* Fairfax, VA: George Mason University.

82 Have open communication with your college-age kid. (1999, September). Cannabis news: Informing the public about cannabis. Retrieved

on April 30, 2009 from http://cannabisnews
.com/news/2/thread2818.shtml.

[83] Parent's, you're not done yet. *The Century
Council.* Retrieved on August 30, 1999 from
http://www.centurycouncil.org/parents/index
.cfm.

[84] Dimeff, L. A., Baer, J. S., Kivlahan, D. R., &
Marlatt, G. A. (1999). *Brief alcohol screening and
intervention for college students: A harm reduction
approach.* New York: The Guilford Press.

[85] Additional Information on Alcohol and Violence: A round-up of current facts and findings.
(2000). *Research Briefs, 13*(54), 2–8.

A Parents' guide to college and drinking. (1999,
September 28) *Higher Education Center: LaSalle
University.* Retrieved on November 24, 1999
form http://www.edc.org/hec/parents/lasalle
.html.

Austin, E., Pinkleton, B., & Fujioka, Y. (2000).
The role of interpretation processes and parental
discussion in the media's effect on adolescents'
use of alcohol. *Pediatrics, 105*, 343–349.

Azar, B. (1995, May). Avoiding alcohol in real-
world settings. *American Psychological Association.*
Retrieved on November 7, 1999 from http://
www.apa.org/monitor/may95/prevent.html.

Borges, G., Cherpitel, C., & Rosovsky, H. (1998).
Male drinking and violence-related injury in the
emergency room. *Addiction, 93*, 103–112.

Branch, D. (1998). Brief counseling of freshmen
may crub student drinking. *Clinical Psychiatry
News, 26*(3), 1.

Davenport, A., Dowdall, G., Grossman, S.,
Wechsler, H., & Zanakos, S. (1996). Binge
drinking, tabacco, and illicit drug use and
involvement in college athletics: A Survey of
Students at 140 American Colleges. *JACH, 44.*

Dimeff, L.A., Baer, J.S., Kivlahan, D.R., &
Marlatt, G.A. (1999). *Brief alcohol screening and
intervention for college students: A harm reduction
approach.* New York: The Guilford Press.

Feigelman, W., Gorman, B., & Lee, J. (1998).
Binge drinkers, illicit drug users and polydrug
users. *Journal of Alcohol and Drug Education, 44*(1),
47–69.

Hilde, P., Rossow, I., & Wichstrom, L. (1999).
Young, wet, and wild? *Addiction, 94*, 1017–1031.

Kilbourne, J. (1991). *Calling the shots: Advertising
and alcohol* (2nd ed.). Produced by Cambridge
Documentary Films. 28 minutes. Videocassette.

Migneault, J., Velicer, W., Prochaska, J., &
Stevenson, J. (1999). Decisional balance for
immoderate drinking in college students. *Substance Use and Misuse, 34*, 1325–1346.

Moss, H., & Tarter, R. (1993). Substance abuse,
aggression, and violence: What are the connections? *American Journal on Addictions, 2*, 149–160.

Nuwer, H. (1999). *Wrongs of passage: Fraternities,
sororities, hazing, and binge drinking.* Bloomington: Indiana University Press.

O'Hare, T., & Sherrer, M. (1999). Validating
the alcohol use disorder identification test with
college first-offenders. *Journal of Substance Abuse
Treatment, 17*, 113–119.

Parker, R., & Auerhahn, K. (1998). Alcohol,
drugs, and violence. *Annual Review of Sociology,
24*, 291–311.

Parker, R., & Cartmill, R. (1998). Alcohol and
homicide in the United States 1934–1995 – Or
one reason why U.S. rates of violence may be
going down. *Journal of Criminal Law and Crimi-
nology, 88*, 1369–1398.

Pernanen, K. (1998). Prevention of alcohol-related violence. *Contemporary Drug Problems, 25*
(fall), 477–509.

Rickgarn, R. (1989). Violence in residence
halls: Campus domestic violence. In J. Sherill
& D. Siegel's (Eds.). *Responding to violence on
campus.* San Francisco: Jossey-Bass Inc.

Rossow, I., Pape, H., & Wichstrom, L. (1999).
Young, wet and wild? *Addiction, 94*(7), 1017–1031.

Veenhuis, P. (1997). Recent developments in alcoholism, vol. 13: alcohol and violence – epidemiology, neurobiology, psychology, family
issues. *American Journal of Psychiatry, 155*,
1453–1454.

Warner, J. (1997). Shifting categories of the social
harms associated with alcohol: Examples from
late medieval and early modern England. *American Journal of Public Health, 87*(11), 1788–1797.

Wechsler, H., Davenport, A., Dowdall, G.,
Grossman, S., & Zanakos, S. (1996). Binge
drinking, tobacco, and illicit drug use and involvement in college athletics. *JACH, 44*, 1–6.

Wechsler, H., Dowdall, G., Maenner, G.,
Gledhill-Hoyt, J., & Lee, H. (1998). Changes in
binge drinking and related problems among
American college students between 1993 and
1997. *Journal of American College Health, 47*,
57–68.

[86] Mountain States Employers Council, Inc. and Nicoletti-Flater Associates. (1996). *Violence Goes to Work: An Employer's Guide.* Denver, Colorado: Mountain States Employers Council, Inc. and Nicoletti-Flater Associates.

[87] Nicoletti, J., Zinna, K., & Spencer-Thomas, S. (1999). *Violence goes to school: Lessons learned from Columbine.* Lakewood, Colorado: Nicoletti-Flater.

[88] Bernstein, E. (2008, May 20). Currents: Schools struggle with dark writings; in the wake of Virginia Tech killings, colleges weigh student's safety vs... *The Wall Street Journal,* A16. Retrieved on May 1, 2009 from http://elibrary .bigchalk.com/libweb/curriculum/do/ documen?set=search&groupid=1&requestid= lib_standard&resultid=1&edition=&ts=09BD6 EA4F7B5BDF604B8BB171A557021_1241304 148799&start=1&urn=urn%3Abigchalk%3 AUS%3BBCLib%3Bdocument%3B152757633.

[89] Redden, E. (2007, September 5). When student writing could be a red flag. Retrieved on September 5, 2007 from http://www.Insidehigh-ered.com.

[90] Cohen, L., & Swift, S. (n.d.) Beyond brochures: Preventing alcohol-related and injuries. *Prevention Institute.* Retrieved on March 6, 2009, from http://www.preventioninstitute.org/alcohol.html.

[91] Zimmerman, R. (2004, February). Campus and community coalitions in AOD prevention. *The Higher Education Center for Alcohol and Other Drug Abuse and Violence Prevention.* Retrieved on March 6, 2009 from http://www.higheredcenter .org/files/product/campus-comm-coal.pdf.

[92] Effective coalitions are flexible, deferential, structured. (2000, January 10). *Join Together Online.* Retrieved on January 11, 2000, from http://www.jointogether.org/sa/default.jtml?0= 261553.

[93] DeJong, W. (2008). Presidential leadership: The catalyst for effective prevention. *Catalyst, 10*(2), p. 1.

[94] DeJong (2008), p. 2.

[95] Denzenhall, E., & Weber, J. (2008). *Damage control. Why everything you know about crisis management is wrong.* New York: Penguin Group, p. 42.

[96] Sherill, J. (1989). Models of response to campus violence. In Sherrill, J. M., & Siegel, D. G. (Eds.), *Responding to violence on campus.* San Francisco: Jossey-Bass, Inc.

[97] Mountain States Employers Council, Inc. and Nicoletti-Flater Associates. (1996). *Violence goes to work: An employer's guide.* Denver, Colorado: Mountain States Employers Council, Inc. and Nicoletti-Flater Associates.

[98] Seidmann, N. (1997). Professors hope teaching violence might help prevent it. Retrieved on March 6, 2009 from http://www.emory.edu/ EMORY_REPORT/erarchive/1997/April/ erapril.14/4_14_97Bellesiles.html.

[99] Katz, J. (1995). Reconstructing masculinity in the locker room. *Harvard Educational Review, 65*(2), 163–174.

[100] Hellstrom, D. (1999, September). Creating a home, making a difference. *The Peer Educator.*

[101] Ibid.

[102] Schuh, J. (1998). Campus vulnerability. In R. H. Fenske, J. H. Schuh, & A. H. (Eds.), *Violence on campus* (pp. 17–28). Gaithersburg, Maryland: Aspen Publications.

[103] Hoover, E. (2008, April 10). Colleges grapple with the "behavioral broken arm." *The Chronicle of Higher Education, 54*(32), p. A10.

[104] Cohen, L., & Swift, S. (n.d.) Beyond brochures: Preventing alcohol-related and injuries. *Prevention Institute.* Retrieved on January 12, 2000 from http://www.preventioninstitute.org/alcohol.html.

[105] Bronner, E. (1999, March 3). In a revolution of rules, campuses go full circle. *The New York Times on the Web.* Retrieved on October 25, 1999 from http://www.nytimes.com/library/ national/030399collegesupervision.html.

[106] Mountain States Employers Council, Inc. and Nicoletti-Flater Associates. (1996). *Violence goes to work: An employer's guide.* Denver, Colorado: Mountain States Employers Council, Inc. and Nicoletti-Flater Associates.

[107] Nicoletti, J., & Spencer-Thomas, S. (1999). *Violence goes to school: Lessons learned from Columbine.* Lakewood, Colorado: Nicoletti-Flater Associates.

[108] Interpersonal violence and alcohol and other drug use. (1999, June). *The Higher Education Center for Alcohol and Drug Prevention.* Retrieved on April 2, 2000 from http://www.edc.org/hec/ pubs/factsheets/fact_sheet4.html.

[109] Campus crime legislation in the 106th congress (1999–2000). *Campus Crime Legislation.* Retrieved on April 17, 2000 from http://www.campus-safety.org/publicpolicy/congress/106/index .html.

110 Gose, B. (1998). Some colleges extend their codes of conduct to off-campus behavior. *Chronicle of Higher Education, 45*(7), A51–A52.

111 Mountain States Employers Council, Inc. and Nicoletti-Flater Associates. (1996). *Violence goes to work: An employer's guide.* Denver, Colorado: Mountain States Employers Council, Inc. and Nicoletti-Flater Associates.

112 Hoffman, A., Schuh, J., & Fenske, R. (1998). Violent crime in the college and university workplace. In R. H. Fenske, J. H. Schuh, J. H., & A. H. Hoffman, (Eds.), *Violence on campus.*
Hunnicutt, K., and Kushibab, P. (1998). The legal response to violence on campus. In R. H. Fenske, J. H. Schuh, & A. H. Hoffman, (Eds.), *Violence on campus.*

113 Mountain States Employers Council, Inc. and Nicoletti-Flater Associates. (1996). *Violence goes to work: An employer's guide.* Denver, Colorado: Mountain States Employers Council, Inc. and Nicoletti-Flater Associates.

114 NASPA (n.d.) In Search of Safer Communities: Emerging Practices for Student Affairs in Addressing Campus Violence.

115 Higher Education Opportunity Act – 2008 (2009). ED.Gov: U. S. Department of Education. Retrieved on May 1, 2009 from http://www.ed.gov/policy/highered/leg/hea08/index.html.

116 Additional information on building policies:
Hansen, M. (1993). An ex-con goes to law school. *ABA Journal, 79*, 19.
Hoffman, A., Schuh, J., & Fenske, R. (1998). Violent crime in the college and university workplace. In *Violence on Campus.* Gaithersburg, Maryland: Aspen Publications.
Hunnicutt, K., and Kushibab, P. (1998). The legal response to violence on campus. In A. Hoffman, J. Schuh, and R. Fenske (Eds.), *Violence on campus: Defining the problems, strategies for action.* Gaithersburg, Maryland: Aspen Publishers.
Mountain States Employers Council, Inc. & Nicoletti-Flater Associates (1996). *Violence goes to work: An employer's guide.* Denver, Colorado: Mountain States Employers Council, Inc. and Nicoletti-Flater Associates.
Nicoletti, J., Zinna, K., & Spencer-Thomas, S. (1999). *Violence goes to school: Lessons learned from Columbine.* Denver, Colorado: Nicoletti-Flater Associates.

Nicoletti, J., Spencer-Thomas, S., & Porter, K. (1998). *Survival-oriented kids in a violent world.* Lakewood, Colorado: Nicoletti-Flater Associates.
Roark, M. (1993). Conceptualizing campus violence: Definitions, underlying factors and effects. In L. Whitaker & J. Pollard (Eds.), *Campus violence: Kinds, causes, and cures.* New York: The Haworth Press, Inc.
Siegel, D. (1994). Summary. In *Campuses respond to violent tragedy.* American Council on Education. Phoenix, Arizona: Oryx Press.

117 Nicoletti, J., Spencer-Thomas, S., & Porter, K. (1998). *Survival-oriented kids in a violent world.* Lakewood, Colorado: Nicoletti-Flater Associates.

118 Nicoletti, J., Zinna, K., & Spencer-Thomas, S. (1999). *Violence goes to school: Lessons learned from Columbine.* Lakewood, Colorado: Nicoletti-Flater Associates.

119 Choi, C. (2007, December 12). Why time seems to slow down in emergencies. Retrieved on December 12, 2007 from www.LiveScience.com.

120 Kates, D. B., & Mauser, G. (Spring 2007). Would banning firearms reduce murder and suicide? *Harvard Journal of Law and Public Policy, 30*(2), 649–694.

121 Ibid.

122 Ibid.

123 Ibid.

124 For recommendations on confronting people carrying weapons see the following article: Bender, W. & McGlaughlin, P. (1997). Weapons violence in schools: Strategies for teachers confronting violence and hostage situations. *Intevention in School and Clinic 32*(4), 211–216.

125 Security on Campus Inc. Retrieved on April 30, 2009 from http://securityoncampus.org/.

126 Nicoletti, J., Zinna, K., & Spencer-Thomas, S. (1999). *Violence goes to school: Lessons learned from Columbine.* Lakewood, Colorado: Nicoletti-Flater Associates

127 Ibid.

128 Ibid.

129 Ibid.

130 Ibid.

131 Ibid.

132 Ibid.

133 Ibid.

134 Ibid.

135 Ibid.

136 Ibid.

137 Ibid.

138 Additional information relating to environmental protection strategies:

Greengard, S. (1999). Zero tolerance: Making it work. *Workforce, 78*(5), 28–34.

Hansen, M. (1993). An ex-con goes to law school. *ABA Journal, 79*, 19.

Hoffman, A., Schuh, J., & Fenske, R. (1998). Violent crime in the college and university workplace. In *Violence on campus: Defining the problems, strategies for action.* Gaithersburg, Maryland: Aspen Publishers.

Hunnicutt, K., & Kushibab, P. (1998). The legal response to violence on campus. In A. Hoffman, J. Schuh, and R. Fenske (Eds.), *Violence on campus: Defining the problems, strategies for action.* Gaithersburg, Maryland: Aspen Publishers.

Mountain States Employers Council, Inc. & Nicoletti-Flater Associates. (1996). *Violence goes to work: An employer's guide.* Denver, Colorado: Mountain States Employers Council, Inc. and Nicoletti-Flater Associates.

Nicoletti, J., Spencer-Thomas, S., & Porter, K. (1998). *Survival-oriented kids in a violent world.* Lakewood, Colorado: Nicoletti-Flater Associates.

Nicoletti, J., Zinna, K., & Spencer-Thomas, S. (1999). *Violence goes to school: Lessons learned from Columbine.* Lakewood, Colorado: Nicoletti-Flater Associates.

Roark, M. (1993). Conceptualizing campus violence: Definitions, underlying factors and effects. In L. Whitaker & J. Pollard (Eds.), *Campus violence: Kinds, causes, and cures* (Chap. 1). New York: The Haworth Press, Inc.

Siegel, D. (1994). Summary. In *Campuses respond to violent tragedy* (Chap. 11). American Council on Education: Oryx Press.

139 Vice President, Dean, and Professor of Law, Stetson University College of Law.

140 David G. Owen. *The Five Elements of Negligence,* 35 Hofstra L. Rev. 1671 (2007).

141 *Id.* at 1676.

142 *Id.* at 1684.

143 *Id.* (citing *Crankshaw v. Piedmont Driving Club,* 156 S.E.2d 208, 209–10 (Ga. App. 1976)).

144 *Id.* at 1684-85.

145 *Id.* at 1676.

146 449 N.E.2d 331 (Mass. 1983).

147 *Id.* at 337.

148 *Id.* at 335.

149 861 P.2d 768 (Kan. 1993).

150 *Id.* at 771.

151 *Id.*

152 *Id.* at 772.

153 *Id.*

154 *Id.* at 780.

155 *Id.*

156 1999 WL 47153 (N.D.N.Y. Jan. 26, 1999).

157 *Id.* at *7.

158 652 S.E.2d 624 (Ga. App. 2007).

159 *Id.* at 626–627.

160 Memorandum and Order, AD 892-2003 (Ct. Com. Pleas, Crawford County, Pa. Dec. 22, 2005).

161 *Id.*

162 *E.g. Knoll v. Board of Regents of the University of Nebraska,* 601 N.W.2d 757 (Neb. 1999).

163 73 Fed. Reg. 15573, 15589 (Mar. 24, 2008).

164 Stone, G. (1993). Psychological challenges and responses to a campus tragedy: The Iowa experience. In L, Whitaker, & J. Pollard, (Eds.), *Campus violence: Kinds, causes, and cures.* New York: The Haworth Press, Inc.

165 Ibid.

166 Ibid.

167 Tunnediffe, M. (1997). Immediate trauma counseling: A roadblock on the path to healing. *Emergency Support Network.* Retrieved on February 2, 2008 from http://www.emergency support.com.au/art18.html.

168 Ibid.

169 Violence on campus: Prevention and recovery. (2000, March 21). *NASPA Task Force on Violence.*

170 Ibid.

171 Hurst, J. (1999). The Matthew Shepard tragedy – Crisis and beyond. *About Campus. 4,* 3.

172 Anonymous. University of Massachusetts rallies against campus attack. *CNN.com* 24 November 1999. Retrieved on February 27, 2000 from http://www.cnn.com/US/9911/24/amherst .rapes.index.html.

173 Janoff-Bulman, R. (1992). *Shattered assumptions: Towards a new psychology of trauma.* New York: The Free Press.

174 Sokolow, B. (n.d.) An op-ed on the media response to the Virginia Tech Tragedy. Retrieved on July 30, 2007, from http://www.ncherm .org/article-vtech.html.

175 This model was developed in consultation with Rebecca Flintoft, Director of Residence Life at the Colorado School of Mines.

176 Koss, M. P. (1988). Hidden rape: Sexual aggression and victimization in a national sample of students in higher education. In A. W. Burgess (Ed.), *Rape and sexual assault*, 3–25. New York: Garland.

177 Kilpatrick, D. G., Resnick, H. S., Ruggiero, K. J., Conocsenti, L. M., & McCauley, J. (2007). *Drug-facilitated, incapacitated, and forcible rape: A national study* (NCJ 219181). Retrieved November 1, 2007, from http://www.ncjrs.gov/pdffiles1/nij/grants/219181.pdf.

178 Kassing, L. R., Beesley, D., & Frey, L. L. (2005). Gender role conflict, homophobia, age and education as predictors of male rape myth acceptance. *Journal of Mental Health Counseling, 27,* 311–328.

179 Abbey, A., Zawacki, T., Buck, P., Clinton, A. M., & McAuslan, P. (2001). Alcohol and sexual assault. *Alcohol Research & Health, 25,* 43–51.

180 Was I raped? (2008). Retrieved January 15, 2008, from http://www.rainn.org/types-of-assault/was-i-raped.html.

181 Waldorf College sexual assault policy. (2008). Retrieved January 15, 2008 from http://www.waldorf.edu/services/studentlife/assault.htm.

182 Kelly, L., Burton, S., & Regan, L. (1996). Beyond victim or survivor: Sexual violence, identity, and feminist theory and practice. In L. Adkins, & V. Merchant, (Eds.), *Sexualizing the social: Power and the organization of sexuality,* 77–101. London: Macmillan.

183 Young, S. L., & Maguire, K. C. (2003). Talking about sexual violence. *Women & Language, 26,* 40–52.

184 Ibid.

185 Ibid.

186 Kilpatrick, D. G., Resnick, H. S., Ruggiero, K. J., Conocsenti, L. M., & McCauley, J. (2007). *Drug-facilitated, incapacitated, and forcible rape: A national study* (NCJ 219181). Retrieved November 1, 2007, from http://www.ncjrs.gov/pdffiles1/nij/grants/219181.pdf.

187 Kilpatrick, D. G., Resnick, H. S., Ruggiero, K. J., Conocsenti, L. M., & McCauley, J. (2007). *Drug-facilitated, incapacitated, and forcible rape: A national study* (NCJ 219181). Retrieved November 1, 2007, from http://www.ncjrs.gov/pdffiles1/nij/grants/219181.pdf.

188 Krebs, C. P., Lindquist, C. H., Warner, T. D., Fisher, B. S., Martin, S. L. (2007). *The campus sexual assault (CSA) study* (NCJ 221153). Retrieved January 23, 2008, from http://www.ncjrs.gov/pdffiles1/nij/grants/221153.pdf.

189 Tjaden, P., & Thoennes, N. (2000). *Full report of the prevalence, incidence, and consequences of violence against women* (NCJ 183781). Retrieved February 3, 2008, from http://www.ncjrs.gov/pdffiles1/nij/183781.pdf.

190 Krebs, C. P., Lindquist, C. H., Warner, T. D., Fisher, B. S., & Martin, S. L. (2007). *The campus sexual assault (CSA) study* (NCJ 221153). Retrieved January 23, 2008, from http://www.ncjrs.gov/pdffiles1/nij/grants/221153.pdf.

191 Ibid.

192 Kassing, L. R., Beesley, D., & Frey, L. L. (2005). Gender role conflict, homophobia, age and education as predictors of male rape myth acceptance. *Journal of Mental Health Counseling, 27,* 311–328.

193 Crowell, N. A., & Burgess, A. W. (1996). *Understanding violence against women.* Washington, D.C.: National Academy Press.

194 Kilpatrick, D. G., Resnick, H. S., Ruggiero, K. J., Conocsenti, L. M., & McCauley, J. (2007). *Drug-facilitated, incapacitated, and forcible rape: A national study* (NCJ 219181). Retrieved November 1, 2007, from http://www.ncjrs.gov/pdffiles1/nij/grants/219181.pdf.

195 Krebs, C. P., Lindquist, C. H., Warner, T. D., Fisher, B. S., & Martin, S. L. (2007). *The campus sexual assault (CSA) study* (NCJ 221153). Retrieved January 23, 2008, from http://www.ncjrs.gov/pdffiles1/nij/grants/221153.pdf.

196 Kilpatrick, D. G., Resnick, H. S., Ruggiero, K. J., Conocsenti, L. M., & McCauley, J. (2007). *Drug-facilitated, incapacitated, and forcible rape: A national study* (NCJ 219181). Retrieved November 1, 2007, from http://www.ncjrs.gov/pdffiles1/nij/grants/219181.pdf.

197 Koss, M. P., Gidycz, C. A., & Widniewski, N. (1987). The scope of rape: Incidence and prevalence of sexual aggression and victimization in a national sample of higher education students. *Journal of Consulting and Clinical Psychology, 55,* 64–170.

198 Carr, J. L., & VanDuesen, K. M. (2004). Risk factors for male sexual aggression on college campuses. *Journal of Family Violence, 19,* 279–289.

199 Kilpatrick, D. G., Resnick, H. S., Ruggiero, K. J., Conocsenti, L. M., & McCauley, J. (2007). *Drug-facilitated, incapacitated, and forcible rape: A national study* (NCJ 219181). Retrieved November 1, 2007, from http://www.ncjrs.gov/pdf files1/nij/grants/219181.pdf.

200 Krebs, C. P., Lindquist, C. H., Warner, T. D., Fisher, B. S., Martin, S. L. (2007). *The campus sexual assault (CSA) study* (NCJ 221153). Retrieved January 23, 2008, from http://www .ncjrs.gov/pdffiles1/nij/grants/221153.pdf.

201 Koss, M. P. (1988). Hidden rape: Sexual aggression and victimization in a national sample of students in higher education. In Burgess, A.W., ed. *Rape and sexual assault*, 3–25. New York: Garland.

202 Ullman, S. E., Karabatsos, G., Koss, M. P. (1999). Alcohol and sexual assault in a national sample of college women. *Journal of Interpersonal Violence, 14,* 603.

203 Krebs, C. P., Lindquist, C. H., Warner, T. D., Fisher, B. S., & Martin, S. L. (2007). *The campus sexual assault (CSA) study* (NCJ 221153). Retrieved January 23, 2008, from http://www .ncjrs.gov/pdffiles1/nij/grants/221153.pdf.

204 Young, I. M. (2000). Five faces of oppression. In M. Adams, W. J. Blumenfeld, R. Casteñeda, H. W. Hackman, M. L. Peters, & X. Zúñiga, (Eds.), *Readings for diversity and social justice,* 35–49. New York: Routledge.

205 Kilmartin, C., & Allison, J. (2007). *Men's violence against women: Theory, research, and activism.* Mahwah, NJ: Lawrence Erlbaum Associates.

206 James, R. K. (2008). *Crisis intervention strategies.* Belmont, CA: Thomson Brooks/Cole.

207 Sokolow, B. (2000). Sexual violence: The legal front. In J. Gold, & S. Villari, (Eds.), *Just sex: Students rewrite the rules of sex, violence, activism, and equality,* 211–222. New York: Rowman & Littlefield Publishers, Inc.

208 Sherry, A. (2007, December 6). CU settles case stemming from recruit scandal. *Denver Post.* Retrieved January 23, 2008 from http://www.denver post.com/search/ci_7645722.

209 Sokolow, B. (2000). Sexual violence: The legal front. In J. Gold, & S. Villari, (Eds.), *Just sex: Students rewrite the rules of sex, violence, activism, and equality,* 211–222. New York: Rowman & Littlefield Publishers, Inc.

210 Ibid.

211 Krebs, C. P., Lindquist, C. H., Warner, T. D., Fisher, B. S., & Martin, S. L. (2007). *The campus sexual assault (CSA) study* (NCJ 221153). Retrieved January 23, 2008, from http://www .ncjrs.gov/pdffiles1/nij/grants/221153.pdf.

212 Kalof, L. (2000). Ethnic differences in female sexual victimization. *Sexuality & Culture, 4,* 75–97.

213 Krebs, C. P., Lindquist, C. H., Warner, T. D., Fisher, B. S., & Martin, S. L. (2007). *The campus sexual assault (CSA) study* (NCJ 221153). Retrieved January 23, 2008, from http://www .ncjrs.gov/pdffiles1/nij/grants/221153.pdf.

214 Koss, M. P., Gidycz, C. A., & Widniewski, N. (1987). The scope of rape: Incidence and prevalence of sexual aggression and victimization in a national sample of higher education students. *Journal of Consulting and Clinical Psychology, 55,* 64–170.

215 Tewksbury, R. (2007). Effects of sexual assaults on men: Physical, mental and sexual consequences. *International Journal of Men's Health, 6,* 22–35.

216 Krebs, C. P., Lindquist, C. H., Warner, T. D., Fisher, B. S., & Martin, S. L. (2007). *The campus sexual assault (CSA) study* (NCJ 221153). Retrieved January 23, 2008, from http://www .ncjrs.gov/pdffiles1/nij/grants/221153.pdf.

217 Struckman-Johnson, C. (1988). Forced sex on dates: It happens to men too. *Journal of Sex Research, 24,* 234–241.

218 Davies, M. (2002). Male sexual assault victims: A selective review of the literature and implications for support services. *Aggression and Violent Behavior, 7,* 203–214.

219 Kassing, L. R., Beesley, D., & Frey, L. L. (2005). Gender role conflict, homophobia, age and education as predictors of male rape myth acceptance. *Journal of Mental Health Counseling, 27,* 311–328.

220 Tewksbury, R. (2007). Effects of sexual assaults on men: Physical, mental and sexual consequences. *International Journal of Men's Health, 6,* 22–35.

221 Kassing, L. R., Beesley, D., & Frey, L. L. (2005). Gender role conflict, homophobia, age and education as predictors of male rape myth acceptance. *Journal of Mental Health Counseling, 27,* 311–328.

222 Fisher, B. S., Daigle, L. E., Cullen, F. T., & Turner, M. G. (2003). Acknowledging sexual

victimization as rape: Results from a national-level study. *Justice Quarterly, 20,* 535–574.

223 Golding, J. M., Siegel, J. M., Sorenson, M. A., & Stein, J. A. (1989). Social support sources following sexual assault. *Journal of Community Psychology, 17,* 92–107.

224 Krebs, C. P., Lindquist, C. H., Warner, T. D., Fisher, B. S., & Martin, S. L. (2007). *The campus sexual assault (CSA) study* (NCJ 221153). Retrieved January 23, 2008, from http://www .ncjrs.gov/pdffiles1/nij/grants/221153.pdf.

225 Fisher, B. S., Cullen, F. T., & Turner, M. G. (2000). *The sexual victimization of college women* (NCJ 182369). Retrieved February 3, 2008, from http://www.ncjrs.gov/txtfiles1/nij/182369 .txt.

226 Kilpatrick, D. G., Resnick, H. S., Ruggiero, K. J., Conocsenti, L. M., & McCauley, J. (2007). *Drug-facilitated, incapacitated, and forcible rape: A national study* (NCJ 219181). Retrieved November 1, 2007, from http://www.ncjrs.gov/pdf files1/nij/grants/219181.pdf.

227 Ibid.

228 Thompson, M., Sitterle, D., Clay, G., & Kingree, J. (2007). Reasons for not reporting victimizations to the police: Do they vary for physical and sexual incidents? *Journal of American College Health, 55,* 277–282.

229 Starynski, L. L., Ullman, S. E., Townsend, S. M., Long, L. M., & Long, S. M. (2007). What factors predict women's disclosure of sexual assault to mental health professionals? *Journal of Community Psychology, 35,* 619–638.

230 Cullen, F. T., Fisher, B. S., & Karjane, H. M. (2001). *Campus sexual assault: How America's institutions of higher education respond* (NCJ 196676). Retrieved January 23, 2008, from http://www.ncjrs.gov/pdffiles1/nij/grants/196676 .pdf.

231 Ibid.

232 Holmes, M. M., Resnick, H. S., & Kilpatrick, D. G. (1996). Rape-related pregnancy: Estimates and descriptive characteristics from a national sample of women. *American Journal of Obstetric and Gynecology, 179,* 336–342.

233 Fisher, B. S., Cullen, F. T., & Turner, M. G. (2000). *The sexual victimization of college women* (NCJ 182369). Retrieved February 3, 2008, from http://www.ncjrs.gov/txtfiles1/nij/182369 .txt.

234 Krebs, C. P., Lindquist, C. H., Warner, T. D., Fisher, B. S., & Martin, S. L. (2007). *The campus sexual assault (CSA) study* (NCJ 221153). Retrieved January 23, 2008, from http://www .ncjrs.gov/pdffiles1/nij/grants/221153.pdf.

235 Kilpatrick, D., Edmunds, C. N., & Seymour, A. K. (1992). *Rape in America: A report to the nation.* Arlington, VA: National Victim Center and Medical University of South Carolina.

236 Kilpatrick, D. G., Resnick, H. S., Ruggiero, K. J., Conocsenti, L. M., & McCauley, J. (2007). *Drug-facilitated, incapacitated, and forcible rape: A national study* (NCJ 219181). Retrieved November 1, 2007, from http://www.ncjrs.gov/pdf files1/nij/grants/219181.pdf.

237 Ibid.

238 Tewksbury, R. (2007). Effects of sexual assaults on men: Physical, mental and sexual consequences. *International Journal of Men's Health, 6,* 22–35.

239 Elliott, D. M., Mok, D. S., & Briere, J. (2004). Adult sexual assault: Prevalence, symptomatology, and sex differences in the general population. *Journal of Traumatic Stress, 17,* 203–211.

240 Burnam, M. A., Stein, J. A., Golding, J. M., Siegel, J. M., Sorenson, S. B., Forsythe, A.B., et al. (1988). Sexual assault and mental disorders in a community population. *Journal of Consulting and Clinical Psychology, 56,* 843–850.

241 Walker, J., Archer, J., & Davies, M. (2005). Effects of rape on men: A descriptive analysis. *Archives of Sexual Behavior, 34,* 69–80.

242 Sokolow, B. (2000). Sexual violence: The legal front. In J. Gold, & S. Villari, (Eds.), *Just sex: Students rewrite the rules of sex, violence, activism, and equality,* 211–222. New York: Rowman & Littlefield Publishers, Inc.

243 U.S. Department of Justice, National Institute of Justice. (2005). *Sexual assault on campus: What colleges and universities are doing about it* (NCJ 205521). Retrieved January 20, 2008, from http://www.ncjrs.gov/pdffiles1/nij/205521.pdf.

244 Littel, K. (2001). *Sexual assault nurse examiner (SANE) programs: Improving the community response to sexual assault victims* (NCJ 186366). U.S. Department of Justice, Office for Victims of Crime. Retrieved January 23, 2008, from http://www.ojp.usdoj.gov/ovc/publications/ bulletins/sane_4_2001/186366.pdf.

245 Cullen, F. T., Fisher, B. S., & Karjane, H. M. (2001). *Campus sexual assault: How America's institutions of*

higher education respond (NCJ 196676). Retrieved January 23, 2008, from http://www.ncjrs.gov/pdffiles1/nij/grants/196676.pdf.

246 Ibid.

247 Kilpatrick, D. G., Resnick, H. S., Ruggiero, K. J., Conocsenti, L. M., & McCauley, J. (2007). *Drug-facilitated, incapacitated, and forcible rape: A national study* (NCJ 219181). Retrieved November 1, 2007, from http://www.ncjrs.gov/pdffiles1/nij/grants/219181.pdf.

248 Ibid.

249 Cullen, F. T., Fisher, B. S., & Karjane, H. M. (2001). *Campus sexual assault: How America's institutions of higher education respond* (NCJ 196676). Retrieved January 23, 2008, from http://www.ncjrs.gov/pdffiles1/nij/grants/196676.pdf.

250 White Kress, V. E., Trippany, R. L., & Nolan, J. M. (2003). Responding to sexual assault victims: considerations for college counselors. *Journal of College Counseling, 6,* 124–133.

251 Ibid.

252 Ibid.

253 Russell, P. L., & Davis, C. (2007). Twenty-five years of empirical research on treatment following sexual assault. *Best Practice in Mental Health: An International Journal, 3,* 21–37.

254 James, R. K. (2008). *Crisis intervention strategies.* Belmont, CA: Thomson Brooks/Cole.

255 Fraser, C., & Fribley, C. (2005). Assessing organizational readiness to provide online advocacy and services. *The Resource,* 4–7.

256 Krebs, C. P., Lindquist, C. H., Warner, T. D., Fisher, B. S., & Martin, S. L. (2007). *The campus sexual assault (CSA) study* (NCJ 221153). Retrieved January 23, 2008, from http://www.ncjrs.gov/pdffiles1/nij/grants/221153.pdf.

257 Berkowitz, A. D. (2002). Working with men to prevent sexual assault. *The Resource,* 2–12.

258 Bell, L. A. (1997). Theoretical foundations for social justice education. In M. Adams, L. A. Bell, & P. Griffin, (Eds.), *Teaching for diversity and social justice: A sourcebook,* 1–15. New York: Routledge.

259 Brecklin, L. R., & Ullman, S. E. (2004). Correlates of postassault self-defense/assertiveness training participation for sexual assault survivors. *Psychology of Women Quarterly,* 28, 147–158.

260 Berkowitz, A. D. (1994). *Men and rape: Theory, research, and prevention programs in higher education.* San Francisco: Jossey Bass.

261 Berkowitz, A. D. (2002). Working with men to prevent sexual assault. *The Resource,* 2–12.

262 Barone, R. P., Wolgemuth, J. R., & Linder, C. (2007). Preventing sexual assault through engaging college men. *Journal of College Student Development, 48,* 585–594.

263 Rothman, E., & Silverman, J. (2007). The effect of a college sexual assault prevention program on first-year students' victimization rates. *Journal of American College Health, 55,* 283–290.

264 Berkowitz, A. D. (1994). *Men and rape: Theory, research, and prevention programs in higher education.* San Francisco: Jossey Bass.

265 From "Don't Erase Your Future" Social Marketing Campaign developed by Better World Advertising, www.donteraseyourfuture.org.

266 American Foundation for Suicide Prevention (n.d.) Facts and figures: National Statistics. Retrieved on September 30, 2007 from www.afsp.org.

267 American Foundation for Suicide Prevention (n.d.) Facts and figures: International statistics. Retrieved on September 30, 2007 from www.afsp.org.

268 U.S. Preventive Services Task Force. (2004, May). Screening for suicide risk: Recommendation and rationale. Agency for Healthcare Research and Quality, Rockville, MD. Retrieved on September 30, 2007 from http://www.ahrq.gov/clinic/3rduspstf/suicide/suiciderr.htm.

269 American Foundation for Suicide Prevention (n.d.) Facts and figures by gender. Retrieved on September 30, 2007 from www.afsp.org.

270 U.S. Preventive Services Task Force

271 Ibid.

272 Ibid.

273 Suicide Prevention Resource Center (n.d.) Fact sheet. Retrieved on September 30, 2007 from www.sprc.org.

274 CDC's WISQARS website "Fatal Injury Reports" and "Leading Cause of Deaths Reports": http://www.cdc.gov/ncipc/wisqars/. Retrieved September 30, 2007.

275 Ibid.

276 Ibid.

277 Kessler, R., Chiu, W., Demler, P., & Walters, E. (2005). Prevalence, severity, and comorbidity of 12-Month *DSM-IV* disorders in the national comorbidity survey replication. *Archives of General Psychiatry, 62,* 617–627.

[278] American Foundation for Suicide Prevention (n.d.) Facts and Figures: National statistics. Retrieved on September 30, 2007 from www.afsp.org.

[279] Center for Disease Control. 2005, United States Suicide Injury Deaths. Retrieved on March 2, 2008 from http://webappa.cdc.gov/cgi-bin/broker.exe.

[280] Shneidman, E. (1993). *Suicide as psychache: A clinical approach to self-destructive behavior.* Northvale, NJ: Aronson.

[281] Joiner, T. (2005). *Why people die by suicide.* Cambridge, MA: Harvard University Press.

[282] Ibid.

[283] Suicide Prevention Resources Center, retrieved from www.SPRC.org on March 2, 2008.

[284] Ibid

[285] Suicide Prevention Resource Center.

[286] American Association of Suicidology. About Suicide. Retrieved on March 2, 2008 from http://www.suicidology.org/displaycommon.cfm?an=2.

[287] The Jed Foundation. (2006). *Framework for developing institutional protocols for the acutely distressed or suicidal college student.* New York: The Jed Foundation.

[288] Lamberg, L. (2006). Experts work to prevent college suicides. *American Medical Association, 296*(5), 502–504.

[289] Suicide Prevention Resource Center. (2004). *Promoting mental health and preventing suicide in college and university settings.* Newton, MA: Education Development Center, Inc., p. 6.

[290] Ibid.

[291] Heron, M. P., & Smith, B. L. (2007). Deaths: Leading causes for 2003. *National Vital Statistics Reports, 55*(10), 1–93. Retrieved June 20, 2007 from http://www.cdc.gov/nchs/data/nvsr/nvsr55/nvsr55_10.pdf.

[292] American Association of Suicidology. (2004). *Youth suicide fact sheet.* Retrieved October 20, 2006 from http://www.jedfoundation.com/libraryNews_alphalist.php.

[293] Kochanek. K. D., Murphy, S. L., Anderson, R. N., Scott, C. Deaths: Final data for 2002. National vital statistics reports; vol 53 no 5. Hyattsville, Maryland: National Center for Health Statistics. 2004.

[294] Haas, A. P., Hendin, H., & Mann, J. J. (2003). Suicide in college students. *American Behavioral Scientist, 46*(9), 1224–1240.

[295] Silverman, M. M., Meyer, P. M., Sloane, F., Raffel, M., & Pratt, D. M. (1997). The big ten student suicide study: A 10-year study of suicides on Midwestern university campuses. *Suicide and Life-Threatening Behavior, 27*(3), 285–303.

[296] Ibid., p. 299

[297] Brener, N. D., Hassan, S. S., & Barrios, L. C. (1991). Suicidal ideation among college students in the United States. *Journal of Consulting and Clinical Psychology, 67*(6), 1004–1008.

Division of Adolescent and School Health, National Center for Chronic Disease Prevention and Health Promotion. Youth Risk Behavior Surveillance: National College Health Risk Behavior Survey – United States, 1995. In: *CDC Surveillance Summaries*, November 14, 1997. Morbidity and Mortality Weekly Report 1997; 46(No. SS-6), 1–56.

[298] Ibid.

[299] Ibid.

[300] Suicide Prevention Resource Center. (2004). *Promoting mental health and preventing suicide in college and university settings.* Newton, MA: Education Development Center, Inc., p. 9.

[301] Ibid., p. 21.

[302] Kitzrow, M. A. (2003). The mental health needs of today's college students: Challenges and recommendations. *NASPA Journal, 41*(1), 167–181.

[303] Ibid., p. 169.

[304] Harvard School of Public Health (n.d.) Means matter. Firearm access is a risk factor for suicide. Retrieved on July 1, 2008 from http://www.hsph.harvard.edu/means-matter/means-matter/risk/index.html.

[305] Zubin, J., & Spring, B. (1977). Vulnerability: A new view of schizophrenia. *Journal of Abnormal Psychology, 86*, 103–126.

[306] Hendrickson, S., & Cameron, C.C. (1975). Student suicide and college administrators: A perceptual gap. *The Journal of Higher Education, 46*(3), 349–354.

[307] Hendin, H. (1975). Growing up dead: Student suicide. *American Journal of Psychotherapy, 29*, 327–339.

[308] Bernert, R., Joiner, T., Cukrowicz, K., Schmidt, N., & Krakow, B. (2005) Suicidality and sleep disturbances. *Sleep, 29*(9), 1039–1040.

[309] National Mental Health Association & The Jed Foundation. (2002). *Safeguarding your students*

against suicide: Expanding the safety net. Retrieved October 20, 2006 from www.jedfoundation.com.

[310] American College Health Association. (2001). *National College Health Assessment: Aggregate report, spring 2000.* Baltimore: Author.

[311] National Mental Health Association & The Jed Foundation. (2002). *Safeguarding your students against suicide: Expanding the safety net.* Retrieved October 20, 2006 from www.jedfoundation .com.

[312] Office of Applied Studies. (2003). Results from the 2002 National Survey on Drug Use and Health: National findings (DHHS Publication No. SMA 03-3836, NHSDA Series H-22). Rockville, MD: Substance Abuse and Mental Health Services Administration.

[313] Lipschitz, A. (1995). Suicides prevention in young adults (ages 18–30). *Suicide & Life-Threatening Behavior, 25*(1), 155.

[314] Silverman, M. M., Meyer, P. M., Sloane, F., Raffel, M., & Pratt, D. M. (1997). The big ten student suicide study: A 10-year study of suicides on Midwestern university campuses. *Suicide and Life-Threatening Behavior, 27*(3), 285–303.

[315] Suicide Prevention Resource Center. (2004). *Promoting mental health and preventing suicide in college and university settings.* Newton, MA: Education Development Center, Inc.

[316] Ibid.

[317] National Institute of Mental Health. (n.d.) Are gay and lesbian youth at high risk for suicide? Retrieved September 5, 2005 from http://par entingteens.about.com/cs/gayteens/a/gay youthsuicide.htm, ¶ 1.

[318] Laumann, E. O., Gagnon, J. H., Michael, R. T., & Michaels, S. (1994). *The social organization of sexuality: Sexual practices in the United States.* Chicago: University of Chicago Press.

[319] Fitzpatrick, K. K., Euton, S. J., Jones, J. N., & Schmidt, N. B. (2005). Gender role, sexual orientation and suicide risk. *Journal of Affective Disorders, 87*, 35–42.

[320] McDaniel, J. S., Purcell, D., & D'Augelli, A. R. (2001). The relationship between sexual orientation and risk for suicide: Research findings and future directions for research and prevention. *Suicide and Life-Threatening Behavior, 31*, 84–105.

[321] Herrell, R., Goldberg, J., True, W. R., Ramakrishnan, V., Lyons, M., Eisen, S., & Tsuang, M.

T. (1999). Sexual orientation and suicidality: A co-twin control study in adult men. *Archives of General Psychiatry, 56*, 867–874.

[322] Bagley, C., & Tremblay, P. (1997). Suicidal behaviors in homosexual and bisexual males. *Crisis, 18*, 24–34.

[323] National Registry of Evidence-based Programs and Practices (NREPP). Retrieved on March 2, 2008 from http://www.nrepp.samhsa.gov/review-criteria.htm.

[324] U.S. Air Force Medical Service (2002). *Air Force Suicide Prevention Program: A Population-based, Community Approach.* D.C: U.S. Department of Health and Human Services.

[325] Masten, A. S., Best, K. M., & Garmezy, N. (1990). Resilience and development: Contributions from the study of children who overcome adversity. *Development and Psychopathology, 2*, 425–444.

[326] McPherson, M., Smith-Lovin, L., & Brashears, M. (2006). Social isolation in America: Changes in core discussion networks over two decades. *American Sociological Review, 71*(3), 353–375.

[327] U.S. Department of Health and Human Services (2001). National Strategy for Suicide Prevention: Goals and Objectives for Action. Rockville, MD: USDHHS.

[328] Stuart, C., Waalen, J. K., & Haelstromm, E. (2003). Many helping hearts: An evaluation of peer gatekeeper training in suicide risk assessment. *Death Studies, 27*, 321–333.

[329] Suicide Prevention Resource Center. Gatekeeper Matrix. Retrieved on March 2, 2008 from http://www.sprc.org/library/SPRC_Gate keeper_Matrix.pdf.

[330] Joiner, T., Kalafat, J., Draper, J., Stokes, H., Knudson, M. Berman, A., & McKeon, R. (2007). Establishing standards for the assessment of suicide risk among callers to the National Suicide Prevention Lifeline. *Suicide and Life Threatening Behavior, 37*(3), 353–365.

[331] Beck, R., Morris, J., & Beck, A. (1974). Cross validation of the suicide intent scale. *Psychological Report, 34*(2), 445–446.

[332] American Psychiatric Association (2003). *Practice guideline for the assessment and treatment of patients with suicidal behaviors.* p. 3.

[333] Brown, G. (n.d.) A review of suicide assessment measures for intervention research with adults and older adults. Retrieved on July 12, 2007

from http://www.nimh.nih.gov/suicideresearch/adultsuicide.pdf.

334 Department of Veterans Affairs: Office of Inspector General (2007, May 10). *Healthcare Inspection: Implementing VHA's Mental Health Strategic Plan Initiatives for Suicide Prevention.* Report No. 06-03706-126. Washington, D.C.: VA Office of Inspector General.

335 Linehan, M., Comtois, K., Murray, A., Brown, M., Gallop, R., Heard, H., Korslund, K., Tutek, D., Reynolds, S., & Lindenboim, N. (2006) Two-year randomized controlled trial and follow-up of Dialectical Behavior Therapy vs Therapy by Experts for suicidal behaviors and borderline personality disorder. *Archives of General Psychiatry, 63*(7), 757–766.

336 Baldessarini, R., Tondo, L., & Hennen, J. (2003). Lithium treatment and suicide risk in major affective disorders: Update and new findings. *Journal of Clinical Psychiatry, 64*(5), 44–52.

337 Meltzer, H., Alphs, L., Green, A, Altamura, A., Anand, R, Bertoldi, A., Bourgeois, M., Chouinard, G., Islam, M., Kane, J., Krishnan, R., Lindenmayer, J., & Potkin, S.. (2003) Clozapine treatment for suicidality in schizophrenia . *Archives of General Psychiatry, 60*, 82–91.

338 Simon, O., Swann, A., Powell, K., Potter, L., Kresnow, M., & O'Carroll, P. (2001). Characteristics of impulsive suicide attempts and attempters. *Suicide and Life-Threatening Behavior, 32*(1 Suppl), 49–59.

339 Swahn, M., & Potter, L. (2001). Factors associated with the medical severity of suicide attempts in youths and young adults. *Suicide and Life Threatening Behavior, 32*(1) 21–29.

340 Spielmann, G. (2005). Means restriction. Retrieved on December 23, 2007 from http://www.omh.state.ny.us/omhweb/savinglives/Volume2/means_rest.html.

341 Carlson, S. (1999, September 24). F.B.I. investigates second bombing at historically black Florida ACMU. *The Chronicle of Higher Education.* Retrieved on September 28, 1999 from http://www.ede.org/hec/.

342 Bollinger, C. (2004). *Practice as pedagogy and the promise of possibility: Exploring the production and formation of hate.* Unpublished doctoral dissertation. Bowling Green State Unviersity, Ohio.

343 Ibid.

344 U.S Department of Justice – Federal Bureau of Investigation (November 2007). FBI releases 2006 hate crime statistics. *U.S. Department of Justice – Federal Bureau of Investigation 2006 Hate Crime Statistics.* Retrieved on February 6, 2008 from http://www.fbi.gov/ucr/hc2006/press release.html.

345 Franklin, K. Psychosocial motivations of hate crime perpetrators. *APA Public Policy Office.* Retrieved on January 24, 2000 from http://www.apa.org/ppo/pi/franklin.html.

346 Levin, J., & McDevitt, J. (2002). *Hate crimes revisited: America's war on those who are different.* Cambridge, MA: Westview.

347 The category structures of perceived psychological, physical, and socio-economic threats and appropriate responses for them were developed in consultation with a colleague, Dr. Tiffiny Sia, who has done extensive research into reducing prejudice towards negatively stereotyped groups.

348 As a general rule, we try to avoid being perceived as taking ideological stands in higher education, even though every position has an ideological stand. We resist the notion of telling someone their values are wrong. However, one person's freedom ends when it takes another person's human status away. We exercise such a position all the time in our policies and practices. When it comes to culturally tense topics, we fear taking the stand even more so. Our research has led us to the conclusion that hate is an issue that will never really be dealt with, unless we are willing to discuss working toward ideological shifts in thinking.

349 Van Dijk, T. A. (1997). Political discourses and racism: Describing others in Western parliaments. In S. H. Riggins, (Ed.), *The language and politics of exclusion: Others in discourse.* Thousand Oaks, CA: Sage.

350 Levin, J. & McDevitt, J. (2002). *Hate crimes revisited: America's war on those who are different.* Cambridge, MA: Westview.

351 There have been a number of criticisms of Allport's Contact Hypothesis since its origin. However, many of them are the result of not meeting all four conditions. All four of the conditions must be met for the theory to hold.

352 Allport, G. W. (1954). *The nature of prejudice.* Reading, MA: Addison-Wesley.

353 Ibid.

354 hooks, b. (1994). *Teaching to transgress: Education as the practice of freedom.* New York: Routledge.

355 Poynter, K. Frequently Asked Questions: What is safe zone? *National Consortium of Directors of LGBT Resources in Higher Education.* Retrieved on February 6, 2008 from http://www.lgbtcampus .org/index.html.

356 Shapiro, N. S., & Levine, J. H. (1999). *Creating learning communities* (p. 54). San Francisco: Jossey-Bass.

357 University of Denver. The living and learning communities at DU. *University of Denver.* Retrieved on February 6, 2008 from http://www .du.edu/livinglearning/index.htm.

358 Shapiro, N. S., & Levine, J. H. (1999). *Creating learning communities* (p. 54). San Francisco: Jossey-Bass.

359 Chaves, C. A. (2003). *Student involvement in the community college setting* (p. 2). (ERIC Document Reproduction Service No. EDO-JC-03-02).

360 Butler, J. (1997). *Excitable speech: A politics of the performative* (p. 80). New York: Routledge.

361 Herek, G. M. The impact of hate crime victimization. *APA Public Policy.* Retrieved on January 5, 2000 from http://www.apa.org/ppo/pi/herek .html.
Herek, G. M., & Cogan, J. C. (1999). Psychological sequelae of hate-crime victimixation among lesbian, gay and bisexual adults. *Journal of Consulting & Clinical Psychology, 67*(6), 945–951.
Levin, J., & McDevitt, J. (2002). *Hate crimes revisited: America's war on those who are different.* Cambridge, MA: Westview.

362 This model is adapted from a model provided by Allan Blattner who is now the Associate Director for Staff and Student Development in the Department of Residence Life and Housing at UNC Charlotte. Over the past ten years, Bollinger has used the model many times with very positive results.

363 Hurst, J. 1999. The Matthew Shepard tragedy – Crisis and beyond. *About Campus, 4*:3.

364 Ibid.

365 Ibid.

366 Ibid.

367 Ibid.

368 Ibid.

369 Ibid.

370 Ibid.

371 Ibid.

372 Ibid.

373 Ibid.

374 Ibid.

375 Ibid.

376 Nuwer, H. (2001). *Wrongs of passage: Fraternities, sororities, hazing, and binge drinking.* Bloomington, IN: Indiana University Press.

377 Hoover, N., & Pollard, N. (1999). *Initiation rites and athletics: A national survey of NCAA sports teams.* Alfred, NY: Alfred University and Reidman Insurance Co. Inc.

378 Allan, A., & Madden, M. (2008). Hazing in view: College students at risk. Retrieved July 17, 2008 from http://www.hazingstudy.org/.

379 Ibid.

380 Lipkins, S. (2006). Preventing hazing: How parents, teachers, and coaches can stop the violence, harassment, and humiliation. San Francisco: Jossey-Bass.

381 Nuwer, H. (1990). *Broken pledges: The deadly rites of hazing.* Marietta, GA: Longstreet Press, Inc.

382 Kimmel, M. (2008). *Guyland: The perilous world where boys become men.* New York: HarperCollins.

383 Nuwer, H. (2004). *The hazing reader.* Bloomington, IN: Indiana University Press.

384 Nuwer, H. (2001). *Wrongs of passage: Fraternities, sororities, hazing, and binge drinking.* Bloomington, IN: Indiana University Press.

385 Allan, E., & Madden, M. (2008). Hazing in view: College students at risk. *National Center for Hazing Research and Prevention.* Retrieved July 18, 2008 from http://www.hazingstudy.org/.

386 Hazing information. (2008). *National Federation of State High School Associations.* Retrieved July 18, 2008, from http://www.nfhs.org/web/2006/ 08/hazing_information.aspx.

387 Nuwer. H. (2001). *Wrongs of passage.* Bloomington, IN: Indiana University Press, pp. 159–171.

388 Janis, I. L. (2004). Groupthink. In H. Nuwer (Ed.), *The hazing reader* (pp. 19-26). Bloomington, IN: Indiana University Press.

389 Nuwer, H. (Ed.) (2004). Cult-like hazing. In *The hazing reader* (pp. 27–50). Bloomington, IN: Indiana University Press.

390 Arnold, J. C. (2004). Hazing and alcohol in a college fraternity. In H. Nuwer (Ed.), *The hazing reader,* (pp. 51–105). Bloomington, IN: Indiana University Press.

391 Associated Press (2007, December 28). Parents suing Rider University over suspected hazing death. *New York Daily News*. Retrieved July 18, 2008 from http://www.nydailynews.com/ny_local/2007/12/28/2007-12-28_parents_suing_rider_university_over_susp.html.

392 Crow, R. B. and Rossner, S. R. (2004). Institutional liability and hazing – Mainly athletics-related. In H. Nuwer (Ed.), *The hazing reader* (pp. 224–251). Bloomington, IN: Indiana University Press.

393 Nuwer, H. (2004). *The hazing reader*. Bloomington, IN: Indiana University Press.

394 Nuwer, H. (1999). *Wrongs of passage: Fraternities, sororities, hazing, and binge drinking* (p. 35). Bloomington, IN: Indiana University Press.

395 Randazzo, M., Borum, R., Vossekuil, B., Fein, R., Modzeleski, W., & Pollack, W. (2006). Threat assessment in schools: Empirical support and comparison with other approaches. In S. Jimerson & M. Furlong (Eds.), *The handbook of school violence and school safety* (p. 146). Mahwah, NJ: Lawrence Erlbaum Associates.
Reddy, M., Borum, R., Vossekuil, B., Fein, R., Berglund, J., & Modzeleski, W. (2001). Evaluating risk for targeted violence in schools: Comparing risk assessment, threat assessment, and other approaches. *Psychology in the School, 38*, 158.

396 Nicoletti, J., Spencer-Thomas, S., & Bollinger, C. (2001). *Violence goes to college: The authoritative guide to prevention and intervention*. Springfield, IL: Charles C Thomas.

397 Wolowitz, H., (1971). Paranoia and power. *Psychiatry, 34*(4), 358–375.
Karson, M. (2001). *Patterns of child abuse: How dysfunctional transactions are replicated in individuals, families, and the child welfare system*. New York: Haworth Maltreatment and Trauma Press.

398 Nicoletti, J., Spencer-Thomas, S., & Bollinger, C. (2001). *Violence goes to college: The authoritative guide to prevention and intervention*. Springfield, IL: Charles C Thomas.
Karson, M. (personal communication, November 18, 2008).

399 Nicoletti, J., Spencer-Thomas, S., & Bollinger, C. (2001). *Violence goes to college: The authoritative guide to prevention and intervention*. Springfield, IL: Charles C Thomas.

400 Vossekuil,B., Fein, R., Reddy, M., Borum, R., & Modezeleski, W. (2002). *The final report and findings of the Safe School Initiative: Implications for the prevention of school attacks in the United States*. Washington, DC: U.S. and U.S. Department of Education, Office of Elementary and Secondary Education, Safe and Drug-Free Schools Program and U.S. Secret Service, National Threat Assessment Center.
Nicoletti, J., Spencer-Thomas, S., & Bollinger, C. (2001). *Violence goes to college*. Springfield, IL: Charles C Thomas.

401 Nicoletti, J., Spencer-Thomas, S., & Bollinger, C. (2001). *Violence goes to college: The authoritative guide to prevention and intervention*. Springfield, IL: Charles C Thomas.

402 Vossekuil, B., Fein, R., Reddy, M., Borum, R., & Modzeleski, W., (2002). *The final report and findings of the Safe School Initiative: Implications for the prevention of school attacks in the United States*. Washington, DC: U.S. and U.S. Department of Education, Office of Elementary and Secondary Education, Safe and Drug-Free Schools Program and U.S. Secret Service, National Threat Assessment Center.
Nicoletti, J., Spencer-Thomas, S., & Bollinger, C. (2001). *Violence goes to college: The authoritative guide to prevention and intervention*. Springfield, IL: Charles C Thomas.

403 Vossekuil, B., Fein, R., Reddy, M., Borum, R., & Modzeleski, W. (2002). *The final report and findings of the Safe School Initiative: Implications for the prevention of school attacks in the United States*. Washington, DC: U.S. and U.S. Department of Education, Office of Elementary and Secondary Education, Safe and Drug-Free Schools Program and U.S. Secret Service, National Threat Assessment Center.

404 Nicoletti, J., Spencer-Thomas, S., & Bollinger, C. (2001). *Violence goes to college: The authoritative guide to prevention and intervention*. Springfield, IL: Charles C Thomas.

405 Vossekuil, B., Fein, R., Reddy, M., Borum, R., & Modzeleski, W. (2002). *The final report and findings of the Safe School Initiative: Implications for the prevention of school attacks in the United States*. Washington, DC: U.S. and U.S. Department of Education, Office of Elementary and Secondary Education, Safe and Drug-Free Schools Program and U.S. Secret Service, National Threat Assessment Center.

[406] Nicoletti, J., Spencer-Thomas, S., & Bollinger, C. (2001). *Violence goes to college: The authoritative guide to prevention and intervention.* Springfield, IL: Charles C Thomas.

[407] Ibid.

[408] Ibid.

[409] Ibid.

[410] Maiese, Michelle. (2003) Dehumanization. In G. Burgess, & H. Burgess, (Eds.), *Beyond intractability.* Conflict Research Consortium, University of Colorado, Boulder.

[411] Carnagey, N. L., Anderson, L. A., & Bushman, B. J. (2007). The effect of video game violence on physiological desensitization to real-life violence. *Journal of Experimental Social Psychology, 43,* 489–496.

[412] Nicoletti, J., Spencer-Thomas, S., & Bollinger, C. (2001). *Violence goes to college: The authoritative guide to prevention and intervention.* Springfield, IL: Charles C Thomas.

[413] Ibid.

[414] Centers for Disease Control and Prevention. (2004). Violence-related behaviors among high school students – United States, 1991–2003. *Morbidity and Mortality Weekly Report (MMWR), 53,* 651–655.

[415] Reddy, M., Borum, R., Vossekuil, B., Fein, R., Berglund, J., & Modezeleski, W. (2001). Evaluating risk for targeted violence in schools: Comparing risk assessment, threat assessment, and other approaches. *Psychology in the School, 38,* 157–172.

[416] Sokolow, B. (n.d.) An op-ed on the media response to the Virginia Tech Tragedy. Retrieved on July 30, 2007 from http://www.ncherm.org/article-vtech.html.

[417] Ibid.
Reddy, M., Borum, R., Vossekuil, B., Fein, R., Berglund, J., & Modezeleski, W. (2001). Evaluating risk for targeted violence in schools: Comparing risk assessment, threat assessment, and other approaches. *Psychology in the School, 38,* 157–172.

[418] Randazzo, M., Borum, R., Vossekuil, B., Fein, R., Modzeleski, W., & Pollack, W. (2006). Threat assessment in schools: Empirical support and comparison with other approaches. In S. Jimerson, & M. Furlong (Eds.), *The handbook of school violence and school safety* (pp. 146). Mahwah, NJ: Lawrence Erlbaum Associates.

Fein, R.A., Vossekuil, B., Pollack, W.S., Borum, R., Modzeleski, W., & Reddy, M. (2002). *Threat assessment in schools: A guide to managing threatening situations and creating safe school climates.* Washington, DC: U.S. and U.S. Secret Service, National Threat Assessment Center.

[419] Reddy, M., Borum, R., Vossekuil, B., Fein, R., Berglund, J., & Modezeleski, W. (2001). Evaluating risk for targeted violence in schools: Comparing risk assessment, threat assessment, and other approaches. *Psychology in the School, 38,* 157–172.
Randazzo, M., Borum, R., Vossekuil, B., Fein, R., Modzeleski, W., & Pollack, W. (2006). Threat assessment in schools: Empirical support and comparison with other approaches. In S. Jimerson & M. Furlong (Eds.), *The handbook of school violence and school safety* (p. 146). Mahwah, NJ: Lawrence Erlbaum Associates.

[420] Reddy, M., Borum, R., Vossekuil, B., Fein, R., Berglund, J., & Modezeleski, W. (2001). Evaluating risk for targeted violence in schools: Comparing risk assessment, threat assessment, and other approaches. *Psychology in the School, 38,* 157–172.
Homant, R., & Kennedy, D. (1998). Psychological aspects of crime scene profiling: Validity research. *Criminal Justice & Behavior, 25,* 319–343.
Randazzo, M., Borum, R., Vossekuil, B., Fein, R., Modzeleski, W., & Pollack, W. (2006). Threat assessment in schools: Empirical support and comparison with other approaches. In S. Jimerson & M. Furlong (Eds.), *The handbook of school violence and school safety* (p. 146). Mahwah, NJ: Lawrence Erlbaum Associates.

[421] Douglas, J. E., Ressler, R. K., Burgess, A. W., & Hartman, C. R. (1996). Criminal profiling from crime scene analysis. *Behavioral Sciences & the Law, 4,* 401–421.
Homant, R., & Kennedy, D. (1998). Psychological aspects of crime scene profiling: Validity research. *Criminal Justice & Behavior, 25,* 319–343.

[422] Reddy, M., Borum, R., Vossekuil, B., Fein, R., Berglund, J., & Modezeleski, W. (2001). Evaluating risk for targeted violence in schools: Comparing risk assessment, threat assessment, and other approaches. *Psychology in the School, 38,* 157–172.

Randazzo, M., Borum, R., Vossekuil, B., Fein, R., Modzeleski, W., & Pollack, W. (2006). Threat assessment in schools: Empirical support and comparison with other approaches. In S. Jimerson & M. Furlong (Eds.), *The handbook of school violence and school safety* (p. 146). Mahwah, NJ: Lawrence Erlbaum Associates.

423 Sewell, K. W., & Mendelsohn, M. (2000). Profiling potentially violent youth: Statistical and conceptual problems. *Children's Services: Social Policy, Research, and Practice, 3*, 147–169.

424 Ibid.
Reddy, M., Borum, R., Vossekuil, B., Fein, R., Berglund, J., & Modezeleski, W. (2001). Evaluating risk for targeted violence in schools: Comparing risk assessment, threat assessment, and other approaches. *Psychology in the School, 38*, 157–172.
Randazzo, M., Borum, R., Vossekuil, B., Fein, R., Modzeleski, W., & Pollack, W. (2006). Threat assessment in schools: Empirical support and comparison with other approaches. In S. Jimerson & M. Furlong (Eds.), *The handbook of school violence and school safety* (p. 146). Mahwah, NJ: Lawrence Erlbaum Associates.

425 Sewell, K. W., & Mendelsohn, M. (2000). Profiling potentially violent youth: Statistical and conceptual problems. *Children's Services: Social Policy, Research, and Practice, 3*, 147–169.

426 Reddy, M., Borum, R., Vossekuil, B., Fein, R., Berglund, J., & Modezeleski, W. (2001). Evaluating risk for targeted violence in schools: Comparing risk assessment, threat assessment, and other approaches. *Psychology in the School, 38*, 157–172.
Randazzo, M., Borum, R., Vossekuil, B., Fein, R., Modzeleski, W., & Pollack, W. (2006). Threat assessment in schools: Empirical support and comparison with other approaches. In S. Jimerson & M. Furlong (Eds.), *The handbook of school violence and school safety* (pp. 147–156). Mahwah, NJ: Lawrence Erlbaum Associates.

427 Borum, R. (2000). Assessing violence risk among youth. *Journal of Clinical Psychology, 56*, 1263–1288.
Otto, R. K. (2000). Assessing and managing violence risk in outpatient settings. *Journal of Clinical Psychology, 56*, 1239–1262.

428 Reddy, M., Borum, R., Vossekuil, B., Fein, R., Berglund, J., & Modezeleski, W. (2001). Evalu-

ating risk for targeted violence in schools: Comparing risk assessment, threat assessment, and other approaches. *Psychology in the School, 38*, 157–172.

429 Reddy, M., Borum, R., Vossekuil, B., Fein, R., Berglund, J., & Modezeleski, W. (2001). Evaluating risk for targeted violence in schools: Comparing risk assessment, threat assessment, and other approaches. *Psychology in the School, 38*, 157–172.

430 Borum, R. (2000). Assessing violence risk among youth. *Journal of Clinical Psychology, 56*, 1263–1288.
Reddy, M., Borum, R., Vossekuil, B., Fein, R., Berglund, J., & Modezeleski, W. (2001). Evaluating risk for targeted violence in schools: Comparing risk assessment, threat assessment, and other approaches. *Psychology in the School, 38*, 157–172.

431 Reddy, M., Borum, R., Vossekuil, B., Fein, R., Berglund, J., & Modezeleski, W. (2001). Evaluating risk for targeted violence in schools: Comparing risk assessment, threat assessment, and other approaches. *Psychology in the School, 38*, 157–172.

432 Litwack, T.R. (2001). Actuarial versus clinical assessments of dangerousness. *Psychology, Public Policy and Law, 7*(2), 409–443.

433 Reddy, M., Borum, R., Vossekuil, B., Fein, R., Berglund, J., & Modezeleski, W. (2001). Evaluating risk for targeted violence in schools: Comparing risk assessment, threat assessment, and other approaches. *Psychology in the School, 38*, 166.

434 Reddy, M., Borum, R., Vossekuil, B., Fein, R., Berglund, J., & Modezeleski, W. (2001). Evaluating risk for targeted violence in schools: Comparing risk assessment, threat assessment, and other approaches. *Psychology in the School, 38*, 157–172.
Randazzo, M., Borum, R., Vossekuil, B., Fein, R., Modzeleski, W., & Pollack, W. (2006). Threat assessment in schools: Empirical support and comparison with other approaches. In S. Jimerson & M. Furlong (Eds.), *The handbook of school violence and school safety* (pp. 147–156). Mahwah, NJ: Lawrence Erlbaum Associates.

435 Sewell, K. W., & Mendelsohn, M. (2000). Profiling potentially violent youth: Statistical and conceptual problems. *Children's Services: Social Policy, Research, and Practice, 3*, 147–169.

436 Fein, R. A., Vossekuil, B., Pollack, W. S., Borum, R., Modzeleski, W., & Reddy, M. (2002). *Threat assessment in schools: A guide to managing threatening situations and creating safe school climates.* Washington, DC: U.S. and U.S. Secret Service, National Threat Assessment Center.

Reddy, M., Borum, R., Vossekuil, B., Fein, R., Berglund, J., & Modezeleski, W. (2001). Evaluating risk for targeted violence in schools: Comparing risk assessment, threat assessment, and other approaches. *Psychology in the School, 38,* 157–172.

Fein, R., Vossekuil, B. (1998). *Protective intelligence & threat assessment investigations: A guide for state and local law enforcement officials* (NIJ/OJP/DOJ Publication No. 170612). Washington, DC: U.S. Department of Justice.

Fein, R., & Vossekuil, B. (1999). Assassination in the United States: An operational study of recent assassins, attackers, and near-lethal approachers. *Journal of Forensic Sciences, 50,* 321–333.

Borum, R., Fein, R., Vossekuil, B., & Berglund, J. (1999). Threat assessment: Defining an approach for evaluating risk of targeted violence. *Behavioral Sciences & the Law, 17,* 323–337.

Randazzo, M., Borum, R., Vossekuil, B., Fein, R., Modzeleski, W., & Pollack, W. (2006). Threat assessment in schools: Empirical support and comparison with other approaches. In S. Jimerson & M. Furlong (Eds.), *The handbook of school violence and school safety* (pp. 147–156). Mahwah, NJ: Lawrence Erlbaum Associates.

437 Fein, R. A., Vossekuil, B., Pollack, W. S., Borum, R., Modzeleski, W., & Reddy, M. (2002). *Threat assessment in schools: A guide to managing threatening situations and creating safe school climates.* Washington, DC: U.S. and U.S. Secret Service, National Threat Assessment Center.

Fein, R., Vossekuil, B. (1998). *Protective intelligence & threat assessment investigations: A guide for state and local law enforcement officials* (NIJ/OJP/DOJ Publication No. 170612). Washington, DC: U.S. Department of Justice.

Fein, R., Vossekuil, B. (1999). Assassination in the United States: An operational study of recent assassins, attackers, and near-lethal approachers. *Journal of Forensic Sciences, 50,* 321–333.

Reddy, M., Borum, R., Vossekuil, B., Fein, R., Berglund, J., & Modezeleski, W. (2001). Evaluating risk for targeted violence in schools: Comparing risk assessment, threat assessment, and other approaches. *Psychology in the School, 38,* 157–172.

Randazzo, M., Borum, R., Vossekuil, B., Fein, R., Modzeleski, W., & Pollack, W. (2006). Threat assessment in schools: Empirical support and comparison with other approaches. In S. Jimerson & M. Furlong (Eds.), *The handbook of school violence and school safety* (pp. 147–156). Mahwah, NJ: Lawrence Erlbaum Associates.

438 Fein, R. A., Vossekuil, B., Pollack, W. S., Borum, R., Modzeleski, W., & Reddy, M. (2002). *Threat assessment in schools: A guide to managing threatening situations and creating safe school climates.* Washington, DC: U.S. and U.S. Secret Service, National Threat Assessment Center.

Reddy, M., Borum, R., Vossekuil, B., Fein, R., Berglund, J., & Modezeleski, W. (2001). Evaluating risk for targeted violence in schools: Comparing risk assessment, threat assessment, and other approaches. *Psychology in the School, 38,* 157–172.

Randazzo, M., Borum, R., Vossekuil, B., Fein, R., Modzeleski, W., & Pollack, W. (2006). Threat assessment in schools: Empirical support and comparison with other approaches. In S. Jimerson & M. Furlong (Eds.), *The handbook of school violence and school safety* (pp. 147–156). Mahwah, NJ: Lawrence Erlbaum Associates.

439 Fein, R. A., Vossekuil, B., Pollack, W. S., Borum, R., Modzeleski, W., & Reddy, M. (2002). *Threat assessment in schools: A guide to managing threatening situations and creating safe school climates.* Washington, DC: U.S. and U.S. Secret Service, National Threat Assessment Center.

Reddy, M., Borum, R., Vossekuil, B., Fein, R., Berglund, J., & Modezeleski, W. (2001). Evaluating risk for targeted violence in schools: Comparing risk assessment, threat assessment, and other approaches. *Psychology in the School, 38,* 157–172.

Randazzo, M., Borum, R., Vossekuil, B., Fein, R., Modzeleski, W., & Pollack, W. (2006). Threat assessment in schools: Empirical Support and Comparison with other approaches.

In S. Jimerson & M. Furlong (Eds.), *The handbook of school violence and school safety* (pp. 147–156). Mahwah, NJ: Lawrence Erlbaum Associates.

440 Fein, R. A., Vossekuil, B., Pollack, W .S., Borum, R., Modzeleski, W., & Reddy, M. (2002). *Threat assessment in schools: A guide to managing threatening situations and creating safe school climates.* Washington, DC: U.S. and U.S. Secret Service, National Threat Assessment Center.

Borum, R., Fein, R., Vossekuil, B., & Berglund, J. (1999). Threat assessment: Defining an approach for evaluating risk of targeted violence. Behavioral Sciences & the Law, 17, 323–337.

Reddy, M., Borum, R., Vossekuil, B., Fein, R., Berglund, J., & Modezeleski, W. (2001). Evaluating risk for targeted violence in schools: Comparing risk assessment, threat assessment, and other approaches. *Psychology in the School, 38,* 157–172.

Fein, R., Vossekuil, B. (1998). *Protective intelligence & threat assessment investigations: A guide for state and local law enforcement officials* (NIJ/OJP/DOJ Publication No. 170612). Washington, DC: U.S. Department of Justice.

Fein, R., Vossekuil, B. (1999). Assassination in the United States: An operational study of recent assassins, attackers, and near-lethal approachers. *Journal of Forensic Sciences, 50,* 321–333.

Randazzo, M., Borum, R., Vossekuil, B., Fein, R., Modzeleski, W., & Pollack, W. (2006). Threat assessment in schools: Empirical support and comparison with other approaches. In S. Jimerson & M. Furlong (Eds.), *The handbook of school violence and school safety* (pp. 147–156). Mahwah, NJ: Lawrence Erlbaum Associates.

441 Fein, R. A., Vossekuil, B., Pollack, W. S., Borum, R., Modzeleski, W., & Reddy, M. (2002). *Threat assessment in schools: A guide to managing threatening situations and creating safe school climates.* Washington, DC: U.S. and U.S. Secret Service, National Threat Assessment Center.

442 Report of the Review Panel. (2007). Mass Shootings at Virginia Tech. Presented to Governor Tim Kaine, August 2007, p. 35.

443 CNN (2007). Killer's manifesto: 'You forced me into a corner'. Retrieved May 19, 2008, from http://www.cnn.com.

444 Report of the Review Panel. (2007). Mass Shootings at Virginia Tech. Presented to Governor Tim Kaine, August 2007, p. 43.

445 Ibid., p. 44.

446 Ibid.

447 Ibid., p. 45.

448 Ibid.

449 Ibid., p. 46.

450 Ibid., p. 47.

451 Ibid., p. 51.

452 Bailey, K., (2006). Legal knowledge related to school violence and school safety. In S. Jimerson & M. Furlong (Eds.), *The handbook of school violence and school safety* (pp. 31–49). Mahwah, NJ: Lawrence Erlbaum Associates.

Tribbensee, N. E., & McDonald, S. J. (2007). FERPA allows more than you think. Retrieved May 19, 2008, from http://insidehighered.com.

453 Tribbensee, N. E., & McDonald, S. J. (2007). FERPA allows more than you think. Retrieved May 19, 2008, from http://insidehighered.com.

454 Levine, A., & Cureton, J. 1998. *When hope and fear collide: A portrait of today's college student.* Somerset, NJ: Jossey-Bass Publishers.

455 Acker, G. (1997, September 10). Students prove they won't be controlled. *The Opinion.*

Lesson in riot control. (1993). *National Review, 45*(1), 14.

Colorado State, city officials to coordinate following incident. (1997, August 30). *Colorado State University News and Information.* Retrieved on May 23, 2000 from http://www.colostate.edu/Depts/PR/releases/news/incident.htm.

Colorado State University establishes hotline to identify students involved in incidents near campus. (1997, September 8). *Colorado State University News and Information.* Retrieved on May 23, 2000 from http://www.colostate.edu/Depts/PR/releases/nes/hotline.htm.

Riot act. (1997, September 9). *The Opinion.*

Student rioters demand the "right to party." (1998). *Chronicle of Higher Education, 44*(36), A46.

Annual OU riot a hit. (1998, April 10). *The Miami Student Online.* Retrieved on May 24, 2000 from http://mustudent.muohio.edu/1997/041098/ou.html.

The yell. (1998, April 9). *The Post: Athens, Ohio.*

Police arrest eight more in July 12 Penn State riot about 1,500 people took part in the melee. (1998, August 28). *York Daily Record.*

Penn State riot reported about 1,500 people flooded streets through the early morning Sunday after the Central Pennsylvania Festival of Arts. (1998, July 13). *York Daily Record.*

Penn State riot damage estimated at $100K. (1998, July 14). *York Daily Record.*

Penn State should expel rioters. (1998, July 14). *Daily Collegian.*

Sober thoughts as Penn State riots show, binge drinking has become the most serious drug problem on campus. (1998, July 19). It's time to address it. *Sunday News.*

Students demonstrate for right to bear beers. (1998, May 13). *Times Union.*

Seventeen arrested in weekend riot. (1998, May 4). *The State News.*

Students involved in summer riot no longer in school. (1998, November 30). *Penn State Online.* Retrieved on May 23, 2000 from http://www .psu.edu/ur/ NEWS/news/riotsanctions.html.

Halloween's a riot again at U. of 0., despite extra police patrols. (1998, November). *The Columbian.*

A brief history of Eugene. (1998, October 28). *Eugene Information.* Retrieved on May 23, 2000 from http://www.ci.eugene.or.us/local/euggov .htm.

University weekend rioters disciplined. (1998, September 21). *University of Connecticut Advance.* Retrieved on May 23, 2000 from http://www .advance.uconn.edu/09219802.htm.

After Web posts, police feared copyright infringement. (1999). *News Photographer, 54*(5), 30.

Campus incident reports. (1999, April 5). *Campus Watch Newsletter Online.* Retrieved on October 25, 1999 from http://campussafety .org/WATCH/watch0499.05.html.

Court tells Michigan newspaper to hand over photos of campus riot. (1999, April 6). *The Freedom Forum Online.* Retrieved on April 13, 2000 from http://www.freedomforum.org/press/ 1999/4/6msuriot.asp.

Enrollment history. (1999, February). *Oregon University System.* Retrieved on May 23, 2000 from http://www.ous.edu/irs/factbook/WEB student/hchist.htm.

About Plymouth State College. (1999, January 19). *Plymouth State College Homepage.* Retrieved on May 23, 2000 from http://www.plymouth .edu/psc/admserv/factbook/general_info.htm.

Three more sentenced for participation in riot. (1999, January 28). *Intercom Online.* Retrieved on May 23, 2000 from http://www.psu.edu/ archives/intercom_1999/Jan28/riot.html.

State College police make eight more riot-related arrests. (1999, September 3). *Intercom Online.* Retrieved on May 23, 2000 from http:// www.psu.edu/ur/archives/intercom_1998/Sept 3/roit.html.

Thumbnail facts. (2000, January). *University of Connecticut.* Retrieved on May 23, 2000 from http://www.uconn.edu/about.html.

College rioters jailed at higher rate than rapists. (2000, March 5). *APB News.* Retrieved on March 15, 2000 from http://www.apbnews .com:80/newscenter/breakingnews/2000/ 03/05/msuriot0305_01.html.

Facts about WSU. (2000, May 23). *WSU Facts.* Retrieved on May 23, 2000 from http://www .wsu.edu/NIS/FactsAboutWSU.html.

Oxford, OH. (n.d.) *U.S. Gazetteer.* Retrieved on July 11, 20000 from http://www.census.gov/ cgibin/gazetteer?city=Oxford&state=0H&zip=.

Prospective students. (n.d.) *Miami University Homepage.* Retrieved on May 24, 2000 from http://www.mohio.edu/prospectivestudents/.

The official Commentator riot guide. (n.d.) *Oregon Commentator.* http://darkwing.uoregon.edu/ ocomment/ocarchive/oc97_98/oc2_97_4.html.

UNH profile 1999. (n.d.) *University of New Hampshire Homepage.* Retrieved on May 23, 2000 from http://www.unh.edu/aboutunh.html.

What Jeanne didn't know. (n.d.) *Security on Campus, Inc.* Retrieved on February 27, 2000 from http://campussafety.org/soc/jac,html.

Just the facts. (n.d.) *University of Colorado at Boulder.* Retrieved on May 23, 2000 from http://www.colorado.edu/Public Relations/ JustTheFacts/jtf.html.

Penn State quick facts. (n.d.) *Penn State Online.* Retrieved on May 23, 2000 from http://www .psu.edu/ur/about/quick.html.

The 1997 University Hill riots. (n.d.) Retrieved on May 23, 2000 from http://www.colorado .edu/geography/COGA/geogweb/university hill/forum/riotpic2.html.

U.S. Gazetteer. (n.d.) U.S. Census Bureau. Retrieved on May 23, 2000 from http://www .census.gov/cgi-bin/gazetteer?city=Boulder &state=CO&zip=.

Applegate, R. (1962). *Kill or get killed.* Boulder, CO: Paladin Press.

Beene, C. (1992). *Police crowd control.* Boulder, CO: Paladin Press.

Applegate, R. (1981). *Riot control.* Boulder, CO: Paladin Press.

Arden-Smith, T. (1998, April 7). Daylight saving is a riot. *Student.com.* Retrieved on May 24, 2000 from http://www.student.com/article/ohioriot.

Austin, D., & Hardy, K. (1999, November 3). Last riot case brings closure. *The State News.*

Beutler, W. (n.d.) Oregon commentator riot guide. *Oregon Commentator.* Retrieved on May 23, 2000 from http://darkwing.uoregon.edu/-ocomment/ocarchive/oc98_99/oc3_98_5.html.

Blair, B., & Cole, P. (1998, July 13). 1,500 riot at Penn State; 20 arrested. *Daily Collegian.*

Bloch, G. (n.d.) Prohibition, part II: At the University, and across the country, students are fighting for their right to party. *Oregon Commentator.* Retrieved on May 23, 2000 from http://darkwing.uoregon.edu/-ocomment/ocarchive/oc9798/oc13974.html.

Bradley, F., & Cichon, F. (2000, July 17). Police end riot near Penn State University. *Daily Collegian.*

Brown, D. (2000, March 24). UNH takes action against possible riots. *The New Hampshire.* Retrieved on May 23, 2000 from http://www.tnh.unh.edu/Issues/032400/News /riots.html.

Brown, J., & Politsky, A. (1997, April 24). *The Post.*

Brunt, J. (1997, September 8). Weekend fracas "total anarchy." *The State News.*

Burden, M. (1999, April 19). Suspended rioter reinstated. *The State News.*

Burden, M. (1999, April 5). Alumni hesitant with gifts after riot. *The State News.*

Byyny, R., & Stump, R. (1998, November 13). Past points to possible solutions. *Carillon.* Retrieved on May 23, 2000 from http://www.colorado.edu/Carillon/volume17/stories/2_alcohol_solutions.html.

Caufield, K. (1999, March 30). Peace groups tried to stop riot, damage. *The State News.*

Chen, H. (1999, June 10). Student jailed for role in campus riot. *APB News.* Retrieved on October 25, 2999 from http://www.apbnews.com/newscenter/breakingnews/1999/06/10/riot0610_01.html.

Cheng, V. (1998, September 3). Community wants to curtail drinking; Students binge drinking was blamed for fueling the July 12 riot at Penn State. *York Daily Record.*

Chronicle of Higher Education, 44(36), A48.

Ripley, T. (1999). Riot control equipment. *Armada International, 23*(2), 40–44.

Clapp, A., & Hardy, K. (2000, March 27). Enforcement helps deter further riots. *The State News.*

Cohen, J., & Pardo, S. (1999, March 29). Riot wasn't spontaneous; students had stockpiled. *The Detroit News.*

Cook, K. (1999). Field of screams. *Sports Illustrated, 91*(10), 32.

Corlene, D. (1998, April 1). Students riot. *The Post.* Retrieved on May 24, 2000 from http://thepost.baker.ohiou.edu/archives/040198/aftop.html.

Couch, G. (2000, March 28). The real March madness. *Chicago Sun-Times.*

Curtin, D. (1999, November 12). CU regent proposes "riot fee." *The Denver Post.*

Curtin, D. (1999, November 23). Anti-riot policy has initial OK. *The Denver Post.*

Curtin, D. (1999, September 21). Mile High will be dry for CU, CSU. *The Denver Post.*

Danchuk, E. (1998, April 14). Riots not a well chosen battle. *The Miami Student Online.* Retrieved on May 24, 2000 from http://mustudent.muohio.edu/1997/041498/riots.html.

Delgado, V. (2000, July 14). Two rioters suspended. *Lansing State Journal.* Retrieved on April 14, 2000 from http://www.lansingstatejournal.com/features/riot/suspended.html.

Donvan, J., Sawyer, F., Tate, R., Zeoli, R., & Coleman, M. (1998, May 11). The right to party. *ABC Nightline.*

Drummond, D. (1999, August 29). School tightens rules to curb alcohol abuse, prevent repeat of riots. *The Toledo Blade.* Retrieved on August 30, 1999 from http://www.toledoblade.com:80/editorial/news/9h29msu.htm.

Durbin, D. (1999, March 31). MSU suspends 2 rioting students. *South Bend Tribune.*

Freile, V., & Mateen, M. (1998, July 27). Conference focuses on PSU riot. *The Digital Collegian.* Retrieved on May 23, 2000 from http://

www.collegian.psu.edu/archive/1998/0 7/07-27-98tdc/07-27-98d01-003.asp.

French, B. (1999, March 29). Booze, rebellion fed rampage. *The Detroit News.*

Gilje, P. (1996). *Rioting in America.* Bloomington: Indiana University Press.

Gonzales, P. (n.d.) Riots at Michigan State University. *Campus Safety Journal.* Retrieved on April 13, 2000 from http://www.campusjournal.com/michigan-state-riot.htm.

Gose, B. (1998). At Connecticut's party weekend, days of music replaced by nights of vandalism. *Chronicle of Higher Education, 44*(36), A47–A48.

Haddock, D., & Polsby, D. (1994, Spring/Summer). Understanding riots. *The Cato Journal, 14*(1). Retrieved on May 23, 2000 from http://www.cato.org/pubs/journal/cj14n1-13.html.

Hamilton, L. (1997, September 9). Riot proves city is full of oppression. *The Opinion.*

Hampshire, K. (1998, April 29). Campus clashes not uncommon occurrences. *The Post-Ohio University.*

Howe, J. (1998, August/September). Reading the riots. *Link Magazine.* Retrieved on May 24, 2000 from http://www.linkmag.com/Link/aug_sept_98/980820Riots.html.

Hudson, M. (1998, August 12). Students pleased by riot workshop. *The State News.*

Hughes, K. (2000, March 24). Churches seek to help heal riot wounds. *The State News.*

Imhof, H. (1999, April 16). WSU students spearhead efforts to curb alcohol abuse. *News from Washington State University.* Retrieved on May 23, 2000 from http://www.wsu.edu/NIS/release2/hi125.htm.

Imhof, H. (2000, April 23). WSU Greeks plan community party. *News from Washington State University.* Retrieved on May 23, 2000 from http://www.wsu.edu/NIS/releases2/hil31.htm.

Jackson, C. (n.d.) Campus riots continue. *Student.com.* Retrieved on May 23, 2000 from http://www.student.com/article/riotupdate.

Kinney, D. (1998, July 8). Police gear up to prevent repeat performance of riot. Some men convicted for their part in the riot last year are being visibly punished. *York Daily Record.*

Kron, M. Fight for your right. (n.d.) *Oregon Commentator.* Retrieved on May 23, 2000 from

http://darkwing.uoregon.edu/ocomment/ocarchive/oc97_98/oc3_97_8.html.

Kuntz, J. (2000, May 4). Riots stupider than daylight saving time. *Student Advantage.* Retrieved on May 24, 2000 from http://www.studentadvantage.com/article_story/1,1075,c2-i39-t0-a25790,00.html.

Levine, A., & Cureton, J. (1998). *When hope and fear collide: A portrait of today's college student.* Somerset, NJ: Jossey-Bass Publishers.

Levine, M. (1999). Rethinking bystander non-intervention. *Human Relations 52*(9), 1133–1155.

Lively, K. (1998). At Michigan State, a protest escalated into a night of fires, tear gas, and arrests. *Chronicle of Higher Education, 44*(36), A46–A47.

McCollum, K. (1999). Hackers attack Web site set up to nab student rioters at Michigan State U. *Chronicle of Higher Education, 45*(33), A38.

Meese, J. (1999, April 1). How to stop a riot: Forum yields ideas. *The State News.* Retrieved on May 23, 2000 from http://www.statenews.com/editionsspring99/040199/p1forum.html.

Methvin, E. (1970). *The riot makers.* New Rochelle: Arlington House.

Michelson, M. (2000, March 6). Potential Washington State U. riot repeat rebuffed. *Daily Evergreen.*

Petura, B. (1998, August 14). Expulsions, suspensions, fines, probation included. *New from Washington State University.* Retrieved on May 23, 2000 from http://www.wsu.edu/NIS/releases/ bp129.htm.

Mills, D. (1998, May 2). Munn field riot latest in long string of uprisings. *The State News.*

Mitchell, K. (1999, February 5). U. Colorado students riot after Super Bowl. *Campus Press-University of Colorado.*

Mitchell, M. (2000, May 5). Official suggestions for safe student celebrations. *Carillon.* Retrieved on May 23, 2000 from http://www.colorado.edu/Carillon/volume43/stories/5official.html.

Morse, J. (1998, May 9). More violence near Miami. *Enquirer Local News Coverage.* Retrieved on May 24, 2000 from http://enquirer.com/editions/1998/05/09/mia mi.html.

Muir, P. (1999, April 22). Riot ordinance empower police. *The State News.* Retrieved on May 23, 2000 from http://www.state-news.com/editionsspring99/042299/ci_ordi-nance.html.

Murphy, P. (1997, September 10). City, 'U' disrespect students' rights. *The Opinion.*

Nault, D. (1998, May 8). Overnight disturbance. *Miami News and Public Information Office.* Retrieved on May 24, 2000 from http://news-info.muohio.edu/news_display.cfm?mu_un_id=298.

Olsen, N. (1998, October 19). Colorado State needs to cut party attendance to avoid police tear gas. *Rocky Mountain Collegian-Colorado State.*

Owen, M. (1999, November 9). Riot footage shows up on 'Real TV' party school piece. *The State News.*

Pardo, J., & Cohen, J. (1999, March 29). MSU vows to expel rioters: Police seek melee videos; students may face charges. *Detroit News.*

Parfitt, M. (1998, July 14). Penn State riot aftermath: Officials clean up, assign blame. *Daily Collegian.*

Phillips, M. (2000, June 20). Washington State U. aims for more students, money. *Daily Evergreen.*

Smylie, M. (1999, May 6). One year later, Washington State U. remember May riot. *Daily Evergreen.*

Piscitelli, A. (1998, May 18). Look around you: There's more to see. *The Post-Ohio University.*

Platt, A. (1971). *The Politics of Riot Commissions 1917–1970.* New York: Macmillan.

Quinn, S. (1998, May 8). Riots spark publicity, animosity. *The New Hampshire.* Retrieved on May 23, 2000 from http://www.tnh.unh.edu/Issues/050898/News/riots.html.

Reilly, R. (1998). And the band fought on. *Sports Illustrated, 89*(14), 112.

Reisberg, L. (1998). Some experts say colleges share the responsibility for the recent riots.

Ritzo, N. (1997, October 14). UNH is a mess, but not because of riots. *The New Hampshire.* Retrieved on May 23, 2000 from http://www.tnh.unh.edu/Issues/101497/Foru m/badrep.html.

Sanchezand, R., & Ebnet, M. (1998, May 5). "Fluke" weekend riot at WSU may be part of trend. *The Seattle Times.* Retrieved on May 24, 2000 from http://seattletimes.com/news/local/htm198/pull_050598.html.

Schlosser, R. (1997, September 23). Riot act: Part II. *The New Hampshire.* Retrieved on May 23, 2000 from http://www.tnh.unh.edu/Issues/092397/News/riot.html.

Schneider, K. (2000, April 13). Video depicts questionable police actions during riot at Ohio U. *The Post.*

Shepardson, D. (1999, April 11). Media fight to demand MSU riot photos. *The Detroit News.* Retrieved on April 13, 2000 from http://www.detnews.com/1999/metro/9904/11/04110046.htm.

Simpson, H. (1998, April 7). What a riot this weekend was! *The Post: Athens, Ohio.* 7 April.

Skertic, M. (1998, May 12). Arrested seniors' status in limbo. *Enquirer Local News Coverage.* Retrieved on May 23, 2000 from http://enquirer.com/editions/1998/05/12/diplomas12.html.

Sowa, J. (1997, November 3). Halloween party turns into riot. *Oregon Daily Emerald.*

Sowa, T. (1998, May 20). Law enforcement cites mistakes in handling riot authorities lacked shields and failed to wait for backup, say officers involved in WSU melee. *The Spokane Review.*

Stebbins, R. (n.d.) Who bath woe? *Plymouth State College English Department.* Retrieved on May 23, 2000 from http://www.ply-mouth.edu/psc/english/special_projects/spir-its/stebbinsl.html.

Steele, J. (1999, March 31). Student look to extinguish negative image. *The State News.*

Stockwell, J. (n.d.) Rioting: The new rage? *Student.com.* Retrieved on May 23, 2000 from http://www.student.com/article/riots.

Swavy, J. (1997, September 11). Gunson residents to challenge tickets. *The State News.*

Swavy, J. (1997, September 9). Police brace for crowds. *The State News.*

Tato, S. (2000, July 14). MSU officials defend riot suspensions. *Lansing State Journal.* Retrieved on April 14, 2000 from http://www.lansingstatejournal.com/features/r iot/msuofficials.html.

Tato, S. (2000, July 14). New policy lets MSU suspend future rioters. *Lansing State Journal.* Retrieved on April 14, 2000 from http://www.lansingstatejournal.com/features/riot/suspend.html.

Terlep, S. (1997, September 11). E.L. at odds with students. *The State News.*

Terlep, S. (1997, September 9). E.L. turmoil angers city. *The State News.*

Terlep, S.(1997, September 10). City designs plans to deter future melees. *The State News.* Retrieved on April 13, 2000 from http// www.statenews.com/editionsfa1197/091097/pl _balance.html.

Tio, A. (1999, April 27). Police hoping to avoid riot repeat. *The Miami Student Online.* Retrieved on May 24, 2000 from http://www.mustu dent.muohio.edu/1999/042799/festival.html.

Viator, J. (1997, October 7). Riot aftermath hits professors. *The New Hampshire.* Retrieved on May 23, 2000 from http://www.tnh.unh.edu/ Issues/100797/News/profriot.html.

Vogt, A. (1998, May 4). Overnight riot injures 23 police at WSU students spill out of party house for fiery showdown with officers. *The Spokane Review.*

Vogt, A. (1998, May 5). We know who you are, police tell WSU rioters investigators review videotapes. *The Spokane Review.*

Vogt, A. (1998, September 11). Ex-WSU student has dim recall of riot Jackson tells court of drinking binge. *Spokesman Review.*

Vogt, A. (1999, October 22). WSU riot trial ends in acquittal Jamie Jackson not guilty of assaulting deputy. *Spokesman Review.*

Vogt, A. (2000, April 16). WSU tries to polish its image. *Spokane.net.* Retrieved on April 17, 2000 from http://www.spokane.net:80/news-story-body.asp?Date=041600&ID=s792186 &cat=.

Whaley, M. (2000, August 29). Three strikes, you're out, CU says. *Denver Post.*

Wise, T. (n.d.) The kids are all-white: Riots, pathology, and the real meaning of color-blindness. Something to Think About. Retrieved on May 24, 2000 from http://www.samrc.com/ news/othernews.htm.

Witkin, G. (1993). Ready for the worst. *US News and World Report, 114*(15), 24–27.

Wolper, A. (1999). Newsies aren't police. *Editor & Publisher, 132*(27), 15.

Wyer, W. (n.d.) Riot retrospective. Oregon Voice. Retrieved on May 23, 2000 from http:// darkwing.uoregon.edu/-ovoice/riots.html.

Xu, S. (1999, March 17). Sentences given in final Penn State U. riot trials. *Daily Collegian-Penn State University.*

Zeigler, P. (1998, July 13). Entertainment value found in riot at Penn State. *Daily Collegian.*

[456] Just the facts. (n.d.) *University of Colorado at Boulder.* Retrieved on May 23, 2000 from http:// www.colorado.edu/Public Relations/JustThe Facts/jtf.html.

Colorado State, city officials to coordinate following incident. (1997, August 30). *Colorado State University News and Information.* Retrieved on May 23, 2000 from http://www .colostate.edu/Depts/PR/releases/news/inci dent.htm.

Colorado State University establishes hotline to identify students involved in incidents near campus. (1997, September 8). *Colorado State University News and Information.* Retrieved on May 23, 2000 from http://www.colostate .edu/Depts/PR/releases/nes/hotline.htm.

The 1997 University Hill riots. (n.d.) Retrieved on May 23, 2000 from http://www.colorado .edu/geography/COGA/geogweb/university hill/forum/riotpic2.html.

U.S. Gazetteer. (n.d.) U.S. Census Bureau. Retrieved on May 23, 2000 from http://www .census.gov/cgi-bin/gazetteer?city=Boulder &state=CO&zip=.

Byyny, R., & Stump, R. (1998, November 13). Past points to possible solutions. *Carillon.* Retrieved on May 23, 2000 from http://www.col orado.edu/Carillon/volume17/stories/2_alco hol_solutions.html.

Mitchell, K. (1999, February 5). U. Colorado students riot after Super Bowl. *Campus Press-University of Colorado.*

Mitchell, M. (2000, May 5). Official suggestions for safe student celebrations. *Carillon.* Retrieved on May 23, 2000 from http:// www.col orado.edu/Carillon/volume43/stories/5official .html.

Olsen, N. (1998, October 19). Colorado State needs to cut party attendance to avoid police tear gas. *Rocky Mountain Collegian-Colorado State.*

[457] Ibid.
[458] Ibid.
[459] Ibid.
[460] Ibid.
[461] Ibid.
[462] Anonymous. (1998, April 10). Annual OU riot a hit. *The Miami Student Online.* Retrieved on May 24, 2000 from http://mustudent.muohio .edu/1997/041098/ou.html.

Prospective students. (n.d.) *Miami University Homepage*. Retrieved on May 24, 2000 from http://www.mohio.edu/prospectivestudents/.

Anonymous. (1998, April 9). The yell. *The Post: Athens, Ohio.*

Arden-Smith, T. (1998, April 7). Daylight saving is a riot. *Student.com.* Retrieved on May 24, 2000 from http://www.student.com/article/ohioriot.

Corlene, D. (1998, April 1). Students riot. *The Post.* Retrieved on May 24, 2000 from http://thepost.baker.ohiou.edu/archives/04019 8/aftop.html.

Danchuk, E. (1998, April 14). Riots not a well chosen battle. *The Miami Student Online.* Retrieved on May 24, 2000 from http://mustu dent.muohio.edu/1997/041498/riots.html.

Hampshire, K. (1998, April 29). Campus clashes not uncommon occurrences. *The Post-Ohio University.*

Nault, D. (1998, May 8). Overnight disturbance. *Miami News and Public Information Office.* Retrieved on May 24, 2000 from http://news info.muohio.edu/news_display.cfm?mu_un_id =298.

Piscitelli, A. (1998, May 18). Look around you: There's more to see. *The Post-Ohio University.*

Platt, A. (1971). *The Politics of Riot Commissions 1917-1970.* New York: Macmillan.

Schneider, K. (2000, April 13). Video depicts questionable police actions during riot at Ohio U. *The Post.*

Simpson, H. (1998, April 7). What a riot this weekend was! *The Post: Athens, Ohio.* 7 April.

Tio, A. (1999, April 27). Police hoping to avoid riot repeat. *The Miami Student Online.* Retrieved on May 24, 2000 from http://www.mustudent .muohio.edu/1999/042799/festival.html.

Morse, J. (1998, May 9). More violence near Miami. *Enquirer Local News Coverage.* Retrieved on May 24, 2000 from http://enquirer.com/ editions/1998/05/09/mia mi.html.

[463] Ibid.

[464] Ibid.

[465] Thumbnail facts. (2000, January). *University of Connecticut.* Retrieved on May 23, 2000 from http://www.uconn.edu/about.html.

University weekend rioters disciplined. (1998, September 21). *University of Connecticut Advance.* Retrieved on May 23, 2000 from http://www .advance.uconn.edu/09219802.htm

Gose, B. (1998). At Connecticut's party weekend, days of music replaced by nights of vandalism. *Chronicle of Higher Education, 44*(36), A47–A48.

[466] Ibid.

[467] Ibid.

[468] Imhof, H. (1999, April 16). WSU students spearhead efforts to curb alcohol abuse. *News from Washington State University.* Retrieved on May 23, 2000 from http://www.wsu.edu/ NIS/release2/hi125.htm.

Imhof, H. (2000, April 23). WSU Greeks plan community party. *News from Washington State University.* Retrieved on May 23, 2000 from http://www.wsu.edu/NIS/releases2/hil31.htm.

Michelson, M. (2000, March 6). Potential Washington State U. riot repeat rebuffed. *Daily Evergreen.*

Petura, B. (1998, August 14). Expulsions, suspensions, fines, probation included. *New from Washington State University.* Retrieved on May 23, 2000 from http://www.wsu.edu/NIS/re leases/bp129.htm.

Phillips, M. (2000, June 20). Washington State U. aims for more students, money. *Daily Evergreen.*

Smylie, M. (1999, May 6). One year later, Washington State U. remember May riot. *Daily Evergreen.*

Anonymous. (2000, May 23). Facts about WSU. *WSU Facts.* Retrieved on May 23, 2000 from http://www.wsu.edu/NIS/FactsAbout WSU.html.

Sanchezand, R., & Ebnet, M. (1998, May 5). "Fluke" weekend riot at WSU may be part of trend. *The Seattle Times.* Retrieved on May 24, 2000 from http://seattletimes.com/news/local/ htm198/pull_050598.html.

Sowa, T. (1998, May 20). Law enforcement cites mistakes in handling riot authorities lacked shields and failed to wait for backup, say officers involved in WSU melee. *The Spokane Review.*

Vogt, A. (1998, September 11). Ex-WSU student has dim recall of riot Jackson tells court of drinking binge. *Spokesman Review.*

Vogt, A. (1998, May 4). Overnight riot injures 23 police at WSU students spill out of party house for fiery showdown with officers. *The Spokane Review.*

Vogt, A. (1998, May 5). We know who you are, police tell WSU rioters investigators review videotapes. *The Spokane Review.*

Vogt, A. (1999, October 22). WSU riot trial ends in acquittal Jamie Jackson not guilty of assaulting deputy. *Spokesman Review.*

Vogt, A. (2000, April 16). WSU tries to polish its image. *Spokane.net.* Retrieved on April 17, 2000 from http://www.spokane.net:80/news-story-body.asp?Date=041600&ID=s792186&cat=.

[469] Ibid.

[470] Ibid.

[471] Ibid.

[472] Ibid.

[473] Ibid.

[474] Ibid.

[475] Ibid.

[476] Vogt, A. WSU tries to polish its image. *Spokane.net.* 16 April 2000. retrieved on 17 April 2000 from http://www.spokane.net:80/news-story-body.asp? Date=041600&ID=s792186&cat=

[477] Ibid.

[478] Anonymous. Penn State quick facts. *Penn State Online.* Retrieved on May 23, 2000 from http://www.psu.edu/ur/about/quick.html.
Penn State riot damage estimated at $100K. (1998, July 14). *York Daily Record.*
Penn State riot reported about 1,500 people flooded streets through the early morning Sunday after the Central Pennsylvania Festival of Arts. (1998, July 13). *York Daily Record.*
Penn State should expel rioters. (1998, July 14). *Daily Collegian.*
Police arrest eight more in July 12 Penn State riot about 1,500 people took part in the melee. (1998, August 28). *York Daily Record.*
Sober thoughts as Penn State riots show, binge drinking has become the most serious drug problem on campus. It's time to address it. (1998, July 19). *Sunday News.*
Students involved in summer riot no longer in school. (1998, November 30). *Penn State Online.* Retrieved on May 23, 2000 from http://www.psu.edu/ur/NEWS/news/riotsanctions.html.
Blair, B., & Cole, P. (1998, July 13). 1,500 riot at Penn State; 20 arrested. *Daily Collegian.*
Bradley, F., & Cichon, F. (2000, July 17). Police end riot near Penn State University. *Daily Collegian.*

Cheng, V. (1998, September 3). Community wants to curtail drinking; Students binge drinking was blamed for fueling the July 12 riot at Penn State. *York Daily Record.*

Parfitt, M. (1998, July 14). Penn State riot aftermath: Officials clean up, assign blame. *Daily Collegian.*

Xu, S. (1999, March 17). Sentences given in final Penn State U. riot trials. *Daily Collegian-Penn State University.*

Zeigler, P. (1998, July 13). Entertainment value found in riot at Penn State. *Daily Collegian.*

[479] Ibid.

[480] Ibid.

[481] Penn State quick facts. (n.d.) *Penn State Online.* Retrieved on May 23, 2000 from http://www.psu.edu/ur/about/quick.html.
Penn State riot reported about 1,500 people flooded streets through the early morning Sunday after the Central Pennsylvania Festival of Arts. (1998, July 13). *York Daily Record.*

[482] Court tells Michigan newspaper to hand over photos of campus riot. (1999, April 6). *The Freedom Forum Online.* Retrieved on April 13, 2000 from http://www.freedomforum.org/press/1999/4/6msuriot.asp.
Gonzales, P. (n.d.) Riots at Michigan State University. *Campus Safety Journal.* Retrieved on April 13, 2000 from http://www.campusjournal.com/michigan-state-riot.htm.
Lively, K. (1998). At Michigan State, a protest escalated into a night of fires, tear gas, and arrests. *Chronicle of Higher Education, 44*(36), A46–A47.
McCollum, K. (1999). Hackers attack web site set up to nab student rioters at Michigan State U. *Chronicle of Higher Education, 45*(33), A38.
Delgado, V. (2000, July 14). Two rioters suspended. *Lansing State Journal.* Retrieved on April 14, 2000 from http://www.lansingstatejournal.com/features/riot/suspended.html.
Tato, S. (2000, July 14). MSU officials defend riot suspensions. *Lansing State Journal.* Retrieved on April 14, 2000 from http://www.lansingstatejournal.com/features/r iot/msuofficials.html.
Tato, S. (2000, July 14). New policy lets MSU suspend future rioters. *Lansing State Journal.* Retrieved on April 14, 2000 from http://www.lansingstatejournal.com/features/riot/suspend.html.

College rioters jailed at higher rate than rapists. (2000, March 5). *APB News.* Retrieved on March 15, 2000 from http://www.apbnews.com:80/newscenter/breakingnews/2000/03/05/msuriot0305_01.html.

Drummond, D. (1999, August 29). School tightens rules to curb alcohol abuse, prevent repeat of riots. *The Toledo Blade.* Retrieved on August 30, 1999 from http://www.toledoblade.com:80/editorial/news/9h29msu.htm.

Durbin, D. (1999, March 31). MSU suspends 2 rioting students. *South Bend Tribune.*

Pardo, J., & Cohen, J. (1999, March 29). MSU vows to expel rioters: Police seek melee videos; students may face charges. *Detroit News.*

Shepardson, D. (1999, April 11). Media fight to demand MSU riot photos. *The Detroit News.* Retrieved on April 13, 2000 from http://www.detnews.com/1999/metro/9904/11/0411 0046.htm.

[483] Ibid.

[484] Ibid.

[485] Ibid.

[486] Gilje, P. (1996). *Rioting in America.* Bloomington, IN: Indiana University Press.

[487] Applegate, R. (1962). *Kill or get killed.* Harrisburg, PA: The Stackpole Company.

[488] Haddock, D., and Polsby, D. (1994, Spring/Summer)Understanding riots. *The Cato Journal, 14,* 1. Retrieved on 23 May 2000 from http://www.cato.org/pubs/journal/cj14n1-13.html.

[489] Methvin, E. (1970). *The riot makers.* New Rochelle, NY: Arlington House.

[490] Ibid.

[491] Beene, C. (1992). *Police crowd control.* Boulder, CO: Paladin Press.

[492] Applegate, R. (1981). *Riot control.* Boulder, CO: Paladin Press.

[493] Applegate, R. (1962). *Kill or get killed.* Harrisburg, PA: The Stackpole Company.

[494] Haddock, D., & Polsby, D. (1994, Spring/Summer) Understanding riots. *The Cato Journal, 14,* 1. Retrieved on 23 May 2000 from http://www.cato.org/pubs/journal/cj14n1-13.html.

[495] Beene, C. (1992). *Police crowd control.* Boulder, CO: Paladin Press.

[496] Methvin, E. (1970). *The riot makers.* New Rochelle, NY: Arlington House.

[497] Kaihla, P. (1992). Concordia's trials. *Maclean's, 105*(45), 52–55.

[498] Ibid.

[499] Kaihla, P. (1992). Concordia's trials. *Maclean's. 105*(45), 52–55.

[500] Death threat found at San Diego State. (1996). *Chronicle of Higher Education, 43*(15), A12.

[501] Ibid.

[502] Rickgarn, R. (1989). Violence in residence halls: Campus domestic violence. In J. Sherrill & D. Siegel (Eds.), *Responding to violence on campus.* San Francisco: Jossey-Bass Inc.

Shook, N., Gerrity, D., Jurich, J., & Segrist, A. (2000). Courtship violence among college students: A comparison of verbally and physically abusive couples. *Journal of Family Violence, 15*(1), 1–22.

Walker, L. (1980). *Battered woman.* New York: HarperCollins.

[503] Ibid.

Schlesinger, L. Murder and sex murder: Psychopathology and psychodynamics. In *Lethal violence: A sourcebook on fatal domestic, acquaintance and stranger violence.* London: CRC Press.

[504] van Wormer, K. Family safety current trends: About domestic homicide and murder-suicide. Social workers: Help starts here. Retrieved on April 29, 2009 from http://www.helpstartshere.org/Default.aspx?PageID=1248.

[505] Campus police kill man as he fatally stabs girlfriend at University of Michigan. (1997). *Jet, 92*(21), 39–40.

Williams. (1997, September 23). *The Michigan Daily.*

Two killed on Michigan cam pus. (1997, September 24). *Black News Today.*

Cohen, J. (1997, September 25). Friend may know reason behind attack. *The Michigan Daily.*

Hepburn, S. (1997, September 24). Best friend shocked, hurt by violent death. *The Michigan Daily.*

Hepburn, S. (1997, September 25). Report details Williams murder. *The Michigan Daily.*

Kosseff, J. (1997, September 24). Campus experts decry, abuse, offer assistance. *The Michigan Daily.*

Plona, K. (1997, September 24). Murder alarms students, sparks parental fears. *The Michigan Daily.*

[506] Ibid.

[507] Columbia woman killed in dorm boyfriend later dies on subway tracks. (2000, February 6). *The Record.*

Mann, E. Columbia student stabbed to death. (2000, February 7). *WSN News.* Retrieved on February 8, 2000 from http://www.nyu.edu/pubs/wsn/00/02/07/NcolumbiaStab.htm.

Mann, E. (2000, February 10). In wake of Columbia U. killing, security changes not foreseen. *Washington Square News.*

Schefrin, N. (2000, February 7). Student found stabbed to death in Columbia U. dorm room. *Columbia Daily Spectator.*

[508] Ibid.

[509] Ibid.

[510] Authorities investigate why Harvard honor student stabbed her roommate to death and later hanged herself. (1995). *Jet, 88*(6), 52–53.

Hewitt, B., Longley, A., Brown, S., & Eftimiades, M. (1995). Death at Harvard. *People Weekly, 43*(23), 40–43.

Prose, F. (1997). Halfway heaven: Diary of a Harvard murder. *People Weekly, 48*(14), 43–48.

Shea, C. (1995). Harvard in shock after junior kills her roommate, then hangs herself, as students leave for summer. *Chronicle of Higher Education, 41*(39), A36.

[511] Hewitt, B., Harmes, J., Clark, C., Williams, K., & Sellinger, M. (2000). Their paradise lost. *People Weekly, 53*(13), 173–177.

Thernstrom, M. (1997). *Halfway heaven.* New York: Doubleday

[512] Thernstrom, M. (1997). *Halfway heaven.* New York: Doubleday.

[513] Ibid.

[514] Ibid.

[515] Ibid.

[516] Howe, R. (1996). A fatal friendship. *People Weekly, 46*(1), 65–71.

[517] Ibid.

[518] Former Hopkins student sentenced in slaying. (1997). *Chronicle of Higher Education, 43*(46), A6.

[519] Stalking, questions, and answers. (1995). *The national center for victims of crime.* Retrieved on April 29, 2009 from http://www.ncvc.org/ncvc/main.aspx?dbName=DocumentViewer&DocumentAction=ViewProperties&DocumentID=32456&UrlToReturn=http%3a%2f%2fwww.ncvc.org%2fncvc%2fmain.aspx%3fdbName%3dAdvancedSearch.

[520] Ibid.

[521] Ibid.

[522] Spence-Diehl, E. (1999). *Stalking: A handbook for victims.* Holmes Beach, FL: Learning Publications Inc.

[523] Geraghty, M. (1997). Hidden pregnancies and babies' deaths raise painful questions for colleges. *Chronicle of Higher Education, 44*(3), A49–A50.

[524] Nicholson, M. E., Wang, M. W., Maney, D., Yuan, J., Mahoney, B. S., & Adame, D. D. (1998). *American Journal of Health Studies, 14*(1), 1–10.

[525] Wanat, T. (1996). Football players' attack on a fraternity house stuns U. of Rhode Island. *Chronicle of Higher Education, 43*(10), A44.

[526] Haworth, K. (1997). Va. Wesleyan suspends 23 athletes after brawl. *Chronicle of Higher Education, 43*(26), A42.

[527] Abel, D. (2000, March 20). UNH brawl raises new doubts about fraternities. Boston Globe. Retrieved on March 20, 2000 from http://www.boston.com/dailyglobe2/080/metro/UNHbrawlraisesnewdoubtsaboutfraternities+.shtml.

[528] Ibid.

[529] Boone, B. (2000). How I could just kill a man. *Oregon Commentator Online.* Retrieved on May 23, 2000 form http://darkwing.uoregon.edu/-ocomment/ocarchive/oc98_99/oc3_6.html.

Campbell, C. (2000, July 30). Violence at Georgetown. *Washington Post.*

Murphy, C. (2000, July 20). Mother calls GU response to son's death ineffective. *The Washington Post.*

Murphy, C. (2000, July 23). GU hears testimony in student's death. *Washington Post.*

[530] Ibid.

[531] Three injured during halftime band brawl between Southern University and Prairie View A&M. (1998). *Jet, 94*(20), 51.

Reilly, R. (1998). And the band fought on. *Sports Illustrated, 89*(14), 112.

[532] Ray, A., & Gold, S. 1996. Gender roles, aggression, and alcohol use in dating relationships. *Journal of Sex Research, 33*:47–55.

Rickgarn, R. (1989). Violence in residence halls: Campus domestic violence. In J. Sherrill & D. Siegel (Eds.), *Responding to violence on campus.* San Francisco: Jossey-Bass Inc.

Schlesinger, L. Murder and sex murder: Psychopathology and psychodynamics. In *Lethal violence: A sourcebook on fatal domestic, acquaintance and stranger violence.* London: CRC Press.

Shook, N., Gerrity, D., Jurich, J., & Segrist, A. (2000). Courtship violence among college students: A comparison of verbally and physically abusive couples. *Journal of Family Violence, 15*(1):1–22.

533 Walker, L. (1980). *Battered woman.* New York: HarperCollins.

534 Ibid.

535 Evans, P. (1992). *The verbally abusive relationship.* Holbrook, MA: Bob Adams, Inc. Publishers.

536 Hunnicutt, K. (1998). Introduction to women and violence on campus. In A. Hoffman, J. Schuh, & R. Fenske (Eds.), *Violence on campus: Defining the problems, strategies for action.* Gaithersburg, MD: Aspen Publishers.

537 Malamuth, N. M., Scokloskie, R. J. Koss, M. P., & Tanaka, J. S. (1991). Characteristics of aggressors against women: Testing a model using a national sample of college students. *Journal of Consulting and Clinical Psychology, 59*(5), 670–681.

538 Tjaden, P., & Thoennes, N. (2000). Prevalence and consequences of male-to-female intimate partner violence as measured by the National Violence Against Women Survey. *Violence Against Women, 6*(2), 142–161.

539 Game stats. (n.d.) *National Coalition Against Violent Athletes.* Retrieved on May 1, 2009 from http://www.ncava.org/stats.html.

540 Alvi, S., & Selbee, K. (1997). Dating status variations and woman abuse: A test of the dependency, availability, and deterrence (DAD) model. *Violence Against Women, 3*(6), 610–628.

541 Bogel-Allbritten, R., & Allbritten, W. (1991). Courtship violence on campus: A nationwide survey of student affairs professionals. *NASPA Journal, 28*(4), 312–318.

542 Renzetti, C., & Miley, C. (1996). *Violence in gay and lesbian domestic partnerships.* Bingham, NY: Harrington Park Press.

543 Ibid.
Dandeneau, C., & Fontaine, J. (1997). Violence in gay and lesbian domestic partnerships. *Sex Roles: A Journal of Research, 36*(5-6), 431–432.
Elliott, P. (1996). Shattering illusions: Same-sex domestic violence. In Claire Renzetti (Ed.), *Violence in gay and lesbian domestic partnerships.* Bingham, NY: Harrington Park Press.
Garnets, L., Herek, G., & Levy, B. (1992). Violence and victimization of lesbians and gay men. In *Hate crimes.* Newbury Park, NJ: Sage.

Hamberger, K. (1996). Intervention in gay male intimate violence requires coordinated efforts on multiple levels. In C. Renzetti & C, Miley (Eds.), *Violence in gay and lesbian domestic partnerships.* New York: Harrington Park Press.
Landolt, M., & Dutton, D. (1997). Power and personality: An analysis of gay male intimate abuse. *Sex Roles: A Journal of Research, 37*(5–6), 335–359.
Merrill, G. (1996). Ruling the exceptions: Same-sex battering and domestic violence theory. In C. Renzetti & C. Miley (Eds.), *Violence in gay and lesbian domestic partnerships.* Bingham: NY: Harrington Park Press.

544 Hamberger, K. (1996). Intervention in gay male intimate violence requires coordinated efforts on multiple levels. In C. Renzetti & C. Miley (Eds.), *Violence in gay and lesbian domestic partnerships.* Bingham, NY: Harrington Park Press.

545 MacDonald, J., Shaughnessy, R., & Galvin, J. (1977). *Bombers and firesetters.* Springfield, IL: Charles C Thomas.
MacDonald, J., Shaughnessy, R., & Galvin, J. (1977) Bombing and firesetting (Chap. 1). In *Bombers and firesetters.* Springfield, IL: Charles C Thomas.
MacDonald, J., Shaughnessy, R., & Galvin, J. (1977). Bombers and their mothers (Chap. 3). In *Bombers and firesetters.* Springfield, IL: Charles C Thomas.
MacDonald, J., Shaughnessy, R., & Galvin, J. (1977). Victims and targets (Chap. 7). In *Bombers and firesetters.* Springfield, IL: Charles C Thomas.
MacDonald, J., Shaughnessy, R., & Galvin, J. (1977). Bomb disposal (Chap. 8). In *Bombers and firesetters.* Springfield, IL: Charles C Thomas.
MacDonald, J., Shaughnessy, R., & Galvin, J. (1977). Bomb threats (Chap. 9). In *Bombers and firesetters.* Springfield, IL: Charles C Thomas.
MacDonald, J., Shaughnessy, R., & Galvin, J. (1977). Criminal investigation (Chap. 11). In *Bombers and firesetters.* Springfield, IL: Charles C Thomas.

546 "Facts on Fire." (n.d.) *U.S. Fire Administration.* Retrieved on April 29, 2009 from http://USFA.dhs.gov.

547 Target arson. (2000, June 21). *Fire Investigators.* http://www.fire-investigators.org/aaw/Arson Fac.htm.

[548] Ibid.

[549] Ibid.

[550] A look at campus crime. (2000). *The Chronicle of Higher Education, 46*(40), A49.

[551] MacDonald, J., Shaughnessy, R., & Galvin, J. (1977). *Bombers and firesetters.* Springfield, IL: Charles C Thomas.

[552] Barker, A. (1994). *Arson: A review of the psychiatric literature.* Oxford: Oxford University Press.

[553] Smoke-bomb Prank Leads to Death. (1996). *Chronicle of Higher Education. 43*(10), A9.

[554] Ex-student's trial in dorm fire at Murray delayed until October. (2000, February 1). *Cincinnati Enquirer.*

Fatal Fire at Murray State ruled arson. (1998). *Chronicle of Higher Education, 45*(6), A10.

Five once charged in Murray dorm fire file suit alleging wrongful arrest. (1999, October 27). *Lexington Herald-Leader.*

Five students charged in Murray State fire. (1998). *Chronicle of Higher Education, 45*(11), A12.

Gerth, J. (1998, October 1). Fatal Murray fire prompts calls for changes. *The Courier-Journal.* Retrieved on June 22, 2000 from http://www.courier-journal.com/localnews/1998/9810/01/19981001dormfire.html.

Malone, J. (1999, February 12). Chandler can't punish prosecutor in dorm-fire case. *The Courier-Journal.*

Murray State student charged in fire death. (1999) *Chronicle of Higher Education, 45*(42), A10.

Patton's sprinkler stance frustrates victim's mother. (1998, November 15). *The Courier-Journal.* Retrieved on June 22, 2000 from http://www.courier-journal.com/localnews/1998/9811/15/19981115pattonsprinkler.html.

Poynter, C. (1998, November 8). Murray fire suspect recall night of pranks. *The Courier-Journal.* Retrieved on June 22, 2000 from http://www.courier-journal.com/localnews/1998/9811/08/19981108dorm.html.

Poynter, C. (1998, October 13). Students move off campus after fire. *The Courier-Journal.* Retrieved on June 22, 2000 from http://www.courier-journal.com/localnews/1998/9810/13/19981013murr.html.

Poynter, C. (1999, January 23). Two agencies left out of arson probe. *The Courier-Journal.* Retrieved on June 22, 2000 from http://www.courier-journal.com/localnews/1999/9901/23/990123murrayprobe.html.

Poynter, C., & Malone, J. (1998, September 23). Murray dormitory fire was arson, police say. *The Courier-Journal.* Retrieved on June 22, 2000 from http://www.courier-journal.com/localnews/1998/9809/23/19980923murrayfire.html.

Vance, D. (1998, November 7). After fire, safety on minds of Murray State students. *World Wide Edition of The Kentucky Post.* Retrieved on June 22, 2000 from http://www.kypost.com/news.murray110798.html.

[555] Ibid.

[556] Ibid.

[557] Ibid.

[558] Ibid.

[559] Three arson fires cause more than $1 million in damage to Clark Atlanta University Buildings. (1995). *Jet, 87*(22), 22–24.

[560] Five fires hit U. of Miami in week; 1 Ruled Arson. (1997). *Chronicle of Higher Education, 43*(22), A8.

[561] Benedict College victim of arson. (1998). *Chronicle of Higher Education, 44*(27), A11.

[562] Wilson, R. (2000). Radical group takes credit for lab fire. *Chronicle of Higher Education, 46*(23), A18.

[563] Levin, B. (1976). *Arson: Some problems and solutions.* Boston: National Fire Protection Association Publications.

[564] Ibid.

[565] MacDonald, J., Shaughnessy, R., & Galvin, J. (1977). *Bombers and firesetters.* Springfield, IL: Charles C Thomas.

[566] Target arson. (n.d.) *Fire Investigators.* Retrieved on June 21, 2000 from http://www.fire-investigators.org/aaw/ArsonFac.htm.

[567] Fire Net International. (n.d.) Retrieved on May 1, 2009 from http://www.fire.org.uk.

[568] MacDonald, J., Shaughnessy, R., & Galvin, J. (1977). *Bombers and firesetters.* Springfield, IL: Charles C Thomas.

[569] University of Georgia. (1989). *How Fast It Burned.* Produced and directed by the University of Georgia. 22 minutes. University of Georgia.

[570] Student Pleads Guilty to April Bomb Threat. (1996). *Chronicle of Higher Education, 43*(17), A9.

571 Eight Students Arrested for Bombs on Two Campuses. (1999). *Chronicle of Higher Education, 45*(33), A14.

572 Bridges, T., & Martin, D. Little information emerges on Lombardi. *Tallahassee Democrat Online.* Retrieved on July 10, 2000 from http://www.tdo.com/local/famubomb/1002.loc .whoheis.htm (10 July 2000).

Green, M. (n.d.) FAMU takes extra measures for safety. *Tallahassee Democrat Online.* Retrieved on July 10, 2000 from http://www.tdo.com/ local/famubomb/famuan/0927famuan.htm.

Hefner, D. (n.d.) On FAMU campus: feelings of justice, safety and relief. *Tallahassee Democrat Online.* Retrieved on July 10, 2000 from http:// www.tdo.com/local/famubomb/0624.loc.verdict reax.htm.

Jury convicts Fla. hate-crime bomber. (2000, June 23). *UPI.*

Pjankuch, T. (1999, September 30). Aid sought in FAMU bomb case, recording photo released; more violence threatened. *Florida Times-Union.*

Pjankuch, T., & Pendleton, R. (1999, October 2). Arrest in FAMU bombs, citizens recognized man's photo, voice in the release recording. *The Florida Times-Union.*

Rosica, J. (2000, July 2). Transcripts Have Bomber Planning Alibi. *Tallahassee Democrat Online.* Retrieved on July 10, 2000 from http://www.tdo.com/local/famubomb/0703.loc .lombardi.htm.

Rosica, J. (n.d.) Bomber guilty on 6 counts. *Tallahassee Democrat Online.* Retrieved on July 10, 2000 from http://www.tdo.com/local/famu bomb/0624.loc.lombardi.htm.

Rosica, J. (n.d.) Ex-friend describes Lombardi. *Tallahassee Democrat Online.* Retrieved on July 10, 2000 from http://www.tdo.com/local/famu bomb/0621.loc.lombardi.htm.

Rosica, J. (n.d.) Trial could go to jury today. *Tallahassee Democrat Online.* Retrieved on July 10, 2000 from http://www.tdo.com/local/famubomb/ 0623.loc.lombardi.htm.

Rosica, J. (n.d.) Witness: He his book on bombs. *Tallahassee Democrat Online.* Retrieved on July 10, 2000 from http://www.tdo.com/ local/famubomb/0622.loc.lombardi.htm.

Shock of FAMU bombings fade as suspects trail nears. (2000, June 16). *Florida Today.*

White Man Arrested in Bombings at Florida A&M University. (1999). *Jet, 96*(20), 18.

573 Ibid.

574 Ibid.

575 Kennish, J. (n.d.) Preparing for bomb threats. Retrieved on June 21, 2000 from http://kennish .com/bombthreat.

AUTHOR INDEX

SUBJECT INDEX

ABOUT THE EDITORS

John Nicoletti, Ph.D.

John Nicoletti received his doctorate in psychology from Colorado State University. Dr. Nicoletti is a Clinical/Police Psychologist who specializes in identifying, assessing and defusing attack-related behaviors and violence in various workplaces, campuses and schools. In his other area of specialization, he provides on-site psychological screenings and consultations at the U.S. bases of McMurdo and the South Pole in Antarctica.

Dr. Nicoletti has written three books in the areas of violence, entitled *Violence Goes to Work* (1994); *Violence Goes to College* (2001), published by Charles C Thomas; and *Violence Goes to School* (2002), National Education Services.

Dr. Nicoletti provides national training and consultation to various university campuses and school districts. In addition, he is also called upon to conduct individual direct and indirect risk assessments for campuses and corporations. Dr. Nicoletti was on-scene at the April 20, 1999 Columbine school shooting and also responded to the Platte Canyon High School shooting in September 2006. Dr. Nicoletti is on the Colorado Governor's Task Force on Expert Emergency Response and is past Chair of the Police Psychologist Section for the International Association of Chiefs of Police. Dr. Nicoletti was an invited participant at the June 2007 National Association of Attorneys General (NAAG) Task Force on School Safety. He currently is a member of The International Association of Chiefs of Police Task Force on the Virginia Tech shootings.

Sally Spencer-Thomas, Psy.D., MNM

As the Executive Director of the Carson J. Spencer Foundation, a mental health advocacy group, and survivor of her younger brother's suicide, psychologist Dr. Sally Spencer-Thomas is an in-demand speaker on the topic of suicide prevention and other mental health issues. Dr. Spencer-Thomas has shared her insights with organizations such as the Federal Bureau of Investigation, the United States Department of Higher Education, and the International Association of Suicide Prevention, among many others. She is currently the Survivor Division Chair for the American Association of Suicidology and the Co-Chair for the Suicide Prevention Coalition of Colorado.

Dr. Sally Spencer-Thomas received her doctorate in psychology from the University of Denver in 1995. For over a decade, she worked for both Regis University and Nicoletti-Flater Associates in the capacities of clinical and health psychologist, programmer and consultant. She served as the Area Consultant (Colorado, Wyoming, Utah, and Montana) for the BACCHUS & GAMMA Peer Education Network and supervised "Choices," the award-winning peer education program at Regis. She also volunteered as the Regional Coordinator for the U.S. Department of Education's "Network Addressing Collegiate Alcohol and Other Drug Issues."

Dr. Spencer-Thomas received specialized training in the areas of violence and trauma. During her work as an employee of the Denver Police Department, she served as a Victim Advocate, counseling and providing resources for families in crisis. Dr. Spencer-Thomas also developed expertise in trauma under the guidance of the National Center for Post-Traumatic Stress Disorder (PTSD) at the Boston VA Medical Center.

Dr. Spencer-Thomas lives in Conifer, Colorado with her three sons and partner and is an avid marathon runner.

Chris Bollinger, Ph.D.

Dr. Bollinger earned his doctorate in Communication Studies from Bowling Green State University in 2004 after completing a dissertation exploring the ways in which hate is conceptualized, formulated, practiced, and resisted within our educational systems. Over the course of his career he has facilitated workshops across the country addressing issues of violence, hate, and education. On occasion, he works as a consultant for student affairs programs.

Dr. Bollinger is currently an Assistant Professor in the Department of English and Communication studies at Texas Lutheran University. Dr. Bollinger brings together nine years of experience working in Residence Life and seven years' experience as a full-time faculty member as he integrates curricular and co-curricular efforts addressing issues of diversity. He works closely with the Women's Studies Center, Black Student Union, Lone Star Scholars Academy, and Center for Servant Leadership.

Dr. Bollinger resides in Seguin, Texas with his partner Dr. Denise Menchaca, who is a cultural studies scholar, performer, and Assistant Professor for Northeast Lakeview College in San Antonio, Texas.

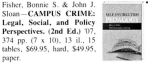